THE ROUTLEDGE COMPANION TO ALTERNATIVE AND COMMUNITY MEDIA

The Routledge Companion to Alternative and Community Media provides an authoritative and comprehensive examination of the diverse forms, practices and philosophies of alternative and community media across the world.

The volume offers a multiplicity of perspectives to examine the reasons why alternative and community media arise, how they develop in particular ways and in particular places, and how they can enrich our understanding of the broader media landscape and its place in society.

The 50 chapters present a range of theoretical and methodological positions, and arguments to demonstrate the dynamic, challenging and innovative thinking around the subject, locating media theory and practice within the broader concerns of democracy, citizenship, social exclusion, race, class and gender.

In addition to research from the UK, the US, Canada, Europe and Australia, the *Companion* also includes studies from Colombia, Haiti, India, South Korea and Zimbabwe, enabling international comparisons to be made and also allowing for the problematisation of traditional – often Western – approaches to media studies.

By considering media practices across a range of cultures and communities, this collection is an ideal companion to the key issues and debates within alternative and community media.

Contributors: Laura Ahva, Stuart Allan, Heather Anderson, Chris Atton, Olga Guedes Bailey, Mary Angela Bock, Megan Boler, Axel Bruns, Jean Burgess, Bart Cammaerts, Nico Carpentier, William K. Carroll, Yiannis Christidis, Nick Couldry, Vaia Doudaki, Tony Dowmunt, John D. H. Downing, Victoria Esteves, Susan Forde, Kerrie Foxwell-Norton, Christian Fuchs, Janey Gordon, Pinar Gurleyen, Robert A. Hackett, Adnan Hadzi, James F. Hamilton, Tony Harcup, Heikki Heikkilä, Arne Hintz, Per Jauert, Richard Lance Keeble, Linda Jean Kenix, Dorothy Kidd, Eun-Gyoo Kim, Risto Kunelius, Peter M. Lewis, Leah A. Lievrouw, Hayes Mawindi Mabweazara, Kirsten MacLeod, Robin MacPherson, Michael Meadows, Graham Meikle, Stefania Milan, Mike Mowbray, Daniel H. Mutibwa, Patrick E. Okon, Mojca Pajnik, Camilo Pérez Quintero, Herbert Pimlott, Thomas Poell, Christian E. Ramírez Hincapié, Jennifer Rauch, Jane Regan, Clemencia Rodríguez, Marisol Sandoval, David Skinner, Christina Spurgeon, Pradip Ninan Thomas, José van Dijck, Kush Wadhwa, Hayley Watson and Wendy Willems.

Chris Atton is Professor of Media and Culture in the School of Arts and Creative Industries at Edinburgh Napier University, UK. His books include *Alternative Media, An Alternative Internet* and *Alternative Journalism*. He has made special studies of fanzines, the media of new social movements, and audiences for avant-garde and other 'difficult' forms of popular music.

THE ROUTLEDGE COMPANION TO ALTERNATIVE AND COMMUNITY MEDIA

Edited by Chris Atton

Routledge
Taylor & Francis Group

LONDON AND NEW YORK

First published 2015
by Routledge
2 Park Square, Milton Park, Abingdon, Oxon, OX14 4RN

and by Routledge
711 Third Avenue, New York, NY 10017

Routledge is an imprint of the Taylor & Francis Group, an informa business

British Library Cataloguing in Publication Data
A catalogue record for this book is available from the British Library

Library of Congress Cataloging in Publication Data

ISBN: 978-0-415-64404-4 (hbk)
ISBN: 978-1-315-71724-1 (ebk)

Typeset in Goudy
by Taylor & Francis Books

Printed and bound in the United States of America by Publishers Graphics, LLC on sustainably sourced paper.

CONTENTS

CONTENTS

CONTENTS

CONTENTS

CONTENTS

LIST OF ILLUSTRATIONS

Figures

Tables

LIST OF CONTRIBUTORS

Laura Ahva is a postdoctoral researcher in the School of Communication, Media and Theatre at the University of Tampere, Finland. She has published in *Journalism: Theory, Practice & Criticism*, *Digital Journalism* and *Journalism Practice*, among others. Her research interests include journalism studies, citizen participation and audience research.

Stuart Allan is Professor of Journalism and Communication in the School of Journalism, Media and Cultural Studies at Cardiff University, UK. Recent books include *Citizen Witnessing* (2013), *The Routledge Companion to News and Journalism* (2012) and *Citizen Journalism: Global Perspectives*, Volume 2 (co-edited with E. Thorsen, 2014).

Heather Anderson is a postdoctoral fellow with the Centre for Communication and Social Change at the University of Queensland in Brisbane, Australia. She has been involved in community radio for over twenty years. She published her first book on prisoners' radio in 2012.

Chris Atton is Professor of Media and Culture in the School of Arts and Creative Industries at Edinburgh Napier University, UK.

Olga Guedes Bailey is based at Nottingham Trent University, UK, where she is co-director of the Inequality Culture and Difference Research Centre. She holds visiting professorships at the Shanghai University of Finance and Economics and the University of Fortaleza. She is researching the politics of communication of ethnic minorities and diasporas.

Mary Angela Bock is an Assistant Professor of Journalism at the University of Texas at Austin. A former television journalist, her research interests include visual rhetoric and photojournalistic practice. She is the author of *Video Journalism* (2012) and a co-author of *Visual Communication* (2014).

Megan Boler is Professor of Media and Education at the Ontario Institute for Studies in Education, University of Toronto. Her books include *Feeling Power: Emotions and Education* (1999); *Democratic Dialogue in Education* (2004); *Digital Media and Democracy: Tactics in Hard Times* (2008); and *DIY Citizenship* (2014).

Axel Bruns is an Australian Research Council Future Fellow and Professor at Queensland University of Technology in Brisbane, Australia. He leads the QUT

Social Media Research Group and is the author of *Blogs, Wikipedia, Second Life and Beyond* (2008) and *Gatewatching* (2005).

Jean Burgess is Associate Professor of Digital Media at the Queensland University of Technology and Director of Research Training for the Creative Industries Faculty. She has published on the cultures, politics and methods for studying social and mobile media platforms, and has worked with government, industry and community organisations.

Bart Cammaerts is Associate Professor and Director of the PhD programme in the Department of Media and Communications at the London School of Economics. He is the former chair of the Communication and Democracy Section of ECREA and vice chair of the Communication Policy and Technology section of IAMCR.

Nico Carpentier is Associate Professor at the Communication Studies Department of the Vrije Universiteit Brussels and lecturer at Charles University, Prague. He is an executive board member of IAMCR and was vice president of ECREA from 2008 to 2012.

William K. Carroll is Professor of Sociology at the University of Victoria. His research focuses on social movements and social change, the political economy of corporate capitalism, and critical social theory and method. His work has appeared in *Capital and Class*, *Critical Sociology* and *Sociology*, among others.

Yiannis Christidis studied Cultural Technology and Communication at the University of the Aegean and holds an MSc in Sound Design from the University of Edinburgh. He researches the social attributes of everyday sounds, and he designs sound and music for radio and audiovisual productions.

Nick Couldry is a sociologist of media and culture. He is Professor of Media, Communications and Social Theory at the London School of Economics. He is the author or editor of eleven books, including *Ethics of Media* (2013), *Media, Society, World* (2012) and *Why Voice Matters* (2010).

Vaia Doudaki is Assistant Professor of Journalism and Media Studies at the Cyprus University of Technology. Her research interests lie in the fields of media, conflict and crisis, theory and practice of newsmaking and journalism, community and participatory media.

Tony Dowmunt is a senior lecturer, and convenes the MA Screen Documentary, at Goldsmiths, University of London. From 2003 to 2006 he held an AHRC Fellowship in the Creative and Performing Arts, which included the production of an experimental video-diary, 'A Whited Sepulchre'.

John D. H. Downing is the author of *Radical Media* (2001) and editor of the *Encyclopedia of Social Movement Media* (2011), among other studies. He has taught at Greenwich University, the University of Texas at Austin and Southern Illinois University. He and his life partner, Ash Corea, live in Brooklyn, New York.

Victoria Esteves is a doctoral researcher at the University of Stirling. Her research focuses on the circulation of participatory cultures online.

Susan Forde is an associate professor of journalism at Griffith University, Brisbane, Australia. She is the author of *Challenging the News* (2011) and co-author of *Developing Dialogues* (2009). Prior to joining academia, she was a journalist and editor in the Australian alternative and community press.

Kerrie Foxwell-Norton is a senior lecturer in Journalism and Media Studies at Griffith University, Australia. Her research investigates the role of local media and communities in addressing global environmental issues.

Christian Fuchs is Professor of Social Media at the University of Westminster's Communication and Media Research Institute, and the Centre for Social Media Research. He is editor of *Communication, Capitalism and Critique*, chair of the European Sociological Association's Research Network 18 and co-founder of the ICTs and Society Network.

Janey Gordon is a principal lecturer at the University of Bedfordshire and founder of Radio LaB 97.1 FM, its on-site community radio station. Her research focuses on community radio and mobile phones. Her publications include *Br(e)aking the News* (2013) and *Community Radio in the Twenty-First Century* (2012).

Pinar Gurleyen is a doctoral candidate in the School of Communication at Simon Fraser University, Canada. Her main research interest is the democratic significance of alternative media, particularly focusing on the news culture of alternative journalism organisations.

Robert A. Hackett is Professor of Communication at Simon Fraser University, Canada. He researches and publishes on media democratisation and journalism paradigms, including *Expanding Peace Journalism* (2011), *Remaking Media* (2006) and *Democratizing Global Media* (2005). He has co-founded media analysis and advocacy initiatives, including Media Democracy Days.

Adnan Hadzi is a researcher at Coventry University and an artist. His research focuses on the influence of digitalisation and new forms of documentary film production, as well as authors' rights in relation to collective authorship. As an artist, Hadzi is part of !Mediengruppe Bitnik and the SPC medialab.

James F. Hamilton is an associate professor in the Grady College of Journalism and Mass Communication at the University of Georgia, USA. His research focuses on the history, theory and practice of alternative media and democratic communication. His books include *Democratic Communications* (2008) and *Alternative Journalism* (2008).

Tony Harcup worked as a staff and freelance journalist in both alternative and mainstream media before moving into journalism education. He now teaches journalism at the University of Sheffield in the UK, and his books include *Alternative Journalism, Alternative Voices* (2013) and *Journalism: Principles and Practice* (2015).

Heikki Heikkilä is a senior research fellow in the School of Communication, Media and Theatre at the University of Tampere, Finland. He is interested in the theoretical and empirical relationships between media organisations and their audiences/users. He has published in *Journalism, Journalism Practice* and *Javnost/The Public*.

Arne Hintz is a lecturer at the School of Journalism, Media and Cultural Studies at Cardiff University, UK. His research connects communication policy, media activism, citizen media and technological change. He is Chair of the Community Communication Section of IAMCR.

Per Jauert is an associate professor in media studies at Aarhus University, Denmark. His research interests include community media, public service media, radio history and digital platforms for radio. His publications include *Digital Radio in Europe* (2010) and *Radio, TV and Internet in the Nordic Countries* (2006).

Richard Lance Keeble has been professor of journalism at the University of Lincoln since 2003. He has produced 29 books on peace journalism, media ethics, literary journalism, investigative journalism and George Orwell. He gained a National Teaching Fellowship in 2011 and a Lifetime Achievement Award from the Association for Journalism Education in 2014.

Linda Jean Kenix is Head of the Media and Communication Department at the University of Canterbury in New Zealand. She has published *Alternative and Mainstream Media: The Converging Spectrum* (2011) and articles in over 30 journals. She has been a visiting scholar at Oxford University, the University of Cambridge and Monash University.

Dorothy Kidd teaches in the Department of Media Studies at the University of San Francisco. Her documentation of many aspects of social movement media can be found at http://usfca.academia.edu/DorothyKidd.

Eun-Gyoo Kim is Associate Professor in the Department of Mass Communication and Journalism at Woosuk University, Korea. He is affiliated with the Korean Society for Journalism and Mass Communication Studies. His research focuses on the relationship between media power and civil society.

Risto Kunelius is Professor of Journalism Research in the School of Communication, Media and Theatre at the University of Tampere, Finland. He currently coordinates an international project on the coverage of climate change politics and has co-edited two books on this topic.

Peter M. Lewis is Senior Lecturer in Community Media in the Faculty of Social Sciences and Humanities at London Metropolitan University. He is currently a member of an international research team whose project *Transnational Radio Encounters* (www.transnationalradio.org) is funded by HERA.

Leah A. Lievrouw is Professor of Information Studies at the University of California–Los Angeles. Her research focuses on the relationship between media and information technologies and social change. Her most recent book is *Alternative and Activist New Media* (2011).

Hayes Mawindi Mabweazara is a senior lecturer in Journalism Studies at Falmouth University, UK. He serves on the editorial board of *Digital Journalism* and is Associate Editor for *African Journalism Studies*. Mabweazara edited *Digital Technologies and the Evolving African Newsroom* (2014) and co-edited *Online Journalism in Africa* (2014).

Kirsten MacLeod is a lecturer in television at Edinburgh Napier University. She is also a producer and director working in broadcast television and community media. Her chapter is based on her practice-led doctoral research in participatory community-based media at the University of the West of Scotland.

Robin MacPherson is Professor of Screen Media and Director of Screen Academy Scotland (a Creative Skillset Film Academy) at Edinburgh Napier University. Formerly head of development at Scottish Screen, he has produced films for cinema and broadcast. He is a board member of Creative Scotland.

Michael Meadows worked as a print and broadcast journalist for ten years before moving into journalism education and communications research in the late 1980s with a particular focus on Indigenous media. He is based at the Griffith Centre for Cultural Research, Griffith University, in Brisbane.

Graham Meikle is Professor of Social Media at the University of Westminster. His most recent book is *Media Convergence: Networked Digital Media in Everyday Life*, co-authored with Sherman Young (Palgrave Macmillan, 2012). His next book, *Social Media: Creativity, Sharing, Visibility*, will be published by Routledge in 2015.

Stefania Milan is curious about activism, the interplay between technologies and society, and communications governance. She is Assistant Professor at the University of Amsterdam, and is the principal investigator of an ERC-funded project on the politics of big data.

Mike Mowbray is a PhD candidate at Simon Fraser University in Vancouver, Canada. His current research focuses on the representation of urban struggles in Vancouver's underground press in the 1960s and 1970s, and on the genre shift from 'underground' to 'alternative weekly' press in North America.

Daniel H. Mutibwa is Research Fellow on an AHRC-funded Digital Transformations in Community Research Co-Production project entitled *Pararchive: Open Access Community Storytelling and the Digital Archive*. He researches and teaches in the School of Media and Communication, University of Leeds.

Patrick E. Okon is a graduate of Edinburgh Napier University. He holds a PhD in Media Policy and Communication Studies. He is currently looking forward to an academic appointment in the Department of Theatre and Media Studies of the University of Calabar, Nigeria.

Mojca Pajnik is a lecturer at the Department of Communication, University of Ljubljana, and senior research associate at the Peace Institute in Ljubljana, Slovenia. She is co-editor of *Alternative Media and the Politics of Resistance* (2008) and *Contesting Integration, Engendering Migration: Theory and Practice* (2014).

Herbert Pimlott worked in alternative and mainstream media before he started teaching communication studies. His writing has been published in *Labour/Le Travail*, *Journalism Studies*, *Socialist Studies*, and *Media, Culture and Society*. His first book, *Wars of Position*, will be published in 2015.

Thomas Poell is Assistant Professor of New Media and Digital Culture at the University of Amsterdam. His research is focused on social media and the transformation of public communication in different parts of the world.

Camilo Pérez Quintero is a PhD student of Media Arts and Studies at Ohio University. His interests focus on participatory and visual research methods, citizens' media, performance studies, sensory ethnography and media for social change. He is a co-founder of Pasolini en Medellin.

Christian E. Ramírez Hincapié is a PhD student at CEDLA–University of Amsterdam. His research interests include citizens' and community media, especially media initiatives operating in areas of armed conflict in Colombia, as well as other communication processes outside mainstream media.

Jennifer Rauch (Long Island University–Brooklyn) examines how media sources and communication models constitute 'alternatives' in terms of their content, practices, uses of technology and engagements with the public. She has studied zine producers and alternative media audiences. Rauch is author of the blog Slow Media (www.slow-media.org).

Jane Regan has co-founded three community- and student-based newsrooms, two in Haiti and one in the US. An investigative journalist and filmmaker, Regan has contributed to several books and taught at universities in Haiti and Boston. She has worked for non-profit media such as PBS and commercial outlets such as the Associated Press.

Clemencia Rodríguez is Professor at the Department of Communication, University of Oklahoma. Her publications include *Fissures in the Mediascape* (2001), *Lo Que le Vamos Quitando a la Guerra. Medios Ciudadanos en Contextos de Conflicto Armado en Colombia* (ed., 2008) and *Citizens' Media Against Armed Conflict* (2011).

Marisol Sandoval is a lecturer in the Department of Culture and Creative Industries, City University London. She is the author of *From Corporate to Social Media* (2014) and managing editor of the open-access journal *tripleC: Communication, Capitalism and Critique*.

David Skinner is an associate professor in the Department of Communication Studies at York University in Toronto, Ontario, Canada. His research focuses mainly on the political economy of communication, media policy, media reform, and independent and community media.

Christina Spurgeon is a senior lecturer in Media and Communication at the Queensland University of Technology. She has published widely on new media and communication industries, and leads an Australian Research Council-funded research project looking at the social functions of storytelling in community media arts contexts.

Pradip Ninan Thomas is currently Acting Head of the School of Journalism and Communication at the University of Queensland. He has an abiding interest in issues related to alternative media, and his book *Negotiating Communication Rights: Case Studies from India* (2011) explores five communication rights movements in India.

José van Dijck is Professor of Comparative Media Studies at the University of Amsterdam. Her research areas include media technologies, digital culture, popularisation of science and medicine, and television and culture. Her latest book, *The Culture of Connectivity*, was published in 2013.

Kush Wadhwa is a senior partner at Trilateral Research & Consulting. He provides independent, non-partisan advisory services with respect to emerging technologies in security, ICT and health, focusing upon issues of strategic policy development related to privacy and data protection, socio-economic issues and inclusion.

Hayley Watson is an associate partner at Trilateral Research & Consulting, a niche research and advisory consultancy bringing together strategy, technology and policy. Her research includes the role of technology in relation to security, the development of citizen journalism and the role of social media in crisis management.

Wendy Willems is an assistant professor in the Department of Media and Communications at the London School of Economics and an honorary research fellow at the University of the Witwatersrand, Johannesburg. She is co-editor of *Civic Agency in Africa* (2014) and Associate Editor of the *Journal of African Media Studies*.

INTRODUCTION

Problems and positions in alternative and community media

Chris Atton

The focus of this *Companion* is on media that bypass the usual channels of commercial production and distribution, and that are most often organised and produced by 'ordinary' people, local communities and communities of interest. It is primarily interested in social and cultural practices that enable people to participate directly in the organisation, production and distribution of their own media, and how these media are used to construct and represent identity and community, as well as to present forms of information and knowledge that are under-represented, marginalised or ignored by other, more dominant media. However, rather than consider alternative and community media as entirely separate, it is also necessary to contextualise them in terms of those dominant, 'mainstream' practices and to examine hybrid and disputed forms of media that exhibit characteristics from both sets of media practices, such as the use of citizen journalism and user-generated content by professional media organisations.

The *Companion* addresses the social, cultural and political value of alternative and community media: how they offer democratic access to the media and how local and global notions of citizenship may be developed through them. It examines issues of social inclusion and community-building initiatives, and explores how amateur and non-professional media producers establish their own alternative frames of participation, political power and creativity. The *Companion* also addresses questions of epistemology and the construction of knowledge, the challenges to expert culture and professionalisation through alternative forms of social and cultural capital, and how alternative media contribute to critiques of media power.

The study of media power is concerned with discourse and with how discourses are constructed. Discourses matter because it is through them that we understand the world; they are social processes and as such are subject to the same conditions as other social processes: they are produced by people working together in groups, communities, organisations and institutions. Discourses are simultaneously ways of living in the world and modes of representing the world. One outcome of media discourse is the text: a news report, an interview, an analysis. Another outcome is the selection and arrangement of texts. A further outcome is the organisation and structuring of those engaged in media discourses: producers and audiences; journalists and readers; managers and consumers. Media discourses with the furthest reach (national and international broadcasters, global media companies) tend towards the hegemonic: their modes of representation have become naturalised and legitimated.

These modes of representation are built from practices that have become 'common sense' and taken for granted: the notion of the journalist as expert and as objective reporter of 'reality'; the structuring and ordering of stories as well as the convention of the telling of stories; the selection and legitimation of experts; news values that determine hierarchies of significance in the selection and presentation of reality. The economic power of national and global media companies might be vast, but arguably it is secondary to their symbolic power, the power to construct reality. To study alternative media is to consider how the world might be represented differently. It is to examine different ways of generating, structuring and presenting those representations. It is to explore how journalism arises and who might be able to generate these different representations. It shows how it is possible for those who are not part of formal media structures to participate in media discourses, to become reporters of their own reality, to become experts in their own social settings.

Alternative media are not simply concerned with presenting *a* different version of the world; taken together, they offer *multiple* versions of the world. Most often, alternative media practices take place within communities, of varying size and composition: most alternative media are community media; hence the title of this *Companion*.

Of names and naming

The construction of alternative media discourses matters because they enable what Alberto Melucci terms 'the construction of social life' (Melucci 1996: 357). If we are to consider the media not as a set of texts but as social processes (an argument made very convincingly by Nick Couldry in his book *The Place of Media Power* 2000), then how we describe, interpret and take part in the world all become aspects of media practice. Media practice is about naming the world; it is a process of 'nomination', to use Melucci's term. Naming matters not simply because it generates categories or enables ordering. To categorise is not to understand the world; neither is it to engage with the world. The act of naming has deeper consequences; it is concerned with questions of who produces discourses about the world and how those discourses shape our ways of living in the world. Alternative media are important because they reveal the structuredness of media discourse and show how the world might be represented differently by different media actors. Writing about social movements, Melucci argues that they (by implication through their media practices)

> strive to reappropriate the capacity to name through the elaboration of codes and languages designed to define reality, in the twofold sense of constituting it symbolically and of regaining it, thereby escaping from the predominant forms of representation.
>
> (Melucci 1996: 357)

I find that a compelling definition of alternative media.

More narrowly, but no less significantly, we need to consider how we name our object of study, what I am calling alternative media, as well as community media. Anyone who spends even a little time reading what is now a very large body of work on alternative media will encounter an array of terms that seem to refer to the same phenomenon. Some readers will argue with my settling on the term 'alternative media'; others will cavil at its equation with community media. While a term such as 'alternative' can seem either infuriately vague (alternative to what?) or appear untenably limiting (there is only one alternative), I present it as an analytical category.

To name, though, is not to settle once and for all. Just as the naming of reality is never definitive and absolutist, the naming of our object of study might be seen as a series of acts of analysis, argument and focus, each of which may be contextualised historically, geographically and culturally.

Other names might contain within them different arguments, suggest a different focus or even obscure arguments and processes. Any term can itself be seen as a 'bounded discourse' (Couldry 2010: 6), one that provides a limit within which cultural practices might be examined. As practices develop and the context around them develops, a term might become redundant or might ossify, capable of referring only to specific practices at particular times and places.

Some examples: the term 'independent media' might enable a study of the political economy of media production, where community engagement is less important than the freedom of journalists to report on topics less regarded by corporate media organisations. A study of independent media might have more to do with exploring the possibilities of the production of critical content by professional journalists, rather than the contributions of 'ordinary people'. To study amateur journalism might mean to study the limits of journalism that is practised outside professionalised environments (in other words, amateur*ish* journalism). Conversely, it might encourage an exploration of the roots of professional journalism in amateur practices, whether through the English Radical Press of the 1800s or through the counter-cultural and underground press of the 1960s. Citizen journalism, considered as an aspect of the mass media, may be viewed variously as a threat to the profession of journalism, a cheap way of filling space and a stop-gap mode of reporting until the professionals arrive on the scene. Citizen witnessing, on the other hand, as Stuart Allan (2013) has shown, can be understood as a public service rendered by citizens in times of crisis. Clemencia Rodríguez (2001) has proposed the term 'citizens' media' to refer to media practices where the living-out of those practices or 'media performances' is at least as important as the media products. For Rodríguez, to report on and to construct one's own reality through media can be a transformative experience. Finally, we might ask: what range of processes and relations are obscured or revealed by the term 'social media'?

These examples are far from exhaustive; they are meant simply to show how naming can reveal as well as hide. Throughout this *Companion* there are numerous examples of naming. Some readers might find the variety bewildering. Bear in mind how those names are mobilised and for what purposes. The name is less important than what goes on behind it. Later in this introduction I shall explore some of these terms in more detail. For now, though, I hope you will forgive a personal digression. How we come to our studies, particularly in the field of media and cultural studies, is often through less than rigorous ways. Brief and unplanned encounters with texts, individuals and events can be as formative as our formal education. The meandering route that led me to the study of alternative media is, I hope, not without relevance. If anything, it shows how encounters with alternative media, both as objects of study and as a personal interest, can be as transforming as they are contentious.

A reflexive history

If I remember correctly, my first introduction to alternative media was as an under-graduate. Perhaps we should call it a fanzine – its focus was precisely on one strand of the peculiar music I had been enjoying since my early teenage years: free impro-visation. Here was an entire magazine devoted to it, called *Musics* (I had never known that the plural form existed and it seemed doubly odd, given its apparently monothematic interest). I came across *Musics* by chance, finding it on the shelves of the university's student shop, alongside the expected copies of *New Musical Express*, *Melody Maker* and *Sounds*. *Musics* was far more satisfying than the three weekly British rock papers and not simply because it ploughed a particularly obscure furrow in detail. What fascinated me were the methods it used. It experimented with styles of reviewing, producing accounts of concerts and records that were very different from those in the commercial music press. I remember one review that comprised a handful of small pen-and-ink abstract drawings, with gnomic captions ('smoke', 'interference', 'framing'). A review of a duo concert by guitarist Derek Bailey and pianist Misha Mengelberg was presented as written during the performance. The review was split into two columns, the first listing Bailey's actions ('single repeated note', 'plays a tremolo on an open 5th'), the second Mengelberg's ('high clusters', 'tinkly stuff, like Messiaen'). For a musical style that relies on spontaneity and unrepeatability, the highly descriptive nature of the review seemed to capture its evanescence and its mundanity, while oddly making it more mysterious (why would musicians do things like this?). Like the performance of the music, *Musics* itself seemed to appear and disappear unpredictably; for weeks, sometimes for months, no new issue would appear. When it did, I would read it repeatedly, as if searching for clues to a hidden world.

Free improvisation was and remains a marginal musical practice, sustained by a micro-ecology of musicians and fans, with no interest from commercial record labels, promoters and very little attention paid to it by the commercial media. Since the early 1970s musician-run and fan-run labels have been the primary means of dis-tributing recordings of free improvisation. The clues I found in the pages of *Musics* came in the form of addresses for labels such as Incus, as well as those of concert organisers and venues, of local musicians involved in promoting as well as practising the music. *Musics* offered me ways into music that I had not experienced before. As a fan I was primarily interested in hearing the music, and this required purchases – to that extent my relationship with the music remained as a consumer, and yet without the addresses my access to the music would have been nigh impossible. Those addresses gave me more than access to consumer goods – they brought me into contact with people, with other fans and with the musicians themselves. *Musics* gave me access to a community; it enabled me to become part of that community, not simply vicariously by reading the privileged accounts of others, but as a participant sharing a lived experience with others. I corresponded with musicians and fans, met them and found that my involvement in the free improvised music scene brought me into contact with writers and editors who were interested in my views. I became a music critic of sorts, writing for publications in the UK, the US, France, Germany and Italy. The notion of an alternative publication started to mean something: it offered different ways of doing (writing about music, producing narratives) and different ways of being (becoming a writer, assuming media power). I found this a remarkable property of publishing; I still do.

A theoretical excursion

My first theoretical exposure to alternative media came through John Downing's 1984 book *Radical Media*. I read this back to back with his earlier work, *The Media Machine* (1980), a critique of the political economy of the mass media and its journalistic methods. If *The Media Machine* stated the problem, *Radical Media* offered the solution. In selecting the term 'radical media', Downing reached back into a history of naming. His title implied a connection between the Radical Press of Britain that flourished in the first half of the nineteenth century and Downing's contemporary examples across the world. 'Radical' pointed to the rooting of politics in the everyday lives of working people and suggested that solutions to those problems would come not from a cadre of professional politicians (of whatever stripe), but from the communities that endured those problems. Downing was careful to distinguish these community-based forms of political action from the centralised and institutionalised forms of political organisation, whether conservative, liberal or revolutionary. Radical media practice was to be located within communities and not to be driven by hierarchical control.

Rather than looking to Communism for an alternative to capitalist media control, as scholars such as Peter Allen (1985) and Colin Sparks (1985) were doing around the same time, Downing looked to the philosophy of anarchism, which he used to generate a broad set of arguments about radical media. Chief among these were:

- an emphasis on the multiple realities of social life;
- the privileging of movements over institutions;
- an emphasis on prefigurative politics;
- a disengagement of media from political parties or groups of intellectuals.

(paraphrased from Downing 1984: 17)

Downing's thesis (one that has been adopted and developed by other scholars in the field) is that media practices that display these features and that may be explained in these ways will tend to engage 'ordinary' people as media producers, will move away from homogeneity and will be able to better represent multiple perspectives of the lived experience within communities. Moreover, radical media practices might be able to show how politics may be practised in the future, as their methods of organisation, process and engagement can be seen as small-scale attempts at new forms of democracy. When I wrote *Alternative Media* (2002), I acknowledged a debt to Downing's work in my own typology of alternative media, where (though neither of us ignored content) I too emphasised organisation, process and social relations.

Nick Couldry and James Curran use the term 'alternative media' for similar ends, to indicate that 'whether indirectly or directly, media power is what is at stake' (2003: 7). Whichever term we use, though, enables us to examine amateur media practices for examples of how the mass media representations we take for granted may be challenged and disrupted. Couldry (2000) argues that alternative media projects result in the de-naturalisation of dominant media spaces (what we might call the 'mainstream'). Amateur media producers play an important role in rebalancing the power of the media. Instead of conceiving of media structures as permanent and immanent, we might, following Couldry, consider them as social processes. They then become open to challenge by other kinds of social processes of media practice, which might lead to more inclusive and democratic forms of media production. In sum, alternative or community media are able to construct realities that oppose the conventions and representations of the mainstream media. To consider alternative media is to recognise the relationship between dominant, professionalised media practices and otherwise marginal, amateur practices. The struggle between them becomes 'the place of media power' (Couldry 2000). Participatory, amateur media production contests the concentration of institutional and professional media power and challenges the media monopoly on producing symbolic forms.

My reason for preferring 'alternative' over 'radical' was out of a desire to range more widely in my examination of media practices. Without wishing to dismiss the explicitly politicised, social movement media that were at the heart of Downing's book, I wanted to introduce publications that dealt with the arts, either as platforms for amateur creative practice itself (short stories, poetry, comic books) or as opportunities for audiences (consumers) to set down their views in writing – to make public what is most often a private or a narrow social activity: talking about music, films, television, books, sport. (In a later work, we find an extremely wide range of media, which includes creative practices such as visual art, street theatre and music, but still locates them within the practices of social movements; see Downing 2001.) Of course, writing about popular culture may also be seen as a political practice to the degree that it might challenge notions of authority (who is an expert and who gets to speak?) and modes of representation (experiments with style, as in the concert reviews from *Musics*), but what we might call 'amateur arts journalism' takes place in spaces (whether ideological or geographical) very different from those where we find social movements or community groups. The dispersed nature of audiences, particularly specialist audiences, means that the medium becomes the space, the community forms itself within and around the medium. In the case of fanzines, for instance, it can be argued that the medium creates a community from a previously dispersed and atomised group of individuals, a very different notion of community from that considered by community media scholars.

Citizens' media: a radical form of community media

Studies of community media tend to focus on actually existing, geographically bounded communities, typically a city neighbourhood, a village, a housing estate. Community media develop to serve the interests of the inhabitants of these 'bounded' communities.

The argument on which the significance of community media rests is again one about media power and questions of media representation. Community media provide a signal example of how amateur media practices may be embedded in everyday life practices; they are already located in broader political, economic, social and cultural contexts. For those who might be tempted to dismiss community media as concerned with local trivia (though it is hard to see how one might think that, given the amount of work that has been done in documenting and exploring case studies across the world, some of which is documented in this *Companion*), Clemencia Rodríguez's (2011) study of rural Colombia stands as a powerful corrective.

Within local communities threatened by guerrilla warfare, paramilitary raids and drug traffickers, Rodríguez finds numerous examples of the creative deployment of community media in the service of local communities. These practices she conceptualises as 'citizens' media', a term that has a particular theoretical power for Rodríguez. First proposed in her *Fissures in the Mediascape* (2001), Rodríguez argues that the practice of citizens' media engages social groups (usually local neighbourhood communities or villages, but also groups of young people or women) in becoming 'active citizens' of their own locale. Building on Chantal Mouffe's notion of radical democracy, Rodríguez argues that by using media technologies to make films as well as radio and television programmes that embody their own situations, fears and dreams, local people trapped in cultures of violence can begin to realise their own methods of coping with that violence. As Rodríguez puts it, citizens' media can be thought of as the "lived experience of nonviolent ways to manage conflict, deal with difference, and interact with one another" (ibid.: 254). In short, local communities become engaged in everyday political action.

There are three key possibilities for citizens' media, Rodríguez argues. First, there is evidence that community media are being used to re-appropriate public spaces, to re-integrate communities and combat the isolation felt by communities in war zones (or war-like zones). Second, and consequently, such activities enable local participation in decision-making to be enhanced. Finally, at the heart of citizens' media is not the use of communication technologies to provide information or to represent experience, but media practice understood in a performative sense, where individuals and groups use media to experience the world as they construct it for themselves. Citizens' media entail a focus on members of a community as reflexive media producers. Audiences, in the sense of a distinct group of listeners, viewers or readers, seem to be absent from the kinds of media production Rodríguez conceptualises as citizens' media, where participation in media production and reflexive engagement in social structures are prioritised over the production of media texts for an 'absent' audience.

Should the absence of an audience trouble us? Does participation in the media ('becoming the media') offer a sufficient understanding of alternative media? Marisol Sandoval (2014) invites us to consider whether alternative media should be characterised by their opportunities for participation or by their potential to effect wider social and political change through critical content. Her question is a useful beginning, but I find its binary distinction a little blunt. Sandoval is quite rightly encouraging us to attend to the content of alternative media and not merely to valorise participation as an end in itself. I am not convinced that researchers have ignored content, but it can at times seem like that. Audiences for alternative media are often local; participation in the production of content can seem remarkable enough for that content to be put in the shade. After all, many studies emphasise – as I am doing in this introduction – questions of media power, social relations, authority and expertise as fundamental to the study of alternative media. Content (news, stories, narratives) are often presented as outcomes of active media participation; only rarely do they seem to be studied in their own right.

Content needs context, of course, and the diversity of alternative media presented in this *Companion* shows how content will always be linked with social, cultural and political contexts. It is a linkage that also suggests that we should view the search for audiences as differentially as we search for alternative media themselves. John Downing (2003) warns against reproducing the assumptions and aims of conventional audience research that focuses on demographics and treats audience research as a form of marketing. The rise of 'active audience' research as a challenge to the positioning of audiences as passive consumers is helpful here, but even that approach will have its limits (and the neologism 'prosumer' seems a little too pat to me). Audiences can be extremely small in number, often inevitably (a highly specialised fanzine might reach only a few dozen readers), at times deliberately (producing a limited number of a publication, whether for economic reasons or to emulate the culture of 'limited editions' in the art world).

It is not only Rodríguez's citizens' media that problematise the audience to the point of disappearance; some of the personal zines that form the subject of Stephen Duncombe's (1997) study seem to be produced almost as personal therapy: an audience (or at least one understood conventionally) seems irrelevant – again, transformation lies in the reflexive act of media production. Social movement media, while looking beyond a local geographic space, will tend to provide content that is orientated towards action ('mobilising information') and rationale (philosophy). Perhaps not intended to convert or even inform a broader audience, they provide platforms for education and information, for solidarity and growth. But we should not assume that audiences for alternative media will be necessarily distinct from other audiences, or that the former will never engage with other media products. A local radical newspaper may set itself up in competition with the local commercial press. Unlikely to compete economically or to take audiences away from its professional counterpart, the content of the radical press presents a comparative (and combative) supplement to dominant narratives. The studies of the Radical English press of the 1970s and 1980s, for example by Tony Harcup (2013) and the Minority Press Group (1980), provide vivid accounts of struggles over media power that are rooted in lived experience, from which springs a content of conviction and confrontation.

Diverse content, diverse audiences – to which we may add diverse practices. While the performativity of citizens' media might also be found in community media more widely (and there are examples in this *Companion*), we also need to take account of media practices that seek to communicate beyond a narrow community of media producers. Often these result in collaborative work between professional journalists and members of a community, where professionals offer training with technology, investigative techniques or writing. The aim here is to produce content that holds a critical position towards its subjects (whether these are people, such as local officials or politicians), but employs some of the narrative and representational conventions of professionalised media, the better to reach a wider audience. Elsewhere, professional journalists working within professional environments have brought together multiple narrative experiences of their readers (Kunelius and Renvall 2010). Rather than relying on the expert assessments of professional experts, the readers were considered experts by virtue of their direct experience (in this case of care homes for the elderly) and as capable of converting their witnessing into narratives. Kunelius and Renvall call this approach 'evocative communication' (ibid.: 518), one that uses a 'language of small pictures' to counterbalance the dominance of professionalised expertise and its 'language of the big picture' (ibid.: 523). It seems possible to practice journalism that brings together the craft skills of professional journalism with less regarded forms of storytelling to ask questions about power, ideology and representation.

This volume

Throughout this introduction I have tried to avoid a reductionist understanding of alternative and community media. It is unhelpful to provide a once-and-for-all definition of the subject. Instead, we need to take account of the situatedness of these media. We should examine them from the perspectives of history, geography, culture, politics and economics. Consequently, any collection of writings on alternative and community media can be neither comprehensive nor definitive. Instead, the *Companion* offers a multiplicity of perspectives. It examines the reasons why alternative and community media arise, how they develop in particular ways and in particular places, and how they can enrich our understanding of the broader media landscape and its place in society. The *Companion* aims to be inclusive in the following ways:

- It presents a range of theoretical and methodological positions and arguments, to demonstrate the dynamic, challenging and innovative thinking around the subject and to avoid reductionist approaches.
- The majority of the chapters engage with the evaluation of media practices, blurring the boundary between theory and practice, and examining the 'real world' implications of media practices. As a consequence, the *Companion* presents numerous case studies that are intended to stimulate dialogue and debate around the key issues identified earlier in this introduction: media power, representation, participation and citizenship.
- The discussion draws on research from different geographical and geopolitical contexts. In addition to research from the UK, the US, Canada, Europe and Australia, the *Companion* includes studies from Colombia, Haiti, India, South Korea and Zimbabwe. This enables international comparisons to be made, as well as enabling the problematisation of traditional (often Western) approaches to media studies.
- The *Companion* considers media practices across a range of cultures and communities, including indigenous media, the media of diasporic communities, experiments with global media and 'small nation' media.
- Many of its contributors demonstrate a reflexive engagement with their subject through direct involvement in a project, whether as journalists, trainers or

members of a community. Hybrid positions such as researcher-journalist and academic-trainer present opportunities for critical thinking that is situated in real-world concerns.

- The *Companion* demonstrates a commitment to interdisciplinarity in its presentation of research that locates media theory and practice in broader concerns of democracy, citizenship, social exclusion, race, class and gender.

In the next section of this introduction, I shall outline the rationale for the structure of the *Companion* and present a brief summary of each of its 50 chapters.

Structure and contents

The *Companion* is divided into six parts, each of which addresses a key theme in the study of alternative and community media. These are:

   I   Concepts
  II   Culture and society
 III   Policies and economies
  IV   Doing alternative journalism
   V   Communities and identities
  VI   Cultures of technology

The thematic organisation of the book is intended to help the reader navigate through what is a very diverse and, it might seem at times, a contradictory subject. Nevertheless, these themes should be not seen as discrete: they overlap and interpenetrate throughout the book. For example, chapters throughout the book deal with the concept of 'voice' in alternative media. Questions of technology do not appear in only one part of the book ('Cultures of technology'): they are present in almost every chapter to some degree. Readers who have an interest in particular media forms (such as television, radio, newspapers, online communication) will find chapters throughout the *Companion* to enable comparative approaches within and across these forms. Readers will also find studies of specific topics in more than one part. For example, those interested in studies of conflict reporting will find relevant chapters in Parts II, IV and V. Issues of media representation are considered most fully in Part IV ('Doing alternative journalism'), but representation is arguably the subject of every chapter. Conceptual and theoretical concerns are to be found in every chapter. That said, the *Companion* begins by setting out key issues in the conceptual and theoretical positioning of alternative and community media in Part I ('Concepts'). The first chapter, by Mike Mowbray, presents a critical overview of the major literature on alternative and community media, thus engaging with a number of other authors whose work appears in the *Companion* (including my own). Mowbray identifies four 'logics' that inform media practices and their theoretical positioning by researchers: participation; the formation of publics; the 'intellectual means of struggle'; and creativity. As the introductory chapter to this section and to the book as a whole, it stands as both overview and intervention, and as such sets the tone for the rest of the *Companion*. Herbert Pimlott's contribution (Chapter 2) might be read as an exploration of one outcome of Mowbray's logics. Arguing for the value of alternative media as strategic communication for social change, he offers a rethinking of the Leninist party newspaper that has conceptual implications for the historicisation and compartmentalisation of political media, as well as highlighting the practice of politics through socialist media.

Alternative media have often been characterised as 'giving voice to the voiceless', but too rarely is that claim defended conceptually. In Chapter 3, Nick Couldry considers the effectiveness of alternative media through a theorisation of voice that argues for a twofold understanding of the term: voice as process and voice as value. It is not enough to simply offer platforms for voice (the process of alternative media); voice must also be valued as part of wider processes that enable social change. In Chapter 4, Robert A. Hackett and Pinar Gurleyen address one of the key issues within the practice of alternative media: how the concept of objective journalism is complicated by 'alternative journalists'. Drawing on a range of practices, they argue that it is necessary to move beyond binary and oppositional thinking, and towards more nuanced and situated approaches to how news reporting is constructed within alternative media. Linda Jean Kenix (Chapter 5) argues for a convergence model of media practices that takes account of how alternative media place themselves (and are placed) within a wide media environment. This is not to ignore the distinctive features of alternative media, but rather to problematise their relationship with more dominant media ideologies and practices. James F. Hamilton (Chapter 6) argues that, in light of social media, features that once made alternative media unique – open access, interactivity, mobility – are now commonplace. Rather than reinventing alternative media, Hamilton argues, we might look to history in order to rethink 'media work' as 'cultural work'.

It has been said that the West provides theory and the rest of the world provides evidence. In Chapter 7, Wendy Willems challenges this notion by offering a rethinking of media theory that derives its power from 'the rest of the world', in this case from Africa. She argues for a 'dewesternising' of alternative media theory that shifts its analytical focus from media outputs to processes of mediation, and from civil society media to 'mediated civic agency'. In the final chapter of this part, John D. H. Downing (Chapter 8) begins by picking up Kenix's argument about avoiding the compartmentalisation of alternative media. He draws our attention to the language of research, in particular the metaphor. He shows how many metaphors encourage a static, structural and functionalist view of social phenomena, including alternative media. Kinetic and fluid metaphors, on the other hand, suggest ways of thinking about processes of change, development and volatility that are particularly appropriate to highly dynamic and emergent forms of media.

The chapters in the *Companion*'s second part, 'Culture and society', deal with the ways in which alternative and community media may be considered integral elements of wider cultural, social and political practices. Mojca Pajnik (Chapter 9) argues that if alternative media are to be effective in their political engagement, they need to engage their readers as 'active' citizens, and to be more than simply vehicles for representation. In Chapter 10, Camilo Pérez Quintero, Christian E. Ramírez Hincapié and Clemencia Rodríguez present case studies of the use of alternative media as performative communication. Based on Rodríguez's concept of citizens' media, they explore how community media are used as forms of resistance in conflict zones and how communities themselves may be transformed through such practices. Pradip Ninan Thomas's (Chapter 11) case study of the Right to Information Movement in India provides an opportunity to critique Westernised notions of alternative media and the public sphere. An acknowledgment of cultural context and the nature of political communication comes to the fore here, where alternative media practices privilege oral communication (both speaking and listening) and the local, collective relevance of that communication is preferred over more diffuse and simplified 'messages'. In Chapter 12, Michael Meadows uses a study of Indigenous broadcasting in Australia to consider the role of radio and television in indigenous cultures across the world, and in particular the maintenance of social networks, language and local traditions. Chapter 13 asks a fundamental question about media participation that has deep social implications: what is it that people become part of through participatory journalism? In this chapter, Laura Ahva, Heikki Heikkilä and Risto Kunelius consider what 'making a difference' through alternative media might mean and critically assess the potential of participation to effect political action. In the final chapter of this section, Christian Fuchs and Marisol Sandoval (Chapter 14) explore the contradictions revealed when a decentralised social movement (Occupy) makes use of highly centralised online communication systems (social media). They argue that, while the internet can benefit social movement media that relies on the effective, global mobilisation of its resources, asymmetrical relations of power and ownership of the medium can threaten autonomy and critical voices. The chapter concludes with a call for radical online media reform that brings together action from states and from civil society within states. In so doing, it forms a bridge to the next section, which deals with the questions of policy and economics.

Part III addresses two key forces with which projects of alternative and community media must often contend: the economics of production and the implications of government policy. Peter M. Lewis (Chapter 15) examines the history of the struggles for the recognition of community media by governments across the world and presents a case study of community radio in the UK to illuminate the challenges faced by community broadcasters. He concludes by arguing for an increased role for academics in the support of community media policy. In Chapter 16, Per Jauert reviews the growth of community media in the Nordic countries and analyses the changing functions and roles of public and private media. He asks a crucial question that is relevant to all forms of community media everywhere: are such media still recognised as important alternatives to the mainstream media by the citizens in the community? David Skinner (Chapter 17) reports on the diverse landscape of alternative and community media across Canada, taking in broadcasting, publishing, and internet sites and examining media set up by and for ethnic groups and aboriginal communities, among others. He notes the economic uncertainty that many endure and argues that more thoroughgoing programmes and policies support initiatives across the country. We turn to sub-Saharan Africa for the next chapter, in which Patrick E. Okon (Chapter 18) reports on efforts by community media activists in Ghana, Nigeria, and South Africa to effect media policy reform. The chapter highlights the interventionist role of alternative media groups beyond their role as news media and shows how different structures and strategies emerge under differing political conditions. William K. Carroll (Chapter 19) develops this theme further in his study of transnational alternative policy groups. These global organisations, he argues, form the 'next step' for alternative media organisations and social movements, acting as think tanks where policy might be developed to counter neoliberal globalisation and to mobilise the knowledge produced through alternative media. Much has been written about the supposed freedoms that the internet can bring to alternative media projects that are under-resourced and subject to government restrictions, particularly in the broadcast sector. Arne Hintz (Chapter 20) reports on the encroachment of the state into cyberspace and the increasing regulation of online communication. However, he also points to initiatives that seek to expand internet freedoms, either by technological experimentation or through policy advocacy.

In Chapter 21 we shift from questions of policy to problems of economics. Janey Gordon illuminates the tensions between the funders of community radio stations and the broadcasters themselves. She explores how community radio stations are funded in a number of countries globally and assesses the extent to which these models provide a degree of autonomy for the stations. Eun-Gyoo Kim (Chapter 22) offers insights into the complexities and particularities of media reform in South Korea. His analysis spans over twenty-five years of political and social change, and shows how forms and functions of alternative media can be intimately tied to civil society and movements for social change. Robin MacPherson (Chapter 23) moves us from the global to the concerns of a single country in his account of the development of radical filmmaking in Scotland. Tracing its history over a fifty-year period, he shows how currents and counter-currents of ideology, identity and institutional policy have come together to create an especially contested terrain of cultural production, one that has implications for creative practice more widely in Scotland and beyond. In the final chapter of this part, Daniel H. Mutibwa (Chapter 24) presents a pragmatic and sobering analysis of third-sector media production. Through four case studies from Germany and the UK, he demonstrates how the socio-political ambitions of media projects are tempered by professional and commercial considerations. Projects that aim to be autonomous and distinctive attempts at communication can often fail in their ambitions, a finding that has implications for theorising alternative media and for how funding of projects might be sustained.

Part IV ('Doing alternative journalism') explores a range of principles and practices of producing the journalism that lies at the heart of much alternative media. This part also provides contextual and comparative material within which alternative journalism may be situated. Susan Forde's (Chapter 25) survey of research in the field identifies key problems and issues central to the planning and practising of alternative journalism. She points to a diversity of approaches, from historical 'heroes' to contemporary, collaborative forms of news sourcing and storytelling, arguing that common to all these approaches is a commitment to journalism as a political act. Digital media are the subject of Leah A. Lievrouw's (Chapter 26) account of the integration of digital technologies and news. She identifies three themes that emerge from integration: news as process; the segmentation and segregation of content and readers; and changing news ethics and values. Significantly, these are as much matters of concern to dominant media institutions as they are to alternative and community media organisations, an observation that illuminates commonalities across a range of practices. That is not to deny important differences: much alternative journalism is distinguished by its rejection of objectivity in favour of an explicitly partisan and personally engaged practice. This does not equate, however, to a rejection of ethics, as Tony Harcup (Chapter 27) argues in his exploration of alternative journalism practices in the UK. Alternative journalism does not always require entirely novel ways of making the news; standard reporting techniques have often been used to uncover stories ignored by the professional media. Harcup draws our attention to the common cause that can exist between the classes of media and concludes that we should not separate the practice of journalism from ethical practice: they can 'perhaps best be understood as being one and the same thing'. Jane Regan (Chapter 28) invokes two hundred years of journalism history in her evaluation of a collaborative news project in Haiti. While 'local' in reach, she argues that the project is global in inspiration and questions the continuing utility of terms such as 'alternative' and 'mainstream' to describe practices that are interwoven from as many different sources as Haiti Grassroots Watch. Richard Lance Keeble (Chapter 29) argues that there are specific topics on which alternative media have reported, which the mass media have tended to ignore, marginalise or belittle. The practice of peace journalism seeks to uncover the 'invisible effects of violence' and, in its focus on the marginalised and the 'voiceless', might be seen as an ideal-typical form of alternative journalism, as well as one that is structurally and ideologically opposed to what its practitioners and advocates see as a reductionist and propagandist mass media.

The notion of citizen journalists is a highly visible (and highly contested) feature in studies of alternative journalism; it is also of great interest to professional journalists, whether sceptics or proponents. Questions routinely asked about citizen journalists include: do they threaten the professional role of the journalist? Are they merely forms of cheap or free labour for the mass media? Are they journalists at all, or merely inexpert commentators? The final five chapters in Part Four explore the role and practices of citizen journalism. Mary Angela Bock (Chapter 30) sees citizen journalism as a practice of 'routine truth-telling' that is best understood by locating it within the interpretative communities from which it develops and where it is of most relevance. Rather than focusing on the status of the reporter as a journalist in the accepted sense, we might consider citizen journalists as bearing witness to human events in the world. Stuart Allan's chapter (Chapter 31) develops his earlier work on citizen witnessing to focus on what has long been the preserve of the professional, photojournalism. But rather than finding a mimicking of professional standards and expectations, Allan argues that citizen photojournalism suggests radical ways of reframing events through its 'authority of presence'. Hayley Watson and Kush Wadhwa (Chapter 32) study what they term 'independent citizen journalists', to distinguish their identities and practices from those whose work is routinely used (and often generated) by the mass media. Watson and Wadhwa present an underresearched topic in the field (reporting on terrorism) to illuminate how independent citizen journalists have developed their news-gathering practices, what challenges they face and what problems their practices might pose for the practice of journalism more widely. Axel Bruns (Chapter 33) explores citizen journalism as a form of social media, drawing attention to its development and transformation through online platforms. Bruns avoids the trap of technological determinism by locating his study historically as the latest manifestation of a sociocultural engagement with technology that goes back centuries; instances of 'citizen journalism' as a social practice always draw on the publishing tools at hand. Kerrie Foxwell-Norton (Chapter 34) highlights the tensions in the citizen reporting of environmental issues. She examines the problematic nature of citizen participation in environmental policy, arguing that if the environment is to have a voice, local community media is a powerful place for that voice. How, though, to reconcile national and international policy-making with local communication structures? In answering this question, Foxwell-Norton argues for a closer relationship of 'ecological democracy' with media democracy.

Part V ('Communities and identities') engages with media practices that are focused on the interests of specific communities, as well as practices that have the capacity to do more than merely report. All the chapters are concerned with media practices that play an active role in identity formation within communities. Some earlier chapters have already touched on similar issues (for example, in Parts II and IV); Part V presents seven case studies that enable a more focused reflection on the nature of community and identity in alternative media. One such approach is that of digital storytelling, intended to help 'ordinary people' marginalised in dominant media cultures develop techniques for self-representation and social participation. Christina Spurgeon and Jean Burgess's (Chapter 35) case study of the Center for Digital Storytelling demonstrates how collaborative workshops are able to build trust, solidarity and narrative capacity among non-professional media producers. Olga Guedes Bailey (Chapter 36) explores the role of the media in diasporic communities. She emphasises the possibilities for alternative media to not only contribute to the maintenance of identity within diasporas, but also to foster multicultural dialogue within and across cultures. Rather than diasporic media encouraging separatism and division, they can offer opportunities for participation and representation in the wider public sphere. In Chapter 37, Heather Anderson reports on a largely unregarded aspect of community media, the use of radio by prisoners and prisoners' support groups. Whether originating within prisons or through public radio stations, prisoners' radio enables prisoners, ex-prisoners and their friends and families to discuss public and private elements of life behind bars. Anderson explores how prisoners' radio also fosters connections to the wider community by producing alternative discourses about prison life that enrich the public sphere. My own contribution (Chapter 38) looks at the history of the fanzine, amateur magazines produced by enthusiasts of various aspects of popular culture. I have two particular interests in this chapter: first, to explore the connections between amateur writing and arts journalism; second, to report on how online platforms are transforming these forms of amateur journalism. Bart Cammaerts (Chapter 39) draws on the work of Michel Foucault to explore the use of media by social movements. The use of media to build the collective identity of a movement tends to be seen as an inward-looking process. By deploying Foucault's notion of technologies of self, Cammaerts argues that this process can also have an important outward aspect, where social movement media play a crucial role in presenting the movement to the world through reflexive processes of disclosure, self-examination and archiving. Social movement media are also examined by Dorothy Kidd (Chapter 40), whose study of the global Occupy movement illuminates aspects of the movement that have tended to be sidelined by commentators who see only a failure to change state or corporate institutions. Instead, Kidd argues for the prefigurative contribution of Occupy to the development of a participatory politics, a contribution that emphasises the principle of democratic communication as fundamental to the struggle for a direct, 'grassroots' democracy. In the last chapter of this part, Tony Dowmunt (Chapter 41) brings his extensive experience of working with indigenous media organisations to bear on a crucial question of community media production: what are the benefits that it brings to indigenous communities? As he looks for an answer, Dowmunt explores disputes about media ideologies and technologies, struggles over representation and, most importantly, whether it is possible to find the value of community media for the communities themselves.

The final part of the *Companion* ('Cultures of technology') presents a range of current thinking about technology. Technology, though, is never considered for its own sake and each chapter locates technological practices within broader discussions of economics, culture and society. Nico Carpentier, Vaia Doudaki and Yiannis Christidis (Chapter 42) explore internal struggles over technology within community media organisations and external struggles within regulatory environments. By applying Chantal Mouffe's notion of agonism to their account of these struggles, the authors argue that conflicts are never transitory or trivial, but instead are a necessary part of developing participatory media. Moreover, the problem-solving strategies of such media have the capacity to enhance a wider democratic culture. In Chapter 43, Hayes Mawindi Mabweazara reports on the latest wave of pirate or underground radio stations that transmit to Zimbabwe. His case studies of two stations illuminate how digital technologies have radically transformed the production, transmission as well as reception practices of traditional pirate radio in Africa. Using visual anthropology as a starting point, Kirsten MacLeod's (Chapter 44) exploration of community media projects in Scotland argues for their status as social processes that nurture knowledge through participation in production. As participants engage in the technical aspects of production, she argues, they come to create their own sites of knowledge production, which in turn are able to develop relations and networks within and across communities. Collaborative media production within digital arts is the focus of Adnan Hadzi's (Chapter 45) study of the use of open-source software by a radical community television project. The open-source platform of FLOSSTV and its materials is available to all participants through a digital commons approach to software and, Hadzi argues, enables collaborative production methods that blur the boundary between producers and consumers. Thomas Poell and José van Dijck (Chapter 46) argue that the rise of communication through social media has led to a shift in the distribution of media power, with activists much less dependent on television and mainstream newspapers to influence public opinion. Drawing on examples from the Arab Spring and the Occupy protests, the chapter shows that social media allow activists, under the right conditions, to directly communicate with very large publics. Nevertheless, activist communication does not remain immune to the dominant technological and commercial mechanisms that drive social media systems and that have the potential to undermine the long-term efficacy of such communication.

Megan Boler (Chapter 47) focuses on an under-researched question in alternative and community media studies: what motivates people to engage in the production of alternative media? She finds that participants often offer complex and articulated reasons that go beyond simple dissatisfaction and distrust with dominant media, instead pointing to a desire to create communities as well as reach out to wider publics. Stefania Milan (Chapter 48) examines the philosophies and practices of a very specific form of collective activism, that of 'hacktivism', a form of protest that deliberately attacks the infrastructure of electronic networks (broadly speaking, the internet) in the interests of social change. She examines the ethics and politics of hacktivists, and explores the extent to which hacktivism may be considered a vanguard that is representative of a wider social movement beyond its own community. A very different form of media practice is unravelled by Victoria Esteves and Graham Meikle (Chapter 49) in their exploration of internet memes. The apparently random images of 'doges' and 'lolcats' are harnessed to many kinds of communication: absurd humour, satire, commercial critique. These images and their accompanying texts can also be seen as exemplifying the 'fundamental aesthetics and production logics of the remix culture' of social media. Beyond their apparent triviality, internet memes may be understood as a powerful means of intercreativity, as collaborative processes of making and sharing meaning. Finally, Jennifer Rauch (Chapter 50) draws the *Companion* to a close with some reflections on the 'Slow Media' movement, whose proponents aim to transform our thinking about mediated communication and digital media through a critique of 'speed' in daily life. Slow Media activism does not take a Luddite approach to digital technology and aim for its removal. Instead, it offers a critique of technological 'progress' as well as a critique of corporate and commercial culture. Seen in this light, the Slow Media movement has much in common with those individuals, communities, organisations and projects that appear throughout the *Companion* as producers, users and proponents of alternative and community media.

References

Allan S. (2013) *Citizen Witnessing: Revisioning Journalism in Times of Crisis*. Cambridge: Polity Press.

Allen, P. (1985) "*Socialist Worker* – Paper with a purpose." *Media, Culture and Society*, 7, 205–32.

Atton, C. (2002) *Alternative Media*. London: Sage.

Couldry, N. (2000) *The Place of Media Power: Pilgrims and Witnesses of the Media Age*. London and New York: Routledge.

——(2010) *Why Voice Matters: Culture and Politics after Neoliberalism*. London: Sage.

Couldry, N. and Curran, J. (2003) "The paradox of media power." In Couldry, N. and Curran, J. (eds.) *Contesting Media Power: Alternative Media in a Networked World*. Lanham, MD: Rowman and Littlefield (pp. 3–15).

Downing, J. D. H. (1980) *The Media Machine*. London: Pluto Press.

——(1984) *Radical Media: The Political Experience of Alternative Communication*. Boston, MA: South End Press.

——(2003) "Audiences and readers of alternative media: The absent lure of the virtually unknown." *Media, Culture and Society*, 25(5), 625–45.

——(Ford, T. V., Gil, G. and Stein, L.) (2001) *Radical Media: Rebellious Communication and Social Movements*. Thousand Oaks, CA: Sage.

Duncombe, S. (1997) *Notes from Underground: Zines and the Politics of Alternative Culture*. London: Verso.

Harcup, T. (2013) *Alternative Journalism, Alternative Voices.* London: Routledge.

Kunelius, R. and Renvall, M. (2010) "Stories of a public: Journalism and the validity of citizens' testimonies." *Journalism: Theory, Practice and Criticism*, 11(5), 515–29.

Melucci, A. (1996) *Challenging Codes: Collective Action in the Information Age.* Cambridge: Cambridge University Press.

Minority Press Group (1980) *Here Is the Other News: Challenges to the Local Commercial Press* (Minority Press Group Series No. 1). London: Minority Press Group.

Rodríguez, C. (2001) *Fissures in the Mediascape: An International Study of Citizens' Media.* Cresskill, NJ: Hampton Press.

——(2011) *Citizens' Media Against Armed Conflict: Disrupting Violence in Colombia.* Minneapolis: University of Minnesota Press.

Sandoval, M. (2014) "Alternative Media – Participation and Critique." Heathwood Press, www.heathwoodpress.com/alternative-media-participation-and-critique-marisol-sandoval/ (accessed 18 June 2014).

Sparks, C. (1985) "The working-class press: Radical and revolutionary alternatives." *Media, Culture and Society*, 7, 133–46.

Part I
CONCEPTS

1
ALTERNATIVE LOGICS?
Parsing the literature on alternative media

Mike Mowbray

A distinct body of academic work has taken shape under the rubric of 'alternative media' and its cognate terms, consolidated and rapidly expanding from roughly 2000–2001. Writing a decade prior to this surge in scholarly production, Jassem (1990: 12) suggested that often "it is not entirely clear" what we mean by the term. Numerous subsequent articles have departed from a similar premise – and despite the volume and variety of work that has come on the heels of this assertion, which has treated a wide variety of objects (texts, practices, forms of organisation) and generated diverse theoretical accounts, the problem has yet to be dispensed with. Andersson (2012: 755), for example, suggests that there still exists an "uncertainty as to whether 'alternative media' … is an analytical construction," or remains in the imprecise realm of 'common-sense' concepts derived from everyday language, thin on coherence and specificity. While some may prefer to move among the abundance of cognate terms suggested to delimit, nuance, and subdivide the conceptual territory (e.g., radical, independent, participatory, community, grassroots, citizens', autonomous, tactical, critical, or social movement media), a pluralism that could be seen to evade the initial definitional quandary, others find the ubiquitous 'alternative' moniker a useful umbrella under which to consolidate broader discussion. On the whole, it seems that questions of differential emphasis and conceptualisation among scholars are (still) in need of some sorting out.

Couldry and Curran (2003: 7) suggest a 'minimal definition' of alternative media: "media production which challenges, at least implicitly, actual concentrations of media power, whatever form those concentrations may take in different locations." 'Alternative' stands as a "more flexible, *comparative* term, since it involves no judgments about the empowering effects of the media practices analyzed" (ibid.). This definition presents a necessary but not sufficient condition for a more explicitly politicised conception. Contesting "media power" is among the basic prerequisites of contemporary social struggle. As Couldry elaborates (2003: 39):

> To contest media power is to contest the way social reality itself is defined or named (cf. Carey, 1989; Melucci, 1996). This is no easy thing, since it involves contesting the prevailing definitions of what is socially contestable; in particular, it means contesting media institutions' preeminent position as our frame onto the 'realities' of the social world.

Theoretical efforts in the field of alternative media studies almost invariably address fundamentally normative problems, whether implicitly or explicitly. The question of 'empowering effects', or of the political implications of certain media practices, forms of organisation, or content, is next to impossible to evade. Indeed, such considerations are intrinsic both to the *raison(s) d'être* of alternative media projects as conceptualised by practitioners and to typical justifications for their study by scholars.

Some authors foreground the specific political valence of 'alternative media' or their preferred cognate. Downing (2001: xi), for example, writes in the introduction to his book *Radical Media* that "alternative media generally serve two overriding purposes: (a) to express opposition vertically from subordinate quarters directly at the power structure and against its behaviour; (b) to build support, solidarity and networking laterally against policies or even against the very survival of the power structure." His general position is echoed by Hackett and Carroll (2006: 58), who indicate a range of content-focused criteria when they assert that:

> in political orientation and content, the 'ideal' alternative medium is progressive, explicitly opposed to particular axes of domination (corporate capitalism, heterosexism, racism, state authoritarianism), openly assumes a stance of advocacy rather than pseudo-'objectivity', experiments with new aesthetic styles, and accesses voices and issues marginalized in hegemonic media.

Others are more circumspect in connecting definitions and examples with counter-hegemonic oppositional struggles (whether at the level of particular axes of domination or aiming at broad socio-political transformation), preferring to focus on more limited normative implications closer to the consensus values of public-sphere liberalism. On both sides of this continuum, we are called upon to attend to two interrelated levels of impact that alternative media projects might have: (1) subjective individual and immediate group-level impacts for participants in production; (2) broad social and political impacts related to public-formation, group representation, political deliberation, contestation and social movement formation/mobilisation. Specific projects, practices and texts in circulation mediate complex social-political processes from the level of subject-formation and individual consciousness to that of the relational status of groups (defined by identity and status criteria or competencies connected to social location: social, cultural and economic capital) as manifest in media systems, and draw attention to fundamental questions over the representation of interests, problems and possibilities for emancipatory change in extant configurations of social and political power.

Uzelman (2011: 29) raises the concern that some work in the field of alternative media studies suffers from what he calls a "determinism of technique" whereby "particular techniques are assumed to have effects (generally positive) independent of the social relations in which they are embedded or the purposes to which they are directed" – a problem exacerbated by fuzzy definitional work and reticence to think examples through in terms of all the key criteria we might adduce to alternative media. Avoiding both determinism and crude instrumentalism, it is necessary to attend not only to the relative novelty of particular examples (of technological developments, aesthetic innovations, original organisational forms) but to the social and political *effects* both aimed at and in fact produced at different levels of scale.

In seeking to parse the numerous and varied emphases and conceptual elaborations in the field of academic literature on alternative media, I propose to consider four 'alternative logics': *participatory logics, logics of (counter-)public-formation and facilitation, critical-emancipatory logics* and *heterodox-creative logics*. I wish to suggest that these 'logics' represent the primary types of impetus embedded in alternative media projects, and stand out as predominant axes of theoretical description and differentiation. Each, albeit occurring and expressed in multiple variants, represents a *relatively* distinct cluster of normative principles orienting action and innovation in particular projects. Importantly, each is also liable to operate in different political registers. By dint of differing conceptualisations loosely consistent with each general logic, a continuum may be identified within each between liberal- and radical-democratic (or counter-hegemonic) concepts and functions.

Those tendencies that I have grouped under the rubric of *logics of (counter-)public-formation and facilitation* and of *logics of participation*, broadly speaking, are manifest in the form and (emergent) structure of communicative relations constituted through practices of media production and/or circulation and engagement with texts. Those loosely assembled as *critical-emancipatory logics* and as *heterodox-creative logics* are manifest in the *form* and *content* of media texts. Their mutual imbrication in practice is such that each 'logic' identified here at times shades into another; considered as an ensemble, the possibilities within each conceptual cluster tending towards the radical-democratic pole of the continuum do so insofar as they imply (or even appear to mutually presuppose) the others, as I will seek to demonstrate in exploring each in turn.

Logics of participation

In the contemporary literature on alternative media, the most basic variant of what I'm calling *logics of participation* is immediately identifiable in Clemencia Rodríguez's description of the "polymorphic ensemble" of so-called *citizens' media* as "expressions of the same drive – citizens attempting to break into the established mediascape, citizens' elbowing their way into a fissure where their own voices – and whatever they have to say can have a presence in the public realm" (2001: 165). Concern for participation as *self-representation* (at an individual level, but perhaps more importantly at the level of oppressed groups) and as the substitution or supplement of a grassroots alternative allowing public voice to those effectively excluded from mainstream media discourse fits well with Couldry and Curran's 'minimal' definition of alternative media cited in the introduction. Such a conceptualisation keys on *access* to the means of media production and to the terrain of media representation, and generally (above and beyond that 'minimal definition') implies *capacity-building* or *empowering* effects.

Uzelman (2011: 27) points out that alternative media's 'accessibility' is a 'crucial characteristic' for scholar James F. Hamilton (2000) (as it is for Rodríguez), citing three important dimensions identified in his work: "(1) low barriers to participation (e.g., time, distance, money and training); (2) a non-corporate, 'spontaneous' mode of organisation requiring little capital; (3) integration with 'other realms of life'."

Accessibility tends to be construed as offering broad-based, *direct* participation in media production, especially to those least well represented in mainstream media and the discourse of dominant publics. Further synthesising Hamilton's work with that of other prominent authors in the field, Uzelman (2011: 28) suggests that "direct participation in media production as opposed to professionalised content creation" and "the need for possibilities of dialogic or horizontal communication rather than hierarchical, point-to-mass communication" are common elements.

In the context of apparent 'communicative abundance' facing many of us in the contemporary world (especially in the Global North), it is important to differentiate *superficial* modes of participation from what I would term *intensive* modes. In a superficial mode, logics of participation end up reduced simply to the possibility for each and all to circulate contributions to an imagined communicative agora (a liberal platitude), as in the case of some less cautious accounts of the significance of networked and mobile communications technologies. Dean (2008: 109–10), along these lines, has sought to describe how 'communicative capitalism' both produces and thrives upon 'a fantasy of participation' in which our individual desire to see our contributions take a place in the circulation of content online works to displace real-world struggles, and technology acts as a fetish "helping us understand ourselves as active" (ibid.).

In marked contrast to notions of participation marked by the fetish of the contribution – or the minimal forms of participation allowed the 'managed public' of call-ins and letters to the editor – are accounts in line with Downing's (2001: 72) presentation of the 'self-management' model of organisation as a site for prefigurative politics, characterised by horizontal forms which actively "develop participation by all historically extruded groups" in decision-making and carve out a microcosm of anti-authoritarian self-organisation that might be seen, as the oft-repeated IWW slogan would have it, "to carve out a new world in the shell of the old". In such *intensive* modes, logics of participation imply relatively direct, reciprocal and dialogic relationships and communicative exchanges among those involved in media production – an emphasis on concrete, collective interactive processes characterised by agonistic exchange and by process-based anti-oppressive practice in the context of particular (often small-scale) projects. They also suggest the possibility, if not the necessity, of implication at multiple levels: participation in the generation of content, in quotidian management, and in overall direction.

Downing, of course, has always been certain to emphasise that his interest lies with media that facilitate broad-based participation – and which also work to perpetuate emancipatory radical-democratic social movements that challenge the state and other privileged sites of power. The question of whether political ends characterised in terms of hegemonic struggle are to be prioritised relative to more immediate (intensive) 'participatory' emphases, however, can be a point of contention. Thus, as Uzelman (2011: 29) summarises, elements of the participatory tendency within recent alternative media studies may be seen as "indicative of a broader shift away from a narrow conception of politics as struggle for control of, or influence on, apparatuses of power and towards one that also emphasises the construction of new, more liberating relationships and emancipated subjectivities in the present".

Taking up the implications of such a rhetorical contrast, recent polemic interventions by the media theorist Christian Fuchs (2010), and by Sandoval and Fuchs (2010), imply a dim view of the implications of an ostensibly excessive focus on such direct and collective forms of intensive participation. Sandoval and Fuchs (2010: 142) argue that participatory approaches "dominate the field of alternative media studies", and that such approaches are "insufficient because they tend to idealize small-scale production and to neglect orientation toward the political public" (Fuchs, 2010: 174). Pointedly, Fuchs points to "the danger that small-scale local alternative projects will develop into psychological self-help initiatives without political relevance that are more bourgeois individualist self-expressions than political change projects" (ibid.: 189). Wishing to move away from the allegedly excessive focus on small-scale projects (and the micro-political implications of prefigurative organisational forms), Sandoval and Fuchs (2010: 143) insist that "[a] statement that does not reach the masses is not a significant statement at all, only an individual outcry that remains unheard and hence ineffective".

Problems such as how to reconcile normative commitment to intensive modes of participation with large-scale political questions are abiding concerns – and any account of alternative media, or any given empirical case, stands to be evaluated in part upon the basis of the degree of emphasis accorded to *logics of participation* over other logics, how 'participation' is conceptualised (as a simple 'reversal of circuits' or as a more substantive reconfiguration of communicative relationships; as a question of the right of each and all to communicate or as a question of unequal access to representation on the basis of social position and status), and how this conceptual cluster of concerns fits in with other prerogatives.

Logics of (counter-)public formation and facilitation

As with *logics of participation*, *logics of (counter-)public formation and facilitation* encompass a loose conceptual cluster across different works/projects, and such logics tend to manifest in different political registers, sometimes in significant tension with one another. A key axis of tension lies along the lines of Christians et al.'s (2009) distinction between *facilitative* and *radical* normative theories of the social and political role of media/journalism. The 'facilitative' role can be expressed effectively in terms supplied by Coleman and Ross (2010: 92), situating alternative media as "enriching the pluralism of the public sphere" and pushing the 'general public' into more-or-less-consensual self-transformation. Emphasis in this register promotes a focus on media projects which seek to account for diversity, polysemy and contention in the construction of mediated publics, and upon fostering attention, engagement, and public dialogue among sectors of the nominal community, typically with an emphasis on working within existing political structures. Such a role is largely consistent with a ubiquitous public sphere liberalism (Hackett and Carroll, 2006) that takes up an idealised notion of Habermas's (1989) concept of public sphere as a site of communicative exchange and rational deliberation, exercising an effective influence on the power of the state, in which particular interests are set aside in the name of the common good.

By contrast, Negt and Kluge's (1993[1972]) notion of the 'counterpublic' can be characterised as "a site filled with struggle, protest, fantasy, and opposition against bourgeois public spheres of production and communication practice" (Goodnight, 1997: 271). Both concepts (public and counterpublic) refer to the construction of collective identity (and identification) across difference, but the emphasis is decidedly different. Rather than a space of consensus-oriented deliberation, the latter conceptualisation emphasises 'an arena of contested meanings', saturated with real power relations (Eley, 1992: 325). Nancy Fraser (1992: 123) theorises the public sphere (writ large) as that of a 'dominant public,' pointing up the illusory nature of formal status equality in situations of structural inequality, and describes counterpublic spheres as "parallel discursive arenas where members of subordinated social groups invent and circulate counterdiscourses to formulate oppositional interpretations of their identities, interests and needs".

The significance of alternative media is highlighted when we consider that the formation of publics or counterpublics as a *communicative social process* is significantly enabled by the circulation of texts (Warner, 2002). Publics, for Warner, are generated and maintained in multiple and overlapping instantiations through common attention, identification and reflexive engagement with texts. Importantly, counterpublics are brought into being by individuals' activity rather than any ascribed characteristic or 'objective' social status or position, and their continued existence depends upon the voluntarily deployed attention and activity of members.

In thinking specifically about *logics of (counter-)public formation and facilitation*, we are also drawn to elucidate more clearly the context of production as a social space extending far beyond the immediate level of the radical newspaper or the community radio station (characterised in terms of class and status group, culture and subculture, indicating questions such as those of speech genre and style raised by Warner). Following Fraser (and with an eye to Fuchs's reservations about excessive focus on *logics of participation*), we are called to consider the degree to which particular projects either facilitate processes internal to counterpublics or serve to expand them and exert meaningful effect at the level of the dominant public sphere. We are led to question exactly what *effects* alternative media in circulation might have through uptake and engagement, highlighting what Downing (2003) and Atton (2009: 274) suggest is an almost completely neglected area: inquiry into the audiences and reception of alternative media output. As Couldry (2010: 26) suggests, it may be useful to "understand better how particular media contribute to everyday practice, and not just that of the producers themselves" – a question manifestly relevant to "the larger disciplinary question of whether alternative media research should be seen primarily as the analysis of social movement or the analysis of processes of mediation".

Critical-emancipatory logics

Critical-emancipatory logics may be considered primarily at the level of *content* and *form*, working though circulation among (potential or nascent) counterpublics and characterised by an alternative political vision. At a basic level (though the cited author here intends to suggest that this is on its own a somewhat reductive vision), we might point to a division by which, as James F. Hamilton puts it, "'mainstream' [may be] seen as maximizing audiences by appealing to safe, conventional formulas, and 'alternative' foregoing the comfortable, depoliticizing formulas to advocate programs of social change" (cited in Elghul-Bebawi, 2009: 21) – a split, as it were, between media 'agents of social reproduction' and 'agents of social change'. Such logics key on what scholars such as Downing (2001) and Bailey, Cammaerts and Carpentier (2008) describe as the 'counter-hegemonic' function of alternative (or radical) media. Such media express "an alternative vision to hegemonic policies, priorities and perspectives" (Downing, 2001: v); they are associated with "educational and transformative possibilities" which may be connected to "sociocultural or sociopolitical projects ... aimed at social change" (Atton, 2002: 153).

Taking a cue from the critical theory of Horkheimer, Marcuse and others, Sandoval and Fuchs (2010: 146) suggest that critical media necessarily "make the judgment that structures of oppression and exploitation benefit certain classes at the expense of others and hence should be radically transformed by social struggles". Following Negt and Kluge, Fuchs (2010: 176) conceptualises 'alternative media' – or 'critical media' – as 'intellectual means of struggle', and argues that in identifying this sort of media (as opposed to primary concern with *organisation* and *process*), "form and content are considered decisive" (ibid.: 188).

An emphasis on content (and its effective circulation at the level of 'the political public') prompts an evaluation of such logics in terms of the symbolic and discursive bases upon which social actors might seek to interpellate and persuade individuals, constitute counterpublics, contribute to the composition of social movements, approach the broader (dominant) public sphere and seek to effect political change. Key questions here turn not only on the substantive analysis of structures of oppression and domination, but on extant *discursive* (as opposed to *structural*) opportunities and constraints (cf. Cammaerts, 2012). Critical or oppositional content, as Fuchs (2010: 179) summarises:

> provides alternatives to dominant repressive heteronomous perspectives that reflect the rule of capital, patriarchy, racism, sexism, nationalism, etc. Such content expresses oppositional standpoints that question all forms of heteronomy and domination. So there is counter-information and counter-hegemony that includes the voices of the excluded, the oppressed, the dominated, the enslaved, the estranged, the exploited, and the dominated. One aim is to give voices to the voiceless, media power to the powerless as well as to transcend the filtering and censorship of information monopolies, state monopolies or cultural monopolies in public information and communication.

Critical-emancipatory logics are instantiated in ideology critique and expressions of radical imagination, explicitly opposed to 'particular axes of domination', and dedicated to connecting diverse struggles; they are, distilled at the level of content and form, resources for a counter-hegemonic project.

Heterodox-creative logics

Heterodox-creative logics are exemplified in a concern with the production of 'culturally radical' content and aesthetic innovations (Atton, 2002: 27). Questions of *aesthetic form* are of primary concern. *Heterodox-creative logics*, in the context of our discussion of the ensemble of *logics* that characterise alternative media, imply attention generally to intersections between (innovative) aesthetic practices and progressive or radical politics. From the outset, a distinction needs to be made between a politically engaged practice of aesthetic creation and an abstruse pursuit of perpetual novelty under the rubric of 'art for art's sake' – a distinction anchored in the history of competing and contra-dictory twentieth-century modernisms. Among twentieth-century avant-garde move-ments, currents committed to the former furnish a number of paradigm cases. Berlin dada, for example, stands out as a politically committed, if inchoate, group repre-senting "one of the first major attempts to bridge and even abolish the gap between 'high' elitist art and 'low' popular culture" (Sheppard, 2000: 171).

Montage, the most distinctive Berlin dada aesthetic technique, was deployed to create cut-and-paste assemblages of photographic fragments and snippets of text pilfered from popular media (newspapers, magazines, print advertisements and propaganda posters), typically questioning the war propaganda of the German state and the ideological claims of wartime reactionaries and Weimar capitalists. The method itself is transparent artifice; examples from this period make no effort to put up a seamless front. It is also an eminently replicable technique, with popular resonance to the present day. James F. Hamilton (2001: 159) identifies montage as "a popularly available means of visual critique" which consists in "the selection, editing or altering of existing images, phrases or symbols, and their reassembly into a new work that expresses a critique of the dominant". Considering the conditions of emergence of the technique – not only in Berlin, but also simultaneously among US radical labour activists and others – Hamilton (ibid.: 163) notes that "the targets of critique were local manifestations of a generalised social, political, and economic order intertwined with the media industries"; examples of politicised montage critiqued both particular ideologies and the mode of their perpetuation via media spectacle. The acts of de- and re-contextualisation, of juxtaposition and recomposition, that this kind of aesthetic practice entails are, he suggests, much more than a *merely* formal innovation.

The influence of Dada on later twentieth-century, politically inflected art movements – and political movements with aesthetic concerns, such as the Situationists who sought a "fluid language of anti-ideology" (Debord, 1994[1967]: §208) in techniques of re-contextualisation and juxtaposition – is well documented, and the view of aesthetic techniques like montage espoused by Hamilton finds resonance with practices well outside the field of art as such. On the one hand, we have accounts such as Duncombe's (2008: 132–34) take on the zines of the 1980s and 1990s, in which he highlights the way the cut-up amateurism of such "cheap, multiple-copy objects" (ibid.: 133) represents a politically important aesthetic form precisely insofar as it stands in contrast to the "slick, polished, seamless" façade of professionalised media production and thus both elicits a distancing effect in contrast to the immersive qualities of consumer spectacle and instantiates, represents, and encourages the diffusion of a participatory 'do-it-yourself' (sub)culture. On the other, we might locate examples such as the *Adbusters* version of culture jamming as neo-Situationist practice. At its best, as Nomai (2008: 31) suggests:

> Culture jamming, by and large, does not directly confront its target of critique.
> Instead, the critique within culture jamming texts shrouds itself in the very

language, symbols and aesthetics of its intended target. Culture jammers, then, rarely present their criticism in a straightforward manner. Instead, viewers of these jams are first confronted by what seems on the surface to be an original, until further inspection reveals it as a copy that is a repudiation of the original.

While the above account presents a lineage often evoked in the contemporary literature on alternative media, and a potent (if sometimes ambivalent) illustration of what I would classify as *heterodox-creative logics*, the emphasis on visual modes of representation should not be taken as exhaustive of the category. The innovative rhetorical form and news values associated with the underground journalism of the 1960s and 1970s (Johnson, 1971) could be presented as another example at the level of written language, where practitioners sought explicitly to work against the grain of traditional journalistic 'regimes of objectivity' (Hackett and Zhao, 1998; cf. Hackett and Gurleyen, Chapter 4, this volume) by taking up an informal mode of address, jettisoning any aversion to evaluative statements, deploying personalised narratives, and taking up an implicit standpoint epistemology or a 'declared bias' in solidarity with those who struggle against oppression and domination. Like other possible examples, it is essential here to consider the possible gulf between *intent* and *effect*, and to recognise that the potential impact of variance in form is highly situational: alternative techniques deployed in some underground journalism shaped a form and practice that was significant in a given historical moment, standing in contrast to the conventional ubiquity of certain mid-twentieth-century journalistic conventions.

In essence, attention to *heterodox-creative logics* leads us to consider the politics of form in connection with different media artefacts and modes of communication. Aesthetic form is undoubtedly significant (whether at the level of the banal taken-for-granted or of showy attempts at cultural intervention), if not always easily evaluated in terms of its effects. The contention that creative aesthetic work holds the potential to trouble or even to topple hegemonic representations of the social world is persistent, if also prone at times to what Uzelman refers to as a "determinism of technique". The "aesthetics of truth", as Michael Lithgow (2013) reminds us, are dynamic, historically and culturally contingent; a range of different genres of communication each imply different problems and possibilities, and appropriate understanding (and practice) requires concern for that context.

Conclusion

This chapter outlines a loose taxonomy that seeks to describe simultaneously the key forms of impetus embedded in alternative media projects and the predominant axes of theoretical description and differentiation, in a fashion intended to illuminate both contrasts and connections – as well as tensions running through particular 'logics'. To a significant extent, this taxonomy is characterised by porous or uncertain borders between categories. As noted, I wish to suggest that the possibilities within each conceptual cluster tending towards the radical-democratic or counter-hegemonic pole of the political continuum (away from a public-sphere liberal perspective which more easily accommodates selective emphasis and compartmentalisation) may to some extent be seen to do so insofar as they imply, or even appear to mutually presuppose, aspects of the others – an argument that cannot be fully articulated in the space of this short chapter. I hope at least that this taxonomy – and, indeed, the rest of this volume – makes some headway in sorting out questions of differential emphasis and conceptualisation in the field of alternative media studies.

Further reading

The comprehensive introduction ('Four approaches to alternative media') to Bailey, Cammaerts and Carpentier (2008) provides a comparable, but different (and more fully elaborated), taxonomy of concerns and concepts in the field of alternative media studies. Uzelman (2011) similarly seeks to draw out relevant contrasts of approach to alternative media studies in elaborating his concerns regarding 'determinism of technique' in the field.

References

Andersson, L. (2012) "There is no alternative: The critical potential of alternative media for challenging neoliberal discourse." *tripleC*, 10(2), 752–64.

Atton, C. (2002) *Alternative Media*. London: Sage.

——(2009) "Alternative and citizen journalism." In K. Wahl-Jorgensen and T. Hanitzsch (eds.) *The Handbook of Journalism Studies*. London: Routledge (pp. 265–78).

Bailey, O., Cammaerts, B. and Carpentier, N. (eds.) (2008) *Understanding Alternative Media*. Maidenhead: Open University Press.

Cammaerts, B. (2012) "Protest logics and the mediation opportunity structure." *European Journal of Communication*, 27(2), 117–34.

Carey, J. (1989) *Communication as Culture*. Boston: Unwin Hyman.

Christians, C. G., Glasser, T. L., McQuail, D., Nordenstreng, K. and White, R. A. (2009) *Normative Theories of the Media: Journalism in Democratic Societies*. Urbana: University of Illinois Press.

Coleman, S. and Ross, K. (2010) *The Media and the Public: "Them" and "Us" in Media Discourse*. Oxford: Wiley-Blackwell.

Couldry, N. (2003) "Beyond the hall of mirrors? Some theoretical reflection on the global contestation of media power." In N. Couldry and J. Curran (eds.) *Contesting Media Power: Alternative Media in a Networked World*. Lanham, MD: Rowman & Littlefield (pp. 39–54).

——(2010) "Introduction." In C. Rodríguez, D. Kidd and L. Stein (eds.) *Making Our Media: Global Initiatives Toward a Democratic Public Sphere: Creating New Communication Spaces*. New York: Hampton Press (pp. 24–28).

Couldry, N. and Curran, J. (2003) "The paradox of media power." In N. Couldry and J. Curran (eds), *Contesting Media Power: Alternative Media in a Networked World*. Lanham, MD: Rowman & Littlefield (pp. 3–15).

Dean, J. (2008) "Communicative capitalism: Circulation and the foreclosure of politics." In M. Boler (ed.), *Digital Media and Democracy: Tactics in Hard Times*. Cambridge, MA: MIT Press (pp. 101–22).

Debord, G. (1994[1967]) *The Society of the Spectacle*. New York: Zone.

Downing, J. D. H. (2001) *Radical Media: Rebellious Communication and Social Movements.* London: Sage.

——(2003) "Audiences and readers of alternative media: The absent lure of the virtually unknown." *Media, Culture and Society,* 25(5), 625–45.

Duncombe, S. (2008) *Notes from Underground: Zines and the Politics of Alternative Culture.* Bloomington, IN: Microcosm Publishing.

Eley, G. (1992) "Nations, publics and political cultures: Placing Habermas in the nineteenth century." In C. Calhoun (ed.), *Habermas and the Public Sphere.* Cambridge, MA: MIT Press (pp. 289–339).

Elghul-Bibawi, S. (2009) "The relationship between mainstream and alternative media: A blurring of the edges?" In J. Gordon (ed.), *Notions of Community: A Collection of Community Media Debates and Dilemmas.* Bern: Peter Lang (pp. 17–32).

Fraser, N. (1992) "Rethinking the public sphere: A contribution to the critique of actually existing democracy." In C. Calhoun (ed.), *Habermas and the Public Sphere.* Cambridge, MA: MIT Press (pp. 109–42).

Fuchs, C. (2010) "Alternative media as critical media." *European Journal of Social Theory,* 13(2), 173–92.

Goodnight, G. T. (1997) "Opening Up the 'Spaces of Public Dissent'." *Communication Monographs,* 64, 271–75.

Habermas, J. (1989) *The Structural Transformation of the Public Sphere.* Cambridge, MA: MIT Press.

Hackett, R. and Carroll W. (2006) *Remaking Media: The struggle to Democratize Public Communication.* London: Routledge.

Hackett, R. and Zhao, Y. (1998) *Sustaining Democracy? Journalism and the Politics of Objectivity.* Toronto: Garamond Press.

Hamilton, J. F. (2000) "Alternative media: Conceptual difficulties, critical possibilities." *Journal of Communication Inquiry,* 24, 357–78.

——(2001) "Visualizing critique: Montage as a practice of alternative media." *Media History,* 7(2), 159–70.

Jassem, H. K. (1990) "The alternative media's values for the 21st century." Retrieved from http://eric.ed.gov/ERICWebPortal/search/detailmini.jsp?_nfpb=true&_&ERICExtSearch_SearchValue_0=ED320185&ERICExtSearch_SearchType_0=no&accno=ED320185 (accessed 15 January 2013).

Johnson, M. L. (1971) *The New Journalism: The Underground Press, the Artists of Nonfiction, and Changes in the Established Media.* Lawrence: University Press of Kansas.

Lithgow, M. (2013) "Aesthetics of legitimacy: Resisting the effects of power with 'grassroots' news & queer sasquatches." *American Communication Journal,* 15(1), 34.

Melucci, A. (1996) *Challenging Codes.* Cambridge, UK: Cambridge University Press.

Negt, O. and Kluge, A. (1993[1972]) *Public Sphere and Experience.* Minneapolis: University of Minnesota Press.

Nomai, A. J. (2008) "Culture jamming: Ideological struggle and the possibilities for social change." PhD Dissertation, University of Texas–Austin.

Rodríguez, C. (2001) *Fissures in the Mediascape.* Cresskill, NJ: Hampton.

Sandoval, M. and Fuchs, C. (2010) "Towards a critical theory of alternative media." *Technics and Informatics,* 27, 141–50.

Sheppard, R. (2000) *Modernism–Dada–Postmodernism.* Evanston, IL: Northwestern University Press.

Uzelman, S. (2011) "Dangerous practices: 'Determinism of technique' in alternative media and their literature." *International Journal of Media and Cultural Politics,* 7(1), 21–36.

Warner, M. (2002) *Publics and Counterpublics.* New York: Zone Books.

2

VANGUARD MEDIA

The promise of strategic communication?

Herbert Pimlott

Introduction

"A spectre is haunting Europe – the spectre of communism."
(Marx and Engels, *The Communist Manifesto*, 1848)

Since the beginnings of the financial crisis in 2007, the spectre of 'communism' has begun to haunt the world for the first time in a quarter century, amidst the tumult of growing social and political unrest, from the 'Arab Spring' to Quebec's 'Maple Spring', from anti-austerity protests in Europe to the spread of Occupy Wall Street (OWS) across the US and beyond. These waves of widespread unrest are evidence that neoliberalism has failed to maintain the 'consent' of the governed, and yet the governed, or at least the 'Left', have been unable to take advantage of the 'crisis'. Some activists, frustrated with the apparent inability of alternative media to move beyond 'tactical media' (Ray and Sholette, 2008), have called (with tongue firmly in cheek) for a 'networked Leninism' (Dyer-Witheford, 2012) or attempted to promote a discussion of strategy (e.g. the OWS periodical *Tidal: Occupy Theory, Occupy Strategy*). Other activists and academics are reassessing the idea of 'communism', including Lenin's 'vanguard party', in the hopes of finding a 'political instrument' that can coordinate, mobilise and organise the various organisations and movements against neoliberalism (e.g. Budgen et al., 2007; Dean, 2012; Panitch et al., 2012). The allure of the Leninist model is understandable because it brings 'certainty'. However, we need to rethink the 'party paper' as 'strategic communication' to move beyond this impasse.

This chapter, therefore, proposes a way for alternative media to move beyond a 'tactical' orientation and engage in strategic communication based upon a rethinking of the 'party paper', the once-dominant model of Leninist political organisations. While the practices of Leninist parties historically have created a considerable degree of mistrust among potential social movement allies, at least since the 1960s and 1970s, activists have overlooked the potential of the 'party paper' as a model for strategic communication. After outlining key aspects of strategic communication and the vanguard party, this chapter will address the strengths and weaknesses of the five functions that make up the concept of 'vanguard media' as strategic communication: 'party paper'; 'organisation'; 'bridge'; 'network'; and 'public relations'.

From vanguard party to vanguard media

Strategic communication has generally been associated with those interested in exercising power via management of government or corporations and has therefore been closely identified with such traditional areas of academic study as 'corporate communication' and 'marketing, advertising, and public relations' (Hallahan et al., 2007: 4). However, recent developments have seen a shift whereby strategic communication includes "activist organizations and social and citizen movements" as part of a move away "from … management studies" (ibid.: 4). Although alternative media practitioners have been uncomfortable with the concept of persuasion because of connotations of "manipulation," persuasion is the essence of influence, which is at the core of strategic communication. If "purposeful influence is the fundamental goal of communications by organizations", then it is not just vanguard parties, corporations or governments that can be said to engage in strategic communication, since alternative media seek to influence others (ibid.: 10).

The vanguard media concept also need not be limited to a singular, historical or narrow understanding of a 'party'. The use of the term 'vanguard' itself does not necessarily indicate that it has to be an authoritarian form of governance or political organisation, despite the legacy of Communist parties. The *Oxford English Dictionary* defines 'vanguard' as simply "leaders of movement, of opinion etc." Most, if not all, alternative media perform one or more functions of 'vanguard' by this definition, whether or not they recognise formal or informal leadership, as they constitute a movement, milieu or organisation by engaging in raising consciousness, highlighting the abuses of power and the powerful and/or challenging the dominant ideology or laws; they are also the primary means for articulating the ideas and perspectives of, and thereby constituting, movements, milieux and organisations. Such communication practices translate effortlessly into rationales for vanguard media, for which "strategic communication" is the "purposeful use of communication by an organisation to fulfil its mission" (Hallahan et al., 2007: 3).

I am therefore proposing to re-conceptualise the strategic aspect of communication, one that is often overlooked by alternative media studies, but is frequently implied in the desire for transformation, by rethinking the 'vanguard party *paper*' as 'vanguard *media*'. While vanguard media can be seen as part of an organisation, movement or milieu, with corresponding control, constraints and hierarchies within the differences in the degree of informal or formal organisational structure, the model is about identifying the five functions for alternative media that make up strategic communication and could contribute to building a counter-public sphere.

The party paper

The 'party paper' in one form or another remained the dominant model for alternative media as long as both print media remained the primary and most accessible means for radical social and political movements to communicate their messages (e.g., in terms of technology and cost) and the vanguard party remained the dominant or preferred model of political organisation among social and political activists.

Lenin's 'party of a new type', or vanguard party, had been a response to try and organise the array of movements, parties and other radical working-class formations that had arisen during the latter half of the nineteenth century. The paper, as Lenin (1973[1902]) argues in *What Is to Be Done?*, is as necessary to a political organisation (or social movement) as scaffolding is to a building, because it provides the means around which the party (or movement) forms: without a paper (or media), there would be no party (or movement).

The party paper was the primary means for reaching out to potential or prospective supporters, a much smaller group than the general public, but larger than an internal audience of party members and sympathisers (thus, different from both the 'bridge' and 'organisation' functions discussed below). In seeking out potential supporters, the party paper functions to support those readers, who act as agitators and propagandists to carry forward alternative news and views via agitation, which is "short-term information tactics to bring immediate abuses and problems to public notice", and propaganda, which is "longer-term communication strategies ... to shape the hearts and minds of the public" in one or other ideological direction (Downing, 2001: 68). The function of the party paper, codified in the Communist International's *Theses*, identifies these two functions, agitation and propaganda, as critical to promote the 'party line' which also enables the organisation of cadres into a party (e.g. Fogarasi, 1979[1921]).

The party paper's function is closely related to both its historical origins during the rise of mass-produced newspapers at the start of the twentieth century and the nature of print media, which is ideally suited to sustaining systematic serial critiques of a political-economic power structure, and vitally necessary to promote a vision of an alternative (e.g. Pimlott, 2006). The tendency for top-down control and one-way communication practices within the Bolshevik Party, and subsequently with the affiliated parties of the Communist International, was only partly related to the nature of print media, which involved a range of skills and the division of labour (and which is similar to the capitalist division of labour). The Bolsheviks had, in point of fact, actually made use of the most advanced communication technologies of their era, which did include mass-produced newspapers *and* film (e.g. Ely, 2013). Even the party papers of vanguard parties, such as the UK's Socialist Workers' Party's weekly, *Socialist Worker*, are not actually modelled on Bolshevik papers, such as *Iskra* or *Pravda*, but rather on a radical version of a popular commercial newspaper, such as the *Daily Mirror* (e.g. Allen, 1985; Pimlott, 2006).

More importantly, it should be recognised that, although the nature of print media practices might lend themselves more readily to the top-down, one-way mode of communication that was widely practiced in Communist media, this central weakness of the party paper is the result of the belief in the need for the organisational discipline based upon the historical example of the Bolshevik Revolution. This perspective ignores the historical situation that Bolsheviks faced between 1900 and 1921: the Tsar's secret police; foreign war and intervention; civil war. The key practice known as 'democratic centralism' was supposed to enable the membership to exert control over the leadership, which would run the party between party congresses, the forum in which members were supposed to be able to exert their influence. As long as the USSR and other Communist regimes existed, this particular understanding of the role of the party paper wielded influence among political radicals on the Left.

Organisation

Whereas the party paper functions in the role of reaching out to the public via the agitation and propaganda of readers, the 'organisation' function is about the process of enhancing and enabling internal communication within a milieu, organisation or movement, and it is vital to building and strengthening that entity's capacities for it to work effectively. This function emphasises the importance of the internal structure for enabling the effective communication between producers and member-readers.

It emphasises the two-way flow of internal communication between those in leadership or decision-making positions and the rank-and-file. This function is as necessary for the smallest organisation as it is for the largest. The Communist Party is an example whereby different media were designated for enabling internal communication between members from the internal 'party review', which highlighted party departments, issues and debates to specialist niche journals, focusing on topics such as art or economics. Since participants engage with members with similar interests, there can be assumed prior knowledge of foundational concepts and ideas, which means more complex arguments can be made around the organisation's ideology, theory, policies, internal operations, tactics and strategy.

Control is a key aspect of the organisation function with the emphasis of many alternative media on the means of democratic control, not always just emphasising the practitioners' control, but also that of movement activists and their audiences. One such long-running example is *Il Manifesto*, which began as a monthly run by a cooperative of journalists during Italy's 'hot autumn' of 1969. *Il Manifesto* broke away from the left political party with which it had been connected and broadened its range of contributors; to connect its audiences with the staff, the paper held congresses where readers and producers could debate and develop the paper's editorial line (Downing, 1984: 237–54). However, an emphasis on extending control to activists and/or audiences can clash with professional standards and marketplace demands, that some forms of alternative media emphasise more than others.

A key weakness in this model is the degree of control that can be exerted over the leadership and staff by the rank-and-file (except where alternative media are organised as cooperatives). Ensuring democratic control involves making the processes of decision-making and the selection of decision-makers transparent and the leadership and staff accountable to the membership. A related weakness is when the internal focus becomes the primary function of an organisation or movement; this can lead to full-time disputes and even all-consuming struggles over an organisation's resources. The CPGB between 1982 and 1985, for example, descended into a full-blown 'civil war', where the internal struggle for control of the party meant factions building bases via taking control of different publications. For example, one tendency took control of the CPGB's daily newspaper, *The Morning Star*, whereas opponents consolidated their control over other periodicals, such as *Marxism Today* or *Comment*. The

Gramscian 'war of position', a strategy that many leading party members argued for to fight Thatcherism, became a 'war of position' within the party.

The bridge

The concept of the 'bridge' function of vanguard media identifies alternative media's most historically pervasive role at least since the rise of the late eighteenth-century and early nineteenth-century 'pauper press' and the socialist and Chartist papers of the nineteenth century. Well before Lenin made the case for the 'party paper', alternative media provided a bridge between radical working-class formations and the 'general public'. The function played by newspapers, periodicals and pamphlets has been crucial in constituting radical working-class movements and spreading their ideas, both among their own publics as well as to the broader public outside their milieux.

Since the 1960s, the bridge model has functioned in a manner similar to that of mainstream news media in providing a range of 'news and views' on the Left or for particular social movements (e.g., environmental, ethnic), and/or between such movements and the national public sphere. There are a number of examples of national alternative newspapers, such as *News on Sunday* (UK), *Il Manifesto* (Italy) and *Die Tageszeitung* (TAZ) (Germany), and broadcast programmes, such as *Democracy Now!* (US) and *The Real News Network* (TRNN) (US), which attempt to function as bridges between alternative and mainstream audiences. Both *Il Manifesto* (launched in 1969) and *Die TAZ* (launched in 1978) have existed for a considerable amount of time and therefore have achieved a level of credibility and reputation, which can enhance their position in reaching a broader audience beyond their immediate organisational bases. *Il Manifesto* provides a considerable amount of coverage of the full range of subjects (and more) that mainstream newspapers do, as does *Die TAZ*. Although both express editorial support for particular Left and environmental political alternatives to mainstream parties, they both maintain an editorial independence from direct affiliation with any party.

In the English-speaking world, there have been few examples since the 1960s of newspapers that are able to bridge between marginal and politically radical audiences and the general public at a national level. In 1986, there was an attempt to start a weekly, the *News on Sunday*, to redress the imbalance in outlets for more left-of-centre views beyond the centre-right of the Labour Party, as provided by such mainstream newspapers as *The Daily Mirror* and *The Guardian*. It survived for about six months amidst a host of problems, where conflicts arose between professional and commercial pressures on one side and democratic political processes and radical values on the other (e.g., Chippindale and Horrie, 1988). The *News on Sunday*'s awkward attempt at merging top-down and bottom-up involvement in its production became a disaster, reinforcing the perception that alternative media cannot compete with corporate media to reach a broader public via mainstream distribution channels.

However, there are a number of web-based news media series that are attempting to act as a bridge between small and marginal audiences of politically informed and motivated citizens, and the general public, as part of an attempt to reach out beyond state and corporate broadcasters. (It should be noted, though, in consideration of the bridge function, that there has been a development of a few well-resourced media in English-speaking countries, such as Al Jazeera English and Russia Today, which offer a much more critical and independent view of dominant elites and ideologies in the West, but which do not represent the politics of alternative media. Interestingly, *The Guardian* in the UK has been able to gain a greater online presence in the US and Canada because of the lack of mainstream, left-of-centre journalism in those countries.) For example, the most enduring broadcast program to date, which had its origins on the alternative Pacifica Radio network (established in 1948), is *Democracy Now!*, hosted by Amy Goodman, which provides both televisual and audio reporting broadcast over airwaves and online by various local stations around the US and abroad, and has built up a wider audience than most alternative media. Both *Democracy Now!* and the web-based TRNN adopt aspects of the professional journalistic techniques, including requesting interviews with government and corporate spokespeople, but retain a critical understanding of how news *and* power works.

A more episodic example of the bridge function is that of Robert Greenwald's Brave New Films (BNF), which produces low-cost single-topic films for rapid distribution and broadcast. These films are professionally produced (though limited resources and time constraints do have some impact on the final quality). BNF was set up in 2002 to react swiftly against New Right propaganda; it is telling that its inaugural film was based on deconstructing the Fox News channel's techniques (*Outfoxed*). By the end of 2010, its videos were reaching 50 million viewers.

While the adoption of professional media techniques raises the potential credibility of alternative media with audiences outside their milieux, there are some potential pitfalls. For example, alternative media could become a vehicle for corporations and governments to reach out into counter-public spheres. *Marxism Today*'s transformation from a dense, jargon-ladened journal into a 'glossy' magazine enabled it to reach a larger public beyond its original party readership. Although it never succeeded as a bridge for radical ideas to reach a broader public beyond the 'radical ghetto', *Marxism Today* did instead provide a bridge for mainstream media professionals to intervene in the Left's counter-public sphere, helping pave the way for New Labour by dismantling the Left's 'shibboleths' (Pimlott, forthcoming).

Thus, while the bridge function offers potential in reaching out beyond the 'radical ghetto' to the general public, it can also enable access to dominant groups that might gain legitimacy with alternative media audiences. It is also the one function that often divides alternative media practitioners over the extent to which one adopts or adapts to the marketplace and mainstream formats to reach the general public. Some see the process of the bridge function as undermining the 'message' of alternative media (Sandoval and Fuchs, 2010).

Network

With the rapid spread of new media technologies since the 1990s, the idea of alternative media operating as a 'network' quickly gained popularity with activists. The network function was seen as overcoming top-down control and one-way communication, and other problems of corporate and state media and older forms of alternative media, such as the Leninist party paper; these media were seen as examples of authoritarian constraints of a bygone era, closely associated with analogue technologies. The new digital media technologies enabled a process of decentralised decision-making and production processes, and two-way, participatory communication that is closely associated with the network's origins in the prefigurative politics of multiple social movements at the 'Battle of Seattle' in 1999. Although it connects different individuals and groups via a non-hierarchical and 'leaderless' form of grassroots democracy, participatory production is not inherently progressive, nor are networks necessarily without hierarchy (Sandoval and Fuchs, 2010).

The first and, for several years, leading network model was the Independent Media Center (IMC) collective across the world, which became known as the *Indymedia* network. The IMC was launched in 1999, when more than 50,000 environmental, alter-globalisation and labour activists protested the World Trade Organization (WTO) meeting in Seattle. The network is closely associated with the alternative media activists using laptops and camcorders to show the world police brutality and that a different perspective on 'globalisation' was possible. The possibilities of the IMC provided considerable interest and engagement from alternative media practitioners, and the IMCs spread, albeit unevenly, to different cities, regions and nations around the world, offering a range of marginalised and radical news and views in several languages.

Indymedia offers an example of how the network functions to enable dispersed and autonomous alternative media to retain their ideological, operational and political independence on one hand and yet link up with social-political movement allies and operate as a coherent entity. It offers a network of alternative news and views to anyone around the world with access to the internet. *Indymedia* raises some of the problems that come with operating such a global network of alternative media. There have been disagreements over content and attempts to prevent some items from being published via the network. However, it has not been without its problems, as with some stories that have been seen as offensive to some groups, yet participants have tried to avoid 'censoring' such stories. A separate page was provided for such stories, but not on IMC pages immediately available via search engines.

Another aspect of the network function points to the potential of a loose 'coalition' or 'coordination' of alternative media, which comes out of developments in the US, where research found that alternative media audiences do not overlap, contrary to what had been assumed. Various alternative media recognised that cooperation was also important because of the dominance of the New Right's juggernaut via Fox News, and the various cable TV and radio outlets for 'shock jocks' and right-wing talking heads like Rush Limbaugh and Glenn Beck (Clark and Van Slyke, 2010). Thus, the Media Consortium, a grouping of alternative media, has begun building a broad, progressive counter-public sphere that has successfully challenged neoliberal and neoconservative ideas, by sharing and coordinating their messaging and framing of issues the way the New Right has done, via its 'echo chamber', over the past thirty-plus years (ibid.: 78). While the range of alternative media in the Media Consortium includes many that might be seen as more mainstream than alternative in terms of internal organisation and decision-making (though this is not always the case, as Sandoval and Fuchs (2010) define alternative media and in Pimlott's (2014) continuum of alternative media), efforts at working together are beginning to have an impact in enhancing the challenge to neoliberal hegemony. This form of the network function eclipses the IMC's emphasis on direct democracy and prefigurative politics in alternative media.

A strong part of the appeal of the network model is its seemingly 'leaderless' and horizontal mode of operations, which is also a potential source of weakness. For example, during the early 1970s, the potential 'tyranny of structurelessness' from the shunning of overt leadership was highlighted as a potential problem for social movements.

> The attempt to do without structure only prevents the formulation of *formal* structures. Structures are inevitable. All groups have *informal* structures; some groups also have *formal* structures. In those with only informal structures power relations are masked and the rules of power ... are only known to the members of the informal elite.
>
> (Landry et al., 1985: 10–11, original emphasis)

Nevertheless, the network function, at least in the abstract, appears to offer the possibility of something more than the sum of its parts. It offers independence and autonomy to each alternative media unit, which while emphasising the media's autonomy makes it difficult to come to any kind of unanimity in terms of objectives, other than to provide a platform for sharing or coordinating messages. Nevertheless, the latter function is a potential strength of counter-hegemonic social movements.

Public relations

The final function that the vanguard media concept encompasses is that of 'public relations', which is the role that alternative media do perform in reaching out to dominant, mainstream media. This function is important because there is a need to establish a presence with mainstream media to counter dominant (mis)representations even when there is little control that can be exerted over the 'message'. Alternative media practitioners can find themselves either acting as 'spokespersons' or 'representatives' of social movements, or providing the platforms for certain activists whom mainstream media will seek out given their prominence, especially when there are no 'leaders'. In addition, establishment media continue to dominate and retain legitimacy in terms of their function as 'opinion leaders', and they do hire high-profile critical commentators to enhance both the perception that a range of opinions are provided as well as attracting and retaining those who would otherwise seek news and views from other mainstream or alternative media. For example, we can find a range of critical commentators, such as George Monbiot, Naomi Klein and Laura Penny, in *The Guardian* (UK).

However, the most interesting engagement in using the PR function, without compromising its politics, is that of the Zapatista Army of National Liberation (Ejército Zapatista de Liberación Nacional, or EZLN) from the launch of its resistance to the North American Free Trade Agreement (NAFTA) on 1 January 1994, the day the three-nation deal came into effect. By attracting the attention of the world and through the use of the internet, the EZLN was able to secure fair coverage from established, international (i.e., non-Mexican) mainstream media, and such coverage prevented the Mexican paramilitary and military forces from carrying out massacres of the poorly armed, indigenous rebels in the state of Chiapas (e.g. Wolfson, 2012).

The PR function is an increasingly important part of the role alternative media play. We can see it in a range of handbooks and manuals that range from simple explanations in one-page leaflets to commercially produced books as a means of extending influence (e.g. Monbiot, 2001; Salzman, 2003; Witt, 2011). Ideally, the adoption of the PR function of vanguard media is thinking about the process of reaching out via professional public relations techniques to mainstream media. In the case of the EZLN, its messages were taken up eagerly by alternative media and non-governmental organisations far beyond the borders of Mexico. The PR function, however, can enhance the position of alternative media where mainstream media recognise the credibility, legitimacy and authority of such media because of their standing with others, even as there can be little control exerted over how mainstream media frame them and their message(s).

Conclusion

By reconceptualising the 'party paper' as 'vanguard media', we can rethink the objectives of communication by and through alternative media, whether to internal or external audiences, whether seeking access to established, mainstream media, other movements or the counter-public sphere. We can also see that some of the five func-tions of 'vanguard media' require or work better with certain media forms, technologies and/or practices which might or might not enhance the means of democratic control, prefigurative politics and/or production of radical and alternative ideas and other content. If we rethink alternative media as vanguard media, we can begin assessing their contribution to the formation and dissemination of news and views with the strategic goal of raising a new awareness or consciousness and/or representations to various publics.

Rethinking vanguard media as strategic communication is to see these functions within a larger milieu, and this activity requires coordinated action. The first stage of such a process is the cross-fertilisation of alternative media audiences that could provide the foundation for alternative media to link across different sectors, including trade unions, social movements and community organisations, to develop a network to bridge issue silos. This interrelationship and networking among different alternative media production and distribution sites could potentially develop into a broad, net-worked counter-public sphere, which would enable greater public visibility for a range of neglected views. For example, the cross-fertilisation of anti-poverty activists and environmental groups via alternative media would go some way in establishing a dialogue that could bring many of these groups together to see how their issues overlap (e.g. Pimlott, 2014: 300–302). While vanguard media as strategic commu-nication might be the best way to rethink how alternative media could ensure that future social change is driven by the grassroots, the renewed interest in communism and Leninism represents what the concept of vanguard media cannot speak to: a single, unifying worldview or ideology (even if this ideology was, and is, subject to differing interpretations).

Further reading

Although the idea of strategic communication and alternative media is relatively new, there are some key readings to build from. For assessing the party paper and more broadly the Leninist vanguard party, L. T. Lih (2008[2005]) provides an exacting reconstruction of the debates and meanings by which he claims *What Is to Be Done?* has been purposely misrepresented by both Stalinists and Western liberal academics. For different perspectives on the strengths and weaknesses of Lih's reassessment of the vanguard party (and by implication the party paper), see the special issue of *Historical Materialism* introduced by P. Blackledge (2010). J. Dean (2012) offers an argument for rethinking organisation for the Left via Leninism, whereas M. Harnecker (2007) provides an interesting account for a way beyond Leninism via rethinking the problems of 'actually existing' Leninism, including most pertinently her chapter on the 'political instrument'. J. Clark and T. Van Slyke (2010) offer an assessment of the US alternative mediascape and identify some possibilities for developing a more coherent alternative media strategy, as does H. Pimlott's (2014) overview of Canadian alternative media.

References

Allen, P. (1985) "*Socialist Worker*: Paper with a purpose." *Media, Culture and Society*, 7, 205–32.

Blackledge, P. (2010) "Editorial introduction: Symposium on Lars Lih's *Lenin Rediscovered*." *Historical Materialism*, 18(3), 25–33.

Budgen, S. et al. (2007) *Lenin Reloaded*. Durham, NC: Duke University Press.

Chippindale, P. and Horrie, C. (1988) *Disaster! The Rise and Fall of the News on Sunday: Anatomy of a Business Failure*. London: Sphere Books.

Clark, J. and Van Slyke, T. (2010) *Beyond the Echo Chamber: Reshaping Politics Through Networked Progressive Media*. New York: New Press.

Dean, J. (2012) *The Communist Horizon*. London and New York: Verso.

Downing, J. (1984) *Radical Media*. Boston, MA: South End Press.

——(with Ford, T.V., Gil, G. and Stein, L.) (2001) *Radical Media: Rebellious Communication and Social Movements*. Rev. ed. Thousand Oaks, CA: Sage.

Dyer-Witheford, N. (2012) "Networked Leninism? The circulation of capital, crisis, struggle, and the common." *Upping the Anti: A Journal of Theory and Action*, 13, 123–35.

Ely, M. (2013) *Sites of a Communist Beginning*. Kasama Project.

Fogarasi, A. (1979[1921]) "The tasks of the Communist press." In A. Mattelart and S. Siegelaub (eds.) *Communication and Class Struggle: Volume 1: Capitalism, Imperialism*. New York: IMMRC/International General (pp. 149–52).

Hallahan, K., Holtzhausen, D., van Ruler, B., Verčič, D. and Sriramesh, K. (2007) "Defining strategic communication." *International Journal of Strategic Communication*, 1(1), 3–35.

Harnecker, M. (2007) *Rebuilding the Left*. London and New York: Zed Books.

Landry, C., Morley, D., Southwood, R. and Wright, P. (1985) *What a Way to Run a Railroad: An Analysis of Radical Failure*. London: Comedia.

Lenin, V. I. (1973[1902]) *What Is to Be Done?* Beijing: Foreign Languages Press.

Lih, L. T. (2008[2005]) *Lenin Rediscovered: What Is to Be Done? in Context.* Chicago: Haymarket.

Monbiot, G. (2001) *An Activist's Guide to Exploiting the Media.* London: Bookmarks.

Panitch, L. et al. (eds.) (2012) *The Socialist Register 2013: The Question of Strategy.* Pontypool, Wales, and Halifax, Nova Scotia: Merlin Press and Fernwood Publishing.

Pimlott, H. (2006) "Marxism's 'communicative crisis'? Mapping debates over Leninist print-media practices in the 20th century." *Socialist Studies*, 2(2), 57–77.

——(2014) "Reality check: The counter-publicity of alternative media." In K. Kozolanka (ed.), *The Publicity State and Canada.* Toronto: University of Toronto Press (pp. 285–313).

——(forthcoming) *Wars of Position: Marxism Today, Cultural Politics and the Remaking of the Left Press, 1979–1990.* Leiden: Brill.

Ray, G. and Sholette, G. (2008) "Introduction: Whither tactical media?" *Third Text*, 22(5), 519–24.

Salzman, J. (2003) *Making the News: A Guide for Activists and Nonprofits.* Rev. and updated ed. Boulder, CO: Westview Press.

Sandoval, M. and Fuchs, C. (2010) "Towards a critical theory of alternative media." *Telematics and Informatics*, 27(2), 141–50.

Witt, M. (2011) "News release tips." *TheWorkSite.org* (accessed 18 January 2014). http://the worksite.org/index.php/media-tips-a-training/news-release-tips/77-news-release-tips.

Wolfson, T. (2012) "From the Zapatistas to Indymedia: Dialectics and orthodoxy in contemporary social movements." *Communication, Culture and Critique*, 5(2), 149–70.

3

ALTERNATIVE MEDIA AND VOICE

Nick Couldry

Introduction

What value motivates the making of 'alternative media', and defines its success or failure? Let us first define 'alternative media' as media whose operations challenge the concentration of resources (particularly the symbolic resource of making and circulating images and information) in large media institutions (Atton and Couldry, 2003; Atton, 2002). This definition by itself does not, however, make clear *why* people should be involved in the enterprise of alternative media. After all, control over many resources, such as basic utilities, is concentrated, but few are interested in challenging the centralisation that allows, say, water to be distributed. Indeed, the idea that 'the media' provide a basic utility in the domain of information held back for decades the idea of building and researching alternative media: the centralisation that came with the size of large media was, some thought, a basic and irreversible fact of large modern societies (Garnham, 1990). Now, however, in the digital age, when it is easy, or at least easily imaginable, to make media, with or without a large institution, the resistance to 'alternative media' is less automatic. But the value that motivates people and communities (rather than large corporations) to make media still has to be explained.

Two things quickly show us that this question of value is far from straightforward. First, value has shaped the competing names for what we research: alternative media, community media, radical media, citizens' media (Atton, 2002; Fuller, 2007; Downing, 2001; Rodríguez, 2001). These varying titles each tell their own story of the purpose and values of small-scale media. Second, the question of value has become an issue within the field of research itself. One form was John Downing's (2003) insistence that alternative media research had neglected the audience: who indeed was watching, reading or listening to alternative media, and how much did this matter? It mattered a lot on some conceptions of these media's purpose, and not so much on others. But some resolution of this point is necessary: if alternative media were just a matter of *making* media without regard to whether anyone was listening, such media would risk being self-serving and irresponsible. The ease of basic media production in a hyperlinked digital world sharpens the issue: no one is served, quite clearly, by a cacophony where everyone is speaking (that is, making media) and no one is listening (Dreher, 2009; MacNamara, 2013). The only way forward is to clarify what value is at stake in such possibilities of listening.

I will develop that insight in this chapter through the concept of 'voice'. Voice, properly understood, is the value that motivates the production of alternative media, and enables us to assess whether such production is *effective* in terms of those media's goals: effectiveness must involve, to some extent at least, the possibility of being listened to. More specifically, I will explain in the next section how voice can be understood in two linked ways: voice as *process* and voice as *value*. It is the understanding of voice as value that was missing, at least as an explicit term, from much earlier debate on alternative media. From that starting point, I will in the chapter's second section explore some contrasting cases which illustrate the multiple ways in which alternative media may, or may not, be seen to embody the value of voice, that is, to succeed or fail.

The concept of voice

Two everyday senses of the word 'voice' are familiar. First, we can mean the sound of a person speaking, but this usage does not capture the range of ways, not necessarily involving sound, in which I can give an account of myself. Second, we have in the sphere of politics become accustomed to equating 'voice' with the expression of opinion or, more broadly, the expression of a distinctive perspective on the world that a political system could acknowledge. This political use of the word 'voice' continues to be useful, especially in contexts where long-entrenched inequalities of representation need to be addressed. But it is in danger of becoming banal: we all have 'voice', we all celebrate 'voice', so how far can using the term in this sense take us?

Voice as process and voice as value

I would like, however, to use the term 'voice' differently, distinguishing between two levels: voice as a *process* (already relatively familiar) and voice as a *value*. The second sense, voice as a value, is particularly important at times when a whole way of thinking about social political and cultural organisation (neoliberalism) operates on the basis that for certain crucial purposes voice as a process does *not* matter. Neoliberal social forms fail to value – indeed, do not choose to value – those specific frameworks for organising human life and resources such as genuine democracy that *themselves* value voice (as a process). Treating voice as a value means discriminating *in favour* of ways of organising human life and resources that put the value of voice into practice. Treating voice as a value means discriminating *against* frameworks of social, economic and political organisation that undermine voice. Valuing voice then involves particular attention to the conditions under which voice (as a process) can be effective, and how broader forms of organisation may subtly devalue voice. Neoliberalism is, of course, not the only form of social or political organisation that closes down voice. The effects of colonialism and postcolonial continuations of colonial power can, in part, be understood this way. Hector Amaya's powerful reading of the racial limitations of US democracy right down to the very operation of law and policy formation (Amaya, 2013, to which I return later) can also be read as diagnosing a profound lack of voice for Latina/o populations in the US.

Voice as a value distinguishes between large-scale ways of organising societies, resources and the world which take account of people's capacities for voice (that is, to participate in voice as a process) from those which do not. Voice, then, is the overarching value which makes sense of why people get involved in, and fight for the possibility of, alternative media: voice as value grounds the possibility of imagining alternative media at all.

Although I have no space to detail this here, the value of voice articulates some basic aspects of human life that are relevant *whatever* our views on democracy or justice. The value of voice potentially establishes common ground between diverse frameworks for evaluating economic, social and political organisation (from the work of philosophers Paul Ricoeur and Judith Butler to that of development economist Amartya Sen and social theorist Axel Honneth: Ricoeur, 1980; Butler, 2005; Sen, 1999; Honneth, 2007). Voice has many connections to contemporary sociology and psychology too (Sennett, 1998; Gilligan, 1982). More generally, the value of voice is connected with recent debates about the crisis of knowledge in 'the West' that derives from its historic exclusion of other knowledges and ways of producing knowledge from outside 'the West' (Connell, 2007; de Sousa Santos, 2005). Let me set out in a little more detail what is involved in voice as a process, connecting it to the practicalities of alternative media.

The process of voice

Voice is the process of giving an account of one's life and its conditions or, as Judith Butler (2005) puts it, 'giving an account of oneself'. To give such an account means telling a story, providing a narrative. It is not often, perhaps, that any of us sits down to tell a story as such, with a formal beginning and end, like a news feature or documentary. But *narrative* is also a basic feature of human action, because the human being, as Charles Taylor (1986) put it, is 'a self-interpreting animal'. Our actions already come embedded in narrative, our own and that of others. To ignore another's capacity for narrative – to deny her potential for voice – is to deny a basic dimension of human life. A form of life that systematically denied voice would be intolerable.

If we define voice as our capacity to make, and be recognised as making, narratives about our lives and the world within which we act, some further general principles follow. First, voice is *socially grounded*. Voice is not the practice of individuals in isolation: voice depends on shared material resources, and the specifically social resources (including language) that enable and sustain practices of narrative. Having a voice requires resources: both practical resources (language) and the (seemingly purely symbolic) status necessary if one is to be recognised by others as having a voice. Media processes (production and distribution) contribute importantly to such resources, and so are part of the materiality of voice, the 'matter' without which voice is impossible. In addition, and more fundamentally, narrative as a process is unimaginable except as part of an ongoing *exchange* of narratives with others. As Alisdair

Macintyre (1981: 203) put it, 'the narrative of anyone's life is part of an interlocking set of narratives'; Cavarero (2000: 88), even more eloquently, writes of 'an identity which, from beginning to end, is intertwined with other lives and needs the other's tale'. Voice as a social process involves, from the start, both speaking *and listening*: the building of alternative media is a social application of that principle.

Second, voice is a form of *reflexive agency*. The exchangeable narratives that constitute our voices are not random babblings, but a form of agency for which we take responsibility as agents: the stories we tell, like our actions more generally, as Hannah Arendt (1958: 193) argues, "disclose" us "as subjects". Voice, therefore, is always more than discourse; it is part of what we, as "'individuals', 'persons', or social movements might want or be able *to do* in the world" (Harvey, 2000: 118, added emphasis). A key part of such agency is reflexivity, the ongoing process of reflection through exchanging narratives back and forth between our past and present selves, and between us and others. Humans have a desire to narrate, as Cavarero (2000: 41) puts it, a *desire* to make sense of their lives. Humans inevitably, therefore, reflect on the adequacy of the stories by and about them, and seek to intervene when they see a misfit between the stories told about them and the story they want to tell. Here is the root of the impulse to alternative media.

This reflexivity concerning voice is connected, also, to voice's necessary plurality: not just external differences between voices, but also the *internal diversity* within a particular voice. The inherent internal plurality of each voice encompasses the processes whereby we think about what one strand of our lives means for other strands. To block someone's capacity to bring one part of their lives to bear on another part – for example, by denying them the capacity to speak on how their family or work life affects their actions as a citizen, or vice versa – is to deny a dimension of voice itself.

Third, *voice requires a material form which may be individual, collective or distributed*. Voice does not simply require social resources, as already noted; it also requires a form. Both are aspects of the materiality of voice. But the material form of voice need not be under the exclusive control of the individual; often I recognise myself in a collectively produced voice such as a media channel or a drama series, but sometimes I cannot do so (we will return to the term 'recognition' later). Sometimes we can recognise ourselves in the outcome of a production where specific individual and collective inputs cannot easily be separated from a broader flow: this form of voice is not individual or collective, but 'distributed'. Networked, distributed voice is increasingly important in a digital age.

If, however, through an unequal distribution of narrative resources and access to narrative forms, people *lack control* over the materials from which they must build their account of themselves, then this represents a deep denial of voice, a type of oppression. As a result, available forms for voice will *fail to fit* the conditions of experience, and, as a result, there will be no effective voice. This can happen in many ways: when collective voices or institutional decisions fail to register individual experience; when institutions ignore collective views; when distributed voice is not reflected in opportunities to redeem voice in specific encounters; or, most generally, when societies become organised on the basis that individual, collective and distributed voice need not be taken into account, because a higher value or rationality (such as market functioning or political expediency) trumps them. Alternative media, in various ways, respond to such deficits in the process of voice, and in so doing, affirm the value of voice.

Applying the concept of voice to alternative media

In this section of the chapter, I want to illustrate the range of ways in which alternative media can instantiate the process and value of voice. I will start with three contrasting examples of the potential benefits, but also the practical limits of alternative media as a process of voice. Alternative media, which initially express voice, may be more or less successful in sustaining the conditions whereby such voice is valued and taken into account in society. In the later part of this section, I will look in detail at Clemencia Rodríguez's account of alternative media in violence-torn Colombia to see how, under difficult conditions, alternative media may instantiate the value of voice.

The resonance of alternative media

As my first example, I will take the 'cultural encyclopedia' produced by the peoples of Chiloé in southern Chile (Fundación Radio Estrella del Mar, n.d.). The Chiloé region is a remote mainland and archipelago region of southern Chile, near the tip of the Latin American continent. Its visionary bishop from the 1970s, Bishop Ysern, obtained a radio licence from Chile's dictator, Pinochet, which enabled the community radio network Radio Estrella del Mar to start in 1981 (Rodríguez, 2003).

In the mid-1990s, the foundation linked to the radio network sponsored and encouraged the process of collective production that generated the *Enciclopedia Cultural de Chiloé*. In 2003, I was given the two parts of its volume 1, which deal with mountain and forest life in this region: since then, volumes 2, 3, 4 and 5 have been published on various themes, including architecture and local history. The whole production is an act of communal memory and of proposing and confirming each participant as what Axel Honneth calls a person with 'capabilities of constitutive value to a concrete community' (2007: 139). As such, the production process enacts a fundamental principle of the value of voice, which is recognition (see Couldry, 2010a: 105–7 for more detailed discussion).

As such, the very idea, as well as the execution of this encyclopaedia project, is itself a form of reflexive challenge to this region's people's long absence from Chile's accounts of itself. The act of producing an exhaustive description of a territory and its ways of life, as Bishop Ysern writes in his preface to volume 1, 'triggers many processes of participation and dialogue by way of reflection on the themes of life' (translation mine: all quotations from the unpaginated preface to the *Enciclopedia Cultural de Chiloé*; Fundación Radio Estrella del Mar, n.d.: volume 1, part 1). It would make no sense to skew our assessment of the value of this process of voice by asking how many people read the encyclopaedia, when and to what purpose. The encyclopaedia of Chiloé itself stands as the outcome of a collective process of voice, of bringing a community's voice into public existence: as Ysern again says, 'these dialogues must be produced as much through the elaboration of each volume, as through its use after publication' (ibid.: Presentación). This sensitivity to the importance of voice as a process *behind* distributed media content acknowledges the harm that comes from mis-recognition when those at a distance fail to listen or care: the peril of disrespect (Honneth, 2007). The ethic of listening that animates the project expresses the value of voice in its purest form: in Ysern's eloquent phrase, 'es necesario que se oigan todas las voces en el concierto de la vida' (all voices in the concert of life must be heard).

For a second and contrasting example, I want to reflect on a network of community reporters that I will call Citizens' Media, which with colleagues I researched during 2011–13. It was run from the north of England, but linked up community reporters from across the UK. The context had some basic similarities to the Chilean context just discussed: this too occurred in a poor region whose voice is rarely heard clearly or positively in national debate. But in most respects the context was very different, since it was not focussed by strong regional identities; the dynamics that make voice necessary are not regional exclusion, but the individualising force of poverty and social isolation. The community reporters we interviewed often carried a vision of the importance of their reporting for community building, but generally they had to act alone and their reports could go unread by many except for themselves and those who run the platform. In our research, we were interested in how a broader narrative exchange could be built from such reports through digital means (Fotopoulou and Couldry, 2015).

In this context, there was no self-validating communal process of producing voice that could anchor wider processes of communal identity and mutual recognition. On the contrary, membership of the network did not bring with it much in the way of social or cultural context, once the initial training workshop was completed. Nor did the current website of the network and training organisation stimulate much discussion or commentary by itself. Our research brought home to us the sheer difficulty of establishing the digital resources to create a supportive long-term context for the brief, generally decontextualised moments of narrative that much online alternative media comprises. The problem goes beyond economic resource (Couldry, 2010b), to encompass the difficulty of sustaining a context of meaning in which individual stories carry weight. The minimum is an effective website that encourages discussion around particular stories and the exchange of stories across contexts. This network, like so much alternative media, must struggle in a wider cultural landscape *saturated* with ever-changing media contents, against which it is difficult to establish a new meaning-context within which such non-institutional sources can be heard at all. In our fieldwork, we were involved, as action researchers, in helping build such a context through the development of the website's metadata and other properties, but for my argument here, I want to emphasise a more basic point. In a time of mass self-broadcasting (Castells, 2009), when everyone in principle has the capacity to express *something* in what is formally a public domain (through being online), the question of *how* every voice can be 'heard in the concert of life' becomes an institutional question of great complexity – unless, that is, one can fall back on the default of a large-scale institution of production with a guaranteed slice of a population's regular attention.

My third example shows that even when that institutional condition is met, the wider dynamics of a large communication landscape may act against it. Hector

Amaya is concerned with alternative media that are not small scale: the networks of Spanish-language media in the US that provide the primary media for US Latinas/os. Two large corporations dominate this landscape: Univision (owned by private equity) and Televisa (owned by NBC): Univision is the larger of these, but even Telemundo cost $2.9 billion when NBC purchased it in 2002 (Amaya, 2013: 129).

Amaya does not deny that Spanish-language media give more coverage to global Latin American news and to Latinas/os voices within the US. But he regards this as falling far short of sustaining a Latina/o voice within the US mainstream media landscape overall. While this itself is part, he argues, of a longer history of pure commercialism in Spanish-language media in the US (ibid.: 131), Amaya's point is different and relates to the deep structural underpinnings necessary to *sustain* alternative media voices on a large scale. Amaya argues that a fundamental barrier to building Spanish-language media as an effective voice for Latinas/os within the US mainstream is the lack of *legal* protection for its cultural and political status; yet, such media play an important and non-substitutable role in representing and recognising Latinas/os within US public culture. It is paradoxical, therefore, that the US regulatory system gives no value to Spanish-language media *as voice*, categorising it merely as commercial commodities which, at best, need no special protection in for example takeover battles, and, at worst, should be limited as a foreign import (ibid.: 124, 131–5). As Amaya writes, "a *pluri*national public sphere will always be in danger of disappearing without adequate legal protection. Spanish-language media should be so protected by the Federal Communication Commission, not as a language for commerce, but as a language for community and politics" (ibid.: 157, added emphasis).

Not all alternative media, of course, are shaped directly by such large-scale legal or regulatory factors, but they are always potentially in play, so much should be taken into account in thinking about the wider space in which alternative media provide effective voice for specific communities.

Alternative media's voice against violence

I want to end this section by counterposing against Amaya's eloquent doubts concerning the effectiveness of Spanish-language media in the US Clemencia Rodríguez's account of community media in Colombia and their role in challenging violence's dominance over a violence-riven country in the 2000s.

Rodríguez is interested in 'citizens' media'. She defines these as "those media that facilitate the transformation of individuals into 'citizens'", following the political theorist Chantal Mouffe's rethinking of citizenship outside formal political structures as an open process whereby individuals and groups discover a political identity for themselves (2011: 24, quoting Mouffe, 1992). This notion of citizenship (and "the culture of citizenship": Rodríguez, 2011: 216) is from the beginning tied to processes of cultural and symbolic transformation: "empowering citizens to name the world in their own terms" (ibid.: 24, added emphasis). The result of such processes is to reconstruct individual and communal identities through symbolic processes in which communally owned and used media have a privileged position, since they are understood precisely as collective means to name the world (compare Freire 1972). As one leading radio station creator, Alirio Gonzáles, puts it: "what we need [through citizens' media] is for this territory to rethink itself as a subject" (quoted in 2011: 76). This broad rethinking of citizens' media as a way of life and an alternative mode of 'social reproduction' has some overlaps with recent accounts of the politics of protest camps such as Occupy (Feigenbaum, Frenzel and McCurdy, 2013: 220, 227).

This need is especially deep when people live under extreme violence: then the conventional role of media – to represent facts, including the facts of conflict – becomes too dangerous (Rodríguez, 2011: 158) and a pervasive culture of violence corrodes basic processes of trust, self-belief and community interaction. Under these conditions, Rodríguez argues, community-owned media can literally enact another way of living, a way of living still in *peace*, that is embedded in the ordinary processes of everyday life: "citizens' media act as loudspeakers for those realities that still exist out of the reach of armed violence, situations not yet permeated by logics of war and aggression" (ibid.: 253).

How this is achieved relates very closely to the features of voice discussed earlier. First of all, the *material means* for voice have to be rethought, by moving the technologies of communication across space in a new way. A key example is the radiobicycle invented by the founder of Radio Andaquí, Alirio Gonzáles, that brings "radio technology to wherever people are, not the other way round" (quoted by Rodríguez, 2011: 55). This reconfiguration of the material infrastructure of voice is linked to new forms of distribution and education. Gonzáles also set up EAIBA (Escuela Audiovisuel Infantil de Belén de los Andaquiés), a media school for local children which allows children who feel they have a story to go to their teachers, who help them take photos, build a soundtrack and put a short *fotovideo* together: media education is built into the basic production process. Similarly with distribution: such programmes by local children are first broadcast in the public streets of the community where the children live, before being broadcast on the radio and archived on YouTube (ibid.: 55). As a result of this reconfiguration, the technologies for wider communication are placed closed to daily processes: they become present "there *with* the community of Belen in its natural and cultural context" (ibid.: 78).

This rethinking of the role of media (ibid.: 233) focuses not on the audiences who may or may not be reached, but on the *subjects* transformed in the process of making media (ibid.: 79). It focuses on how citizens' media can change people's 'communicative competence' and so their sense of themselves. Gonzáles puts it eloquently: "we narrate what we do and who we are, so that we can discover where we want to go" (quoted, ibid.: 56). Narrative and storytelling under these circumstances become profoundly political, but this is not an aberration: rather, it grasps the potential of media infrastructures, as technologies for voice, from the beginning as a means by which a community can "emerge as a collective of active agents with a voice" (2011: 62).

This process necessarily involves the *social process* of listening: not passive registering of sound, but active listening in dialogue with the different identities of others. Here, Rodríguez draws on Colombian cultural theorist Jesus Martin-Barbero and his vision for rethinking the contemporary cliché of 'diversity': "diversity is not just there, it has to be constructed as we become interlocutors, when we seriously listen to others, even if doing so means risking our own certainties" (quoted, ibid.: 218). This *reflexive process* is clearly a contrast with the usual aims of commercial media, and this was understood by the producers Rodríguez interviewed (ibid.: 206–7). Producing citizens' media is not a matter simply of setting up a new station with a community broadcasting licence. On the contrary, it is an ongoing process of building voice: "these media are not born as community media; we have to make them into community media, and this is a long and arduous process. A real community radio station should include *the entire community*" (ibid.: 224, added emphasis). On this civic conception, community media literally become the collective processes for the production, sustaining and enacting of collective *voice*, so transforming our sense of the values at stake in media production.

The resulting transvaluation of media processes is not, in its details, a simple recipe for how media can be everywhere. Indeed, Rodríguez emphasises the extremity of the conditions under which her radio producers and communities collaborate and the distinctiveness and vulnerability of each solution found locally to war's profound corrosion of peaceful life. But her fieldwork offers the clearest expression of how the motivation of alternative media (in a broad sense) is grounded in the value of voice, as a counter-value to broad forms of oppression. Such an approach does not reject the importance of audiences (the question of who is listening), but builds it more deeply into the *social* processes that go into producing and distributing media themselves.

Conclusion

In this chapter, I have tried to make explicit one key element in the normative foundations of alternative media research: the concept of voice. That principle is in turn related to another concept, recognition. Voice, as we have seen, is a multilayered process, and so the conditions under which voice is effectively realised are complex. Seriously enacting the value of voice means not just proclaiming the importance of exercising voice in isolation, but building processes for social, civic and political change, which increase the likelihood of processes of voice being sustained and *taken into account* in wider public culture and decision-making.

The implications of voice as a concept – and alternative media fully committed to enacting voice as a process – for societies, whether officially democratic or not, are potentially radical. Unfortunately there has been no space to explore those implications here. Instead, the chapter has concentrated on illustrating the range and diversity of the factors that shape whether voice is effectively achieved and sustained (or not). It is perhaps on the full understanding of such positive conditions for voice that the long-term success of alternative media research depends.

Further reading

Chapter 1 of Couldry's *Why Voice Matters* (London: Sage, 2010) provides a more detailed account of the concept of voice in the specific context of Western neoliberal democracies, with chapter 5 explaining the philosophical background of the concept of voice. Chapter 1 of Rodríguez (2011) is a vivid, detailed account of the process of voice in practice in rural Colombia. Dreher (2009) explores the limits of voice, understood in isolation, and supplements voice with the concept of listening. Readers interested in the concept of listening specifically should read Susan Bickford's book *The Dissonance of Democracy: Listening, Conflict and Citizenship* (Ithaca, NY: Cornell University Press, 1996), especially chs. 1, 3 and 5.

References

Amaya, H. (2013) *Citizenship Excess*. New York: New York University Press.

Arendt, H. (1958) *The Human Condition*. Chicago: Chicago University Press.

Atton, C. (2002) *Alternative Media*. London: Sage.

Atton, C. and Couldry, N. (2003) "Introduction to special issue on alternative media." *Media Culture and Society*, 25(5), 579–88.

Butler, J. (2005) *Giving an Account of Oneself*. New York: Fordham University Press.

Castells, M. (2009) *Communication Power*. Oxford: Oxford University Press.

Cavarero, A. (2000) *Relating Narratives*. London: Routledge.

Connell, R. (2007) *Southern Theory*. Cambridge: Polity.

Couldry, N. (2010a) *Why Voice Matters*. London: Sage.

Couldry, N. (2010b) "New online news sources and writer-gatherers.'" In N. Fenton (ed.), *New Media, Old News*. London: Sage (pp. 138–52).

de Sousa Santos, B. (ed.) (2005) *Democratizing Democracy*. London: Verso.

Downing, J. (with Villareal Ford, T., Gil, G. and Stein, L.) (2001) *Radical Media: Rebellious Communication and Social Movement*. Thousand Oaks, CA: Sage.

——(2003) "Audiences and readers of alternative media: The absent lure of the virtually unknown." *Media Culture and Society*, 25(5), 625–46.

Dreher, T. (2009) "Listening across difference: Media and multiculturalism beyond the politics of voice." *Continuum*, 23(4), 445–58.

Feigenbaum, A, Frenzel, F. and McCurdy, P. (2013) *Protest Camps*. London: Pluto.

Fotopoulou, A. and Couldry, N. (2015) "Telling the story of the stories: Online content curation and digital engagement." *Information Communication and Society*, 18(2), 235–49.

Freire, P. (1972) *Pedagogy of the Oppressed*. Harmondsworth: Penguin.

Fuller, L. (ed.) (2007) *Community Media: International Perspectives*. New York: Palgrave MacMillan.

Fundación Radio Estrella del Mar (n.d.) *Enciclopedia Cultural de Chiloé. Volume 1: El Monte*. Chiloé: Fundación Radio Estrella del Mar.

Garnham, N. (1990) *Capitalism and Communication*. London: Sage.

Gilligan, C. (1982) *In a Different Voice*. Cambridge, MA: Harvard University Press.

Harvey, D. (2000) *Spaces of Hope*. Edinburgh: Edinburgh University Press.

Honneth, A. (2007) *Disrespect*. Cambridge: Polity.

Macintyre, A. (1981) *After Virtue*. London: Duckworth.

MacNamara, J. (2013) "Beyond voice: Audience-making and the work and 'architecture of listening' as new media literacies." *Continuum*, 27(1), 160–75.

Mouffe, C. (1992) *Dimensions of Radical Democracy*. London: Verso.

Ricoeur, P. (1980) "Narrative time." In W. Mitchell (ed.), *On Narrative*. Chicago: Chicago University Press (pp. 165–86).

Rodríguez, C. (2001) *Fissures in the Mediascape*. Creskill, NJ: Hampton Press.

——(2003) "The bishop and his star: Citizens' communication in southern Chile." In N. Couldry and J. Curran (eds), *Contesting Media Power*. Lanham, MD: Rowman and Littlefield (pp. 177–94).

——(2011) *Citizens' Media Against Armed Conflict: Disrupting Violence in Colombia*. Minneapolis: University of Minnesota Press.

Sen, A. (1999) *Development as Freedom*. Oxford: Oxford University Press.

Sennett, R. (1998) *The Corrosion of Character*. New York: Norton.

Taylor, C. (1986) "Self-interpreting animals." In C. Taylor (ed.), *Philosophical Papers* (Vol. 1). Cambridge: Cambridge University Press (pp. 45–76).

4
BEYOND THE BINARIES?
Alternative media and objective journalism

Robert A. Hackett and Pinar Gurleyen

What is the orientation of alternative media to journalism objectivity? Do journalists in alternative media endorse, negotiate or challenge the practices and concept of objectivity as a guiding ethos? These questions are complex, since both 'alternative media' and 'journalism objectivity' are contested concepts that denote shifting, diverse, malleable and sometimes contradictory practices and organisations. They are questions worth untangling, however, as they can shed light on commonality and difference within the realm of alternative media, and relations between hegemonic and alternative media, including the possibility of reciprocal influence. Answers to these questions can also help us assess the comparative effectiveness of different editorial philosophies within alternative journalism, in terms of earning credibility and sustainability, shaping public discourse and promoting social justice. They are also relevant to understanding the status of contending paradigms within journalism, at a time of political, economic and technological flux.

In this chapter, we first outline objectivity as a central characteristic of 'mainstream' journalism, particularly in the US. We then briefly survey existing research regarding different orientations of alternative journalism, and then approach the question more conceptually, through a fourfold schema of alternative media. We then 'concretise' the analysis by considering three specific types of alternative journalism – IndyMedia, Wikinews, and journalistic blogs. We conclude by considering current media developments that further challenge the equation of mainstream media with objectivity, and alternative media with advocacy or subjectivity.

Journalism's regime of objectivity

Objectivity can be regarded as a multifaceted paradigm that informs news production by professionals. Hackett and Zhao (1998) argue that it comprises a discursive 'regime' with five aspects. First, objectivity is a normative ideal, indicating values and goals that journalists should strive for. These can be divided into values concerning journalism's capacity to impart information about the world (separation of fact from opinion, accuracy, completeness), and values concerning the stance reporters should take toward the value-laden meanings of news: neutrality, detachment, impartiality and independence, avoiding partisanship, personal biases, ulterior motives or outside interests (McQuail, 1992: 196–204).

Second, these values imply an epistemological stance – assumptions about knowledge and reality. The assumption that news can and ought to report on the world as it is, without 'bias', implies a positivist confidence in the possibility of accurate descriptions through careful observation and recording of events and facts, perceivable through the senses (Hackett, 2008: 3347). By contrast, other practices that are taken as hallmarks of objectivity – notably, quoting 'both sides' of a controversial issue, such as climate change, without attempting to ascertain the truth of the matter – imply the quite different epistemological stance of conventionalism. Conventionalism holds that human perception of the world is always mediated by our mental categories and procedures of knowledge production; news production is thus as much a construction as a reflection of the social world. Journalism cannot live up to the objectivity ideal, because knowledge of the world independent of the observer's standpoint is impossible.

The objectivity regime's third dimension is a mutable set of newsgathering and presentational practices. Bennett (2009: 192–208) identifies six such practices. Journalists assume the role of a politically neutral adversary, critically examining both sides of each issue to ensure impartial coverage; observing prevailing social standards of decency and good taste; using documentary reporting practices, based on reporters' direct observation or information from credible sources; using a standardised story format; training reporters as generalists rather than specialists; and enforcing the above practices through editorial supervision, to prevent violations of professional norms. A different list is offered by Peace Journalism theorists, who see a link between the incentivisation of conflict escalation by the media, and conventional 'objective' war reporting on timely events (like battles) rather than broader contexts or long-term processes; a bias in favour of official rather than grassroots sources; and a deep-rooted dualism that portrays conflicts as two-sided zero-sum games (Lynch and McGoldrick, 2005: 209–12).

Some of these practices may seem almost quaint in this age of infotainment, but as characteristics of American journalism's twentieth-century era of 'high modernism' (Hallin, 1992; Baym, 2010), they still constitute benchmarks by which 'serious' journalism is evaluated. This indicates a fourth dimension of the objectivity regime: it is an ingredient in public discourse about news. Objectivity provides the language for everyday assessments of journalistic performance, including synonyms like 'fairness' and 'balance', and opposites, like 'bias' (Hackett, 2008: 3346).

Finally, objectivity is embodied in an institutional framework. As manifested in American 'high modernist' journalism, news organisations are formally independent from the state, with legal guarantees of press freedom. They separate internal editorial and marketing functions to minimise owners' and advertisers' influence. Reporting is undertaken by socially responsible professionals with requisite skills and ethics. Historically, the American metropolitan daily newspaper and British public service broadcasting can be considered citadels of the objectivity regime. Under the impact of conglomeration and hypercommercialism in media industries, and broader cultural and political currents, faith in journalism objectivity is eroding in those citadels. But in many non-Western 'transition societies', the objectivity regime may be burgeoning under the impact of media globalisation, and as an alternative to the state-oriented authoritarianism of the past.

Alternative media, diverse stances

At first sight, one might assume that journalists in alternative media would oppose the objectivity regime. Perhaps alternative journalism would favour either open advocacy or unabashed subjectivity (the expression of personal experience, outside and against official channels – the voice of victims of war, for instance). Some research supports this interpretation. Thus, Atton and Hamilton (2008) argue that alternative journalists "seek to challenge objectivity and impartiality from both an ethical and practical standpoint" (ibid.: 85) and exhibit openly proclaimed biases and selectivity, with generally little interest in 'balanced' reporting (ibid.: 86). Ethically and epistemologically, alternative journalists reject both the possibility and desirability of separating facts from values (ibid.: 85), and they see themselves counterbalancing the dominant media's elite-oriented hierarchy of sources and viewpoints. The philosophy is summarised by David Barsamian (interview with Hackett, 15 April 2012), the Colorado-based producer of Alternative Radio: "I reject objectivity because I don't want to give a voice to injustice." Similarly, Susan Forde's interviews with alternative journalists in the US, UK and Australia reveal a widespread rejection of neutrality and detachment, in favour of open advocacy (Forde, 2011: 114).

Scholarship on journalism objectivity also sets up a *prima facie* case for the objective/alternative journalism binary. Critical scholars have argued that overall, news objectivity tends to "systematically favour the reporting of official perspectives" (Bennett, 2009: 187), or even more broadly, to provide a smokescreen for ideological accounts of the world that appear to be neutral, representing 'universal' perspectives. In that vein, Hackett and Zhao (1998: 206) argue that alternative media are an especially likely venue for "positive alternatives to the regime of objectivity", partly because their very existence "implicitly challenges the dominant news media's claims to speak to and for everybody". Research on the historical origins of news objectivity provides similar grounds for such binarism. Various catalysts have been identified (Maras, 2013: 22–38), including technology, the pursuit of professional status by journalists, the economic interests of advertisers and commercial press owners in seeking broad multipartisan readerships, and the emergence of capitalist social relations, particularly alienation, commodity fetishism and modernity's self-reflexive gaze (Calcutt and Hammond, 2011).

These historical explanations are much debated, but they share an implication that journalism objectivity serves vested commercial or political interests, and/or functions to maintain relations of domination. One could reasonably suppose that in opposing domination and giving voice to movements for social change, alternative media would reject journalism objectivity as well.

The question is not so simple, however. One historical interpretation sees a quite progressive impulse in objectivity's emergence. Schiller (1981) links it to the democratic and populist discourse of the pre-commercial labour press in nineteenth-century America, and its claim to constitute a politically independent voice for all citizens, against the vested elite interests expressed through the era's partisan papers. Such a stance bears some similarity to today's alternative media. One can imagine hybrid positions between wholesale rejection and adoption of objectivity. It is possible to accept some aspects of the objectivity regime, especially its goals (such as truth-telling in the public interest, fairness, reportage based on investigation, careful observation and rejection of propaganda) – while avoiding others (such as artificial balance between truth and lies, or excessive dependence on official sources). Below, we infer different potential orientations to objectivity from researchers' categorisations of alternative media.

A schema of alternative media

Bailey, Cammaerts and Carpentier (2008: 6–33) offer a fourfold schema of theoretical perspectives on alternative media. Their schema implies differing orientations to objectivity. *Community-oriented participatory media*, such as those represented by AMARC, the World Association of Community Radio Broadcasters, would presumably tend to reflect the values of geographically or interest-based communities. In their public affairs programming, commitment to objectivity might vary with the degree and type of training that volunteer participants in programming receive. Even when objectivity is adopted as a norm, it is likely to be strongly influenced by the political opinions and cultural values of the audience. Susan Forde's research (2011: 53) implies a stance of attachment rather than neutral observation, in that alternative media journalists often belong to the various movements they report on. They also claim an "overriding commitment to their public sphere".

Analysing Al Jazeera's Arab-language coverage of the US-led war in Iraq, Iskandar and el-Nawawy (2004) describe the network's approach as 'contextual objectivity'. This concept registers the tension between journalists' pursuit of objectivity, and the imperative of resonating with their cultural context. That concept might well apply to journalism produced within and for other, smaller communities: multiple perspectives may be accessed, but within a framework of orientation to shared values. Within these communities, journalists may recognise a plurality of truths. At the same time, though, those outside the community's value system may be considered ideologues (as in the online community constituted by the Wikinews project, discussed below). Indeed, this argument might well be extended to 'mainstream' media as well: objectivity is *always* contextual, but it is easier for hegemonic media to render their biases natural, to make them seem 'the way it is'. Not that all community-oriented media are themselves progressive or democratic (Downing, 2001: 39, 88–95). The rejection of objectivity in ultra-nationalist or fundamentalist religious platforms could well help legitimise exclusionary practices or even hate propaganda.

A second conception of alternative media, in Bailey et al.'s schema, highlights *challenges to hegemonic media and their representations*. This notion parallels Downing's focus on progressive 'radical media' that build solidarity laterally among subordinate groups, and express their opposition to power structures (Downing, 2001: xi). It also accords with Fuchs's emphasis on alternative media's oppositional and transformational *form and content*, rather than their participatory *processes*. In his view, such 'critical media' promote a participatory, co-operative society and express the interests of the dominated, among other goals (Fuchs, 2010: 177, 181–2). Given such explicit orientations, counter-hegemonic media would presumably seek to counterbalance the perceived biases of mainstream media, in favour of marginalised or under-represented groups. To some extent, such radical media have reinvigorated the tradition of the nineteenth-century British and American partisan press. At the hard-left edge of the spectrum, alternative media that are tied to particular political organisations may generate the 'tightly unified vision' of Leninist-style 'agit-prop', which combines short-term publicising of immediate social problems (agitation) with long-term political indoctrination (propaganda) (Downing, 2001: 68). Such media may well claim the mantle of objectivity, to the extent that they purport to offer a 'correct' interpretation of politics from the standpoint of subordinate classes. In Western countries, however, this kind of radical partisan media has declined along with the sectarian political Left since the 1970s. More commonly, contemporary critical media acknowledge pluralism within the spectrum of counter-hegemonic perspectives and voices.

A third approach envisages alternative media as *helping activate and democratise civil society*, promoting active citizenship and maintaining independence from both state and market forces. In this view, alternative media contribute to democratisation *of* the media, enabling citizens "to be active in one of many (micro-) spheres relevant to daily life, to organize different forms of deliberation, and to exert their rights to communicate" (Bailey, Cammaerts and Carpentier, 2008: 24). They also contribute to democratisation *through* the media, facilitating participation in civil society beyond the media field. Unlike the two previous categories, such civil society or citizens' media (Rodríguez, 2001) are not necessarily oppositional, or oriented towards particular communities. Nevertheless, in the pursuit of extensive participation and self-representation in the public sphere(s) for various social groups, civil society/citizens' media would likely share a scepticism towards "the absolutist interpretation of media neutrality and impartiality" (ibid.: 25).

The fourth approach defines alternative media as '*rhizomatic*', a botanical metaphor suggesting that such media can spread roots and sprout in unexpected places and times. Such media often function as a nexus – "the crossroads where people from different types of movements and struggles meet and collaborate" – and that deepen democracy by linking them. Such media are organisationally fluid and contingent; diverse and elusive; and destabilising of the rigidities and certainties of public and corporate media, while leaving open the door to 'transhegemonic collaborations' with those same hegemonic media (ibid.: 31). By contrast with the first three perspectives, the rhizome metaphor challenges the alternative-versus-mainstream binarism, and highlights the potential for reciprocal influence and hybridisation. Accordingly, rhizomatic media may or may not pursue objectivity, depending on the cultural context and the political conjuncture in which they find themselves. A sketch of three examples of alternative journalism in practice indicates diverse orientations to objectivity.

Indymedia

Independent Media Centers (IMCs) have sprouted in various countries alongside the anti-corporate globalisation movement since 1999. The IMCs are 'alternative' in both their processes (participatory and consensus-based decision-making) and their content ('open' publishing, but in close relationship with global justice movements). The IMCs clearly reject objectivity, and indeed journalists from Indymedia's free newspaper in New York define objectivity as one of the mainstream media's key problems (Forde, 2011: 120). Instead, they emphasise 'accuracy' as a guiding principle (Scatamburlo-D'Annibale and Chehade, 2004). Indymedia's implicit epistemology is pluralist: "truth is not seen as an absolute but as an infinite sampling of perspectives of a given situation" (Platon and Deuze, 2003: 346). Indymedia journalists adopt a journalism style that favours the participation of groups "systematically marginalized by mainstream media". Refusing a "false sense of objectivity", Austin Indymedia embraces open publishing, community collaboration and non-hierarchical and consensus decision-making to deploy media-making as tools "for social, economic and environmental justice" (http://blip.tv/austin-indymedia-center).

From his research in Ontario, Canada, Hanke (2005: 59) sees Indymedia journalists as "participant, rather than detached, observers of the movement scene and direct actions", with their epistemological 'perspectivism' being based on "their social position and experience of the world, as well as their political commitments". Arguments for the necessity of the mainstream media's standards of balance and caution about reporting rumours ignore the 'practical ethics' that do govern Indymedia practice. For instance, one Indymedia maker said that "people destroying bank machines" should probably not be videotaped at demonstrations because "you're working in solidarity with the protesters" (ibid.: 59).

Wikinews

Wikinews provides an instructive contrast to Indymedia. Established in 2004 as a parallel project to Wikipedia, Wikinews offers both articles synthesised from other media sources, and original first-hand reports of events from contributing citizen journalists. Regarding content, it is not a "critical" medium in Fuchs's sense, but rather "independent" (of state or corporate control). Yet it can be considered an alternative medium in the sense of participatory processes and orientation to an online community of contributors. Wikinews embraces objectivity as embodied in its Neutral Point of View (NPOV) principle (Vis, 2009: 67). Given the association between objectivity and journalistic professionalism, that embrace may seem paradoxical. On the one hand, it challenges professionalism through its reliance on citizen reporting (Wikinews, n.d. a). On the other hand, while citizens are trusted to help set the news agenda, their presentation of articles is guided by NPOV, a policy that arguably mimics hegemonic media. According to Wikinews founder Jimmy Wales, NPOV "attempts to present ideas and facts in such a fashion that both supporters and opponents can agree", provided they are 'essentially rational people', as distinct from 'ideologues' forcefully stating their own viewpoint (Wikinews, n.d. b).

The practice of NPOV entails avoiding bias towards particular identifiable viewpoints; debates are to be 'described fairly' rather than 'advocating any side' (Wikinews, n.d. c). Certain editorial practices are applied in pursuit of this kind of objectivity, including removal of apparent cultural, personal or political bias, and the addition of counter-information (Thorsen, 2008: 940–44). Contributors can also use the inverted pyramid style of writing, a hallmark of objectivity in the conventional press; quotes can be sequenced in articles according to writers' own interpretation of the 'hierarchy of credibility' among sources (ibid.: 945). Wikinews's NPOV approach to objectivity has a democratic aspect: it represents different viewpoints and enables readers' participation. Yet it can also be criticized for undermining deliberative journalism by reducing "the multiple perspectives of its contributors into a single, coherent narrative" (Atton and Hamilton, 2008: 81) and on the grounds that "anyone who does not agree with the community consensus, or at least the way in which this is being represented, is effectively positioned as an 'ideologue'" (Thorsen, 2008: 939).

Blogs

To the extent that they are participatory and often oriented towards particular communities, blogs can be considered another form of alternative media. Their hallmark is subjectivity, the expression of individual authors' experience and opinions. Blog-based journalism has been described as a new form "infused with post-modern sensibilities" and "a narrative style characterized by personalization and an emphasis on non-institutionalized status; audience participation in content creation; and story forms that are fragmented and interdependent with other websites" (Wall, 2005: 153).

In journalistic blogs, orientations to objectivity vary with the organisational context, level of professionalisation and author(s)' status – journalist, ordinary citizen or activist. Domingo and Heinonen (2008: 7–11) offer a fourfold typology: (a) Citizen Blogs, written by the public outside media organisations; (b) Audience Blogs, written by the public but moderated or facilitated by news organisations; (c) Journalist Blogs, written by journalists outside the rubric of media institutions; and (d) Media Blogs, written by journalists within media institutions. Media Blogs would generally be the most objective. In Citizen Blogs, however, transparency often overrides fairness, accuracy or objectivity as ethical values (Blood, 2003: 63; see also Singer, 2007: 86; Phillips, 2010: 379). What accounts for this value shift? Possible factors include emphasis on speed, and lack of journalistic resources and training (Domingo and Heinonen, 2008: 8). Even in blogs produced by journalists, there is greater scope for creativity and interpretation compared to conventional news media (ibid.: 10). Robinson (2006) observes that in countering the threat of independent weblogs, professional journalists' blogs surrender such traditional routines as fact-checking, conversely giving room to subjectivity and rumour. Robinson arguably exaggerates the rigor of conventional reporting, underestimating the recent impact of conglomerate ownership, cutbacks in newsroom resources, and growing reliance on public relations hand-outs, among other symptoms of what critics regard as a crisis in American journalism (McChesney and Nichols, 2010).

Nevertheless, journalistic blogs can be seen to pose a double challenge to objectivity. First, by contrast with the production of ostensibly authoritative accounts by the journalist as an expert in dispassionate observation, blogs typically enable audiences to be a "vital part of the storytelling process"; news stories are iterative, as participants take on the editorial role of correcting 'inaccuracies' in successive versions (St. John III and Johnson, 2012: 4). Such a process arguably replaces journalistic gatekeeping with 'gatewatching', a term coined by Bruns (2005) to indicate that interested parties can aggregate news to present it online, leaving the content unfinished for readers to interact if they so wish (St. John III and Johnson, 2012: 4).

The blogosphere's second challenge to objectivity relates to the political culture of the internet more broadly. As a networked medium that facilitates the emergence of virtual communities and discursive worlds segregated from others, blogs in a sense reincarnate the nineteenth-century partisan press. Ryfe (2012: 189) argues that journalistic objectivity cannot be maintained as online journalists vie for the attention of "committed, like-minded people".

Such a view may be exaggerated; the very fragmentation of the internet may create a demand for independent, public interest-oriented journalism that can transcend factional polarisation, albeit a journalism that may be difficult to monetise and sustain in market terms. Still, arguably the very concepts of reality and truth are being transformed, or at least rendered fluid, in the blogosphere. Robinson (2006: 71) suggests that definitions of reality are based on the perception of the community (readers), and the accumulation of reader comments that "present as many 'truths' as possible" serves to construct the story. Ryfe (2012: 202) foresees that community values may be displacing objectivity, as online journalists "adopt whatever practices and values are useful for making themselves valuable nodes in their networks". In this respect, as well as others discussed below, the dichotomy of mainstream and alternative or participatory journalism may be blurring. Some observers see audience/citizen contributions to news as a 'counterbalance' to some of the limitations of objective reporting, such as over-reliance on official sources (St. John III and Johnson, 2012: 5). They also propose a cautious embrace of subjectivity and a careful acknowledgment of its benefits and dangers. With consumers increasingly valuing subjectivity, a new "post-objective" approach may be necessary, one that would (1) acknowledge wider spectrums of viewpoints; (2) embrace transparency; and (3) engage the public through active education and updates to issues germane to their lives (ibid.).

Conclusion

As discussed, any attempted equation of dominant media with objectivity, and of alternative media with its rejection, is untenable. The picture is further complicated in two ways. First, in the citadels of Western journalism, the objectivity regime is in crisis, if not defunct. One study of American broadcast journalism posits a fundamental paradigm shift related to shifts in the political economy of media and the broader political culture (Baym, 2010). The "objective effort to record the occurrence of the actual" (ibid.: 3), associated with high modernism and a triumvirate of television networks, shifted during the 1980s and 1990s to a 'postmodern' paradigm characterised by a multichannel mediascape, profit-oriented conglomerate ownership, deregulation, the commodification of the public sphere, the displacement of 'serious' news by infotainment and an "epistemological relativism that rejects the possibility of objectivity while suspecting that all normative standards are culturally located and historically contingent" (p. 15). In more recent satirical news programs like Jon Stewart's *Daily Show*, Baym sees an emergent 'neo-modernism' that combines postmodernist forms – sarcasm, irony, subjective viewpoints – with the modernist ideal of informed citizenship.

Baym's analysis arguably overburdens Stewart and his fellow satirist Stephen Colbert, but it does suggest powerful processes of hybridisation and 'discursive integration' – the conjunctural rearticulation of styles, standards and genres (p. 18). Such processes challenge the mainstream/alternative and objective/subjective binaries – an argument extended by Kperogi (2013). Like Baym, he sees an epochal retreat from objectivity by (American) professional journalism, but he regards it as a profit-driven strategic co-optation of alternative media practices that have gained prominence in the new digital media environment. He instances corporate media-enabled citizen journalism projects and sites, the participatory 'crowdsourcing' of news agendas, the "journalism of attachment" enabled by j-blogs (discussed above), the practice of "fact-checking" sources' statements, and the open ideological orientations – redolent of the press's partisan origins – of corporate media like Fox News. Whether such corporate practices always derive from alternative media is debatable, but Kperogi's argument explicitly challenges the mainstream/alternative binary, and raises for research the dialectic between alternative media's influence within the overall system, and obversely, the potential for co-optation that would look more like a 'symbiosis' than mutual exclusivity. This arguably signals "the birth of postobjectivism in mainstream reportorial practices and the erasure of the distinctiveness of alternative media practices" (Kperogi, 2013: 60). If so, such unparalleled "hegemonic containment of alternative media" would have real consequences for the role, conception, and future of both journalism and emancipatory politics (ibid.).

A second factor complicates the equation of alternative media with opposition to objectivity. In many countries, popular movements struggling against authoritarian regimes clamour for a press that can speak truth to power, that has sufficient independence to counter the propaganda of regime-oriented media. From our own observation as researchers, objective journalism is both a popular demand, and a goal pursued by at least some alternative media, in countries as diverse as Fiji, Serbia and Turkey. As one example, consider *140 Journos*, a popular Turkish citizen journalism site on Twitter. Defining itself as a 'counter media movement', it works to offset the perceived shortage of fact-based objective news reporting in the dominant Turkish media. Its detached tone and neutral language do not render it apolitical, however; it collaborates with social change organisations to transform the news into social responsibility campaigns, giving citizens a voice on issues that affect them (Engin Onder and Cem Aydogdu, interview with Gurleyen, 19 August 2013). Further comparative research, especially in non-Western media and political systems, would doubtless reveal further articulations.

In summary, the diversity of both objectivity and alternative media suggests the possibility of various orientations. Some alternative media reject objectivity as an ideological smokescreen for the status quo and a barrier to social change. Many alternative media might well accept the ideal, and see themselves as the real inheritors of objectivity, in contrast to corporate or state media that fail to provide watchdog journalism or 'real' news. To the extent that they do pursue objectivity, however, alternative media are likely to pursue it with more collective, dialogic, egalitarian and multiperspectival methods than was conventional in the corporate press. The corporate press may not be able to co-opt everything, and some basis for a binary distinction may remain.

Acknowledgements

The authors acknowledge research funding from the SFU/SSHRC Institutional Grants Committee, Simon Fraser University; and research or editorial assistance from Angelika Hackett, Kavya Joseph, Wendee Lang and Rebecca Visser.

Further reading

Atton, C. and Hamilton, J. F. (2008) *Alternative Journalism*. Los Angeles: Sage. Analyses diverse forms and genres of journalism challenging mainstream news, including a section on objectivity.

Forde, S. (2011) *Challenging the News: The Journalism of Alternative and Community Media*. Houndmills, UK, and New York: Palgrave Macmillan. A historical and comparative analysis of alternative and community journalism, based on extensive empirical research and offering a theoretical view of its distinct continuities.

Hackett, R. A. (2011) "New vistas for peace journalism: Alternative media and communication rights." In I. S. Shaw, J. Lynch and R. A. Hackett (eds.) *Expanding Peace Journalism: Comparative and Critical Approaches*, Sydney: Sydney University Press (pp. 35–69). Situates alternative journalism in relation to both the objectivity regime and other movements for more democratic communication.

Maras, S. (2013) *Objectivity in Journalism*. Cambridge: Polity Press. While not addressing alternative media, a comprehensive overview of research literature on news objectivity.

References

Atton, C. and Hamilton, J. F. (2008) *Alternative Journalism*. Los Angeles: Sage.

Bailey, O., Cammaerts, B. and Carpentier, N. (2008) *Understanding Alternative Media*. Maidenhead, UK: McGraw-Hill/Open University Press.

Baym, G. (2010) *From Cronkite to Colbert: The Evolution of Broadcast News*. Boulder, CO: Paradigm.

Bennett, W. L. (2009) *News: The Politics of Illusion*. 8th ed. New York: Pearson/Longman.

Blood, R. (2003) "Weblogs and journalism: Do they connect?" *Nieman Reports*, 57(3), 61–63. Retrieved from http://www.nieman.harvard.edu/reports/03-3NRfall/V57N3.pdf (accessed 23 December 2009).

Bruns, A. (2005) *Gatewatching: Collaborative Online News Production*. New York: Peter Lang.

Calcutt, A. and Hammond, P. (2011) *Journalism Studies: A Critical Introduction*. London and New York: Routledge.

Domingo, D. and Heinonen, A. (2008) "Weblogs and journalism: A typology to explore the blurring boundaries." *Nordicom Review*, 29(1), 3–15.

Downing, J. (with Ford, T. V., Gil, G. and Stein, L.) (2001) *Radical Media: Rebellious Communication and Social Movements*. Thousand Oaks, CA: Sage.

Forde, S. (2011) *Challenging the News: The Journalism of Alternative and Community Media*. Houndmills, UK, and New York: Palgrave Macmillan.

Fuchs, C. (2010) "Alternative media as critical media." *European Journal of Social Theory*, 13(2), 173–92.

Hackett, R. A. (2008) "Objectivity in reporting." In W. Donsbach (ed.), *The International Encyclopedia of Communication*, 7. Malden, MA: Blackwell (pp. 3347–3350).

Hackett, R. A. and Zhao, Y. (1998) *Sustaining Democracy? Journalism and the Politics of Objectivity*. Toronto: Garamond.

Hallin, D. C. (1992) "The passing of the 'high modernism' of American journalism." *Journal of Communication*, 42, 14–25.

Hanke, B. (2005) "For a political economy of Indymedia practice." *Canadian Journal of Communication*, 30(1), 41–64.

Iskandar, A. and el-Nawawy, M. (2004) "Al-Jazeera and war coverage in Iraq: The media's quest for contextual objectivity." In S. Allan and B. Zelizer (eds), *Reporting War: Journalism in Wartime*. London and New York: Routledge (pp. 315–32).

Kperogi, F. (2013) "News with views: Postobjectivism and emergent alternative journalistic practices in America's corporate news media," *Review of Communication*, 13(1) (January), 48–65.

Lynch, J. and McGoldrick. A. (2005) "Peace Journalism: A global dialog for democracy and democratic media." In R. A. Hackett and Y. Zhao (eds), *Democratizing Global Media: One World, Many Struggles*. Lanham, MD: Rowman & Littlefield (pp. 269–88).

Maras, S. (2013) *Objectivity in Journalism*. Cambridge: Polity Press.

McChesney, R. W. and Nichols, J. (2010) *The Death and Life of American Journalism: The Media Revolution That Will Begin the World Again*. Philadelphia: Nation Books.

McQuail, D. (1992) *Media Performance: Mass Communication and the Public Interest*. London: Sage.

Phillips, A. (2010) "Transparency and the new ethics of journalism." *Journalism Practice*, 4(3), 373–82.

Platon, S. and Deuze, M. (2003) "Indymedia journalism: A radical way of making, selecting, sharing news?" *Journalism*, 4(3), 336–55. Retrieved from http://jou.sagepub.com/cgi/content/abstract/4/3/336

Robinson, S. (2006) "The mission of the j-blog: Recapturing journalistic authority online." *Journalism*, 7(1), 65–83.

Rodríguez, C. (2001) *Fissures in the Mediascape: An International Study of Citizens' Media*. Cresskill, NJ: Hampton Press.

Ryfe, M. D. (2012) "Why objectivity is impossible in networked journalism and what this means for the future of news." In B. St. John III and K. A. Johnson (eds), *News with a View: Essays on the Eclipse of Objectivity in Modern Journalism*. Jefferson, NC, and London: McFarland & Company (pp. 189–204).

Scatamburlo-D'Annibale, V. and Chehade, G. (2004) "The revolution won't be televised, but it might be uploaded." Retrieved 5 June 2013 from http://www.policyalternatives.ca/publications/monitor/june-2004-indymedia-phenomenon

Schiller, D. (1981) *Objectivity and the News*. Philadelphia: University of Pennsylvania Press.

Singer, J. B. (2007) "Contested autonomy: Professional and popular claims on journalistic norms." *Journalism Studies*, 8(1), 79–95.

St. John III, B. and Johnson, K. A. (2012) "Introduction: Challenges for journalism in a post-objective age." In B. St. John III and K. A. Johnson (eds), *News with a View: Essays on the Eclipse of Objectivity in Modern Journalism*. Jefferson, NC, and London: McFarland & Company (pp. 1–9).

Thorsen, E. (2008) "Journalistic objectivity redefined? Wikinews and the neutral point of view." *New Media & Society*, 10(6), 935–54. Retrieved from http://nms.sagepub.com/content/10/6/935 (accessed 11 May 2012).

Vis, F. (2009) "Wikinews reporting of Hurricane Katrina." In S. Allan and E. Thorsen (eds), *Citizen Journalism: Global Perspectives*. New York: Peter Lang (pp. 65–74).

Wall, M. (2005) "Blogs of war: Weblogs as news." *Journalism*, 6(2), 153–72.

Wikinews (n.d. a) "Mission statement." Retrieved from http://en.wikinews.org/wiki/Wikinews:Mission_statement (accessed 17 October 2013).

Wikinews (n.d. b) "Neutral point of view." Retrieved from http://en.wikinews.org/wiki/Wikinews:Neutral_point_of_view (accessed 17 October 2013).

Wikinews (n.d. c) "Neutral point of view." Retrieved from http://meta.wikimedia.org/wiki/Wikinews/Open_English/Neutral_point_of_view (accessed 17 October 2013).

5

COMMERCIALISM AND THE DECONSTRUCTION OF ALTERNATIVE AND MAINSTREAM MEDIA

Linda Jean Kenix

This chapter aims to deconstruct previous categorisations of alternative and mainstream media by arguing for a convergence of the media spectrum. The collapse of alternative and mainstream distinctions in the media is the result of several contributory factors that are converging across the journalistic profession: the rise of internet technologies; an interdependency of sources and resources; reduced journalism standards met with rising standards of alternative journalism; and increased expectations for transparency as well as 'relatability' across all media. This chapter argues that all of these factors are interrelated within an omnipresent commercial ideology that has revised economic mandates across journalism and has led to a widespread collapse of meaningful distinctions between the alternative and mainstream press. It is important to stress that essential differences do remain at the individual level between generalised conceptions of alternative and mainstream media. However, the aim of this chapter is to problematise the common tendency toward mutually exclusive classifications and to investigate the complexities that now exist in categorising our present media system within the context of an omnipresent commercialism found throughout contemporary culture.

The ideological pervasiveness of commercialism in media runs counter to previous research, which has argued that alternative media articulate an ideological position (Atton, 2009) that is oppositional to the dominant mainstream (Fenton, 2007; Hamilton, 2000). It has been argued, for example, that the alternative press serve as the central instigator for social change in democratic societies (Atton, 2002b; Curran and Couldry, 2003; Ostertag, 2008) – often in direct contrast to mainstream media (Albert, 2006). Such research has been bolstered by historical examinations of media, which have found prominent differences between alternative media that offer a particular ideological brand of content quite different from mainstream media

(Makagon, 2000). These differences have been attributed, in large part, to the commercial imperatives that were seen to be unique to mainstream news operations and subsumed within corporate capitalistic media conglomerations (Atkinson, 2006). In contrast, it has been argued that alternative media have not succumbed to the same capitalistically directed markers of success that have been embedded in the practices of mainstream journalism (Armstrong, 1981).

While recognising these stark differences outlined in a portion of the academic literature, this chapter builds upon research that highlights certain areas of overlapping interests between the mainstream and the alternative press (most notably Atton, 2002a; Downing, 2001; Hamilton, 2006; Dowmunt and Coyer, 2007). This chapter argues that a much more complex and fluid continuum of norms, practices, communication models and ideologies have emerged in response to consumerist mandates, which are increasingly important to a media system driven by a ubiquitous, fundamentally commercial imperative to gain market share across a converged media platform (Kenix, 2011).

At the forefront of this examination is the recognition of a mass culture (Bennett, 1982), which infers that no media are situated completely outside the ideological mainstream, carrying distinctive identities completely excluded from elite systems of power. Thus, in a hypercommercialised culture, all media coexist in this mass culture regardless of whether the media outlet is directed explicitly towards non-commercial outcomes. Any media, which aim to attract any audience, do so within the same capitalistic framework. It is that framework which is driving the rapidly dissolving boundaries between alternative and mainstream media.

Alternative versus the mainstream

There have been a variety of labels advanced to help identify any media not within the generally perceived mainstream: radical, activist (Waltz, 2005), participatory, citizen (Rodríguez and El Gazi, 2007), tactical (Atkinson, 2004), community and autonomous are but a few. However, alternative media is the term most widely used to categorise media that are not considered mainstream. It is important to note that what defines a section of media within any of these groupings at any particular moment of culture and time might be labelled mainstream within a different cultural time and place (Dowmunt and Coyer, 2007). Definitions and labels cannot be fixed, given the inherent subjective flexibilities within contemporary culture. In relation to the more generally used term 'alternative' media, there are also contradictions embedded within the label itself. For example, Downing (2001: ix) has argued that the label alternative is actually "oxymoronic", given that everything is an alternative to something else in the world.

While accepting the potential discursive contradiction of alternative media as a defining label, this research aims to build upon the use of 'alternative' in exploring differences among two ownership models that are used to define what it is to be part of mainstream media and what it is to be non-mainstream. Thus, while 'alternative media' may be problematised as a discursive term when considering the myriad possibilities across all media (Kenix, 2011), its usage is useful in exploring a truncated model of ownership, divided between conglomerate and independent ownership.

Given only two options, one must be the alternative of the other. Due to the relative power of conglomerately owned mainstream media, the independent press are positioned as the alternative choice, hence the usage of the term 'alternative' in this context is appropriate.

Although independent and conglomerate ownership models are quite different, alternative media owners must also be fiscally focused with at least an ancillary goal for economic sustainability, if they are to survive within the contemporary commercialised capitalist media system. For example, Jason Kottke, owner and content-manager of the widely read liberal arts 2.0 current affairs blog kottke.org, states plainly that he created the site "for fun *and income*" (2010: italics added). He creates the site for his own pleasure, but also hopes to provide a sustainable income for himself. In aiming for an economic return, Kottke must gain a sense of what his readers expect from his blog in the hope that he can fill that need and potentially earn an income. This interest in the audience is manifestly part of any economic equation. Being commercially minded does not necessarily mean that alternative media were created with the specific aim to make a profit. Rather, commercially minded alternative media are naturally cognisant of economic pressures and fiscally plan their operations in such a way to (hopefully) ensure their own continued existence – even if the chance of economic sustainability is quite small. It should go without saying that commercially minded media may share this important facet of operations but then can still operate in strikingly different ways. It is that point of difference (or potential similarity) which is the focus of this chapter.

There are alternative media that exist for their own sake, such as media created explicitly for artistic purposes or media with a strictly altruistic intent. However, one would expect a performance art piece, for example, to be different from a mainstream news article, given the widely different modes of expression and the creator's intent as either art or commerce. Such differences lose their meaning in a comparative context. Commercially minded operations share a fundamental perspective on self-sustainability that necessitates a certain level of audience awareness. This may be where the resemblance ends, but it is a point of similarity from which it might be possible to draw more evocative conclusions about the nature of alternative and mainstream media. Creating a comparison based on this categorisation also recognises the overwhelming preponderance of commercial news media that audiences engage with – for example, the most popular fifteen blogs in August 2013 were divided among independent (six blogs) and conglomerate (nine blogs) media outlets (eBiz, 2013). All fifteen were viewed as commercially minded, based on omnipresent consumer-friendly logos, gift subscriptions, donation calls, visual design based on professional graphic displays, and related merchandising products available through the familiar commercially savvy online shopping cart.

Media convergence

Technological and professional convergence is undeniably intertwined in the conflation of alternative and mainstream media and the continued rise of commercialism in Western societies. The convergence of news media may be the result of several broader social contexts (Deuze, 2008), such as the move away from individual expertise to collective intelligence (Levy, 1997) or the shift from solid modernity to liquid modernity (Bauman, 2000). Yet, commercialism cannot be removed from these larger social contexts. Media are converging through two interdependent trends: the convergence of multimedia newsrooms and the integration of citizens into the creation of content (Deuze, 2008). These two phenomena mutually inform the other and are both intrinsically related to commercialism, which is having a profound impact on the professionalism of journalism across alternative and mainstream media.

As citizens become more engaged in the newsmaking process, they are helping co-create converged multimedia newsrooms around the globe. This convergence is changing journalism as a profession and further problematising any distinctions between alternative and mainstream media. This seemingly organic and mutual construction of an entirely converged industry has a "cultural logic of its own" (Deuze, 2008: 103). Such cultural logic is steeped in shared consumerist motives to simultaneously participate in the creation of one's own consumed product (acting as a prosumer) while also decreasing operational costs in the hope of eventual increased profits. Thus, convergence is "both a top-down corporate-driven process and a bottom-up consumer-driven process" (Jenkins, 2004: 34). Commercialism is central to understanding the reasons why convergence across the media spectrum has been so successful and also why the normative tropes of journalism as a profession have changed so drastically in that time across the media spectrum.

There is a widespread acknowledgment that 'good' journalism is too expensive when balanced against the glut of information available online. The deconstruction of journalism within a commercialised context equates value to an increased economic return on investment. Thus, convergence facilitates a shift away from more expensive and laborious activities that are involved in objective, investigative pursuits and towards what Matheson (cited in McCrone, 2013) calls 'relatable' journalism. Audiences have embraced relatable journalism as a counterpoint to the onslaught of cross-referenced content, duplicated from one source to another, across internet outlets. Audiences are searching for something (or someone) to connect with, which generally means more opinion-based narratives and emotive subject matter in both the mainstream and alternative press. What emerges is a converged spectrum of sources for audiences who select their content from a variety of like-minded opinionated alternative and mainstream outlets online. Examples across mainstream media are numerous: CNN's Freedom Project that campaigns to end slavery and Christiane Amanpour's personal tweets are representative of what audiences expect through 'relatable' mainstream journalism. In the alternative press, audience members are asked to 'take action' and 'support' specific causes in independent outlets such as The Nation, while individuals not employed as journalists are invited as contributors to sites such as the Huffington Post and Kiwiblog. This type of journalism has exploded in popularity on the internet as audiences flock to relatable information steeped in opinion-based narratives. Amanpour has over 770,000 Twitter followers, while the Huffington Post recently reported 4.5 million unique monthly viewers (Quantcast, 2013).

A comparative study examining globalisation coverage in the alternative and mainstream press found that alternative media share more than just a 'relatable' approach. Alternative media are often "fragmented, non-responsive and even more exclusionary than the mainstream media" (Groshek and Han, 2011: 1537). Elitist and episodic journalism has long thought to be the result of a conglomerated mainstream media structure, but it is increasingly found in the alternative press. This is because all media have increasing needs for capital in converged, commercialised media environments that demand a multitude of expertise (Fountain, 2007). Radical experiments in alternative journalism that have been found in historical research (Harcup, 2003) may not be as frequent in the commercialised context of contemporary journalism. Thus, scholarship must be mindful to not idealise alternative media as "free spaces" that are completely liberated from the day-to-day structural considerations in the practice of journalism (Atton, 2002a: 154).

There are shared norms, routines and goals for success that are mutually hinged on commercial outcomes. Mainstream websites, such as CNN's iReport, co-opt the 'ethos' of citizen journalism while obviously also sourcing free content (Kperogi, 2008). Citizens uploading journalistic content are engaged in a commercial exchange that they receive no economic benefit from – they provide free labor to media outlets, generating content that will then be profiteered through advertising, but receive no compensation in return. *The New York Times* has recently partnered with local blogs in Brooklyn and New Jersey to create local content in those two communities while also forging relationships with City University of New York's Graduate School of Journalism to create a collaborative blog titled The Local, which provides local content and examines citizens' contributions to news. In absorbing a role that was previously the domain of alternative media, mainstream outlets such as *The Times* have been building upon converged social media to create relationships with readers – while also placating audiences who have relied on alternative media in the past: "professional journalism, with its veneer of autonomous and independent reporting in the public interest, allows corporate news entities to further solidify their place in society" (St. John III, 2008: 112). The intensively competitive market frames this relatable exchange in the mainstream press as facilitating democratic participation and citizen participation. However, one cannot ignore that the pursuit of these readers is intrinsically a commercial one and, if successful, results in increased market share.

Within a commercialised culture, only that which can be bought has value. This widespread commercial perspective can be seen as an inversion from what was once treasured in society. At one time, as Immanuel Kant (1985) argued, items for sale did not occupy the same space as that which was viewed as honourable, dignified or beautiful. The expansion of consumerism, which celebrated the markets and commercial exchanges, has devalued that which exists outside market forces (Kuttner, 1997). This process has continued to the point that now only what can be bought and sold is what is revered as the most beautiful within society. The hegemonic power of money rests in the fundamental acceptance that "we use money to express our identities" (Churchill, 2007: 410). Commercial representations of identity are more valued than non-commercial representations. This inter-relational process between the celebration of specific economically sustained values and fiscal returns has been called the "hegemony of money" (ibid.). Given such a widespread acceptance of commercialism within audiences, producers and 'prosumers' (Toffler, 1970) of media content all existing within one consumer culture, it is perhaps not surprising that recent research found alternative media visually expressing commercial interests at the same rate as, and in some instances with even more enthusiasm than, the mainstream press (Kenix, 2013). Visual imagery in the alternative press has become much more commercialised to sell that media as a product to consumers who are hyper-aware of consumptive cues that induce a commercial exchange. The visual construction of commercial interests in the alternative press suggests a move towards commercially based ideology that sees the consumerist message itself as symbolic capital. Commercial design and images, and not challenging iconography or design, are rewarded in such an environment, which helps explain its presence in the alternative press. Alternative media elevated commercial messaging above all else in an effort to increase their value within such a system (ibid.).

It is now assumed that a commercial perspective is essential to survival – a notion that has not historically been as widely accepted in the alternative media community. The contemporary media system, whether that is within the alternative or mainstream media, appears prestructured to include consumption. Therefore, the act of marketing oneself is fundamental to the process of communication, and that marketing message is not viewed within a necessarily conceptual framework but within the confines of the media message as a product.

The audience as consumer

The media spectrum of 'choices' has shifted focus towards a consumable set of ideologically driven products, rather than tools for public discussion (Kellner, 2006). The result of these commercial changes is that editorial content is aimed to be 'useful' to audiences within the consumerist system with stories about consumer choices and issues deemed to be important to consumers (Kunelius and Ruusunoksa, 2008) that are "in response to market demands" (Bennett, 1996). Integral to this commercialism is that individuals now consider the news and media content to be a product to be consumed (Kunelius and Ruusunoksa, 2008).

Within a commercial marketplace, whether that is in mainstream media or the alternative press, "quality and value are defined by consumers". Media maintain a hyper-reflexive "responsiveness to consumers"; they must offer immediate "self-correction" according to customer desires, have a "constant motivation to excel", an "efficient allocation of society's resources" and operate within an environment of "freedom of choice" (McManus, 1994: 4–5). These are the qualities that define a commercial media marketplace. Any competition that depends upon economic incentives will have these qualities present.

In the newsroom, these commercial qualities herald "a move away from reliance on craft norms defining what is newsworthy and how to report, toward a journalism based on serving the marketplace" (McManus, 1995: 301). Contemporary journalism is now situated within the confines of a commercial media system, whereby "market concerns now determinate operation and content" (Picard, 2004: 54). Entertaining story elements take precedence over objectivity, accuracy and relevance (Allern, 2002). The news in particular is now "packaged" (Kunelius and Ruusunoksa, 2008) and branded. There is also much more attention on commercially driven visual aesthetics across both alternative and mainstream media in order to gain audience share

(Kenix, 2007). For example, widely known alternative media such as *Alternet*, *The Sleuth Journal*, Alex Jones's *Infowars*, *Naturalnews* and *Utne Reader* all have advertising on their websites with obvious marketing orientations throughout – logos, gift subscriptions, donation calls and related merchandising products all with the familiar consumer-savvy online shopping cart. These markers of prestige within a consumer-oriented culture are presumably used to encourage consumerism through a unified, commercialised 'high-pressure' sales pitch. These commercialised approaches to communication suggest an embrace of consumerist ideology and part of a continual shift towards the "inevitable subordination of ideals to material progress" (King, Grinter and Pickering, 1997: 5).

Commercialism and the media spectrum

The main constraints on media are no longer political, but are economic and commercial (Croteau and Hoynes, 2001). Widespread consumerism has transformed the media system. The ideology of capitalism and the free market requires an implicit assumption from audiences that capitalism is needed within Western societies for growth and prosperity (Christians, 2002). Such an ideologically driven assumption on the part of audiences obviously fuels audience preferences, but also informs advertisers' financial interests, market technological capabilities and institutional profitability (Hamilton, 2004). These interconnected economic outcomes are intrinsic to capitalism itself – and help explain contemporary media. As all media outlets attempt to standardise and find more efficient, converged modes of telling stories, content becomes homogenised (Underwood, 1993). This omnipresent economic mandate in a commercialised media marketplace (Gentzkow and Shapiro, 2010) encompasses alternative news organisations – even those who aim to be outside commercial forces (Forde, 2011).

Alternative media organisations, like their mainstream counterparts, are also in desperate pursuit of larger market share. The result is a media system homogeneous in its opinion-based journalism, which aims to build relationships with readers in return for increased market share. Research examining content originating from outlets with different ownership models has confirmed a lack of pluralism in perspectives (Valcke, 2009). This lack of plurality is because "media outlets – even those that editorially oppose 'corporate media' – are themselves corporations" (Pritchard, Terry and Brewer, 2008: 13). The nearly universal economic model of profiteering as a marker of success within capitalism suggests that meaningful differences in content are likely to be indiscernible across the media spectrum.

One of the central defining characteristics of alternative journalism has been to "turn journalism from a lecture into a conversation" (Gerlis, 2008: 126). However, within a commercially driven culture, defined by branding and 'relatable' moments, every interaction between a writer and a reader is aimed at directing the conversation toward a potentiality of financial rewards. Recent examinations of community-based alternative media found that it was actually conglomerate community media that have been at the forefront in urging communication with readers and depending more on native reporting – not the independently owned alternative media (Kenix, forthcoming). The producers of these conglomerately owned community outlets are drawing upon investigative, thematic reporting and non-elitist perspectives to create narrative fragments that support a non-conglomerate, or alternative, ideology – the same journalistic qualities have all been indicators of alternative media as defined by previous scholars. It is likely that within a capitalistic system, independent ideologies may 'sell' better to those interested in community media and are therefore celebrated by the conglomerate press. Conglomerate media have historically been far better at discovering hidden markets and finding unique communication models to exploit them. In the case of community media, they have more general access to resources, so they can do more investigative journalism, community building and original reporting – journalistic approaches appreciated within the community media market.

Conglomerated media have an imperative, within this context, to build a sense of community through their journalistic work that they can then sell back to advertisers as a larger share of the market and therefore receive larger advertising dollars and support. Thus, the evidence of independent ideologies in conglomerate community media may represent accurate market research on the part of the parent company, which recognises that such ideologies 'sell' better for a certain section of society seeking out community 'independent' media. In contrast, local community media that are independently owned may be much more dependent upon outside forces and therefore less inclined to offend corporate entities or government officials. Their economic constraints may translate into journalistic practice that is potentially not as appealing to the community-minded readers they are presumably hoping to attract in this market. As this example illustrates, the distinction between alternative and mainstream media, even when truncated along two distinct ownership models, remains complex.

Conclusion

The commercial model of media has always existed, but has intensified as corporate consolidations have increased. Alternative media have responded to this structural shift by promoting mainstream conventions, thereby limiting open-access participation and embracing commercial models of communication. There is some irony in this circuitous equation. As alternative media adopt more corporate organisation models, they require more professionalised modes of production, which implicitly lock out voices that were part of what made alternative media 'alternative' in the first place (Solomon and McChesney, 1993).

Generally, though, alternative media remain less commercially minded and more ideologically driven than the mainstream; they still operate in ways that are distinct from mainstream media. Although the capitalistic structure tends to legitimise the commercial behaviour of all media, there are examples of community-minded, engaged media that value readers as citizens and not as consumers – even within a commercial structure of operation. Yet, as I hope this chapter has illustrated, it is increasingly contradictory to compartmentalise mainstream media as uniformly distinct from the alternative press.

Further reading

The first chapter of Kenix's *Alternative and Mainstream Media: The Converging Spectrum* (2011) gives a detailed overview of how and why alternative and mainstream media have been increasingly drawing from the other in practice and ideology. Kenix provides several additional case studies exploring the structural and ideological similarities between mainstream media and independent political news blogs (2009), community media (forthcoming) and alternative news websites (2013). Readers interested in examining the complicated definitional categorisations of both alternative and mainstream media should examine the important work of Sandoval and Fuchs (2010), Curran and Couldry (2003), Coyer, Dowmunt and Fountain (2007), Rodríguez (2001) and Downing (2001). All of these texts problematise the simplistic demarcations that are often placed between alternative and mainstream media. Those interested in the confluence across audiences of alternative media should explore the work of Jennifer Rauch (2013), who provides an insightful analysis of how audiences negotiate a converged marketplace of media through a framework of what she calls the "alternative-mainstream dialectic", whereby alternative media audiences strongly critique but also heavily use mainstream media.

References

Albert, M. (2006) "Mass media: Theirs and ours." *Z Magazine*.

Allern, S. (2002) "Journalistic and commercial news values: News organizations as patrons of an institution and market actors." *Nordicom Review*, 23, 137–52.

Armstrong, D. (1981) *A Trumpet to Arms: Alternative Media in America*. Boston, MA: South End.

Atkinson, J. (2004) *Building a Resistance Performance Paradigm: An Analysis of the Roles of Alternative Media in the Social Construction of Reality in Social Justice Movements*. Columbia: University of Missouri Press.

——(2006) "Analyzing resistance narratives at the North American anarchist gathering: A method for analyzing social justice alternative media." *Journal of Communication Inquiry*, 30, 251–72.

Atton, C. (2002a) *Alternative Media*. London: Sage.

——(2002b) "News cultures and new social movements: Radical journalism and the mainstream media." *Journalism Studies*, 3(4), 491–505.

——(2009) "Alternative journalism: Ideology and practice." In S. Allan (ed.), *The Routledge Companion to News and Journalism*. Abingdon: Routledge (pp. 169–78).

Bauman, Z. (2000) *Liquid Modernity*. Cambridge and Oxford: Polity Press & Blackwell.

Bennett, T. (1982) "Theories of the media, theories of society." In M. Gurevitch, T. Bennett, J. Curran et al. (eds), *Culture, Society and the Media*. London: Methuen (pp. 30–55).

Bennett, W. L. (1996) "An introduction to journalism norms and representations of politics." *Political Communication*, 13, 373–84.

Christians, C. G. (2002) "Justice and the global media." *Studies in Christian Ethics*, 13, 76–92.

Churchill, L. (2007) "The hegemony of money: Commercialism and professionalism in American medicine." *Cambridge Quarterly of Healthcare Ethics*, 16, 407–14.

Coyer, K., Dowmunt, T. and Fountain, A. (eds) (2007) *The Alternative Media Handbook*. New York: Routledge.

Croteau, D. and Hoynes, W. (2001) *The Business of Media: Corporate Media and the Public Interest*. Thousand Oaks, CA: Pine Forge Press.

Curran, J. and Couldry, N. (2003) *Contesting Media Power: Alternative Media in a Networked World*. Lanham, MD: Rowman and Littlefield.

Deuze, M. (2008) "The professional identity of journalists in the context of convergence culture." *Observatorio (OBS) Journal*, 7, 103–17.

Dowmunt, T. and Coyer, K. (2007) "Introduction." In K. Coyer, T. Dowmunt and A. Fountain (eds), *The Alternative Media Handbook*. New York: Routledge (pp. 1–12).

Downing, J. (with others) (2001) *Radical Media: Rebellious Communication and Social Movements*. Thousand Oaks, CA: Sage Publications.

eBiz (2013) "Top 15 most popular blogs." Retrieved from http://www.ebizmba.com/articles/blogs (accessed 31 August 2013).

Fenton, N. (2007) "Getting alternative messages in the mainstream media." In K. Coyer, T. Dowmunt and A. Fountain (eds), *The Alternative Media Handbook*. London: Routledge (pp. 143–54).

Forde, S. (2011) *Challenging the News: The Journalism of Alternative and Community Media*. Basingstoke, UK: Palgrave Macmilan.

Fountain, A. (2007) "Alternative film, video and television 1965–2005." In K. Coyer, T. Dowmunt and A. Fountain (eds), *The Alternative Media Handbook*. New York: Routledge (pp. 29–46).

Gentzkow, M. and Shapiro, J. M. (2010) "What drives media slant? Evidence from US daily newspapers." *Econometrica*, 78, 35–71.

Gerlis, A. (2008) "Who is a journalist?" *Journalism Studies*, 9, 125–28.

Groshek, J. and Han, Y. (2011) "Negotiated hegemony and reconstructed boundaries in alternative media coverage of globalization." *International Journal of Communication*, 5, 1523–1544.

Hamilton, J. (2000) "Alternative media: Conceptual difficulties, critical possibilities." *Journal of Communication Inquiry*, 24, 357–78.

——(2004) *All the News That's Fit to Sell: How the Market Transforms Information into News*. Princeton, NJ: Princeton University Press.

——(2006) "Rethinking communication, media and activism." *International Journal of Media and Cultural Politics*, 2, 220–25.

Harcup, T. (2003) "The unspoken – said: The journalism of alternative media." *Journalism: Theory, Practice and Criticism*, 4, 356–76.

Jenkins, H. (2004) "The cultural logic of media convergence." *International Journal of Cultural Studies*, 7, 33–43.

Kant, I. (1985) *Foundations of the Metaphysics of Morals*. New York: Macmillan.

Kellner, D. (2006) *Habermas, the Public Sphere, and Democracy: A Critical Intervention*. Retrieved from http://www.gseis.ucla.edu/faculty/kellner/papers/habermas.htm (accessed 12 December 2010).

Kenix, L. J. (2007) "The homogenized imagery of non-profit organizations on the internet." *Visible Language*, 41, 127–62.

——(2009) "Exploring political blogs as a form of alternative media." *Journal of Computer-Mediated Communication*, 14, 790–822.

——(2011) *Alternative and Mainstream Media: The Converging Spectrum*. London and New York: Bloomsbury Academic.

——(2013) "A converging image? Commercialism and the visual identity of alternative and mainstream news websites." *Journalism Studies*, 14(6), 1–22.

——(Forthcoming) "The influence of ownership on independent and conglomerate community newspaper websites." *Newspaper Research Journal*.

King, J. L., Grinter, R. E. and Pickering, J. M. (1997) "The rise and fall of Netville: The saga of a cyberspace construction boomtown in the great divide." In S. Kiesler (ed.), *Culture of the Internet*. Mahwah, NJ: Lawrence Earlbaum Associates (pp. 3–33).

Kottke, J. (2010) "The exciting About page." Retrieved from http://kottke.org/about/ (accessed 8 August 2010).

Kperogi, F. A. (2008) "Cooperation with the corporation? CNN and the hegemonic cooptation of citizen journalism through iReport.com." *New Media and Society*, 13, 314–29.

Kunelius, R. and Ruusunoksa, L. (2008) "Mapping professional imagination – On the potential of professional culture in the newspapers of the future." *Journalism Studies*, 9, 662–78.

Kuttner, R. (1997) *Everything for Sale: The Virtues and Limits of Markets*. New York: Alfred A. Knopf.

Levy, P. (1997) *Collective Intelligence: Mankind's Emerging World in Cyberspace*. New York: Perseus.

Makagon, D. (2000) "Accidents should happen: Cultural disruption through alternative media." *Journal of Communication Inquiry*, 24, 430–47.

McCrone, J. (2013) "Did journalism fail in Afghanistan?" *The Press*, 17 August. Retrieved from http://www.stuff.co.nz/the-press/news/9054102/Did-NZ-journalism-fail-in-Afghanistan/ (accessed 21 January 2015).

McManus, J. H. (1994) *Market-Driven Journalism: Let the Citizen Beware?* Thousand Oaks, CA: Sage.

——(1995) "A market-based model of news production." *Communication Theory*, 5, 301–38.

Ostertag, B. (2008) "Social movements and the printed and electronic word." In S. P. Gangadharan, B. De Cleen and N. Carpentier (eds), *International Communication Association*. Montreal: Tartu University Press (pp. 31–40).

Picard, R. G. (2004) "Commercialism and newspaper quality." *Newspaper Research Journal*, 25, 54–65.

Pritchard, D., Terry, C. and Brewer, P. R. (2008) "One owner, one voice? Testing a central premise of newspaper-broadcast cross-ownership policy." *Communication Law and Policy*, 13, 1–27.

Quantcast. (2013) Huffington Post. Retrieved from https://www.quantcast.com/huffingtonpost.com (accessed 28 August 2013).

Rauch, J. (2013) "Exploring the alternative-mainstream dialectic: What 'alternative media' means to a hybrid audience." Paper presented to the Critical and Cultural Studies Division of the 2013 Meeting of the Association for Education in Journalism & Mass Communication. Washington, DC, 8–11 August.

Rodríguez, C. (2001) *Fissures in the Mediascape: An International Study of Citizens' Media*. Cresskill, NJ: Hampton Press.

Rodríguez, C. and El Gazi, J. (2007) "The poetics of indigenous radio in Colombia media." *Culture and Society*, 29, 449–68.

Sandoval, M. and Fuchs, C. (2010) "Towards a critical theory of alternative media." *Telematics and Informatics*, 2, 141–50.

Solomon, W. and McChesney, R. (1993) *Ruthless Criticism: New Perspectives in US Communication History*. Minneapolis: University of Minnesota Press.

St. John III, B. (2008) "Not biting the hand that feeds them: Hegemonic expediency in the newsroom and the Karen Ryan/Health and Human Services Department video news release." *Journal of Mass Media Ethics*, 23, 110–25.

Toffler, A. (1970) *Future Shock*. New York: Random House.

Underwood, D. (1993) *When MBA's Rule the Newsroom: How the Marketers and Managers Are Reshaping Today's Media*. New York: Columbia University Press.

Valcke, P. (2009) "From ownership regulations to legal indicators of media pluralism: Background, typologies and methods." *Journal of Media Business Studies*, 6, 19–42.

Waltz, M. (2005) *Alternative and Activist Media*. Edinburgh: Edinburgh University Press.

6
WHAT'S LEFT?
Towards a historicised critique of alternative
media and community media

James F. Hamilton

Alternative media and community media have always confronted sizeable challenges. Yet maybe these challenges should now succeed. This sentiment may seem a bit unusual, coming as it does from someone who has written and argued for years on behalf of alternative media and community media, so let me be clear. My admiration for the commitment and creativity of these varied projects and the people who engage in them (and who study and write about them) remains undiminished. I make the opening point not about the projects and people so much as about conceptions of 'alternative media' and 'community media', whose dated pedigree is being revealed most starkly today by commercial social media. Consider for a moment how many long-standing goals of alternative media and community media they seem to meet, such as virtually open access (granting users' literacy skills), no direct financial cost to users, real-time interactivity, mobility, seamless scalable reach from the local to the global and multimedia capability. Given these features, it would seem that social media have forever rendered conventional conceptions of alternative media and community media as a means by which regular people can communicate outside the constraints of the media industries quaint if not delusional. After all, given what social media can do, who in their right mind would prefer mimeographed underground newspapers or public-access channels on local cable television?

However, all is not as it seems. While these technical goals have been met, digital communications also enable unprecedented levels of data monitoring by national intelligence organisations (Greenwald, 2013). And the larger problem of sustaining progressive-left coalitions with traction in today's world remains as difficult as ever, as the recent experiences of Egypt, Libya, Syria and others suggest. While digital communications have changed how these efforts take place, they have not been any more decisive.

The increasingly questionable relevance of established conceptions of alternative media and community media given present conditions provides the impetus for this chapter. It is a first step into a critical inquiry of conceptions of alternative media and community media, with an eye towards retheorising the practices they label and generate. This exploratory effort starts to recover and clarify what constituted alternative media and community media as distinctively progressive-left practices. The chapter does not argue in favour of going back to an ostensibly better or 'purer' time, but of recovering its contributions more fully so as to remake them today. Due to space limitations, such an expansive topic can only be sketched, but future work can probe more fully the argument suggested here.

Dilemmas

While the practices labelled as 'alternative media' and 'community media' have never been more important, these received concepts should never delimit or fix the practices. As historical products themselves, these concepts were formulated in a pre-digital media landscape and in a specific historical context. The intentions driving them continue to be exceptionally relevant in today's world of ever-expanding wealth disparity, social inequality and looming ecological catastrophe. However useful they have been, they have had from the start a key shortcoming, which is in defining these practices as 'media', thus as kinds of technologies or tools, betraying their relation to the study of 'mass communication' and 'mass media' and to the media-effects tradition such study legitimates (Williams, 1980: 50–53). The problem in turn with defining media as tools is that they can be used by anyone for any purpose. To define alternative media and community media as neutral tools, easily appropriated for virtually any purpose, is not only to dilute their relevance and usefulness for progressive-left social change. It is to define the use itself as the distinctly undemocratic media-effects effort to get people to do what communicators want them to do (Hamilton, 2008: 3–4).

One way this can be seen is in the many examples of neoliberal or radical-right incorporation of alternative media and community media (Downing, 2001: vii–viii; Atton, 2004: 61–90; Mazepa, 2012). A US example that spans the 1960s to the 2000s is that of conservative agitator Richard Viguerie, who used what he calls 'alternative media' (in this case, direct mail rather than conventional media relations and political advertising) to usher in the conservative revolution of the 1980s by ostensibly delivering, as he puts it, "power to the people" (Viguerie and Franke, 2004: 1). In yet another US example, conservative political prankster James O'Keefe characterises his work in progressive-left terms as "a guerrilla war to expose fraud and save democracy" (O'Keefe, 2013: 6). In addition, this self-styled radical-right warrior uses tactics inspired by US labour and community organiser Saul Alinsky, whom Conservapedia brands as a communist while also disparaging the degree to which "the enemies of conservatism and Christianity (or indeed any Religion) have practiced without end Alinsky's 'rules'" (ibid.; see also Alinsky, 1971; Conservapedia, 2013).

These and many other examples today bring to mind progressive-left commentary of the 1970s that addressed the theme of 'what's left?', a phrase that signified fears that the reservoir of progressive-left intellectual resources had run dry, as well as doubts about what counted as a left political position (Hobsbawm, 2002: 275–76; but compare Williams, 1989a: 175 and Williams, 1989b: 175–85). The phrase's relevance today comes from the ease with which the radical right incorporates progressive-left media practice, as well as how transnational commercial social media deliver capabilities long aspired to by the progressive left. It also comes from the degree to which self-styled progressive-left media projects aspire to the size, design and operation of commercial media projects. What's left, indeed.

In this vertiginous situation, it is crucially important to revisit critically the theory, method and practice of alternative media and community media (Couldry and Curran, 2003). One way of doing this is to recover more fully the progressive-left bases of radical media practices in order to reground each in the other. Granting the historical range, variety and international or transnational extent of such bases and practices (Hamilton, 2008), a fruitful time regarding the US and Britain on which to focus is the decade of the 1960s. Three reasons can be offered for doing so. First, media practices that emerged in this decade are cited routinely as paradigmatic examples of alternative media and community media, such as underground radical newspapers, hand-held film and video activist vérité documentary, pirate radio and radical theatre and public art 'happenings' as street protest (Downing, 2001). Second, radical movements of the New Left emerged in this decade, both in the US and in Britain, which provided the cultural reservoir of resources and energy for these media practices, and that persist today in many ways. Third, in this decade there emerged two key intellectual formations of each respective New Left. In the US, the philosophy of participatory democracy loomed large, while in Britain the radical historical rehabilitation of past popular political action legitimised contemporary action, as the participation and prominence of radical historians such as Edward Thompson attests (Hamilton, 2011).

Formations

What proved exceptionally difficult for the respective New Lefts was not which medium to use and how to use it, but much more fundamentally how to formulate a workable critical position vis-à-vis capitalist consumerism. In the US and Britain of the late 1950s and early 1960s, dominant resources for this effort existed in two very different philosophical positions. One position derived from liberalism, and can be expressed in 1960s parlance as 'do your own thing'. Its inadequacy as a critical position is due to its relativism and the resulting inability to provide any grounds for valuing one programme or position over another: all positions are equally legitimate. A second position was derived from vanguardism, expressed (perhaps too flippantly) as 'do our thing, or else'. Its inadequacy as a progressive-left stance is due to the fetishisation of a revolutionary orthodoxy and the narrow rigidity of its resulting prescriptions for society. Where liberalism suffers from extreme individualism, vanguardism suffers from its 'command politics' and the very undemocratic restriction of meaningful participation to party elites.

Yet, these positions did not exhaust all options. In addition to varieties of critical European theorising throughout much of the twentieth century (Anderson, 1976), what gained most traction in the US New Left was philosophical pragmatism and, in the British New Left, working-class radical socialism. These largely indigenous political-philosophical responses to liberalism and vanguardism came about in the wake of widespread recognition of the structural ills of laissez-faire capitalism (Westbrook, 1991; Bevir, 2011). They sought to provide an open, non-dogmatic position (much the opposite of a command politics), but one that enabled critique and concentrated action instead of simply inchoate flashes of resistance.

Of greater relevance to this chapter than the emergence of these positions is their re-emergence in the late 1950s and 1960s. It was the immediate need for strategies and tactics that proved to be fertile ground for their renewed relevance as part of new progressive-left politics worthy of the moniker 'new left'. Newly visible and sizeable movements of progressive social change at the time included the civil-rights and anti-war movements in the US and, in Britain, the Campaign for Nuclear Disarmament as well as opposition to the US-led war on Vietnam. As will be argued, intellectual work that developed conceptions of participatory democracy as well as radical popular social resistance reverberated on both sides of the Atlantic as an energising horizon of formative thinking and action.

Kaufman and participatory democracy

As only one of many contributors to the emergence and character of the New Left in the US, the work of philosopher and University of Michigan faculty member Arnold Saul Kaufman (1927–1971) proved to be formative (Wiener, 1991: 232; Westbrook, 1991: 548–50). By using the philosophical pragmatism of Dewey to reject distinctions between means and ends, and between culture and society, Kaufman argued that open-ended, non-dogmatic but creative and effective social change consists of understanding means as also ends, and that both means and ends were best seen as the practice of participatory democracy (Dewey, 1927).

Debates that informed the New Left in the US in its formative years were conducted largely through sociology, a discourse that, as a *Labour Monthly* reviewer of the 1960 compilation *Out of Apathy* claimed, was "all the rage" at the time (Nandy, 1960). Academic figures such as the radical sociologist C. Wright Mills loomed large, particularly by 1962, with the drafting and circulation of the Port Huron Statement (Tilman, 1984; Gamson, 2005; Hayden, 2005; Geary, 2009; Treviño, 2012). However, in addition to figures such as Mills, Tom Hayden and others of the New Left in the US drew upon philosopher and University of Michigan faculty member as well as 'teach-in' creator Arnold Kaufman and his concept of participatory democracy as the manifestation of radical-democratic social change (Rothman, 1972; Hayden et al., 2006; Hilmer, 2010; Hayden, 2012).

Although seeing himself as working within the liberal tradition from J. S. Mill onwards, Kaufman also drew upon Marx in an unlikely pairing that mirrored not only the severe defects he saw in liberalism as manifest in the postwar US but also the experimental, innovative times in which he worked (Rodewald and Wasserstrom, 1972: 9–12). Although different in many ways, both Dewey and Marx put great importance on direct participation, something that traditional theories of representative democracy dismissed as too unwieldy in all but the smallest groups and, even if engaged in, too intellectually taxing for most people. To these criticisms, Kaufman argues that participatory democracy is a necessary if not essential supplement and complement to representative democracy, not its replacement. And, while certainly no Pollyanna when it came to recognising what some people are capable of, Kaufman nevertheless argued that, ultimately, "participation contributes to individual personal development, while nonparticipation stifles it" (Rodewald and Wasserstrom, 1972: 15–16).

Kaufman's conception of direct participation was central to his sense of a workable process of radical democracy, one that remained as open as it was inclusive. In this, he echoed Dewey, who placed participation centrally in his conception of democratic social order. To escape the no-win choice between liberalism and vanguardism (and the drawbacks of each), Dewey regarded direct participation not as a means to a goal, or a neutral tool or tactic, but as both the means and the goal. This point needs to be emphasised. What matters for Dewey is not achieving specific goals through the application of neutral techniques and tools (and thus the separation of means from ends), but achieving the process as a way of concretely addressing ever-changing problems. Expanding on this point, Visnovsky (2007) argues that, for Dewey, partici-patory "democracy is a high cultural, moral and spiritual ideal first, and a procedure, a method, a technique second ... It is a process first, and a [political] state second. It is a value in-itself first, and an instrument second."

Kaufman not only valorised broad-based popular and direct deliberation. He also emphasised it as a necessarily creative activity, a feature that characterises social protest throughout the 1960s. To do so, Kaufman refused foundational distinctions between ideas and actions, or what today we might call culture and society (Williams, 1958). Recalling his writing on this topic helps clarify this point. In 1954, Kaufman had already launched his scholarly writing career while at the College of the City of New York (Eddins, 1972: 4). An article published in *The Journal of Philosophy* lays out what Kaufman calls the "instrumental function" of political theory, which viewed ideas as action in contradistinction to a positivist position which kept them separate (Kaufman, 1954). Kaufman recognises that ideals and hopes exist not just in minds, but in the world and in action taken. The "accretion of private, personally significant meanings" to abstract ideals such as "freedom" energises activists to take action in the world (ibid.: 6). In an influential essay published six years later, Kaufman expands this point by referring to an argument by the US pragmatist philosopher William James, a contemporary of Dewey. In his paraphrase, Kaufman argues that "making an effort to achieve a possible good depends on our belief in the possibility of that achievement" (Kaufman, 1960: 283–84). No guarantee exists that any particular goal will be achieved. However, what is guaranteed is failure if one were never to believe that a goal might be achieved, even if only in part. As Kaufman argues, "pessimism, while it protects us from disappointment, blinds the individual to possible lines of advance". Thus, "it is necessary to encourage and renew man's [sic] efforts to improve himself [sic] and his [sic] world, not wither the will to try, by subjecting it to a bombardment of sophisticated and somewhat cynical arguments which never actually prove the extreme conclusion they either affirm or, more likely, insinuate" (ibid.: 283–85).

Finally, Kaufman emphasised the necessity of a continually critical approach to formulating and enacting programs of social change, one that would subject the manifestation of ideals and hopes to continual empirical validation and revision, rather than encase them in the armour of unquestionable orthodoxy. He argued that it is not enough simply to assert and work toward a normative goal. "Necessarily vague" abstractions need to be specified in the form of "statistical indices" derived from "empirical investigation." Empirical measures need to be designed to accurately evaluate whether these ideals have actually been achieved and to what degree their achievement corresponds with their intention (Kaufman, 1954: 11).

By working through liberalism, pragmatism and Marxism to reach new insights and syntheses, Kaufman came to propose a social theory that avoided the problems of liberalism and vanguardism. He put his work to the test not only in the classroom, but on campus and nationally (Eddins, 1972: 4). That much of its persuasiveness seemed to be lost by the late 1960s in the rise of street riots, nihilist drug-fuelled gratification and paranoia in the "days of rage" is not to detract from it or its contribution to the now long-running debate about how to concretely realise participatory democracy (Gitlin, 1987: 285–408; Hilmer, 2010). While efforts on the other side of the Atlantic took a very different form, they embodied a similarly popular, holistic and critical approach.

Hobsbawm and radical popular culture

While clear lines between the New Left in the US and the New Left in Britain are impossible to fix or set exactly, a useful way to distinguish them nevertheless is to note the form of intellectual work that sustained each. In the US New Left, Mills's, Kaufman's and others' critiques tended towards philosophical, theoretical arguments and abstract logical-structural analyses, a tendency that Kaufman sought to change later in his life (Wasserstrom, Robischon and Furth, 1974). By contrast, finding more of a home in the British New Left was concrete radical historical work that, while grounded in theoretical reflection, stressed the creative, lived making of critical positions that were equally worldviews, and organisational and cultural forms of practice. Its relevance to the times was its affirmative redefinition of popular political action of the past and by implication its validation of emergent, contemporary popular political action.

Much of this work in Britain was done by academic Marxist historians, which is not surprising given the centrality of historical analysis in Marx. Yet, this work was refracted through an indigenous working-class radicalism as well as an Anglo historicist empiricism. As a result, rather than mechanically legitimise party orthodoxy, such work prized rigorous use of documentary evidence to open up new understandings of past processes and their relevance for the present.

This Popular-Front approach can be seen clearly in the radical history journal *Past and Present* and later in the *History Workshop Journal* (Editorial Collective, 1976; Taylor, 2008). *Past and Present* was expressly a non-dogmatic, open journal of critical historical work judged, in co-editor Hobsbawm's words more recently, "not by the badge in the authors' ideological buttonhole, but by the contents of their articles" (Hobsbawm, 2002: 230). Its inaugural editorial statement from 1952 quoted French Annales historians Marc Bloch and Lucien Febvre by stating that the journal would practice critical-historical scholarship "'not by means of methodological articles and theoretical dissertations, but by example and fact'" (*Past and Present*, 1952: i). To do so from the start, the editorial board put into place various organisational means of providing "a visible guarantee against 'Marxist domination'," as a retrospective account ironically put it to poke fun at feverish fears at the time of the "Red menace" active at a miniscule academic journal (Hill, Hilton and Hobsbawm, 1983: 9).

Despite differences between logical-abstract arguments and concrete historical work, American radical social theory and radical historical work shared key ways of overcoming the drawbacks of liberalism and vanguardism. For example, the editors of *Past and Present* argued as Kaufman did against distinguishing ideas from actions, and culture from society. They did so by critiquing two common approaches to historical work. On the one hand, they criticised doing history wholly inductively as "a 'laborious' accumulation of fact" that somehow produces "a photographically exact reconstruction of an 'objective' past," because doing so relegates culture to being only a by-product or symptom of an already constituted society (*Past and Present*, 1952: iii). On the other hand, the editors also critiqued doing history through a "philosophical idealism" that treats history simply as "merely the subjective [pattern] we put into it from the present", because doing so ignores the real, concrete social conditions that constitute social life (*Past and Present*, 1952: iii). In contrast to these two extremes, culture and society had to be addressed holistically and concretely, although with due recognition to inconsistencies, multiplicities and incompleteness (del Valle Alcalá, 2013: 75–80). Similar to efforts by American radical social theorists who sought to address pressing, current problems rather than engage in abstract speculation for its own sake, the editors of *Past and Present* sought as well to meld the study of the past with the present on behalf of efforts to make a better future. They argued that "history cannot logically separate the study of the past from the present and the future, for it deals with objective phenomena, which do not stop changing when we observe them" (*Past and Present*, 1952: iii).

One can see this perspective put to use in Hobsbawm's study of "'primitive' or 'archaic' forms of social agitation" (Hobsbawm, 1959: 1). The book draws its examples from Western and Southern Europe, especially Italy, examples that are archaic in form, based as most are on kinship and honour instead of abstract political ideology, but that take place in the 'modern' nineteenth and twentieth centuries. For all the qualifications regarding the book's tentative nature and limited scale and scope, it addresses historically the general processes by which popular resistance coalesces and activates. Understood in this broad way, many New Left readers faced with the challenge of social change in the early 1960s recognised the parallels between what they faced and what Hobsbawm's various "primitive rebels" of the book faced. The task within both the cases of the book and the New Lefts generally was to, as Hobsbawm quotes Gramsci, transform "the inchoate strivings" against intrusive new systemic pressures into "an effective expression of these aspirations" in favour of greater equality and control over ones' lives (ibid.: 10). Due to this relevance, the book resonated with many unintended readers at the time. Hobsbawm notes in his pub-lished memoir that, in the early 1960s, he was "astonished and a little baffled to be told by a colleague from the University of California, Berkeley, the epicenter of the student eruption, that the more intellectual young rebels there read the book with great enthusiasm *because they identified themselves and their movement* with my rebels [emphasis original]" (Hobsbawm, 2002: 250).

This resonance was due in no small part to the valorisation of the creativity of popular experience through its emphasis on *"pre-political* people who have not yet found, or only begun to find, a specific language in which to express their aspirations about the world [emphasis original]" (Hobsbawm, 1959: 2). The book also places culture and lived experience on centre stage in a concluding chapter on ritual in social movements as a means of consolidating and effectively expressing an emerging movement's aspirations. Finally, the book makes clear that these inchoate strivings were made into social movements by the participants themselves, a contention that Thompson would develop later in his influential historical study of the making of the English working class (Thompson, 1963).

From media theory to social theory

A legitimate objection to the above account of key intellectual projects that supported the two New Lefts in the 1960s might very well be 'but where is alternative media or community media in all this?' Such an objection is of course accurate. But the absence of media as standalone, isolated concerns is precisely the point to be underscored. The value of this work in its day is precisely in *not* essentialising and *not* ghettoising as separate and isolated concerns the use of particular media 'tools'. Intellectual work done by Kaufman, Hobsbawm and countless others of the respective New Lefts both within and outside the academy gave shape to the radical needs and questions of the day, providing not prescriptive step-by-step plans about which media tools to use and how, but an open horizon of creative possibilities of thinking and acting, including radical communications practice.

This horizon displays at least three characteristics. First, it places popular participation at the centre of progressive projects, in order to prevent elite and undemocratic direction. Second, it argues in favour of holistic conceptions of intellectual work that merge means and ends, and holistic conceptions of society that understand culture as a constituent, material social process. Third, it emphasises the need for a fully critical project, one that requires at all points and at all times a confrontation between theory and practice. Most importantly for the argument of this chapter, it refuses to separate, isolate and ghettoise media practice as 'alternative media' and 'community media'. Rather than propose a standalone theory about the effectiveness of a particular communications medium or kind of message, this horizon understands cultural practice broadly as constituent of human life and action in the world (Williams, 1975). These efforts of the early 1960s deserve attention today, not because they have the answers, but because of their effort to critically rethink new possibilities for a workable radical democracy. In their creative retheorising and responsiveness to their own pressing conditions along with the degree to which they enabled significant social movements of the day, these efforts are a high-water mark of progressive-left thinking of the past sixty years. As a result and perhaps paradoxically, this horizon, which did not isolate media as exclusive or pre-eminent concerns, nevertheless enabled and supported the emergence of what are seen as paradigmatic alternative-media and community-media practices.

Such a horizon informs activist work today, which continues to reformulate what progressive-left social challenge can be, and what 'alternative media' and 'community media' theory and practice might be replaced by within a broad program of progressive social challenge. For example, experimentation in direct participation as a means and goal can be seen in the recent Occupy movements. In a Boston encampment in 2011, thousands of people "camped out in tents, all arranged in rows, even marked with street signs". One of the protester-residents reflected that "we've created this intentional community where we take care of everyone in this community, and you have a voice. So for us, living this process was the best example that we had of what our fix was" (Smith, 2011). And radical historical work is again relevant in such ways as the "New Putney Debates" held in London during fall 2012, which occurred in "the 365th-year anniversary of the original Putney Debates of 1647". As "inspired by the Levellers and the Diggers demands for social justice, civil rights and equal access to the land", this 2012 version sought to "focus on the challenges facing us now and what is needed now for a more just and equal society" (Occupy London, 2012). Compare this to technology-centred conceptions of social change that all too easily fit commercial and state interests and concerns (Li and Bernoff, 2011; Shirky, 2009).

It is time for scholars of alternative media and community media to catch up with times and with current practice, and to continue to reformulate, recalibrate and reconceptualise what radical-democratic cultural work might yet be and become. While posing no answer even in the times of their formulation, the transatlantic experience of the 1960s New Lefts discussed here provides a compelling exemplar of efforts to do so.

Further reading

Kaufman's most prominent work is *The Radical Liberal, New Man in American Politics* (New York: Atherton Press, 1968). A useful examination of the intellectual substance of the US New Left at the time is Massimo Tedori (ed.), *The New Left; a Documentary History* (New York: Bobbs-Merrill, 1969). Radical historical work of relevance in addition to what is cited here includes George Rudé, *The Crowd in History; a Study of Popular Disturbances in France and England, 1730–1848* (New York: Wiley, 1964); and (although appearing later than the time period discussed here) Christopher Hill, *The World Turned Upside Down; Radical Ideas During the English Revolution* (London: Temple Smith, 1972).

References

Alinsky, S. D. (1971) *Rules for Radicals; A Practical Primer for Realistic Radicals.* New York: Random House.
Anderson, P. (1976) *Considerations on Western Marxism.* London: New Left Books.
Atton, C. (2004) *An Alternative Internet; Radical Media, Politics and Creativity.* Edinburgh: Edinburgh University Press.
Bevir, M. (2011) *The Making of British Socialism.* Princeton, NJ: Princeton University Press.
Conservapedia (2013) "Saul Alinsky." Retrieved from http://www.conservapedia.com/Saul_Alinsky (accessed 20 October 2013).

Couldry, N. and Curran, J. (2003) "The paradox of media power." In N. Couldry and J. Curran (eds), *Contesting Media Power; Alternative Media in a Networked World*. Lanham, MD: Rowman and Littlefield (pp. 3–15).

del Valle Alcalá, R. (2013) "A multitude of hopes: Humanism and subjectivity in E. P. Thompson and Antonio Negri." *Culture, Theory and Critique*, 54(1), 74–87.

Dewey, J. (1927) *The Public and Its Problems*. New York: Henry Holt.

Downing, J. (with Ford, T., Gil, G. and Stein, L.) (2001) *Radical Media: Rebellious Communication and Social Movements*. Thousand Oaks, CA: Sage.

Eddins, B. (1972) "In memoriam." *Social Theory and Practice*, 2(1), 3–4.

Editorial Collective (1976) "Editorials; History Workshop Journal." *History Workshop Journal*, 1, 1–3.

Gamson, W. (2005) "Afterword." in D. Croteau, W. Hoynes and C. Ryan (eds.) *Rhyming Hope and History; Activists, Academics, and Social Movement Scholarship*. Minneapolis: University of Minnesota Press (pp. 265–79).

Geary, D. (2009) *Radical Ambition: C. Wright Mills, the Left, and American Social Thought*. Berkeley: University of California Press.

Gitlin, T. (1987) *The Sixties: Years of Hope, Days of Rage*. New York: Bantam.

Greenwald, G. (2013) "XKeyscore: NSA tool collects 'nearly everything a user does on the internet'." *The Guardian*, 31 July. Retrieved from http://www.theguardian.com/world/2013/jul/31/nsa-top-secret-program-online-data (accessed 14 November 2003).

Hamilton, J. F. (2008) *Democratic Communications: Formations, Projects, Possibilities*. Lanham, MD: Lexington Books.

Hamilton, S. (2011) *The Crisis of Theory: E. P. Thompson, the New Left and Postwar British Politics*. Manchester, UK: Manchester University Press.

Hayden, T. (2005) *The Port Huron Statement: The Visionary Call of the 1960s Revolution*. New York: Thunder's Mouth Press.

——(2012) "Tom Hayden on Port Huron at 50." *Rolling Stone*, 30 July. Retrieved from http://www.rollingstone.com/politics/blogs/national-affairs/tom-hayden-on-port-huron-at-50-20120730 (accessed 14 November 2013).

Hayden, T., Flacks, R., Aronowitz, S. and Lemert, C. (2006) *Radical Nomad: C. Wright Mills and His Times*. Boulder, CO: Paradigm Publishers.

Hill, C., Hilton, R. H. and Hobsbawm, E. J. (1983) "Past and present: Origin and early years." *Past and Present*, 100, 3–14.

Hilmer, J. (2010) "The state of participatory democratic theory." *New Political Science*, 32(1), 43–63.

Hobsbawm, E. (1959) *Social Bandits and Primitive Rebels: Studies in Archaic Forms of Social Movement in the 19th and 20th Centuries*. Glencoe, IL: Free Press.

——(2002) *Interesting Times: A Twentieth-Century Life*. New York: Pantheon.

Kaufman, A. (1954) "The nature and function of political theory." *Journal of Philosophy*, 51(1), 5–22.

——(1960) "Human nature and participatory democracy." In C. J. Friedrich (ed.), *Responsibility; Nomos III: Yearbook of the American Society of Political and Legal Philosophy*. New York: Liberal Arts Press (pp. 266–89).

Li, C. and Bernoff, J. (2011) *Groundswell; Winning in a World Transformed by Social Technologies*. Boston, MA: Harvard Business Review Press.

Mazepa, P. (2012) "Regressive social relations, activism, and media." In K. Kozolanka, P. Mazepa and D. Skinner (eds), *Alternative Media in Canada*. Vancouver: University of British Columbia Press (pp. 244–63).

Nandy, D. (1960) "Review of *Out of Apathy*, by Edward P. Thompson (ed.)." *Labour Monthly*, October, 479–80.

O'Keefe, J. (2013) *Breakthrough: Our Guerilla War to Expose Fraud and Save Democracy*. New York: Threshold.

Occupy London (2012) "The New Putney Debates – A series of public debates about democracy." 25 October. Retrieved from http://occupylondon.org.uk/occupy-londons-the-new-putney-debates-a-series-of-public-debates-about-democracy (accessed 31 October 2012).

Past and Present (1952) "Introduction." *Past and Present*, 1, i–iv.

Rodewald, R. and Wasserstrom, R. (1972) "The political philosophy of Arnold S. Kaufman." *Social Theory and Practice*, 2(1), 5–31.

Rothman, J. (1972) "The radical liberal strategy in action." *Social Theory and Practice*, 2(1), 33–45.

Shirky, C. (2009) "How social media can make history." TED.com. Retrieved from http://www.ted.com/talks/clay_shirky_how_cellphones_twitter_facebook_can_make_history.html (accessed 5 October 2013).

Smith, N. (2011) "Wall Street protesters turn Boston park into a village." *National Public Radio*. Retrieved from http://www.npr.org/2011/10/13/141301949/wall-street-protesters-turn-boston-park-into-a-village (accessed 17 September 2013).

Taylor, B. (2008) "History workshop journal." *Making History*. Institute of Historical Research, University of London. Retrieved from http://www.history.ac.uk/makinghistory/resources/articles/HWJ.html (accessed 1 October 2013).

Thompson, E. P. (1963) *The Making of the English Working Class*. New York: Pantheon.

Tilman, R. (1984) *C. Wright Mills: A Native Radical and His American Intellectual Roots*. University Park: Pennsylvania State University Press.

Treviño, A. (2012) *The Social Thought of C. Wright Mills*. Thousand Oaks, CA: Pine Forge Press.

Viguerie, R. and Franke, D. (2004) *America's Right Turn: How Conservatives Used New and Alternative Media to Take Power*. Chicago: Bonus Books.

Visnovsky, E. (2007) "The Deweyan conception of participatory democracy." *Americana: E-Journal of American Studies in Hungary* 3(2). Retrieved from http://www.americanaejournal.hu/vol3no2/visnovsky (accessed 24 October 2013).

Wasserstrom, R., Robischon, T. and Furth, M. (1974) "1974, University of California: In memoriam: Arnold Saul Kaufman, philosophy: Los Angeles." University of California (System) Academic Senate, Berkeley Division. Retrieved from http://content.cdlib.org/view?docId=hb6h4nb3q7&brand=calisphere (accessed 1 October 2012).

Westbrook, R. B. (1991) *John Dewey and American Democracy*. Ithaca, NY: Cornell University Press.

Wiener, J. (1991) "The New Left as history." In J. Wiener (ed.), *Professors, Politics and Pop*. London: Verso (pp. 228–43).

Williams, R. (1958) *Culture and Society, 1780–1950*. New York: Columbia University Press.

——(1975) *Television: Technology and Cultural Form*. New York: Schocken.

——(1980) "Means of communication as means of production." In R. Williams (ed.), *Problems in Materialism and Culture*. London: Verso (pp. 50–61).

——(1989a) "The uses of cultural theory." In T. Pinkney (ed.), *Politics of Modernism: Against the New Conformists*. London: Verso (pp. 163–76).

——(1989b) "Socialists and coalitionists." In *Resources of Hope: Culture, Democracy, Socialism*. London: Verso (pp. 175–85).

7

ALTERNATIVE MEDIATION, POWER AND CIVIC AGENCY IN AFRICA

Wendy Willems

Introduction

A number of terms have been invoked in order to refer to those forms of media distancing themselves from mainstream media, including 'community media' (Howley, 2005), 'grassroots media', 'autonomous media' (Langlois and Dubois, 2005), 'citizen journalism' (Allan and Thorsen, 2009), 'alternative media' (Atton, 2002; Couldry and Curran, 2003; Bailey, Cammaerts and Carpentier, 2008), 'tactical media', 'citizens' media' (Rodríguez, 2001), 'small media' (Sreberny and Mohammadi, 1994), 'radical media' (Downing, 2001), 'underground media', 'pirate media', 'social movement media' (Downing, 2008, 2011) and 'civil society media' (Carpentier, Lie and Servaes, 2003). While all these terms have different analytical implications, what they share is a commitment to media that serve the interests of citizens (and particularly those on the margins), and a belief in alternative funding structures of media institutions. For example, for Atton (2002: 4), alternative media "are crucially about offering the means for democratic communication to people who are normally excluded from media production", whereas for Hamilton (2000: 373), the value of these media lies "in their exploration of new forms of organizing more participatory techniques of media and more inclusive, democratic forms of communication".

A second feature that characterises the body of literature above is the intimate entanglement between forms of media which distinguish themselves from the mainstream, and civil society organisations and networks. Generally, studies in the subfield of 'alternative media studies' tend to be positive about the supportive role of media to various sections of civil society. For some, this almost leads to a disappearance of the analytical distinction between media and civil society. Downing's (2008, 2011) term 'social movement media' suggests a blurring between social movements and media institutions where civil society organisations engage in content production and *become* media producers, and vice versa, where media institutions because of their opposition to both state-run and corporate media *become* part of civil society.

The emergence of new media has produced a new body of media research that has continued to investigate the – often deemed productive – relationship between new media and civil society. In this regard, scholars have pointed to the important role of the internet in making possible collective action by citizens, also known as 'cyber-activism' (Hill and Hughes, 1998; McCaughey and Ayers, 2003). Mobile phones have been credited with enabling seemingly spontaneous 'smart mobs' (Rheingold, 2002) as well as popular uprisings against Philippine President Joseph Estrada in January 2001 (Paragas, 2003; Rafael, 2003; Pertierra, 2006; Qiu, 2008), mass demonstrations in the aftermath of the 2004 Madrid bombings in Spain (Castells et al., 2006), and mobilisation in the aftermath of the 2004 Indian Ocean tsunami (Robinson and Robison, 2006). The success of the Zapatista Army of National Liberation (EZLN), a revolutionary leftist group based in southern Mexico, in running networked campaigns via the internet has often been cited as exemplary of the way in which the internet gave way to new forms of online activism.

New media have thus enabled innovative – often transnational – forms of organising and have made possible mobilising in contexts where it was deemed difficult for activists to organise themselves offline, hereby arguably leading to new forms of 'networked politics' (Kahler, 2009) or 'connective action' (instead of collective action; Bennett and Segerberg, 2012). The empowering potential of social media such as Twitter and Facebook has been particularly highlighted in post-election protests in Iran in June 2009 (Sreberny and Khiabany, 2010; Khiabany, 2012) and, even more famously, the role of Facebook in enabling the so-called 'Arab Spring' in North Africa and the Middle East in early 2011 (Hounshell, 2011; Axford, 2011; Khondker, 2011; Nanabhay and Farmanfarmaian, 2011; Cottle, 2011; Khiabany, 2012).

The rise of new media has had a number of implications for debates in the subfield of 'alternative media studies'. To some extent, earlier work was often characterised by an interest in both alternative media *institutions* such as Indymedia or community radio stations, and the use of media by civil society *organisations*. Because of their ability to forge relatively spontaneous networks between people distanced by space and time, the rise of social media – and as Castells (2009) has argued, the emergence of 'networked power' more generally – is posing challenges to our understanding of notions such as 'civil society', 'collective action', 'community', 'institution' and 'organisation', and their role in contesting dominant forms of state or corporate power. The need to go beyond media-centric analyses of alternative media institutions has been recognised, for example, by scholars who have drawn on Deleuze and Guattari's (1987) metaphor of the 'rhizome'. They have argued that considering alternative media as part of civil society has ignored the manner in which these media institutions frequently form links with both the state and the market for tactical reasons. Hence, they do not completely operate in the realm of civil society, that is, the domain outside market and state. Instead, the rhizomatic approach to alternative media aims to shed light on how alternative media have forged 'horizontal' alliances with a range of like-minded organisations in order to challenge 'vertical' relations of power vis-à-vis a range of hegemonic institutions such as the church, the state or 'the market' (Carpentier, Lie and Servaes, 2003: 61). While the rhizomatic approach to alternative media is useful in gaining a better, contextual understanding of the pragmatic and always evolving alliances between alternative media, state and market, it still retains a focus on alternative media *institutions* and civil society *organisations*.

In this chapter, I will suggest that a further broadening of terms may be useful in order to gain a fuller understanding of the multiple ways in which different forms of media are involved in resisting different forms of power. I will propose a shift from an analytical focus on 'alternative media' to 'alternative mediation', and from 'civil society media' to 'mediated civic agency'. Such a shift, I will argue, enables us to appreciate a fuller spectrum of the different modes in which citizens have contested, opposed or resisted power. Furthermore, it also helps us understand these contestations in contexts in which Eurocentric forms of 'civil society' are not omnipresent, or are themselves part of crucial transnational power relations that have not always been put under critical scrutiny in academic literature. Focusing on mediated civic agency and alternative mediation in Africa, this chapter aims to contribute to the broader debates on 'dewesternising', 'internationalising' or 'decolonising' the field of media, communication and cultural studies (Downing, 1996; Curran and Park, 2000; Abbas and Erni, 2004; McMillin, 2006; Thussu, 2009; Shome, 2009; Wang, 2013).

From civil society media to mediated civic agency

The concept of civil society regained popularity in the post–Cold War context. Against the background of processes of democratisation – that is, the fall of military dictatorships and transitions from one-party rule to multiparty democracy – taking place on the African continent in the late 1980s and 1990s, it began to be seen as the crucial "missing key to sustained political reform, legitimate states and governments, improved governance, viable state-society and state-economy relationships, and prevention of the kind of political decay that undermined new African governments a generation ago" (Harbeson, Rothchild, and Chazan, 1994: 1–2, quoted in Lewis, 2001: 5). In donor policy circles, a particular, oppositional notion of civil society emerged which largely equated civil society to the so-called 'non-governmental organisations' (NGOs). The typical NGO on the continent was dependent on foreign donor funding, established relatively recently in the 1990s, involved either in advocacy and campaigning targeting the state, or in delivering services such as education, healthcare or social welfare. This narrow, normative discourse on civil society has not only profoundly masked the rich historical legacy of civil society organisations and activities on the continent, but it has also excluded other forms of organising which did not neatly fit with the assumptions made about the social composition of civil society and its normative obligations. For example, organisations which were not defined in opposition to the state, or organised along the lines of kinship, religion, ethnicity or local 'tradition', were not considered to be part of 'good civil society'. Furthermore, the discourse failed to apprehend the global power structures within which NGOs were embedded as a result of funding dependencies.

Within this larger discourse on a particular kind of civil society in Africa, scholars have tended to examine the role of media in two ways (Willems, 2013). First of all, they have approached media *as part of* civil society and examined the role of privately owned media in holding the state to account in the transition from one-party rule to multiparty democracy (Ansah, 1988; Hydén, Leslie and Ogundimu, 2003; Kasoma, 1995, 1997; Tettey, 2001). Much of this literature has uncritically adopted liberal democracy as a normative ideal (Willems, 2012a, 2012b). In this perspective, the media must act as watch-dogs, guarding against abuses of power by governments, and fulfil their role as the 'fourth estate'.

Second, scholars have examined the relation *between* media and civil society organisations. This instrumentalist approach has considered the supportive role of media in NGO practices. It is part of a broader professional discourse within the Western donor community that often measures organisational impact through media coverage and visibility. Closely tied to this approach is academic research – often commissioned by donors and therefore firmly 'embedded' within the development industry – that seeks to assess the impact of NGO's media strategies. Scholars adopting this approach have focused on the strategic use of media by non-governmental organisations, hereby often examining the deployment of internet and mobile phones (Mercer, 2004; Mudhai, 2004, 2006, 2012). This approach tends to be based on "the assumption that new media enhance the efficiency of civic actors in carrying out their routine functions that may or may not result in their exercise of 'soft power'" (Mudhai, 2012: 7). It advances a depoliticised, technocratic/techno-determinist perspective which implies that media can help make the work of African NGOs more effective and aid them in achieving a bigger impact in their advocacy work. While for some, this discourse is part of a broader 'ICT fetishism' among Western donors interested in 'engineering an elite civil society' in Africa (Mercer, 2004: 49), the assumption made is still that civil society largely is equal to the activities of NGOs.

Both approaches therefore assume a particular kind of civil society that is found in a specific sector of society, separated from market and state. However, as Fowler (2009: 153) has argued, this has masked other ways in which citizens engage politically:

> Much enquiry into civic agency exhibits a logical inconsistency. It does so by 'locating' civic agency primarily within and as a distinctive attribute of civil society. This location is often understood as a Habermasian public space for communication, information, debate, and exchange bounded by state, market, and family. However, as sociopolitical categories, citizenship and civic agency are not amenable to reframing in terms of location within a particular institutional 'sector' or 'space' ... Sectoral differentiation within a society distorts the essence of what citizenship and civicness are about. It does so in ways that recast their ontology toward a particular political project associated with liberal capitalism. Disembodied from the enduring rights and duties of citizenship and fixated on civil society organizations, placing civic agency in institutional category introduces a potentially narrowed and apolitical separation from roots of politics and rights.

Elsewhere, we have suggested that there is a need for a broader conception and examination of civic agency in Africa which transcends the study of NGOs which have since the 1990s been assigned a key role in processes of social change and frequently been seen as exemplifying agency and resistance on the continent (Willems and Obadare, 2014). In situating these forms within global, regional and national

socio-economic and political milieus, we can gain a better understanding of processes of "social change *actually* taking place" (Chabal, 2009: 11) on the continent
instead of drawing attention to processes donors want to see taking place. The concept of mediated civic agency points to a wider spectrum of actions in which citizens
engage power through a range of media forms, whether formal or informal.

For example, in the case of Africa, music has been particularly crucial in mobilising
citizens to resist oppression in colonial regimes such as in colonial Mozambique (Vail
and White, 1978, 1983), apartheid South Africa (Drewett, 2003, 2004; Drewett and
Clegg, 2006; Gilbert, 2007; Olwage, 2008) but also in postcolonial times such as during
military rule in Nigeria (Hungbo, 2014) or under an authoritarian state in Zimbabwe
(Mano, 2007). In the 1970s guerrilla war in Zimbabwe, liberation songs urged young
men and women to join the struggle for independence (Pongweni, 1982). These modes
of expression were not always directly linked to formal civil society organisations but
were initiated by individual musicians or music groups and spread through guerrilla
radio stations operating in neighbouring countries (Mosia, Riddle and Zaffiro, 1994).
Similarly, Nigerian musician Fela Kuti used his music to critique both the military
regime in power in Nigeria and the flawed power balance between Global North and
Global South within the United Nations system (Hungbo, 2014).

The concept of mediated civic agency therefore is able to capture a wider range of
actions aimed at different forms of power. Non-governmental organisations on the
continent are often primarily supported or funded by international donors to contest
the African nation-state. They consider misgovernance, corruption and lack of
accountability and transparency as key causes of Africa's 'underdevelopment'. However, it is problematic to treat African nation-states as fully fledged, self-governing
entities, given the fundamentally, inequitable global system within which African
states are situated. African states largely operate as 'quasi-states' (Jackson, 1990)
within a context of what we have elsewhere called 'fractured sovereignty' (Willems
and Obadare, 2014). Concentrating one's attention on the actions of donor-funded,
oppositional non-governmental organisations ultimately does not only mask the
global power relations that they represent but also silences the way in which Africans
like Fela Kuti have questioned a fundamentally unequal global system.

From alternative media institutions to alternative mediation

As indicated earlier in this chapter, early work in the subfield of alternative media
studies has drawn our attention to a range of media institutions operating outside, or
in opposition to mainstream media institutions. These organisations did not only
differ in terms of the content and coverage they produced but also adopted organisational cultures that were not driven by the same principles as their mainstream
counterparts. In the African context, a number of scholars have also highlighted the
role of alternative media institutions such as the practice of 'guerilla journalism' in
the context of Nigeria under military rule between 1993 and 1998 when the country
was subject to General Sani Abacha's regime (Olukotun, 2002a, 2002b, 2004; Dare,
2007; Adebanwi, 2008, 2011). Far from the type of 'fourth estate' journalism carried
out by privately funded, professionally run media houses described above,

underground publications such as *Tempo* and *NEWS* magazine and pirate radio stations like *Radio Kudirat* practiced "a hit-and-run style in which journalists operating from hideouts continued to publish opposition and critical journals in defiance of the state" (Olukotun, 2004: 78). This approach, in many ways, was also adopted by the 'resistance press', 'alternative press' or 'progressive press' in apartheid South Africa, which included newspapers such as *South*, *Weekly Mail* and *New African*, and grassroots publications such as *Grassroots* and *Saamstaan* that sought to counter the apartheid state of the 1980s (Tomaselli and Louw, 1991; Switzer, 1997; Switzer and Adhikari, 2000).

While this work on alternative media institutions has provided us with important insights into the work of institutions operating outside, or in opposition of, mainstream media, an institutional focus has also prevented us from acknowledging other ways in which alternative media content has been spreading. This is particularly important in the context of new media but is also relevant in relation to much older forms of communication, such as interpersonal communication. In the context of Africa, scholars have pointed to the crucial sharing of information not via mass media but through debates and discussions in public spaces, referred to by Ellis (1989: 321) as "*radio trottoir*" ('pavement radio' in English), which he defined as "the popular and unofficial discussion of current affairs in Africa" (ibid.: 321). Verbal, interpersonal forms of communication such as popular rumour, humour and jokes have been crucial in challenging those in power in postcolonial Cameroon, Nigeria and Zimbabwe (Mbembe, 2001; Obadare, 2009, 2010; Willems, 2008, 2010, 2011b, 2011c).

For example, in my own work on political humour in Zimbabwe, I have discussed how jokes profoundly challenged the credibility of the state broadcaster Zimbabwe Broadcasting Corporation (ZBC) in the early 2000s (Willems, 2010, 2011a, 2011b, 2011c). Unlike many other African countries, Zimbabwe's broadcasting landscape was still dominated by one state-controlled broadcaster. While satellite television became more widely available in the period after 2005 made possible through cheap decoders, ZBC occupied a dominant position in broadcasting in the early 2000s. On 30 November 2001, ZBC launched its new 'Vision 30' strategy, and was renamed to Zimbabwe Television (ZTV). Its mission was announced as "to provide world-class quality programmes and services that reflect, develop, foster and respect the Zimbabwean national identity, character, cultural diversity, national aspirations and Zimbabwean and Pan-African values" (advert in ZBC relaunch supplement, *The Herald*, 30 November 2001). Soon after the introduction of Vision 30 in December 2001, ZTV stopped its regular broadcasts of CNN news bulletins and the broadcaster began to implement local content regulations which stipulated that 75 percent of its programming comprise local television content and material from Africa.

This new policy resulted in the introduction of a range of new television programmes which largely supported the agenda of the ruling party Zimbabwe African National Union-Patriotic Front (ZANU-PF). The screening of documentaries about the liberation war, the emergence of nationalist talk shows, the recycling of liberation war songs through the state-commissioned *Third Chimurenga* music albums and the introduction of commemorative music galas all helped remind Zimbabweans of ZANU-PF's historical legacy and served to delegitimise the opposition Movement for Democratic Change (MDC) which was formed in 1999 (Ndlovu-Gatsheni and

Willems, 2009). Given that the majority of television viewers were urban Zimbabweans who were most likely to vote for the MDC, as their stronghold was in the cities, more and more Zimbabweans became disillusioned with the heavy bias towards ZANU-PF on the national broadcaster. Letters to the editor in private newspapers complained about the 'declining standards' at ZBC. In its weekly media column 'What's on Air', *The Standard* regularly referred to 'Dead BC' when discussing television content. The growing disillusionment with the national monopoly broadcaster was also expressed in jokes which commented on the declining standards at the national broadcaster. Jokes commented on the way in which the broadcaster was increasingly instrumentalised by the ruling party, and were shared orally, via online discussion forums, e-mail listservs and SMS messages.

The concept of alternative mediation is able to capture both the way in which Zimbabwe's state broadcaster aimed to offer an alternative perspective to Western-driven media and the manner in which ordinary Zimbabweans ridiculed the growing appropriation of ZBC by the ruling party through the popular jokes they circulated in public spaces, through e-mail listservs and via SMS messages. Hence, a key advantage of the concept of mediation is that it refers to the dynamic process of communication as compared to a more static understanding of institutions (Martin-Barbero, 1993; Silverstone, 2005; Livingstone, 2009). For Martin-Barbero (1993) in particular, mediation refers to the process of production and reception, and his specific interest is in the way in which people counter and resist the content of mainstream media. This is not only relevant in a context in which new media are increasingly offering ordinary people – rather than formal media institutions and referred to by Castells (2009) as mass self-communication – the opportunity to produce content but also suits a context in which power itself is multilayered and in which the nation-state cannot simply be seen as an oppressive force exercising power but should simultaneously be treated as subject to other relations of power such as those represented by global media conglomerates such as BBC and CNN.

Conclusion

Drawing examples from Africa, I have proposed a double shift in this chapter from, on the one hand, civil society media to mediated civic agency, and on the other hand, alternative media to alternative mediation. I have argued that this shift is necessary first of all in order to grasp the changing nature of power which is no longer simply vested in institutions and organisations – whether nation-states or mass media institutions – but increasingly challenged by informal, networked forms of resistance enabled not only by new media but also by other forms of arguably more affective forms of communication such as music and humour, which have been particularly crucial on the African continent. The concept of mediated civic agency is able to draw our attention to those forms of resistance not located in a specific institutional, collective and oppositional realm outside the state and market.

Second, such a shift is important in order to account for the process in which different forms of media struggle for power and engage in resistance on behalf of the state or its citizens. Power is not simply something that institutions own or have, but it is something that actors continually will have to fight for in the face of impending resistance always on the lure. The concept of alternative mediation helps us map this dynamic and dialogical process, which is even more important in the context of the postcolony which does not only exercise power but is also subject to the power of global forces that continue to threaten and fracture the sovereignty of the African nation-state, and its ability to communicate.

Further reading

Chapter 1 of Obadare and Willems's *Civic Agency in Africa: Arts of Resistance in the 21st Century* (Oxford: James Currey) offers an empirical and conceptual overview of the way in which scholars have discussed civic agency and resistance in the context of Africa. Mbembe's (2001) seminal book provides a highly original theoretical approach to the aesthetics of power in Africa and the relation between rulers and ruled. Readers interested in case studies of alternative media in Africa may wish to consult Olukotun (2002a, 2002b, 2004), Dare (2007) and Adebanwi (2008, 2011) on Nigeria, or Tomaselli and Louw (1991), Switzer (1997), and Switzer and Adhikari (2000) on apartheid South Africa.

References

Abbas, M. A. and Erni, J. N. (2004) *Internationalizing Cultural Studies: An Anthology.* Oxford: Blackwell.

Adebanwi, W. (2008) *Trials and Triumphs: The Story of the NEWS.* Lagos, Nigeria: West African Book Publishers.

——(2011) "The radical press and security agencies in Nigeria: Beyond hegemonic polarities." *African Studies Review*, 54(3), 45–69.

Allan, S. and Thorsen, E. (2009) *Citizen Journalism: Global Perspectives.* New York: Peter Lang.

Ansah, P. A. V. (1988) "In search of a role for the African media in the democratic process." *Africa Media Review*, 2(2), 1–16.

Atton, C. (2002) *Alternative Media.* London: Sage.

Axford, B. (2011) "Talk about a revolution: Social media and the MENA uprisings." *Globalizations*, 8(5), 681–86.

Bailey, O., Cammaerts, B. and Carpentier, N. (2008) *Understanding Alternative Media.* Maidenhead: Open University Press.

Bennett, W. L. and Segerberg, A. (2012) "The logic of connective action." *Information, Communication and Society*, 15(5), 739–68.

Carpentier, N., Lie, R. and Servaes, J. (2003) "Community media: Muting the democratic media discourse?" *Continuum: Journal of Media and Cultural Studies*, 17(1), 51–68.

Castells, M. (2009) *Communication Power.* Oxford: Oxford University Press.

Castells, M., Qiu, J. L., Fernandez-Ardevol, M. and Sey, A. (2006) "The mobile civil society: Social movements, political power, and communication networks." In M. Castells, J. L. Qiu, M. Fernandez-Ardevol and A. Sey (eds), *Mobile Communication and Society: A Global Perspective.* Cambridge, MA: MIT Press (pp. 185–214).

Chabal, P. (2009) *Africa: The Politics of Suffering and Smiling.* London: Zed Books.

Cottle, S. (2011) "Media and the Arab uprisings of 2011: Research notes." *Journalism*, 12(5), 647–59.

Couldry, N. and Curran, J. (eds.) (2003) *Contesting Media Power: Alternative Media in a Networked World.* Lanham, MD: Rowman & Littlefield.

Curran, J. and Park, M.-J. (2000) *De-Westernizing Media Studies.* London: Routledge.

Dare, S. (2007) *Guerrilla Journalism: Dispatches from the Underground.* Bloomington, IN: Xlibris.

Deleuze, G. and Guattari, F. (1987) *A Thousand Plateaus: Capitalism and Schizophrenia.* Minneapolis: University of Minnesota Press.

Downing, J. (1996) *Internationalizing Media Theory: Transition, Power, Culture: Reflections on Media in Russia, Poland and Hungary, 1980–95.* London: Sage.

——(with others) (2001) *Radical Media: Rebellious Communication and Social Movements.* London: Sage.

——(2008) "Social movement theories and alternative media: An evaluation and critique." *Communication, Culture & Critique,* 1, 40–50.

——(2011) Encyclopaedia of Social Movement Media. London: Sage.

Drewett, M. (2003) "Battling over borders: Narratives of resistance to the South African border war voiced through popular music." *Social Dynamics,* 29(1), 78–98.

——(2004) "Remembering subversion: Resisting censorship in apartheid South Africa." In M. Korpe (ed.), *Shoot the Singer! Music Censorship Today.* London: Zed Books (pp. 88–93).

Drewett, M. and Clegg, J. (2006) "Why don't you sing about the leaves and the dreams? Reflecting on music censorship in apartheid South Africa." *Popular Music Censorship in Africa.* Aldershot, UK: Ashgate (pp. 127–36).

Ellis, S. (1989) "Tuning into pavement radio." *African Affairs,* 88(352), 321–30.

Fowler, A. (2009) "Civic agency." In H. K. Anheier and S. Toepler (eds), *International Encyclopedia of Civil Society.* New York: Springer (pp. 150–55).

Gilbert, S. (2007) "Singing against apartheid: ANC cultural groups and the international anti-apartheid struggle." *Journal of Southern African Studies,* 33(2), 421–41.

Hamilton, J. (2000) "Alternative media: Conceptual difficulties, critical possibilities." *Journal of Communication Inquiry,* 24, 357–78.

Harbeson, J. W., Rothchild, D. S. and Chazan, N. (1994) *Civil Society and the State in Africa.* Boulder, CO: Lynne Rienner.

Hill, K. A. and Hughes, J. E. (1998) *Cyberpolitics: Citizen Activism in the Age of the Internet.* Lanham, MD: Rowman & Littlefield.

Hounshell, B. (2011) "The revolution will be tweeted." *Foreign Policy,* 187, 20–21.

Howley, K. (2005) *Community Media: People, Places, and Communication Technologies.* Cambridge: Cambridge University Press.

Hungbo, J. (2014) "'Beasts of no nation': Resistance and civic activism in Fela Anikulapo-Kuti's music." In E. Obadare and W. Willems (eds.) *Civic Agency in Africa: Arts of Resistance in the Twenty-First Century.* Oxford: James Currey (pp. 167–81).

Hydén, G., Leslie, M. and Ogundimu, F. F. (2003) *Media and Democracy in Africa.* Uppsala: Nordiska Afrikainstitutet.

Jackson, R. H. (1990) *Quasi-States: Sovereignty, International Relations and the Third World.* Cambridge: Cambridge University Press.

Kahler, M. (2009) *Networked Politics: Agency, Power, and Governance.* Ithaca, NY: Cornell University Press.

Kasoma, F. (1995) "The role of the independent media in Africa's change to democracy." *Media, Culture and Society,* 17(4), 537–55.

——(1997) "The independent press and politics in Africa." *Gazette: International Journal for Communication Studies,* 59(4–5), 295–310.

Khiabany, G. (2012) "Arab revolutions and the Iranian uprising: Similarities and differences." *Middle East Journal of Culture and Communication,* 5(1), 58–65.

Khondker, H. H. (2011) "Role of the new media in the Arab Spring." *Globalizations*, 8(5), 675–79.

Langlois, A. and Dubois, F. (2005) *Autonomous Media: Activating Resistance and Dissent.* Montreal: Cumulus Press.

Lewis, D. (2001) *Civil Society in Non-Western Contexts: Reflections on the "Usefulness" of a Concept.* London School of Economics Civil Society Working Paper 13. London: London School of Economics, Centre for Civil Society.

Livingstone, S. (2009) "On the mediation of everything." *Journal of Communication*, 59(1), 1–18.

Mano, W. (2007) "Popular music as journalism." *Journalism Studies*, 8(1), 61–78.

Martin-Barbero, J. (1993) *Communication, Culture and Hegemony: From the Media to Mediation.* London: Sage.

Mbembe, A. (2001) *On the Postcolony.* Berkeley: University of California Press.

McCaughey, M. and Ayers, M. D. (2003) *Cyberactivism: Online Activism in Theory and Practice.* New York: Routledge.

McMillin, D. C. (2006) *International Media Studies.* Oxford: Blackwell Publishers.

Mercer, C. (2004) "Engineering civil society: ICT in Tanzania." *Review of African Political Economy*, 31(99), 49–64.

Mosia, L., Riddle, C. and Zaffiro, J. (1994) "From revolutionary to regime radio: Three decades of nationalist broadcasting in Southern Africa." *Africa Media Review*, 8(1), 1–24.

Mudhai, O. F. (2004) "Researching the impact of ICTs as change catalysts in Africa." *Ecquid Novi*, 25(2), 313–35.

——(2006) "Exploring the potential for more strategic use of mobile phones." In J. Dean, J. Anderson and G. Lovink (eds), *Reformatting Politics: Information Technology and Global Society.* New York: Routledge.

——(2012) *Civic Engagement, Digital Networks, and Political Reform in Africa.* Basingstoke, UK: Palgrave Macmillan.

Nanabhay, M. and Farmanfarmaian, R. (2011) "From spectacle to spectacular: How physical space, social media and mainstream broadcast amplified the public sphere in Egypt's 'Revolution'." *Journal of North African Studies*, 16(4), 573–603.

Ndlovu-Gatsheni, S. J. and Willems, W. (2009). "Making sense of cultural nationalism and the politics of commemoration under the *Third Chimurenga* in Zimbabwe." *Journal of Southern African Studies*, 35(4), 945–65.

Obadare, E. (2009) "The uses of ridicule: humour, 'infrapolitics' and civil society in Nigeria." *African Affairs*, 108(431), 241–61.

——(2010) "State of travesty: Jokes and the logics of socio-cultural improvisation in Africa." *Critical African Studies*, 4, 1–21.

Olukotun, A. (2002a) "Authoritarian state, crisis of democratization and the underground media in Nigeria." *African Affairs*, 101(404), 317–42.

——(2002b) "Traditional protest media and anti-military struggle in Nigeria 1988–1999." *African Affairs*, 101(403), 193–211.

——(2004) *Repressive State and Resurgent Media under Nigeria's Military Dictatorship, 1988–1998.* Research Report 126. Uppsala: Nordic Africa Institute.

Olwage, G. (2008) *Composing Apartheid: Music for and against Apartheid.* Johannesburg: Wits University Press.

Paragas, F. (2003) "Dramatextism: Mobile telephony and people power in the Philippines." In J. K. Nyíri (ed.), *Mobile Democracy: Essays on Society, Self and Politics.* Vienna: Passagen Verlag (pp. 259–83).

Pertierra, R. (2006) *Transforming Technologies, Altered Selves: Mobile Phone and Internet Use in the Philippines.* Manila: De La Salle University Press.

Pongweni, A. J. C. (1982). *Songs That Won the Liberation War*. Harare, Zimbabwe: College Press.

Qiu, J. L. (2008) "Mobile civil society in Asia: A comparative study of People Power II and the Nosamo movement." *Javnost – The Public*, 15(3), 39–58.

Rafael, V. L. (2003) "The cell phone and the crowd: Messianic politics in the contemporary Philippines." *Public Culture*, 15(3), 399–425.

Rheingold, H. (2002) *Smart Mobs: The Next Social Revolution*. Cambridge, MA: Perseus Publishing.

Robinson, W. and Robison, D. (2006) "Tsunami mobilizations: Considering the role of mobile and digital communications devices, citizen journalism, and the mass media." In A. P. Kavoori and N. Arceneaux (eds), *The Cell Phone Reader: Essays in Social Transformation*. New York: Peter Lang (pp. 85–104).

Rodríguez, C. (2001) *Fissures in the Mediascape: An International Study of Citizens' Media*. Cresskill, NJ: Hampton Press

Shome, R. (2009) "Post-colonial reflections on the 'internationalization' of cultural studies." *Cultural Studies* 23(5–6), 694–719.

Silverstone, R. (2005) "The sociology of mediation and communication." In C. Calhoun, C. Rojek and B. S. Turner (eds), *The Sage Handbook of Sociology*. London: Sage (pp. 188–207).

Sreberny, A. and Khiabany, G. (2010) *Blogistan: The Internet and Politics in Iran*. London: I. B. Tauris.

Sreberny, A. and Mohammadi, A. (1994) *Small Media, Big Revolution: Communication, Culture, and the Iranian Revolution*. Minneapolis: University of Minnesota Press.

Switzer, L. (1997) *South Africa's Alternative Press: Voices of Protest and Resistance, 1880s–1960s*. Cambridge: Cambridge University Press.

Switzer, L. and Adhikari, M. (2000) *South Africa's Resistance Press: Alternative Voices in the Last Generation under Apartheid*. Athens: Ohio University Center for International Studies.

Tettey, W. J. (2001) "The media and democratization in Africa: Contributions, constraints and concerns of the private press." *Media, Culture and Society*, 23(1), 5–31.

Thussu, D. K. (2009). *Internationalizing Media Studies*. London: Routledge.

Tomaselli, K. and Louw, P. E. (eds) (1991) *The Alternative Press in South Africa*. Belville: Anthropos.

Vail, L. and White, L. (1978) "Plantation protest: The history of a Mozambican song." *Journal of Southern African Studies*, 5(1), 1–25.

——(1983) "Forms of resistance: Songs and perceptions of power in colonial Mozambique." *American Historical Review*, 88, 883–919.

Wang, G. (2010) *De-Westernizing Communication Research: Altering Questions and Changing Frameworks*. London: Routledge.

Willems, W. (2008) "Mocking the state: Comic strips in the Zimbabwean press." In J. Abbink and A. van Dokkum (eds), Dilemmas of Development: Conflicts of Interest and Their Resolutions in Modernizing Africa. Leiden: Africa Studies Centre (pp. 151–61).

——(2010) "Beyond dramatic revolutions and grand rebellions: Everyday forms of resistance in the Zimbabwe crisis." *Communicare*, 29, 1–17.

——(2011a) "At the crossroads of the formal and popular: Convergence culture and new publics in Zimbabwe." In H. Wasserman (ed.), *Popular Media, Democracy and Development in Africa*. London: Routledge (pp. 46–62).

——(2011b) "Comic strips and 'the crisis': Postcolonial laughter and coping with everyday life in Zimbabwe." *Popular Communication*, 9(2), 126–45.

——(2011c) "Political jokes in Zimbabwe." In J. Downing (ed.), *Encyclopaedia of Social Movement Media*. London: Sage (pp. 410–12).

——(2012a) "Interrogating public sphere and popular culture as theoretical concepts: On their value in African studies." *Africa Development*, 37(1), 11–26.

——(2012b) "The ballot vote as embedded ritual: A radical critique of liberal-democratic approaches to media and elections in Africa." *African Studies*, 71(1), 547–63.

——(2013) "Theorising media as/and civil society in Africa." In E. Obadare (ed.), *The Handbook of Civil Society in Africa*. New York: Springer (pp. 43–59).

Willems, W. and Obadare, E. (2014) "Introduction: African resistance in an age of fractured sovereignty." In E. Obadare and W. Willems (eds), *Civic Agency in Africa: Arts of Resistance in the 21st Century*. Oxford: James Currey (pp. 1–23).

8

CONCEPTUALISING SOCIAL MOVEMENT MEDIA

A fresh metaphor?

John D. H. Downing

Introduction: The headache

Given the vast continent of alternative media objectives and formats, it is unsurprising that conceptualising them has taken very different forms. The multidimensionality of 'alternative media' is indicated (Downing, 2011, 2014) by the pullulating terms in use – not only 'alternative' media, but 'counter-information' media, 'tactical' media, 'social movement' media, 'community' media, 'citizens' media, 'independent' media, and still others. This multiplicity does not evince intellectual confusion, but rather the ineluctably Protean media practices and purposes under our lens.

Yet, if we take Linda-Jean Kenix's recent exploration of the interpenetrations among 'mainstream' and 'alternative' media (Kenix, 2011) as an important encouragement to eschew rigid compartmentalisation of media into those two categories, then the task of definition becomes more complex still. Her research is very much tilted towards journalism and news, but the point is well made. A robust illustration of Kenix's argument is Håkan Thörn's splendid study of the transnational anti-*apartheid* movement, which traces four overlapping modes of media communication, from mainstream to independent, deployed over a period of four decades (Thörn, 2006). We should not rely on either media scale or funding sources in order to pinpoint our object of study.

My own work has been rather narrowly obsessed with the relation between media of all kinds and struggles for social justice, and against racism and war. I have never envisaged the much more macroscopic agenda that Chris Atton, for example, has addressed in his *Alternative Media* (2001) and elsewhere, engaging in the study of small-scale media as a dimension of the anthropology of culture. Nonetheless, some definition, conceptualisation and/or metaphors are needed. In what follows, my primary concern is with metaphors relevant to the subset of alternative media that I have concentrated on, namely social movement media – but I think the discussion will also be relevant to a wider zone still, if not to the entire 'continent'.

Overused metaphors

For too long, attempts at social scientific metaphors to capture societal processes have drawn for preference on ones implying immobility. I am far from alone in observing this, but the point, given the resilience of metaphors in shaping our *Fragestellungen/problématiques*, bears quite steady repetition. I shall critique four of them briefly, and then gingerly propose a different one, based – of all things – on hydrodynamics and kinematics. I shall only try to apply this metaphor to the kind of radical media – social movement media – I have always focused upon, not to the much larger dimensions that Atton and Kenix address, though it may be that there too this fresh metaphor may turn out to have heuristic consequences.

The most obvious of the static metaphors is 'structure', which inevitably conjures up architectural solidity (which of course, in that instance, one hopes will indeed prove stable, not least in earthquakes and floods). Even when Raymond Williams wrenched the term away from its moorings in Second and Third International Marxist thought to insist on the parity of *feelings'* power with that of political-economic forces, and coined the term "structures of feeling", he appears to have relied on the irreducible solidity that 'structure' conveys to underscore the full weight of his 'heterodox' argument (Williams, 1977: II.9).

The use of the body metaphor in functionalist sociology – where the notion of a working assembly of integrated body organs latches on to the interconnections among social institutions and processes – is implicitly a pitch for continuity and calm, virtually for stasis; and against conflict or change, seen as pathological. Even when Lewis Coser (1964) famously pointed out that conflict could be societally functional, it was the goal of equilibrium that appeared to prevail in his argument. Vilfredo Pareto's concept of societal equilibrium was drawn from engineering rather than biology. It visualised mutually balancing forces – for instance, in a suspension bridge, or a cathedral roof held in place by flying buttresses – as the source of societal stability, rather than the cosy health of the body-metaphor. Nonetheless, equilibrium was the greatest good.

But must we be chained forever to the radically pessimistic premise of Thomas Hobbes's Civil War–derived dystopia ("the war of all against all")? Does social equilibrium *have* to be our secular *credo quia absurdum*? Civil war has *not* been a permanent or normal human condition. Even from the very civil war that transfixed Hobbes's attention, Christopher Hill's *The World Turned Upside Down* (1975) excavated a very different face – including a media face.

Structure and equilibrium are not the only static metaphors in frequent use. The German term *Öffentlichkeit* is certainly 'out there', initially deployed fifty years ago by Jürgen Habermas and then subsequently, following its English translation as 'the public sphere' or 'public realm', by a heavenly host of academic writers. The German term has no single English equivalent and can designate – according to context – publicity, the public at large, activity conducted in public; and in its adjectival form can apply to open court, state schools, public opinion, the public good, the public sector, even public toilets. In other words, not a location such as the Athenian agora, but a kinetic process, a series of activities.

In English, 'public sphere' perpetually prompts us to be trying to identify 'the' public sphere's location or visible institutional identity. 'Are' mainstream media 'the public sphere'? If they are not, then what or where 'is' it? – and then, how are they situated in relation to 'it'? Location, location, location ...

In an extra twist on the term, US sociologist Todd Gitlin lamented what he saw as the fragmentation of contemporary political life into political "sphericules". He was then quizzed by two Australian media researchers for neglecting the important contribution of minority-ethnic media "sphericules" to a pluralistic multicultural polity (Gitlin, 1998; Cunningham and Sinclair, 2000). In an interesting set of edited essays on the French polity, Bastien and Neveu (1999) proposed that 'the' public sphere was in reality best conceived as a mosaic of overlapping rhetorics and discourses characteristic of separate governmental policy arenas. All these contributions had the merit of refocusing back on to the kinetic dimensions inherent in Habermas's original deployment of the term. But despite them, a very great deal of the metaphor's English-language usage is very one- or two-dimensional, and correspondingly static.

The fourth tendentially static metaphor, I would propose, is 'network'. In the end, a network is either something fixed, akin to a spider's web, or a grid, or the infrastructure of computer terminals, cables, satellites, cell phones and cell towers. The web may shift slightly in the breeze, the satellites may be doing seven thousand miles an hour but still in geo-stationary orbit, the phones and laptops may be being carried around, but the rest of the grid stands still. Very still. The rhizome metaphor has the merit of stressing spontaneity and the significance of the growth of connectedness invisible to the naked eye, but still represents a spatially anchored network. Now, it may be objected, the point of networks is not that they sit there, but that they enable the colossal contemporary mass of inter-human connections in action that we call the internet and telephony. But this argument would be akin to calling traffic a road. The terms 'networking' and 'networked' do have a kinetic sense, though they tendentially evoke interpersonal connectedness.

What, though, about the 'space of flows' notion so well known through the work of Manuel Castells on the 'network society' (Castells, 2000: 407–59)? In this notion, I would suggest there are not one but two problems. One is the splendidly ambiguous term 'space', which Henri Lefebvre (1991), himself a stern critic of sloppy uses of the word, pinned down into three separate dimensions: perceived, conceived and lived space. Although influenced by Lefebvre, Castells's "space of flows" does not engage with this specification. The other is 'flows', which implies a spontaneous, simultaneous and unblocked process. Castells recruits the metaphor, but does not develop it any further (it is absent from the index to his three-volume work). It serves in practice simply as a synonym for 'process/processes'. He writes at one point:

> ... our society is constructed around flows: flows of capital, flows of information, flows of technology, flows of organizational interaction, flows of images, sounds and symbols ... they are the expression of processes dominating our economic, political and symbolic life ... By flows I understand purposeful, repetitive, programmable sequences of exchange and interaction

between physically disjointed positions held by social actors in the economic, political and symbolic structures of society.

(Castells, 2000: 442)

In the pages following (ibid.: 442–45), he argues that the "space of flows" has three levels: "[a] a circuit of electronic exchanges … [b] nodes and hubs … [c] the spatial organization of the dominant, managerial elites … " Slightly further on (ibid.: 453), Castells claims that a majority of humans still experience and conceive of their lives simply in terms of 'place', not in connection to these flows. None of these formulations put very much flesh on flows. Yet, it may be that a deeper exploration of the term 'flows' may generate something useful. I attempt an initial foray in the rest of this essay.

We need to be cautious, though. Every term we have looked at – structure, organism, public sphere, network (up to and including rhizome and flows) – has a potentially fatal common, still more profound flaw, namely the application to human society and its communicating processes of an inanimate reality. Thus, we need to be careful *never* to stray beyond the heuristic application of a metaphor to pinpoint and highlight key social processes, into using it as a concept actually endowed with explanatory sociological power.

A kinetic fluidity metaphor?

The media research literature is hardly a stranger to terms derived from liquid flows. The term 'channels' (and 'canals', in French, German, Russian and many other European languages) has long been used to denote broadcasting, cable and satellite diffusion. Corporate media have conventionally been referred to as 'mainstream'. Some studies of citizens' media have used the metaphor of 'waves', as in Gumucio Dagron's *Making Waves* (2001), which in its French publication is *Ondes de Choc* (Shock Waves), also the title of a book on movement radio activism in the 1960s–1980s in parts of Europe (Collin, 1982).

Those metaphors vary in focus. 'Channels', and especially 'canals', implies a one-way, steady, laminar communication movement inside clearly defined banks; indeed, the banks/edges are as important as the movement, as broadcast frequency regulations indicate. 'Mainstream' implies steady unidirectional movement, but this time of a sizable and consistently predictable laminar river, with eddies, rills and slower-moving side channels as also-rans. 'Shock waves' suggests intermittent, unpredictable turbulence of considerable force, but again unidirectional. Both the latter metaphors engage implicitly with issues of power and size, whereas 'channels' does not address the agency by which the metaphorical river- or canal banks were formed, or suggest anything other than unidirectional movement. Indeed, when Bertolt Brecht, in his much-cited 1932 essay on radio (Brecht, 1983[1932]), proposed recasting the technology from its unidirectional 'vertical' application into "an enormous canal system (*ein ungeheures Kanalsystem*)", he was perhaps the very first to push the 'canal' metaphor into the interactive realm, though aside from radio's marginal CB (citizen band) and 'ham' uses, it was only with the emergence of the internet that his vision became realised.

Pursuing the flow/water metaphor in a different sense, Zygmunt Bauman (2000) coined the term 'liquid modernity' to denote what he argues to have become a seismic cultural shift since the late twentieth century away from stable identities and towards a consumerism-driven quest for a series of temporary commodity-purchase-generated identities, where media branding and advertising are central forces. 'Liquid modernity' is his attempt to avoid the conceptual confusion surrounding the term post-modernity.

For some, however, the post-modernist assertion of the collapse of so-called grand narratives and the dissolution of established projects and strategies has even become something to celebrate, as in a study of Australian and American global social justice movement activists entitled "From solidarity to fluidarity" (McDonald, 2002). (McDonald uses 'solidarity' to denote closely defined collective goals and disciplined organisation, not international solidarity activism.) 'Fluidarity' is a term drawn from one of his interviews with activists, which McDonald adopts to characterise the unplanned, un-programmatic energy evident in short-run street upsurges to protest corporate domination. The refusal of political platforms and the rejection of institutional leadership formats, marking many moments within both the global social justice movements of the 2000s and the 2011 Occupy and *indignados* movements, echoed that philosophy, although as Gerbaudo (2012) rightly points out, in actual practice certain forms of leadership were both in action and indispensable.

This embrace, almost, of instability is visible in the discourse of 'tactical media' (Lovink, 2002; Raley, 2009), and enthroned in the Temporary Autonomous Zone notion of Hakim Bey (1991). At its best, this viewpoint acknowledges the validity of temporary upsurges against exploitation and repression – 'upsurges' being yet another water metaphor, here alluding to the *force* in water – and refuses to dismiss them as trivial just because they do not, overnight, revolutionise the planet. Point taken; but this viewpoint risks a fatalistic subjection to the existing order, a conviction that we are permitted a little 'fun' now and then, effectively kowtowing to the powers that be (who can certainly cope with that level of insubordination). Is it so different from a more or less bloodless version of a *jacquerie*? The bloodstained version may have hung around in aristocratic *Angst* for quite a few centuries, but those centuries also saw the most glacial change in farmers' options ('glacial' – another water metaphor).

Let us, then, take stock for a moment of the water metaphor as a category. While there is no reason to junk the static conventional metaphors reviewed above, there is no question but that water is an infinitely more agile metaphor, embracing kinetic variations from torrent and tsunami to glacial and stagnant, all of which imply considerable force in one way or another. We can be discussing rivers, oceans, currents, waves, tides, surges, turbulence, floods, trickles, seepage, ponds, lagoons, waterfalls, wells, vortices, rain, hail, snow, ice, thaw, steam, silt, delta, dams. We can be discussing turbidity or viscosity. We can be talking about reflection, refraction or recharge, about diffraction, slack water – or even sea puss. We are certainly not confined to unidirectionality. Rather, we are confronted with dialectically operating forces in the extreme, including in laminar situations.

The options spin beyond even these. So far we have been talking H_2O. There are many other fluids: blood, oil, honey, sap … Moreover, flows do not only consist of fluids. Air flows are omnipresent, from wind chill to twisters to jet-streams to pleasing zephyrs. They whip up oceans into monster waves. Over time, they cut huge rocks into fantastic shapes. The fact that neither fluids nor air have the bony formations of structure, the calibrated mutuality of an animal organism, the spatial connotation of 'public sphere' or the stability of a network does not entail that power and force are blissfully absent, that water only runs peacefully through our fingers and air through our hair.

In their emphasis on motion and change, such metaphors do offer an escape from the metaphors implying stasis; yet, in their inclusion of sometimes quite overwhelming force, they engage with power, one of the core aspects of life in human society. The mighty Mississippi River creates its own course over time (even briefly flowing backwards in some stretches in both 1812 and 2012), despite human efforts to steer and corral it. Its course-making is an act of power, exemplified over long periods of time, and involving the totality of its volume and processes, enormous and tiny. Longitudinal dimensions, change dimensions, power dimensions, expansion and contraction dimensions, pattern dimensions, conflict dimensions, are all encompassed.

In other words, the metaphoric lake of fluidity offers a motherlode which could illuminate our thinking on a whole range of social and cultural processes and liberate us from the confines of our conventional static metaphors, yet without plunging us into a post-modernist *tohu wa bohu*. Let me conclude by suggesting some brief examples of how elements of this frame might illuminate the nano-media of social movements.

Time-frame. Thinking about social movements (and their media) is typically dominated by short-run spectacularity. The lens is something like this: a desperate Tunisian street vendor tragically immolates himself; for the Tunisian public, which gets to hear about it through Facebook, this is the last straw, they take to the streets, and their dictator of twenty-three years flees with his family to the cosy confines of Saudi Arabia. Two countries east, the dictator of forty years is arrested and jailed, with America's Facebook a tasty tool in his demise. In between these countries 'it' all takes a bit longer, but after generous bombing it's bye-bye to another one. Hey presto! Democracy in north Africa! And now for Syria …

The pre-existence of overt and subterranean oppositional movements stretching back over decades, of clan networks and loyalties, of varying and often clashing religious ties, of consistent Washington, London, Paris and Rome regime support (in the latter years of Libya's Gaddafi regime), is not in this lens. Nor of course the vortical aftermath. Only the razzmatazz.

Yet, in an excellent forthcoming study of the Tunisian process, Mohamed El Zayani of Georgetown University, Qatar (Zayani, 2015), traces the unanticipated interconnected consequences of everyday Tunisian life as, very gradually, internet applications and then cell phones became part of the quotidian fabric, with zero expectation of their relevance to regime change. Except on the part of the regime, which both kick-started digital network connectivity and maintained a highly trained internet and cell phone surveillance agency.

Applying a riverine metaphor to this process would push our attention almost effortlessly away from the spectacular momentariness of flood, and towards the ongoing flows, large and small, whose combined laminarity might over a substantial period of time be shifting direction, but almost imperceptibly at any given moment.

Within these long-term and shorter-term flows, a range of social movement media and regime-friendly or -tolerant media are integral elements of the fluid mass and drive. One of the besetting sins of Media Studies is its typically ahistorical bent. Only contemporary news, new Hollywood, latest TV series, next year's digital killer app seem to figure large. In the study of social movement media, this vice compounds with the razzmatazz-fixation of many social movement studies. It is as though eddies and rills constituted a river.

The very long-term consequences of labour nano-media, feminist nano-media, abolitionist nano-media, anti-colonial nano-media, to take just four instances, easily disappear from view if our understanding of causes and consequences gets so dramatically foreshortened. The German government in 2011 announced that no new nuclear power stations would be built on German soil, and the remaining ones would be de-commissioned by 2022. This followed no less than thirty years of Germany's anti-nuclear power movement and its multiple nano-media steadily refreshing public debate and activism. In other words, a further instance of the utility of long-term analysis of the roles of social movement media, and an illustration of the potential pay-off of fluidity metaphors if appropriately deployed.

Stagnancy. In hydrological terms this is different from inertia, which can also describe a large plane sustaining itself in flight, or water running downhill. In order to illustrate how the stagnancy metaphor might usefully be applied, allow me to cite a study I undertook way back of Britain's Marxist press during the 1970s (Downing, 1980: 187–99). I analysed one Eurocommunist daily, and two rival Trotskyist weeklies. They principally covered economic struggles of one kind or another, reflecting the long domination of Second, Third and Fourth International Marxism's economic reductionism. Their self-perceived roles were that of *Iskra* (*The Spark*, newspaper of Russia's Bolsheviks), as set out by Lenin in 1902, namely the organisational tool of a disciplined revolutionary party. (In the case of the Communist daily, a little less absolute.)

With these twin *mantras*, the stage was indeed set for stagnancy. Week by week, year by year, it appeared as though they had bottled up the great variety of progressive social currents and significant conflicts in play, and carefully set them on one side. The issue was not that the various economic struggles on which they then concentrated were figments of their imagination, let alone unimportant. It was that in focusing almost entirely upon them, much of human life was swept aside. They did not warmly resonate beyond rather small assemblies of convinced activists, somehow able to munch their wooden prose. And yet these papers were offered for sale at pretty well every demonstration, presumably because their political parties' leaders thought they would ... well, strike a spark. Thatcherism, notwithstanding its continued detestation in many parts of British life, succeeded in ringing bells in zones of social imagination with which that press simply did not engage.

Stagnancy in the contemporary era of extremely fast change is crippling, and generational issues perhaps play more of a role than ever. This does not mean that patronising forays into "appealing to 'the youth'" are recipes for stagnancy. Self-run youth media themselves have a far better chance of resonance (Khalil, 2011; Rennie, 2011). But this media stagnancy has power, the power to box in, almost to dam – but not channel – social movement vitality.

Turbulence. One of the practical problems in analysing social movements and their media is that conducting systematic interviews when they are in full flood is difficult logistically, though not impossible (Tufekci and Wilson, 2012; Gerbaudo, 2012).

Interviewing Portuguese radio activists many years back, I asked why they had not sought some kind of feedback for their broadcast practice during the tumultuous years 1974–1976. They pointed to two reasons: the nonstop fluctuation of events; and their only-too-evidently high level of public support at times of crisis. But it does mean that analysing social movement organisations and leadership is much more feasible, and can have routine methods of investigation applied (e.g., Smith, 2008), than researching the various levels of movement periphery. It is here, especially, that metaphors of fluidity of one kind or another may serve us better, and certainly avoid fusing leader perspectives with grassroots ones.

Applying a water or air turbulence metaphor to the processes from Tunisia to Bahrain at the outset of the current decade might illuminate the combination of determinacy and indeterminacy which seems to be at the heart of crisis periods. No one feels secure as to what the outcome will be, and even whether a particular outcome will serve their interests. Huge surges in different directions represent ferocious struggles to sway the final outcome, yet they may and likely will generate 'reflective' counter-surges. All kinds of media uses are intensively engaged in this dynamic.

In this regard, the following brief encapsulation of water and air turbulence processes by Homsy et al. (2004: 740) may spark some productive reflection:

> [The] chaotic, or random, aspect of turbulence is due to strong nonlinearities in the three-dimensional flow, and results in turbulence having very broad ranges of time and length scales. Even though turbulent flows are random, they still possess identifiable flow structures … These structures, while occurring in a somewhat unpredictable manner, have certain identifiable features. Finally, not all turbulent flows are homogeneously turbulent in time or space. Some regions of the flow may have velocity fields that are random, but not turbulent.

As a heuristic model of social and mediatic flux, this formulation may be found quite evocative, not least in its simultaneous combination of ranges, regularities, structure and randomness. So might the notion of a 'shear layer', namely where a higher speed flow passes over a lower speed flow, creating an unstable shear layer which can break down into turbulence (Homsy et al., 2004: 742). Or the turbulence may last for quite a few kilometres, as with the visible confluence of the muddy Amazon River and the black, colder, faster Rio Negro just east of Manaus, and then they gradually merge.

For example, perhaps, we might take the interactions in the tumultuous events of May–June 1968 between the established Communist left in France and the multitudinous Trotskyist, Maoist and anarchist splinters and *groupuscules*. All of them had media activists aplenty, using graffiti, murals, fliers, placards, painted slogans, newspapers, street theatre, music, demonstrations, occupations, teach-ins. They were certainly moving at sharply different 'speeds', with the Communist Party establishment determined to retain its long-term ascendancy over the Left at large and the rest equally determined to shake that domination. For a while all over France, not just Paris, frozen public life thawed and developed intense turbulence, and the ripples spread out for decades.

Slack water and sea puss. In tidal terms, slack water signifies a temporary juncture at which incoming and ebbing tides are more or less balancing each other. Sea puss is a dangerous longshore current, a rip current caused by return flow. Loosely, the term may also refer to a submerged channel or inlet through a bar caused by those currents (South West Washington Coastal Erosion Survey, 2012). In their different ways, this apparent stasis and these almost invisible but potentially lethal currents might serve as metaphors for the extreme unpredictability that can ensue during a highly volatile period of political and cultural struggle. Examples, though quite distinct from each other in their specifics, could include Italy immediately after the 1918–1920 *biennio rosso* (Red Biennium); Weimar Germany; and Egypt, from the initial 2011 explosion in Cairo and other cities through the military coup of 2013.

Concluding comment

There is a considerable amount of more thought and research needed in order to establish the utility of metaphors of fluidity for conceptualising social movement media. This essay is simply an initial draft of a working hypothesis. It is probably stronger in pointing out the deficiencies of our conventional static metaphors than in establishing the complementary metaphor lake of fluidity. But in addressing issues of social movements and their media, where so often the analysis makes no effort to be comparative across the planet, or is single-mindedly obsessed with more recent communication technologies, or is pivoted on establishing simplistic and overly deterministic patterns and 'laws', hopefully this may be a little breath of fresh air. Insofar as such media are part of the larger public communication dynamic, hopefully some refreshing zephyrs are there too.

Acknowledgements

To fit the 5000-word limit for this volume, some points in my argument had to be addressed rather briefly. I would like to thank Professor John Sinclair of Melbourne University for his comments while preparing this essay, and Professor Mohamed El Zayani of Georgetown University, Qatar, for sharing his book manuscript on Tunisia with me before publication.

Further reading

For a very informative short comparison of differing uses of digital connective media – a better term by far than 'social media' – in the 2011 social upheavals in Egypt, Spain and Wall Street Occupy, see Paolo Gerbaudo's *Tweets in the Streets* (2012). For a fascinating look at an earlier epoch, namely the civil war and revolutionary movement in England in the mid-1600s, and the important part that printed fliers and pamphlets, and unorthodox religious views, played in the tumults, see Christopher Hill's classic *The World Turned Upside Down* (1975). Turning back to the present, Rita Raley's *Tactical Media* (2009) presents and discusses a number of videogames developed to challenge racist immigration policies, the war against Iraq (2003–) and the transnational finance system. For further information on 250 examples of, and perspectives on, media of these kinds from 1900 on around the planet, browse my *Encyclopedia of Social Movement Media* (2011). For a review of social and cultural theories which make some sense of these media, take a look at the first section of my *Radical Media* (2001, 2nd edition).

References

Atton, C. (2001) *Alternative Media*. London: Sage.

Bastien, F. and Neveu, E. (eds.) (1999) *Espaces Publics Mosaïques: Acteurs, arènes et rhétoriques, des débats publics contemporains*. Rennes: Presses Universitaires de Rennes.

Bauman, Z. (2000) *Liquid Modernity*. Cambridge: Polity.

Bey, H. (1991) "The temporary autonomous zone." In *T.A.Z.: The Temporary Autonomous Zone, Ontological Anarchy, Poetic Terrorism*. New York: Autonomedia (pp. 95–141).

Brecht, B. (1983[1932]) "Der Rundfunk als Kommunikationsapparat." *Blätter des Hessischen Landestheaters Darmstadt* 16, July 1932. "Radio as a means of communication." In A. Mattelart and S. Siegelaub (eds), *Communication and Class Struggle 2: Liberation, Socialism*. Bagnolet, France: International Mass Media Research Center (pp. 169–71).

Castells, M. (2000) *The Rise of the Network Society* (2nd edn). Malden, MA: Blackwell Publishing (pp. 407–59).

——(2012) *Networks of Outrage and Hope: Social Movements in the Internet Age*. Cambridge: Polity.

Collin, C. (1982) *Ondes de Choc: De l'usage de la radio en temps de lutte*. Paris: Éditions l'Harmattan.

Coser, L. (1964) *The Functions of Social Conflict*. Glencoe, IL: Free Press.

Cunningham, S. and Sinclair, J. (eds.) (2000) *Floating Lives: The Media and Asian Diasporas*. Lanham, MD: Rowman & Littlefield.

Downing, J. D. H. (1980) *The Media Machine*. London: Pluto Press.

——(with others) (2001) *Radical Media: Rebellious Communication and Social Movements*. 2nd rev. ed. Thousand Oaks, CA: Sage Publications.

——(ed.) (2011) *Encyclopedia of Social Movement Media*. Thousand Oaks, CA: Sage Publications.

——(2014) "Social movement media in the process of constructive social change." In K. Wilkins, T. Tufte and R. Obregón (eds), *Handbook of Development Communication and Social Change*. Boston, MA: Wiley-Blackwell (pp. 331–50).

Gerbaudo, P. (2012) *Tweets from the Streets*. London: Pluto Press.

Gitlin, T. (1998) "Public sphere or public sphericules." In T. Liebes and J. Curran (eds), *Media, Ritual and Identity*. London: Routledge (pp. 168–74).

Gumucio Dagron, A. (2001) *Making Waves*. New York: Communication for Social Change Consortium, Rockefeller Foundation.

Hill, C. (1975) *The World Turned Upside Down*. Harmondsworth: Penguin.

Homsy, G. M., Aref, H., Breuer, K. S. and Hochgreb, S. (2004) *Multimedia Fluid Dynamics* CD-ROM. New York: Cambridge University Press.

Kenix, L.-J. (2011) *Alternative and Mainstream Media: The Converging Spectrum*. London: Bloomsbury Academic Press.

Khalil, J. F. (2011) "Youth-generated media." In J. D. H. Downing (ed.), *Encyclopedia of Social Movement Media*. Thousand Oaks, CA: Sage Publications (pp. 559–62).

Lefebvre, H. (1991) *The Production of Space*. Malden, MA: Blackwell.

Lovink, G. L. (2002) *Dark Fiber: Tracking Critical Internet Culture*. Cambridge, MA: MIT Press.

McDonald, K. (2002) "From solidarity to fluidarity: Social movements beyond 'collective identity' – the case of globalization conflicts." *Social Movement Studies*, 1(2), 109–20.

Raley, R. (2009) *Tactical Media*. Minneapolis: University of Minnesota Press.

Rennie, E. (2011) "Youth media." In J. D. H. Downing (ed.), *Encyclopedia of Social Movement Media*. Thousand Oaks, CA: Sage Publications (pp. 552–55).

Smith, J. (2008) *Social Movements for Global Democracy*. Baltimore, MD: Johns Hopkins University Press.

South West Washington Coastal Erosion Survey (2012) "Glossary of coastal terminology: S–T." Retrieved from http://www.ecy.wa.gov/programs/sea/swces/products/publications/glossary/words/S_T.htm (accessed 15 January 2015).

Thörn, H. (2006) *Anti-Apartheid and the Emergence of a Global Civil Society*. London: Palgrave Macmillan.

Tufekci, Z. and Wilson, C. (2012) "Social media and the decision to participate in political protest: Observations from Tahrir Square." *Journal of Communication*, 62, 363–79.

Williams, R. (1977) *Marxism and Literature*. Oxford: Oxford University Press

Zayani, M. (2015) *Networked Publics and Digital Contention: The Politics of Everyday Life in Tunisia*. New York: Oxford University Press.

Part II
CULTURE AND SOCIETY

9

CHANGING CITIZENSHIP, PRACTISING (ALTERNATIVE) POLITICS

Mojca Pajnik

Introduction

There are various understandings of citizenship stemming from different historical and political contexts and ideologies. With the depoliticisation of society (Habermas, 1972), citizenship has become increasingly apolitical and technicist, with some speaking of the "marketization of citizenship" (Somers, 2008). In the media and web spheres, marketisation and commercialisation have resulted in a gap between the digital citizen, including the young, the educated, the political and the economic elite who have acquired social and cultural "digital capital" on the one hand, and large populations of the excluded "non-digitals" on the other.

While in the past two decades research into citizenship has soared, the popularisation of citizenship theories has been growing since the 1950s and the publication of Marshall's *Citizenship and Social Class* (1992[1950]). Marshall's triad of rights comprises civic, political and social rights. The first refers to personal liberty, freedom of speech and property rights; the second to decision-making rights, such as the right to vote and to be elected; and the third to notions of the welfare state, such as social rights, education and employment rights. Since Marshall's model, of particular relevance to my arguments in this chapter is the more ambivalent notion of cultural citizenship (Miller, 2006). On the one hand, cultural citizenship was a response to the civic movements from the 1960s, and it focused attention on the inequalities that are reproduced at the intersection of gender, sexuality, ethnicity, nationality and class. Addressing inequalities, cultural citizenship claimed the importance of minority rights. On the other hand, cultural citizenship can be used to celebrate the consumerist orientation of citizenship. From the perspective of more established ideals of political citizenship that refer to the participation of citizens in public debate (Habermas, 1972, 1989[1968]), the notion of "citizen-consumer" (frequently seen in media and cultural studies) is perhaps a contradiction in terms. The very notion of citizenship presupposes political activity, and the attempts to "widen" it to the extent of including the mere acts of consumption leads to a deflation of the concept.

In its "mutated" form, the notion of citizen-consumer risks over-celebrating consumerism at the expense of sharpening meanings of citizenship originally related to democracy and citizen participation.

Therefore, theorising citizenship in the context of alternative media should be careful to capture distinctions and contradictions in terms, and also analyse concepts with historic sensitivity. For instance, the crude libertarian argument that the web is simply democratic in its expansion of free choice should be carefully considered against the views of the web as a "political web" (Dahlgren, 2013), one that is judged against the norms of democracy. Arguing that all citizenship today is more or less consumerist, or that citizenship practices are actually everyday consumerist choices, is an administrative claim that serves the financial interests that dominate the media and the web. Such approaches contribute little to our understanding of citizenship as citizens' activity. Literature from the field of alternative and radical media provides examples to counteract such narratives.

Many authors have claimed that the time has come to change the meaning of citizenship, arguing that the "old" models don't work anymore (Isin, 2009; Deuze, 2008). Proposing an alternative analysis of citizenship is a useful attempt to capture the multiplicity of "emerging citizenships". What I propose here is, however, different – rather than inventing a new vocabulary, my approach is to think about citizenship through the antagonisms that exist within apparently stable conceptualisations.

An example of this approach is provided by Bennett, Wells, and Freelon (2011) in their analysis of the youth web sphere, where they contrast "dutiful citizenship" and "actualizing citizenship". While the civic style of the dutiful citizenship is orientated around citizens' input to government or formal institutions and is channelled through membership, actualising citizenship is open to civic input, ranging from government to global activism, and is channelled through personal interests and networks. If dutiful citizenship adopts an orientation towards consumption in its communication logic and treats citizens as target audiences, actualising citizenship engages citizens in the production processes, and includes looser engagement of individuals and peer networks (ibid.: 840). The study shows that websites that target youth predominantly tend to address their audience by pursuing the ideals of dutiful citizenship. Employing the "contrasting approach", the study thus shows (ibid.: 851) that website producers in their communication of citizenship to young people embrace narrow citizenship ideals and neglect a range of expressing opportunities for civic engagement that young people more or less routinely encounter in other online environments (such as Facebook).

Research such as this points to gaps between the narrow citizenship ideals and the broader range of civic engagement that can and does occur. In this chapter, I explore citizenship in its relation to the media and the web by analysing differences in how we might understand media-related citizenship. I explore the notion of mediatised citizenship, and contrast political and consumerist models of citizenship. By analysing antagonisms in the concepts of citizenship, I will also explore controversies between the notions of alternative or radical media and the mass media. My aim is to contribute to a "realist" (Zolo, 1992) conceptualisation of citizenship that is open to various citizens' social and political activities, by focusing on those that emerge in alternative media projects.

Mediatisation of citizenship against media/cultural citizenship

The meanings of citizenship have been various in the past decades. The 1950 model of citizenship that expressed the need of citizens to inform themselves about the political establishment so that they could then vote based on informed decisions, as argued by Schudson (1999), embraced the notion of being informed, resulting in a dependency on sources that one could not question or interact with. The notion of the "informed citizen" (ibid.), therefore, expresses an individualised, private and rational citizenship that is informed by the "objective" press. The construction of citizenship was largely the domain of experts and professionals whose roles were to deliver "objective" information, leaving citizens detached from deliberation. The first rupture in the informed citizen paradigm emerged with the various civil rights revolutions from the 1960s to the 1980s when rights were claimed by individuals and groups in the context of identity. The "informed citizen" model was, second, affected by the rise of consumerist culture in this same period, while the development of internet and other ICTs had the effect of integrating media strongly into everyday lives of citizens, blurring the public-private and the offline-online divides. Today, citizens develop a "monitorial" (Schudson, 1999; Deuze, 2008) or "browsing" (Deuze, 2008: 852) attitude to information, integrating professionalism with their own competence and interest. Citizens scan all sorts of media sources, engage in online and offline social networks, tailor these to their own needs, and by so doing seem to act simultaneously as citizens and consumers (ibid.).

Hartley (2012) and Miller (2006) present these changes as a form of "media citizenship" and deploy the term "active audiences" to refer to practices that use "leisure entertainment to inform themselves and to connect with co-subjects" (Hartley, 2012: 143). While we can acknowledge that notions of cultural and media citizenship can enable participation by excluded groups – research into migrant media (Madianou and Miller, 2012) provides a good example – cultural and media citizenship should not be viewed simply as liberating for its capacity for self-organisation, participation and tolerance. Other processes should also be considered, such as those captured by the term "mediatized citizenship" (Blumler and Gurevitch, 1995; Dahlgren, 2000; Pajnik, 2005), where there is an emphasis on the less desirable processes of unequal power relations, exclusion, distorted representation and financial manipulation. To consider "mediatised citizenship" is to raise serious doubts over the possibility of citizens to truly express their concerns and be heard in decisions that concern public life. Mediatised politics, permeation of politics with the media and the media with the politics, reduces the view of reality, produces more and more groups of excluded citizens, which results in increased distance of politics from citizens and in decreased trust of citizens in politics (Blumler, 2014).

The notion of DIY/DIWO citizenship (do it yourself/do it with others) with which Hartley (2012) supplements Marshall's model captures contemporary social and media changes that result in more privatised, both individuated and collective media use. This notion of citizenship may be applied to alternative media projects. Such "contributory citizenship" (ibid.: 144) should, however, not only be described for its potential to engage citizens and communities in "new" ways. For example, the use of media in the Arab Spring has shown that the web can offer much political and participatory potential, but it is far from clear that its use fosters democracy. On the contrary, it might be used for anti-democratic projects and result in a continuation of totalitarian regimes. This, of course, does not counter the analysis of the democratic potential of the web. As I shall show in the second half of this chapter, research into alternative and radical media provides one route to analysing the politically meaningful practices of citizens.

In conceptualising alternative, digital or DIY/DIWO citizenship, we should be aware of the "digital libertarian discourses" (Dahlberg, 2007) that deploy a narrow understanding of citizenship and that picture the digital citizen as a self-actualising individual who creatively and freely chooses his or her likes. Dahlberg warns that libertarian discourse has gained currency in the literature of media and cultural studies that centralises around the ideology of free choice and risks the collapse of citizenship into consumerism or into prosumerism, where citizens become producers and consumers acting in corporate-owned web platforms. Such warnings are, of course, not new: Habermas himself warned against the collapse of public speech and action into the consumer culture of mass media. With media and ICT developments, such a critique remains relevant (if not more relevant), despite some recent dismissals (see Lovink's otherwise challenging book, 2011).

Citizens: Devalued as political actors, praised as consumers

As Habermas (1989[1968]) argued, reasoning and public debate is giving way to consumption and consumer-driven exchange of opinions and experiences. Political activity on the web, if compared to the commercial, is still negligible; commercial websites are dominating and keep representing the fastest-growing domain category. For example, in the year 2000, 25 million.com sites dominated, as compared to 6 million.edu sites (Sunstein, 2001: 117, 118). We not only observe how the web is used for commercial and marketing purposes, but the web is largely used for economic transactions for multinational companies such as Amazon, Google, Apple, etc., to earn huge profits and avoid taxes that are then paid by growingly impoverished citizens. Free from control policy that governs the web has shown some negative consequences for citizens, such as oligopoly of big owners, increased control of online navigation by companies, risks of misuse of personal information for commercial and other non-intended purposes, spread of online hate, etc. The web that was initiated as a public sphere facilitating citizens' interaction was analysed with lots of hope for its democratic potential, and the debates around e-democracy reflect the optimist atmosphere of the 1980s–1990s. Recently, several critics, especially from the field of political economy of communication, have pointed to more contested achievements of the web. In the past few decades, we've been witnessing the rise of media conglomerates – Google, Microsoft, Yahoo, Facebook, News Corporations, Time Warner – which are, according to the IDATE reports, among some at the top who have nearly doubled in size between 1998 and 2010. Largest portions of revenue don't come from political or educational activity but from advertising and entertainment, stimulating the rise of global infotainment (Thussu, 2007). The big companies have been critically analysed for accumulating capital at the expense of unpaid labour online, where for example bloggers and Google and Facebook users create content that is then used to increase the profit of companies (Scholz, 2013). Moreover, the disempowerment of citizens is believed to take place with the rise of cloud computing and big data that are strongly marketed around the globe while raising privacy, security and surveillance concerns (Mosco, 2014).

A narrative has emerged in the past two decades that problematises the retreat of citizens into individual mediated spaces. It has been argued that political engagement appears as a minor activity online, one that is giving way to citizens' consumerist involvement in the industries of entertainment, gaming, shopping, chat rooms and so on (Murdock, 1992; Sunstein, 2001; Mosco, 2004). Furthermore, it has been argued that mediatised citizenship has produced an incomprehensible jumble of voices that cannot come to the aid of the citizen. The result of continuous individualisation, isolation and self-expression in private communication spaces cannot produce more than "enclave deliberation" (Sunstein, 2001: 75) that results in a cacophony of voices impeding any meaningful discussion (Hardt, 2008). "Hyperindividual personal information spaces" (Deuze, 2008: 850) that dominate the web have been shown to narrow citizens' interests and concerns. Such circumstances are ideal for the rise of consumers' culture that devalues political citizenship.

Alternative media and movements: Hope for citizenship?

Research from the field of radical and alternative media and social movement studies has documented that what we might term the "political web" is used by movements, NGOs, groups of citizens and journalists at the global level as a space for exercising citizenship, for articulating positions that would otherwise be invisible, silenced or suppressed in predominant political debate.

The value of alternative media for citizenship theory is in bringing the individual, the personal and the particular into public debates, as a counterpart to historical developments when certain (minority) discourses were banned from public appearances. Valuing public communication only by granting validity to universal claims has always emerged at the expense of suppressing the particular, and has accelerated the alienation of citizens from themselves and from politics (Pajnik, 2005). This is not to say that a proliferation of voices does not create more problems; it certainly complicates any analysis of communication and citizenship. But it also points to important shifts in contemporary democracy and the media sphere, where a need has emerged to move from a representational model of citizenship to models that incorporate more actual citizens' practices and the concerns they articulate.

Alternative media and alternative journalism (Atton, 2002; Atton and Hamilton, 2008; Pajnik and Downing, 2008) offer challenging responses to the notion of "changing citizenship" and speak to a democratic deficit in the mass media, in their attempts to readdress the divide between the professional journalist and the amateur audience reporter. By challenging the interpellation of audiences as passive consumers, alternative media and their journalisms engage citizens in media-making. By so doing, alternative media projects aspire to be more responsive to communities and to encourage 'ordinary people' to actively engage in public life through taking on roles as journalists (Rodríguez, 2001).

Alternative journalism can be exemplified by the journalism of the Independent Media Centers or "Indymedia journalism" (Platon and Deuze, 2003), which functions to give space to activists to express their views and debate issues of political value, locally and globally. Indymedia journalism is defined in contrast to mainstream practices that are subjected to corporate and commercial interests; encouraging citizens to "become the media" "allows for experiments with the concept of 'news' in an international non-profit networked setting, with its roots in volunteer and non-profit work" (ibid.: 339). In other words, the journalism of Indymedia embodies the need for a "close and non-hierarchical relationship between reader and writer" (Platon and Deuze, 2003).

Roles in alternative journalism are not fixed; distinctions between producers and receivers are blurred, as they are all responsible to the community. The roles are not predetermined as in traditional journalism, where clear hierarchies exist between media executives, editors, journalists and audiences. Alternative journalism not only enables the practising of reasoning by citizens, but it can also function to empower citizens and local public spheres where they live and engage (corresponding well with the idea of political citizenship). This is not to say that the practice of alternative journalism need be entirely separate from that of more traditional, hierarchical media. In their social demographic survey of alternative journalists, Atton and Hamilton (2008: 42–59) present alternative journalism as a mixed economy, as a hybrid mode of practising journalism where professionals and amateurs might work together (as in their the example of the Korean website *OhmyNews*, which engages media professionals alongside with intellectuals and citizen reporters).

Historical analyses offer examples that reveal the ethics of alternative journalism. Eastern European *samizdat* in 1970s were often based on workers as correspondents. Refusing the professionalism of traditional journalism, *samizdat* favoured personal accounts in various forms such as philosophical essays, short stories, literary criticism, conversations among friends and other forms of informal and imaginative acts of protest – key to this method was the individual's self-expression as a way of doing journalism (Downing, 1984). Atton and Hamilton (2008: 30) point to other examples, such as *Ordine Nuovo* (1919–1925, edited by Antonio Gramsci), which aimed at overcoming the distance between communist readers and writers by exchanging their roles. Rather than simply negate traditional media, alternative journalism moves beyond professionalised models towards new forms of engagement that seek to include citizens in their creation.

Alternative sourcing and self-organisation

It is a distinct characteristic of alternative journalism that it tends to avoid validating its reports by consulting powerful sources within political and economic elites. By contrast, alternative journalism produces its news "from below" using voices of activists, members of minorities or local residents – news sources that are typically placed at the bottom of the news hierarchy of mass media, where elite groups are the usual spokespersons (Atton and Hamilton, 2008: 86).

In his study of *Leeds Other Paper*, Harcup (2003) analyses the approach of this British alternative newspaper in contrast to the mainstream *Yorkshire Evening Post* by examining their coverage of the Chapeltown riots in 1981. Whereas the latter reported the riots as a law-and-order story and gave priority to elite sources, *Leeds Other Paper* contextualised the events within a frame of poverty and unemployment, foregrounding the first-person accounts. We find similar approaches in other alternative journalism. In Ljubljana, the street paper *Kralji Ulice* (*Kings of the Street*) points to a very different representation of the homeless from that found in the country's mainstream newspapers. Another example from Slovenia would be the LGBT paper *Narobe* (*Wrong*), which engages with citizens by disrupting mainstream representations of gender and nation, and by critically addressing heteronormativity and homophobia.

If alternative journalism is alternative in that it priorities "ordinary people" to elites as news sources, this definition should not lead us to idealise alternative journalism as detached from social relations characterised by hierarchy and imbalanced power relations. In their analysis of sourcing practices at *SchNEWS* (a weekly activist newspaper from Brighton, UK) Atton and Wickenden (2005: 353–4) note that "native reporters" strongly identify with the individuals and groups they choose as sources. *SchNEWS* constructs its own hierarchy of sources that seems to operate similarly to sourcing strategies of mainstream media. If mainstream journalism prioritises elite sources, alternative journalism might well privilege remarkable individuals, activist groups and organisations that share a specific ideology with the journalists.

Contrary to the hierarchical organisation of mass media, alternative media seek more egalitarian ways of organising. They are, of course, not immune to the political and economic constellations of society, even though their placement is usually that of "the edge" or "beyond" the dictates of contemporary capitalism. While it appears that a general suspicion towards capitalism or neoliberalism prevails in alternative media, they do vary in the ways in which they oppose capitalism. In principle, it is part of the ethics of alternative media, or even the basis of its foundation, not to allow the elite instrumentalisation of media. In opposing elite influence, alternative media is surely more radical if compared to the mass media and their modest and understated claims for autonomy. However, there are examples of alternative media that are financed by the help of advertising. But a closer look reveals that, often in contrast to mainstream media, alternative journalism tend not to change their agenda to fit the advertisers' goals. The presupposition of alternative media is that they do not accept just any advertising; they are more attentive and aware of its influence and so more radical in dealing with its pressure. For example, in order to preserve its autonomy, Catalonian citizens' television adopted a policy where advertising must be reserved only for local business and cannot exceed five percent of the total broadcasting time (Rodríguez, 2001: 102).

A notable historical example where an alternative publication was substantially financed by advertisers is the political periodical that emerged from the suffrage movement in Britain. In the early 1900s, *Votes for Women* was still able to promote votes for women and an early form of feminism, despite running advertisements that promoted women's fashion (Atton and Hamilton, 2008: 31, 40). More recently, *OhmyNews* attracts advertising but at the same time publishes citizens' news that are independent of advertising and its pressures (Kim and Hamilton, 2006). Though not financed by advertising, *Tribuna* in Slovenia relies on funding from a student organisation that has been criticised publicly by several intellectuals, students and activists for being profitable, depoliticised and ignorant to alternative media. To date, though, it seems that *Tribuna* has retained its autonomy and critical edge, while it faces uncertainty in funding. Similar is the position of Radio Student, one of Europe's oldest non-commercial, alternative radio stations, established in 1969, that has for decades promoted independent thought, social and political critique, cultural diversity and tolerance and has recently (2013–14) seen severe cuts in funding and attempts to undermine autonomy by restructuring governing bodies.

That alternative media are often based on self-organisational practices of certain groups of citizens is at the heart of engaged and community-sensitive journalism. But this approach is not without problems. There are "problems of voluntarism" in alternative media (Atton and Hamilton, 2008: 52) that often engage young activists, while the pressures of earning a living and family life significantly affect the ability or willingness of activists in their thirties and into middle age to engage in such projects. One of the founders of *Avtonomija* (*Autonomy*), launched in 2009 in Ljubljana as a newspaper of the Federation of Anarchist Organizing, notes that the federation mostly engages the young while older generations are in a minority. Voluntarism is frequently a reason for the short duration of many alternative media projects, though this should not prevent us from considering these projects as contributing to a form of engagement that struggles against the notion of mediatised citizenship.

Conclusion

In this chapter, I have explored citizenship by contrasting the conceptualisations of media and mediatised citizenship and by examining the devaluation of political citizenship and the praising of the "consumer citizen". I have discussed alternative media as examples of the advancement of citizenship and of the embracing of citizens' engagement with the world. Alternative media are presented here as a hope that points to possibilities for the future of citizenship, where mutual learning between the elites and the citizens, the professionals and the public might be advanced.

The question of political participation, especially by young people, prompts contradictions in contemporary society. Although young people's participation in the period of transnationalisation of politics might have increased, political agency is still narrowly defined as a subject of institutional politics only. Citizens use alternative media to establish alternative political communities, and a "new politics" emerges in non-institutional frameworks in the context of horizontal communication. The impact of alternative media projects on democratic processes might well be underestimated in research, and consequently dismissed or ignored by a political elite that seems preoccupied with other concerns.

The prospects of citizenship for the present and the future require a greater understanding of political action (Pajnik, 2014), of a kind of political engagement that softens the dichotomised position between citizens and elites, between professionals and audiences. The failure to address active citizenship in relation to mass media is reproduced on the web. What, we might ask, is new about new media, if we leave aside technological advancement, and the celebration of consumers and e-voters? To discuss citizenship and media today requires us to move beyond the liberal ideals of representation, both in perceiving as well as in analysing political action. We need to focus urgently on citizens' actions rather than on their reactions, on a civic and political life beyond consumerism and elections.

Further reading

Isin and Nielsen in *Acts of Citizenship* (London: Zed Books, 2008) provide an interesting analysis of citizenship as a political and participatory concept. Readers interested in citizenship and participatory democracy would also enjoy Dahlgren's book *The Political Web: Media, Participation and Alternative Democracy* (Basingstoke: Palgrave, 2013). A challenging critique of mediatisation and the analysis of its undermining effects on democracy is Mazzoleni and Schulz's 1999 analysis "Mediatization" of politics: A challenge for democracy? (*Political Communication*, 16(3), 247–62). I've also written about this in 2005, in "Citizenship and mediated society" (*Citizenship Studies*, 9(4), 349–67) and have addressed larger problems of depoliticisation of citizenship in "Reconstructing citizenship for the future of polity", in F. Anthias and M. Pajnik (eds), *Contesting Integration, Engendering Migration: Theory and Practice* (Basingstoke: Palgrave, 2014).

References

Atton, C. (2002) *Alternative Media*. London: Sage.

Atton, C., and Hamilton, J. F. (2008) *Alternative Journalism*. London: Sage.

Atton, C. and Wickenden, E. (2005) "Sourcing routines and representation in alternative journalism: A case study approach." *Journalism Studies*, 6(3), 347–59.

Bennett, W. L., Wells, C. and Freelon, D. (2011) "Communicating civic engagement: Contrasting models of citizenship in the youth web sphere." *Journal of Communication*, 61, 835–56.

Blumler, J. G. (2014) "Mediatization and democracy." In F. Esser and J. Strömbäck (eds), *Mediatization of Politics: Understanding the Transformations of Western Democracies*. New York: Palgrave.

Blumler, J. G. and Gurevitch, M. (1995) *The Crisis of Public Communication*. London: Routledge.

Dahlberg, L. (2007) "'Do it yourself' digital citizenship: A preliminary interrogation." *New Zealand Sociology*, 22(1), 104–11.

Dahlgren, P. (2000) *Television and the Public Sphere*. London: Sage.

——(2013) *The Political Web: Media, Participation and Alternative Democracy*. Basingstoke: Palgrave.

Deuze, M. (2008) "The changing context of news work: Liquid journalism and monitorial citizenship." *International Journal of Communication*, 2, 848–65.

Downing, J. (1984) *Radical Media: The Political Experience of Alternative Communication*. Boston, MA: South End Press.

Habermas, J. (1972) *Theorie und Praxis: Sozialphilosophische Studien*. Frankfurt am Main: Suhrkamp Verlag.

——(1989[1968]) *The Structural Transformation of the Public Sphere*. Cambridge, MA: MIT Press.

Harcup, T. (2003) "'The unspoken – said': The journalism of alternative media." *Journalism*, 4(3), 356–76.

Hardt, H. (2008) "Talk, or the decline of conversation in the age of mass communication." In M. Pajnik and J. Downing (eds), *Alternative Media and the Politics of Resistance: Perspectives and Challenges*. Ljubljana: Peace Institute.

Hartley, J. (2012) *Digital Futures for Cultural and Media Studies*. Malden, MA: Wiley-Blackwell.

Isin, E. F. (2009) "Citizenship in flux: The figure of the activist citizen." *Subjectivity*, 29, 367–88.

Kim, E. G. and Hamilton, J. W. (2006) "Capitulation to capital? *OhmyNews* as alternative media." *Media, Culture & Society*, 28(4), 541–60.

Lovink, G. (2011) *Networks Without a Cause: A Critique of Social Media*. Cambridge: Polity.

Madianou, M. and Miller, D. (2012) *Migration and New Media: Transnational Families and Polymedia*. New York: Routledge.

Marshall, T. H. (1992[1950]) *Citizenship and Social Class*. London: Pluto Press.

Miller, T. (2006) *Cultural Citizenship*. Philadelphia: Temple University Press.

Mosco, V. (2004) *The Digital Sublime: Myth, Power, and Cyberspace*. Cambridge, MA: MIT Press.

——(2014) *To the Cloud: Big Data in a Turbulent World*. Boulder, CO: Paradigm Publishers.

Murdock, G. (1992) "Citizens, consumers, and public culture." In M. Skovmand and K. C. Schroder (eds), *Media Cultures: Reappraising Transnational Media*. London: Routledge.

Pajnik, M. (2005) "Citizenship and mediated society." *Citizenship Studies*, 9(4), 349–67.

——(2014) "Reconstructing citizenship for the future of polity." In F. Anthias and M. Pajnik (eds), *Contesting Integration, Engendering Migration: Theory and Practice*. Basingstoke: Palgrave.

Pajnik, M. and Downing, J. D. H. (eds.) (2008) *Alternative Media and the Politics of Resistance: Perspective and Challenges*. Ljubljana: Peace Institute.

Platon, S. and Deuze, M. (2003) "Indymedia journalism: A radical way of making, selecting, and sharing news?" *Journalism*, 4(3), 336–55.

Rodríguez, C. (2001) *Fissures in the Mediascape: An International Study of Citizens' Media*. Cresskill, NJ: Hampton Press.

Scholz, T. (ed.) (2013) *Digital Labour: The Internet as Playground and Factory*. New York: Routledge.

Schudson, M. (1999) *The Good Citizen: A History of American Civic Life*. Cambridge, MA: Harvard University Press.

Somers, M. R. (2008) *Genealogies of Citizenship: Markets, Statelesness, and the Right to Have Rights*. Cambridge: Cambridge University Press.

Sunstein, C. (2001) *Republic.Com*. Princeton, NJ: Princeton University Press.

Thussu, D. (2007) *News as Entertainment: The Rise of Global Infotainment*. London: Sage.

Zolo, D. (1992) *Democracy and Complexity: A Realist Approach*. University Park: Pennsylvania State University Press.

10
CAMERAS AND STORIES TO DISARM WARS
Performative communication in alternative media

Camilo Pérez Quintero, Christian E. Ramírez Hincapié and Clemencia Rodríguez

Since the 1950s, Colombia has lived in a semi-permanent state of war. Between 1958 and 2012, the lives of 220,000 Colombians were lost to armed conflict (Grupo de Memoria Histórica, 2013: 31). The Colombian war has its own idiosyncrasies: war is waged where people live; antagonist armed groups invade neighbourhoods, towns, farms, and streets. Leftist guerrillas, right-wing paramilitaries, the Colombian armed forces, drug traffickers and criminal gangs compete for control of people and territory. While legal and illegal armed groups wage war, civilians are caught in the crossfire; as a result, 81.5 per cent of all casualties since 1958 have been civilians (ibid.: 32).

When civilian communities have to co-exist with armed groups, the negative impact on civilian life goes far beyond the visible markings of war, such as the destruction of lives and infrastructure. The presence of armed groups gradually erodes the social, democratic and cultural fabric of communities. The groups recruit children and inject massive doses of mistrust, individualism, fear and uncertainty into the lives of regular citizens. Traditional bonds of solidarity, togetherness and trust crumble. Aggression and the resolution of everyday conflicts with violence and force are normalised. After decades of historical research in Colombia, Daniel Pécaut observed that, against their will, Colombia's "population finds itself inscribed in the logics of war" (Pécaut, 2001: 18); it is an involuntary conscription of the daily lives of communities, in a war that is not their own.

Despite the normalisation of silence and isolation, communities are able to develop strategies of resistance. In this chapter, we explore how media technologies are being used by communities in contexts of war, as practices of resistance against isolation, notions of self and place as violent, and other cultural codes imposed by war.

Although localised in Colombia, our findings can be applied to many other communities forced to live in contexts of armed violence. In our time, wars take new and different shapes, and it is time to revise our – sometimes colonial – interpretations of wartorn places as faraway communities in the Global South. In the same way that a small town in southern Colombia or a neighbourhood in Medellín is silenced and terrorised by armed groups, Latino immigrants in Arizona and black communities in Ferguson, Missouri, are terrorised by a police force emboldened by racism and anti-immigration laws; North African immigrants in Barcelona and Sydney are persecuted, tortured and inhumanely detained by local security forces; Mexican towns and neighbourhoods are caught between corrupt security forces and drug trafficking mafias; and youth are recruited by armed gangs in Baltimore and Los Angeles.

This chapter documents two different Colombian initiatives in which media are used to buffer the negative impact of armed groups on the social fabric of local communities: Pasolini en Medellín (PeM – pasolinienmedellin.wordpress.com/about/) and the Escuela Audiovisual Infantil de Belén de los Andaquíes (EAIBA – http://escuelaaudiovisualinfantil.blogspot.com/). Although very different, these two initiatives share certain characteristics that make them exceptionally interesting in the field of alternative and community media research.

First, both of these initiatives are deeply rooted in their local communities. Founded by people *from* the community, they interact with external donors, state agencies, international organisations and NGOs, but their founders are born and raised in the communities. This explains why both projects privilege local communication needs, legitimise local languages and aesthetics, honour local rhythms and schedules and are passionate about finding beauty, poetry and value in local everyday life. Second, both PeM and EAIBA exhibit a profound commitment to collective participation and ownership. In the case of EAIBA, the land title to the school's building is held in the name of the entire community. At PeM, the boundaries of what or who the project is are always blurry. PeM is not an NGO with a clear structure; any local youth can easily become a PeM leader. Third, both PeM and EAIBA are about much more than dumping media technologies into marginalised communities. In these times of naïve excitement for C4D and social media driven by corporate interests trying to open new markets in the Global South, it is important to re-position the key question of "media for what?" In this sense, we intend to demonstrate how PeM and EAIBA have developed their own media pedagogies. Issues of voice, narrative and re-signification of the local are at the centre of these strategies. Ultimately media production is merely a pretext for addressing issues of political agency, both individual and collective.

And finally, both PeM and EAIBA disrupt narrow definitions that limit communication to persuasion, transmission of information, or empowerment. In general, the field of alternative and community media research embraces narrow understandings of communication – mostly inherited from mass communication research. This creates a context in which alternative and community media are examined as community senders that use participatory communication to either inform, persuade or empower community receivers. However, PeM and EAIBA demonstrate that, in the hands of communities, media can have many other uses. In these pages, we intend to explain the performative uses of media implemented by PeM in the neighbourhoods of Medellín and EAIBA in a small town in southern Colombia.

Pasolini en Medellín: Art and culture to disarm minds

Today, Medellín has become a model of urban planning. Several progressive mayors (i.e. Sergio Fajardo, 2004–7, and Alonso Salazar, 2008–11) shifted public policy to benefit the less wealthy neighbourhoods in the city. At the same time, since the 1980s and 1990s, Medellín's marginalised neighbourhoods have become the battleground of drug lords, paramilitary groups, leftist guerrillas, and territorial gangs (Riaño-Alcalá, 2006). The markings of war were felt by everyone in these neighbourhoods as armed groups normalised a series of war codes and practices. Young men and women were particularly targeted. Drug lords, guerrilla *comandantes* and gang leaders heavily recruited young men as combatants; young women were pushed further into the private, domestic sphere, as parents feared the gaze of armed men on their daughters' bodies. A young masculine body walking down the street became a signifier of armed violence, a threatening presence to be feared and avoided. In this context, there is a need to re-live the backup of experiences and stories inscribed in people's bodies; there is a need to reopen the possibility of naming, creating and sharing, to reopen the realm of narratives.

In 2003, Germán Arango and Camilo Pérez, two young anthropology students who grew up in the city, were inspired by the cinematic principles of Italian filmmaker Pier Paolo Pasolini and Jean Rouch's concept of "shared anthropology" to begin a project called Pasolini en Medellin (PeM). Soon, they were joined by Ana Maria Muñoz, César Tapias, Jose Leonardo Cataño, Duvan Londoño, Diego Gómez and Andrés García, other Medellín youth who shared their passion for filmmaking and their enthusiasm for ethnography. Other young activists, artists, students and professionals joined PeM (i.e. María Ochoa, current director of PeM), bringing their own talents and ideas, making PeM a dynamic and growing non-profit that transforms itself continually. Today, PeM is a non-profit organisation with hundreds of projects and videos under its belt (PeM's YouTube Channel: www.youtube.com/user/pasolinienmedellin).

The name of the organisation is derived from Pier Paolo Pasolini, an Italian writer, poet and filmmaker. The founders of PeM found inspiration in both Pasolini's literary work and his proposal for a poetic cinema, particularly his filmmaking in Roman slums. In opposition to realism, and responding to his passion for local aesthetics and narratives, Pasolini proposed a cinema engaged in finding the poetry in local realities (Pasolini, 2005; Pasolini and Rohmer, 1970). In this sense, PeM was born as an initiative created to explore local contexts through poetic lenses that open the possibility of creating one's own meanings rather than remaining locked into given chains of signification (Pasolini, 2005). PeM understands that to poetise reality is to open aesthetic spaces where people can break the veil of a reality hijacked by war, as they use media to re-frame their everyday lives and re-signify the world around them, through the poetic appropriation of their own experiences. PeM's motto derives from these ideas: "Art and Culture to Disarm Minds."

PeM's goals are twofold: first, to explore the power of storytelling as a strategy to break silences, poetising life in the midst of a complex context of armed conflict; and second, to build bridges between anthropology and communication, academic research and media practice, art and politics (Pérez Quintero, 2013). Towards these goals, PeM has developed its own media pedagogy based on a series of participatory media production workshops rooted in the following principles: experimentation, specificity, reflexivity, dialogue, knowledge sharing, collective construction and 'RE' (see below).

PeM sets in motion a series of collaborative active learning processes with youth, inciting *experimentation* and creative ways of seeing. *Specificity* means that every PeM project is context specific, deeply rooted in local situations, responding to local needs and possibilities. War impacts communities differently, thus one side of a neighbourhood may experience the presence of armed groups differently from the other side of the neighbourhood; the markings of war are local and distinct. PeM's media practices are never a recipe, nor a template. Instead, they are open works, guided by *reflexivity*, and sensitive to interaction with local conditions. *Dialogue* is the cornerstone of PeM. One of the less visible effects of the presence of armed groups in communities is the normalisation of mistrust, with the ensuing reduction of people's capacity to listen to each other. PeM counters isolation and mistrust with media production practices centred on inclusion:

> Sometimes [we end up including] even people from the community, onlookers who are watching what we do. Frequently we are surrounded by children laughing and old ladies hanging around while we are shooting a scene ... and sometimes we just want to ask for silence, or say: "just move a little behind the camera so we can shoot", but then we realize that they feel like part of the story, so we can't push them out ... we include them in the story.
>
> (Benítez, 2012)

Ana Maria Muñoz, one of PeM's founders, explains:

> In Medellín, violence has trapped us in certain mental codes, the opinions of others are always felt as competition, or as an offense. We are taught to annihilate and disappear the other, in the literal and metaphorical sense ... so, I think dialogue is key in the workshops, to generate processes where listening has a central place.
>
> (Muñoz, 2013)

Dialogue guides PeM's media pedagogy, making *knowledge sharing* crucial, as it engages participants in horizontal relationships, thus disrupting authoritarian and hierarchical interactions normalised by armed groups. Every single media production workshop convened by PeM recognises every participant as a subject with his/her own storytelling style; every participant is seen as an owner of knowledge with whom to exchange views. César Tapias, former director of PeM, says:

> Sharing experiences is at the center of PeM's proposal. We know that each participant comes with their own knowledge. It is in practice, in dialogue, where such knowledge is exchanged. We could be producing stage theatre [instead of media], or writing poems, rap lyrics, movies, whatever, but the process has validity as long as there is another subject with whom you can share or create.
>
> (Tapias, 2012)

Ideally, each participant experiences PeM's media workshops as an opportunity to re-frame their ideas of difference and shift from viewing difference as a threat to seeing it as an opportunity for *collective construction*. Even though each film produced by PeM has a director, all participants experience the production process as a collective construction:

> When I am the director of one of the videos, all the others are involved too. with the scenery, photography, or in different areas ... For example, who has a bowl we need for one of the scenes? Or, who owns a skirt for the peasant scene? Who has the chalk we need to draw on the street?
>
> (Benítez, 2012)

Ethnography and visual anthropology are brought into PeM's media pedagogy in the form of practical exercises that invite participants to observe, inscribe and describe the world around them. PeM designed a series of exercises that shift the participants' points of view, "re-positioning them in front of their own otherness" (Vega in Pérez Quintero, 2013: 66). Using field diaries, first-time participants are asked to make the familiar strange:

> Sounds of my neighborhood: Brushing, sneezing, blender, chickens, cough, phlegm, the screaming cooking pot, washing clothes, snoring, dishes, pigs, cries, bikes, the metro, urination, refrigerator, iron, sex, groans, the creek, bathing, death and its mourning, flush the toilet, football, belching, babies, weekends, yawning.
>
> (Carlos Santos's field diary, in Pérez Quintero, 2013: 69)

In a different exercise, participants bring in a family photograph and develop two narratives about the images in the photo. The first is an emotional narrative about the people in the photo. The second narrative is meant to shift the narrator's point of view to one of an ethnographer. PeM's media production workshops also include tasting, listening, viewing, feeling, mapping and walking exercises. The experience of observing the world through a cardboard frame leaves quite an impact on participating youth:

> The exercises with the cardboard frame, uff that really marked my life! We looked through the cardboard frames at our church, our block, or *la negra* [dog's name], which is also a main character in all of our stories ... and by doing so, we became sort of researchers, but also the researched, that was one of the most intense exercises I can recall.
>
> (Benítez in Pérez Quintero, 2013: 74)

All these strategies push participants to critically view their surroundings, experiences, and practices, constituting what PeM calls "to narrate in code RE". Designed around these RE strategies, PeM's media production workshops trigger sensory, aesthetic, and political processes of re-signification. PeM's RE strategies include:

- **RE-visiting** one's own life experiences;
- **RE-discovering** the stories hidden in everyday life;
- **RE-calibrating** one's senses;
- **RE-framing** one's social reality;
- **RE-cognising** one's own voice and the voices of others;
- **RE-writing** one's own stories collectively;
- **RE-signifying** one's role in the social context.

PeM is a creative lab intended to re-signify life through the poetic appropriation of reality. PeM believes that learning to poetise one's own reality is much more important than accessing media technology. From the start, PeM understood that communication extends far beyond information transmission, persuasion or even empowerment. Based on Pasolini's teachings, PeM believes that media should allow people to re-signify themselves, their own reality, and their own experience. In a context like Medellín's neighbourhoods, where war has imposed meanings, ways of understanding, and cultural codes, media are used as performative tools to *make things happen*. PeM's leaders describe themselves as vultures, "flying in the periphery of what has been said, looking for stereotypes and established signifiers as carrion" (Pérez Quintero, 2013, 58). As a case in point, PeM's media practices "digest" and transform the cultural code of young masculinity as a sign of aggression. Duvan Londoño, one of PeM's filmmakers, recalls:

> I remember seeing two kids in my neighborhood pretending they had guns. They were playing *Bazuquito* and *Lucho*, two real thugs that terrified the neighborhood during the 90s. These thugs were gang leaders of enemy militias. What struck me was that one of the kids yelled that bullets could not harm him, which is actually one of the myths that circulated in the neighborhood, that this gang leader was protected by sorcery and spells and bullets could not harm him. I realized the power these myths have over the neighborhood: when *Bazuquito* and *Lucho* controlled the neighborhood, these kids were not even born.
>
> (Londoño, 2013)

Years later, Duvan came back to his neighbourhood to shoot *Click Obtura Gallo*, a documentary about Villa Niza, the neighbourhood where he grew up. By this time, people in the neighbourhood were used to seeing PeM's youth shooting in the streets, setting up lights and arranging actors in a scene. What he finds is a testimony to PeM's performative power:

> What I saw is that, over time, my role as a filmmaker began to attract the kids' attention in the neighborhood. Seeing what we were doing had a seductive force on them. Toward the end of the shooting, I found several of these kids playing in the street. At first I thought they were setting up their usual games of guns and warriors, but I was surprised when I saw that the game was about a team making a film; it was quite a performance. When I saw that, I remembered those other kids I had seen, and I came to a little

understanding, which is that our practice is displacing the violence that unfortunately has occupied such a central place in our neighborhoods.

(Londoño, 2013)

This is what we mean here by *the performative power of media*. In this case, even before any content is produced, PeM's media practices make things happen in these communities. PeM's approach to media-making reaches far beyond the use of media to produce content that communicates; instead, PeM appropriates media technologies as opportunities for intervention, performative spaces that allow people in the community to re-frame their reality, re-write their present and future and re-cognise who they are.

Escuela Audiovisual Infantil de Belén de los Andaquíes: Without a story, there's no camera

Belén de los Andaquíes, with over twelve thousand inhabitants, is a municipality located in Caquetá, in southern Colombia, on the edge of the Andean foothills, the gateway to the Amazon. Belén is composed of a small town by the same name, surrounded by rural areas. The country's central regions (Bogotá, Antioquia) have historically stigmatised this part of southern Colombia as a war zone, a territory known only for its guerrilla fighters and illicit crops (mainly coca).

In the late 1990s and early 2000s, Belén de los Andaquíes experienced an intense period of armed violence (Ramírez Hincapié, 2013; Rodríguez, 2011). Guerrilla groups fought against paramilitary groups to gain control of the area. People living on the mountainside were regularly marked as *guerrilleros* (leftist guerrilla fighters), while people living in the valley were considered *paracos* (right-wing paramilitary). This arbitrary division cracked Belén's social fabric as it forced people to cut any social relations with family or friends living on the "opposite" side (Ramírez Hincapié, 2013). Trusting relationships suddenly turned into fear and mistrust, breaking social bonds and cutting fluid communication channels (Rodríguez, 2011).

After Colombian peace negotiations with the guerrillas failed in 2001, the Uribe administration decided to try a military strategy to solve the guerrilla problem. Thanks in part to funds from Plan Colombia (an aid package that made Colombia the recipient of the second largest amount of military aid from the United States, after Israel) the Colombian government started a process of strengthening the armed forces and increasing manpower in areas that usually had no military presence. Belén de los Andaquíes went from having one police station to having a military garrison at the town's entrance and a base perched on the mountain behind the town's center. Today, military and police personnel, all armed to the teeth, regularly pass through the town's streets and neighbourhoods. They usually move in small groups, exuberant with the sense of pride and arrogance that uniforms and weapons instil. Belén's children and youth, although too young to vividly remember the most intensely violent years around 2000, have grown up in an environment where weapons and uniforms are signs of power and respect. In a region where employment is scarce and poverty can seem inescapable, legal and illegal armed groups (i.e., armed forces, guerrillas, militias subsidised by drug lords) are tempting options for professional careers and individual identities. This is roughly the context in which Escuela Audiovisual Infantil de Belén de los Andaquíes (EAIBA), the 'Children's Audiovisual School of Belén de los Andaquíes' has developed as a successful community media project.

EAIBA was born in 2005, an offshoot of Radio Andaquí, one of the first Colombian community radio stations to receive a community broadcasting license in 1996 (see Rodríguez, 2011). In less than ten years, EAIBA has produced hundreds of videos designed, directed, acted, and animated by children and youth. In 2013, EAIBA was awarded an *India Catalina*, the Colombian equivalent of an Oscar, for its children's television series *TeleGordo*. Founded by Alirio González, a local cultural leader and public intellectual, EAIBA survives by selling audiovisual services, applying for grants and funded initiatives, and employing a variety of other creative funding tactics. Between their grants and the name they have made for themselves as a quality audiovisual producer, EAIBA has proven to be an example of sustainability. The school does not depend directly on any public, private, or international donor. Like PeM, EAIBA has developed its own idiosyncratic media pedagogy based on a series of principles tailored to local conditions and responding to local communication needs:

> EAIBA does not work like a regular school. At EAIBA, there are no teachers, classrooms, assignments, calendars or schedules, grades, graduation or tuition fees. Children cannot be enrolled by their parents. Rather, they must become members by their own means and out of their own interest, which is both a simple and difficult task. Simple because the only requirement for EAIBA membership is the child's willingness to tell a story – any story – and, once they have a finished product, to share it with their peers, family and community.
>
> (Ramírez Hincapié, 2013)

The school's façade sports a colourful mural that changes from time to time, but the school's motto always appears at the center: 'Without a Story, There's No Camera'. Telling a story, committing to it, and being able to transform it into an audiovisual product for sharing is a difficult task; and yet, the school believes that each child, by means of his or her own motivation, can become a storyteller. Once a child enters the school with a story in hand, they are pushed through the creative process of thinking, drawing, sketching, photographing, shooting video, animating and editing. EAIBA's media pedagogy is designed from beginning to end to push children to explore and express the world around them as they understand it. In this pedagogical strategy, the process of exploration will enable children and youth to re-frame the place where they live.

EAIBA is not meant to be a place for children to spend their free time. Instead, it is meant for children to use media technologies and cameras and microphones to explore their surroundings, cherish their own local languages and aesthetics and, most importantly, create life projects other than those usually available in Colombia's armed conflict regions (i.e., joining one of the armed groups, succumbing to growing illicit crops or resigning themselves to the poverty of subsistence agriculture). In their videos, children acknowledge the presence of war, but they invariably re-frame its centrality: war is present, but it does not exhaust their lives or who they are. In one of EAIBA's videos, titled *Click*, over images of the children swimming in the river, hanging out and riding bikes, children rap: "we are neighbors of the forest, we are neighbors of the war". Repeatedly clicking the shutter of a camera, a boy states: "running from fear I began to shoot [images]. War chases me, I keep shooting. I seek stories to chase fear away" (all videos can be seen on EAIBA's YouTube channel, www.youtube.com/channel/UCer3UXTAJgmOp5D-5Cj4CWA).

For EAIBA to meet its goals in a difficult context of war like Caquetá, it has to offer children and youth a real cultural alternative. Thus, EAIBA operates under a broadened understanding of media practice that includes complex performative functions that extend far beyond producing media content. EAIBA teaches children how to operate cameras, microphones and computers, but more importantly, the school uses media production practice to trigger new ways of looking and understanding. For example, a Sunday afternoon trip to the nearby river becomes a journey of re-examining and re-signifying local contexts, as children point cameras and microphones to capture the songs of local birds, the fluid shapes of water over boulders or their own images as savvy underwater swimmers. EAIBA affirms the validity and value of children's narratives. This has been achieved by adapting technologies to children's narratives and not the other way around, and by allowing children to be children, giving them the freedom to re-signify everything, never forcing them to express an adult's perspective as their own.

EAIBA uses media production to build emotional and cultural bonds between the child and his/her surrounding world, elicit new understandings, and invite children to disrupt normalised conceptions of their region as a wartorn area where the taken-for-granted assumption is that everyone is a *guerrillero* or a *paraco*. At EAIBA, stories are the goal and technologies are the means. Stories recount the complexity of the region, how war has left its mark but never entirely colonised all identities and interactions. Stories tell what is important to people, how they remember their lived experiences and how they want to recount those experiences. EAIBA seems to share García Márquez's (2004, epigraph) notion of storytelling: "Life is not what one lived, but what one remembers, and how one remembers it in order to tell the tale." EAIBA assumes that in telling a story, bonds are created and communities are built. In contrast with more traditional participatory media initiatives that first teach children how to use media technologies and leave the 'technology for what' question for the end, EAIBA privileges the process of storytelling, or creating representations of how children relate to their communities. Access and connectivity are secondary.

In their stories, children explore how they perceive their town, and how they want to see it. In *La Vida en la Pesca*, EAIBA's children show what it is to be a local fisherman; *Lleva en el Río* recounts their favourite pastime, playing in the river; in *La Película del Lunes*, a girl narrates how her friends laughed at her and made her cry; in *Papá es una Madre*, a child describes his single dad's life. In *Divertimento Andaquí*, the creators explain: "While we practice different camera movements, we discover all kinds of things about our town." One of their favourite genres is transforming *corridos* or rap – rhythms stigmatised as representing drug lords or gangs, into their own music videos, creating beautiful representations of their own aesthetic perceptions of place.

EAIBA has accomplished the goal of incorporating children's narratives into Belén's public spheres. Public presentations of the videos are organised periodically:

a large screen and projector are set up in a public space and the friends, families and teachers of the video creators are invited. EAIBA also made a deal with the local cable company, so one of the cable channels is managed by the school as a venue for presenting their productions. In EAIBA, the moment of media reception is as carefully designed as the moment of media production.

Rather than using technology to represent the world, EAIBA uses media as what Jesús Martín-Barbero (2002) explains as "*contar para contar*". According to Martín-Barbero, the power of communities to name the world on their own terms is directly linked to their power to enact political actions. In Spanish, Martín-Barbero plays with a linguistic pun around the double meaning of the terms '*contar*' (to narrate) and '*contar*' (to have a strong presence, to count) and explains that only those who can '*contar*' (narrate) will '*contar*' – only those able to name their identities and the world on their own terms will have a strong presence as political subjects. Martín-Barbero's ideas point to the need for public spaces for deliberation and encounter, where people can be heard and listen to others recounting, spaces where people can feel and experience what recounting really means as a member of a community. In other words, what it feels like to be a citizen (Rodríguez, 2011). In the act of doing, EAIBA's children have found ways to open social spaces where their voices are taken into account, enabling them to perform as recounters and to encounter recounting as a vivid experience.

Since its birth in December 2005, EAIBA has helped carve out a path for children to conceive of their futures apart from the war industry. Some of the children in the three generations that have participated in the first ten years of the school are the first in their families to finish high school (Ramírez Hincapié, 2013); others are the first generation considering higher education, while several others are already enrolled in universities. Some have made a conscious decision to step away from what their older siblings have done with their lives (i.e. getting married, having children at a very young age, joining one of the local armed groups) and have decided that they want something different for their futures. Probably the most astonishing fact, however, is that EAIBA's children and youth do not want to leave Belén; they have found that it is possible to make a living in the place they love, where they grew up, thanks to their expertise in media technologies. EAIBA has shown them that they don't have to migrate.

Conclusion

War impacts social and cultural fabrics in a multitude of ways, some of which are tangible (maimed bodies, destroyed structures) and many of which leave intangible scars. PeM and EAIBA demonstrate that, if well designed, alternative media initiatives can be used to counter the damage caused by war. We can learn to see PeM and EAIBA's creative pedagogies as strategies of resistance against silence, mistrust and crass individualism. Meanings and cultural codes normalised by years of war can be replaced by alternative meanings created by those who did not take up arms.

From PeM and EAIBA we can also learn that war does not conquer all, even in communities that may appear to be engulfed in armed conflict. Even if marginal and subtle, identities, practices and ways of interaction not permeated by the logics of war survive in every context of armed conflict. If strongly rooted in the local, community media have great potential to magnify these sites of peaceful co-existence. Weapons and armed violence wreak havoc in communities. Social bonds are broken, invisible ties that knit the social fabric disintegrate, relationships collapse. In these contexts, media can play roles that reach far beyond the production and dissemination of content. Media can take on performative functions, triggering new ways of observing and interpreting, activating alternative ways of interacting and normalising different notions of self, other, place, history and memory. PeM and EAIBA have learned to master the performative function of alternative media, making things happen in their communities.

Further reading

Chapter 1 of Rodríguez (2011) provides a detailed account of community radio – the precursor of EAIBA – in Caquetá. Chapter 5 in the same book explains the theoretical foundation behind the concept of 'performative media'. In *Cine de Poesía contra Cine de Prosa* (Editorial Anagrama, 1970), Italian filmmaker Pier Paolo Pasolini and French filmmaker Eric Rohmer propose filmmaking as a strategy to poetise reality (unfortunately, this text has not been translated into English).

References

Benítez, S. (2012) Interview with author. Medellín, Colombia. Audiorecording.

García Márquez, G. (2004) *Living to Tell the Tale*. New York: First Vintage International.

Grupo de Memoria Histórica (2013) *BastaYa! Colombia: Memorias de guerra y dignidad*. Bogotá: Centro de Memoria Histórica. Retrieved from http://www.centrodememoriahistorica.gov. co/micrositios/informeGeneral/descargas.html (accessed 11 June 2014).

Londoño, D. (2013) Interview with author. Medellín, Colombia. Audiorecording.

Martín Barbero, J. (2002) "Identities: Traditions and new communities." *Media Culture and Society*, 24(5), 621–41.

Muñoz, A. M. (2013) Interview with author. Medellín, Colombia. Audiorecording.

Pasolini, P. P. (2005) *Heretical Empiricism*. Washington, DC: New Academia Publishing.

Pasolini, P. P. and Rohmer, E. (1970) *Cine de Poesía contra Cine de Prosa*. Barcelona: Editorial Anagrama.

Pécaut, D. (2001) *Guerra Contra la Sociedad*. Bogotá: Editorial Planeta.

Pérez Quintero, C. (2013) "Images to disarm minds: An examination of the 'Pasolini in Medellín' experience in Colombia." M.A. thesis, Communication and Development, Ohio University.

Ramírez Hincapié, C. E. (2013) *Recounting Stories, Disrupting Mediascapes: The Case of Belén de los Andaquíes Children's Audiovisual School in the Mi(d)st of Colombia's Long Lasting Armed Conflict*. Master's thesis, University of Amsterdam.

Riaño-Alcalá, P. (2006) *Dwellers of Memory: Youth and Violence in Medellín, Colombia*. New Brunswick and London: Transaction Publishers.

Rodríguez, C. (2011) *Citizens' Media Against Armed Conflict: Disrupting Violence in Colombia*. Minneapolis: University of Minnesota Press.

Tapias, C. (2012) Interview with author. Medellín, Colombia. Audiorecording.

11

THEORISING VOICE IN INDIA

The *jan sunwai* and the Right to Information Movement

Pradip Ninan Thomas

What possibilities are there for Voice to become the basis for meaningful social change in India? And in what sense can Voice become the basis for a renewal of specifically Indian public spheres? What are the performative conditions that facilitate Voice making and indigenous means that are supportive of Voice in the making of local public spheres in India? These questions related to the location of Voice, its conditions of operationalisation, its means and its politics of possibility, correspond to an issue that has remained of critical importance to theorists of alternative and community media – specifically, the meaning of and conditions for empowerment. Scholars working on societal issues in India, just as scholars in other parts of the non-Western world, have had little choice but to employ theoretical and conceptual frameworks that are Western in origin. With the benefit of hindsight, it is clear that many of these frameworks have generated knowledge on Indian realities, although 'translation' has by no means been unproblematic. The inability of scholars from a Marxian persuasion to ignore caste and privilege class is just one example of the failure of theorists to adapt theories to the local and for theory itself to be informed by the local. Recent conversations, mainly in the *Economic and Political Weekly*, on the nature of 'Dalit intellection' by the Dalit scholar Gopal Guru (2013), Sarukkai (2007), Dilip Menon (2013) and others point to the limitations of theory solely informed by the project of mimesis and which discounts experience and the need for another theorising based on experience (see also Guru and Geetha, 2000; Guru, 2009; Gurukkal, 2013). 'Humiliation studies' is one attempt to generate a "new conceptual language" capable of capturing "complex dimensions of social reality" that do not fall within the purview of established social and political theorising (Guru, 2009: 19). Such interventions expose the fault-lines in the social sciences in India that are caught between the *doxa* of the academy and the perceived universality of received theory.

This chapter explores issues related to the Right to Information Movement in India, specifically in relation to the public sphere, a concept that is habitually invoked to describe spaces for deliberation and communication. However, this concept too, as much as its cognate concept 'civil society', lends itself to very contextual interpretations that are far removed from the notion of the bourgeois public sphere that is ascribed to Habermas (1991) or that of the space between the economy and the state that civil society is most often considered to inhabit. One can argue that the issue is not merely that of 'translation' – although that is an important issue – it also has to do with experience, culture, traditions, formations and ways of seeing and knowing the world. Theorising 'self-respect' is of particular significance to Dalit theorists, and there are a host of individuals and movements in India – including Ambedkar, EVR Periyar, Jyotirao Phule, Iyothee Thass, the anti-Brahmin movements in India and the Namashudra Movement in East Bengal (now Bangladesh) that have thrown light on the specificities of untouchability and the theorising of Dalit consciousness.

In other words, it can be argued that 'organic' public spheres are bound to emerge from a variety of contexts as the result of a variety of communicative and cultural shapings. Scholars from India, most notably Neera Chandhoke (2003, 2005), Susanne and Lloyd Rudolph (2003), Partha Chatterjee (1993), Sudipta Kaviraj (2011) and Amir Ali (2001), have highlighted the fraught nature of the translation of concepts such as the public sphere and civil society. Chandhoke's assessment and critique in particular raises a number of issues specifically with respect to the public sphere, regarding the limitations of genuine dialogue when a dominant language is employed by dominant interlocutors to set the terms for any given debate. Using the example of indigenous groups in India (officially known as 'tribals') in India negotiating with officialdom for compensation for traditional land that has been slated to be 'dammed', she observes that customary ownership of land outside the property regime articulated by a relatively 'weak' language is not on a level playing field given the power of the dominant discourse and language. As she observes (Chandhoke, 2005: 342), power "identifies and privileges the language that *constitutes* the public sphere of deliberation" and "power in the deliberative form has to do with *epistemic* authority inasmuch as it privileges one system of meaning over another". It is unlikely that, with the exception of the Maoris in New Zealand, whose language, culture and political economy are robust enough to compete with the dominant discourse, there are indigenous groups in a position to negotiate from a position of strength. The power of official discourse, in other words, often is dominating and dominant precisely because it is the constitutive basis of the public sphere.

While Chandhoke's critique of the structural contradictions of the Habermasian public sphere highlights the reality of exclusive public spheres in hierarchical societies, she nevertheless does not entertain the possibility of counter public spheres or the spaces and channels for deliberation, dissent and agonism that have certainly contributed to the project of social change in India. One can argue that there have been moments in India's post-Independent history that have been characterised by robust counter public spheres, as was the case with the Non-Brahmin movements in the states of Maharashtra and Tamil Nadu in the 1940s and 1950s and the Right to Information Movement that took root in the late 1990s before becoming a national movement. These movements crystallised distinct public spheres – the former around the lower castes and their cultural and economic emancipation from the dominance of Sanskritic Brahmanism, and the latter around the rural poor in India who used the power of 'Voice' to denounce corruption and announce an ethic of governance based on transparency and accountability. It is arguable that in post-Independent India, the only movement that has become truly national in scope, on par with the Independence Movement, is the Right to Information Movement. The strength of this movement can be gauged from the fact that its imprint has progressively impacted the public sector at all levels and, in some instances, led to a redefinition of citizen–state relationships of India.

The Mazdoor Kisan Shakti Sangathan (MKSS)

The Right to Information Movement began in the 1990s against the background of endemic corruption in government services and in the provisioning of entitlements. This finely calibrated system of corruption was based on different levels of graft committed by entire public sector bureaucracies in the allocation and provisioning of public services from kick-backs at a higher level to petty corruption at lower levels. Rural India, characterised by high rates of illiteracy, small farmers and a variety of land tenures overlaid by caste hierarchies, is the focus for national development projects, and it is in this context that access to information and its actioning assumes criticality for the simple reason that for many of India's rural population, survival including access to food, shelter, health and employment is closely connected to their regular access to an array of public entitlements. In addition, there was no obligation by the government to disclose information:

> in spite of India's status as the world's most populous democratic state, there was not until recently any obligation at village, district, state or national level to disclose information to the people – information was essentially protected by the colonial Secrets Act 1923, which makes the disclosure of official information by public servants an offence. The colonial legacy of secrecy, distance and mystification of the bureaucracy coupled with a long history of one party dominance proved to be a formidable challenge to transparency and effective government.
>
> (Rai, n.d.)

While there had been a number of previous initiatives in India aimed at introducing right-to-information legislation – such as the draft Right to Information (RTI) bill circulated by the Press Council of India in 1996, by the Consumer Educational Research Council (CERC), the Freedom of Information Act 2002 and *sui generis* bills passed by the Tamilnadu and Goa state governments in 1996 and 1997 – the moral force and strength of the Right to Information Act (2005) can be traced back to the struggles waged by the MKSS. The MKSS was officially formed in 1990 by activists including Aruna Roy, Nikhil Dey and Shankar Singh in Devdungri, a village in the state of Rajasthan. Initially, their advocacy focussed on struggles by landless labourers for minimum wages, land and women's rights and initiatives related to making the Public Distribution System accountable. In Aruna Roy's (2000: 22) words, "The Right to Information therefore began with the right to earn a daily wage, to live with dignity, indeed *a right to survive*" (original emphasis). Very early on in their work, they realised that the key obstacles to development at the village level were the lack of information on a variety of entitlements to rural people, in the areas of employment, rural infrastructure such as dispensaries, clinics, schools, roads, and irrigation along with information on the many government initiatives related to poverty alleviation, including access to pensions and the public distribution system.

The MKSS launched a campaign based on consultation, street-based discussions and popular theatre performances throughout the state. In 1994, and in the face of official recalcitrance and unwillingness to cooperate with people's demands, the MKSS decided to organise public hearings (*jan sunwais*), with the first hearing held in the village of Kotkirana in the Pali District. These hearings took the form of an audit of local-level development projects, especially the social audit of 'employment muster rolls' and expenses related to public works and wages paid to workers. This led to the demand for all copies of documents related to public works to be made public. However local government officials were not, in the beginning, cooperative, and launched their own counter-campaigns against the Right to Information Movement. These hearings, however, took on a life of their own. As more and people throughout the state began to hear the literally hundreds of stories of corruption, they became empowered to act on this information. In district after district, these hearings exposed the vast gaps between official expenditures on development projects and actual expenditures. These hearings unearthed evidence of widespread corruption and the systemic links between local officials and politicians who were also involved in a variety of scams. This evidence discussed at the public hearings led to non-violent civic actions, boycotts and sit-ins at government offices that were systematically used to wear down the opposition and elicit a response from the government.

In other words, here is evidence of the creation of a public sphere based on the local idiom, a local means of communicative and performative traditions that enabled a balance between speaking, listening and actioning. The priorities of the hearing were established by local people. And these *jan sunwais* arguably functioned as a medium of communication and public opinion. One of the often overlooked aspects of Habermas's theory of the public sphere is his critique of the take-over of the bourgeois public sphere by big media and the resulting creation of citizens as mere consumers of mediated information within a re-feudalised public sphere. In Habermas's words (1991: 188), "To the extent that they were commercialised and underwent economic, technological, and organisational concentration, however, they have turned during the last hundred years into complexes of societal power, so that precisely their remaining in private hands in many ways threatened the critical functions of publicist institutions." Mediated public spheres were limited in their ability to provide spaces for agonistic deliberations precisely because of the interests and agendas that they had as profit-making cultural industries. While some media in India have played an active role in maintaining the best traditions of democracy, it can be argued that the majority of media have been supportive of the status quo. One can argue that in such a context, the people created their own media, with public hearings becoming the space for public communication and public opinion making that is representative of people's interests and not that of the mainstream media. This is in some ways analogous to the situation described by Julie Frederikse (1984) in her study of the freedom struggle in Rhodesia in a context in which the media was controlled by the apartheid government while the freedom fighters shaped their own counter media, including *chimurengas*, late-night gatherings that featured local songs for the new nation, and *pungwes*, spaces for political education. The *jan sunwai* arguably is a communication channel that intentionally provides the space for the engendering of localised public spheres.

In 2002, the then central government introduced the Freedom of Information Act. This was amended by the present government to become the Right to Information Bill (2004). This led to the Right to Information Act (2005) that has influenced and in turn been moulded by prior right-to-information legislation in a number of states in India, inclusive of Rajasthan, Madhya Pradesh, Maharashtra, Goa, Tamil Nadu, Karnataka, New Delhi and Andhra Pradesh. The RTI Act 2005 (3) explains the meaning of this right as follows:

- The right to seek information from any public authority,
- The right to take certified copies of records held by public authorities,
- The right to inspect records held by public authorities, take notes,
- The right to information also means the right to inspect any work being carried out by an public authority,
- The right to take certified samples of material and the right to take information in the form of tapes, floppies or held in any electronic format

Valorising communication rights: The *jan sunwai* as a public sphere

The *jan sunwai* is an important indigenous means and pedagogical device used by this movement to mobilise, radicalise and give voice to marginalised people who have traditionally been expected to remain silent, even in the face of the most atrocious atrocities committed by the forward castes and wealthy. The *jan sunwai* is often used by traditional organisations in India such as guilds and associations of small traders and manufacturers to make themselves accountable to their publics. As Jenkins (2007: 60) describes it:

> The MKSS's key innovation ... was to develop a novel means by which information found in government records could be shared and collectively verified: the *jan sunwai* (public hearing). A *jan sunwai* is a publicly accessible forum, often held in a large open-sided tent pitched on a highly visible spot, at which government records are presented alongside testimony by local people with first-hand knowledge of the development projects that these records purpose to document. Key pieces of information from project documents are read aloud. Those with direct knowledge of the specific government projects under investigation are invited to testify on any apparent discrepancies between the official record and their own experiences as labourers on public-works projects or applicants for means-tested antipoverty schemes.

The *jan sunwai* is, as pointed out by Guru in the Lokniti Newsletter (2005), "an empowering process in that, it not only does away with civil society structures that are stacked against the marginalised but also inverts power equations in favour of the marginalised, by making them the centre of the discussion. There are no experts and 'hence on chance of objectification of the victim' and the 'victim represents his case without any technical assistance." In the words of Gopal Guru, "The *sunwai* is a public hearing but it is different from legal and procedural hearings instituted by the state which by its official, legal, and almost pompous nature, place the victim at an inherent disadvantage. The *sunwai* restores to a person his place in the system by allowing him to represent himself and make himself heard." Most importantly the *jan sunwai* is a mechanism that affirms Voice and strengthens self-confidence, often in contexts where caste and class collude to silence people. In the context of the RTI movement, these public hearings allowed local people to examine both the information and dis-information on local development, the collusions, the silences, the corruption and the political economy of under-development.

These hearings unearthed evidence of widespread corruption and the systemic links between local officials and politicians who were also involved in a variety of scams. This evidence discussed at the public hearings led to non-violent civic actions, boycotts and sit-ins at government offices, which was systematically used to wear down the opposition and elicit a response from the government. These local resistances reinforced what the public already knew, the fact that there was gross misappropriation of funds – wages paid to fictitious people, even to workers who had died years back, recorded in local employment registers, incomplete public works projects such as roads and buildings that that were listed as complete when these were either partially complete, abandoned or non-existent and often made from sub-standard building material.

The *jan sunwai* as a local/plebian public sphere stands in stark contrast to the 'rational', bourgeois and rather exclusive public sphere that Habermas highlighted. The *jan sunwai* is deliberately inclusive in that its strength is drawn from local people giving an account of their experiences with development and non-development. No voice is considered unworthy in a full public hearing. This public sphere can be contrasted with other public spheres in India shaped by the literate, associational caste groups and Catholic, cross-caste and religious public spheres that evolved in India as a response to colonial projects in British India. Bayly (1999), in his classic study *Empire and Information,* has a chapter on the Indian Ecumene in which he attempts to describe indigenous public spheres in North India in which respectable, literate men played an important role in contesting colonial excesses and providing moral moorings. But Bayly also writes of "dense networks of social communication" that brought "butchers, flower-sellers, bazaar merchants and artisans into political debates and demonstrations" (ibid.: 204). Such correspondences do indicate that public spheres were inclusive, although Bayly also observes that these relational continuities were by no means seamless and that it was also characterised by discontinuities – most notably between the Brahmanic elite whose ecumenism and dialogue was bounded and Hindu noblemen who were open to writing in Persian and Urdu and to the challenges posed by dialogue (ibid.: 210). The *jan sunwai* is indicative of a public sphere that is grounded in the rhythms of locality animated by ordinary people who are the agents of a collective, shared memory that refuses to be erased or forgotten. In other words, the *jan sunwai* fundamentally provides a spatial framework within which the simultaneous recognition of individual voices and that of the collectivity is highlighted and reinforced. This tradition is consonant with public sphere traditions in India that have deliberately been shaped by the idioms of locality and that went beyond literate cultures of the 'word'. Susanne and Lloyd Rudolph (2003) have explored the Gandhian ashram (meditation retreats) as a public sphere and the repertories of protest that were intentionally linked to making mass movements associated with civil disobedience a dynamic public sphere: "The problem of creating a public sphere, a self-automating civil society, among non-literates propelled Gandhi and his ashram associates to enact, exemplify, amplify political goals in theatrically visible forms, and to create participatory contexts – marches, sit-ins, boycotts – which required political understanding and commitment to goals more than the word" (Rudolph and Rudolph, 2003: 399). This need for political understanding and appropriate repertories of protest is clearly illustrated in the Right to Information Movement's support for and enabling of Voice.

Theorising Voice

An important recent contribution to understanding the public sphere is the theorising of Voice, particularly in the work of Nick Couldry (2009, 2010) and others such as Charles Husband (2009), who has made a case for the right to be understood. In their way of conceptualising Voice, its validation is linked to the human imperative to deepen the human tryst with freedoms and the fulfilment of the human potential to respect, listen and understand the other through inter-subjectively defined projects. As Couldry points out, neo-liberalism plays down the need for people to give an account of themselves and instead devalues Voice while privileging the voices of power. In this context, Couldry's (2010: 2) definition of Voice as value and process goes beyond the traditional understanding of Voice as simply the right to speak:

> voice as a value ... refer(s) to the act of valuing, and choosing to value, those frameworks for organising human life and resources that *themselves* value voice (as a process) ... .Valuing voice then involves particular attention to the conditions under which voice as a process is effective ... "voice" as used here, is a value *about* values or what philosophers sometimes call a second-order value. (original emphasis)

The right to speak was used powerfully to counteract the right of established voices such as that of politicians who in the early 1990s used *Rath Yatras* (motorised chariots) and other means to consolidate the Hindu vote against minorities, in particular against Muslims. The MKSS empowered villagers to use their voices in *yatras* of their own, demonstrating to people that Voice is not a privilege but a right. Aruna Roy (2000: 17) describes the 'truck *yatras*' that were used by the MKSS:

> Called the "Jan Nithi" and "Jan Adhikar Yatra", 40 to 50 volunteers travelled through several districts in Rajasthan in the back of a truck. One objective was to lampoon political *yatras* themselves. Street theatre, music and other forms of cultural expression were used to take the debate about democracy

and participatory governance to the people. The *yatras* have been extremely useful in starting genuine debates, emanating from the common people's concern about their future, and the future of the country.

The RTI is an essential aspect of the Right to Know – knowing and being able to act on what is known as consequences of access to information is what is ultimately significant. The ordinary meaning of 'information' tends to be technical; it refers to data transmitted through any means of communication. However, the information that people access in the context of the RTI is information that can make a difference in their lives – in this sense it is information vital to the leveraging, facilitation and knowledge of change processes. Such knowing can result in empowerment; empowerment on a national scale can have a major impact on the project of substantive democracy and citizenship. Even on a local scale, empowerment can be powerful, simply because submerged or marginalised Voices can now be heard. One of the fundamental contributions of the RTI in India is the valorisation of Voice. Voice needs to be seen not simply in terms of the human capacity to create sounds but the politics of speaking in contexts in which the right to speak is a privilege associated with the structures of domination undergirded by caste, class and gender. Taken in this sense, the spoken Voice in the context of public hearings popularised by the RTI movement in India is an invitation to listen and dialogue.

The empowerment that results from 'naming' corruption and non-accountability is an act of freedom precisely because that act connects self, and the obligations of self, to the community, thus strengthening the larger environment of a communicating public. Eric Watts (2001: 185, original emphasis) has argued that

> "voice" is a particular kind of speech phenomenon that pronounces the ethical problems and obligations incumbent in community building and arouses in persons and groups the frustrations, sufferings and joys of such commitments ... It is itself a *happening* that in invigorated by a public awareness of the ethical and emotional concerns of discourse. ... "Voice", then, is the *sound* of specific experiential encounters in civic life.

In the context of the public hearings examined in this chapter, the public acknowledgment of Voice has led to the validation of agency. These public hearings demonstrate in a profound manner ideal environments for communication rights – environments in which any given person's right to speak is no less than the right of others. These are also environments that are conducive to listening.

Conclusion

What is the larger meaning of the *jan sunwai* as a mechanism for Voice and as a framework for localised public spheres?

The *jan sunwai* is representative of repertories of protest in post-Independent India that specifically reinforce the primacy of orality and traditions of listening, hearing, speaking, denouncing and announcing. While it is certainly the case that these voices are amplified through traditional, print and mobile cultures – it begins with and in and through validations of Voice.

This accent on Voice makers as change agents is a welcome addition to the often technology-mediated forms of protest that are a feature of communication in social change in India. The *jan sunwai* is a scalable form of alternative communications precisely because its methodology can be easily replicated. This stands in contrast to the many examples of the non-replicability of alternative forms of communication in India.

In very critical ways the *jan sunwai* establishes identity, community and solidarity through the primacy of Voice. As a cultural practice it is based on the recognition of agency and the validity of local meanings. This public sphere is intentionally collective; it is based on the 'we' of a community that is united by their experiencing of commonly shared deficits. It is also a community that is united by their desire to make the relationship between the state, development and people accountable and transparent. While this community may consist of members belonging to contiguous villages and different caste groupings they do exhibit, this "principle of community" informs their "fundamental constitutive character as the purposive political acts of a collective consciousness" (Chatterjee, 1993: 163).

While this quotation from Chatterjee is taken from his reading of the Indian historian Ranajit Guha's understanding and work on peasant insurgency in colonial India, it is clear that the success of the *jan sunwai* is tied to a shared sense of dispossession and loss in an era characterised by exploitation and graft.

This brings us to Guha's work, and in particular, to his strong validation of peasant consciousness. While *jan sunwais* are typically organised by activists and peasant communities and are strictly not connected to an 'insurgency' (such as the Maoist struggles in parts of Central and East India), it connects to a form of protest nevertheless that is directed towards throwing off the yoke of the old order and ushering in the new through non-violent means. The *jan sunwai* as an event is not a spontaneous and un-premeditated happening. On the contrary, it is based on collectives understanding that the denouncing of the old order is a risky undertaking given that their "subalternity was materialised by the structure of property, institutionalised by law, sanctified by religion and made tolerable – and even desirable – by tradition" (Guha, 2009: 194). These are intentional spaces for deliberation that reflect the fact that the consciousness of the rural poor is as grounded in rational ways of thinking as others more fortunate in India.

Further reading

Bayly, Chandhoke, Chatterjee and Guha offer the means to understand 'plebian' public spheres in India. Guha's *Elementary Aspects of Peasant Insurgency*, in particular the chapter entitled 'Transmission', provides an excellent introduction to the role played by 'Voice' in the making of plebian public spheres in colonial India. Also see the writings of Aruna Roy and Nikhil Dey, who played a key role in the making of the RTI movement in India.

References

Ali, A. (2001) "Evolution of public sphere in India." *Economic and Political Weekly*, 36(26), 2419–25.

Bayly, C. A. (1999) *Empire and Information: Intelligence Gathering and Social Communication in India, 1780–1870*. New Delhi: Cambridge University Press.

Chandhoke, N. (2003) "The 'civil' and the 'political' in civil society." In C. M. Elliott (ed.), *Civil Society and Democracy: A Reader*. New Delhi: Oxford University Press (pp. 238–61).

——(2005) "Exploring the mythology of the public sphere." In R. Bhargava and H. Reifeld (eds), *Civil Society, Public Sphere and Citizenship: Dialogues and Perceptions*. New Delhi: Sage (pp. 327–47).

Chatterjee, P. (1993) *The Nation and Its Fragments: Colonial and Postcolonial Histories*. Princeton, NJ: Princeton University Press.

Couldry, N. (2009) "Rethinking the politics of voice." *Continuum*, 23(4), 579–82.

——(2010) *Why Voice Matters*. London: Sage.

Frederikse, J. (1984) *None but Ourselves: Masses vs. the Media in the Making of Zimbabwe*. Johannesburg: Raven Press.

Guha, R. (2009) "The prose of counter insurgency." In P. Chatterjee (ed), *The Small Voice of History: Ranajit Guha*. Ranikhet: Permanent Black (pp. 194–238).

Guru, G. (ed.) (2009) *Humiliation*. New Delhi: Oxford University Press.

——(2013) "Freedom of expression and the life of the Dalit mind." *Economic and Political Weekly*, 48(10), 39.

Guru, G. and Geetha, V. (2000) "New phase of Dalit-Bahujan intellectual activity." *Economic and Political Weekly*, 35(3), 130–34.

Gurukkal, R. (2013) "On mirroring the social: Can felt ontology alone inform the theory?" *Economic and Political Weekly*, 48(14), 27–31.

Habermas, J. (1991) *The Structural Transformation of the Public Sphere: An Enquiry into a Category of Bourgeois Society*. Cambridge, MA: MIT Press.

Husband, C. (2009) "Between listening and understanding." *Continuum: Journal of Media and Cultural Studies*, 23(4), 441–3.

Jenkins, R. (2007) "Civil society versus corruption." *Journal of Democracy*, 18(2), 55–68.

Kaviraj, S. (2011) *The Enchantment of Democracy and India*. Ranikhet: Permanent Black.

Menon, D. M. (2013) "Minding one's words." *Economic and Political Weekly*, 48(16), 58–9.

Rai, S. (n.d.) *Transparency and Accountability in Governance and Right to Information in India (1–14)*. Retrieved from http://rti.img.kerala.gov.in/RTI/elearn/GovernanceandRTIinIndiaSHEILA_RAI.pdf (accessed 27 August 2010).

Right to Information Act (2005) Retrieved from http://rti.gov.in/rti-act.pdf (accessed 7 July 2014).

Roy, A. (2000) *Information, Democracy and Ethics*. Twelfth Shri B. V. Narayana Reddy Memorial Lecture, 1 February. Bangalore: MKSS/Indian Institute of World Culture (pp. 1–35).

Rudolph, S. H. and Rudolph, L. I. (2003) "The coffee house and the ashram: Gandhi, civil society and public spheres." In C. M. Elliott (ed.), *Civil Society and Democracy: A Reader*. New Delhi: Oxford University Press (pp. 377–404).

Sarukkai, S. (2007) "Dalit experience and theory." *Economic and Political Weekly*, 42(40), 4043–8.

Watts, E. K. (2001) "Voice" and 'Voicelessness' in rhetorical studies." *Quarterly Journal of Speech*, 87(2), 179–96.

12
BLACKFELLA LISTENING TO BLACKFELLA
Theorising Indigenous community broadcasting

Michael Meadows

Introduction

At the centre of life in Western democracies are the public spheres in which private citizens engage with issues that concern them. This activity takes place in varied settings – classrooms, associations, unions, community meetings, and in provincial and national arenas, including the media. While most citizens take access to these spaces for granted, a great many 'others' are systematically excluded. The advent of mass democracy and mass media has seen the concept of the "imagined community" (Anderson, 1984) – the nation – meld into one which conceives of *societies* made up of multiple-connected public spheres. These spheres have evolved in unique social, political, economic and cultural contexts. In this discussion, I want to consider the idea of Indigenous public spheres and their potential to both empower and inform.

Rather than adopting the idea of a single, all-encompassing public sphere, we should think of the existence of a series of parallel and overlapping public spheres – spaces where participants with similar cultural backgrounds engage in activities of importance to them. Each of us simultaneously has membership in several different public spheres – or public arenas – moving between and within them in our everyday lives according to desire and obligation. In this way, these multiple spheres of activity articulate their own discursive styles and formulate their own positions on issues that are then brought to a wider public sphere, where they are able to interact "across lines of cultural diversity" (Fraser, 1993: 13; see also Avison and Meadows, 2000; Forde, Foxwell and Meadows, 2003, 2009; Meadows, 2005).

However, despite the existence of alternative ideas and assumptions, there is no guarantee that any will be taken up as part of a broader democratic process such as policymaking, for example. Indeed, the ephemeral nature of the policy process means that change might occur only "when the stars align" (Meadows, 2012).

The fear of *further* cultural and language loss is fuelling the impetus for the development of Indigenous media production globally. Western-style media for most Indigenous people represent a double-edged sword. Although sometimes identified as the vanguard of cultural imperialism, media technologies and media practices have the *potential* to be powerful community cultural resources enabling public sphere activity (Michaels, 1986; Kulchyski, 1989; Meadows, 1994, 1995). A range of authors have argued that alternative media practices extend contemporary ideas of the public sphere and democracy (Downing, 2001; Rodríguez, 2001; Atton, 2002; Forde, Meadows and Foxwell, 2002; Rennie, 2002; Howley, 2005; Meadows et al., 2007; Chitty and Rattichalkalakorn, 2007; Kidd, Stein and Rodríguez, 2007; Forde, Foxwell and Meadows, 2009; Forde, 2011). This can be seen in Indigenous media producers appropriating various media technologies to suit their own social and cultural needs. The basis for successful applications of media technologies is 'functionality' – in other words, there must be a clear benefit flowing from the adoption of such technologies. This is especially the case in remote Indigenous communities, which are commonly required to confront issues of survival on a daily basis (Meadows and Morris, 2003). Indigenous media production – or "invention", as Michaels (1986) has described it – suggests the need to reconceptualise the notion of the public sphere through an examination of the unique relationship between Indigenous media producers and their audiences.

A wide range of audiences access Indigenous radio and television in Australia. Both Indigenous and non-Indigenous listeners and viewers say these unique services offer an essential service to communities and play a central organising role in community life. Indigenous radio and television help maintain social networks and play a strong educative role in communities, particularly for young people. These media offer an alternative source of news and information which avoids stereotyping Indigenous people and issues, thus helping break down inaccurate perceptions prevalent in mainstream Australia. The Indigenous media sector also represents crucial platforms for specialist music and dance (Meadows et al., 2007; Forde, Foxwell and Meadows, 2009).

Audiences for Indigenous radio and television around Australia define them in many ways (Meadows et al., 2007: 54); for example: "the electronic message stick of the new millennium"; "our voice"; the "Murri grapevine" ('Murri' is a term used by Indigenous people in Queensland to describe themselves); and the "bush telegraph". One passionate listener on Palm Island in far north Queensland explained simply: "Because it's blackfella listening to blackfella. You know you want to communicate with them. You know!"

There is little doubt of the globalising impact of mainstream media to transform the wider public sphere, and it is within such a context that Indigenous people continue to seek access to their own media for political, educational and cultural reasons. Global media processes have perhaps inadvertently acted as a catalyst for grassroots' action, and many disadvantaged groups have recognised the potential of a wide range of media as tools for cultural and political intervention – effectively, allowing the dispossessed to "speak as well as hear" (Girard, 1992: 2). In Australia, this response has emerged as a result of several influences – combating stereotypes, addressing information gaps in non-Indigenous society, and reinforcing local community languages and cultures. The impact on Indigenous communities who are able to hear their own voices and languages is profound (Michaels, 1986; Meadows, 1993, 2001; Aboriginal and Torres Strait Islander Commission, 1999; Productivity Commission, 2000;

Molnar and Meadows, 2001; Meadows et al., 2007; Forde, Foxwell and Meadows, 2009; Meadows and Foxwell, 2011).

Audiences for Indigenous broadcasting in Australia identify empowerment as a central element of the nature of this relationship, and thus the success of Indigenous-produced media in providing a first level of service to their many and varied communities. It highlights the importance of a process of cultural resource management that is a defining characteristic of Indigenous broadcasting in communities where community media are active (Meadows, 2001). Grossberg (1987: 95) defines empowerment as "the enablement of particular practices, that is ... the conditions of possibility that enable a particular practice or statement to exist in a specific social context and to enable people to live their lives in different ways". It is clear from recent studies of Indigenous broadcasting audiences that this process is a catalyst for community organisation around communication hubs such as community radio and television stations.

In this chapter, I want to consider some of the theoretical issues around the public sphere and the ways in which Indigenous media producers and audiences have created spaces for themselves at the level of not only local, but also broader community activity.

Indigenous media and their audiences in Australia

Community radio and television remain the major communications outlet for Indigenous voices in Australia, with more than 100 licensed radio stations in remote regions and a further 20 radio stations in regional and urban areas producing around 1,400 hours of Indigenous content weekly. This includes two Indigenous radio networks: the satellite-delivered National Indigenous Radio Service (NIRS) and the National Indigenous News Service (NINS) (Molnar and Meadows, 2001; Community Broadcasting Foundation, 2009).

In addition, in 2012, 80 Remote Indigenous Broadcasting Services (RIBS) produced radio and/or television content for isolated communities in various parts of the continent. These RIBS units also re-broadcast a National Indigenous Television (NITV) service, launched in 2007. Most of the small stations based in remote townships are engaged in re-transmitting available satellite programming, both mainstream and community produced. In 1988, Imparja Television became the first Indigenous-owned and -managed *commercial* television service in Australia and, arguably, the world. However, since its launch, largely for financial reasons, Imparja has been able to produce minimal Indigenous content.

An Aboriginal-owned and -run Indigenous community television service, ICTV, began broadcasting to several remote regions in central, northern and western Australia from one of Imparja's spare satellite channels in 2001. This innovative service featured close to 100 percent Indigenous content, produced mostly by small bush communities and often in the 15–20 local or regional Aboriginal languages which are still active. It was initiated by Aboriginal-controlled Pitjantjatjara-Yunkantjatjara (PY) Media and produced around 300 hours of new content annually from 2005 on. ICTV ran on an annual budget of about AU$70,000 and included contributions from PY Media, Pintubi-Amatyerre-Warlpiri (PAW) Media, Pilbara and Kimberley Aboriginal Media (PAKAM), Ngaanyatjarra Media, Top End Aboriginal Bush Broadcasters Association

(TEABBA) and other local Indigenous producers. Former PY Media general manager Will Rogers (personal communication, email, 18 August 2009) reflects on the ICTV experience:

> ICTV was a real project started from the grassroots; an opportunity for the un-heard to have the freedom to say what it needed to. Another funny thing was, what was said was OK – it wasn't said in anger but just an opportunity to say something and show the pride of people that live in the bush and their lifestyles.

A federal government policy decision led to the launch of NITV in 2007, displacing ICTV from the airwaves. This caused great concern for remote Indigenous media audiences at the time but has led to some creative responses, including the launch of *Indigitube*, a database of Indigenous-produced videos available for viewing online. NITV merged with Australia's national multicultural broadcaster, the Special Broadcasting Service (SBS), in December 2012 and began transmitting through one of its digital channels. Following some intense lobbying by the Indigenous Remote Communication Association (IRCA), ICTV re-launched on its own digital television channel also in late 2012. However, it can be seen only by remote and regional communities that have access to the existing television satellite network (Meadows et al., 2007; Forde, Foxwell and Meadows, 2009; Meadows, 2010; Featherstone, 2011; D. Featherstone, IRCA general manager, personal communication, 2012).

About AU$16 million each year is distributed by the Community Broadcasting Foundation (CBF) for Indigenous community radio and television program production around Australia. NITV's annual budget is around AU$15 million. The multifarious roles played by Indigenous radio and television in their communities make this investment by government seem modest, particularly when compared with funding for comparable Indigenous media organisations globally. For example, in Canada in 2012, the Aboriginal People's Television Network had an annual budget of AU$40 million, with an additional AU$9 million distributed for National Aboriginal Broadcasting program production by the Department of Canadian Heritage. In the same year, Maori Television in New Zealand received AU$34 million, with an additional AU $1 million allocated for Maori television programming (Aboriginal People's Television Network, 2012; Maori Television, 2012; Department of Canadian Heritage, 2012).

Although Indigenous broadcasting in Australia remains on the periphery of the Australian mediascape, a study of the sector in 2007 revealed that audiences identify Indigenous media as essential community services which play a central organising role in community life. Indigenous media help maintain social networks and play a strong educative role in communities in supporting languages and cultures, particularly for young people. They offer alternative sources of news and information without the pre-valent stereotyping present in mainstream media, and in doing so, help break down prejudices for non-Indigenous audiences. The stations offer a crucial medium for Indigenous music and dance, and arguably are the primary supporters of the vast Indigenous music industry. It is evident that Indigenous radio and television is playing a key role in facilitating cross-cultural dialogue between Indigenous and non-Indigenous Australia (Meadows et al., 2007; Forde, Foxwell and Meadows, 2009; Meadows, 2010). This extraordinary and diverse contribution to the democratic process continues to pass almost unnoticed by the broader Australian public and its political servants.

The public sphere

Jurgen Habermas's theorisation of the public sphere provides a useful framework for development of the idea of an Indigenous public sphere, centred primarily on media production and process. A central focus of Habermas's idea draws on the shifting role of the mass media as centres of rational-critical discursive activity to commercialised vehicles for advertising and public relations, within the context of the nineteenth-century decline of the liberal public sphere (Habermas, 1974, 1989, 1992). Habermas describes the public sphere as "a realm of our social life in which something approaching public opinion can be formed" – unrestricted access to the public sphere is a defining characteristic, with the mass media playing a central role in this process (1974: 29). The decline of the *liberal* public sphere was hastened with a shift from the media being a forum for rational-critical debate for private citizens assembled to form 'a public', to a privately owned and controlled institution that is easily manipulated by media owners. For Habermas (1989: 185), this came about as a result of the absence of a barrier between editorial and advertising – a process that continues unabated, extending to ethical collapse in modern mass media systems (Herman and McChesney, 1997; Hamilton, 2004; Davies, 2008; Finkelstein, 2012; Leveson, 2012). Thus, the central role of mass media – particularly broadcasting – as a primary element of public sphere formation has thrown up challenges to Habermas's ideal.

Nancy Fraser's critique of Habermas's model – which excludes women, 'plebian' men and all people of colour – nevertheless prompts a rethinking rather than a rejection of his ideas. For Fraser, the important theoretical task is to "render visible the ways in which societal inequality infects formally exclusive existing public spheres and taints discursive interactions with them" (1993: 13). So her reconceived public sphere model theorises it as a space where participants with similar cultural backgrounds *can* engage in discussions about issues and interests important to them, using their own discursive styles – and genres – to formulate their positions on various issues. Such ideas and assumptions can then be shared through a wider public sphere where "members of different more limited publics talk across lines of cultural diversity" (ibid.: 7). This theorises the existence of multiple public spheres where members of society who are subordinated or ignored – "subaltern counterpublics" – are able to communicate (ibid.: 14).

It is precisely this empowering process that has acted as a catalyst for the rise of community media around the world, and it is nowhere more evident than in Australia, which has become the most researched globally in terms of its community radio and television sector. But while community radio and television offer alternatives and a level of empowerment for media audiences in the broader community, they repre-sent *an essential service* for those on the periphery. And that is the focus of my argument here.

Indigenous public spheres

Indigenous public spheres are not a non-dominant variant of the broader public sphere. Although they develop both within and alongside mainstream society, they should be seen as discrete formations that exist in a unique context as the product of contestation with the mainstream public sphere. While they operate *within* a dominant context, it is their 'Indigenousness' that is the defining characteristic (Avison, 1996; Meadows, 2005). This is evident in audience descriptions of why Indigenous radio and/or television matters. Extending Fraser's (1993) notion of the existence of multiple public spheres, Indigenous public spheres can be seen as providing opportunities for people who are regularly subordinated and ignored by mainstream public sphere processes. This is akin to Grossberg's (1987) notion of empowerment. These spheres enable Indigenous people to deliberate together, to develop their own counter-discourses, and to interpret their own identities and experiences. Albeit speaking about Canada's Native peoples, Valaskakis underlines the importance of Indigenous people controlling their own representations, concluding (1993):

> ... otherness is related to issues of identity and cultural struggle entrenched in representation and appropriation, in how they are represented, and how these representations are appropriated by others in a political process which confines their past as it constructs their future.

Representation is a crucial site of struggle over identity; a dynamic process that functions through dialogue (Langton, 1993; Avison, 1996; Meadows, 2001). And it is the very nature of the dialogue between Indigenous producers and their audiences that offers a unique insight into the creation and maintenance of Indigenous identity. The *absence* of a barrier between producers of Indigenous media and their audiences has been suggested before (Michaels, 1986; Kulchyski, 1989). But without access to significant audience data, such claims have relied primarily on anthropological methods such as participant observation and ethnography. The data from an extensive national audience study of the Indigenous media sector offered new insights into the processes of the Indigenous public sphere (Meadows et al., 2007). One media worker in the remote Indigenous community of Yuendumu described the relationships in producing local media like this (ibid.: 53):

> The audience are the producers and ... we get constant feedback from them as to what they want. And also ... they're prepared to just get up there and do it themselves ... it's a unique situation [and] it's something that the government should treasure.

In locations around Australia, audiences for Indigenous radio and television expressed this sentiment in different ways: a sense of ownership, communication, identification with the grassroots, access and the innate ability by stations to relate to their listeners socially, culturally and linguistically. One of the most persuasive came from an elderly Pitjantjatjara woman during a cultural festival at Umuwa in the central desert. She was determined to have her say about the importance of Indigenous-produced radio and television in her community (ibid.: 61):

> Travelling in any way in the country they can listen to music; they can put a TV there and make everybody happy, make everybody awake and think

about the land: this is my grandmother's land; this is my *tjamu's* land, this is my *kami's* land, my grandmother's, and grandfather's, uncle's, mother's. The media we started for *Anangu* children. We can't give it to anybody.

For this Indigenous woman, like many others around the country, Indigenous media is *inherent in* local culture: there is no division between media and community. It underlines that the communication network facilitated by Indigenous media is expansive and unique. This is the Indigenous public sphere in action.

Indigenous public spheres are frames of understanding existing on a variety of levels: clan, community/reserve, provincial/territorial, regional, urban, national/international. They are also constituted to an extent by mainstream media through agenda-setting functions and the processes of 'local talk' – the ways in which people 'make sense' of ideas and assumptions concerning Indigenous affairs represented in mainstream media (McCallum, 2007, 2010). Indigenous public spheres are places where Indigenous people find the information and resources they need to deliberate on issues of concern to them. In keeping with Habermas's principle of publicity, they are accessible to all citizens and, ideally, are spaces where the views of participants are judged and authorised, according to traditional, local protocols. For example, the very nature of non-Indigenous journalistic inquiry is often in direct conflict with traditional knowledge-management processes in Indigenous societies making understanding of Indigenous public sphere processes critical for journalists (O'Regan, 1990: 68; Ginsburg, 1991, 1993: 574; Meadows, 1993; Avison, 1996; Meadows, 2005).

Storytelling, art and music – and even silence – are important ways in which Indigenous people make their positions known, as are the ways in which they are presented. An 'ideal' Indigenous public sphere – one which takes account of the inevitable complications inherent in cross-cultural communication – accommodates such varied and culturally specific communicative styles (Meadows, 2005). One unexpected outcome of the national study of the Indigenous media sector was the important role being played by community radio and television in promoting mental health. The promotion of emotional and social well-being is enabled, particularly because of the absence of a barrier between audiences and producers of local radio and television in Indigenous communities – another example of an Indigenous public sphere in action in unexpected ways (Meadows and Foxwell, 2011).

The particular relationship that defines audiences and producers of Indigenous community broadcasting has created a "more engaged and participatory culture" which enhances the communication process at various levels (Deuze, 2006: 271). Indigenous community radio, in particular, has the potential to enhance social cohesion and social gain – arguably the markers of successful social media activity. It suggests, too, that perhaps it is only at the level of the local that such critical social processes are best managed.

Conclusion

The continuing circulation of ideas and assumptions about Indigenous communities – through Indigenous media – contributes to the development of a national Indigenous public sphere by highlighting common experiences and issues and facilitating dialogue about them. Leakage 'across lines of cultural diversity' into the mainstream public sphere enable ideas to be considered as part of a broader democratic process – theoretically, at least. Indigenous media serve as an important cultural bridge between the Indigenous and non-Indigenous worlds, linking these 'parallel universes'. Indigenous-produced radio and television – particularly at the community level – provide sites for public opinion formation; sites where citizens can engage in collective efforts to bring their issues to the dominant public sphere; and sites where Indigenous people can attempt to influence the policies of various governments through the pressure of public opinion. Valaskakis (1993) eloquently articulates this process, facilitated by the very existence of Indigenous public spheres that enable the voices of such 'subaltern counterpublics' to be heard:

> It is through the prism of parallel voices, of competing narratives, expressed in public text – in literature, art, music, ceremony, and media – that we can access the subaltern experience, expand our concepts of inquiry, and approach our points of connectedness.

And surely, any activity that enhances the ability to 'connect' – socially, culturally and politically – is an admirable contribution to the democratic process.

Further reading

Forde, S., Foxwell, K. and Meadows, M. (2009) *Developing Dialogues: Indigenous and Ethnic Community Broadcasting in Australia*. London: Intellect; Chicago: University of Chicago Press. A comprehensive analysis of the Indigenous and ethnic community broadcasting sector based on a national audience study and two decades of additional research.

Meadows, M., Forde, S., Ewart, J. and Foxwell, K. (2007) *Community Media Matters: An Audience Study of the Australian Community Broadcasting Sector*. Brisbane: Griffith University. Retrieved from http://cbonline.org.au/news-and-publications/community-media-matters-report/ (accessed 30 August 2013). The full report of the first national audience study of a community media sector globally with an extensive analysis of Indigenous broadcasting.

Meadows, M. and Molnar, H. (2002) "Bridging the gaps: Towards a history of Indigenous media in Australia." *Media History*, 8(1), 9–20. A history of the idea of Indigenous media development in Australia.

Michaels, E. (1986) *Aboriginal Invention of Television Central Australia 1982–1985*. Canberra: Australian Institute of Aboriginal Studies. A seminal study of the 'invention' of Aboriginal television by the Warlpiri community in Yuendumu by anthropologist Eric Michaels.

Rennie, E. and Featherstone, D. (2008) "The potential diversity of things we call TV: Indigenous community television, self-determination and NITV." *Media International Australia*, 129, 52–66. A more recent analysis of new developments in the Indigenous media sector in Australia.

References

Aboriginal and Torres Strait Islander Commission (1999) *Digital Dreaming: A National Review of Indigenous Media and Communications – Executive Summary*. Canberra: Aboriginal and Torres Strait Islander Commission.

Aboriginal People's Television Network (2012) *Financial Statements*. Retrieved from http://www.aptn.ca/corporate/PDFs/Financial-Statements-APTN-2012.pdf (accessed 30 August 2013).

Anderson, B. (1984) *Imagined Communities: Reflections on the Origin and Spread of Nationalism*. London: Verso.

Atton, C. (2002) *Alternative Media*. London: Sage.

Avison, S. (1996) *Aboriginal Newspapers: Their Contribution to the Emergence of an Alternative Public Sphere in Canada*. Unpublished Master of Arts thesis. Montreal: Department of Communication Studies, Concordia University.

Avison, S. and Meadows, M. (2000) "Speaking and hearing: Aboriginal newspapers and the public sphere in Canada and Australia." *Canadian Journal of Communication*, 25, 347–66.

Chitty, N. and Rattichalkalakorn, S. (2007) *Alternative Media: Idealism and Pragmatism*. Penang: Southbound.

Community Broadcasting Foundation (CBOnline) (2009) *Community Broadcasting and Media: Year 2015, A Five-Year Plan to Create the World's Most Innovative, Accessible Community Media Sector*. Retrieved from http://www.cbf.com.au/files/3013/5546/5327/Community_Broadcasting_and_Media_2015.pdf (accessed 30 August 2013).

Davies, N. (2008) *Flat Earth News*. London: Chatto and Windus.

Department of Canadian Heritage (2012) *Analysis of National Aboriginal Broadcasting Financial Information and Aboriginal Content, Fiscal Year 2010–2011* (personal communication).

Deuze, M. (2006) "Ethnic media, community media and participatory media." *Journalism*, 7(3), 262–80.

Downing, J. D. H. (with others) (2001) *Radical Media: Rebellious Communication and Social Movements*. Thousand Oaks, CA: Sage.

Featherstone, D. (2011) "The Ngaanyatjarra Lands telecommunications project: A quest for broadband in the Western desert." *Telecommunications Journal of Australia*, 61(1), 1–25.

Finkelstein, R. (2012) *Independent Inquiry into Media and Media Regulation*. Canberra: Department of Broadband, Communications and the Digital Economy.

Forde, S. (2011) *Challenging the News: The Journalism of Alternative and Independent Media*. London: Palgrave Macmillan.

Forde, S., Foxwell, K. and Meadows, M. (2003) "Through the lens of the local: Public arena journalism in the Australian community broadcasting sector." *Journalism*, 4(3), 317–42.

——(2009) *Developing Dialogues: Indigenous and Ethnic Community Broadcasting in Australia*. London: Intellect; Chicago: University of Chicago Press.

Forde, S., Meadows, M. and Foxwell, K. (2002) *Culture, Commitment, Community: The Australian Community Radio Sector*. Brisbane: Griffith University.

Fraser, N. (1993) "Rethinking the public sphere: A contribution to the critique of actually existing democracy." In B. Robbins (ed.) *The Phantom Public Sphere*. Minneapolis: University of Minnesota Press (1–32).

Ginsburg, F. (1991) "Indigenous media: Faustian contract or global village?" *Cultural Anthropology*, 6(1), 92–112.

——(1993) "Aboriginal media and the Australian imaginary." *Public Culture*, 5, 557–78.

Girard, B. (1992) *A Passion for Radio: Radio Waves and Community*. Montreal: Black Rose Books.

Grossberg, L. (1987) "Critical theory and the politics of empirical research." In M. Gurevitch and M. Levy (eds), *Mass Communication Review Yearbook 6*. London: Sage (pp. 86–106).

Habermas, J. (1974) "The public sphere: An encyclopedia article." *New German Critique*, 3, 29–35.

——(1989) *The Structural Transformation of the Public Sphere: An Inquiry into a Category of Bourgeois Society.* Cambridge, MA: MIT Press.

——(1992) "Further reflections on the public sphere." In C. Calhoun (ed.), *Habermas and the Public Sphere.* Cambridge, MA: MIT Press (pp. 421–61).

Hamilton, J. T. (2004) *All the News That's Fit to Sell: How the Market Transforms Information into News.* Princeton, NJ: Princeton University Press.

Herman, E. and McChesney, R. (1997) *The Global Media: The New Missionaries of Corporate Capitalism.* Cassell: London.

Howley, K. (2005) *Community Media People, Places and Communication Technologies.* Cambridge: Cambridge University Press.

Kidd, D., Stein, G. and Rodríguez, C. (2007) *Mapping Our Media.* Cresskill, NJ: Hampton Press.

Kulchyski, P. (1989) "The postmodern and the Paleolithic: Notes on technology and native community in the far north." *Canadian Journal of Political and Social Theory*, 53(3), 49–62.

Langton, M. (1993) "'Well, I heard it on the radio and I saw it on the television': An essay for the Australian Film Commission on the politics and aesthetics of filmmaking by and about Aboriginal people and things." Sydney: Australian Film Commission.

Leveson, B. (2012) *An Inquiry into the Culture, Practice and Ethics of the Press.* London: Stationery Office.

Maori Television (2012) *Annual Report.* Retrieved from http://www.maoritelevision.com/sites/default/files/attachments/M%C4%81ori%20Television%20Annual%20Report%202012.pdf (accessed 30 August 2013).

McCallum, K. (2007) "Public opinion about Indigenous issues in Australia: Local talk and journalistic practice." *Australian Journalism Monographs* 8. Brisbane: Griffith University.

——(2010) "News and local talk: Conversations about the 'crisis of Indigenous violence' in Australia." In S. E. Bird (ed.), The Anthropology of News and Journalism. Evansville: University of Indiana Press (pp. 151–67).

Meadows, M. (1993) "The way people want to talk: Media representation and Indigenous media responses in Australia and Canada." Unpublished PhD thesis. Brisbane: Faculty of Humanities, Griffith University.

——(1994) "The way people want to talk: Indigenous media production in Australia and Canada." *Media Information Australia*, 3, 4–73.

——(1995) "Ideas from the bush: Indigenous media in Australia and Canada." *Canadian Journal of Communication*, 20(2), 197–212.

——(2001) *Voices in the Wilderness: Indigenous Australians and the News Media.* Westport: Greenwood Publishing.

——(2005) "Journalism and Indigenous public spheres." *Pacific Journalism Review*, 11(1), 36–41.

——(2010) "Conducting conversations: Exploring the audience-producer relationship in Indigenous media research." *Observatorio*, 4(4), 307–24.

——(2012) "When the stars align: Indigenous media policy formation 1998–2008." In K. McCallum (ed.), *The Media and Indigenous Policy: How News Media Reporting and Mediatized Practice Impact on Indigenous Policy.* Canberra: University of Canberra (pp. 23–32).

Meadows, M., Forde, S., Ewart, J. and Foxwell, K. (2007) *Community Media Matters: An Audience Study of the Australian Community Broadcasting Sector.* Brisbane: Griffith University. Retrieved from http://cbonline.org.au/news-and-publications/community-media-matters-report/ (accessed 30 August 2013).

Meadows, M. and Foxwell, K. (2011) "Community broadcasting and mental health: The role of local radio and television in enhancing emotional and social wellbeing." *Radio Journal*, 9(2), 89–106.

Meadows, M. and Molnar, H. (2002) "Bridging the gaps: Towards a history of Indigenous media in Australia." *Media History*, 8(1), 9–20.

Meadows, M. and Morris, C. (2003) "Framing the future: Indigenous communication in Australia." In N. Couldry and J. Curran (eds), *Contesting Media Power*. Boulder, CO: Rowman and Littlefield Publishers (pp. 71–88).

Michaels, E. (1986) *Aboriginal Invention of Television Central Australia 1982–1985*. Canberra: Australian Institute of Aboriginal Studies.

Molnar, H. and Meadows, M. (2001) *Songlines to Satellites: Indigenous Communication in Australia, the South Pacific and Canada*. Leichhardt: Pluto Press.

O'Regan, T. (1990) "TV as cultural technology: The work of Eric Michaels." *Continuum* 3(2), 53–98.

Productivity Commission (2000) *Broadcasting*, Report No. 11, 3 March. Canberra: Ausinfo. Retrieved from http://www.pc.gov.au/projects/inquiry/broadcasting/docs/finalreport (accessed 30 August 2013).

Rennie, E. (2002) "The other road to media citizenship." *Media International Australia*, 103, 7–13.

Rennie, E. and Featherstone, D. (2008) "The potential diversity of things we call TV: Indigenous community television, self-determination and NITV." *Media International Australia*, 129, 52–66.

Rodríguez, C. (2001) *Fissures in the Mediascape: An International Study of Citizens' Media*. Creskill, NJ: Hampton Press.

Valaskakis, G. G. (1993) "Parallel voices: Indians and others – Narratives of cultural struggle." *Canadian Journal of Communication*, 18(3). Retrieved from http://www.cjc-online.ca/view article.php?id=179&layout=html (accessed 30 August 2013).

13
CIVIC PARTICIPATION AND THE VOCABULARIES FOR DEMOCRATIC JOURNALISM

Laura Ahva, Heikki Heikkilä and Risto Kunelius

Introduction

The link between civic participation and journalism is a twofold question. First, it concerns the participatory quality of the *discourse of journalism*. How does journalism help, control or hinder the opportunities of people to practice their citizenship? Which story types, interactive platforms, reporting routines and uses of language are applied to this? How well does journalism represent the public, that is, people, interests or groups, as they try to enter the public domain? Second, there is the question about the quality of the discourse *about journalism*. What normative vocabularies are applied to critical evaluations of journalism? Which assumptions about citizens, professionals and power relations are incorporated into our language about democracy and the role of media and journalism in it? How well does our critical language adjust to new developments?

Thus, ideas about journalism's ability to enable civic participation are dependent on the tension between practical imagination and normative-democratic imaginaries about journalism. Today, as we find the practices of journalism in dramatic flux, it is ever more important to look at how participatory impulses within journalism are changing the profession. It is equally crucial to think how their justification is argued for in terms of critical vocabulary. As Dahlgren puts it:

> We should be wise not to anticipate any swift resolution to the force-field between professional and civic ideals of online journalism; it is a dynamic that will continue to play out intensely in the years ahead, shaped and

altered as circumstances evolve. But for the sake of democracy, we need a positive unfolding.

(Dahlgren, 2013: 169)

When talking about participation, a core question must be: What do people *become part of* through journalism – and why? Democratic participation always aims at 'making a difference' in the public domain, whether this refers to one's own local community or to a broader domain of political processes. Thus, a critical assessment of *participation through* journalism must go beyond opportunities for self-presentation: it assumes that collective action also bears consequences (Carpentier, 2011: 193–4). From this perspective, a critical vocabulary of participation needs to be linked to the hierarchy or *scale of power*.

This essay invokes a discussion about such vocabularies in the rapidly changing contexts of civic participation through journalism. We base our discussion on three key concepts – access, dialogue and deliberation (Heikkilä and Kunelius, 1998). The threesome is linked back to the conditions in which participation was contained and defined in the mass media framework. Compared to our image of that era, the current digital environment appears to be in many ways 'flatter' than the earlier mass media one. We try to grasp this changing landscape by judging to what extent the earlier conceptualisations of participation are still useful. Shortly put, we argue that they are, albeit they need to be slightly re-thought. Their persistent validity stems from the fact that they are critically sensitised not only to the media environment but also to hierarchies of power which are not likely to disappear in the digital landscape.

The mass media framework: Access, dialogue, deliberation

Journalism is about representation in both senses of the word. It claims to offer trustworthy reports on what is happening. But it also claims to catalyse the formation of public opinion by bringing forth voices and viewpoints of citizens and institutions. Journalism sets out to 'stand for' the social reality and 'act for' those who want to have a say and influence the course of social developments (Heikkilä and Kunelius, 1998: 71–2). Journalism's performance in fulfilling these functions has significantly shaped the forms of participation in public life.

What makes participation difficult and complex in modern societies is that democratic politics takes place in circumstances that exceed way beyond the scale where citizens can gather together and speak to each other (e.g. Peters, 1999). This has resulted in the bureaucratisation of politics, whereby political life is often described as a pyramid "with leaders at the apex and followers at the base where political participation seldom takes place" (Barnhurst, 2011: 582). Democracy is organised into different levels or platforms of participation. At each one, from local to national and global, civic actors are faced with three consecutive obstacles: How to get in? How to establish contact and have exchange with the others? How to make a difference politically?

Access: How to get in? In the era of mass communication, journalists occupied a distinct position as gatekeepers (see, for example, Shoemaker, 1991). At least technically, they had the power to control which actors got their views through to the public sphere via journalism. A number of classic studies on newsroom practices pertaining to *access* proved that news organisations prioritised institutional sources over the less established ones, such as 'ordinary citizens', and the majority viewpoints over the minorities (Ericson, Baranek and Chan, 1989).

The recurring experiences of the systemic bias within mainstream journalism triggered demands for a better access for citizens to the public discussions mediated by journalism. This was insisted to a degree that the parts of the media should be owned, created and distributed by the very people for whom they exist (Atton, 1999: 72). Such demands had also practical impacts: alternative routes of 'public access' were developed around the world, particularly in the electronic media. While public access radio and television channels helped challenge the mainstream media logic, their social impact remained limited before the emergence of the internet.

Dialogue: How to produce exchange? In the context of the mass media, civic participation tended to face another structural obstacle: the difficulty of citizens in engaging in mutually responsive, two-way communication with decision-makers, experts or political opponents. Journalism's role in facilitating dialogue was criticised in two ways. On the one hand, it was asked how well news organisations organise dialogue between different stakeholders on a given issue. On the other hand, more dialogue was demanded between journalism and its audiences.

Both arguments highlight the same criticism: rather than creating dialogue across boundaries, journalism tends to compartmentalise opinions and prevent exchanges between them. The internal (generic) hierarchy of a newspaper illustrates this: the prime minister and ordinary citizens may indeed be talking about the same topic in the paper – but the former can have his say on the front page and the latter in the letters to the editor. The popularity of less paternalistic media genres and formats, such as audience discussion programs on television, helped researchers see how journalism may redeem its dialogic potential. For instance, Livingstone and Lunt (1994, 36) noted that discussion programs helped draw together ordinary people and representatives of established power to discuss the same topics in public. These programs also backed up the assumption that it was indeed actually possible to unpack the one-way and top-down modes of communication.

Deliberation: How to make a difference? In addition to assessments about authenticity (access) and reciprocity (dialogue), civic participation can also be evaluated against its efficacy: What *difference* does the dialogue make? Such a question, often drawing from the ideal of *deliberation*, situates the evaluation of participation into a broader framework of political and social consequences. At the core of deliberation is a trust in that citizens are entitled to – and capable of – participating in problem-solving through public discussions (e.g. Bohman and Rehg, 1997). Rather than limiting its claims to discussions in the media (such as audience discussion programs on TV), a deliberative framework looked into whether public exchanges bring about changes, either on actual policies or on those actors who participate in the intersubjective, civic communication.

Ultimately, the notion of deliberation situates journalism to the 'epistemic' dimension of democracy: How does a society come to know how to act collectively, and what is the role of journalism in this participatory process (Habermas, 2006)? Against this backdrop, the objective for journalism expands from the management of access and facilitation of dialogue to creating public narratives about how citizens leave their mark on public policies and democratic processes. An example of how such a vocabulary inspired practical reforms is the 1990s idea of 'public' or 'civic journalism' that called professional mainstream journalism to enhance democracy as "something that people do, not something that is done to them" (Rosen, 1999: 299; see also Glasser, 1999; Friedland, 2003). Despite the diffusion of such ideas and practices, the movement itself started to wane by the shift of the millennium. While there are many reasons for this (economic, professional, political), a major cause was the technological change, whereby journalism began to gradually lose its imagined centrality. The core question became: How are journalists and news organisations to reposition themselves in the new media environment where they are no longer the privileged hubs of public communication?

Participation in the flat media environment

Digital tools and platforms have seemed to transfer us into 'flatter' and more open media environment for civic participation (Benkler, 2006; Castells, 2009). This shift has triggered many changes in journalistic practice and discourse about journalism. In contemporary research, this is tagged with titles such as 'hybrid' (Chadwick, 2013), 'networked' (Beckett, 2010) or 'ambient' (Hermida, 2010) journalism. Ongoing changes and challenges can be discussed at both the level of *discourse of journalism* and *discourse about journalism* by asking to what extent the concepts of access, dialogue and deliberation still carry their critical weight in the seemingly flat digital environment.

Better access? Probably the most profound change in the relationship of news organisations and citizens is marked by the introduction of UGC, user-generated content. Both everyday experience and studies of participatory journalism suggest that the new forms of UGC have indeed changed the terms of access. The participatory user role is especially noticeable at the "access and observation stage of the news process", that is, in the initial information gathering phase of online journalism (Singer et al., 2011: 18–19). At the same time, it is noted that the contributions of users are in most cases treated as new means of *sourcing* (Thurman, 2008: 149; Thorsen, 2013: 127). Thus, the question of citizens' access to the public sphere is often flipped over and translated as journalists' access to information and raw materials emanating outside the institutional domains.

Consequently, the use of UGC – especially the visual citizen material – does not necessarily lead to enhancement of citizens' political participation but rather to the enrichment of authentic and emotionally captivating presentation of news (Pantti, 2012). Such narratives and roles are important in expanding the potential repertoires for citizens to become part of the public, but they seem to remain subordinate to editorial control. Singer et al. (2011) have observed that despite being labelled as participatory or collaborative journalism, the actual agenda-setting power in this context remains out of reach for citizens. Ordinary people and the content they provide are currently prevalent in the media as 'material'. This problem cannot be circumvented simply by translating the issues of access into questions of 'openness' (Bowman and Willis, 2003; Lewis, 2012).

Scholars point to yet another problem: In the era of the mass media, access to news meant gaining at least some *public attention*, but today, access and public attention are not necessarily linked to each other. There is no guarantee that citizens' ability to publish their views actually makes them 'public' in the sense that the messages were heeded by others. Thus, as the structural constraints of access to online news services and platforms have been relaxed, more attention should be paid to, as Jönsson and Örnebring (2011: 140) suggest, how people get recognised as public actors. In this sense, the problem of access is transformed into problems of visibility and public attention (Goode, 2009: 1295).

The increased use of UGC in journalism, then, includes important potential for civic participation at the initial level. But the notion of access maintains its validity as part of the critical discourse about journalism. It helps clarify 'whose' access is being enhanced (journalists' or the citizens). It underlines that 'opening up' a digital platform does not solve issues of recognition. Situated into this new dynamics, critique of access may have to be rephrased, but the underlying idea still helps us capture some of the inequalities of public participation.

Better dialogue? In addition to the promise of eliminating hierarchies of access, participatory journalism portends enhanced dialogue between citizens, journalists and institutions of power. The new technical opportunities for dialogue go well beyond the capacities of printed newspapers or broadcasted audience discussions. Two practices adopted by news organisations have caught particular attention among news organisations and journalism researchers: user comments and live blogs.

Discussion boards and comment fields attached to news articles were among the earliest and still most popular forms of participatory journalism (Singer et al., 2011). They provide a platform for lively and reciprocal (albeit not always very civic) dialogue in which participants respond to each other's opinions and arguments (Graham, 2013). As journalists seldom monitor reader comments, let alone respond to them (Thurman, 2008; Wardle and Williams, 2010), the dialogic potential of comment fields is often reduced to a peer-to-peer dimension, and the news organisations merely provide a platform for this dialogue (Graham, 2013). The audience contributions to public communication are not insignificant (Fairclough and Fairclough, 2012), but the metaphor of platform easily emphasises role of journalists merely as hosts.

Another practice bearing on the notion of dialogue is live blogging (Thurman and Walters, 2013), where the collaboration of journalists and users extends to the selection of the materials submitted to public exposure (Thorsen, 2013: 139). However, the professional objective in live blogging within news organisations is not always set out to increase the dialogic quality of public communication. Rather, users are more often encouraged to take part in the quality control of news production by giving feedback and correcting errors (Thurman and Walters, 2013: 83; Domingo and Heikkilä, 2012: 280).

The increasing interaction with audiences clearly demonstrates that online news organisations indeed try to reach collaboratively beyond the issues of access or attention management. This ambition is, however, mostly directed at increasing citizens' participation *in journalism*. It is often linked to enhancing the credibility of journalism itself rather than to building interfaces for effective participation *through journalism*. This reflects the newsrooms' preoccupation with being able to sustain a loyal readership in the volatile media environment. What often matters most in digital dialogic journalism is the symbolic presence of 'people' configuring in the coverage. Lively interaction with the audience is thought of as a symbol of the popular acceptance of journalism (in other words, legitimacy). In this context, the demand for better dialogue still retains its critical edge. It reminds us of the more demanding aspects of interaction – reciprocity, authenticity and mutual recognition – that could enrich the professional imagination of journalists to be better attuned to the 'voice' of citizens in its full meaning (see, for example, Couldry, 2010).

Better deliberation? Deliberation raises the stakes in the evaluation of participation by shifting the focus from the moments of dialogue in the media to the efficacy of participation beyond the immediate mediated interaction. Most concretely, such efficacy can refer to political decisions which would be influenced by citizen participation. In participatory journalism, new features aimed at mutual problem-solving are explicit, for instance, in wikijournalism and crowdsourcing, wherein citizens are assigned to gather information and refine it into knowledge as it is published (Muthukumaraswamy, 2010).

In wikijournalism, online platforms enable multiple authors to add, remove and edit content in a collaborative process of news production. Technically, wikis hold the promise of moving away from the linear models of call-response communication to simultaneous, parallel and many-to-many communications (Bradshaw, 2009). Given that wikis aim at bringing diffuse debates to a single platform and producing coherent representations, they could indeed be regarded as a means for reaching the states of temporary consensus, the ideal goal of deliberation (ibid.: 251). Experiences with wikijournalism show that reaching such consensus requires active coordination for being genuinely deliberative. Despite the fact that there is some empirical evidence of how news organisations have assumed a role in coordination, this task is not as yet treated as central to professional journalism.

Similar ideas can be seen in the practice of journalistic crowdsourcing that aspires to "harness collective intelligence of users rather than merely collecting user-generated content" (Vehkoo, 2013: 5). Crowdsourcing thus rests on the idea that citizens can collectively know more than journalists, especially if they are not regarded as 'amateurs' (Brabham, 2012). Another important feature is the idea of open-endedness. Journalism is seen as an unfinished process, a set of tentative factual versions of reality that require elaboration through citizen participation. McNair (2013: 83) notes that in crowdsourcing, users take part in the "transformation of raw or half-cooked data into processed news or commentary", and Bradshaw (2007: 3) reports that the most successful efforts of wikijournalism have been based on "something that is slightly unfinished".

It seems feasible to say that the goals for deliberative processes appear more easily attainable in the context of digital journalism than, for instance, through the designs of public journalism projects in the 1990s. Even if wikijournalism and crowdsourcing projects have not as yet lived up to their potential, there are a number of examples where crowdsourcing has been incorporated to impressive collaborative fact-checking and analysis. *The Guardian*'s investigation of the expenses of MPs in the UK is probably the best-known test case (Daniel and Flew, 2010), but there are others (Vehkoo, 2013).

However, despite the many radical promises of re-scaling citizen participation and providing new ways of 'knowing together', the developments in digital landscape have not emptied out the critical potential of the 'deliberative' framework. While wiki-platforms and crowdsourcing experiments can inspire and mobilise citizens, they may still run short of the *intersubjective* exchanges that are at the core of deliberative theory. A demanding notion of deliberation assumes that participators recognise the differences in each other, try to look at the world from the perspective of others and thereafter submit themselves to the negotiated transformations. This intersubjective dynamics is not very strongly articulated in wikis and crowdsourcing experiments. Thus, they may result in a transformation of journalism, but not necessarily that of citizens. Critical discourse about journalism should still remind us that while the wisdom of the 'crowd' in the new journalism may be collective, it is not necessarily deliberative.

Conclusion

In the current context of rapid change, it is useful to think of journalism as a *practice of public participation in the present moment*. This notion is broad enough to cover different journalistic traditions while retaining the core that ties together alternative, community and mainstream media. Without designating to journalism the task of fostering participation and its efficacy, journalism would lose its democratic potential. Without a critical vocabulary that identifies how journalistic practices impede or enable effective participation, journalism would cease to be public and accountable. Thus, the fate of civic participation in digital journalism will depend on both: the practical innovativeness and fearlessness of citizens and journalists, and the ability of other stakeholders – including scholars – to recognise the democratic affordances in these experiments.

Clearly, the old conceptualisations inherited from the mass media age do not capture exhaustively the democratic potentials embedded in new forms of journalism. Nonetheless, these concepts are not connected merely to particular versions of journalism or media structures but also to a broader and historically informed understanding of democracy, power and participation. Therefore, rethinking them – rather than abandoning them – helps us assess the democratic potential of new forms of 'participatory journalism'. This is much needed if we do not merely want to consider the impact of new participatory practices on journalism, but also their potential impact on society.

A cross-examination of the new and old vocabulary can help us ask sharper questions. An appropriate case for such scrutiny is the ambitious new journalism venture *The Intercept*, established in the aftermath of the Snowden–NSA revelations by the founder of eBay, Pierre Omidyar, and a group of renowned journalists and documentarists such as Glenn Greenwald and Laura Poitras. In addition, NUY professor Jay Rosen briefly joined the team as an adviser. Rosen, who in the public journalism movement of the 1990s had gained prominence by rethinking a democratic role for journalism and who has since become a proponent of internet-based citizen journalism, reflected on this venture with a new vocabulary.

In a blog post corroborating his role in *The Intercept* (still unnamed at that time) in November 2013, Rosen (2013) stayed committed to the link between journalism and public participation. But rather than envisioning journalism as an active facilitator of better access, dialogue and deliberation, he endorsed the role of individual journalists and their capacities to create 'a following' in the face of a new type of attention economy. He envisioned that many citizens joining the audience as followers would be happy to just read and monitor the coverage, but a small part of them could also become contributors and producers and join the team in confronting the powers that be. While suggesting a sort of 'franchising journalism', Rosen seemed to move beyond the vocabulary we have been working on above by replacing access, dialogue and deliberation with *attention, identification* and *confrontation*. This articulation retains a connection to the older vocabulary. At the same time, it is clear that its deliberative ethos is apparently thinner and more individualistic.

This quick analysis is arguably an oversimplification of what is to emerge out of the new landscape of media and democracy. However, for the time being, it leads us to two troubling questions to conclude with: Should we be concerned about the democratic language with which such journalism can be called accountable? Or should we simply celebrate that here the discourse about journalism increasingly becomes a discourse about politics and political action?

Further reading

Singer, J. B., Hermida, A., Domingo, D., Heinonen, A., Paulussen, S., Quandt, T., Reich, Z. and Vujnovic, M. (2011). *Participatory Journalism: Guarding Open Gates at Online Newspapers*, Chichester: Wiley-Blackwell. This book discusses the practices of participatory journalism at various stages of the journalistic production in ten countries.

Habermas, J. (2006). "Political communication in media society: Does democracy still enjoy an epistemic dimension? The impact of normative theory on empirical research." *Communication Theory*, 16(4), 411–26. This article elaborates theoretically on how the media system may enhance deliberative democracy.

Dahlgren, P. (2009) *Media and Political Engagement: Citizens, Communication and Democracy*. Cambridge: Cambridge University Press. This book provides a useful overall conceptual model to think about media and participation, also synthesising different theoretical discourses about the topic.

Carpentier, N. (2011) *Media and Participation: A Site of Ideological-Democratic Struggle*. Bristol: Intellect. This book provides a rich theoretical discussion on the notion of participation, arguing also for the link between participation and power.

References

Atton, C. (1999) "A reassessment of the alternative press." *Media, Culture and Society*, 21(1), 51–76.
Barnhurst, K. (2011) "The new 'media affect' and the crisis of representation for political communication." *International Journal of Press/Politics*, 16(4), 573–93.

Beckett, C. (2010) *The Value of Networked Journalism*. London: London School of Economics and Political Science.

Benkler, Y. (2006) *The Wealth of Networks: How Social Production Transforms Markets and Freedom*. New Haven, CT: Yale University Press.

Bohman, J. and Rehg, W. (eds) (1997) *Deliberative Democracy*. Cambridge, MA: MIT Press.

Bowman, S. and Willis C. (2003) *We Media: How Audiences Are Shaping the Future of News and Information*. Reston, VA: Media Center at the American Press Institute.

Brabham, D. C. (2012) "The myth of amateur crowds." *Information, Communication and Society*, 15(3), 394–410.

Bradshaw, P. (2007) "Wiki journalism: Are wikis the new blogs?" Presented at the Future of Newspapers Conference, Cardiff, UK, 12–13 September.

——(2009) "Wiki journalism." In S. Allan and E. Thorsen (eds), *Citizen Journalism: Global Perspectives*. New York: Peter Lang (pp. 243–54).

Carpentier, N. (2011) "New configurations of the audience? The challenges of user-generated content for audience theory and media participation." In V. Nightingale (ed.), *The Handbook of Media Audiences*. Chichester: Wiley-Blackwell (pp. 190–212).

Castells, M. (2009) *Communication Power*. Oxford: Oxford University Press.

Chadwick, A. (2013) *The Hybrid Media System: Politics and Power*. Oxford: Oxford University Press.

Couldry, N. (2010) *Why Voice Matters: Culture and Politics after Neoliberalism*. London: Sage.

Dahlgren, P. (2013) *The Political Web: Media, Participation and Alternative Democracy*. Basingstoke: Palgrave.

Daniel, A. and Flew, T. (2010) "The *Guardian* reportage of the UK MP expenses scandal: A case study of computational journalism." Presented at the Communications Policy and Research Forum, Sydney, Australia, 15–16 November.

Domingo, D. and Heikkilä, H. (2012) "Media accountability practices in online news media." In E. Siapera and A. Veglis (eds), *The Handbook of Global Online Journalism*. Chichester: Wiley-Blackwell (pp. 272–89).

Ericson, R., Baranek, P. and Chan, J. (1989) *Negotiating Control: A Study of News Sources*. Toronto: University of Toronto Press.

Fairclough, I. and Fairclough. N. (2012) *Political Discourse Analysis: A Method for Advanced Students*. London: Routledge

Friedland, L. A. (2003) *Public Journalism: Past and Future*. Dayton, OH: Kettering Foundation.

Glasser, T. (ed.) (1999) *The Idea of Public Journalism*. New York: Guilford Press.

Goode, L. (2009) "Social news, citizen journalism and democracy." *New Media and Society*, 11(8), 1287–1305.

Graham, T. (2013) "Talking back, but is anyone listening? Journalism and comment fields." In C. Peters and M. Broersma (eds), *Rethinking Journalism: Trust and Participation in a Transformed News Landscape*. Abingdon: Routledge (pp. 114–27).

Guru, G. (2005) *Jan Sunwai: A new instrument for democracy in India, Democracy Asia: State of democracy in South Asia Study*. Available at: www.democracy-asia.org/casestudies_studies_gopal_guru_pz.htm

Habermas, J. (2006) "Political communication in media society: Does democracy still enjoy an epistemic dimension? The impact of normative theory on empirical research." *Communication Theory*, 16(4), 411–26.

Heikkilä, H. and Kunelius, R. (1998) "Access, dialogue, deliberation: Experimenting with three concepts of journalism criticism." *Nordicom Review*, 19(1), 71–84.

Hermida, A. (2010) "Twittering the news: The emergence of ambient journalism." *Journalism Practice*, 4(3), 297–308.

Jönsson, A. M. and Örnebring, H. (2011) "User-generated content and the news: Empowerment of citizens or interactive illusion?" *Journalism Practice*, 5(2), 127–44.

Lewis, S. (2012) "The tension between professional control and open participation." *Information, Communication and Society*, 15(6), 836–66.

Livingstone, S. and Lunt, P. (1994) *Talk on Television: Audience Participation and Public Debate*. London: Routledge.

McNair, B. (2013) "Trust, truth and objectivity: Sustaining quality journalism in the era of the content-generating user." In C. Peters and M. Broersma (eds), *Rethinking Journalism: Trust and Participation in a Transformed News Landscape*. Abingdon: Routledge (pp. 75–88).

Muthukumaraswamy, K. (2010) "When the media meet crowds of wisdom: How journalists are tapping into audience expertise and manpower for the processes of newsgathering." *Journalism Practice*, 4(1), 48–65.

Pantti, M. (2012) "Getting closer? Encounters of the national media with global citizen images." *Journalism Studies*, 14(2), 201–18.

Peters, J. (1999) "Public journalism and democratic theory: Four challenges." In T. Glasser (ed.), The Idea of Public Journalism. New York: Guilford Press (pp. 99–117).

Rosen, J. (1999) *What Are Journalists For?* New Haven, CT: Yale University Press.

——(2013) "Out of the press box and onto the field." *Pressthink*, November 17. Retrieved from http://pressthink.org/ (accessed 15 January 2015).

Shoemaker, P. (1991) *Communication Concepts 3: Gatekeeping*. Newbury Park, CA: Sage.

Singer, J. B., Hermida, A., Domingo, D., Heinonen, A., Paulussen, S., Quandt, T., Reich, Z. and Vujnovic, M. (2011) *Participatory Journalism: Guarding Open Gates at Online Newspapers*. Chichester: Wiley-Blackwell.

Thorsen, E. (2013) "Live blogging and social media curation: Challenges and opportunities for journalism." In K. Fowler and S. Allan (eds), *Journalism: New Challenge*. Bournemouth: Centre for Journalism & Communication Research Bournemouth University (pp. 123–45).

Thurman, N. (2008) "Forms for citizen journalists? Adoption of user-generated content initiatives by online news media." *New Media and Society*, 10, 139–57.

Thurman, N. and Walters, A. (2013) "Live blogging – digital journalism's pivotal platform? A case study of the production, consumption, and form of Live Blogs at Guardian.co.uk." *Digital Journalism*, 1(1), 82–101.

Vehkoo, J. (2013) *Crowdsourcing in Investigative Journalism: Report*. Reuters Institute for the Study of Journalism. Oxford: University of Oxford.

Wardle, C. and Williams, A. (2010) "Beyond user-generated content: A production study examining the ways in which UGC is used at the BBC." *Media, Culture and Society*, 32(5), 781–99.

14

THE POLITICAL ECONOMY OF CAPITALIST AND ALTERNATIVE SOCIAL MEDIA

Christian Fuchs and Marisol Sandoval

This chapter provides an overview of political economy questions that arise when discussing the relationship of capitalist and alternative social media. We begin by clarifying the notion of social media, before going on to examine aspects of the political economy of alternative media. We then apply these aspects to the realm of social media in order to discuss the relationship between capitalist and alternative social media. This includes a discussion of the contradictory character of social media in the Occupy movement.

What are social media?

During the past fifteen years, a number of new platforms have become prominent and now range among the 50 most-accessed World Wide Web (WWW) sites in the world (alexa.com 2013). They include:

- social networking sites: Facebook (#2, founded in 2004), LinkedIn (#8, 2003), VKontakte (#22, 2006);
- video-sharing platforms: YouTube (#3, 2005), XVideos (#41, 1997);
- wikis: Wikipedia (#6, 2001);
- blogs: Blogspot (#12, 1999), Wordpress (#15, 2003), Blogger (#38, 1999);
- microblogs: Twitter (#10, 2006), Sina Weibo (#34, 2009);
- online pinboards: Tumblr (#25, 2007), Pinterest (#27, 2010); and
- photo-sharing sites: Instagram (#37, 2010).

These platforms allow users to generate and share texts and multimedia contents and/or to collaboratively create and edit content and/or to communicate with a self-defined network of contacts and friends. Given the focus on sharing, communication and collaboration, some observers have argued that the Internet and the WWW have fundamentally changed. The notions of Web 2.0 and social media have been introduced in this context (Levinson, 2012; Mandiberg, 2012; O'Reilly, 2005; O'Reilly and Battelle, 2009; Shirky, 2011). Levinson (2012) has termed these platforms "new new media".

Is it not the case, though, that all media are social, if only because they enable the organisation of society and the communication of information? The question that therefore needs to be asked is: What does it mean to be social? Finding answers requires engagement with social theories and theories of society (Fuchs, 2014c). Depending on which concept of the social one utilises – for example, Karl Marx's notion of collaborative work, Ferdinand Tönnies's concept of communities, Max Weber's notions of social action and social relations, Émile Durkheim's concept of social facts and so on – we might find different ways to differentiate social media from 'non-social' media.

An integrated model of sociality distinguishes various levels of sociality that are dialectically interconnected (Fuchs, 2014c). For the media world, this means that specific media support specific information processes and do not support others – the telephone, for example, supports communication, but is not well suited for collaborative work.

The internet has for a long time supported processes of cognition, communication and collaboration (Fuchs, 2008, 2014c). Online collaboration has not emerged with wikis, but was much earlier enabled by Computer-Supported Collaborative Work (CSCW) systems. Blogs, microblogs, wikis, social networking sites, content-sharing platforms and pinboards are therefore not radically new. They do, however, often offer integrated forms of cognition, communication and collaboration on one platform, with the consequence that modes of sociality converge within platforms (Fuchs, 2014c). With the rise of the above-mentioned platforms, community maintenance and collaborative work have become more important on the internet (ibid.). These sites do not constitute a fundamental digital revolution, but rather simultaneously sustain and transform the social online so that the social media world has become more complex (ibid.).

The political economy of alternative media

Definitions of alternative media can be categorised into more subjective and more objective approaches (Sandoval and Fuchs, 2010; Fuchs, 2010). Subjective approaches stress the active participation in the production and circulation of media content; people organise and control the media themselves in DIY processes – alternative media are considered as participatory, as 'citizens' media' (Atton, 2002; Carpentier, 2011; Rodríguez, 2001). Objective approaches are more interested in content. They argue that alternative media diffuse content and worldviews that question dominant realities, provide critical information and give voice to critical viewpoints that tend to be marginalised in the mainstream media – especially the views of progressive social movements and activists – and have a vision of an alternative society without domination (Downing, 2001; Negt and Kluge, 1993; O'Sullivan, 1995).

Table 14.1 Characteristics of alternative media and capitalist media (based on Sandoval and Fuchs, 2010; Sandoval, 2009).

		Capitalist mass media	*Ideal alternative media*	
Media structure	Economic form of media products	Media product as commodity	Non-commercial media product	
	Content of media products	Ideological content	Critical content	
Media actors	Consumers	Many consumers	Critical consumers	Critical prosumers
	Producers	Few producers	Critical producers	

Table 14.1 provides an ideal-typical model of alternative media. It identifies various potential dimensions of alternative media and contrasts them to capitalist 'mainstream' media. The model is based on a media communication model that distinguishes between media actors (media producers, media consumers, audiences and users) and media structures (structures of ownership and control, form and content structures) that are interconnected in a structure-agency dialectic. Media producers create contents under specific organisational structures and media forms that are distributed in society and thereby reach media consumers who react to the provided content in different ways, providing further incentives for media production.

Capitalist mass media are privately owned and accumulate capital by selling media content as well as audiences for that content. These media often disseminate ideological content that does not question, but rather affirms capitalist society or that advances reductionist views and prejudices against minorities (Fuchs, 2011; Golding and Murdock, 1997; Wasko, Murdock and Sousa, 2011). These media also tend to marginalise critical voices and activists who struggle for a participatory democracy that replaces capitalism. The commercial structure of these media can often act as a form of economic censorship: the profit mechanism is not questioned because corporate media operate on this principle themselves; companies are important advertising clients and the rich important consumers that are especially interesting for advertisers (ibid.). Given these conditions, capitalist media are more likely to affirm capitalism and domination than to be critical of it.

In capitalist mass media, there is typically a division between professional media producers and media consumers. In the ideal type of alternative media, media consumers are also media producers who create engaging, multidimensional, dialectical and critical content, and collectively own and control media organisations. Ideal alternative media also include an engaged critical public that is active in vivid critical public debates about politics, culture and society. In the alternative media model, there is no separation between media producers and consumers. The ideal type of alternative media combines what we have termed subjective and objective definitions of alternative media (Fuchs, 2010; Sandoval, 2009; Sandoval and Fuchs, 2010).

The critical political economy of the media and communication is an approach that studies the production, circulation and consumption of information in the context of capitalism, power structures, domination and inequality (Mosco, 2009). It is a normative approach to the extent that it relates the created knowledge to the ideal of a society and to a media system that benefits all and that practices sympathy with progressive social movements. Given that alternative media exist within capitalist society, a society based on fundamental inequalities, it is therefore not just important to study alternative media practices and structures, but to relate such studies to a critical political-economic analysis of alternative media and corporate media. Not all dimensions of alternative media are always present in one particular alternative medium because of the contradictions of the political economy of capitalism that makes influence dependent on the control of money and political power, which are resources that alternative media tend to criticise. The model of alternative media presented in Table 14.1 is therefore an ideal type with analytical dimensions that may or may not be observed in reality. It enables us to provide answers to the question of what the term 'alternative' in the category of 'alternative media' can actually mean: alternatives do not just have one, but multiple dimensions and meanings.

The political economy of capitalism imposes a fundamental limit on contemporary alternative media: within capitalism, to reach the broader public requires money, people, reputation and political influence, but capitalism is a society grounded in the asymmetric distribution of political, economic and cultural resources. The ruling political-economic class, albeit inherently antagonistic itself and therefore split up into competing factions, tends as a contradictory united hegemonic bloc to dominate society. Alternative media tend to be critical of the ruling class and therefore often face resource inequalities: the history of alternative media is a history of precarious voluntary work. Such media tend to lack money, attention, influence and other resources. If, on the one hand, alternative media adopt the predominant mechanisms of power, such as advertising, intellectual property rights, for-profit sales, association with political parties or state funding, they are facing the danger of losing their autonomy and their capacity to be critical. If, on the other hand, they reject these mechanisms, they face the problem of how to mobilise resources. Their voices then tend to remain marginal, and their organisations tend to be based on unpaid and voluntary work of people who in addition to media activism must earn a living in the capitalist economy, which threatens the stability and existence of alternative media.

Alternative media exist against and cannot truly exist within capitalism. *They face a fundamental antagonism between critical autonomy and voice* (Fuchs, 2010; Sandoval and Fuchs, 2010). As Atton and Hamilton (2008: 26) put it, the "general political-economic dilemma for any critical project is that it needs resources with which to work, but those crucial resources are present only in the very society that it seeks to change or dissolve".

Capitalist social media

Herbert Schiller (1991) revised his early concept of cultural imperialism as American empire by arguing that contemporary cultural imperialism predominantly takes the form of transnational corporate domination, in which transnational capitalist companies tend to control the media and culture, colonise these realms by the logic of capital accumulation and exert pressure in order to make states liberalise, privatise and deregulate media and culture and to create deregulated precarious working conditions for cultural workers.

Dal Yong Jin (2013) analysed the political economy of the most frequently used web platforms and found that 98 per cent are for-profit and only 2 per cent non-profit; 88 per cent use targeted advertising as capital accumulation model, and 10 per cent other models such as the sale of products and services, subscriptions/pay-per-view and classified ads. Jin concludes that the capitalist domination of the internet constitutes a form of cultural imperialism in Schiller's (1991) understanding of the term. Jin calls this 'platform imperialism'. Although there was also a minority of Chinese, Japanese, Russian, British, Brazilian and French platforms, 72 per cent of the sites in the sample are owned by transnational US companies. Most non-American platforms also use the targeted advertising model that has resulted in major concerns about users' privacy, the exploitation of digital labour and the commercialisation of life (ibid.). Chinese companies owned 17 per cent of platforms analysed in the sample, but given the dominance of neoliberalism with Chinese characteristics (Harvey, 2005; Zhao, 2008) it is no surprise that "Chinese platforms, including Baidu, QQ, and Taobao, utilize the targeted advertising capital business model, which is not different from US Internet capitalism" (Jin, 2013: 166).

Social media and protest movements

An important question about contemporary politics is what role social media have played in contemporary political and revolutionary movements, such as the Arab Spring, Occupy, 15-M in Spain, the Indignant Citizens Movement in Greece, Yo Soy 132 in Mexico, the Taksim Gezi Park movement in Turkey, the Free Fare Movement in Brazil and the opposition in the Syrian civil war. Whereas some scholars' claims that contemporary revolutions and rebellions are social media movements or networked protests of connective action (Castells, 2012; Bennett and Segerberg, 2013; see Fuchs, 2014c: chapters 4 and 8 and 2014b for a detailed criticism) reflect the populist and techno-determinist sentiments of the tabloid press about 'Facebook and Twitter revolutions', other scholars have warned that such arguments are technologically determinist and neglect that social media are not only activists' tools, but are also shaped by state and capitalist power (Fuchs, 2012, 2014b, 2014c; Morozov, 2013). In addition, social media do not seem to result in democratic networked organisation structures, but are embedded into hierarchies, internal power structures and the formation of elites within social movements (Gerbaudo, 2012).

The optimism that surrounds social media overestimates the role of digital media in protest movements; we argue that optimism should be substituted by an approach that uses a combination of critical theories of society and empirical social research. This approach would ground a dialectical theory of media and society, and inform empirical studies of the role and relationship of capitalist and non-capitalist media and of digital and non-digital media in contemporary social movements.

Activists' use of social media

OccupyMedia! The Occupy Movement and Social Media in Crisis Capitalism (Fuchs, 2014b) presents the results of a survey in which 429 respondents who described themselves as Occupy activists participated. Studying activists' experiences with and attitudes towards corporate and alternative social media was one of the study's main tasks. The survey confirmed that contemporary movements tend to use capitalist social media as well as activist-run alternative digital media platforms and that there is a contradiction between their use of these two types of media; 48.9 per cent of the respondents say that during the protests they at least once per month shared photos in Facebook–Occupy groups, whereas only 15.3 per cent did the same on alternative social networking sites such as Diaspora*, N-1 or Occupii. Furthermore, 62.8 per cent of the respondents used Facebook at least four times a month during the protests for communicating or discussing with other activists, whereas 30.0 per cent used various Occupy chats for the same purpose at least four times per month and 16.6 per cent Riseup communication tools for the same number of times. Whereas 61.5 per cent of the respondents had at least four personal face-to-face conversations per month during the protests that aimed at mobilising others, 54.3 per cent at least four times a month posted announcements on their Facebook profile for the same purpose. And 43.2 per cent posted at least four times a month mobilisation communications in Occupy groups on Facebook. In contrast, 6.5 per cent at least four times per month posted mobilisation-oriented announcements to their own profile on the alterative social networking site Occupii. The share of the same activity was 4.2 per cent on N-1 profiles and 1.4 per cent on Diaspora* profiles.

The data indicate that contemporary political activists tend to use capitalist social media to a much higher degree than they do activist-run alternative social media, whether for activist communication, reaching the public or protest mobilisation. Why is this the case? One respondent argued: "All the activists are already there, but so are regular people. I think it's one of the main goals of the Occupy movement to reach out to the rest of the 99% … Facebook is the only place where we can speak to the people." Also, 69.5 per cent of survey respondents said that the big advantage of commercial social media such as Facebook, YouTube and Twitter is that activists can reach out to the public and everyday people.

Activists' use of corporate social media seems to face a contradiction between the possibilities for better communication and the risk of corporate and state control of protest communication. Facebook, Google and other corporate social media are making billions of dollars in advertising revenue every year (Fuchs, 2014c). They are part of the 1 per cent of rich owners and managers that dominate the economy. Why do the rest of the people – what Occupy calls the 99 per cent – trust that these companies will deal with their data in a responsible manner and not censor them? Edward Snowden's revelation of the PRISM surveillance system shows the dangers of the surveillance-industrial complex, in which Google, Facebook and others support and provide data to the National Security Agency (NSA). Evidence has indicated that social media surveillance has also been directed at protestors and civil society activists (Hodai, 2013). State intelligence institutions and private corporations have long collaborated, but access to social media has resulted in new qualities of the surveillance-industrial complex: it is now possible to obtain detailed access to a multitude of citizens' activities in multiple roles conducted in multiple spaces that all converge on social media profiles that contain a lot of data about the everyday life, activities and movements of billions of people. Another economic dimension is that the NSA has subcontracted and outsourced surveillance tasks to around 2,000 private security companies, such as Booz Allen Hamilton.

Activists are aware of the reality of corporate and state surveillance on corporate social media; 55.9 per cent of the respondents indicate that state and corporate surveillance of activist communication is a huge disadvantage of commercial social media. Activists expressed this fear in various ways:

> My Twitter account was subpoena'd, for tweeting a hashtag. The subpoena was dropped in court.

> Individuals I have supported have had Facebook accounts suspended, tweets catalogued as evidence against them, and this available information used for police to pre-emptively arrest them.

> The other risk is that commercial sites might collaborate with government or corporate interests to close down sites if a threat to their interests became apparent.

> Facebook = Tracebook. We're contributing to capitalism by putting our content for free [on these sites].

The contradiction of corporate social media that activists are facing is that, while they enable activists to communicate easily among themselves and to the public, at the same time the same media expose activists to police surveillance, corporate control, corporate censorship and the exploitation of digital labour (Fuchs, 2014a).

Alternative social media

There are only two not-for-profit platforms among the 100 most-accessed platforms in the world: Wikipedia (#6) and the BBC's website (#52). These are non-capitalist media run by civil society (Wikipedia) and the state (BBC), a circumstance that can be explained with the help of Graham Murdock's (2011) distinction between three modern political economies that are controlled by (a) capital, (b) the state and (c) civil society, and based on (a) commodities, (b) public goods and (c) gifts. Wikipedia is an expression of the gift economy: it is run by a non-profit civil society organisation (the Wikimedia Foundation), is based on the collaborative work of volunteers and provides its content without payment to the public. The BBC is a classic public service broadcaster that is organised by the British state, is funded by a license fee and has no profit imperative. Analyses show that in the political economy of the internet and social media, alternatives to the capitalist internet and capitalist social media are small minorities (Fuchs, 2014c; Jin, 2013; Sandoval, 2012).

Wikipedia can be considered as an alternative social and digital medium in respect to its organisational model, the role of users as producers and its non-profit imperative (Fuchs, 2014c: chapter 10). Public service media have at least one potential alternative dimension in comparison to capitalist media: they reject the for-profit imperative and are not the private property of capitalists. They may or may not (or only from time to time) advance critical content, depending to which level the logic of capital, commercial culture and tabloidisation has affected public service media or left them unaffected (the BBC, for example, broadcasts critical documentaries such as *The Virtual Revolution: The Cost of Free* on the one hand tabloid programmes such as *Bargain Hunt* and on the other hand that are in no way different from many entertainment programmes on commercial channels such as Channel 4). Despite both being non-profit, Wikipedia and the BBC have two very different online models and understandings of social media. Wikipedia encompasses many of the ideals of online participatory culture, whereas the BBC often sees the internet and social media as an extension of broadcasting.

The data from the OccupyMedia! survey (Fuchs, 2014b) presented earlier indicates that contemporary activists tend to use their own profiles and protest group pages and profiles on Facebook, Twitter and YouTube much more than separate non-commercial social media platforms. Progressive social movements seem to prefer corporate social media to communicate counter-hegemonic critical content (a key dimension of alternative media). At the same time, these media platforms are controlled by corporate and state power, which renders the organisational form and the political economy of protest movements' use of corporate social media not alternative at all.

By contrast, non-commercial social media platforms such as Diaspora*, N-1, Occupii, Riseup and the various Occupy fora and networks are alternative in terms of organisational structures, content and actors. They are non-profit media: activists produce, control, own and maintain them. They are relatively independent from state and corporate power, and designed as platforms for the dissemination of critical information and for activist communication. In short, there is a convergence of users and producers. They are ideal-typical examples of alternative social media. However, they face the same problem that confronts all alternative media in capitalist society: the antagonism between critical autonomy and voice.

The OccupyMedia! Survey asked activists what they consider the main advantages and disadvantages of alternative social media (Fuchs, 2014b). A significant share of the respondents (34.1%) could not name any advantages because they were unaware of the existence of alternative platforms. The most frequently mentioned advantages were that alternative social media provide more privacy for activists, that there is less censorship and surveillance and that they are non-profit and non-commercial. One respondent commented: "We own them, and so risks about monitoring etc. are diminished." Another one said that these platforms are "more ethical in that they're probably not putting money into the pockets of the 1%".

Of the respondents, 27.3 per cent said there are no disadvantages if the Occupy movement uses alternative social media; 30.7 per cent argued that alternative social media only have a low reach and do not allow reaching out to the general public. These respondents fear that by using alternative social media, the Occupy movement isolates itself; it does not speak to the public, only to itself. Of those surveyed, 19 per cent mentioned that operating and using these platforms requires that the movement mobilises significant resources: time, money, donations, workforce, software development and maintenance skills, servers, computers, webspace. One respondent felt that "many … [alternative social media] are too small to make a difference". The activists realise the political-economic limits that alternative media face in capitalism: Twitter and Facebook are monopoly capitalists that have centralised social media communication; it is extremely difficult to build alternative channels to challenge these monopolies. At the same time, running alternative media is expensive and work intensive, which poses the problem of resource scarcity for movements. One respondent pinpointed this antagonism:

"Alternative platforms ... seem to suck up time, energy and resources, and are ultimately less convenient to use because they are SO SPECIFIC to the movement" (original emphasis).

Conclusion

Alternative media, online and offline, are facing a political-economic dilemma. On the one hand, their self-management renders them more independent from the interests of the power elite whose domination activists want to challenge, but on the other hand, alternative media face the power of media monopolies and oligopolies, as well as the problem of mobilising resources without state support and advertising. Alternative media confront contradictions between *critical voice and autonomy on the one hand and resource scarcity and lack of visibility on the other*. As a consequence, the history of alternative media is a history of voluntary self-exploited labour, the consequence of a political economy that limits the possibilities for civil society because hearing alternative voices is a matter of money and political resources that afford visibility. The oligopoly structure of social media has resulted in a few large transnational companies (Facebook, Google, Twitter) controlling the vast majority of social media use. Given this control, it is very difficult to establish alternatives that question the very principles on which the capitalist media exist. Capitalist media structures limit the liberal freedoms of speech, opinion, expression, association and assembly. Liberalism is its own limit and immanent critique: liberal freedom of ownership limits citizens' liberal rights.

Are non-corporate social media in particular and non-commercial media in general doomed to failure in capitalism? If this were to be the case, could social movement activism ever expect an alternative communicative dimension that could reach beyond an alternative ghetto?

How to resource alternative media is a crucial democratic question of our times. The conclusion from the arguments in this chapter is to overcome capitalist media oligopolies, which requires major media reforms. Large multinational companies, including Google, Facebook, Amazon and Apple, are avoiding paying taxes in a lot of the countries where they operate. This is not only unfair; it also increases the pressure for austerity measures in times of crisis. We suggest taxing large media (and other) corporations and channelling this income into non-commercial media. This requires combining the increase of corporate taxation with elements of participatory budgeting that allow every citizen to donate a certain amount per year to a non-commercial media project. Elements of state action and civil society action could be combined: the power of the state would guarantee taxation of large companies; the distribution of this income to media projects would, however, be decentralised and put in the hands of citizens. This measure is far from ideal and has its own limits, but it may be a step forward in order to strengthen alternative media.

Further reading

Sandoval, M. (2014) *From Corporate to Social Media? Critical Perspectives on Corporate Social Responsibility in Media and Communication Industries.* London: Routledge. This book studies the political economy and ideologies of eight global capitalist media corporations and argues for alternatives.

Fuchs, C. (2014) *OccupyMedia! The Occupy Movement and Social Media in Crisis Capitalism*. Winchester: Zero Books. This author presents the result of an empirical survey that studied how the Occupy movement uses and thinks about corporate and alternative social media.

Fuchs, C. (2014) *Social Media: A Critical Introduction*. London: Sage. This title shows how critical theory and political economy can be used for analysing and understanding social media.

Fuchs, C. and Sandoval, M. (eds.) 2014. *Critique, Social Media and the Information Society*. New York: Routledge. The authors discuss how capitalism, power structures and social media are connected, and what an alternative internet can look like.

References

alexa.com (2013) *alexa Internet Statistics*. Retrieved from http://www.alexa.com (accessed 14 September 2013).

Atton, C. (2002) *Alternative Media*. London: Sage.

Atton, C. and Hamilton, J. (2008) *Alternative Journalism*. London: Sage.

Bennett, W. L. and Segerberg, A. (2013) *The Logic of Connective Action: Digital Media and the Personalization of Contentious Politics*. New York: Cambridge University Press.

Carpentier, N. (2011) *Media and Participation*. Bristol: Intellect.

Castells, M. (2012) *Networks of Outrage and Hope: Social Movements in the Internet Age*. Cambridge: Polity Press.

Downing, J. (with others) (2001) *Radical Media: Rebellious Communication and Social Movements*. Thousand Oaks, CA: Sage.

Fuchs, C. (2008) *Internet and Society: Social Theory in the Information Age*. New York: Routledge.

——(2010) "Alternative media as critical media." *European Journal of Social Theory*, 13(2), 173–92.

——(2011) *Foundations of Critical Media and Information Studies*. London: Routledge.

——(2012) "Some reflections on Manuel Castells' book *Networks of Outrage and Hope: Social Movements in the Internet Age*." *tripleC: Communication, Capitalism and Critique*, 10(2), 775–97.

——(2014a) *Digital Labour and Karl Marx*. New York: Routledge.

——(2014b) *OccupyMedia! The Occupy Movement and Social Media in Crisis Capitalism*. Winchester: Zero Books.

——(2014c) *Social Media: A Critical Introduction*. London: Sage.

Gerbaudo, P. (2012) *Tweets and the Streets*. London: Pluto Press.

Golding, P. and Murdock, G. (eds.) (1997) *The Political Economy of the Media*. Cheltenham: Edward Elgar.

Harvey, D. (2005) *A Brief History of Neoliberalism*. Oxford: Oxford University Press.

Hodai, B. (2013) *Dissent or Terror: How the Nation's "Counter Terrorism" Apparatus, in Partnership with Corporate America, Turned on Occupy Wall Street*. Retrieved from http://www.prwatch.org/files/Dissent%20or%20Terror%20FINAL.pdf (accessed 10 January 2015).

Jin, D. Y. (2013) "The construction of platform imperialism in the globalization era." *tripleC: Communication, Capitalism and Critique*, 11(1), 145–72.

Levinson, P. (2012) *New New Media*. Upper Saddle River, NJ: Pearson Education.

Mandiberg, M. (ed.) (2012) *The Social Media Reader*. New York: New York University Press.

Morozov, E. (2013) *To Save Everything, Click Here*. London: Penguin.

Mosco, V. (2009) *The Political Economy of Communication* (2nd edn). London: Sage.

Murdock, G. (2011) "Political economies as moral economies: Commodities, gifts, and public goods." In J. Wasko, G. Murdock and H. Sousa (eds), *The Handbook of the Political Economy of Communications*. Chichester: Wiley-Blackwell (pp. 13–40).

Negt, O. and Kluge, A. (1993) *Public Sphere and Experience: Towards an Analysis of the Bourgeois and Proletarian Public Sphere*. Minneapolis: University of Minnesota Press.

O'Reilly, T. (2005) "What is Web 2.0?" Retrieved from http://www.oreillynet.com/pub/a/oreilly/tim/news/2005/09/30/what-is-web-20.html?page=1 (accessed 10 January 2015).

O'Reilly, T. and Battelle, J. (2009) *Web Squared: Web 2.0 Five Years On*. Special report. Retrieved from http://assets.en.oreilly.com/1/event/28/web2009_websquared-whitepaper.pdf (accessed 10 January 2015).

O'Sullivan, T. (1995) "Alternative media." In T. O'Sullivan, J. Hartley, D. Sounders, M. Montgomery and J. Fiske (eds), *Key Concepts in Communication and Cultural Studies*. London: Routledge (p. 10).

Rodríguez, C. (2001) *Fissures in the Mediascape: An International Study of Citizens' Media*. New York: Hampton Press.

Sandoval, M. (2009) "A critical contribution to the foundations of alternative media studies." *Kurgu Online: International Journal of Communication Studies*, 1(2009), 1–18.

——(2012) "A critical empirical case study of consumer surveillance on Web 2.0." In C. Fuchs, K. Boersma, A. Albrechtslund and M. Sandoval (eds), *Internet and Surveillance*. New York: Routledge (pp. 147–69).

Sandoval, M. and Fuchs, C. (2010) "Towards a critical theory of alternative media." *Telematics and Informatics*, 27(2), 141–50.

Schiller, H. I. (1991) "Not-yet the post-imperialist era." In D. K. Thussu (ed.), *International Communication: A Reader*. London: Routledge (pp. 247–61).

Shirky, C. (2011) *Cognitive Surplus: How Technology Makes Consumers into Collaborators*. London: Penguin.

Wasko, J., Murdock, H. G. and Sousa, H. (eds.) (2011) *The Handbook of the Political Economy of Communications*. Chichester: Wiley-Blackwell.

Zhao, Y. (2008) *Communication in China: Political Economy, Power, and Conflict*. Lanham, MD: Rowman & Littlefield.

Part III
POLICIES AND ECONOMIES

15
COMMUNITY MEDIA POLICY

Peter M. Lewis

Definitions and scope

This chapter is concerned with policies involving official recognition and financial support (or the lack of it) for community media, and with the regulation of media (radio, television) which use the airwaves in addition to using the internet. The rapid growth of social media has affected both mainstream and community media, and its relationship to the latter is discussed towards the end of the chapter.

Community media is a term which embraces a range of media – press, photography, film, graphic arts, theatre, radio, video – to name the media which up till recently have been the most prominent. All have in common three features: they are not run for profit but for social gain and community benefit; they are owned by and accountable to the communities they seek to serve; and they provide for participation by the community in production and in management. In the words of AMARC and Panos, "[It] is not about doing something for the community, but about the community doing something for itself, i.e., owning and controlling its own means of communication" (AMARC Africa and Panos Southern Africa, 1998).

The communities concerned may be geographically defined or, more commonly in this digital age, communities of interest, linked for example by language and ethnic origin, by gender or sexual orientation, by political ties, by lifestyle or by artistic and musical tastes. Community media can be seen as a subset of Atton's 'alternative media' (Atton, 2001), and other labels that have been proposed for this type of media are 'participatory' (Servaes, 1999; Gumucio Dagron, 2001), 'citizens' (Rodríguez, 2001) and 'radical' (Downing, 2001). The last label points to the use of media by oppressed or marginalised groups in political struggle.

The timeline of this discussion reaches back to the late 1940s when Radio Sutatenza began broadcasting in Colombia and Pacifica's KPFA came on air in Berkeley, California. Neither at that time used the prefix 'community' which, as a notion, expresses both coherence and difference, is both imagined and experienced materially. By the late 1960s, a period in which rebellion against the scale of corporate institutions was widespread, 'community' became attached to health, housing and law projects, to name but a few examples. In the same period, its use in relation to electronic media was canonised by the regulatory authorities in Canada and the US to describe cable TV channels set aside for use by community groups. By the mid-1970s, Australia had joined the US and Canada in making official space for community radio, but it was community video that first crossed the Atlantic in the same decade and enjoyed brief official recognition on cable networks in Europe. By the end of the 1970s, radio had become the most prominent expression of community media in Europe, whether in the *radios libres* of Italy, France and Belgium, or in the more ordered devolution in Scandinavia and the Netherlands. By the mid-1980s, the French radio landscape included, alongside a burgeoning commercial sector, a sector of community radio (*radios associatives*), officially regulated and funded by a levy on the profits of the commercial sector. Community radio developed in various guises and with differing means of support across Europe, struggling in post-communist Eastern and Central Europe, and finally, after three decades of campaigning, achieving recognition in the UK at the turn of the millennium. The campaign to achieve official recognition in the UK is used as a case study in the section that follows.

Alongside this timeline should be laid the international support for community media. The MacBride Report, commissioned by UNESCO, upheld the complaint of the developing world about the unjust effects of allowing information to be at the mercy of the free play of market forces and asserted the need for communication to be regarded as a matter of human rights (UNESCO, 1980: 172). The same injustice was to be found at the national level, where the absence of space for a voice in mainstream media led to a search for alternatives. UNESCO's concern to address the situation at both global and local levels was, during the 1970s, underpinned by seminars and by studies commissioned for its series *Reports and Papers on Mass Communication*. In the same period, the Council of Europe commissioned reports on a range of community media projects. The nascent research community formed by the authors of these reports was consolidated by the creation in 1982 of the Local Radio and Television Group (now the Community Communication Section) within the International Association for Media and Communication Research (www.iamcr. org). The following year saw the founding conference in Montreal of AMARC (the French acronym now generally used for the World Association of Community Radio Broadcasters, www.amarc.org), a meeting that was important in establishing global connections not only for academic researchers, but between community radio practitioners and activists in different parts of the world. The European branch of AMARC, AMARC-Europe, published a community radio charter in 1994 (Lewis, 2006: 27).

Discursive space: The case of the UK campaign for community radio

Activism has been as necessary in this field as in other alternative movements. To gain a place on a government's policy agenda, it is necessary to win over public opinion, which in turn means gaining mainstream media attention. The campaign over three decades to establish community radio on a permanent basis in the UK will be used to illustrate the problems of creating a discursive space enabling the phenomenon to be recognised and debated by different sectors of opinion (for a fuller account of the campaign, see Lewis, 2012). The campaign had its origins in the experimental cable TV pilots in the early 1970s. Influenced by North American experience, British community video practitioners took advantage of the licences awarded to commercial cable companies by a Conservative government to experiment in community programming. The cable companies were losing subscribers as improved broadcast coverage rendered their service redundant. Local TV, they calculated, might win back viewers, and good behaviour might earn the eventual reward of pay TV. The return of a Labour government in 1974 put an end to those hopes, and all but one of the pilots were abruptly closed down. The consequent anger and frustration led to the founding in 1977 of the Community Communications Group (COMCOM), whose comments on an official report (the Annan Report) on future directions for broadcasting included radical proposals for a community radio sector (COMCOM, 1977). COMCOM's Local Radio Working Party gave evidence to a Parliamentary Select Committee resulting in the recommendation for future provision of "low-power transmission facilities for voluntary community radio services within small communities" (SCNI, 1978: xlix). The Annan Report took sufficient notice of COMCOM's comments to suggest that the expansion of commercial local radio should include some licence awards to local community trusts. In a number of cities, groups were formed to apply for such licenses, but only in Cardiff was such a group successful – and there too community control was short lived, ending in take-over by a commercial chain (Lewis and Booth, 1989: 108–9).

These two attempts to introduce community programming into mainstream media had contradictory results: on the one hand, they raised consciousness among community groups across the country, launched a campaigning movement and gained the attention of officialdom. On the other hand, mainstream media reported the results as a failure: the collapse of the cable industry's hopes due to political change were attributed to ineffective communication at the community level. After the Cardiff episode, word went out in the radio industry that community programming was an audience loser. In any case, most mainstream broadcasters dismissed these new forms of media intervention as 'amateur', while their trade union regarded them as a threat to professional standards. It was decades before the arrival of the internet facilitated 'user-generated content' and 'citizen journalism' and obliged professional media to notice and co-opt the genre.

Community radio advocates had to confront a series of interlinking objections to their proposals. Legislation did not allow for such a type of broadcasting. How would it be regulated? How would stations be financed? How could frequencies be found? Was there sufficient demand to justify such an extension of existing services?

At this time, COMCOM profited from presence in the capital of several Australian activist/practitioners whose experience (Australia had officially recognised community radio in 1974) and radical approach helped launch a number of ad hoc campaigns. Perhaps the two most effective interventions were the commissioning of a report from a former broadcasting engineer which refuted the official claim that there were no spare frequencies in London, and the exposure by COMCOM's ally, the Local Radio Workshop, of the failings in the public consultation procedures of the then regulator, the Independent Broadcasting Authority (IBA), and the inadequacy of the coverage of local affairs by London's local radio stations (Local Radio Workshop, 1983).

After COMCOM ran out of energy, the formation in 1983 of the Community Radio Association (later to become the Community Media Association) helped build a relationship over a long period with officials in the government department responsible for media and with successive regulators. The offer by the government of a pilot experiment in 1985 attracted over 200 applications. Even though the scheme was cancelled, the question about demand had received an answer. An increasing volume of pirate radio, most broadcasting musical genres but including some social, linguistic and political groups, supported the argument that the needs of certain communities were not being met. The popularity of pirate radio also caused some concern to commercial local radio stations which demanded response from the IBA and the government.

Before the IBA was replaced by the Radio Authority in 1990, it was able to satisfy some of the demand through its 'incremental franchise' scheme which allowed a few community radio stations to operate within already existing coverage areas. The introduction by the Radio Authority of a temporary license scheme (RSLs) for up to a 28-day period for the broadcasting of cultural events and religious festivals also went some way towards meeting demand, as well as allowing experience to develop among a wide range of communities (Stoller, 2010).

The final stages of the progress towards the creation of a community radio sector were, first, the Radio Authority's Access Radio Project, launched initially for one year in 2001 and extended until 2003; from nearly 200 applications, 15 were chosen. And second, following the positive evaluation of that project (Everitt, 2003a, 2003b), the Community Radio Order of 2004, which gave legislative status to the notion of the 'social gain' community radio stations were expected to deliver. Its main objectives were: "the provision of broadcasting services to those otherwise underserved; the facilitation of discussion and the expression of opinion; the provision of education or training of volunteers; and the better understanding of the particular community and the strengthening of links within it" (Ofcom, 2010: 7). A decade later, more than 200 community radio stations are licensed and broadcasting (Ofcom, n.d.).

We can now summarise the elements that led to the successful conclusion of the campaign. There had been persistent pressure from the Community Media Association and, in the past decade, sympathetic response and constructive ideas from civil servants and regulators. But for politicians to be persuaded, there needed to be a level of favourable public opinion that reached a tipping point. It helped that the successful record of the RSL scheme had brought community radio to the attention of local media and local MPs and that commercial radio was willing to accept the creation of a separate sector given certain constraints (limitation of coverage area and advertising).

But the role of the academic community should not be overlooked. The growing volume of international attention and research translated into a new wave of published studies of community media on both sides of the Atlantic around the turn of the millennium: the marketing decisions of publishers complemented the funding strategies of research agencies, all of which contributed to a discourse that promoted community radio to a matter of public debate.

Policy issues

Policy issues will continue to be discussed here from the perspective of broadcast community radio, the medium which most prominently impinges on national media policies because frequency space is a consideration. Community television is less common; in Europe, it is often found on cable networks which do not affect frequency allocation, and in significant numbers only in the Netherlands, Italy and Germany. A mapping exercise by the Community Media Forum for Europe (CMFE) in 2012 recorded 2,237 community radio stations and 521 community television stations on the continent (http://communitymedia.se/europe/table.htm).

A key issue is the recognition of community radio as a separate sector of broadcasting. The US, Canada and Australia (where 'public radio' was the label at first used for community radio) were the first countries where this occurred. A famous policy statement of 1978 by the Australian Minister responsible for broadcasting included the words "it is accepted that public broadcasters have a better appreciation of the interests, hence needs, of their broadcasting communities than anyone else, including government" (cited in Lewis and Booth, 1989: 134). The Australian and North American examples provided encouragement for British activists, and may have contributed to South Africa's post-apartheid licensing framework in 1993. In Europe, the Scandinavian countries, France, Germany and the Netherlands found their own separate ways to this important step in the early 1980s, but many countries still do not have legislation which recognises community radio as a separate sector, for example Spain and Poland. This is the case in other Eastern European countries, while Hungary, which led the way in Central Europe, has recently experienced a worsening of government relations with this sector.

Recognition for community radio as a separate sector is a necessary, though not always a sufficient, condition for the fair and transparent award of licenses and should make possible a funding system which does not compete unfairly with mainstream broadcasting. The most significant source of funding for community media is volunteer labour, an expression of community support and participation. Alongside that, local sources are an essential reflection of that support but a search for a variety of sources of funding is regarded as a sensible strategy and a national source of funding is an important guarantee of the stability of the sector. The French system for supporting *radios associatives* involves a levy on the commercial audio-visual sector which supplies a fund administered by the regulator, the CSA. In the Netherlands, the central government transfers funding to local authorities for support for community media – though not all municipalities make use of it effectively. In the UK, a Community Radio Fund is disbursed by the regulator, Ofcom. Despite the recommendation by the evaluator of the pilot Access Radio project that some £8 million would be necessary to support the sector, the £0.5 million shared among the original 15 stations in 2004 has not been increased to match the needs of the 200 stations now in operation.

In most countries, the license fee for community radio is considerably lower than that for mainstream radio, and tax concessions are another method of central government support. What is not common is to find a recognition of the wide spread of social needs met by community radio reflected in sources of government funding *other* than that of a Media Department. One might expect work done by stations in education, public health and social cohesion, for example, to be officially recompensed through continuous support from the respective government departments, although many stations do succeed in winning grants for specific projects in such fields. South Africa's creation of a Media Development and Diversity Agency (MDDA) is an unusual attempt to organise funding from a wide range of sources for the community radio sector (Buckley et al., 2008: 224). A comparative European study for the UK's Community Media Association on factors which contribute to a successful sector noted that countries where there was a strong representative association, in receipt of funding from central government, is an important asset (Edmonds and Buckley, 2005). A similar point is made by Rüdiger Maack, of Deutsche Welle Akademie, interviewed by Mersch (2014).

European measures

Advocacy on behalf of community media at a European level began in the late 1980s with the lobbying of the European Parliament by the Féderation Européenne des Radios Libres (FERL) as a result of which a resolution by an Italian MEP, Barzanti, called on member states to support community radio, described, confusingly, as independent local radio. In the 1990s, AMARC-Europe made a number of submissions to the European Commission's calls on media policies concerning concentration of ownership and media plurality. On AMARC-Europe's temporary decline at the end of the millennium, the Community Media Forum for Europe (CMFE) took up the leading advocacy role at this level. Founded in 2004, the CMFE participated along with other civil society organisations at the 7th European Ministerial Conference on Mass Media Policy in Kiev in March 2005, at which conference themes included freedom of expression and information in times of crisis; cultural diversity and media pluralism in times of globalisation; and human rights and regulation of the media and new communication services in the information society.

Since then, the CMFE has played a key role in securing the European Parliament Resolution (European Parliament, 2008) and the Council of Europe Declaration (Council of Europe, 2009). Both of these are strong and detailed statements, summarising the social benefits of community media for, among other things, strengthening cultural and linguistic diversity, as instruments of social cohesion, media pluralism and local creativity, as well as a means of encouraging civic dialogue; member states are called upon to give their support to this form of media. Subsequent interventions of the CMFE have attempted, with some success, to use these statements to affect national policies in Europe. A recent initiative was the ranking of European states in relation to their treatment of community radio and television.

An area of concern to the CMFE and to their members across Europe is the planned move to digital transmission. Whatever technical system is adopted, digital transfer poses problems for community radio. The geographical area covered by digital platforms is too large to be useful for smaller stations, and the entrance fees are likely to be beyond their budgets – as is the case in the current UK scheme. Moreover, the switchover from the FM band does not necessarily promise additional gains for community radio given the desire of other interests, such as mobile telephony, to move into the vacated frequencies. Not all European governments accept the need for digital transfer, and there is disagreement about the most effective system, with the UK in the awkward position of having been the first to adopt a system, DAB, which has since lagged behind the more recently developed systems (DAB+, DRM) in efficiency. The future possible distribution platforms for community radio in Europe are the subject of a useful study by by Christer Hederström of the CMFE (Hederström, 2014).

Community media and social media

The growth in the use of social media raises in more acute form the question that distribution of community media over the internet has already posed: what is the relationship between virtual and local communities (Fenton, 2012)? Most community radio stations now combine online and over-the-air presence with social media, but there are important differences between the two forms. Community media are collective enterprises owned by the communities they serve, and often their overall contact, both in listenership and production, is with a range of different constituencies who must argue and compromise to achieve a democratically agreed solution. Co-presence is an important feature of this interaction, and so is the physical availability of a meeting place and the technology used to train volunteers. These volunteers can participate at different levels in the organisation, as presenters, producers, trainers or members of management. While social media, on their own, are unlikely to be able to offer any equivalent opportunities, most community projects, like most organisations in general, now maintain a presence on Facebook and Twitter (see, for example, Johnston, 2014).

As the CMFE put it in a paper to a Ministerial Conference of the Council of Europe:

> Community media have a recognized name and established network of active citizens, experience in promoting social justice, integration and social change ... What is important is the growing availability of different media, with different strengths and weaknesses, with different infrastructural and regulatory needs. Also important is that these media need each other to build strong communications.
>
> (CMFE, 2013)

Academics and policy

In conclusion, the role of academics in policy formation is worth a brief mention. A widely held view among British media academics is that current government reliance on specialist research agencies and polling organisations is marginalising critical academic policy intervention of a kind that was possible in the period that led to the creation of Channel 4 at the end of the1970s (Freedman, 2008: 102). Georgina Born, for example, has noted the increasing difficulty academics experience in intervening in policy debates. In policy-making circles, Born claims, academic research suffers from a "waning public profile and legitimacy", an indication of which is the fact that "the role of the public intellectual and policy adviser has been taken over by the increasing numbers of freelance consultants and think tanks" (Born, 2008: 692). Another reason, according to Born, for the failure of academics to make an impression in the policy arena is "the closure of channels previously available to academics for communicating policy-relevant findings in the press and political weeklies" (ibid.: 691). She singles out *The Guardian* and *The Independent*, whose media sections are "staffed by editors whose 'common-sense' falls within the neo-liberal consensus and for whom there is comfort and kudos in speaking the same language as the industry – pro-market and pro-corporate ... the quality of the media coverage is superficial, collusive and unanalytical" (ibid.: 693).

Like Freedman, Rennie makes a comparison between academic policy input in the 1970s and the present. A changed political climate, she notes, nowadays favours business and community partnerships, yet there is still a relegation to the inferior status of community media due to the continuing legacy of the public service broadcasting ethos. This attitude can no longer be justified, given the "decentralized broadcasting environment" within which public service broadcasting now exists (Rennie, 2006: 89).

In the UK, academics interested in media policy have formed a Policy Network within MeCCSA, the Media Communications and Cultural Studies Association, the representative organisation of the subject area in the UK (www.meccsa.org.uk). Prompted in the first instance by the need to counter the proposal in the government's *Digital Britain* report to 'top-slice' some of the TV licence for funding services outside the BBC, the Leveson enquiry and its aftermath are now a main focus for the Policy Network. MeCCSA, since its founding a little over a decade ago, has maintained important contacts with government research policy. Several members of MeCCSA's Policy Network have formal consultancy relations with official parts of government, *pace* the arguments of Freedman and Born. The concentration of the Policy Network's effort on defence of the BBC and on the Leveson enquiry has sidelined consideration of the community radio sector and the case that could be made for improved funding, given its role as a local public service. That omission serves to make the point that the impact of academic policy intervention as a whole may be limited, but even more so are the voices within that sector which speak for community media interests. Community media is still a minority interest in academic media study, demonstrating the truth of Rennie's comments about the status of community media vis-à-vis public service broadcasting.

Further reading

Howley, K. (ed.) (2010) *Understanding Community Media* (London, Los Angeles: Sage) discusses a wide range of theoretical and policy aspects by contributors from across the world.

Lewis, P. M. (2008) *Promoting Social Cohesion: The Role of Community Media*, Report prepared for the Council of Europe's Group of Media Specialists on Media Diversity (MC-S-MD), retrieved from http://www.coe.int/t/dghl/standardsetting/media/Doc/H-Inf(2008)013_en.pdf. A survey of community media at the time including arguments for its place in a broadcasting ecology.

Articles on community radio can often be found in both the *Journal of Radio and Audio Media* (http://www.tandfonline.com/toc/hjrs20/.U4dLY_RDs2Y) and *The Radio Journal: International Studies in Broadcast and Audio Media* (http://www.intellectbooks.co. uk/journals/view-journal,id=123/).

Key websites: AMARC (World Association of Community Radio Broadcasters), http://www2.amarc.org/, and Community Media Forum for Europe, http://www. cmfe.eu/.

References

AMARC Africa and Panos Southern Africa (1998) "What is community radio? A resource guide." Retrieved from http://www2.amarc.org/?q=node/47 (accessed 28 October 2013).

Annan, N. (1977) *Report of the Committee on the Future of Broadcasting*. Chair: Lord Annan. London: HMSO.

Atton, C. (2001) *Alternative Media*. London; Thousand Oaks, CA; New Delhi: Sage.

Born, G. (2008) "Trying to intervene: British media research and the framing of policy debate." *International Journal of Communication*. SSRC Special Feature: *Making Communications Research Matter*. Retrieved from http://essays.ssrc.org/mcrm/?p=11 (accessed 31 October 2013).

Buckley, S., Duet, K., Mendel, T. and Ó Siochrú, S. (2008) *Broadcasting, Voice, and Accountability: A Public Interest Approach to Policy, Law, and Regulation*. Ann Arbor: University of Michigan Press.

CMFE (2013) "Community media and social media: Active citizenship in a changing media environment." Input paper to the Council of Europe Conference of Ministers responsible for Media and Information Society, Belgrade, 7–8 November.

COMCOM (1977) *Comments on the Recommendations of the Annan Committee on the Future of Broadcasting*. London: Community Communications Group.

Council of Europe (2009) Declaration by the Committee of Ministers on 11 February 2009. Retrieved from https://wcd.coe.int/ViewDoc.jsp?id=1409919 (accessed 31 October 2013).

Downing, J. (with others) (2001) *Radical Media: Rebellious Communication and Social Movements*. London: Sage Publications.

Edmonds, N. and Buckley, S. (2005) *Making It Work: Learning from Successful Community Radio Stations*. A CM Solutions Report for the Community Media Association. Sheffield: Community Media Association.

European Parliament (2008) *European Parliament Resolution of 25 September 2008 on Community Media in Europe*. Retrieved from http://www.europarl.europa.eu/sides/getDoc.do?type= TA&reference=P6-TA-2008-0456&language=EN&ring=A6-2008-0263 (accessed 31 October 2013).

Everitt, A. (2003a) *New Voices: An Evaluation of 15 Access Radio Projects*. London: Radio Authority. Retrieved from http://www.ofcom.org.uk/static/archive/rau/radio-stations/access/ NewVoices/New%20Voices.pdf (accessed 30 October 2013).

——(2003b) *New Voices: An Update on the Access Radio Projects*. London: Radio Authority. Retrieved from http://stakeholders.ofcom.org.uk/binaries/broadcast/radio-ops/nvu_oct03. pdf (accessed 30 October 2013).

Fenton, N. (2012) 'The internet and radical politics.' In J. Curran, N. Fenton and D. Freedman (eds), (2012) *Misunderstanding the Internet*. London and New York: Routledge (pp. 149–76).

Freedman, D. (2008) *The Politics of Media Policy*. Cambridge: Polity.

Gumucio Dagron, A. (2001) *Making Waves: Stories of Participatory Communication for Social Change*. A Report to the Rockefeller Foundation. New York: Rockefeller Foundation.

Retrieved from http://www.communicationforsocialchange.org/pdf/making_waves.pdf (accessed 28 October 2013).

Hederström, C. (2014) *Community Radio: FM and Digitalization*. CMFE. Retrieved from http://www.cmfe.eu/ (accessed 13 January 2015).

Johnston, A. (2014) "Community and social media." In J. Hunsinger and T. M. Seft (eds), *The Social Media Handbook*. London: Routledge.

Lewis, P. M. (2006) "Community media: Giving 'a voice to the voiceless'." In P. M. Lewis and S. Jones (eds), (2006) *From the Margins to the Cutting Edge – Community Media and Empowerment*. Cresskill, NJ: Hampton Press.

——(2012) "'It's only community radio': The British campaign for community radio." In J. Gordon (ed.), *Community Radio in the 21st Century*. Oxford: Peter Lang.

Lewis, P. M. and Booth, J. (1989) *The Invisible Medium: Public, Commercial and Community Radio*. London: Macmillan.

Local Radio Workshop (1983) *Nothing Local About It: London's Local Radio*. London: Commedia.

Mersch, Sara (2014) "Strengthening community radio." *onMedia*. Retrieved from http://onmedia.dw-akademie.de/english/?p=17889 (accessed 17 February 2014).

Ofcom (2010) *Notes of Guidance for Community Radio Licence Applicants and Licensees*. Retrieved from http://licensing.ofcom.org.uk/binaries/radio/community/nogs_r23.pdf (accessed 31 October 2013).

——(n.d.) 'Community radio stations.' Retrieved from www.ofcom.org.uk/static/radiolicensing/html/radio-stations/community/community-main.htm (accessed 19 March 2015).

Rennie, E. (2006) *Community Media: A Global Introduction*. Oxford: Rowman & Littlefield.

Rodríguez, C. (2001) *Fissures in the Mediascape*. Cresskill, NJ: Hampton Press.

SCNI (1978) *House of Commons Select Committee on Nationalised Industries, Session 1977–78, Tenth Report, Vol. I*, Report and Proceedings of the Committee (637-I).

Servaes, J. (1999) *Communication for Development: One World, Multiple Cultures*. Cresskill, NJ: Hampton Press.

Stoller, T. (2010) *Sounds of Your Life: The History of Independent Radio in the UK*. New Barnet: John Libbey Publishing.

UNESCO (1980) (International Commission for the Study of Communication Problems) *Many Voices, One World: Communication and Society Today and Tomorrow* (MacBride Report). London: Kogan Page.

16

COMMUNITY MEDIA IN THE NORDIC COUNTRIES

Between public service and private media

Per Jauert

From the perspective of international research, it is not possible to give unequivocal definitions of the broadcast activity in the third media sector. Community media is the most commonly used term, but in a global perspective it includes a widely ranged diversity of terms and practices. A specific national or regional context often appears in the term, used in national languages. In Europe, for instance, we find 'associatif' and 'libre' (France and Italy), in Spain 'comunitarias' and in the five Nordic countries 'lokal' (local) and 'near to you'/neighbourhood media. This diversity in national terminology reflects the specific legislative conditions, and the political, social and cultural contexts for locally based and often 'alternative' media (Rodríguez, 2001; Carpentier, Lie and Servaes, 2007; Howley, 2013).

The principle of subsidiarity, the importance of the media for the local, democratic debate, the construction of local identity and the sense of belonging were the key factors for the establishment of the independent community media (radio and television) in the Nordic countries from the 1970s and onwards, parallel to the break of the monopoly of the public service broadcasting institutions. But in recent decades, both commercial and public service media have expanded into the regional and local markets. Not least due to webcasting, and a general expansion of user-generated content and user interaction on different distribution channels and on social media, the first and second broadcasting sectors seem to have established competing fora within community media.

Nordic community media: Between public and private media

The Nordic countries are often acknowledged for their common social and cultural characteristics, but a more detailed approach finds differences between them, depending on different historical features, different priorities in media and cultural policies and not least in the balance of power between the public service and the private media. But it must be emphasised that behind those differences we will find shared values, common for the Nordic welfare societies. In return for relatively high taxation, there is free access to education, health and social services. Political systems are stable, based on close, collaborative links to societal stakeholders, such as the labour movement and the industry (Nissen, 2013: 11).

From an international perspective, the Nordic public broadcasting institutions have kept a unique position, compared to private media. With the exception of Finland, national monopolies on radio and television were not broken until the 1980s, and they still hold a very strong market position. Four out of the five Nordic countries' public service radio have market shares well above 50 per cent. The extremities are Iceland (47 per cent) and Denmark (80 per cent). For television, Sweden has 35 per cent and Denmark 66 per cent (Harrie, 2013: 35 and 31).

Among the Nordic countries there are no equal and strict definitions of community broadcast media, but over the years it is possible to trace a tendency to distinguish between *private radio* – commercial and privately owned stations (regional or national) as counterparts to the nationwide and regional public service broadcaster; *local or community radio* as privately owned commercial and non-commercial counterpart stations to (mainly) regional stations, run by the national public service broadcaster; and finally, *community radio* as the 'idealistic', privately owned stations, run by institutions (churches), associations, civic movements, etc., anchored in and addressing a local community or a non-geographically defined 'community of interests' (Jauert and Prehn, 1995).

The common ground for the Nordic community broadcast media was a move towards a more open democracy. Participation, access and political decentralisation was put on the agenda, not only by civic movements or 'the youth revolt' in the aftermath of 1968, but also by a number of political parties, from those with left-wing orientations to more liberal, traditional parties (Jankowski, Prehn and Stappers, 1992; Jauert and Prehn, 1994; Jauert and Prehn, 1995; Jauert and Prehn, 2002; Hederström, 2004). But it was not only the political left or the 'grassroot' movements that defined the agenda for the legal framing of community broadcasting. In Denmark and Norway in the early 1980s, a pragmatic political alliance formed between the civic movements and their wish for a non-commercial, open-accessible and participatory community radio and television combined with private, commercial local radio and television stations. This alliance was reinforced by anti-monopolistic companies and political forces that wanted weaker and more narrowly defined public service media, as well as an expansive private commercial broadcast sector. For some time these two very different radio types even shared frequencies in Norway and Denmark, a weird kind of 'arranged marriage', caused mainly by a complicated political atmosphere, related to the break of the monopoly of the broadcast media, nationally as well as in local areas (Jauert and Prehn, 2002).

Mission and organisation

Sweden was the first of the Nordic countries to launch community radio and television, labelled '*naerradio*' (neighbourhood radio) and '*lokal TV*' (local television). The first community radio was established in 1979, and already after a year 341 associations had licences, dominated by religious congregations. The state committee behind the initiative stressed that the mission was "to utilize radio for information, education and agitation", an important part of the concept of public access to media (Hederström, 2004: 35). All frequencies for 'naerradio' were shared, mainly in 60-minute schedules, so during the day the public could be presented with a very differentiated (and non-coherent) programming. The licence was allocated to non-commercial, idealistic associations only, and commercials were not allowed until 1993 (ibid.). Local television was launched in 1983 in cable television networks on the same legal basis as community radio (ibid.).

Commercials and sponsorships were allowed in 1993 for community radio, for local television-only sponsorships. The number of community stations has grown over the years, and in 2011 there were 863 community radio licences on 157 local frequencies and 30 local cable television stations (Jauert, Degn and Taylor Hansen, 2013: 14, based on Nordicom, 2013).

In Finland, there are presently very few community radio stations, established and run on the same principles as in Sweden, financially dependent mostly on local, private and municipal funding (ibid.). Iceland does not have community radio, but a strong commercial nationwide radio (Bylgjan) as a counterpart to the national public service radio and television institution, Ríkisútvarpið (RÚV).

Community media in Norway and Denmark have in many ways developed in similar ways. In both countries, local radio and local television were launched in the beginning of the 1980s for experimental periods, and were at the end of the decennium replaced by permanent schemes (Skogerbø, 1988; Prehn, Nordahl Svendsen and Petersen, 1992; Jauert and Prehn, 1995). Also in both countries the political background was to be found in a widespread tendency in the Nordic countries for decentralisation and locally based involvement in the democratic processes. For instance, in Denmark a structural reform of the municipality structure generated a focus on local democracy, involvement, participatory processes, etc. (Christensen, 2000).

Compared to other European initiatives to establish community media, the Norwegian and Danish approaches were not mainly the result of pressure from below, that is, from grassroots movements, pirate stations or similar forms of 'alternative' organisations (what have been characterised as 'rhizomatic media'). The significance of this type is the highlighting of a struggle for deepening democracy, exposing the rigidities and certainties of public and commercial media (Carpentier, Lie and Servaes, 2007: 222). Broadly speaking, the Nordic approach was dominated by the endeavour to validate and strengthen the local communities by introducing an alternative to mainstream media, and thus facilitate democratisation through media, by open-access channels and opportunities for self-representation in the public arenas (ibid.). However, in Norway and Denmark this approach was combined with other political agendas, set by the conservative and liberal political parties in the two countries, having struggled for decades to break the monopolies of the public service broadcasters.

The battlefield state of community and local media was intensified after the experimental periods and developed into a major challenge for the legislator and the regulators. Key problem areas were funding (public funding, commercials, sponsorships) and regulation (central or decentralised). The experimental periods of community media in the two countries can be regarded as a compromise between right and left in the parliaments, opening up possibilities for a wide range of participants: community radio and television organisations, religious communities, newspapers, political parties, schools and universities, cable network organisations (Prehn, Nordahl Svendsen and Petersen, 1992). Through this open and almost unrestricted access to establish electronic community media, a way was paved for a three-tiered system of local broadcasting: non-commercial community radio and television; commercial, private community radio and television; and regional radio stations, run by the national public service broadcasters, DR and NRK.

Regulation and funding

In what follows, I shall concentrate on the Danish community media sector, for two reasons. First, recent research on community media in the Nordic countries has been very scarce, almost non-existent. Second, the Danish case seems to be the most convincing to display the important present challenges for the community broadcast media. A contributory force to the disputes over media policy in the 1980s was due to the concurrent establishment of the second nationwide public service channel, TV 2, financed partly from advertising and partly from licence fees, together with the struggle to expand the opportunities for private broadcast media on all levels, including community media (Jauert and Prehn, 2003). One of the most important lessons to learn from the experimental period was the turmoil caused by the breaking of DR's monopoly. Although advertising was prohibited for community stations, programming and formats in many community stations to a large extent resembled those of commercial stations, especially music formats and the styles of presentation. These elements, combined with a focus on local news and events, listener contact and involvement, quizzes and so on, made these stations very popular, and in certain areas they succeeded in approaching or actually outdoing the ratings of DR's channels (Prehn, Nordahl Svendsen and Petersen, 1992; Jauert and Prehn, 1995). Another aspect of what we might term a 'commercial deficit' was the competition among the commercial media players (national and international) to achieve a prominent position in the upcoming tender for TV 2 and a further liberalisation of broadcast policy. Significant sums of money were invested – during and after the experimental period – in 'professional' community television, especially in the Copenhagen area. It was estimated that about 23 million Euros were spent on these efforts, compared to the fact that the state and municipalities combined only reached 1.6 million Euros for the whole experimental period. Commercials were banned during the experimental period, but many community stations with 'professional' aspirations to become popular private commercial stations experimented with more or less concealed sponsorships and company portraits in order to make a business out of it (Jauert and Prehn, 2003).

The experimental period in itself, however, was based not on the idea of a 'commercial deficit', but instead on the notion of a 'democratic deficit', expressed both through the mission statements of the legislator and the local civic movements in the communities. The tension between the commercial and the democratic contributed to media policy frictions in the years to come, until a more stable legal framework was initiated in the mid-1990s. The construction of a new Act for community radio and television produced a growing number of different problems because of the conflicting interests between the non-commercial and the commercially oriented stations. Many stations in the local areas had to share transmitters and frequencies, preventing 'flow' during the day, which restricted the income from commercials. On the other hand, this was seen as an advantage by the non-commercial stations, because they could benefit from the high audience numbers produced by the commercial partner. Furthermore, the decentralised regulation of the Act, enforced by the local boards in the municipalities, which were now responsible for distribution of licences and legal control, resulted in inconsistent practices from municipality to municipality: what was considered allowed in one place were prohibited in another.

In 1994 the non-commercial local radio stations gained access to financial support, derived from state soccer and lottery pools, previously intended for cultural projects, to an amount of 1 million euros per year (Jauert and Prehn, 2003). The Ministry of Culture then initiated a review (Jauert and Prehn, 1995) of the whole situation for non-commercial community stations that was to lay the groundwork for reforming the law. In 1997 the bill was passed, mainly based on the recommendations in the report, including its view on these stations as part of an extended concept of public service. Consequently, a subsidy scheme was established, with funds partly coming from the licence fee previously reserved for DR and TV 2. Other funding came from a tax on the commercial community television stations, which the new Radio and Television Act allowed to enter into nationwide networks.

The subsidy scheme is still in operation, most recently with an annual distribution of 6.7 million euros. The principles for distribution have changed several times, but for the past five years it has been reserved for subsidising production and distribution costs for a certain number of weekly produced hours. Local boards administrated the scheme until the end of 2006, when all administration and regulation of non-commercial community radio and television was taken over by the Radio and Television Board, an independent regulatory body, serviced by the Danish Agency for Culture. (A similar subsidy scheme has been established in Norway, which in 2013 has reached 2 million euros (Medietilsynet, 2014).)

Challenges for non-commercial community radio and television

Following the establishment of the permanent subsidy scheme, several legal and administrative obstacles arose, related mainly to criteria for approval of application, and to possibilities for legal control: In short, were the subsidies being spent according to the objectives of the scheme? In 1999, the Ministry of Culture commissioned Jauert and Prehn to carry out an evaluation of the subsidy scheme: its administrative aspects, each station's view of the new scheme and an analysis of a number of stations, including which programmes had received support. (The analysis and the methodology is documented in Jauert and Prehn, 2002, and described in Jauert and Prehn, 2003.)

The report concluded that administratively, the supervision of funds was unsatisfactory. Only a few local boards had systematised the obligatory supervision, and in general it was not possible to discover if the programmes for which the money was granted were actually being produced and broadcast. The analysis of the stations' programming showed a great variety of different programme types, and focus group research revealed that the main part of what was produced did not relate directly to political issues, traditionally connected to the public sphere or the public arena. Instead, programmes were more related to the audience/user sense of belonging, and to the sustaining of identity shaping: "You must be able to identify with the programme content – it must be relevant for me", one of the participants stressed (Jauert and Prehn, 2002: 199). Many of the station managers who were interviewed, as well as viewers and listeners taking part in the focus groups, were keen to point out that community radio and television are no longer driven by "more or less left-wing grassroots movements". Instead, they felt, community broadcasting was a media sector in its own right, one which supplemented other locally based media, though often with different objectives: to present narratives about the diversity of life in the local area. These elements were not sufficiently covered in the subsidy criteria, the report concluded.

The report also examined programme quality by asking: Has the subsidy scheme positively influenced positively the production and content of programming? All stations were positive in their evaluation of the support for programme production, which enhanced the skills of volunteers through professional training courses to improve the conditions for community media production. For listeners and viewers, the quality criteria have to be adapted to the specific community context – not to flawless or 'professional' standards. The sense of proximity, the thoroughness and not least the specific 'lingering' or slow pace of many programmes was accentuated. But if a programme tried to imitate a genre or a specific 'professional' format, the critique from focus-group participants was straightforward: it does not matter if a programme is unprofessional, but it must not be amateurish or dilettantish. Some of the findings and the recommendations of the evaluation report were included in the following amendments of the subsidy scheme.

Some years later the Ministry of Culture and members of the Danish Parliament became increasingly concerned about the state of the community media sector in general and especially the subsidy scheme. From 2000 onwards, the number of subsidies granted to community radio stations were annually about 150 to 175; by 2012, it was 217 (Danish Agency for Culture, 2013). For community television stations, the corresponding numbers were 90 and 215 (ibid.). This was seen as a sign of income speculation, with stations related to religious movements and sects particularly under suspicion. In order to increase their portion of the grant, the organisations behind these and other stations split the original organisation into a number of similar and cooperating organisations, each having a transmission licence – and each therefore qualifying for a subsidy. A further problem was to identify to what extent a station served a distinct community, in the sense of a geographically defined, local community – referring to the specific Danish and Norwegian term for community broadcaster: *local* radio and television. The legislators wanted to stress this aspect of the Act. Even though communities of interest (such as gay and lesbian people, religious associations, student organisations and so on) were allowed, the problem for the legislators especially pointed to evangelical groups that distributed some locally produced content but a majority of foreign content.

A third matter of concern was the audience. Non-commercial community stations are not covered by the Danish PPM (People Portable Meter) surveys but by TNS Gallup, whose audience surveys of radio and television have judged that numbers are so low that they cannot be measured using standard survey methods. In the mission statements for community media stations, audience size has never previously been a matter of great concern, since community media serve minority groups and smaller parts of the population. But as a core element of a revision of the subsidy scheme, the Ministry of Culture and politicians found it necessary to discover whether the 6.7 million euros spent each year 'gives value for money'.

A fourth concern was the consequences for community radio in the future Danish broadcasting landscape. In 2009, television had a digital switchover, and community television was included in a separate switchover covering the eight regions in Denmark, and furthermore possibilities to access a nationwide channel for a restricted number of hours. For community radio the situation is different, even though digital radio transmission (DAB) has been quite successful, similar to the development in the UK and Norway. Around 40 per cent of all households in Denmark have a DAB receiver, and around 15 per cent of listening takes place through DAB and on web radio (DR, 2012). In the Media Agreement of 2012–14, it was declared that the digital switchover would take place in 2019, presupposing that by 2018, 50 per cent of listening takes place on digital platforms. At that time, community radio stations can decide whether they will continue to distribute on FM, or shift to DAB+.

All these concerns were included in the Media Agreement for 2012–14. In Media Agreements, a majority of, and sometimes all, political parties define the aims and goals media policy for radio and television as covered by the Radio and Television Act and outlines initiatives for a defined period of time, normally four years. The Danish Agency for Culture was required to present proposals on a number of specific issues for later revisions of the Act. It was also required to include representatives from the community radio and television organisations in the preparation for proposals. The main issues for the proposals were: How can the subsidy scheme be reserved for programming that has an audience and that deals only with local content? Should non-commercial radio and television still use the FM band for broadcasting or is it more suitable to use internet distribution only? How might the subsidy scheme be allocated to community television and radio that only uses the internet?

Consequently, I was commissioned by the Danish Agency for Culture to deliver two background reports and to take part in the seminars and consultations with the representatives from the community media sector (Jauert, Degn and Taylor Hansen, 2013; Jauert, Degn and Saabye, 2014). The 2014 report consisted of an analysis of the present state in the non-commercial community media sector, based on a quantitative survey among all licence holders (179 radio licences and 214 television licences) concerning programme production, distribution experiences on FM and digital television and on the internet, and finally interaction and contact with the audiences/users. Before the survey, ten representatively selected stations participated in in-depth qualitative interviews. From the analysis of the empirical studies, conclusions were drawn about the viewpoints and experiences among the licence holders, and a number of scenarios for the future regulation and legislation were composed.

The focus of the 2014 report was on the possible shift of community media to internet distribution only, as well as in relation to ongoing activities on the FM band and with digital television. The focus of the 2013 report was the subsidy scheme, related to the overall economic situation for community media, its locally based content production and its audiences: Do the stations really have an audience, and how can they be documented? The report was based on qualitative in-depth interviews with station managers from fifteen stations, supplemented by statistical material from the Nordic regulatory bodies and other European countries.

As a result, amendments were made to the Radio and Television Act (a Consolidation Act). For new non-commercial community television licences (38 across the country's eight regions), it is required that all programmes are produced by the licence holder or by persons from the local area, and targeted to the citizens in that area. This reduction in licences is immense, but takes account of the several former independent licence holders who have formed cooperative associations. Former licence holders without a new licence are directed to internet broadcasting and receive no subsidies. In order to sustain the licence, the station must have a minimum audience size. The Danish Agency for Culture will initiate special television audience biannual surveys in the regions, and in the second half of 2014 the achieved reach must be at least 5,000 persons (of 12 years and over) or 3per cent of the population in the licence area, increasing to 15,000 persons or 7.5 per cent of the population in the second half of 2016. A similar Consolidation Act for non-commercial community radio will be established in 2016, after a new round of licences are issued in 2015. No reduction of the number of licences is planned, since the decision about a digital switchover has not been taken yet.

A new situation for community media: For better or for worse?

The dominant theme among the stations taking part in the surveys was a harsh critique of income speculation by companies working together to receive greater subsidies. It was therefore considered necessary to specify tighter criteria for subsidies, but there was also a common lament that stations based on community of interest (and not on a geographical criterion of 'localism') were excluded from television licences. For new radio licences, all criteria for approval have not yet been decided, but it is likely that the requirement of local presence – production for, by and to the local community – will appear, together with biannual audience research with specified minimum percentages or absolute numbers of listeners.

The lesson learned from these changes in the conditions for community radio and television is that a dependence on public support will always influence and may also restrict the practices for a free, independent community media sector. In order to meet the requirements for public support, stations will have to tailor their profile accordingly. The question about presence on the internet seems quite complicated. A majority of the radio stations are sceptical, since most of their audiences are older people and/or not heavy internet users. However, a double presence on FM and the internet appears acceptable for the majority of the stations. It also appears that television stations are far more experienced in using the internet, both for streaming and downloading, and consider it a unique opportunity to develop new formats. Ultimately, it is evident that the community radio and television sector will have to adjust to the new media landscape, and accept the fact that their activities will need to go beyond traditional broadcasting to embrace a presence on different but combined platforms.

Further reading

C. Hederström, *Community Radio: FM and Digitalization. Future Distribution Platforms for Community Radio in Europe* (Green Paper for Community Media Forum Europe, Stockholm, 2014) presents an overview of the plans for a digital turnover of radio and the options and threats for community radio. L. Hallett and A. Hintz (2009) focus on the often neglected technological, economic and practical obstacles for the digitalisation of radio to accommodate the full range of broadcast services, that exist today. O'Neill et al. (eds.), *Digital Radio in Europe. Technologies, Industries and Cultures* (Bristol: Intellect, 2010) offer a comprehensive review of the complex environment in which European digital radio operates. Articles, books, media trends statistics, and databases in English about broadcast and community media in the Nordic countries can be found in *Nordicom – the Nordic Information Centre for Media and Communication Research* (http://www.nordicom.gu.se/en).

References

Carpentier, N., Lie, R. and Servaes, J. (2007) "Multitheoretical approaches to community media: Capturing specificity and diversity." In L. Fuller (ed.), *Community Media: International Perspectives.* New York: Palgrave Macmillan (pp. 219–36).

Christensen, J. G. (2000) "The dynamics of decentralization and recentralization." In *Public Administration*, (78)2, Wiley Online Library, 389–408.

Danish Agency for Culture (2013) "Rapport om ny ordning for lokal radio og – tv" [Report on a new organization of community radio and television]. Retrieved from http://www.kulturstyr elsen.dk/nyheder/rapport-om-ny-ordning-for-lokalradio-og-tv/ (accessed 15 October 2014).

DR (2012) *DR: Medieudviklingen 2012* [DR–The Media Trends 2012]. Retrieved from http:// www.dr.dk/php/drmu/omdr/Medieudviklingen.pdf (accessed 3 October 2014).

Hallett, L. and Hintz, A. (2009) "Digital broadcasting – Challenges and opportunities for European Community Radio Broadcasters." *Telematics and Informatics*, 27(2), 151–61.

Harrie, E. (2013) *A Nordic Public Service Media Map.* Gothenburg: Nordicom.

Hederström, C. (2004) *Öppna radion och televisionen. Kartläggning och analys av icke-kommerciel lokal radio och tv* [Open radio and television: Mapping and analysis of non-commercial radio and television]. Kulturdepartementet [Swedish Ministry of Culture].

Howley, K. (2013) "Community media studies." *Sociology Compass*, 7(10), 818–28.

Jankowski, N., Prehn, O. and Stappers, J. (eds) (1992) *The People's Voice: Local Radio and Television in Europe.* London: John Libbey.

Jauert, P., Degn, H.-P. and Taylor Hansen, A. (2013) *Forslag til ny ikke-kommerciel lokalradio og – tv-ordning* [Proposal for a new organisation of non-commercial local radio and television].

Kulturstyrelsen [Danish Agency for Culture]. Retrieved from http://www.kulturstyrelsen.dk/ fileadmin/user_upload/dokumenter/KS/medier/radio/Tilskud/Korrigeret_baggrundsrapport_ Per_Jauert.pdf (accessed 15 October 2014).

Jauert, P., Degn, H.-P. and Saabye, S. (2014) *Lokalradio og – tv på Internettet – muligheder og udfordringer. Rapport udarbejdet til Kulturstyrelsen* [Local radio and television on the Internet – opportunities and challenges]. Report made for the Danish Agency for Culture. Retrieved from http://www.kulturstyrelsen.dk/fileadmin/user_upload/dokumenter/KS/medier/mediepro jekter/Rapport_om_lokalradio_og_tv_paa_nettet/Bilag_D_-_Lokalradio_og_-tv_paa_internettet_ af_Per_Jauert_m.fl.pdf (accessed 15 October 2014).

Jauert, P. and Prehn, O. (1994) "Local radio policy in Europe and Scandinavia." *Nordicom Review*, 1, 137–62.

——(1995) *Lokalradio og lokal-tv. Nu og i fremtiden* [Local radio and local television: From now on and in the future]. Kulturministeriet [Danish Ministry of Culture].

——(2002) *Mangfoldighed og kvalitet. Evaluering af tilskudsordningen for lokalradio og – tv* [Diversity and quality: An evaluation of the subsidy scheme for local radio and television]. Kulturministeriet [Danish Ministry of Culture].

——(2003) "The Danish subsidy scheme for non-commercial local stations." *Javnost – The Public*, 10(1), 63–84.

Medietilsynet (2014) [*The Norwegian Media Authority–Subsidy Schemes*]. Retrieved from http:// www.medietilsynet.no/Stotteordninger/Lokalkringkasting/ (accessed 15 October 2014).

Nissen, C. S. (2013) "What's so special about Nordic Public Service Media? An introduction." In U. Carlsson (ed.) *Public Service Media from a Nordic Horizon: Politics, Markets, Programming and Users*. Nordicom, University of Gothenburg (pp. 9–16).

Nordicom (2013) *Media Statistics*. Retrieved from http://www.nordicom.gu.se/en/media-trends/ media-statistics (accessed 14 September 2014).

Prehn, O., Nordahl Svendsen, E. and Petersen, V. (1992) "Denmark: Breaking 60 years of broadcasting monopoly." In N. Jankowski, O. Prehn and J. Stappers (eds), *The Peoples Voice: Local Radio and Television in Europe*. London: John Libbey (pp. 45–61).

Rodríguez, C. (2001) *Fissures in the Mediascape: An International Study of Citizens' Media*. Cresskill, NJ: Hampton Press.

Skogerbø, E. (1988) *Demokratiperspektiv på lokalfjersyn [Democracy Perspectives on Local Television]*. Rapport no. 2. Institutt for medier og kommunikasjon, Universitetet i Oslo [Report no. 2. Department of Media and Communication, University of Oslo].

17

ALTERNATIVE AND COMMUNITY MEDIA IN CANADA

Structure, policy and prospects

David Skinner

'Alternative media' is a difficult term to define. On one side, there are considerations of content. Should the field be confined to only media that challenge dominant ideas and social interests? Should it only consider media that allow citizen participation in production or media that are managed collectively? Should only non-profit media be considered? Should it only include progressive media, or should conservative media be encompassed as well? On another side there are considerations of form. Should only traditional media such as newspapers, television, radio, and online media be included? What about non-traditional media such as zines, street theatre, postering and culture jamming? The definition of 'community media' offers similar problems. What exactly is meant by the term 'community'? What kinds of characteristics or interests comprise a community? Might such media be based upon geographic, political, ethnic, linguistic lines? Or perhaps gender, or sexual preference? And finally, are community media a type of alternative media?

Scholars have dealt with these issues in a number of ways. John Downing (2001: v–xi), one of the early researchers in this field, focuses on what he calls "radical alternative media", that is, media which explicitly challenge dominant institutions, ideas and values. Taking a broader view, Clemencia Rodríguez (2001: 20) argues that we should avoid binaries such as 'mainstream' and 'alternative' and instead see such media as involved in cultural politics and working to empower communities through actively "intervening and transforming the established mediascape". Here, she seems to point to an overlap between alternative and community media and calls such media "citizen's media". Developing a different but somewhat similar position, Nick Couldry and James Curran (2003: 7) define alternative media as "media production that challenges, at least implicitly, actual concentrations of media power, what ever form those concentrations may take in different locations". Here, the key feature of "media power" is the "power to represent the reality of others" (ibid.). Taking a harder line,

Sandoval and Fuchs (2010: 145) offer that alternative media "provide non-commercial products instead of commodities" that focus on "critical content" rather than "ideological content in a standardized form". Echoing a number of other writers, they also emphasise that "ideal typical alternative media abolish the distinction between producers and consumers" and allow consumers "to actively engage in the production process" (cf. Atton, 2002).

Although it is difficult to find a specific set of characteristics that all these definitions share, perhaps the key difference they point to is that alternative and community media provide a range of ideas and opinions that are not readily available in the corporate press, or that serve the needs of a particular group or community that is poorly served by dominant commercial media outlets. To the extent that these media help animate or create a place in which "experiences, critiques, and alternatives" to dominant social forms might be developed, they can also be seen as helping animate alternative "public spheres" or communities in which traditions, ideas and values that differ from the dominant culture might grow and flourish (Downing, 2001: 29–30). This points to a possible distinction between 'alternative media', which look to be active agents of social change, and 'community media', which either explicitly or implicitly challenge dominant ideas and values but do not necessarily advocate for change (Jacob, 2001). Set further to the margins of media markets than their community cousins, alternative media are guided by purposes other than the profit motive, are generally independently owned and are operated on a non-profit or cooperative basis. In some instances, they do not accept advertising and, when they do, the income it provides is seen as secondary to serving specific community or social purposes. For our purposes, what brings alternative and community media together is that they both work to challenge concentrations of media power. From this perspective, Canada has a rich history of alternative and community media.

Alternative media: Setting the frame

Towards the end of the nineteenth century, poor working and social conditions spawned a vibrant labour-based press in Canada. These papers challenged the dominant partisan political newspapers of the time, criticising social inequalities and advocating progressive change – particularly for white, male workers (Verzuh, 1988; Hackett and Zhao, 1998: 20–25). During the years between the First and Second World Wars, the radical admonitions of the socialist and communist press so alarmed governments that measures were taken to censor their views (Weinrich, 1982). Through the late 1960s and early 1970s, the civil rights, student, women's and environmental movements fuelled an explosion of radical newspapers in cities across the country (Woodsworth, 1972). Here, too, governments often reacted with lawsuits and other forms of censorship to material that was perceived as threatening to the social and political order of the time.

The enthusiasm for overthrowing the top-down pattern of communication that characterised conventional mass media overflowed into other media as well, and through this period radio, television and cable all became proving grounds for new forms of citizen- and community-controlled communication. Meanwhile, in the

1960s and 1970s, Quebec nationalism helped provide even greater impetus to the development of a range of media alternatives in that province than in the rest of the country (Raboy, 1984).

In the 1970s and early 1980s, growing concern for community and economic development in Aboriginal communities provided for a burgeoning Aboriginal media (Roth, 2005). Through the 1980s, efforts by a range of interests resulted in changes to the federal Broadcasting Act, and in 1991 new legislation that recognised that the media should reflect a broad range of community, multicultural and Aboriginal perspectives. The 1990s brought the internet and, by the close of the century, the web was home to a wide range of sites that not only extended the reach of traditional alternative media forms but also created new alternative media practices.

Today's mediascape was given form by these events and circumstances. And while many of the original publications and programmes spawned by activist and community movements of the past are gone, many of the marks they left upon the social landscape remain.

Broadcasting

Broadcasting in Canada falls under federal jurisdiction and is regulated by the Canadian Radio-Television and Telecommunications Commission (CRTC). The CRTC maintains a range of policies in the areas of community, student, ethnic and Aboriginal broadcasting. While, for the most part, these broadcasters are much more community oriented than radical in nature, to varying degrees they can be seen as alternatives to commercial media. In an effort to create film and videos that would inspire positive social change, the National Film Board created the 'Challenge for Change' programme in the late 1960s. A key focus of the project was to create horizontal lines of communication between members of disadvantaged communities and thereby help develop and strengthen them. While controversial, the program was key in getting people across North America to advocate for including community channels in the cable systems that were being built at that time. By 1972, more than 100 cable systems in Canada had community channels, and in 1975 the CRTC made the provision of a community channel – complete with a small studio and equipment – a condition of license for most cable operators (Halleck, 2002: 146–47; Goldberg, 1990: 15). In 2013, there were 109 community channels operating in Canada (CRTC, 2013: 76).

While many cable companies provide training and public access to the community channel, the degree of public involvement in these facilities varies dramatically from place to place. As Goldberg (1990: 18) points out, in the 1970s and 1980s, "[c]ontrol over programming decisions, productions, and equipment use was gradually shifted out of the hands of community members and into the hands of the cable licensee and its employees hired to 'run' the community station". This ownership structure made it particularly difficult for community groups to gain access to the channel. Further exacerbating the situation, in 1997 the CRTC ruled that cable companies would no longer be required to provide a community channel. In the face of these concerns, a new community television policy was announced in 2002. But it largely left control of the channel in the hands of cable operators, and numerous complaints that large cable companies were increasingly utilising programming formats similar to those of commercial broadcasters followed (Vallantin, 2008).

Following mounting public pressure, the CRTC held a review of the 2002 policy in 2010. During these hearings, a new organisation – the Canadian Association of Community Television Users and Stations (CACTUS) – presented a model for community broadcasting that would have taken the channels out of the hands of cable companies and set them on an independent footing (Edwards, 2010). But while this plan garnered strong support during the hearings, the CRTC made only minor changes to the policy and the concerns of interveners went largely unaddressed (Lithgow, 2012).

Community television broadcasting in Quebec is organised quite differently than in other Canadian provinces. While in some instances the channel is operated by cable companies, in others cable operators provide access for non-profit, community-based associations as well as some financial support. Programming becomes the responsibility of the associations. There are about 50 such associations in Quebec, 44 of which are represented by the Fédération des télévisions communautaires autonomes du Québec (FEDETVC). The associations provide training, and financing comes from a combination of advertising, government funding, bingo revenues and membership campaigns. Production is undertaken by both employees and volunteers. While for the most part programming is not 'radical', it does place the power of representation in local hands and, in that way, challenges the power of nationally and regionally focused corporate media.

While in recent years, regulators have not been particularly supportive of community television, new technologies have also presented challenges, as satellite broadcasters are not required to carry a community channel (Lithgow, 2012). Perhaps the best hope for the future of community television in Canada is the development of non-profit community-based community television associations similar to the Quebec model, or independent community media centres like those proposed by CACTUS.

Community radio

While commercial radio is by far the dominant model in Canada, in the wake of decades of pressure from supporters and activists, the country now boasts a small but well-entrenched community radio sector. The CRTC defines a 'community radio station' as a station that is "owned and controlled by a not-for-profit organization, the structure of which provides for membership, management and programming primarily by members of the community at large" (CRTC, 2000: 13). The term 'community' is generally defined in geographic terms, and licensees are expected to be welcoming of all members of the community and to both promote community access to the facility and provide training to those who may wish to participate in it. Community stations generally face much stronger limits on advertising than their commercial cousins and raise funds through a variety of means, including membership fees and fund-raising drives. Outside Quebec, community stations usually only have one or two paid staff – often part-time – and the programming is delivered by volunteers.

In 2012, there were 118 community radio stations operating in Canada (CRTC, 2013: 56). Depending upon where they are located, however, they can have quite different mandates. Those located in the downtown core of large urban centres are often more radical than those operating in smaller cities and towns. CFRO, for instance, located in the heart of Vancouver's poverty-stricken Downtown Eastside, sets their sights on providing "information that is not covered by the conventional media or perspectives that challenge mainstream media coverage" (Co-Op Radio, n.d.). Others, such as Regina's CITR, take a more centrist approach and strive to broadly contribute to the city's "cultural and community life" (CITR, n.d.).

Stations located on university campuses are regulated somewhat differently than their off-campus cousins. These 'campus community' stations carry a range of programming, and their political affiliations can vary. In 2012, there were 41 operating in Canada (CRTC, 2013: 56). Founded in 1981, the National Campus and Community Radio Association/Association nationale des radios étudiantes et communautaires (NCRA/ANREC) represents stations from both regulatory categories. With 82 members, it works with government and related industry groups on issues such as licensing, regulatory fairness and copyright. The NCRA's Statement of Principles recognises "that mainstream media fails to recognize or in many instances reinforces social and economic inequities that oppress women and minority groups of our society" (NCRA, n.d.). Member stations also produce a news programme – GroundWire – that the NCRA distributes (GroundWire, n.d.).

Community radio also enjoys a stronger, more entrenched presence in Quebec than in the rest of the country. The Association des radiodiffuseurs communautaires du Quebec (ARC) has 35 member stations in 17 regions of the province (ARC, n.d.). Revenue comes from a combination of advertising, community contributions and government support. In 2007, Canada's largest community radio associations founded the Community Radio Fund of Canada/Fonds canadien de la radio communautaire (CRFC), an independent not-for-profit funding organisation focused on the community radio sector. Seeded by a $1.4 million commitment by Astral Media as part of an ownership transfer community benefits package, money from the CRFC has been available to community stations across the country to bolster programming and other services (CRFC/FCRC, n.d.). However, while the CFRC has brought a much-needed source of revenue to community radio in Canada, because the funding is largely derived from the proceeds of transfers of ownership in the corporate sector it is undependable and not well suited to the long-term stability of this sector.

Publishing

While sex, drugs and rock and roll may have been key themes of the weekly papers of the 1960s and 1970s, such papers were also on the edge of a shifting cultural politics. Carrying news and opinion pieces on the anti-war movement, native rights, the women's movement, justice for workers and environmental and anti-nuclear concerns, proprietors and vendors were often harassed, and sometimes charged, by police and other authorities (Leibl, 1970; Verzuh, 1986). Vancouver's Georgia Straight, for instance, was consistently targeted by police and had its licence suspended in 1967.

In 1969 22 charges – ranging from libel, to publishing obscene material, to "counseling another person to commit an indictable offense" – were laid against the paper and its employees (Sullivan, 1970: 283). In Montreal, the *Logos* suffered similar treatment. Some of these underground papers operated as collectives, while others had more traditional hierarchical management structures (Lipton, 1980; Ladner, 1986; Verzuh, 1989). While most solicited advertising, they generally flaunted accepted commercial production standards in terms of layout and design, story form, and advertising placement. But financing was a problem for almost all of them, and by the mid-1980s shifting social currents drove most of these publications from the market and a new genre of glossy, business-savvy 'news and entertainment' weeklies replaced them. While these papers sometimes still have a political edge, their focus is on the bottom line.

Although too numerous to enumerate here, a broad range of newspapers and magazines continue to be published across the country. These are set between the principles of community service and the imperatives of the marketplace, and focus on a broad range of issues: local and regional politics, gay and lesbian perspectives, feminist and environmental concerns. Several cities also have street papers dedicated to helping the homeless, such as Montreal's *L'Itineraire* and Vancouver's *Megaphone*. There are also a small number of not-for-profit magazines, such as *This Magazine*, *Canadian Dimension* and *Briar Patch*, that carry on the progressive political tradition of alternative newspapers. But financial problems continue to plague these publications, and with the changing economics brought on by the internet, many struggle to survive.

The province of Quebec offers more support for community publications than they receive in other parts of the country. For over 30 years, the provincial government has offered various forms of support to the members of l'Association des médias écrits communautaires (AMECQ), an association representing more than 80 newspapers, magazines, and web-based media in that province. Under the terms of the organisation's charter, member publications must be collectively owned and democratically managed, and while all member publications are not radical per se, they are explicitly mandated to be both accessible by and responsible to a specific geographic or cultural community (AMECQ, n.d.).

Student newspapers

Student newspapers have long been a place where neophyte journalists, social activists and pundits honed their critical skills (Ryerson Review of Journalism, 2013). More recently, however, the activist politics of the student press have themselves been the subject of debate and many papers have lost their radical edge. Established in 1938 as a national non-profit cooperative news-gathering organisation for student newspapers, the Canadian University Press (CUP) has been a key player in the development of the student press for over 75 years. CUP's 1977 Statement of Principles declared that "the major role of the student press is to act an agent of social change", that it should "support (other) groups serving as agents of social change" and that "the student press must use its freedom from commercial and other controls to ensure that all it does is consistent with its major role and to examine issues which other media avoid" (CUP, 1977). At times, CUP has also worked to encourage democratic management practices among its member papers, as well as encouraged student journalists to seek 'alternative' rather than 'official' news sources. Today, the organisation presents a less radical face and is focused on running a not-for-profit newswire, promoting internship opportunities and retaining membership in an increasingly difficult economic climate (Birchard, 2013).

Ethnic media

As Fleras (2011: 136) points out, while the dominant media's track record in dealing with diversity has improved over the years, "messages about what is acceptable or who is desirable" in the context of immigrant and ethnic communities are still deeply embedded in the ways in which they portray them. However, a large number of media have grown up to serve these communities, and the 'ethnic' or multi-cultural press has a history that stretches back to the mid-nineteenth century in Canada (McLaren, 1973). Today, there are over 400 ethnic newspapers and magazines published in a range of languages across the country and, although the federal government has been criticised for not adequately accommodating ethnic minorities in broadcasting policy, there are now a number of ethnic radio and television stations in cities across the country, as well as a growing number of pay and specialty television services (NEPMCC, n.d.; Hayward, 2012). While the larger newspapers and broadcast outlets are part of national and transnational media corporations and decidedly commercial in focus, many do provide content and perspectives not available in the dominant corporate media and, in this way, at least implicitly work to challenge dominant social codes and conventions (Karim, 2012).

Aboriginal media

From being ignored by the press to the use of negative stereotypes, for years the corporate media's representation of Canada's first peoples has been particularly problematic (Bredin, 2012; Roth, 2005; Alia, 1999). Moreover, in the north, where native peoples often live in small remote communities, communication both within and between those communities can be difficult. Through the 1970s and 1980s, a number of efforts were made to address these concerns. In 1970, the federal government created the Native Communication Program to help spur the growth of Aboriginal news-papers. While, over the years, budget and programme cuts have illustrated the federal government to be a fickle and unpredictable partner in such enterprise, today there are over 25 Aboriginal newspapers and magazines serving national, regional and local audiences (White, 1990).

To help fund the production and distribution of Aboriginal television and radio programming in the north, the Northern Native Broadcast Access Program (NNBAP) was instituted in 1983. As Mohr (1992: 36) notes, radio in particular plays an important role in isolated communities with programs that "focus on international, national, and regional news, culture and traditions, children and youth, and impor-tant issues such as native self-government, the education system and the extremely high (youth) suicide rate(s)". At the same time, programming in Aboriginal languages encourages their use and survival. In 2005, the NNBAP was consolidated along with several other programs into a larger policy package designed to support Aboriginal culture and language (Canada, Department of Heritage, n.d.). In 1999, the launch of the Aboriginal Peoples Television Network (APTN) gave Aboriginal broadcasters national reach. In part financed by a small subscription fee, APTN is carried by all licensed program distributors and available to over 10 million Canadian households. Linking large metropolitan centres in Canada's south with small northern communities, it broadcasts in English, French and a variety of Aboriginal languages. Through serving and developing the interests of Aboriginal peoples, these media operate as agents of cultural power and provide both Aboriginal people and the public at large alternative perspectives on Aboriginal communities.

The internet

While the mediascape is being made over by the internet, it has not provided the cornucopia of media opportunities promised by some. Access is still a problem in many areas and for many people, and creating content is costly and time consuming. But the web is a growing source of new kinds of alternative media. Rising out of protests over World Trade Organization talks in Seattle in 1999, Independent Media Centers (IMCs) or Indymedia were set up to provide a counterpoint to the corporate media. Foregrounding participatory, citizen-based journalism, their success quickly led to the creation of a network of centres stretching around the world, and by July 2004 there were a dozen centres operating in Canada. Some Canadian IMCs were established to provide coverage and support for protests against corporate globalisation; others developed out of local concerns (Skinner et al., 2010). However, between the travails of volunteer labour and the proliferation of myriad blogs and websites for posting news and opinion, today there is very little, if any, activity on Canadian IMC sites. But they have left their mark on the mediascape.

For instance, the Media Co-Op has utilised some basic IMC principles to build a non-commercial operation for independent citizen journalists. The Co-Op is "reader-funded and member-run" and has a unique structure that allows for three types of members – readers, contributors and editors – each with their own interest and role in the association. It has 'locals' in Halifax, Montreal, Toronto and Vancouver and also publishes *The Dominion* – a national newspaper that is produced both electronically and in hard copy (Media Co-Op, n.d.). On another front, rabble. ca combines news with activist tools and resources. It is a non-profit organisation, financed through donations from 'sustaining partners', readers and advertising. The site is operated through a combination of paid and volunteer labour and publishes both original and reprinted materials.

On the West Coast in British Columbia's Lower Mainland area, the independent thetyee.ca provides a news alternative in one of the most heavily concentrated media markets in Canada. As a private company, thetyee.ca is not alternative in the way I have defined the term in this chapter. However, it has yet to generate a profit and, with an emphasis on investigative reporting, it goes head-to-head with corporate media and provides a challenge to the generally conservative tone of the dominant media in the area. While web-based alternatives to dominant corporate media may present well on the screen, financing is almost always a challenge and the threat of closing up shop looms large over day-to-day operations (cf. Houpt, 2013).

Conclusion

There is a wide range of media operating in Canada that, to varying degrees, meet with definitions of alternative and community media. But such media should not be seen as directly opposed to corporate media. Rather, the range of media available in Canada should be viewed as a continuum, with alternative and community media working to engender modes of communication that are foreclosed by dominant, market-driven media forms (Hamilton, 2008). For the most part, these kinds of media are economically precarious – particularly those that tend toward the 'alternative' end of the spectrum – and more information is needed on the range of alternative and community media that are currently operating in the country, as well as the kinds of programmes and policies necessary to help them become more economically viable (Skinner, 2012).

Further reading

A more detailed account of the field of alternative media in Canada can be found in David Skinner (2014), "Media on the margin? Alternative media in Canada." Both Kirsten Kozolanka et al. (2012), *Alternative Media in Canada*, and Andrea Langlois and Frederic Dubois (2005), *Autonomous Media: Activating Resistance and Dissent*, provide snapshots of several different dimensions of the field of alternative media in Canada.

Andrea Langlois et al.'s (2010) collection *Islands of Resistance: Pirate Radio in Canada* documents the little-known history of resistance in an otherwise quite heavily regulated industry. Lorna Roth's (2005) *Something New in the Air* documents the growth of indigenous television. And Kim Goldberg's (1990) *The Barefoot Channel: Community Television as a Tool for Social Change* provides an account of the early history of community cable television in Canada.

References

Alia, V. (1999) *Un/Covering the North: News, Media and Aboriginal People*. Vancouver: UBC Press.

AMECQ (n.d.) *Admissibilite* [online]. Retrieved from http://www.amecq.ca/association/admissibilite/ (accessed 8 October 2013).

ARC (n.d.) *Portrait* [online]. Retrieved from http://radiovision.ca/stations (accessed 8 October 2013).

Atton, C. (2002) *Alternative Media*. Thousand Oaks, CA: Sage Publications.

Birchard, K. (2013) "Several student newspapers quit Canadian University Press." *University Affairs* [online], 18 September. Retrieved from http://www.universityaffairs.ca/several-student-newspapers-quit-canadian-university-press.aspx (accessed 12 October 2013).

Bredin, M. (2012) "Indigenous media as alternative media: Participation and cultural production." In K. Kozolanka, P. Mazepa and D. Skinner (eds), *Alternative Media in Canada*. Vancouver: UBC Press (pp. 184–204).

Canada, Department of Heritage (n.d.) "Northern Aboriginal broadcasting" [online]. Retrieved from http://www.pch.gc.ca/eng/1267292195109/1305897413896#a1 (accessed 12 October 2013).

CITR (n.d.) *About* [online]. Retrieved from http://cjtr.ca/about (accessed 2 October 2013).

Co-Op Radio (n.d.) *About* [online] Retrieved from http://www.coopradio.org/content/about-co-op-radio (accessed 8 October 2013).

Couldry, N. and Curran, J. (2003) *Contesting Media Power: Alternative Media in a Networked World*. New York: Rowman and Littlefield.

CRFC/FCRC (n.d.) "Community Radio Fund of Canada" [online]. Retrieved from http:// http://www.communityradiofund.org/en/ (accessed 8 October 2013).

CRTC (2000) "Community radio policy, Public Notice CRTC 2000-13" [online, 28 January]. Retrieved from http://www.crtc.gc.ca/archive/ENG/Notices/2000/PB2000-13.HTM (accessed 28 January 2012).

——(2013) "Communications monitoring report" [online]. Retrieved from http://www.crtc.gc.ca/eng/publications/reports/policyMonitoring/2013/cmr.htm (accessed 11 October 2013).

CUP (1977) *CUP Editor's Manual* (2nd ed.). Ottawa: Canadian University Press.

Downing, J. D. H. (with Ford, T., Gil Villarreal, G. and Stein, L.) (2001) *Radical Media: Rebellious Communication and Social Movements*. Thousand Oaks, CA: Sage Publications.

Edwards, C. (2010) "A new vision for community TV" [online]. Retrieved from http://cactus.independentmedia.ca/node/401/ (accessed 18 January 2012).

Fleras, A. (2011) *Media Gaze: Representations of Diversities in Canada*. Vancouver: UBC Press.

Goldberg, K. (1990) *The Barefoot Channel: Community Television as a Tool for Social Change*. Vancouver: New Star Books.

GroundWire (n.d.) *Mandate* [online]. Retrieved from http://groundwire.ncra.ca/page.cfm/Mandate (accessed 20 January 2012).

Hackett, R. A. and Zhao, Y. (1998) *Sustaining Democracy: Journalism and the Politics of Objectivity*. Toronto: Garamond Press.

Halleck, D. D. (2002) *Hand Held Visions: The Impossible Possibilities of Community Media*. New York: Fordham University Press.

Hamilton, J. F. (2008) *Democratic Communications*. Lanham, MD: Lexington Books.

Hayward, M. (2012) "Ethnic broadcasting: A history." In I. Wagman and P. Urquhart (eds), *Cultural Industries.ca*. Toronto: Lorimer.

Houpt, S. (2013) "We wanted to believe in OpenFile's community journalism – but the dream is dead." *The Globe and Mail*, 21 February [online]. Retrieved from http://www.theglobeandmail.com/report-on-business/we-wanted-to-believe-in-openfiles-community-journalism—but-the-dream-is-dead/article8953664/ (accessed 17 October 2013).

Jacob, Kokila (2001) "Canada's ethnic newspapers provide critical multicultural perspective." *CJFE Reporter*, no. 1, 3.

Karim, H. (2012) "Are ethnic media alternative?" In K. Kozolanka, P. Mazepa and D. Skinner (eds), *Alternative Media in Canada*. Vancouver: UBC Press (pp. 125–44).

Kozolanka, K., Mazepa, P. and Skinner, D. (eds.) (2012) *Alternative Media in Canada*. Vancouver: UBC Press.

Ladner, P. (1986) "A case study in alternates." *Content*, March–April, 7–8.

Langlois, A. and Dubois, F. (2005) *Autonomous Media: Activating Resistance and Dissent*. Montreal: Cumulus Press.

Langlois, A., Sakolsky, R. and van der Zon, M. (2010) *Islands of Resistance: Pirate Radio in Canada*. Vancouver: New Star Books.

Leibl, A. (1970) "Canada's underground press." *Canadian Library Journal*, 27 (January), 16–20.

Lipton, B. (1980) "'Prairie fire' history illustrates struggles of the alternate press." *Briarpatch*, 9(4), May, 35ff.

Lithgow, M. (2012) "Transformations of practice, policy, and cultural citizenships in community television." In K. Kozolanka, P. Mazepa and D. Skinner (eds), *Alternative Media in Canada*. Vancouver: UBC Press (pp. 125–44).

McLaren, D. (1973) *Ontario Ethno-Cultural Newspapers, 1835–1972: An Annotated Checklist*. Toronto: University of Toronto Press.

Media Co-Op (n.d.) *About* [online]. Retrieved from http://www.mediacoop.ca/about accessed 6 October 2013.

Mohr, L. (1992) "To tell the people." In B. Girard (ed.) *A Passion for Radio*. Montreal: Black Rose Books (pp. 23–38).

NCRA (n.d.) *About C/C Radio* [online]. Retrieved from http://www.ncra.ca/about-cc-radio accessed 12 September 2013.

NEPMCC (n.d.) *About* [online]. Retrieved from http://www.nepmcc.ca/ accessed 6 October 2013.

Raboy, M. (1984) *Movements and Messages: Media and Radical Politics in Québec*. Toronto: Between the Lines Press.

Rodríguez, C. (2001) *Fissures in the Mediascape: An International Study of Citizens' Media*. Cresskill, NJ: Hampton Press.

Roth, L. (2005) *Something New in the Air*. Montreal and Kingston: McGill-Queen's University Press.

Ryerson Review of Journalism (2013) *Canadian University Press: 75 Years of Student Journalism* [online]. Retrieved from http://www.rrj.ca/m27383/ accessed 11 October 2013.

Sandoval, M. and Fuchs, C. (2010) "Towards a critical theory of alternative media." *Telematics and Informatics*, 27, 141–50. Retrieved from http://fuchs.uti.at/wp-content/uploads/2009/12/alt_media.pdf accessed 14 September 2013.

Skinner, D. (2012) "Sustaining independent and alternative media." In K. Kozolanka, P. Mazepa and D. Skinner (eds), *Alternative Media in Canada*. Vancouver: UBC Press (pp. 25–45).

——(2014) "Media on the margin? Alternative media in Canada." In L. Regan Shade (ed.), *Mediascapes: New Patterns in Canadian Communication* (4th ed.). Toronto: Nelson Education (pp. 344–63).

Skinner, D., Uzelman, S., Langlois, A. and Dubois, F. (2010) "Independent Media Centres in Canada: Three case studies." In D. Kidd, C. Rodriguez and L. Stein (eds), *Making Our Media: Mapping Global Initiatives toward a Democratic Public Sphere*. Cresskill, NJ: Hampton Press (pp. 275–93).

Sullivan, S. (1970) "The student press in Canada." In *Special Senate Committee on the Mass Media Report*, vol. III. Ottawa: Queens Printer (pp. 271–86).

Vallantin, C. (2008) "Fade to black: How cable companies and the CRTC's lenience are killing what's left of community TV." *Fast Forward Weekly*, 19 June [online]. Retrieved from http://www.ffwdweekly.com/article/life-style/ television/fade-black/ accessed 16 August 2008).

Verzuh, R. (1986) "Alternates: Moving uptown?" *Content*, March–April, 2–6.

——(1988) *Radical Rag: The Pioneer Labour Press in Canada*. Ottawa: Steel Rail Publishing.

——(1989) *Underground Times: Canada's Flower Child Revolutionaries*. Toronto: Deneau Publishers.

Weinrich, P. (1982) *Social Protest from the Left in Canada, 1870–1970*. Toronto: University of Toronto Press.

White, G. (1990) "Cuts showed little concern for natives." *The Calgary Herald*, 2 March, A4.

Woodsworth, A. (1972) *The 'Alternative' Press in Canada*. Toronto: University of Toronto Press.

18

COMMUNITY MEDIA AND MEDIA POLICY REFORM IN ANGLOPHONE SUB-SAHARAN AFRICA

Patrick E. Okon

Introduction

This chapter explores the interventionist role of community media groups in contemporary media policy developments of Anglophone sub-Saharan Africa. It is broadly located within the discourse about the 'shapers' of media policy development and aims to respond to the enduring tensions in scholarship with regard to the actual role of and the difficulty of mapping the impact of grassroots policy actors in media policy reforms (Humphreys, 1994; Hortwitz, 2001; Chakravartty and Sarikakis, 2006). The empirical materials draw upon various case studies of media deregulation and campaigning activities of community print and broadcast media groups in South Africa, Ghana and Nigeria.

Structurally, I reconceptualise media policy in line with the vision of alternative journalists; highlight the value of alternative 'public spheres' to participatory policy-making; streamline trends in media policy debates and the political economy of community media in the sub-Sahara; and identify the campaigning 'platforms' of community media institutions for policy reforms, indicating some of their achievements and enduring challenges. My fundamental argument is that governments and their political institutions are not the exclusive players in contemporary media policy developments. There are other significant and sometimes unacknowledged decision-makers. However, the effectiveness of community media groups is often conditioned by political, legislative and economic processes, differences in business philosophies, available funding regimes and structures for audience participation.

Understanding media policy

Media policy addresses a wide range of issues that include the structural, ethical, censorship, regulatory and economic principles employed to organise media systems and institutions across national and transnational contexts. Different ideological, technological and economic value systems provide the necessary contexts for media policy articulation and realisation. And the specific approach adopted by each scholar also determines the differences and the specific individual definition of the concept (Freedman, 2008; Braman, 2010; Duff, 2010).

For the purpose of this chapter, I propose an 'ethical-political' approach to media policy conception. The 'ethical-political' recognises the importance of 'affective' and 'critical-rational' contents to policy-making. The approach is premised on David Hutchison's "sceptical liberalism" (1999: 4); that is, a right-based theoretical framework that questions the absolute agency of governments to determine political and legal truths.

The 'ethical-political' vision requires the integration of the 'administrative approach' of governments, the 'objectivity vision' of professionalised media, and the 'politicised interests' of civil society groups. Such an approach, it is argued, will enable the conception of the interests of governments, professionalised media and the life contexts of disadvantaged groups, not just as possibilities, but as rights and as legitimate ends (Negt and Kluge, 1983). The three elements of the integrative policy vision must, however, be realised within the ideological and the production fields. Additionally, the goal of the 'ethical-political' framework is to appeal to policy-makers to continue to recognise the values of 'policy community' and 'policy networks' (Humphreys, 1994) in enabling accountability and new entrants into the policy-making arenas of nation-states.

The proposed approach, therefore, offers a distinctive conceptual framework for understanding the kind of policy vision community media groups bring to bear on national and transnational regulatory and deregulatory processes. In this regard, I define media policy, not only in terms of normative principles, but as the mechanisms (ethical, political, economic, legal and social) through which media systems and institutions are regulated and funded against the backdrop of the mundane and rational politics of bureaucratic and corporate life (cf. Moran, 1996).

The value of this conception is grounded in a broader view of the general determinants of State and Corporate actions and how these affect the packaging of information "with alternative labels" (Duff, 2010: 49). In this regard and drawing from different theoretical traditions, I further differentiate between two models of media policy – *mainstream industrial media policy* and *small-scale alternative media policy* (Garnham, 2000; Hackett and Carroll, 2006). Both policy frameworks are, however, impacted by the Enlightenment and post-Enlightenment political thoughts of the seventeenth through mid-twentieth centuries. They are also united around their shared critique of the 'objectivity' logic of professionalised popular journalism and how this could be better actualised by alternative media institutions.

The mainstream model is largely grounded on 'liberal' and 'neoliberal' policy values, whose respective roots stem from the Anglo American decentred political subsystems of policy-making and from its free markets communication project that emphasises media concentration, commercialism and limited media regulations. The alternative media policy paradigm is rooted in emancipatory or socialist ideologies of citizenship that often find expression through the instrumentality of experimental media practices and citizenship social movements.

But just like the dominant policy model, the alternative model also has two value strands: 'the ideologically and culturally radical' (the *reformative* and *subversive* policy visions) that advocates a complete over-oiling and democratisation of the mainstream media sector and the 'not too ideologically and culturally radical' (the *incorporation* and *supplementary* policy visions) that advances minimal reforms within the mainstream media sector (Atton and Hamilton, 2008). These policy trends of alternative journalism can particularly be detected in the ideological and production fields, as well as in the specific proposals offered by community media groups for the resolutions of practice dilemmas tied around the subjects of institutionalisation, capitalisation, the encroachment of political economy into media contents, as well as around the diasporic experiences of alternative journalists.

The alternative policy perspective, therefore, offers to the politics of media regulation and deregulation some benchmarks that transcend that of liberal pluralists. Among them are the demands for the expansion, through statutory reforms, of direct participation in decision-making by which existing media and representative democratic systems could be rejuvenated; the prioritisation of equality (in terms of 'voice' and 'access' to resources) as the central principle of democracy; individual freedom from State and/or Corporate power; and emphasis on social solidarity and community, egalitarian social changes, and on the need to adopt a self-reflexive approach to all forms of injustices imbedded in national social and political orders (Hackett and Carroll, 2006).

But within the two distinctive media policy perspectives, I make a further distinction between 'external' and 'internal' institutional media policy frameworks. While the 'external' framework refers to the set of official (constitutional and legislative) rules imposed by governments on media institutions to guide public communication practices, the 'internal' policy framework refers to the set of institutional practice guidelines formulated internally by media proprietors and editors in response to specific needs for discipline (Oosthuizen, 2001).

Community media as public spheres

The integrative conception of media policy notwithstanding, the understanding of the interventionist potency of community media in media policy formations requires that a certain model of community media be adopted. In this regard, I propose the conception of community media in Anglophone sub-Saharan Africa in terms of *public spheres*; that is, those public arena where citizens can engage critically with one another and with government through deliberations to influence the affairs of the State (Habermas, 1962; Negt and Kluge, 1983; Sholle, 1995; Curran, 1991; Hackett and Carroll, 2006).

A consideration of community media in terms of the *public sphere* model is, therefore, important for the following reasons: it locates the different formats of community media within the framework of media activism and of the global movements to transform communications, so that communications and representations can be less constrained by bureaucracy or commercial interest and remain increasingly open to positive social values and to the public good; it provides spaces for the articulation of media deregulations in terms of State-citizens relationships and offers prospects for understanding the interactive platforms necessary for media policy formations within nation-states. Additionally, the model offers the theoretical parameter for critiquing how the development of contemporary media policy agendas have been destroyed by large-scale commercial organisations that are primarily concerned with fragmentation and commodification, rather than facilitating the realisation of the everyday life concerns of private citizenship.

Trends in media policy in the Anglophone sub-Sahara

An overview of the contemporary media policy environments in Ghana, Nigeria and South Africa is meant to provide the necessary political and regulatory contexts for understanding the empirical data on the growth and political economy of community media, as well as on community media activism for contemporary media policy reforms. As noted by Sholle, "what is alternative about alternative media ... can be answered only by describing the structure and operation of the mainstream media" (1995: 22) environments.

Key 'drivers' of media deregulation and debates across the three countries are rapid technological developments and transfers of the pre- and post-1980s that brought about the need "to fill a regulatory vacuum in several areas" (Hamelink, 1994: 30); the political economy of communication that outlines the constraints of diversification and globalisation on communication managements; the crucial role of colonialism and modernisation process; the development initiatives of international institutions (especially UNESCO) in the area of media deregulations; the NWICO regulatory politics that emerged with the Non-Aligned movements of the pre-1990s; and the dynamics of the emerging democratic politics that advance decentralisation, privatisation and popular participation in public policy decision-making. African scholars, in particular, have also placed emphasis on the importance of African ethical values and communitarian systems to media managements (Nyamnjoh, 2003).

This chapter, however, recognises the crucial role of community media institutions, as the neglected elements, in the debates about 'shapers' of media policy developments.

While the 'drivers' of deregulatory debates across the three countries are fundamentally the same (with differences only in the degrees of technological developments, corporate economic activities, as well as empowering political orientations), the actual media regulatory experiences of the three countries are never homogeneous. And, while there are now expanded legislative frameworks for media liberalisation and democratisation across the three countries, it is the media policy experiences of Ghana and South Africa that now hold out, through established constitutional and legislative means, expansion in community media and greater hopes for the continuing broad-based participation of minority groups in media management. Nigeria's broadcasting policy environment, by not enabling 'grassroots communities' to gain greater access to the technologies of public communication, is still weak in this regard.

Again, apart from the fact that the media policy orientations of the three countries are now relatively progressive, the degree of activism and civil society engagements with national governments to bring about changes in favour of 'leftist' policies has been impacted principally by their different political histories, the level of rural mobilisations, and socio-economic contexts. While the State has remained the principal legitimator and administrator of media policy for decades, with the transition to democracy across the three countries, the participatory frameworks for the legitimisation of policy have relatively expanded over the years to include civil organisations, radical movements and disadvantaged groups.

Additionally, though the media deregulatory environments of the three countries now favour community media developments, their regulatory experiences are united in the common reliance, not only on colonial and postcolonial State media policy legacies to inform policy changes in the twenty-first century, but also on the adoption of transnational media policy frameworks as benchmarks for constitutional and legislative reforms. These, among others, include the various United Nations resolutions on the media and human rights; the 1990 African Charter for Popular Participation in Development and Transformation (Arusha); the 2001 African Charter on Broadcasting (Windhoek); and the 2002 Declaration of Principles on Freedom of Expression in Africa (Banjul). These documents, among others, urge the adoption of development communication policies that support access and participation, freedom of expression, social changes and the preservation of African languages and cultural heritages.

The state of community media in the sub-Sahara

There is now a robust and complex culture of community print and broadcasting media in South Africa, Ghana and Nigeria. The complexity admits of differences in size, type, ideology, technology, economy and professional imperatives. But because of governments' strategic dispositions towards community radios, this sector is better developed across the three countries than the community television (CTV) sector.

South Africa currently has about 480 community newspapers and magazines; over 127 community radio stations; four CTV channels; and a couple of campus media. Out of the four CTVs, only the Cape Town CTV operates at the grassroots and outside satellite networks. Others licensed as 'grassroots' CTVs, due to their inability to withstand the initial financial recessions, now operate as affiliates and advertisement outlets of Kagiso Media – a situation that demonstrates the adoption of an 'absorption' or 'parallel' general policy orientation and questions their competency to educate the citizens in civil cultures. The complexity of community media in South Africa is, therefore, particularly about the split among 'corporately affiliated media' with commercial business interests, the 'authentic community media' at the suburbs with interests in service deliveries and education and the 'radical democratic media' (e.g., *The Mail* and *Guardian*) with business interest in the exposition of corruption and the promotion of democracy.

There are also a number of community newspapers and magazines in Nigeria. A few function to serve community-specific interests. Others serve primarily the interests of commerce or regional politics. Those owned by religious organisations serve principally socialist interests. Though a few of these small publications just come up and after a while disappear, they generally function to empower the citizens at the local information level. However, the 'knock-and-drop' experience and the big industrial production capacity evident in some community press in South Africa is not a general experience for Nigeria. Most small newspapers are sold to interested readers. But voluntarism within the press sector of the two countries is now an exception, rather than a rule.

'Grassroots' community broadcasting is non-existent in Nigeria at the moment. Legislation favours only the licensing of 'campus broadcasting' for universities. The development of over 19 campus broadcasting stations, though good for apprenticeship, is only a partial and strategic official response to the need for broader media democratisation. NBC, the broadcasting regulatory body, confirms that the government is favourably disposed towards 'grassroots' community broadcasting (e.g., Chapter Nine of the NBC Code) and that over 1,000 applications for 'grassroots' broadcasting licenses have so far been received. But unless a letter of authorisation is received from the presidency, the regulatory body is constrained from issuing licenses.

Unlike Nigeria, 'grassroots' community broadcasting is thriving very well in Ghana. The situation is comparable to the development in South Africa. There are about 12 community radios currently on air and only one CTV (Coastal TV). The Ghana Community Radio Network (GCRN) is working to get 12 more radios on air. These are in addition to a couple of campus radios already in operation. These broadcast stations generally show distinctive interests in environmental protections and the empowerment of local populations towards socio-cultural developments.

One of the primary factors militating against further development in 'grassroots' community broadcasting in Ghana is the willingness of NCA to grant operational frequencies. How the functioning community media are firmly rooted in the local communities to minimise elite influence also remains contestable. And how poor and unstable social infrastructures (electricity, telephone and road services) negatively impact the capability of small media was also recognised by respondents.

Except for *specialist* and a few faith-based community publications, evidence shows that there is the demise of community press in Ghana today. There were some 'authentic' community newspapers in the past. But most have died out. Though there are some newspapers whose production centres are now locally based, they are mostly newspapers sympathetic to either the ruling or the opposition political party. They are not community newspapers as conceptualised by UNESCO.

The structural organisations of community media to ensure local participation and accountability to the regulators are diversified across the two industrial sectors. While the management structures are better organised within the community broadcast sector of the three countries in the form of 'Board of Trustees' or its equivalent for the participatory benefit of local communities, they are somewhat 'loosely' organised within the community press sector around an 'Executive Board' primarily for the benefit of business stakeholders. But generally without the existence of such structures, evidence suggests that the sustainability of community media outside elitist political and commercial influences could be difficult. Also, the funding mechanism for community media across the three countries is gradually shifting from 'patronage' towards 'commercial' or 'mixed' funds arrangements. The shifts are necessitated by a combination of factors: the poor economic conditions of African countries; reductions in international developmental supports; the impact of globalisation; and the changes in the way audiences access news. The availability of diversity of funding models is particularly significant in understanding the capability of small media to engage in ongoing trainings and productions geared towards activism for reforms. Though a large percentage of 'corporately affiliated' community press in South Africa still leans strongly on a purely 'business' model for survival, the possible danger this holds for editorial competencies and campaigning practices needs to be recognised.

Audience participation strategies in the three countries, in varying ways, draw on three emerging practice patterns: the engagements of different cadres of audiences in the ownership and management of community media stations through diversity of representational structures; the provision of access to technologies and technicalities of programming; and the partial delivery of audiences from the informal economic sectors to advertisers. The outstanding thing about the participatory models adopted by community media is that it encourages private producers to benefit from their creativity in terms of the actualisation of talents and equitable revenue distributions. The use of participatory models in relation to audiences also implies a deliberate rejection of the top-bottom model operational within commercial media and the strengthening of the interventionist ability of local communities, through community media, in media policy reform.

Campaigning for media policy reform

Because of the media deregulations of the 1990s that enable expansions in community media, campaigning for media-related reforms in the three countries has, in the past two decades, moved beyond the known parliamentary or District Assembly representative processes to include community media processes. Three main community media 'platforms' have been identified: 'programming', 'capacity-building', and 'deliberative social forums'. Also important are the 'horizontal' and 'vertical' linkages that community media groups have maintained over the years.

Bush Radio (Cape Town) organises, in partnership with GCIS, a discursive programme called "Talk to the Ministers". In bringing issues (e.g. the 'Protection of State Information' and the 'Media Appeal Tribunal' Bills) for public debates, the station is always conscious of the split of opinion between government and the communities within the Cape Flat. The management admit that in facilitating dialogue, the radio station is not the 'Voice', but the 'Mediator' of consensus among communities and between local communities and governments. The justification for this role rests on the conception of the radio station as a conduit for social change and on the need to extend discussions on sensitive policy issues from the parliament to the local communities.

The capability of diversity of 'programming' (news, articles, editorials, discussions, etc.) to pressure governments for policy changes, through agenda setting and opinion formations, generally depends on adopted institutional programme philosophies, the chosen programme languages, the availability of necessary funding and expertise for sustainability, the kind of organisational structures adopted to ensure participation and division of labours, co-production agreements with audiences, as well as the use of professional and non-professional skills. Strong emphasis is also placed on the importance of 'follow-ups' on stories and eye-witness testimonies in the construction of credible information to help citizens find resources to question political authorities.

'Capacity-building' that enables community media to connect with the experiences of local populations and experts often comes in the form of organised trainings, community-based researches, and feasibility studies. The significance of capacity-building rests fundamentally on its literacy, empowerment and greater outreach potencies. The process enables local communities to make informed decisions, design their media processes and sustain peaceful working partnerships. Training in competency in media arts, participatory planning and management and skills in accessing financial resources, as well as literacy in social relation process, is therefore vital to the success of community media's interventions in the complex manipulations of symbols and culture and in influencing media policy developments.

GCRN's (Accra) participatory research is essentially field based. It draws on the benefits of oral testimonies from community members and the power of audio-visuals to engage marginalised groups in discursions and decision-making at every level of community radio initiatives. The interconnected layers of the research include the need to help the people understand themselves, the developmental needs of their communities and the potentials of community media in responding to those needs.

'Deliberative social forums' (conferences, workshops, seminars and retreats), in turn, are important in providing opportunities, not only for social interactions, but also for paper presentations, discussions and exchange of views on practice and policy challenges. They also enable collective articulations of unified policy positions for onward submissions to regulatory agencies of governments. Deliberative forums also have the capacity of bringing about joint advocacy visits to ministers, parliamentarians and media regulators or in generating force for minimal street actions and open protests in partnership with unionist and human rights movements to pressure for policy changes.

The two-day annual 'retreat' organised by the Forum of Community Journalists (Mpumalanga Province) provides Lowveld Media (Nelspruit) and other provincial community newspaper publishers the opportunities to impact media policy issues. The most recently reformed press rules undertaken by the provincial community-based journalists in partnership with other stakeholders are the current *South African Press Code* (2011). The revisions of industrial Codes in South Africa since the late 1990s have always remained a collective industrial responsibility.

But in order to deepen conversations, expand self-reflexive joint actions and broaden campaigning impacts, community media groups do consciously sustain broader 'horizontal' and 'vertical' links with national and transnational individuals, communities and groups. Data identify three dimensions of such cross-relationships: the 'horizontal' links with civil rights organisations, donor agencies and NGOs; the 'vertical' relationship with government departments; as well as the 'vertical' (and sometimes 'horizontal') relationship with mainstream media institutions. While some of the organisations are merely programming partners, others are simply funding, training or lobbying partners. Again, while deliberation, cultural practice for the purpose of visibility, philanthropy and social interactions still remain the primary defining qualities of the three modes of cross-partnership, the networking ability of community media groups has, however, changed irrevocably over the years with the advent of the World Wide Web and the surge in social media and virtual community membership. However, community media groups in sub-Saharan Africa must always remain conscious of how the diversity in cross-partnerships could inadvertently lead to a loss in their distinctive humanist and emancipatory objectives if they become completely subsumed in elite totality (Negt and Kluge, 1983; Okon, 2006).

Media policy activism: Achievements and challenges

While it would be unrealistic to assume that all the achievements of the community media groups of the three countries could be completely captured in this small chapter, it is nevertheless important to note that they have, in varying ways, recorded significant victories in their campaigns for media policy changes over the past two decades. Three different criteria have been used by respondents to measure their successes: the number of awards and trophies received; the level of participation in policy debates and decisions; and the positive policy outcomes recorded. But generally, respondents admit that the successes recorded are indicative of not only the strengths of their adopted participatory mediatory processes, but also organised street activism to influence policy changes at all levels.

The community radio initiatives of Ghana, working under GCRN and COTA, have made policy recommendations towards the formation of a comprehensive broadcasting law and local language Code for the purpose of media programming and political campaigns. They have mobilised for the inclusion of local ethical values in media deregulations as safeguards against the neo-liberal policies entrenched in the country by the NDC-led government. GCRN successfully obtained from the government a 'waiver' on taxation imposed on imported equipment for community broadcasting and a 'lowering' ($100 in US dollars) of the licensing tariff for community media. The network has worked with other stakeholders to overturn NCA's initial regulations on political programming and the generation of minimal income in favour of community media. It has ensured the inclusion of an 'exceptional clause' in NCA's 2007 Guidelines on community radio, whereby a 25km coverage radius could be granted to community radios operating under exceptional terrestrial circumstances. And under COTA, GCRN is working through street actions to promote press freedom and checkmate implicit official attempts to strengthen the monopoly of broadcasting spaces by commercial media.

The community media institutions in South Africa, working under CODESA, FAWO and NCRF, have brought about the establishment of a diverse sector of community media. With other stakeholders, they have facilitated the formation of MDDA, the establishment of ICASA and the formation of the 2005 Electronic Communications Act (No. 36). Under OWN, they negotiated with SABC, prior to 2004, for a 'natural partnership' between emerging CTV studios and SABC for capacity development purpose. They have made policy recommendations to ICASA and to the Portfolio Committee on Public Communication in relation to digital migration, laws dealing with payment of royalties to SAMRO for music played by community radio stations and the high cost imposed by SENTECH on signal distribution, enabling the subsequent reviews of some of the situations. Under SASFED, the groups are working with DTI for the amendments of section 21 of the copyright law that regulates audiovisual creativity and benefits. And under the Right-to-Know Campaigns, they are pressurising the parliament not to legislate on the 'State Information Secrecy' and 'Media Appeal Tribunal' Bills put forward by the conservative wing of the ANC-led government.

The community radio initiatives in Nigeria have, under NCRC, contributed to research and the capacity developments of community broadcasters. They have worked with NBC to establish modalities for community media operations. NCRC is also working with its partners to minimise clientelistic tendencies in campus broadcasting and to promote extensive use of local languages in media programming. They also made policy recommendations towards the revisions of the National Mass Communication Policy, the National Broadcasting Policy and the convergence of ministerial and broadcast regulatory agencies to best manage public resources, just to mention a few.

The successes recorded notwithstanding, empirical data indicate that there are still enduring challenges facing community media groups in the three countries, problematising what brings additional pressures on them. While the majority of the challenges are general to either two or three of the countries, a few are unique to each legislative country or are specific to the needs of each community media sector.

The challenges are tied, among others, around the difficulties community broadcast media have in documenting political impacts on the national level informed by the 5km coverage radius imposed on them; lack of equitable frequency allocations in line with the requirements of ITU; and the 'closed' approaches adopted by media regulators to inform broadcast licensing procedures. Others are the limitations in official funding supports; the failure of national media policy to provide for equal advertising benefits for all media sectors; the poor social infrastructures that impede stable and quality programming in Ghana and Nigeria; attempts by governments in Ghana and South Africa to impose media ethics for mere political gains; the frustrations of community newspaper establishments in South Africa in securing immediate official responses to media enquiries in line with the 48 hours dateline stipulated by existing national policy; and the problem of digital contents regulations and how this impacts community media active engagements with end-users.

Conclusion

In view of these challenges, I wish to make the following recommendations in prospect of the future activist role of community media: the need to reconceptualise media policy in terms of the 'ethical-political' policy framework so as to sustain a meaningful balance between government and ordinary citizens' policy processes; the adoption of 'open' administrative approaches in terms of 'policy community' (durable and official rules of participatory engagements in policy-making) and 'policy network' (less durable and less official mode of relationships) that can enable a more effective management of the complex web of interactions and resource dependencies in policy-making (Humphreys, 1994).

I also suggest broader uses of social media to enable community media groups to improve participation, mobilisation and documentation of impacts at all levels; the continuing digitalisation of community broadcast media to enable the sector to effectively bypass governments' frequency scarcity arguments and strengthen the education of citizens through compressed and multiple electronic transport modes (Kleinsteuber, 1998); and the protection of thinly resourced small media. This could be achieved by expanding common-law defences to enable media groups to better manage defamation suits, the provision of sustainable 'mixed' funding supports, improvements in social infrastructures and a more effective management of the political and commercial influences on community media to prevent the possible subversion of their transformative agendas.

At the heart of this chapter was the need to explore how community media intervene and impact media policy-making in Anglophone sub-Saharan Africa. I have argued that the community media groups of Ghana, South Africa and Nigeria have played (and are playing) substantial interventionist roles in progressive media policy developments. Their active involvement, however, clearly requires greater official and academic acknowledgment.

Further reading

C. Calhoun's *Habermas and the Public Sphere* (Cambridge, MA: MIT Press, 1992) provides other dimensions for public sphere reconceptualisation; C. Carter and S. Allan's "If it bleeds, it leads: Ethical questions about popular journalism", in D. Berry (ed.), *Ethics and Media Culture: Practices and Representations* (Oxford: Focal, 2000: 132–53), offers another critical framework for integrating alternative and mainstream news policy concerns; Kwame Boafo's *Promoting Community Media in Africa* (Paris: UNESCO, 2000) further explores community media development in Africa; and R. A. Rhodes's *Understanding Governance: Policy Networks, Governance, Reflexivity and Accountability* (Buckingham: Open University, 1997) offers a comparative approach to the notions of policy community.

References

Atton, C. and Hamilton, J. (2008) *Alternative Journalism*. London: Sage.

Braman, S. (2010) "Mediating the public through policy." In S. Papathanassopoulos and R. Negrine (eds.) *Communications Policy: Theories and Issues*. New York: Palgrave (pp. 22–48).

Chakravartty, P. and Sarikakis, K. (2006) *Media Policy and Globalization*. Edinburgh: Edinburgh University.

Curran, J. (1991) "Rethinking the media as a public sphere." In P. Dahlgren and C. Sparks (eds), *Communication and Citizenship: Journalism and the Public Sphere in the New Media Age*. London: Routledge (pp. 27–57).

Duff, A. (2010) "The age of access? Information policy and social progress." In S. Papathanassopoulos and R. Negrine (eds), *Communications Policy: Theories and Issues*. London and New York: Palgrave (pp. 49–64).

Freedman, D. (2008) *The Politics of Media Policy*. Cambridge: Polity.

Garnham, N. (2000) *Emancipation, the Media and Modernity: Arguments About the Media and Social Theory*. Oxford: Oxford University Press.

Habermas, J. (1962) *The Structural Transformation of the Public Sphere* (T. Burger, Trans.). Cambridge: Polity.

Hackett, R. and Carroll, W. (2006) *Rethinking Media: The Struggle to Democratize Public Communication*. New York: Routledge.

Hamelink, C. (1994) *The Politics of World Communication: A Human Rights Perspective*. London: Sage.

Horwitz, R. (2001) *Communication and Democratic Reform in South Africa*. Cambridge: Cambridge University Press.

Humphreys, P. (1994) *Media and Media Policy in Germany: The Press and Broadcasting since 1945* (2nd edn). Oxford: Berg.

Hutchison, D. (1999) *Media Policy: An Introduction*. Oxford: Blackwell.

Kleinsteuber, H. (1998) "The digital future." In D. McQuail and K. Siune (eds), *Media Policy: Convergence, Concentration and Commerce*. London: Sage (pp. 60–74).

Moran, A. (1996) "Terms for a reader: Film, Hollywood, national cinema, cultural identity and film policy." In A. Moran (ed.), *Film Policy: International National and Regional Perspectives*. London: Routledge (pp. 1–20).

Negt, O. and Kluge, A. (1983) "The proletarian public sphere." In A. Mattelart and S. Siegelaub (eds), *Communication and Class Struggle 2: Liberation, Socialism, An Anthology in 2 Volumes*. New York: Bagnolet (pp. 92–94).

Nyamnjoh, F. (2003) "Media pluralism and diversity: A critical review of competing models." In T. Kupe and J. Barker (eds.) *Broadcasting Policy and Practice in Africa*. London: Article 19 Africa Programme (pp. 114–37).

Okon, P. (2006) "Community radio and political education through news formats." Dissertation, Catholic Institute of West Africa, Port Harcourt: CIWA.

Oosthuizen, L. (2001) "The external media policy framework: From restrictive policy to the democratisation of communication." In P. Fourie (ed.), *Media Studies: Institutions, Theories and Issues* (vol. 1). South Africa: Juta (pp. 163–86).

Sholle, D. (1995) "Access through activism: Extending the ideas of Negt and Kluge to American alternative media practices." *Science Communication: An International and Interdisciplinary Journal of Social Philosophy*, 2(4), 21–35.

19
ALTER-GLOBALISATION AND ALTERNATIVE MEDIA
The role of transnational alternative policy groups

William K. Carroll

Within contemporary capitalist democracies, movements and media are inter-dependent actors. In a media-saturated world, "the political" and "politics" are "articulated through, and dependent on", media that both reflect and constitute social practice (Dahlberg and Phelan, 2011: 4–5). Media, no less than social movements, comprise "a pivotal site for broader political and cultural struggles" at the "seam" between system and lifeworld (Hackett and Carroll, 2006: 203). Alternative media in particular are seen by many analysts as key actors in the formation of the counter-publics that sustain oppositional politics (e.g. Milioni, 2009; Groshek and Han, 2011; Kelly, 2011). Community radio, alternative newspapers, internet initiatives and the like provide communicative infrastructure for discussions, debates and (some-times) consensus formation outside and beyond the mainstream. Such media give voice to alternative perspectives and social visions and nurture radical sensibilities. By underwriting a "radical habitus" (Crossley, 2003), they help sustain subaltern communities as potential collective actors. In all these aspects of alternative media, social movements figure integrally. As Bob Hackett and I have suggested (Carroll and Hackett, 2006; Hackett and Carroll, 2006), alternative media comprise part of a variegated movement politics of media democratisation, which offers a communicative nexus for a fledging counter-hegemonic political assemblage.

A wide range of progressive movements makes use of alternative media, both as cognitive resources and as means to spread their messages. In social movement communication, alternative media serve several functions. They provide informa-tion, assist action and mobilisation, promote interaction and dialogue, make lateral linkages across domains, serve as outlets for creative expression and promote fund-raising and resource generation. Moreover, movements themselves are increasingly producers of such media, often online (Stein, 2009: 752–3).

The link between movements and alternative media is also evident at the transna-tional level where, since the 1970s, an increasingly crisis-ridden neoliberal globalisation has fuelled concerns that democracy is being hollowed out as governments lose the capacity to pursue policies that stray from what has been called the corporate agenda. In response, transnational social movements have developed as advocates of a "democratic globalization" (Smith, 2008) that endeavours to enrich human relations across space by empowering communities and citizens to participate in the full range of decisions that shape and govern their lives. Della Porta and Mosca define the global justice movement as "a loose network of individuals and organizations (with varying degrees of formality), engaged in collective action of various kinds, on the basis of the shared goal of advancing the cause of justice (economic, social, political, and environmental) among and between peoples across the globe" (2009: 773). The 263 websites they analysed evidenced the use of the internet not only for instrumental purposes in mobilising and coordinating action, but for identity-building and "multilateral interactivity through the creation of open spaces for discussion among diverse people" (ibid.: 778).

As collective actors within global civil society, transnational social movements face the challenge of framing a politics of alter-globalisation that inspires activists and movement sympathisers to look beyond national theatres of contention and siloed, single issues. This requires the *production and mobilisation of counter-hegemonic knowledge*: knowledge that critiques dominant political-economic practices and relations while promoting alternative strategies and visions which, as taken up in practice, might foster a cathartic shift from the episodic, fragmented resistances typical of subalternity to a shared ethico-political project that can become "a source of new initiatives" (Gramsci, 1971: 367). As they contest relations of domination, activist groups themselves generate the rudiments of such knowledge, through what Eyerman and Jamison (1991: 55) call "cognitive praxis": "it is precisely in the creation, articulation, formulation of new thoughts and ideas – new knowledge – that a social movement defines itself in society".

However, activists' primary focus on collective action channels their limited resources into campaigns, protests and direct action, lobbying, etc. The alternative media they produce is typically instrumentalised within these action-oriented domains. For their part, alternative media organisations such as Indymedia, while important carriers of counter-hegemonic perspectives, concentrate on *reportage* of events, commentary on current issues and the *mobilisation* of alternative knowledge within publics and counter-publics, through various one-way or interactive channels. Such a focus distinguishes alternative media from the subject of this chapter: alternative policy groups, whose activities centre upon the *production of counter-hegemonic policy perspectives and visions*.

An important aspect of the alter-globalisation or globalisation-from-below that has developed since the 1970s are *transnational* alternative policy groups (TAPGs): 'think tanks' that research and promote democratic alternatives to the corporate agenda of top-down globalisation. This chapter focuses on these groups and their links to alternative media on the one hand and to the global justice movement on the other. In contrast to movement organisations, the groups featured here focus their efforts not on collective action in the immediate sense but on the production and mobilisation of alternative knowledge – a crucial resource for building the counter-publics that vitalise alter-globalisation politics. In contrast to such alternative media as Indymedia, TAPGs direct their efforts less to reportage and dialogue than to producing in-depth, critical analyses of neoliberal globalisation and intellectual resources for radical political alternatives. Their projects entail distinctive forms of cognitive praxis, through which critical-reflexive knowledge is produced and mobilised.

The chapter takes a neo-Gramscian perspective in theorising TAPGs as key agencies of counter-hegemony. In producing and mobilising alternative knowledge, they strive to 'connect the dots' between various forms of injustice and between the movement/media agencies that address such maladies, so as to facilitate a convergence of perspectives and affiliations into an alternative historical bloc. Such a bloc might be seen as forming around a networked configuration of social movement organisations, alternative media and alternative policy groups – bearing a similarity to what Coopman, in an exploration of community radio, calls a "dissent network", namely, the "perpetual mobilization, involving the action of constructing and maintaining an alternative structure" (2011: 160).

As collective 'organic intellectuals' of alter-globalisation, TAPGs are think tanks of a different sort from the conventional ones that advise political and corporate elites. TAPGs create knowledge that challenges existing corporate priorities and state policies, and that advocates alternative ways of organising economic, political and cultural life. They disseminate this knowledge not only via mainstream media but particularly through activist networks and alternative media, and they often work collaboratively with social movements in advocating and implementing these alternative proposals that prefigure a transformed future.

This chapter sketches (1) how TAPGs form a collaborative network with alternative media and movement organisations and (2) their importance as creators of alternative media in their own right. On both counts, transnational alternative policy groups may be seen as significant collective actors in nurturing counterpublics that transect national borders and single-issue politics.

An overview of TAPGs

My analysis is centred upon a judgment sample of 16 major TAPGs, eight head-quartered in the Global North and eight in the Global South. Each group satisfies these criteria: (1) its core function is *production and mobilisation of knowledge* (including research) that challenges existing political-economic hegemonies and that presents alternatives, creates new paradigms, etc.; (2) a significant part of that activity takes up *transnational issues* and speaks to *transnational counterpublics*; (3) it engages a wide range of issues, i.e., it is not narrowly specialised.

Viewing Table 19.1 from top to bottom, we can see that four groups formed in the mid-1970s, at the culmination of the 1960s protest wave, and as the crisis of the postwar era set in. After 1976 there was a near-hiatus of 13 years, during which just three TAPGs were established (each in the Global South), as neoliberal globalisation established itself as a dominant political-economic form. From the mid-1990s to 2005, TAPGs proliferated, as an intellectual aspect of the global democracy movement, but also in response to the crises and contradictions of neoliberal globalisation (see Carroll, 2014).

What is most important for our purposes here are the knowledge-production projects that these groups take up, as left 'think tanks' within transnational political fields. These projects are complementary to the central concerns of alternative media. Unlike many alternative media, TAPGs are not primarily concerned with news

Table 19.1 16 key transnational alternative policy groups.

Est'd	Name	Acronym
1974	Transnational Institute (Amsterdam)	TNI
1975	Third World Forum (Dakar)	TWF
1976	Tricontinental Centre (Louvain-la-Neuve, Belgium)	CETRI
1976	Centre de recherche et d'information pour le developpement (Paris)	CRID
1982	Society for Participatory Research in Asia (New Delhi)	PRIA
1984	Third World Network (Penang)	TWN
1984	Development Alternatives with Women for a New Era (Manila)	DAWN
1989	Third World Institute/Social Watch (Montevideo)	ITeM
1990	Rosa Luxemburg Foundation (Berlin)	RosaLux
1994	International Forum on Globalization (San Francisco)	IFG
1995	Focus on the Global South (Bangkok)	Focus
1997	Network Institute for Global Democratization (Helsinki)	NIGD
1998	People's Plan Study Group (Tokyo)	PPSG
2001	Centre for Civil Society (Durban)	CCS
2005	Alternatives International (Montreal)	Alter-Inter
2005	India Institute for Critical Action: Centre in Movement (New Delhi)	CACIM

reporting, giving voice to the marginalised or jamming dominant hegemonies, although at various points they may engage in these activities. Their primary remit is to present coherent, critical analyses that have strategic and visionary value. That said, the dividing line between TAPGs and alternative media is blurry, since the production of alternative knowledge directly implies its mobilisation through various forms of media, and its application in political practice.

For instance, ITeM/Social Watch mobilises a vast transnational network of 'watchers' who report on state noncompliance with international covenants. The ITeM/Social Watch website serves as a nodal point for a transnational counterpublic, sharing information from local contexts. Yet, apart from these quotidian practices, the group's main work is dedicated to a yearly publication that synthesises national-level knowledge into a global perspective, which is widely distributed in intergovernmental organisational (IGO) and NGO circles as well as back to the various grassroots communities of watchers. In this way, the group combines practices of alternative knowledge production, movement activism and alternative journalism ('watching'). Similarly, Focus on the Global South produces extensive critical policy analysis and proposes alternatives framed in terms of 'deglobalisation' and *buen vivir*. This knowledge is disseminated both face-to-face and through various media, including the information-rich Focus website, which features a growing collection of videos. Yet, much of Focus's work involves grassroots capacity building in dialogue with movements, through which the group tries out political ideas. Focus staff are deeply embedded in movements; their cognitive praxis is a dialectical venture in transformative politics which is simultaneously a process of counter-hegemonic knowledge production and mobilisation.

Although each alternative policy group pursues a specific project, their efforts converge around an overarching "master frame" (Snow and Benford, 1992), a counter-hegemonic nodal point. This frame contains five elements: (1) the critique of neoliberalism – of the class power and disparities it reinforces and the problematic implications of endless, unregulated accumulation by dispossession (Harvey 2005); (2) the importance of social justice and ecological sustainability as paramount values – a nascent social vision of global justice and sustainable human development; (3) the belief that such an alternative future can be achieved only through grassroots democratic movements; (4) the ethical and strategic importance of North-South solidarity; and (5) the value of critical analysis to inform effective and appropriate strategies for creating change. This frame delineates the contours of counter-hegemonic knowledge, as produced and mobilised by transnational alternative policy groups (Carroll, 2014). In what follows, I consider the networks and practices through which that knowledge is mobilised, often in partnership with alternative media and social movement groups. I first consider how TAPGs interact with alternative media and then discuss how TAPGs function as alternative media outlets in their own right.

TAPGs, alternative media and movements: Mapping the global network

Networks are integral to both social movements and alternative media (Diani, 2011; Barassi, 2013), as fundamental elements of lateral social organisation and communication. Our interest here lies in the specific network of relations linking TAPGs to alternative media on the one hand and to key transnational movement organisations on the other. Figure 19.1 depicts this transnational political-cultural field as a network of 82 organisations.[1] The sociogram has been constructed using a snowballing approach, beginning with the 16 TAPGs and then including the 45 alternative media organisations and the 21 international civil society groups most extensively linked to them, 16 of which are social movement organisations or NGOs and five of which are other alternative policy groups. The entire set of organisations forms a single, connected network.[2]

The sociogram gives us a basic representation of how TAPGs connect and collaborate with alternative media and international activist-oriented organisations. Since the network has been abstracted from the larger global civil society network as a set of (overlapping) social circles centred around the TAPGs, the latter appear as relatively central *articulation points* between alternative media and movement activism (the size of each point is proportionate to the number of ties it has with others in the network). For instance, the most central TAPG in the network, Focus on the Global South, has ties to two alternative media groups, nine alternative policy groups and seven movement organisations (including the World Social Forum, which is the most central node in the network, with ties to 21 other groups). The Transnational Institute includes within its social circle eight alternative media organisations, three other TAPGs and three movement organisations. The Centre for Civil Society links to eight alternative media organisations, five alternative policy groups and one movement organisation. From interviews at TAPGs, the nature of some of these ties can be clarified. The line between TNI and the UK-based *Red Pepper* magazine, for instance, signifies a strong collaborative relationship that is carried by Hilary Wainwright, editor of the magazine and a fellow of TNI. At CCS, the link to the Cape Town-based *Amandla* magazine is multifaceted. At the level of intellectual production, CCS Director Patrick Bond contributes occasional articles, but CCS also helps in distribution, through the efforts of its Community Scholars, some of whom sell the

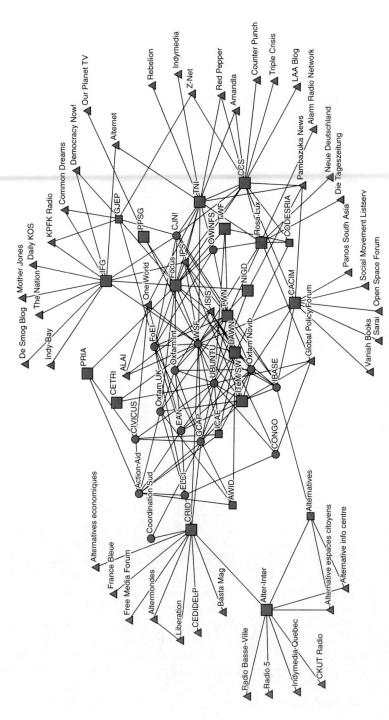

Figure 19.1 The network of TAPGs, alternative media and movement organisations. Squares signify TAPGs; triangles signify alternative media; cirlces signify movement organizations.

magazine in local communities. CCS and TNI are both linked to these two alternative media, and to each other, but also to *Pambazuka News*, which often features analyses by CCS and has good relations with TNI, NIGD and CACIM. Several TAPGs work with Inter Press Service (IPS), a member of the WSF's International Council which is in spirit alternative yet also hooks into mainstream media circuitry. Third World Network has a relationship of mutual aid with IPS in which each uses the other's material. ITeM/Social Watch, DAWN, TNI, CCS, Focus and IFG all use IPS as an important media outlet. There is an intriguing dearth of ties to the polycephalous Indymedia (only two TAPGs, IFG and TNI, show such connections). This may indicate that TAPGs and Indymedia produce and mobilise different genres of alternative knowledge – grassroots reportage versus critical-reflexive knowledge – but it may also pose a challenge – how to integrate the concrete news reportage with more abstracted forms of cognitive praxis.

Overall, some TAPGs participate extensively in the network, linking to other organisations that are themselves centrally positioned, thereby forming a network core. TAPGs at the network core include Focus, TNI, CCS, RosaLux, TWN, DAWN and ITeM/SW; alternative media include IPS, Pabazuka and ISIS; core movement groups include the World Social Forum, UBUNTU World Forum, Friends of the Earth International, Climate Justice Now!, Our World Is Not for Sale and IBASE. These movement groups have highly networked structures that help defray the high transaction costs of transnational activism (Della Porta and Mosca, 2009), enabling them to maintain a more global presence. Other TAPGs are less central to the network overall, and in some cases (e.g., Paris-based CRID, San Francisco-based IFG) manifest ties to nationally oriented alternative media. These various connections integrate the work of alternative policy groups with alternative media and with movement organisations and NGOs, creating the basis for a transnational community of counter-hegemonic praxis.

TAPGs as alternative media producers

As I have emphasised, in addition to networking with alternative media and movements, TAPGs are themselves producers of alternative media. Their products range from books, reports and regular or occasional analytical papers through magazines, newspapers, newsletters and bulletins, pamphlets and flyers, to films, radio and other media (see Table 19.2). At most TAPGs, many of these products (with the partial exception of books) are available *gratis* on the website or to subscribers (TNI's free e-news goes out to approximately 10,000 subscribers). Books often take the form of collaborative, edited volumes, as in CACIM's series on the World Social Forum (Sen and Waterman, 2012) and TNI's volume of case studies on alternative water provision (translated into 13 languages), which helped launch the Reclaiming Public Water Network (Balanyá et al., 2007). In the Global South, where a digital divide continues to exclude many from internet access, groups like RosaLux and Focus have used radio to reach communities. In Durban, CCS uses the SMS messaging system to reach a subaltern constituency that lacks internet connectivity but often has access to mobile phones.

Table 19.2 TAPGs and the types of media they produce.

TAPG	Reports	Books	Magazines	Newsletter	Video/ DVD	Radio/ podcast	Web news	Listserv	Facebook	Twitter	Youtube	SMS	Knowledge Commons	Library
Alter-Inter			x	x			+		x	x				x
CACIM	x	x						x					x	
CCS	x	x			+		+	x	x		x	x		x
CETRI	x		x	x			x	x						x
CRID			x	x			x							x
DAWN	x	x	x	x	x	x	x	x	x		x			
Focus	x	x	x	x	+		x		x	+	x			
IFG	x	x					x	x	x	x	x			
ITeM/SW	x			x			+		x	x				
NIGD		x							x	x				
PPSG		x	x				x	x	x	x				
PRIA	x	x	x	x	x		x		x	x	x		x	+
RosaLux	+	x	x	x	x	x	x		x	x	x		x	+
TNI	x	+	x	x		x	+		x	x	x			+
TWF								x						
TWN	x	x	x				x		x		x			

Note: **x** denotes active production of the media; **+** denotes an especially high level of activity. All TAPGs maintain websites.

The table shows great diversity in the range of media initiatives. Some of the more modestly resourced groups, such as CACIM, NIGD and TWF, produce a narrow range of media; larger groups such as RosaLux, PRIA, TNI and Focus communicate with their publics in many formats and media. Of course, all TAPGs use internet-based communication in their media production, and some have developed elaborate websites embellished with infographics and social media initiatives. Listservs are common; blogging has become more common, along with micro-blogging via Twitter. Focus's Executive Director Pablo Solon is a frequent Tweeter to more than 2,000 followers; other Focus activists are also quite active on Twitter. Focus also has an extensive collection of short videos on Blip; many of CCS's videos can be downloaded from its website; other TAPGs have their own YouTube channels or use Vimeo as a video platform. Most TAPGs maintain their own social network media sites, typically through Facebook, though LinkedIn and http://disqus.com/ are also used. Breaking with the hegemony of English, Social Watch's website and Facebook, updated daily, is in English, Spanish and French; TNI's website includes a considerable amount of material in Spanish; Delhi-based PRIA's website offers machine translation in 58 languages.

Social media have been very effective in drawing people into engagement with TAPGs. Several years ago, as part of its participatory policy research, PRIA started an e-campaign on sexual harassment, which is still ongoing, to which were added Facebook, Twitter and a website: PRIA CASH. At Tokyo-based PPSG, in the aftermath of the Fukushima nuclear disaster, a younger generation of activists has been joining in numbers through the website, in stark contrast to the way PPSG formed a decade and a half ago, out of face-to-face networks. Focus's IT expert and librarian, Raffy Simbol (aka Qiqo), has set up automatic links among Facebook, Twitter and the Focus website, which have proven very useful in outreach, communications and low-intensity political mobilisation. As Focus's Climate and Environmental Justice Programme Coordinator Dorothy Guerrero told me, the social media presence helps recruit support for internet campaigns, eliciting "support from groups that never heard of Focus before, or have never attended a Focus event before".

Clearly, these various communications platforms are now crucial to alternative knowledge mobilisation, particularly as many of them break decisively from the mass media, monological form, and allow for dialogue and discussion. A good example of the latter is the WorldSocialForum-Discuss mailing list, lightly moderated by Jai Sen of CACIM, which includes activist intellectuals from North and South. Increasingly, the work of producing and mobilising counter-hegemonic knowledge implies extensive resort to interactive, digital media.

This is not to deny the continuing importance to alternative knowledge of monological communication, which of course is the means by which critical analysis is typically conveyed, whether in print or electronically. Here, too, new communications technologies open opportunities to innovate. For instance, during my interviews at RosaLux in October 2012, Michael Brie, Director of the Institute for Critical Social Analysis, told me of a collaborative initiative under way to place content, including the *ABCs of Alternatives*, on (German) Wikipedia, taking advantage of Wikipedia's open-source policy. Brie expressed the solidaristic desire, common at TAPGs, to see if, using internet resources, "other groups and foundations, think tanks, initiatives can better combine their knowledge". CACIM's publishing arm, OpenWord (www.

openword.in), promotes "a culture of open publishing" by critically engaging with such emerging practices as copyleft and non-conventional models of content ownership.

As media producers, TAPGs often work in partnership with other progressive groups; but alongside collaborative efforts to develop radical counterpublics, communication also gets directed to the mainstream, through press releases and press conferences, short articles, op-ed pieces and sometimes columns in local or national newspapers. These engage the general public in an accessible manner, introducing some critical ideas without going beyond the breach of mainstream thought. Focus's Walden Bello has had a regular column in a major newspaper. Patrick Bond, referring to the CCS's Eye on Civil Society column in the Durban *Mercury*, said, "those little 800-worders, if they're done properly to reach the audience where they're at, [are] a sort of Saul Alinsky, then you feel you've done something: you've got a little pithy kind of column out". The challenge TAPGs face in getting mainstream play was seen by TNI's Satoko Kishimoto as a trade-off between dealing with issues "in a very complex or comprehensive way" – making it more difficult to reach media "because they don't want to see that kind of complexity" – and creating simpler messages in a strategy geared towards getting covered by the mainstream. This is a dilemma that pervades counter-hegemonic activism.

Conclusions

As key collective intellectuals within alter-globalisation politics – profusely connected to both alternative media and activist groups – transnational alternative policy groups present an instructive site of cognitive praxis that illuminates the relationship between movements, media and counter-hegemony. TAPGs straddle a number of boundaries – between general public and counterpublics, between alternative media and social movements, and across nation-states. Despite the difficulties in translating complex ideas into mainstream news discourse, the counter-hegemonic aspirations of TAPGs mandate them to address the general public (and the dominant institutions of the integral state), and to resist relegation to the cultural margins. TAPGs are alternative media producers, but to realise their projects, the knowledge they produce must carry into the mainstream public sphere, around which corporate media are dominant gatekeepers. Influencing public opinion is an integral goal for all TAPGs, and here they differ from many alternative media groups that address mainly or exclusively subaltern counterpublics.

With regard to activism, TAPGs generally stay one remove from direct-action politics, yet some of their activities amount to internet-based action with a 'high threshold', that is, action occurring online and requiring a commitment of extensive resources (Van Laer and Van Aelst, 2010: 13). Often TAPGs produce and disseminate online counter-hegemonic knowledge that figures directly in movement campaigns, as an integral part of political mobilisation. What distinguishes TAPGs from other high-threshold internet initiatives (e.g., protest and whistleblowing websites such as Wikileaks and alternative media like Indymedia) is the emphasis placed upon producing *critical-reflexive knowledge* – of the forces behind contemporary maladies, of strategies and practices for socio-political transformation, of the enabling conditions for collective action, and of alterative visions and policies.

The example of transnational alternative policy groups suggests further that our understanding of the "mediation opportunity structure" – the media-and-communication environment that provides opportunities for activists "to resist, to exert their agency, to self-represent themselves and to defy the structural constraints" – needs to be broadened beyond instrumental logics (Cammaerts, 2012: 122). In Cammaerts's analysis, contemporary movements strive in their collective action to produce "numbers" (e.g. of bodies at a demonstration), "damage" (e.g. to property or institutional functioning) and "witnessing" (e.g. of injustice), all of which confine activism to the immediacies of direct-action, resistant politics (ibid.). The cognitive praxis of TAPGs, as articulated with and embedded in movements and alternative media, points beyond these instrumentalities. TAPGs produce the intellectual ballast and coherence of social vision to go beyond resistance, into the realm of counter-hegemonic politics. This is not to say that transnational alternative policy groups can afford to ignore the cut-and-thrust of specific campaigns. One of their challenges is to connect counter-hegemonic knowledge into more concrete, conjunctural developments, through dialogue and collaboration with movements. As Marx (1844) put it, critical thought "becomes a *material force* as soon as it has gripped the *masses*". The corollary is equally important: ideas that remain abstract formulations, disembedded from practice, amount to no more than what Gramsci called "castles in the air" (quoted in Germino, 1990: 19). In view of these caveats on theory and practice, it is not surprising that TAPGs are extensively embedded in the transnational movement network. As many of my interviewees emphasised, these groups need to develop knowledge from the grassroots and to communicate it within practices of movement activism. Their highly dialogical mode of knowledge production and mobilisation creates space for the critical reflection that is indispensable in moving from episodic campaigns and micro-political resistance to a transformative politics pointing beyond the hegemonic order. In these ways, TAPGs may be said to provide intellectual leadership for alter-globalisation. Nestled among the movements and the alternative media, they have come to occupy a unique niche within global justice politics.

If the struggle to democratise media (of which alternative media form a component) comprises a crucial nexus, with the potential to establish communicative and practical relations across movements and beyond borders, transnational policy groups may be seen in a complementary light. They produce the counter-hegemonic strategies, visions and policies that facilitate convergence of these social forces into "a new ethico-political form and a source of new initiatives" (Gramsci, 1971: 367).

Notes

1 The *Yearbook of International Organizations* was used as a primary source for the inter-organisational ties (see Carroll and Sapinski, 2013, for details). Additional ties between TAPGs and alternative media groups were added on the basis of 91 in-depth interviews with key activists at the 16 TAPGs conducted between July 2012 and June 2013.

2 To make the sociogram highly legible, only the 21 most central organisations, with direct ties to at least 12 other network members, are shown. The entire network includes 144 NGOs/SMOs directly linked to TAPGs. See Carroll and Sapinski (2013) for a detailed analysis.

Further reading

For more detailed analysis of transnational alternative policy groups as sites for counter-hegemonic knowledge formation, see Carroll (2014) and Carroll and Sapinski (2013). Hackett and Carroll (2006) offer a study of the struggle to democratise public communication as a nexus of social movements that includes within it alternative media. Barassi (2013), Coopman (2011) and Van Laer and Van Aelst (2010) provide strong empirical studies of alternative media, activist networks and social movements. More theoretical discussion can be found in Dahlberg and Phelan (2011) and Sandoval and Fuchs (2010).

References

Balanyá, B., Brennan, B., Hoedeman, O., Terhorst, P. and Kishimoto, S. (eds.) (2007) *Reclaiming Public Water: Achievements, Struggles and Visions from Around the World*. Amsterdam: Transnational Institute.

Barassi, V. (2013) "Ethnographic cartographies: Social movements, alternative media and the spaces of networks." *Social Movement Studies*, 12, 48–62.

Cammaerts, B. (2012) "Protest logics and the mediation opportunity structure." *European Journal of Communication*, 27, 117–34.

Carroll, W. K. 2014. "Alternative policy groups and transnational counter-hegemonic struggle." In Y. Atasoy (ed.) *Global Economic Crisis and the Politics of Diversity*. New York: Palgrave Macmillan (pp. 259–84).

Carroll, W. K. and Hackett, R. A. (2006) "Democratic media activism through the lens of social movement theory." *Media, Culture and Society*, 28, 83–104.

Carroll, W. K. and Sapinski, J. P. (2013) "Embedding post-capitalist alternatives? The global network of alternative knowledge production and mobilization." *Journal of World-Systems Research*, 19, 211–40.

Coopman, T. M. (2011) "Networks of dissent: Emergent forms in media-based collective action." *Critical Studies in Media Communication*, 28, 153–72.

Crossley, N. (2003) "From reproduction to transformation: Social movement fields and the radical habitus." *Theory, Culture and Society*, 20, 43–68.

Dahlberg, L. and Phelan, S. (2011). "Discourse theory and critical media politics: An introduction." In L. Dahlberg and S. Phelan (eds.) *Discourse Theory and Critical Media Politics*. New York: Palgrave Macmillan.

Della Porta, D. and Mosca, L. (2009) "Searching the Net." *Information, Communication and Society*, 12, 771–92.

Diani, M. (2011) "Social movements and collective action." In J. Scott and P. Carrington (eds), *Sage Handbook of Social Network Analysis*. London: Sage.

Eyerman, R. and Jamison, A. (1991) *Social Movements: A Cognitive Approach*. State College: Pennsylvania State University Press.

Germinio, D. L. (1990) *Antonio Gramsci: Architect of a New Politics*. Baton Rouge: Louisiana State University.

Gramsci, A. (1971) *Selections from the Prison Notebooks*. London: Lawrence and Wishart.

Groshek, J. and Han, Y. (2011) "Negotiated hegemony and reconstructed boundaries in alternative media coverage of globalization." *International Journal of Communication*, 5, 1523–44.

Hackett, R. A. and Carroll, W. K. (2006). *Remaking Media: The Struggle to Democratize Public Communication*. London: Routledge.

Harvey, D. (2005) *A Brief History of Neoliberalism*. New York: Oxford University Press.

Kelly, D. M. (2011) "The public policy pedagogy of corporate and alternative news media." *Studies in the Philosophy of Education*, 30, 185–98.

Marx, K. (1844) "Introduction to a contribution to the critique of Hegel's *Philosophy of Right*." Retrieved from http://www.marxists.org/archive/marx/works/1843/critique-hpr/intro.htm (accessed 29 September 2013).

Milioni, D. L. (2009) "Probing the online counterpublic sphere: The case of Indymedia Athens." *Media, Culture and Society*, 31, 409–31.

Sandoval, M. and Fuchs, C. (2010) "Towards a critical theory of alternative media." *Telematics and Informatics*, 27, 141–50.

Sen, J. and Waterman, P. (2012) *World Social Forum: Critical Explorations*. New Delhi: OpenWord.

Smith, J. (2008) *Social Movements for Global Democracy*. Baltimore, MD: Johns Hopkins University Press.

Snow, D. A. and Benford, R. D. (1992) "Master frames and cycles of protest." In A. D. Morris and C. M. Mueller (eds), *Frontiers in Social Movement Theory*. New Haven, CT: Yale University Press.

Stein, L. (2009) "Social movement web use in theory and practice: a content analysis of US movement websites." *New Media and Society* 11(5), 749–71.

Van Laer, J. and Van Aelst, P. (2010) "Internet and social movement action repertoires: Opportunities and limitations." *Information, Communication and Society*, 13, 1146–71.

20
INTERNET FREEDOMS AND RESTRICTIONS
The policy environment for online alternative media

Arne Hintz

Introduction

The rise of the internet has been accompanied by the promise of free communication and a borderless cyberspace where states and businesses have fewer capacities than in the offline world to intervene into free expression. This platform has been particularly suitable for community, alternative and citizen media, as it has increased dramatically the opportunities of participatory and interactive communication – a goal which had been pursued by media activists and community organisations since the early radio experiments and alternative print publications (Brecht, 1927; Atton, 2001; Downing, 2001; Coyer, Dowmont and Fountain, 2008). As a global network, it has allowed alternative media producers to break out of their niches and marginalisations and address a global audience. And as an open platform that requires neither expensive broadcast equipment nor a broadcast licence, it has offered new possibilities for non-profit and radical media that have typically suffered from chronic lack of resources and have rarely been recognised by policymakers (Hintz, 2009; Coyer and Hintz, 2010). Many innovative projects and organisations have not only exploited but expanded these possibilities, from alternative internet service providers to alternative social media platforms, and from the open posting innovations of Indymedia to the broader range of citizen journalism (Atton, 2004; Allan and Thorsen, 2009; Milan, 2013; Hintz, 2014).

However, these freedoms are under attack. Since the early 2000s, states have extended their sphere of influence into cyberspace and have regulated a growing share of online communication. Content is being blocked and filtered, both states and businesses are using the net for data-mining and surveillance, and rules on copyright, libel and defamation increasingly affect online publications. Private intermediaries, such as internet service providers and social media companies, are increasingly enlisted by states to implement restrictive policies and are intervening into online communication and content distribution. These challenges emerge across the globe, both in 'authoritarian' and in 'democratic' states. Yet they are heavily contested, both by digital rights advocacy initiatives and by the relentless innovations of digital activism developing new tools and circumventing restrictions (Deibert et al., 2012).

In this chapter, I will explore these various dimensions of internet freedoms and restrictions as they concern grassroots media activists and citizen journalists. In particular, I will discuss the issues of content filtering, surveillance and commercial forms of censorship, and I will situate these practices in the recent trend of the privatisation of internet policy.

Internet freedoms

In his Declaration of the Independence of Cyberspace, John Perry Barlow described a new world "where anyone, anywhere may express his or her beliefs, no matter how singular, without fear of being coerced into silence or conformity" (Barlow, 1996). The apparent borderlessness and anonymity of the internet allowed citizens to communicate freely and in real time regardless of the geographic demarcations of the offline world, and activists and dissidents to raise their concerns without being censored and with fewer risks for their safety. As a prominent example, the global Indymedia network was created in 1999, expanded around the globe over the following years, and brought alternative news to a global audience. With its open posting mechanism that allowed every internet user to publish their stories and contribute to a user-generated news platform, Indymedia pioneered citizen journalism and social media. It was followed by the rise of blogging as a mass phenomenon and by the widespread practice of 'citizen witnessing' (Allan, 2013) of key news events, with citizen reports, pictures and audiovisual footage complementing or even replacing traditional journalist reporting. WikiLeaks spearheaded an emerging trend of publishing raw data and source material, provided by whistleblowers and often exposing corruption and malpractice (Mitchell, 2011; Brevini, Hintz and McCurdy, 2013). The various forms of citizen journalism as well as new organisations such as WikiLeaks are increasingly recognised as core features of a "networked fourth estate" (Benkler, 2013) in which the traditional mass media have to share their role and space with a range of new alternative and citizen-based information providers.

Online activism has used the affordances of cyberspace to intervene into social and political conflicts. Electronic civil disobedience moved classic protest repertoires such as demonstrations and blockades into the online world (Meikle, 2002), and Anonymous picked up tactics such as denial-of-service attacks and applied them widely (Coleman, 2014). From the SMS protests in Spain and the Philippines in the early 2000s to the alleged Twitter and Facebook revolutions in the Middle East, social media and other digital platforms have enabled "citizens to report news, expose wrong-doing, express opinions, mobilize protest, monitor elections, scrutinize government, deepen participation, and expand the horizons of freedom" (Diamond, 2010: 70). While over-enthusiastic and technologically deterministic notions of social media 'revolutions' have been criticised (Morozov, 2011), digital platforms have been recognised as "effective catalysts" (Khamis and Vaughn, 2011: 1) of change and amplifiers of social movement activism, as they have generated forums for free speech and shared critical discourses.

The nature of the internet as an open and neutral platform, based on the end-to-end principle, has given control to the edges of the network (i.e. the user), rather than central nodes (such as broadcasting stations and internet service providers). For the most part, the standards and protocols that form the basic logical infrastructure of the net were developed in a decentralised, informal and experimental fashion by technologists rather than governments and as "bottom-up, grassroots processes" (Kahn, 2004: 18).

Censorship online: Blocking access, filtering content

Since the start of the new millennium, the state has (re)gained influence over the new virtual landscapes and has used the internet as a means to expand its control (Goldsmith and Wu, 2006). The most prominent example has been the 'Great Firewall of China', which has demonstrated that control over major backbones and access points can allow governments to draw a virtual fence around a state territory and restrict access to both services and information from outside that territory (e.g., Deibert et al., 2008). The Egyptian government, at the height of the Arab Spring uprising in January 2011, proved that internet access in a country can be reduced or even shut down during protest situations, and other governments have applied this new capability with increasing frequency and flexibility (Webster, 2011).

Inside a country's borders, filtering and blocking certain content has become common practice (Open Net Initiative, 2012). Information that transcends moral, religious or political limits set by governments has been blocked, most prominently in the Middle East and Asia, but increasingly also in Western countries.[1] Alternative and citizen media may be directly targeted by such efforts, or they may be affected by the common problem of over-blocking and 'collateral filtering' (Deibert, 2009), as blocking often affects unrelated websites because of the imperfections or technical configuration of the software (Villeneuve, 2006). Child protection filters in the UK have blocked access to, for example, sexual education websites, the support site childline.org.uk and the website of the Electronic Frontier Foundation, an important digital rights organisation (Robbins, 2013).

Even when alternative media are not initially targeted, the creation of an extensive censorship architecture for, for example, restricting child pornography, typically raises demands for wider content restrictions. As Ron Deibert notes, "once the tools of censorship are in place, the temptation for authorities to employ them for a wide range of purposes are large" (Deibert, 2009: 327). In Thailand, for example, the initial blocking of pornographic material was gradually extended to politically sensitive material. Some of the UK child protection filters have included vague categories such as 'extremist-related content' and 'esoteric material', which are open for wide interpretation. The adoption of a child pornography filtering law in Germany in 2009 was quickly followed by demands to extend the law to a broader range of content deemed illegitimate.[2] Websites publishing dissident information, for example criticising governments, may be particular targets as filtering is expanded.[3]

App stores and social media platforms have created their own rules and practices of what content is acceptable. Apple, for example, deleted an app from its app store that marked US drone strikes on a geographic map. The app was not illegal but certainly politically sensitive (Bonnington and Ackerman, 2012). Facebook has taken down activist pages in the run-up to protest events as well as dissident pages such as 'Anarchist memes', a page dedicated to anti-capitalist, anti-racist, feminist and pro-LGBT rights, "as part of a growing effort by Facebook to crack down on the presence of political groups on its network" (Dencik, 2014). Close relations between these (typically US) companies and the US administration as well as other Western governments have allowed protest movements elsewhere to use these platforms, but activist groups closer to home may receive less supportive treatment.

A more indirect form of content restrictions has emerged with the debate on net neutrality. As a network of cables and wireless connections that move data packages from A to B regardless of their content, the internet has largely been a neutral platform for information exchange, rather than a broadcaster that makes editorial decisions (Loeblich and Musiani, 2014). However, ISPs and telecommunications services increasingly block and/or throttle (i.e. slow down) some content, and speed up the delivery of other content and services. This form of content discrimination through infrastructure control provides particular challenges for non-commercial content and small businesses that may not be able to pay the fee required to be on a 'fast lane', and for oppositional and dissident news sources whose exposure a network provider may want to limit (Balkin, 2009).

Surveillance

Electronic communication has vastly increased the capabilities of governments and corporate actors to monitor citizens' interactions, exchanges, locations and movements. In contemporary 'surveillance societies', "all manner of everyday activities are recorded, checked, traced and monitored" (Lyon, 2007: 454). The revelations by whistleblower Edward Snowden about mass surveillance by security agencies such as the NSA and the GCHQ have demonstrated this impressively. Programmes such as Prism, Tempora, Muscular, Endgehill, Bullrun and Quantumtheory have provided evidence of mass surveillance of our social media uses; interception and monitoring of most online and phone communication; state-sponsored hacking into telecommunications services; the sabotage of security tools; and the compromising of internet infrastructure. A range of laws and regulations (e.g., the EU Data Retention Directive) allow governments to monitor citizens' communication and require telecommunications operators and internet service providers to store detailed communications data. Social media companies track and analyse all our activities on their platforms. Whereas a cartoon from the 1990s famously declared that "on the Internet, nobody knows you're a dog", our identity and our preferences are now closely monitored.

Blanket surveillance and the feeling (and certainty) to be constantly observed inevitably undermine critical debate and dissident voices. Critical and investigative reporting is challenged by surveillance, as it requires confidential communication with sources and, occasionally, the anonymity of authors (Rusbridger, 2013). The monitoring of communication therefore puts particularly those forms of journalism at risk which are exercised by alternative and activist media. Activists and dissidents

in countries like Syria, Tunisia and Iran have been targeted by governmental surveillance of social media platforms and digital communication tools, as authorities
have used Facebook to scrape user data and have distributed malware that installs
spying software on the infected computer, for example to capture webcam activity
(Villeneuve, 2012). After the London riots in the UK in August 2011, protesters
were identified through their use of social networking, and merely communicating
about the riots on social media led to severe punishment, including prison sentences
(Bowcott, Carter and Clifton, 2011).

Direct restrictions: Repression, violence and legal contexts

Interest by authorities in bloggers and internet activists can lead to physical repression, violence and death. In 2012, 48 citizen journalists were reported killed, and in
at least 19 countries they were tortured, disappeared, beaten or assaulted as a result
of their online activity (Article 19, 2013: 26). Infrastructure of media activist groups
has been seized repeatedly. For example, servers used by the Indymedia network were
confiscated by authorities in 2004 (following investigations by the FBI) and 2005 (by
British police because of alleged incitement to criminal damage) (Salter, 2009). Internet
activists who provide communications infrastructure for social movements or publish oppositional content have been subject to further police operations such as
house raids or have been incriminated through the use of anti-terrorism legislation
(Hintz and Milan, 2009).

Citizen journalists and media activists typically do not enjoy the privileges of traditional journalists, such as access rights to restricted institutions or areas, protection
against libel charges and the right to protect a source and collect certain types of
information. Their legal position remains precarious, as they are not employed by
recognised media organisations and may not be eligible for membership in journalist
unions and thus to hold a press card (Salter, 2009). Organisations such as Article 19 and
international institutions such as the UN Human Rights Committee have therefore
argued that the same protections and privileges should apply to professional and citizen
journalists. This includes prohibiting licensing and registration schemes for bloggers
that exist in countries such as Iran, Saudi Arabia and Singapore; the right to anonymity;
and protections of the safety of citizen journalists (Article 19, 2013).

Tighter restrictions to speech that may include incitement have provided further
challenges. Many recent laws against the incitement to violence, crime and terrorism
have been vague and open to subjective interpretations, which has led, for example
in the UK, to a steep rise in prosecutions against bloggers and social media users for
comments posted online. In some countries, special criminal sanctions have been
introduced for online defamation, and the so-called 'repetition rule' makes it
impossible, in some jurisdictions, to refer to statements made by others or include
links to defamatory statements without being held liable under defamation laws.
Sanctions like these have restricted, particularly, freedom of expression in blogs and
social media (ibid.).

Finally, restrictions have also emerged through the increasingly rigid interpretation
(and enforcement) of intellectual property. While the internet is a "gigantic, globally

distributed, always-on copying machine" (Mueller, 2010: 131) and a huge library that allows us to share files, share knowledge, and benefit from an abundance of ideas, control over these ideas and this knowledge through the means of intellectual property has become a key economic resource and source of power, and is therefore enforced fiercely. In what has been termed the "second enclosure" (Boyle, 2003), intellectual creativity has been commodified, as we have witnessed "the making of knowledge and information into property" (May, 2009: 364). The state has regulated and supported this process through the draconic punishment of intellectual property violations and multiple attempts to develop international agreements (such as ACTA). Alternative media, citizen journalists and cultural activists have been particularly concerned about these developments, partly because their work requires strong foundations of openness and free expression, and partly because their often experimental nature has involved exploring new forms of culture that relate creatively to established cultural products (Atton, 2001; Lessig, 2008). Subverting existing resources, culture jamming and mesh-ups are all part of current activist practices and are threatened by restrictive interpretations of intellectual property.

Locations of control: Private intermediaries and the state

The intellectual property debate demonstrates "a shift of the responsibility for monitoring and policing Internet conduct onto strategically positioned private sector intermediaries" (Mueller, 2010: 149). For example, the Copyright Alert System in the US, an agreement between the copyright holder industry and ISPs, puts both the definition of, and the punishment for, copyright infringement in the hands of the business sector and thereby by-passes governmental and judicial processes (Flaim, 2012). Private sector entities are increasingly enlisted to implement content restrictions and set their own rules on core issues affecting freedom of expression. When Facebook takes down activist content (such as the Anarchist Memes Facebook group), it acts as a "proxy censor" (Kreimer, 2006: 13) with significant power to reduce alternative voices, and it transforms from an open platform into a "social media police force" (Dencik, 2014).

Private sector policing extends to infrastructure, including server space, domain registration and funding, as was demonstrated in December 2010 when Amazon, Paypal and others closed the services they had previously provided for WikiLeaks, depriving the leaks platform of its domain name and of access to necessary funds in the middle of a major release (the Cablegate leaks). This 'denial of service' (Benkler, 2011) showed how 'cloud' services act as gatekeepers and regulate the activities of alternative media providers.

Commercial social media platforms such as Facebook, Twitter and YouTube have enabled critical debate and protest mobilisations, but also vast data collection. As the so-called 'Green Revolution' in Iran in 2009 (and many protests since then) demonstrated, they could help mobilise the public and spread information internationally, but they are also used to identify, monitor and eventually repress protesters. As Hofheinz (2011: 1420) notes: "While people in New York cafés were forwarding tweets that gave them the thrilled feeling of partaking in a revolution,

Iranian conservatives tightened their grip on power using YouTube videos and other Internet evidence to identify and arrest opposition activists." This emerging 'dark side' of social media platforms has dampened the enthusiasm for digital tools and has called into question their increasing use by activists. Whereas a protester may have uploaded their video and their written account of a protest to Indymedia in the early 2000s, they would have opted for YouTube and Facebook ten years later to allow for wider exposure. However, while a self-organised platform like Indymedia does not log user data and is unlikely to exert political censorship, the use of commercial platforms for both internal communication and spreading information to the public has exposed social movements and activist networks to monitoring and detailed network analysis, and has made them dependent on the goodwill of the company not to censor the information.

Turning the tide: Reactions against internet restrictions

The trend towards the limitation of internet freedoms has led to growing campaigns for digital rights and protests against restrictive internet policies. The surveillance scandal revealed by Edward Snowden, for example, has triggered street protests and international campaigns by digital rights organisations worldwide, such as 'Stop Watching Us'.[4] The protests against the 'Stop Online Piracy Act' (SOPA), a US bill to combat online copyright infringement, led to large mobilisations in 2012, as a "transnational coalition of engineers, academics, hackers, technology companies, bloggers, consumers, activists, and Internet users" (Sell, 2013: 67) managed to defeat the bill in a "David and Goliath story in which relatively weak activists were able to achieve surprising success against the strong" (ibid.: 68). Larger organisations that advocate for digital rights, such as the Association for Progressive Communications (APC), have brought their concerns to debates at international institutions and have participated in multi-stakeholder fora such as the Internet Governance Forum (IGF) and the Internet Corporation for Assigned Names and Numbers (ICANN). They have also developed elaborate policy documents, such as the APC's Internet Rights Charter, which demands that the internet become "a global public space that must be open, affordable and accessible to all" (APC, 2006).

However, a more typical approach in internet activism has been the development of technological alternatives and changes in individual communication practices. Responses to the surveillance scandal have included the increased use of encryption and anonymisation tools, such as PGP and TOR, and their promotion through 'Cryptoparties'. Non-profit activist-based internet services such as Riseup.net offer secure email accounts, mailing lists and online spaces such as blog and pad platforms, and collaborate with similar groups across the globe to create networks of activist communication that are less prone to censorship and surveillance. Efforts to create alternative forms of social networking, such as Lorea.org, have added to a strategy that focuses on the development of autonomous and civil society–based media infrastructure. This approach is informed by the individualism of cyberpolitics, which emphasises the right of the individual to explore all information in cyberspace – unimpeded and uncensored – and to contribute and share knowledge (Jordan, 1999).

It also draws from the rather loose and often temporary forms of association and "connective action" (Bennett and Segerberg, 2013) that online activists and other 'netizens' have developed and experimented with and that focus on values such as autonomy, subsidiarity, expertise and loose networked interactions (Dean, Anderson and Lovink, 2006).

Rather than advocating for policy change, many internet activists thus see their job as creating "self-managed infrastructures that work regardless of 'their' regulation, laws or any other form of governance" (Indymedia activist, quoted in Hintz and Milan, 2009: 31). They operate 'beyond' the classic divisions of social movement activism in 'insider' and 'outsider' approaches (i.e. in collaborative and participatory advocacy versus protest and disruption). Instead, their strategies focus on prefigurative action that constructs alternative infrastructure and circumvents policy obstacles, rather than seeking to influence a hegemonic system that is governed by existing powers (Hintz and Milan, 2013). Incorporating this 'beyond' approach of prefigurative action, some activists have engaged in new forms of do-it-yourself policy-making and 'policy hacking'. As part of 'policy hackathons' as well as established campaigns, they have analysed existing policy and developed new model laws and regulatory proposals (Hintz, forthcoming).

Conclusion

Cyberspace has provided a useful platform for media activists, citizen journalists and alternative media, as it has allowed them to publish information easily, make it accessible to a global audience, create and strengthen international networks and remain comparably safer from censorship than other media forms. Not least, it has enabled them to implement and further develop the ideas and practices of participatory, collaborative and interactive media production that have been at the centre of alternative media for a long time. However, and in contrast to the "policies of liberation" which early cyberspace and cyberlaw thinkers had envisioned, "policies of control" (Sarikakis, 2006: 171) have become more prominent in recent years. The deterritorialised spheres of the internet have partly been re-territorialised by states; the practice of filtering and blocking content is expanding; digital surveillance has become pervasive; and legislative restrictions as well as repression and violence persist. Both the private and state sectors have strengthened their grip on technical infrastructure and its uses. In particular, we can observe the trend of privatising internet policy in which commercial intermediaries are enlisted to police the net and often develop and implement new rules that deeply affect freedom of expression.

Internet activists, digital rights advocates and online alternative media have developed demands for privacy, free expression, an open internet and unrestricted exchange of knowledge, and have underlined those through campaigns, protests, advocacy, and, perhaps most significantly, the creation of technological alternatives that embody and implement these values. Their goals have been similar to those of other self-organised and civil society-based media (e.g., community radio) in that they describe an enabling environment in which such projects can exist and operate, and in which alternative information can be expressed and shared. However, operating in an environment with traditionally less regulation, and with a stronger political and ideological background in libertarian thought and loose association, their emphasis lies more strongly on freedom from interference, an open and neutral technological environment and the practice of developing alternative infrastructure and bypassing regulatory obstacles. Their policy preferences and their practical approach constitute an important building block for the creation of an enabling environment for alternative media.

Notes

1 The UK has occupied a questionable pioneer role as internet service providers, mandated by the government, have established 'Parental Control Filters' that censor a range of different content types deemed inappropriate for minors.
2 Within hours of the adoption, German politicians suggested including filtering of hate speech, violent online games and other content deemed illegitimate (Hintz and Milan, 2013).
3 The publication of the blacklists from several Western countries on WikiLeaks has shown that such lists may include a variety of other sites, including content targeted for political reasons, such as critical and oppositional civil society–based websites and alternative media.
4 See https://rally.stopwatching.us.

Further reading

Challenges to internet freedoms have been discussed in a series of books by Deibert et al., *Access Denied* (2008), *Access Controlled* (2010) and *Access Contested* (2012). The broader context of internet governance is described, for example, in Mueller's *Networks and States* (2010) and DeNardis's *The Global War for Internet Governance* (Yale University Press, 2014). Different forms of activist interventions into policy processes have been analysed, for example, in Milan's *Social Movements and Their Technologies* (2013). For current news and analysis on internet restrictions and repression against online activists, it is useful to check the websites of organisations such as Global Voices, the Electronic Frontier Foundation and the Association for Progressive Communication.

References

Allan, S. (2013) *Citizen Witnessing: Revisioning Journalism in Times of Crisis*. Cambridge: Polity.
Allan, S. and Thorsen, E. (2009) *Citizen Journalism: Global Perspectives*. New York: Peter Lang.
APC (2006) *APC Internet Rights Charter* (November). Melville: APC. Retrieved from http://www.apc.org/en/node/5677/ (accessed 18 January 2015).
Article 19 (2013) *The Right to Blog*. Policy Brief. London: Article 19.
Atton, C. (2001) *Alternative Media*. London: Sage.
——(2004) *An Alternative Internet: Radical Media, Politics and Creativity*. Edinburgh: Edinburgh University Press.
Balkin, J. M. (2009) "The future of free expression in a digital age." *Pepperdine Law Review*, 36(2), 427–44.
Barlow, J. P. (1996) "A declaration of the independence of cyberspace." Retrieved from http://homes.eff.org/~barlow/Declaration-Final.html (accessed 18 January 2015).

Benkler, Y. (2011) "A free irresponsible press: WikiLeaks and the battle over the soul of the networked fourth estate." Working draft. Retrieved from http://www.benkler.org/Benkler_Wikileaks_current.pdf (accessed 18 January 2015).

——(2013) "WikiLeaks and the networked fourth estate." In B. Brevini, A. Hintz and P. McCurdy (eds), *Beyond WikiLeaks: Implications for the Future of Communications, Journalism and Society*. Basingstoke: Palgrave MacMillan (pp. 11–34).

Bennett, L. and Segerberg, A. (2013) *The Logic of Connective Action: Digital Media and the Personalization of Contentious Politics*. Cambridge: Cambridge University Press.

Bonnington, C. and Ackerman, S. (2012) "Apple rejects app that tracks US drone strikes." *Wired*, 30 August. Retrieved from http://www.wired.com/2012/08/drone-app/ (accessed 18 January 2015).

Bowcott, O., Carter, H. and Clifton, H. (2011) "Facebook riot calls earn men four-year jail terms amid sentencing outcry." *The Guardian*, 16 August. Retrieved from http://www.guardian.co.uk/uk/2011/aug/16/facebook-riot-calls-men-jailed (accessed 18 January 2015).

Boyle, J. (2003) "The second enclosure movement and the construction of the public domain." *Law and Contemporary Problems*, 66(1–2), 33–74.

Brecht, B. (1927) "The radio as an apparatus of communication." In A. Gumucio Dagron and T. Tufte (eds), (2006) *Communication for Social Change Anthology*. South Orange, NF: CFSC (pp. 2–3).

Brevini, B., Hintz, A. and McCurdy, P. (eds.) (2013) *Beyond WikiLeaks: Implications for the Future of Communications, Journalism and Society*. Basingstoke: Palgrave MacMillan.

Coleman, G. (2014) *Hacker, Hoaxer, Whistleblower, Spy: The Story of Anonymous*. New York: Verso.

Coyer, K., Dowmunt, T. and Fountain, A. (eds.) (2008) *Alternative Media Handbook*. London: Routledge.

Coyer, K. and Hintz, A. (2010) "Developing the 'third sector': Community media policies in Europe." In B. Klimkiewicz (ed.), *Media Freedom and Pluralism: Media Policy Challenges in the Enlarged Europe*. Budapest: CEU Press (pp. 275–98).

Dean, J., Anderson, J. W. and Lovink, G. (2006) "Introduction." In J. Dean, J. W. Anderson and G. Lovink (eds), *Reformatting Politics: Information Technology and Global Civil Society*. New York: Routledge (pp. xv–xxix).

Deibert, R. J. (2009) "The geopolitics of internet control: Censorship, sovereignty, and cyberspace." In A. Chadwick and P. Howard (eds), *The Routledge Handbook of Internet Politics*. London: Routledge (pp. 323–36).

Deibert, R. J., Palfrey, J. G., Rohozinski, R. and Zittrain, J. (2008) *Access Denied: The Practice and Policy of Global Internet Filtering*. Cambridge, MA: MIT Press.

——(2010) *Access Controlled: The Shaping of Power, Rights, and Rule in Cyberspace*. Cambridge, MA: MIT Press.

——(2012) *Access Contested: Security, Identity and Resistance in Asian Cyberspace*. Cambridge, MA: MIT Press.

Dencik, L. (2014) "Why Facebook censorship matters." *JOMEC Blog*, 13 January. Retrieved from http://www.jomec.co.uk/blog/why-facebook-censorship-matters/ (accessed 18 January 2015).

Diamond, L. (2010). "Liberation technology." *Journal of Democracy*, 21(3), 69–83.

Downing, J. D. H. (with others) (2001). *Radical Media: Rebellious Communication and Social Movements*. London: Sage.

Flaim, S. M. (2012) "Op-ed: Imminent 'six strikes' Copyright Alert System needs antitrust scrutiny." *ars technica*, April. Retrieved from http://arstechnica.com/tech-policy/news/2012/03/op-ed-imminent-six-strikes-copyright-alert-system-needs-antitrust-scrutiny.ars (accessed 18 January 2015).

Goldsmith, J. and Wu, T. (2006) *Who Controls the Internet? Illusions of a Borderless World*. Oxford: Oxford University Press.

Hintz, A. (2009) *Civil Society Media and Global Governance: Intervening into the World Summit on the Information Society*. Münster: Lit.

——(2014) "Independent Media Center." In K. Harvey (ed.), *Encyclopedia of Social Media and Politics*. London: Sage.

——(forthcoming) "Policy hacking: Citizen-based policymaking and media reform." In D. Freedman and R. McChesney (eds), *Strategies for Media Reform: International Perspectives*. New York: Fordham University Press.

Hintz, A. and Milan, S. (2009) "At the margins of internet governance: Grassroots tech groups and communication policy." *International Journal of Media and Cultural Politics*, 5(1), 23–38.

——(2013) "Networked collective action and the institutionalised policy debate: Bringing cyberactivism to the policy arena?" *Policy and Internet*, 5(1), 7–26.

Hofheinz, A. (2011) "Nextopia? Beyond Revolution 2.0." *International Journal of Communication*, 5. Retrieved from http://ijoc.org/ojs/index.php/ijoc/article/view/1186 (accessed 18 January 2015).

Jordan, T. (1999) *Cyberpower: The Culture and Politics of Cyberspace and the Internet*. London: Routledge.

Kahn, R. E. (2004) "Working code and rough consensus: The Internet as social evolution." In D. MacLean (ed.), *Internet Governance: A Grand Collaboration*. New York: United Nations ICT Task Force, 16–21.

Khamis, S., and Vaughn, K. (2011) "Cyberactivism in the Egyptian Revolution: How civic engagement and citizen journalism tilted the balance." *Arab Media and Society*, 14, 1–37. Retrieved from http://www.arabmediasociety.com/?article=769 (accessed 18 January 2015).

Kreimer, S. F. (2006) "Censorship by proxy: The First Amendment, internet intermediaries, and the problem of the weakest link." *University of Pennsylvania Law Review*, 155(1), 11–101.

Lessig, L. (2008) *Remix: Making Art and Commerce Thrive in the Hybrid Economy*. London: Bloomsbury.

Loeblich, M. and Musiani, F. (2014) "Net neutrality and communication research: The implications of internet infrastructure for the public sphere." In E. L. Cohen (ed.), *Communication Yearbook 38*. London: Routledge (pp. 536–65).

Lyon, D. (2007) "Surveillance, power, and everyday life." In R. Mansell, C. Anthi Avgerou, D. Quah and R. Silverstone (eds), *The Oxford Handbook of Information and Communication Technologies*. Oxford and New York: Oxford University Press (pp. 449–72).

May, C. (2009) "Globalizing the logic of openness: Open source software and the global governance of intellectual property." In A. Chadwick and P. Howard (eds), *The Routledge Handbook of Internet Politics*. London: Routledge (pp. 364–75).

Meikle, G. (2002) *Future Active: Media Activism and the Internet*. New York: Routledge.

Milan, S. (2013) *Social Movements and Their Technologies: Wiring Social Change*. Basingstoke: Palgrave MacMillan.

Mitchell, G. (2011) *The Age of WikiLeaks: From Collateral Murder to Cablegate (and Beyond)*. New York: Sinclair Books.

Morozov, E. (2011) *The Net Delusion: The Dark Side of Internet Freedom*. New York: Public Affairs.

Mueller, M. (2010) *Networks and States: The Global Politics of Internet Governance*. Cambridge, MA: MIT Press.

Open Net Initiative (2012) "Global internet filtering in 2012 at a glance." Blog post, 3 April. Retrieved from http://opennet.net/blog/2012/04/global-internet-filtering-2012-glance (accessed 18 January 2015).

Robbins, M. (2013) "Cameron's internet filter goes far beyond porn – and that was always the plan." *New Statesman*, 23 December. Retrieved from http://www.newstatesman.com/politics/2013/12/camerons-internet-filter-goes-far-beyond-porn-and-was-always-plan (accessed 18 January 2015).

Rusbridger, A. (2013) "David Miranda, schedule 7, and the danger that all reporters now face." *The Guardian*, 19 August. Retrieved from http://www.theguardian.com/commentisfree/2013/aug/19/david-miranda-schedule7-danger-reporters (accessed 18 January 2015).

Salter, L. (2009) "Indymedia and the law: Issues for citizen journalism." In S. Allan and E. Thorsen (eds), *Citizen Journalism: Global Perspectives*. New York: Peter Lang (pp. 175–86).

Sarikakis, K. (2006) "Mapping the ideologies of Internet policy." In K. Sarikakis and D. K. Thussu (eds), *Ideologies of the Internet*. Cresskill, NJ: Hampton Press (pp. 163–78).

Sell, S. (2013) "The revenge of the 'nerds': Collective action against intellectual property maximalism in the global information age." *International Studies Review*, 15(1), 67–85.

Villeneuve, N. (2006) "The filtering matrix: Integrated mechanisms of information control and the demarcation of borders in cyberspace." *First Monday*, 11(1–2). Retrieved from http://firstmonday.org/htbin/cgiwrap/bin/ojs/index.php/fm/article/view/1307/1227 (accessed 18 January 2015).

——(2012) "Fake Skype encryption software cloaks DarkComet Trojan." *Trend Micro Malware Blog*, 20 April. Retrieved from http://blog.trendmicro.com/fake-skype-encryption-software-cloaks-darkcomet-trojan/ (accessed 18 January 2015).

Webster, S. C. (2011) "Vodaphone confirms role in Egypt's cellular, Internet blackout." *The Raw Story*, January 28. http://www.rawstory.com/rs/2011/01/28/vodafone-confirms-role-egypts-cellular-internet-blackout/ (accessed 18 January 2015).

21
THE ECONOMIC TENSIONS FACED BY COMMUNITY RADIO BROADCASTERS

Janey Gordon

Community broadcasters come to radio with enormous enthusiasm for the medium and for programme content; they also bring a strong desire to serve their local community of listeners. In the first rush of passion, new community radio stations may also find the capital to set up the studio and transmission requirements in order to get on-air. However, economic preparations for long-term sustainability, financial expertise and business acumen may not be at the forefront of the station's planning. As they obtain funding, they are likely to discover that all resources come with obligations and that the community-based programmes they envisaged at the start may become skewed.

The economics of running a community radio station, of raising and managing the necessary funds, as well as negotiating radio programming with funders, are a pragmatic reality for community radio activists. All funding methods will carry associated obligations, but it may be observed that there are economic models which are more supportive of the ideals of the community radio movement than others. These ideals were forged by activists and articulated by AMARC (the World Association of Community Radio Broadcasters) at their first conference in 1983 and restated in later declarations. Crucially, community radio broadcasters believe that their stations should give listeners a voice and that the divide between broadcaster and listener should blur. Community radio stations broadcast material which reflects cultures, information, views and languages which have little or no platform elsewhere. Twenty years after their first conference of community radio broadcasters, AMARC in their Kathmandu declaration of 2003 re-endorsed the definition of community broadcasting as being "that which is for, by and about the community, whose ownership and management is representative of the community, which pursues social development agenda and *which is not for profit*" (AMARC, 2003, emphasis added).

The snag to this final distinguishing characteristic, *not-for-profit*, is that there are economic costs that must be covered, even when broadcasters extol and seek to function with the highest ideals. Not-for-profit does not mean that money cannot be taken for broadcasting services, but that the radio station is not primarily driven by the need to make a profit for shareholders or other owners. Any potential profits made can be reinvested back into the station's activities. The problem that community stations face is how to remain economically viable, while avoiding being commercially driven and still providing their communities with appropriate radio. Community radio broadcasters need to be pragmatic about their sources of funding, while acknowledging ethical constraints. One UK community station manager, Andrew David (Siren FM), recalled the words of General William Booth, who founded the Salvation Army in the early part of the twentieth century. When Booth was criticised for receiving 'tainted' money for his social welfare projects from wealthy industrial donors, he replied, "We will wash [their money] in the tears of the widows and orphans and lay it on the altar of benevolent effort" (Booth, 1907). Similarly, David felt that any funding coming to his community radio station would ultimately be put to good use for the local community.

This chapter investigates the economic tensions faced by community radio broadcasters. I draw on my own research and personal experiences, as well as recent work by scholars in the field and discussions with community radio broadcasters and activists. The common models that fund community radio stations are explored, along with the economic tensions which each method presents to broadcasters.

Definitions and history

The regulatory body in the country in which a community radio station operates will define how community radio will function under that country's statutory system. These do vary, but the AMARC principles summarise what is at the heart of all community radio.

It has been suggested that community radio began with the development of radio as a medium and even early experimental radio, such as the University of Wisconsin's 9XM in 1916, had an underlying regard for serving its local community (Gordon, 2012: 372–3). Later in the United States, Lewis Hill started KPFA in 1949, which became the Pacifica organisation and which may be considered one of the first stations to consciously adhere to principles that came to be adopted by AMARC and the community radio movement (ibid.). By the 1970s and 1980s, Europe and South America had radio stations considering themselves community stations, which were part of wider political movements (see Lewis and Booth, 1989; O'Connor, 2004; Light, 2012). These were frequently unlicensed stations and considered pirates by their own authorities but were providing platforms for voices unheard on mainstream broadcasts. In Australia, stations, which came to be regarded as a part of their community radio movement, first had licenses in the 1970s and were related to educational broadcasts (Gordon, 2012: 370–71).

More recently there has been a liberalisation of broadcasting regulation in many Eastern European and Asian countries, with community radio stations being legitimised, although some governments are still wary and see community stations as a possible political threat. There seems to be a concern that this type of station may be linked to political activism, which may challenge existing administrations. In Bangladesh, for example, community radio was legitimised in 2008 and the regulation meant that the stations are tightly aligned to governmental or non-governmental organisations, at least at the outset. This has meant that the development of community radio has been slow.

Costs

The costs of running a community radio station will vary depending on where the station is in the world. The sophistication of the station and its technologies, the regulatory framework that it is operating under and the initial funding that oversaw its development will further influence the costs of running the station. The financial costs common to all community radio stations no matter where they are in the world include premises, studio and transmission equipment and the electrical power to support the technical facilities. In addition to these, there may be other costs: rent; local rates; insurance for both the buildings and equipment, and public liability for the volunteer broadcasters; the adaptation of the building for audio use and for community access; staffing costs; and not least publicity, a mechanism to let the community of listeners know that the station exists. This is the basic outlay before the price of any projects that the station may want to initiate in its local area, such as educating volunteers to use the broadcast facilities, which will require both broadcasting and teaching expertise. In addition, there may be an annual license fee payable to the regulatory body and copyright fees for content such as music. In the UK, for example, the annual transmission licenses for a community station are about £1000 and music copyright fees are about another £2500. Who pays for this and what might they want in return?

In order to be successful and provide a radio service for their community, sustainable funding must be found that is not overwhelmingly arduous in terms of reporting to the funders and ensuring compliance with the terms of their economic support. In the United States, small radio stations have been serving niche communities from the very beginnings of radio in the early twentieth century. Some of these have developed into public radio stations using professional staff, and others have become fully commercial stations. But in October 2013, following the enactment of the Community Radio Act, not-for-profit groups have been able to apply for low-power licences. The Prometheus Radio Project is a campaigning organisation that has led the way in this new tier of broadcasting and is helping groups apply for licenses and set up the stations (see Prometheus, 2013). Its advice is straightforward: "If you want money you have to ask for it ... Most people have no idea how much it costs to run a non-profit community radio station or how non-profit organizations get money. If you don't ask them, they will simply assume you are getting the money somewhere" (Klein in Prometheus and KYRS, 2007: 3). Community broadcasters try not to rely on any one method or source of funding but have a mixed financial portfolio, so that if a source withdraws, the whole station does not fold. There are a number of common methods and each has its advantages, but each will create tensions for the broadcaster.

JANEY GORDON

Community funding

The community itself might fund the radio station serving it. This is the ideal, given AMARC's principles that a community radio station should reflect the needs and broadcasting wishes of its audience and some of that audience will take part in the station as volunteer broadcasters. The local community may also support the station by giving "in-kind" support, for example by providing labour or materials to build the fabric of the station or professional expertise to help with legal matters or engineering. Station volunteers themselves are also an actual resource, and in some countries such as the UK and Australia, volunteers' time may be accounted for in the annual financial report.

Direct funding by listener membership subscriptions or fund-raising events is also common in some areas of the world. In Australia, there are around 350 community radio stations operating on a wide range of financial bases. One of the most successful community stations economically is 3RRR, which is based in Melbourne, Victoria. Along with a range of income streams, the station is well supported by its local community, both by subscription and by fund-raising. According to the station website, it has over 12,000 subscribers paying about AU$75 a year and a listenership of around 330,000 per week (3RRR, 2013). 3RRR is able to employ a paid manager and small staff to organise its large group of volunteer broadcasters. The advantage of this type of funding is that it demonstrably shows that the community station is supporting and supported by its community. This builds a strong audience and may lead to further funding opportunities from several of the methods discussed below.

The problem with this type of funding is that the community needs to be sufficiently affluent to be able to provide this type of economic support for their station. It will not work in areas where poverty or a lack of disposable income means that there are no spare funds or free time within the community to give to their station. Community radio frequently is serving the poorest in society and those with the most limited means; they may simply be unable to provide it with any kind of sustainable income.

Patronage

A second model is for the community radio station to have a patron, where the station is a part of a larger organisation, for example an arts centre, communications centre or university. The patron may also host the station within its premises, providing secure accommodation and adequate utilities. Community radio stations based on university campuses are among the oldest and most established (see Gordon, 2012). In addition to the premises, they may often provide an enthusiastic core of volunteers from among the student and academic body, and if the station has links to the university's educational courses, the patron organisation may provide some basic funding and staffing. Having a patron supporting a community station can work well, providing the host organisation is reasonably liberal and does not impose too many strictures on the station. Undoubtedly there are occasions when the opinions or requirements of the radio station and the larger host are at odds, but research seems to show only a few such experiences.

Other common patrons include religious or charitable organisations involved in socially beneficial activities, which use the community station as an addition to their work. This patronage may have benefits beyond the simply economic. In some parts of the world, community radio broadcasters are operating under the same risks as their professional counterparts, and having a patron organisation to defend them may be essential. Brooten (2012: 66–8) gives the example of Radyo Cagayano, a community station in the Philippines. This station was a true community radio station built by funds raised by a local farming community and run by local people to inform and educate themselves and their neighbours. On 2 July 2006, the station had been functioning for just a short time when armed men broke in, tied up the volunteers and burned down and destroyed the station. The Philippines has an unenviable reputation for journalists and broadcasters being abducted and murdered. Small broadcasting organisations such as community radio stations have found the need to associate themselves with larger organisations or patrons to ensure their long-term survival both financially and literally. The Catholic Media Network operates small radio stations across the country on the AM and FM wavebands. It is the largest broadcaster in the Philippines in terms of the total number of stations and its transmission power (CMN, 2013). The stations are supported financially by the CMN and serve the many small communities across the numerous mountainous islands of that country. The CMN has the stated mission of development and Christian evangelism, and its stations must adhere to these overarching principles. However, the backing of the church does help ensure the physical safety of the radio station's premises and their broadcasters in a country where they are part of a perilous business.

Advertisements and sponsorship

In common with many community radio stations globally, the CMN stations accept advertising promotions and other business-related activities, while retaining a generally not-for-profit status. However, local regulations may restrict a community radio station's ability to undertake this type of commercial activity. National regulatory bodies sell broadcasting frequencies to commercial media companies for considerable sums. Having done so, they are then obliged to protect the commercial interests of these companies by restricting the advertising and sponsorship sold by community broadcasters, who will either not have paid for their broadcast frequencies or have paid much less than the commercial organisations. For example, in the UK, a community station applying for a licence in an area with a potential audience of less than 150,000 aged fifteen and over, and that is also served by a commercial radio station, is prohibited from using commercial advertising and sponsorship as a source of income. In addition, no UK community station may earn more than 50 percent of their income from advertising and sponsorship (Ofcom, 2011: 9–15). (Following consultation in 2014, these rules may change.) In Australia, community stations may not take spot advertising, only sponsorship (ACMA, 2008: 1).

As well as any regulatory constraints on this income, some community stations consciously avoid taking funds from advertising and sponsorship, as they feel that doing so may ethically compromise them. Others will accept local advertising but avoid larger corporations, and some will refuse advertising if it will involve them with companies whose pursuits concern alcohol, gambling or activities which may prove detrimental to the community they serve.

In reality, community stations often find it difficult to obtain commercial advertising and sponsorship and, without volunteers with marketing expertise, this type of funding can be time consuming to generate. The station audiences are often small and very distinctive by area or culture, and they may be economically poor, making them unattractive to large advertisers. Ironically, some stations have made commercial advertising and sponsorship a successful financial income stream, for exactly these reasons. Their audiences may be considered 'hard to reach' for advertisers, who may want to target a community due to its culture, ethnicity or language. The advertisers may also appreciate the high regard held by the station locally and wish to be associated with it.

An advantage of commercial advertising and sponsorship for the station is that, once obtained, it can be a simple method of funding to maintain. The companies involved want to sell their products and services and, having agreed with the station exactly what they want to purchase in terms of the number and length of the spot adverts or sponsorship messages, allow the station to fulfil their end of the contract without interference.

Grants

A further source of funding is competitive grants, where stations bid to a central fund managed by a range of organisations, governmental, quasi-governmental and non-governmental, and they are likely to be in competition with other community or socially worthy activities. Despite the arduous nature of making grant applications to funding bodies, there are sizeable amounts of money that may be accessed by a successful bid. In the UK, community stations may apply for grants from organisations such as the Big Lottery Fund, which gains its resources from the weekly National Lottery. This kind of large-scale input of cash undoubtedly benefits community radio broadcasters who are successful. But there are problems of sustainability. A UK community radio station which received a grant of over £300,000 in September 2010 from the Reaching Communities Programme (which aims to help those most in need and build stronger communities) was able to move to more suitable premises and provide a good technical infrastructure, as well as initiate community projects. However, they reported in 2013 that "Big Lottery funding has helped the project to grow to a scale that will experience severe difficulties in sustaining the same level of work once the funding runs out in September 2013" (Diverse, 2013: 11).

The Irish Republic provide a Broadcasting Fund (known as the Sound and Vision Scheme), through a seven percent levy on the television licence. All broadcasters may apply to this fund to make certain kinds of programming, though not for capital projects. While this has proved very beneficial for a number of community radio stations, a recent report noted:

> Whereas the Sound and Vision Scheme is broadly accepted as having had a beneficial impact on the community media sector in Ireland, concerns about

the shortcomings of the schemes have also been voiced. Criticisms emerging in previous research relating to structural and procedural deficits of the scheme were re-stated in consultative seminars undertaken for the present research. In summary, the fund has been criticised for not taking into account the unique characteristics of community radio.

(Murphy et al., 2011: v)

Grant applications are time consuming to write, there are likely to be robust restrictions on the uses of any funding gained and recipients will have to service their grants with meetings and reports, which may also be time consuming. A further problem that community radio stations may have is that managing a large sum of money is a skill in its own right and such expertise may need to be sought externally. Community broadcasting is not immune to poor financial management, fraud, theft or dishonesty. Indeed, the final reports of funding initiatives are almost invariably positive and demonstrate that the project outcomes have been amply fulfilled. More detailed investigation may show that this is not always the case.

Service contracts

Rather than sell advertising time, a broadcaster might sell its skills and services. A community station may deliver courses to educate local young people in media skills or provide audio services for outside events. It may also gain funds by promoting the services of non-commercial organisations. For example, a local health clinic may wish to promote antenatal care among a group of women in the community who previously have not used it and have funds available to purchase Public Service Announcements (PSAs) on their local community radio station. This type of contract can be financially beneficial, but it can restrict programme content by limiting the station's ability to be reactive or imaginative for other events or activities. However if the service contract is well within the overarching remit of the station and its resources, it can not only be financially valuable but also demonstrate the station's social awareness towards its community. A further benefit of this type of funding is that some national regulatory bodies, for example Ofcom in the UK, exempt this type of 'Service-Level Agreement' with non-commercial organisations from their commercial advertising and sponsorship rules (see Ofcom, 2011: 15).

NGOs

In some parts of the world, non-governmental organisations (NGOs) are the initiators and managers of community stations, using broadcasting to further their aims. In Asia and Africa, NGOs support and use community radio widely to promote their work. In Bangladesh, the NGOs Network for Radio and Communication (BNNRC) represents the community media sector to the government, industry, regulatory bodies, media and development partners. The funding model is complex, and some surprising funders are found to have provided capital and support to the new stations. Shameem Reza showed that Radio Mahananada, which started in January 2012, obtained initial funding from the Japanese embassy in Bangladesh. Listeners were also interviewed as to the kind of programming that they wanted to hear on their station, and it was found that they favoured "music, sport, entertainment and information on mango cultivation" (2012: 103–9). Further investigation showed that Bangladesh is a major producer of mangoes and Japan a major importer.

Pavarala and Malik detail the early development of community radio in India (2007: 34) and the assistance that UNESCO gave the first stations through NGOs. UNESCO has been very supportive of community radio and believes that it is a crucial method of reaching poor and remote societies. In 2011, UNESCO initiated World Radio Day on 13 February each year to draw attention to the importance of the medium globally (UNESCO, 2011). However, more recently Pavarala has expressed concern over what he considers such a heavy involvement of NGOs in community radio broadcasting in Asia, which he calls "NGOization" (Pavarala, 2013):

> Well-endowed NGOs and well-meaning donor agencies have upped the ante for smaller groups struggling to put out a few hours of original programming a day. Content is often closely tied to the programmatic agendas of NGOs, and the imperative of putting together a "fixed-point-chart" of more and more hours of daily broadcast forces many stations to a stultifying adoption of standardized genres and formats.
>
> (Pavarala, 2013: 2–4)

While it can be advantageous for a local community to have an experienced organisation involved in the startup and training for a community radio station, what happens when the organisation involved loses its own funding, moves to another area or even loses interest in community radio as a means to an end? A station might not be financially sustainable once the NGO moves on and might be unable to reflect local interests comprehensively.

Government agencies

In some countries, government funds are available for community radio broadcasters, whether from the government itself or through overseas aid from a foreign government. The Australian authorities consider community broadcasting an excellent way of supporting its own diverse communities that may be isolated by geography, language or culture. In particular, successive governments have directly and indirectly funded the Indigenous Broadcasting Program to provide Australian aboriginal communities with radio stations to reflect their particular needs. The budget, though, is dependent on the interests of different administrations and actual amounts are not always assured. In the UK, there is an annual Community Radio Fund of about £400,000 financed by the Department of Media Culture and Sport and managed by Ofcom, the national regulator. Community broadcasters may apply to this fund for small amounts, averaging about £15,000. Some UK community broadcasting activists have argued that this fund is inadequate for the 200 or so stations and that UK community broadcasters should be more generously funded centrally. However, no central government funding comes without keen scrutiny and prescriptive regulation to accompany it. It might also be argued that for a broadcaster, being government funded runs counter to the independent principle of the community radio movement.

Foreign governments may also fund community radio as a way of giving aid to another country. This may be part of a 'hearts and minds' initiative in a country where there has been conflict. In Afghanistan, for example, a number of international organisations and government agencies have been involved in seeking to provide stability in that country. Paywand Radio is a small station broadcasting to and providing training for Afghan women who wish to pursue a career in broadcasting. The station is funded by the US Agency for International Development, or USAID, which in turn is funded by the US government (USAID, 2012). USAID fund a great many small-scale radio stations around the world, and although the local communities gain from the stations, the background to this generosity is political.

Conclusion

Community radio broadcasters obtain economic support from a variety of sources. During my discussions with community radio broadcasters and activists, there was a general expression of pragmatism towards the economic tensions they faced in running their stations. Their programme content may need to be suitable not only for their local communities but also for the agencies and organisations that support them. However, frequently the greatest tension was simply getting enough funds to operate effectively. They found the strain of a constant lack of funds gruelling, and there were often concerns about the sustainability of their stations.

The methods of funding described above are not mutually exclusive; one station might use all the methods to attain economic viability. However, community radio volunteers tend to consider themselves first and foremost broadcasters, and they do not always have the expertise in economic management needed to effectively maintain the station. While a stated goal of being not-for-profit need not prevent the acquisition of funds, there is a sense that too much of a focus on finance is ethically improper for community radio. Funding that is closely linked to programming, such as service contracts, works well if the content required is appropriate to the station's aims, but there are concerns that close links with funding providers could skew the programme content of a station towards what the funders want to hear, rather than the community.

The economic tensions faced by community broadcasters and activists vary with their funding, but the paucity of income means that they are often not able to be too particular about the sources. Earlier in this chapter, I quoted General Booth on the subject of 'tainted money'. He also said: "There's nothing wrong with tainted money. There jus' tain't enough." A community radio station manager – engaged in a struggle for funds to cover costs and maintain the station's output, to keep to the terms of their license while preserving their ethical values and the support of their community – would no doubt agree.

Acknowledgements

Discussion of the themes of this chapter with some of the world's leading community radio activists was facilitated by meetings and dialogue at the following academic conferences: MeCCSA, January 2013, University of Ulster, NI; IAMCR, June 2013, Dublin City University, Republic of Ireland; the Radio Conference, July 2013, University of Bedfordshire, UK; ECREA Radio Research, September 2013, University of Sunderland, UK. My thanks to all those who contributed their experiences and views, although due to the occasionally sensitive nature of the topic, stations and broadcasters are sometimes kept anonymous.

Further reading

Reflection on community radio tends to be nationally specific; for further contemporary accounts of the extraordinary tensions that community radio activists operate under, see the examples in *Community Radio in the 21st Century* (ed. J. Gordon, Oxford: Peter Lang, 2013). For discussion of the ethical issues of community radio funding in the UK and Australia, see chapter 3 of *Notions of Community* (ed. J. Gordon, Oxford: Peter Lang, 2009). Community broadcasters seeking advice on funding models will find that AMARC's "The African community radio manager's handbook: A guide to sustainable radio" (2000) remains a comprehensive and highly readable document (http://www.amarc.org/documents/manuals/The_African_CR_Manager.pdf). For a more global view, see also UNESCO's "Community radio handbook" (2001) (http://www.unesco.org/webworld/publications/community_radio_handbook.pdf). Both provide excellent advice for would-be community broadcasters in any part of the world.

References

3RRR (2013) "Triple R station profile." Retrieved from http://www.rrr.org.au/about/profile/ (accessed 31 October 2013).

ACMA (2008) "Community broadcasting sponsorship guidelines 2008." Retrieved from http://acma.gov.au/webwr/_assets/main/lib310667/community_bcasting_sponsorship_guidelines _2008.pdf (accessed 31 October 2013).

AMARC (2003) "The Katmandu declaration." Retrieved from http://www.amarc.org/index. php?p=The_Kathmandu_Declaration (accessed 31 October 2013).

Booth, W. (1907) "Gen. Booth here with big plans." *New York Times*, 6 March. Retrieved from http://query.nytimes.com/mem/archive-free/pdf?res=FB0F11FC395A15738DDDAF089 4DB405B878CF1D3 (accessed 31 October 2013).

Brooten, L. (2012) "When commercialisation and militarization prevail: Examining community radio in the Philippines." In J. Gordon (ed.), *Community Radio in the 21st Century*. Oxford: Peter Lang Publications (pp. 55–76).

CMN (2013) "Vision mission and profile." http://catholicmedianetwork.org/cmn/About_Us. html (accessed 31 October 2013).

Diverse (2013) "Community radio annual report 2012." Luton: Ofcom.

Gordon, J. (2012) "The role of university radio in the development of community radio stations – a history." In J. Gordon (ed.), *Community Radio in the 21st Century*. Oxford: Peter Lang Publications (pp. 367–84).

Lewis, P. and Booth, J. (1989) *The Invisible Medium: Public, Commercial and Community Radio*. London: Macmillan.

Light, E. (2012) "From pirates to partners: The legalization of community radio in Uruguay." In J. Gordon (ed.), *Community Radio in the 21st Century*. Oxford: Peter Lang Publications (pp. 77–96).

Murphy, K., Murray, C., Farren, N. and Titley, G. (2011) "Cross-national comparative analysis of community radio funding schemes." Retrieved from http://www.bai.ie/?p=1143 (accessed 31 October 2013).

O'Connor, A. (2004) *Community Radio in Bolivia: The Miners' Radio Station*. New York: Edwin Mellen.

Ofcom (2011) "Notes of guidance for community radio licence applicants and licensees." Retrieved from http://licensing.ofcom.org.uk/binaries/radio/community/thirdround/noteso fguidance.pdf (accessed 31 October 2013).

——(2013) "Community radio stations." Retrieved from http://www.ofcom.org.uk/static/radio licensing/Community/community-main.html (accessed 31 October 2013).

——(2013) "Community radio fund guidance notes." Retrieved from http://stakeholders. ofcom.org.uk/binaries/broadcast/radio-ops/crf/crfguidancenotes.pdf (accessed 31 October 2013).

Pavarala, V. (2013) "Ten years of community radio in India: Towards new solidarities." In *EduComm Asia*, 17(2) (April). Retrieved from http://www.col.org/PublicationDocuments/Edu CommAsiaAPRIL2013.pdf (accessed 31 October 2013).

Pavarala, V. and Malik, K. K. (2007) *Other Voices: The Struggle for Community Radio in India*, New Delhi: SAGE.

Prometheus (2013) "A guidebook for low-power community radio applicants." Retrieved from http://www.prometheusradio.org/sites/default/files/lpfmguide.pdf (accessed 31 October 2013).

Prometheus and KYRS (2007) "Fundraising for people-powered community radio." Retrieved from http://www.prometheusradio.org/media/pdf/KYRS_Fundraising_Handbook.pdf (accessed 31 October 2013).

Reza, S. M. S. (2012) "From elite perceptions to marginal voices: Community radio in Bangladesh." In J. Gordon (ed.), *Community Radio in the 21st Century*. Oxford: Peter Lang Publications (pp. 97–113).

UNESCO (2011) "Proclamation of a World Radio Day." General Conference 36th Session, Paris. Retrieved from http://unesdoc.unesco.org/images/0021/002131/213174e.pdf (accessed 31 October 2013).

USAID (2012) "Afghan women's voice on the radio." Retrieved from http://reliefweb.int/ report/afghanistan/afghan-women's-voice-radio (accessed 31 October 2013).

22
DYNAMIC PRACTICES AND THEIR POTENTIAL FOR THE ALTERNATIVE PUBLIC SPHERE IN KOREA

Eun-Gyoo Kim

The emergence of alternative media in Korea

In Korea, the advent of alternative media began as a communication strategy of the civic movement and the new social movement that rose after the 1987 civil uprising, which was an important turning point in the democratisation of Korean society. The oppressive government system was transformed into government where the arena of civil society has expanded, to include not only the existing class-struggle movements, but also movements for economic justice and environmental issues. Alternative media became significant voices for these new social movements (Kim, 1992; Park, 2000).

The appearance of a new public sphere that takes advantage of internet-based decentralised and open communication structures has created a diverse range of alternative media (Yoon, 1998; Kang, 1999). Internet newspapers such as *OhMyNews* (launched in 2000) have introduced the citizen reporter system, increased readers' choice and eliminated the borderline between reporters and readers. These newspapers are able to develop topics from the bottom up, to deliver new types of news based on diverse points of view and to lead open discussion and communication. As alternative media they are able to challenge the structure of the conventional media systems that have tended to monopolise the production and distribution of the media and to enhance the democratisation of communication (Park, 2001).

A further category emerging within the alternative public sphere is that of civic media. Civic media are premised on the strengthening of citizens' access to media, dealing with subjects that reflect the public interest and forming and nurturing the participation of citizens. In a narrow sense, civic media suggest media owned and operated by citizens; in a broader sense, they are media in which citizens can participate regardless of who owns them (Choi, 2005: 61–2). Civic media can be considered as a democratic communication system that enables the diverse voices of civil society, while the system itself may continue to be owned and operated by capital.

Practices within the alternative public sphere before 1987

Although the concept of alternative media became a main part of discussions around the alternative public sphere after 1987, before this date reference was most often made to terms such as resistance media, *minjung* media, counter media and underground media. These terms signify the relationship between a ruling system based on oppressive political power and social movement media that struggled to overcome such oppression before 1987. 'Resistance media' refer to media that resist institutionalised mainstream media (whose goal is to keep intact the interests of the ruling class) and resist the ruling power (Jo, 1995). In Korea, the term had been used in the 1970s and 1980s by the free press movement. The free press movement began in the 1960s when a dictatorship prevailed; the movement struggled for freedom of speech, stressing social democratisation rather than class consciousness (Jung, 1990).

'Counter media' refer to media that advocate class consciousness to those who are alienated politically, economically, socially and culturally. Counter media function as a 'stronghold' based on Leninism against the mainstream media, which are considered to reproduce the ruling ideology. Counter media seek to take part in a social revolution and situate themselves as propagandists, instigators and organisers for social change (Jo, 1990). Therefore, counter media are different from alternative media in an important way: while counter media propagate, instigate and organise a revolutionary ideology against the ruling class, alternative media criticise the media systems that pursue capitalistic profits and mediate the values of new social movements with the citizens' life-world (Kim, 1998).

'Minjung media' was a key concept in the Korean social movements of the 1980s. 'Minjung' refers to the lower classes and includes the labouring class, the peasantry and the urban poor (Choi, 1991). Minjung media manifested based on the partisan interests of the lower classes (Jo, 1995; Park, 1991). In discussing minjung media in Korea, some argued for the media to be thought of as an embodiment of 'national-democratic media' that included a range of lower-class action and interests, with the labouring class at the centre of the social movement (Jung, 1990), while others saw minjung media as solely a product of the labouring class (Sung, 1990).

'Underground media' generally refers to media that publish their news without a legal permit and has its origins in the West, rather than in Korea. In the 1960s, the underground media of the US centred on human rights, the anti-war movement, the anti-racism and anti-discrimination movements, and women's rights (Kim, 2005). In Korea, underground media may include the labourers' newspapers or political newspapers that were illegally published during the early 1980s.

As Korean society changed after 1987, terms such as counter media, minjung media and underground media tended to lose their usefulness, due to two main factors surrounding the dominant media structures. First, as the democratisation of Korean society progressed, media structures gradually recovered their independence from political power. Thus, many practices within what was an alternative public sphere became legal alternative media based within civil society and new social movements. Second, the ebb tide of the revolutionary social movement and its ideologies also affected an alternative public sphere. After the 1987 civil uprising, the Korean revolutionary social movement underwent significant change. The social movements united under the flag of social democratisation split after 1987 to become two distinct movements: a class-based, revolutionary movement and a broader civic movement. As the centre of activism shifted towards the civic movement, the importance of counter media or minjung media faded away. Accordingly, the nature of the alternative public sphere also gradually changed.

The 1987 civil uprising: The expansion of civil society and a change of media structure

As Korean civil society developed, the structure of Korean media was able to break away from the guardianship of the state. The administration that emerged after the civil uprising implemented a media policy that was geared specifically towards "weak oppression and strong allurement" (Yoon, 1995: 190). The ultimate aim of this media policy was to form a compromise between political power and the power of the media. Newspapers that cooperated with the administration were strongly supported, while those that criticised or did not cooperate with the administration were excluded. In a sense, capital functioned as media control. This media policy led to the expansion of the influence of capital on media structures. However, the 1993 government considerably reduced its intervention in the media. This reflected the social circumstances where it was more necessary to attain the agreement of civil society, due to the increase in self-regulation of the civil society. The relationship between the state and the media changed from one of guardianship to one of corporatism (Park and Jang, 2001), and the mainstream media's status changed from an instrumental power based on alliance with the state to a more independent, institutional power (Kang, 2004).

After 1987, the media industries moved from market control to regulation and we witness a significant expansion of the influx and influence of capital (ibid.). In the newspaper industry, capital expanded its power in ownership and as advertising. In this process, a few conservative newspapers that succeeded in accumulating capital during the times of the state's guardianship went on to secure dominant positions in the newspaper industry. In the case of the broadcasting industry, commercial broadcasting companies once again arose in 1991, following their forced merger and abolition by the military government in 1980. Consequently, the introduction of new media broadcasting, such as cable TV, satellite broadcasting and DMB, enabled the expansion of the broadcasting industry, and transformed the industry into a highly competitive market.

In conclusion, the Korean media structure after 1987 shows two striking changes compared to that before 1987: the biggest factor that influences the autonomy of the media moved from state power to capital power, and the media broke away from the guardianship of the state and mainstream media – especially a few conservative newspapers, which became a pseudo-political power. Mainstream media as a public sphere in Korea thus function as members of the ruling alliance, and do not perform their role for the civil society. Therefore, the mainstream media still need to be reformed and such a demand on reforming the media is being consistently raised within civil society.

The alternative public sphere after 1987:
From confrontation to citizens' participation

The Civil Uprising in 1987 has resulted in the expansion of Korean civil society, and thus the alternative public sphere has also faced changes, qualitatively and quantitatively. The alternative public sphere after 1987, however, shows a multifaceted process of change according to the process of the transition of the leading powers in civil society, the relationship between civil society and the state and the advent of new media.

In Korea, the alternative public sphere receives its driving force from civil society and therefore, depending on what characteristics the goals and strategies of social movements within civil society might have, the contents of the alternative public sphere will also change. Thus, it is necessary to discuss the changes in the leading powers in civil society after 1987 in Korea. At the turn of the year, the leading power in civil society was a revolutionary social movement based on class partisanship. But, since the late 1980s and into the 1990s, the leading role of the social movements moved towards a civil movement led by civil organisations. After the mid-1990s, this movement became even further divided into a wide range of specialised civil movements (Kim, 2003: 161–5).

As the 1990s unfolded, the alternative public sphere transformed from counter media or minjung media to alternative media. The advent of the concept of alternative media can be seen as an indication that the leading power of the Korean social movement had moved away from revolution and towards civil reform. The civil movement focused more on healing problems and issues related to ordinary lives and less on class partisanship. As new social movements like economic justice, women, environment and ecology became very active, the civil movement camp used its own alternative media to present its ideals and issues and to communicate within itself.

At the same time, diverse practices for alternative media emerged in the late 1980s and 1990s. A representative case was *Hankyoreh*, a daily newspaper launched in 1988 based on the people's funding. *Hankyoreh* was considered alternative media within the mainstream media structure in that it was independent from capital and political power. Led by journalists made redundant mainly due to political struggle in the 1970s and 1980s and the democratisation movement, *Hankyoreh* received much attention as a kind of alternative sphere. After its establishment, *Hankyoreh* met the expectation of the progressive camps by reporting daringly forbidden issues or subjects that the mainstream media could not. However, *Hankyoreh* has now lost its original identity in order to survive in the intense competition of the media market (Kang, 2004: 328).

Another practice also appeared in local newspapers. Some local weekly newspapers can also be considered within the scope of the alternative media that appeared in the late 1980s and 1990s. The biggest advantage of the local newspapers is that they reflect diverse political, economic, social and cultural aspects of local communities. In addition, they can be established and operated with a small amount of funding (Jang, 2001). These 'grassroots' local newspapers have all the elements of a democratic public sphere for local communities.

At the beginning of the 2000s, the alternative public sphere of Korea has grown to include civic media based on broadcasting and internet practices. While the domain of the alternative media that appeared in the 1990s remains important, this latest expansion results from combining the broadcasting and internet media with the participation of citizens. Expansion has been made possible through the efforts of the civic media movement and the public access movement, as well as through the development and effective use of media technology.

Since 1987, social movement groups have consistently promoted media reform through collective activities, and these civil activities gradually developed into a legal reform movement. As a result, they yielded results such as the 2000 Broadcasting Act and 2005 Newspaper Act. The 2000 Broadcasting Act incorporated citizen participation programmes, programmes produced by citizens and citizens' evaluation programmes into the broadcasting system. Accordingly, public broadcasting company KBS, local channels in cable broadcasting companies and citizens' channels in satellite broadcasting companies secured programmes that people could public access. While not all were owned and operated by citizens, such outcomes secured the range of citizens' participation and expanded the alternative public sphere in Korea.

Moreover, the appearance of internet newspapers based on the participation of citizens, such as *OhMyNews*, also expanded the alternative public sphere. The key feature of *OhMyNews* is that it broke away from the mainstream media model centred on specialists and created a voluntary association of citizen reporters. This new communication network of citizen reporters is a model of civic media that discovers life-world problems in diverse jobs, classes and regions and makes news from them (Hong, 2001).

The return of conservatism and media control

After 1987, the key feature of the Korean media structure is that control shifted from politics to capital. That is, before 1987, the media were the control of a repressive political regime; after 1987, this political power weakened due to social democratisation and capital replaced the regime as a system of media control. However, in 2008, South Korea underwent a very important political shift. Lee Myung-Bak, the candidate of the conservative regime, won the presidential election in 2007 and the conservative MB administration (named after Myung-Bak) was inaugurated in February 2008. Since then, the Korean media structure has also changed conservatively. In particular, the MB administration regards broadcasting as a means of holding the government power. The administration controls public service broadcasting through its governance system, and as a result the independence and the public nature of broadcasting has collapsed. Moreover, the MB administration and the ruling party permit the conservative newspaper companies to enter broadcasting system as general service channels. These newspaper companies were grown under an alliance between the repressive regime state and the media, and as we have seen, became a pseudo-power and finally grew into an oligopoly of a nationwide newspaper market. The consequence is that the diversity of public opinion available through the media has weakened seriously, and competition within the broadcasting market has strengthened irrationally. Since 2008, due to the return of the conservative regime in South Korea, public service broadcasting has become an instrument for the conservative administration, and conservative newspaper companies have expanded their control into the broadcasting sector.

2008 candlelight demonstrations and personal media

In this conservative social atmosphere, new types of alternative media have appeared in South Korea. First, personal media based on the internet became prominent. Power bloggers and personal internet broadcasts operate as an alternative media. Ironically, the advent of personal media as alternative media have also shown up the weaknesses of the conservative administration's control of the media. In 2008, there were large public rallies called 'candlelight demonstrations'. The Korean people demonstrated against the government's import policy of beef from the US. At that time, the MB administration restricted the freedom of speech, so many Korean people, especially young people, reported the rallies and people's opinion on the street through web-based personal media and SMS. The marvel is that almost all of the reporting was conducted by citizens working alone or in small groups (Kim, 2009).

Dynamic practices through podcast and internet

In 2011, another alternative media practice has appeared, a popular podcast titled *Naneun ggomsuda* or *Na-ggom-su*, meaning 'I'm a petty-minded creep'. This is a lampooning talk show that brings together a publicist, a former lawmaker, an investigative journalist and a political satirist (who runs the website). They profess to dedicate their show to 'His Highness', President Lee Myung-Bak, but their real address is to their audience: "Let's not be intimidated! Let's say whatever we want!" (*New York Times*, 2011). The podcast started in April 2011 and closed in December 2012, after 71 shows. During its life, *Na-ggom-su* was the most popular alternative podcast and became more influential than even some mainstream media. Almost 10 million people downloaded the podcast, and the audience comprised not only young people in their twenties and office workers in their thirties and forties, but also the middle aged. Eventually, the Democratic media prize by the National Union of Mediaworkers was awarded to the *Na-ggom-su* podcast in 2011 to celebrate its excellent achievement as an alternative programme.

There are two factors behind the *Na-ggom-su* craze and its success (Mediatoday, 2012). First, the contemporary sociopolitical atmosphere formed an important base. At that time, there was growing popular dissatisfaction with the MB administration, particularly with its policy of favouring the affluent and the privileged. Korean people were greatly disappointed by the MB administration and the privileges it handed out as the conservative regime. The people also distrusted broadcasting controlled by government and the conservative newspapers, because they issued reports biased towards the conservative regime. Therefore, many people prefer the *Na-ggom-su* podcast for catharsis. Second, *Na-ggom-su* applied new media technology successfully. Its programmes were delivered through a podcast platform available on the internet and through smartphones. Korea has an excellent ICT infrastructure, which the programme was able to use. In 2011, internet use was 78 per cent and smartphone use was 45 per cent, the latter of which rose to 62 per cent in 2013 (NIA, 2013).

In January 2012, another alternative media experiment started. *NewsTapa*, which means 'news breaking', was launched by a former journalist forcibly dismissed for political reasons during the MB administration. The main motto of *NewsTapa* is 'breaking the unfaithful news' of the mainstream media and 'truthful reporting with no sanctuaries'. *NewsTapa* can be seen as an alternative news broadcaster of investigative journalism that seeks to express a quite different view than that of conservative, mainstream broadcasting news. *NewsTapa*'s programmes are distributed through the internet, using YouTube and podcasting. Like *Na-ggom-su*, *NewsTapa* has been gradually gaining popularity by reporting issues ignored by the mainstream media. During its first season from January to July 2012, *NewsTapa* updated total 21 news programmes, and it recorded 5,442,511 hits through YouTube and 5,911,177 hits through podcasting (NewsTapa, 2012). *NewsTapa* has been evolving gradually. In its second season, from July to December 2012, famous directors and retired journalists joined the *NewsTapa* team, and the news content became updated weekly. Since March 2013, *NewsTapa* has become a not-for-profit organisation and renamed itself as *NewsTapa/KCIJ* (Korea Center for Investigative Journalism). Currently, *NewsTapa/KCIJ* is able to recruit permanent staff and deliver news broadcasting twice a week (NewsTapa, 2013).

Another alternative media, *KukminTV/CooperationMedia*, launched in April 2013 (*Kukmin* means 'the people'). *KukminTV* shares *Na-ggom-su*'s perspective and for Korea is an entirely new kind of practice in its organisation and participants. Above all, *KukminTV* is a media cooperative based on the people's copartnership. As of November 2013, there were about 17,800 copartners in *KukminTV*, a number that is expected to grow. The purpose of *KunkminTV* as a media cooperative is to produce independent news broadcasting that is free from political power and the capital. *KukminTV* produces radio programmes through the internet and podcasts, as well as a *KukminTV-News* website and an on-air TV project that involves 50,000 copartners in its media cooperative (KukminTV, 2013).

Community radio

In 2014, there are now seven community radio stations operating in Korea. The characteristics of these stations are that they are non-profit, rely on the participation of citizens and offer a community communication system as a public service. They have the merit of lower entry barriers due to small media, without the high costs of broadcasting. In 2004, a community radio project called 'Low-Power Radio' was introduced, becoming 'Community Radio' in 2009. As a result, the broadcasting agency licensed these seven community radio stations, which operate on a regional basis.

The activation of community radio is propelled by public-access movement groups. For a long time, they have been trying to spread public-access programming and channels as an alternative public sphere in the media structure. As a result, about 30 Civic Media Centers were established in major cities across the country during 2002 and 2013. Civic Media Centers offer media education programmes to develop citizen's media competence and also offer an equipment rental service. The centres are funded by various executive organisations; some centres are supported by a branch of national government or by local government; some are supported by the public service broadcasting agency and by civic organisations (Kim, 2010). In parallel with the efforts to establish Civic Media Centers, public-access movement groups have also been working to launch legal community radio stations. As a result of their efforts, community radio was formally recognised as part of Korea's broadcasting policy in 2009.

However, there are still some issues for expansion and development. The Korean broadcasting agency permits just 1kW output power for each community radio station, limiting coverage to within a 1.5 to 2km radius in built-up areas; consequently, community radio is often referred to as 'inaudible broadcasting'. The regulation of community radio means that stations are only permitted to broadcast local cultural content such as music, but not local news and political issues. Through community radio is based on a non-profit system, there are no public funds to support it (Kim and Choi, 2013). All these barriers are caused by the Korean broadcasting agency's policy for community radio: community radio must adhere to the administration's media policy. Unfortunately, the conservative administration maintains a market-driven media policy, and community radio is also forced to adopt a market-driven competitive approach without considering its public function. Therefore, the public-access movement groups and the community radio groups insist on a change of community media policy.

Conclusion

The spectrum of alternative media in Korea is very active and varied. Grassroots weekly newspapers, community radio, internet newspapers, internet broadcasting and podcasting all operate as channels of alternative media. The background of alternative media is intertwined with sociopolitical changes and new media technologies. Before 1987, in the times of oppressive political regime, alternative media revealed its features against an oppressive regime and mainstream media that were supported by that oppressive regime. Consequently, alternative media were called resistance media, counter media, minjung media and underground media and were often based on illegal newspapers or pamphlets. The first turning point was the civil uprising of 1987 and the expansion of Korean civil society. After 1987, following sociopolitical changes and developments in communication technologies, new types of alternative media and civic media appeared with a legal foundation and were produced by various civic groups. These new alternative media served as communication networks for civil society and presented alternative viewpoints against mainstream media. A second turning point was the return of conservatism in 2008, together with more developed media platforms, such as podcasting. In short, the conservative administration has been controlling broadcasting, and some oligopoly and conservative newspapers have been dominating public opinion on behalf of the conservative regime. New types of alternative media based mainly on internet and podcast technologies were launched and continue to be active across civil society. Finally, grassroots local, weekly newspapers and community radio stations have been operating for local communities across the country. In Korea, it appears that alternative media practices are ongoing and are set to continue.

Further reading

E.-G. Kim's *Media and Civic Participation* (Seoul: Communication Books, 2003) explains the sociopolitical background and the diverse types of civic media in South Korea. Chapters 3–6 of Y.-M. Choi's *Civic Media* (Seoul: Arche, 2005) also explore the landscape of South Korea's civic media, as well as making international comparisons. S.-Y. Yu's *Alternative Media in Korea* (Seoul: Korea Press Foundation, 2005) provides a critical view of South Korea's alternative media, evaluates their position after the social democratisation of 1987 and suggests what key issues remain to be resolved. S.-E. Choi's *Community Radio* (Seoul: Communication Books, 2014) focuses on legal community radio that provides opportunities for civic participation as part of the public sphere in South Korea.

References

Choi, J.-J. (1991) "The condition and direction of MinJung democracy." *Society Critics*, 6, 326–52.
Choi, Y.-M. (2005) *Civic Media*. Seoul: Arche.
Hong, S.-G. (2001) "Deliberative democracy and internet." *Media and Society*, 9(4), 173–208.
Jang, H.-S. (2001). *The Hope Is the Small Media*. Seoul: GaeMaGoWon.
Jo, H.-J. (1990) "The theory and prospect of counter media." In Korean Social Media Study Association (eds.) *Modern Society and Mass Communication*. Seoul: HanUl (pp. 337–54).
Jo, Y.-C. (1995). "The prospect and possibility of mainstream media and counter media." In J.-B. Bang and M.-N. Kim (eds), *Media and Modern Society*. Seoul: NaNam (pp. 281–319).
Jung, Y.-J. (1990) "The theory of national democracy media movement." In W.-S. Kim, W.-S. and D. U. Lim (eds), *Political Economy of Korean Media*. Seoul: AChim (pp. 291–333).
Kang, M.-G. (2004) "Media war and the crisis of journalism practices." *Korean Journal of Journalism and Communication Studies*, 48(5), 319–48.
Kang, S.-H. (1999) "Cyberspace as an alternative media: Its potentialities and limits." *Korean Journal of Broadcasting and Telecommunication Studies*, 14(1), 7–40.
Kim, E.-G. (2003) *Media and Civic Participation*. Seoul: Communication Books.
——(2005) "Beyond the David vs. Goliath: Exploring the identity of alternative media." *Korean Journal of Journalism and Communication Studies*, 49(2), 225–82.
——(2009) "Personal media." In Media Public Interest Forum (eds.) *Media Public Interest*. Seoul: Communication Books (pp. 264–70).
——(2010) "Civic media as the social capital for local community." *Korean Political Communication Association*, 19, 47–72.
Kim, E.-G. and Choi, S.-E. (2013) "The study on broadcasting regulation of community radio in Korea: Based on broadcasting experts' view." *Journal of Communication Science*, 13(3), 184–214.

Kim, T.-H. (1992) "New social movement and alternative media." *Korean Journal of Journalism and Communication Studies*, 27, 97–119.

——(1998) "The status and prospect of independence media in Korea." In National Union of Mediaworkers (ed.), *The Media Independence and Internal Control in Korea*. Seoul: National Union of Mediaworkers.

KukminTV (2013) "A prospectus of KukminTV." Retrieved from http://kukmin.tv/ver01/m63.php?pagecode=m63 (accessed 1 November 2013).

Mediatoday (2012) "Adieu, *Na-ggom-su* [What did they leave behind?]" 31 December. Retrieved from http://www.mediatoday.co.kr/news/articleView.html?idxno=106915 (accessed 1 June 2013).

New York Times (2011) "By lampooning leaders, talk show channels young people's anger." 1 November. Retrieved from http://www.nytimes.com/2011/11/02/world/asia/lampooning-leaders-talk-show-channels-young-peoples-anger-in-south-korea.html?pagewanted=1&_r=5& (accessed 1 November 2013).

NewsTapa (2012) "NewsTapa, launching season 2 on 17 August." 15 August. Retrieved from http://newstapa.com/126 (accessed 1 October 2013).

——(2013) "Introduce NewsTapa." Retrieved from http://newstapa.com/743 (accessed 1 October 2013).

NIA (2013) *2013 National Informatization White Paper*. Seoul: National Information Society Agency.

Park, C.-S. (2000) "Civic movement and alternative media." *Korean Journal of Journalism and Communication Studies*, 44(3), 190–221.

Park, S.-G. and Jang, G.-S. (2001) *Media Power and Agenda Dynamics*. Seoul: Communication Books.

Park, S.-H. (2001) "Characteristics of online newspapers as an alternative communication channel." *Korean Journal of Journalism and Communication Studies*, 45(2), 117–55.

Park, S.-R. (1991) "The study on the real configuration of the MinJung media in Korea." Master's thesis, SeoGang University.

Sung, J.-H. (1990) "The study on the labour media in the 1980s." Master's thesis, Seoul University.

Yoon, Y.-C. (1995) "Social changes and media control." in J.-C. Yu (ed.) *Korean Social Changes and Media*. Seoul: SoWha (pp. 181–225).

——(1998) "PC communication as alternative media." *Korean Journal of Journalism and Communication Studies*, 43(1), 184–218.

23
PERIPHERAL VISIONS?
Alternative film in a stateless nation

Robin MacPherson

Scotland's media address a stateless nation of over five million people who possess considerable autonomy within the UK yet have received little attention from media studies or related disciplines, generating only two collected volumes in the past four decades (Hutchison, 1978; Blain and Hutchison, 2008). Individual sectors such as publishing, with 500 years of history and considerable international reach, have fared better than, say, television, for which, like the arts in an earlier era, the specificity of the Scottish experience "if not entirely obliterated, then at least [is] mediated through an English lens" (Maley, 1994: 79). In contrast, Scotland has garnered much greater interest from film studies both inside and outside its borders, reflecting a historical screen presence that extends well beyond its own domestic output. However, this growing bibliography simply highlights the paucity of attention given Scotland's alternative media. Excepting Chris Atton's work (2000, 2003), it is largely absent from the literature. Undoubtedly Scotland's relatively modest contribution to alternative media as a whole provides part of the explanation, but this doesn't wholly explain the gap in domestic (Scottish) scholarship. Rather, there appears to be a certain discursive marginalisation, or misrecognition, of the challenge posed by alternative media and its history in Scotland, not just to the dominant media but to how we think about them. Indeed, the relegation of Scottish alternative media to the scholastic margins is, I suggest, symptomatic of a tendency to treat mainstream Scottish media as the *de facto* alternative to UK media. This may be necessary, but it is hardly sufficient.

As we shall see, alternative filmmaking in Scotland has suffered from just this kind of elision and consequently, while this is not the place to set out its history in any detail (see MacPherson, forthcoming), some account of its development in relation to the wider film sector is needed.

For the avoidance of doubt, I employ Atton's characterisation of alternative media to signify "wider social participation in the[ir] creation, production and dissemination than is possible in the mass media" (Atton, 2002: 25) and 'film' to include technologies from celluloid to digital video and consumption contexts from cinemas to smartphones. Though television is indeed an important part of the picture, space constraints allow only the briefest account of broadcasting and especially Channel 4's pivotal influence on alternative film in the 1980s.

The core argument I advance in this chapter is that alternative filmmaking in modern Scotland developed later, more erratically and across a narrower range of genres than in England because of Scotland's subordinate position within the political economy of UK (and indeed global) media. This has given the dominant, but in crucial respects also subordinate, Scottish media a dual identity as partly mainstream, partly alternative, complicating an already inadequate dichotomy.

Mainstream alternative? National cinema in Scotland

Compared to publishing, Scotland's film industry was from the outset much more subordinate to a British and indeed global system. The technological, economic, regulatory and discursive forces that shaped British film and television in the twentieth century continue today to restrict the volume, diversity and reach of Scottish film and television, whether for domestic or wider consumption. This has become fairly evident in the case of mainstream cinema and television (Blain and Hutchison, 2008; Murray et al., 2009) and I hope will become clearer here in the case of their much less documented alternatives.

The overarching narrative of Scottish cinema's development is relatively easily traced. Following early explorations in locally controlled production, distribution and exhibition, by the 1930s Scotland had an extensive cinema network and one of the highest levels of cinema in Europe (Griffiths, 2012) but practically no domestic film output. The postwar British and global cinematic order permitted Scotland only a minor role as an intermittent provider of literary source material, locations or talent (both on- and off-screen). The position today has changed only in so far as domestic feature production has become established and visiting film and television productions generate substantial revenue and employment (Petrie, 2000; Blain and Hutchison, 2008; Murray, Farley and Stoneman, 2009). However, compared to similar-sized countries such as Norway, Demark or Finland, Scotland continues to have one of the lowest levels of domestic feature film output and audience share in Europe – averaging between three and six films per year. Even its closest comparator, Ireland, which like Scotland is both English speaking and historically part of the same distribution market, has in the past decade regularly produced two to three times as many films and secured a significantly higher audience share (BOP Consulting, 2014).

Contemporary Scottish cinema traces its origins to the late 1930s and concerted efforts, personified by 'father of the documentary' John Grierson, to ensure that Scotland was represented on cinema screens at home and abroad. However, the resulting documentary film sector did not constitute an *industry*, unlike the critical mass of finance, production and distribution in and around London. Notwithstanding their aspirations to make feature films, until the 1980s Scottish filmmakers were almost wholly confined to making sponsored documentaries extolling the country's achievements in industry, public works or social development. Training was 'on the job', until a small craft training scheme was established in 1982 and, with no film school until well into the 1990s, talent inevitably migrated south in search of experience and work (Scott, 2009).

Although the UK National Film Finance Corporation (NFFC) had been established in 1949 and the British Film Institute (BFI) began funding 'experimental' films in 1953 (Dupin, 2012), a Scottish cinema only became imaginable following the success of Bill Forsyth's self-funded *That Sinking Feeling* (1979) and the NFFC-supported *Gregory's Girl*

(1980). Concerted lobbying by a small band of documentary filmmakers from the mid-1970s and Forsyth's success finally persuaded the existing cultural bodies to back a Scottish Film Production Fund in 1982. Additional film-related bodies supporting skills, heritage and locations were created in addition to the SFPF and the education- and exhibition-orientated Scottish Film Council. Finally in 1997, after ten years of discussion increasingly focused on economic issues (McIntyre, 1994), they merged into Scottish Screen, which in 1999 assumed responsibility for the National Lottery finance which had significantly boosted film production across the UK since its introduction in 1995.

Domestic feature film production in Scotland grew from fewer than one a year in the 1970s to three in the 1990s, including international hits *Local Hero* (1983) and *Trainspotting* (1997).

However, as the intrinsic case for arts funding in the UK gave way to an increasingly hegemonic 'creative industries' discourse (and as independent television producers became a more powerful lobby), both Scottish Screen and the filmmaking constituency in Scotland retrenched around the economic case for film funding despite its evident underlying weakness (MacPherson, 2009).

Despite the acquisition of a Parliament in 1999 and prior devolution of cultural policy from the rest of the UK, the continuing lack of domestic finance or distribution has ensured that Scotland remains an undifferentiated part of the UK (and Irish) cinema market and that local producers must compete directly for investment and distribution with their counterparts in London. Despite filmmakers' best efforts, Scottish films secure an average 1 per cent annual share of the local cinema audience (MacPherson, 2010), giving contemporary force to Petrie's observation that by the 1930s "in cinematic terms Scotland was effectively colonized by a metropolitan film industry" (Petrie, 2000: 28).

Given this history of economic and cultural marginalisation, even without considering the films themselves, it is not difficult to see why scholars often treat Scottish cinema as a countercultural alternative to mainstream British cinema. Thus, 'post devolutionary' Scottish filmmaking (Blandford, 2007) has been described as an attempt to "conceive of a new kind of national identity ... to break free of the dominant discourse's representation of the native population" (Martin-Jones, 2009: 229) or as "providing a space for social criticism and imagination of alternative possibilities" (Petrie, 2000: 226) These claims resemble those made for the former Soviet bloc countries where "most media could be said to be ... alternative" (Deane, 2007) or post-colonial Australasian film (Featherstone, 2005).

This treatment of recent Scottish cinema as a progressive alternative to hegemonic 'outsider' representations of Scotland is valid up to a point. But it elides the largely unquestioned acceptance of orthodox paradigms of film production, distribution and consumption which characterises Scottish professional, policy and critical discourse. Yet, alternatives to those discourses exist and have been posed by filmmakers in Scotland since the early days of film.

A more radical alternative?

Evidence of film being used in support of radical causes in Scotland can be found as early as 1917, when suffragists screened film of Scottish women's field hospitals in war-torn France in support of votes for women. By 1930, workers' film societies had been established across Scotland to screen progressive films and especially the new Soviet cinema (Allen, 1982). As elsewhere in the UK, they quickly progressed to making short films highlighting local and international issues in the prewar period (Hogenkamp, 1986). After 1945, with the election of a Labour government and the Communist Party of Great Britain's adoption of parliamentarianism, 'oppositional' filmmaking declined across the UK, virtually disappearing in Scotland until the 1970s, though one celebrated exception, the Dawn Cine Group, produced several documentaries in the 1950s on issues from the nuclear threat to rural depopulation (Stewart, n.d.).

During the 1960s and 1970s, the little alternative filmmaking evident in Scotland was confined to a few individuals operating outside the small professional filmmaking community. They include 'experimental' filmmaker Margaret Tait, recently re-evaluated by feminist scholarship (Neely, 2008), and the 'underground' filmmaker Enrico Cocozza, whose recently rediscovered films deal with themes such as unemployment, crime, parental neglect and arguably the first instance of 'queer' filmmaking in Scotland (Neeley and Riach, 2009).

In 1970s England, by comparison, alternative filmmaking at a professional level was well established (Dickinson, 1999; Hogenkamp, 2000) among both individual filmmakers and the growing 'film co-op' sector. They made common cause through the Independent Filmmakers Association (IFA, est. 1974), which espoused a philosophy of the 'cinema of social practice'. They helped influence the BFI's turn towards support of a British 'art cinema', including its direction of capital investment in a way which "ultimately favoured a few small groups of radical filmmakers" (Porter, 2010: 64), including the London Filmmakers Cooperative, Birmingham Arts Lab and Amber Film Collective in Newcastle. The fact that such groups prospered in English cities which lacked even the small film infrastructure Scotland possessed might indicate there was no real obstacle to developing alternative film practices outside London. However, unlike Scotland, those already based in the regions, or relocating there from London (as did Amber Films in Newcastle, which had actually considered Glasgow as a potential base; Martin, 1999), faced little competition from established filmmakers. This made it easier for them to secure support from the regional arts agencies, the BFI and, after 1982, Channel 4. With the film technicians union ACTT, the IFA, the English Regional Arts Associations and the BFI joining forces in 1982 to promulgate the 'Workshop Declaration', organised alternative filmmaking bloomed in the 1980s (Dickinson, 1999). When 'cultural industries' started to feature in English regional strategies, the English groups were already well positioned to benefit from urban regeneration funds.

In stark contrast, the limited infrastructure and funding available to filmmakers in 1970s Scotland ensured that, despite the Edinburgh Film Festival promoting oppositional film culture (Lloyd, 2011), its engagement with Scotland depended almost entirely on visiting filmmakers from the south. Hence the shop stewards at Glasgow's Upper Clyde Shipyard turned to the London-based collective Cinema Action to document their historic 'work-in', resulting in UCS1 (1971) and Class Struggle – Film from the Clyde (1977). Similarly, Birmingham Film and Video Workshop profiled Scottish radical filmmaker and theatre worker Helen Biggar in its film Traces Left (1983). And although the 1915 women-led Glasgow Rent Strikes inspired 7:84 Theatre Company's 1975 play Little Red Hen, it was Sheffield Film Cooperative that brought it to the screen in Red Skirts on Clydeside (1984).

Alternative Scottish filmmaking having been largely in abeyance since the 1950s, its rebirth and growth in the late 1970s became possible partly due to a new technology – video – and a new (to Scotland) organisational form – the Film and Video Workshop. Video was cheaper, easier to use and better suited than film to intensive 'process' work in working-class communities such as Glasgow's Castlemilk housing estate (Wade, 1980). Starting with Film Workshop Trust in Edinburgh (EFWT) in 1977, the Workshop model drew on the pioneering Canadian 'Challenge for Change' programme (Warren, 1973), community arts principles and the radical, collectivist ethos of the English film co-ops. Their influence had spread through publications such as *Afterimage* (1970), *SCREEN* (1960–) and *Framework* (1974–92) and events such as 'Film and Politics' at the 1975 Edinburgh Film Festival (see Bauer and Kidner, 2013).

As with other cultural responses to Thatcherism and postindustrial decline in 1980s Scotland (Gardiner, 2005), alternative filmmaking experienced a revival with the founding of Red Star Cinema in 1980, Video in Pilton (VIP) in 1981 and Glasgow Film and Video Workshop (GFVW) in 1983. By the late 1980s two more workshops, one in the central Scotland town of Alva and the other, *Fradharc Ur*, on the Hebridean island of Lewis, and community video projects in Glasgow's Drumchapel and Cranhill brought the total number of groups to around a dozen. Though by no means uniform in philosophy, they shared a broad commitment to community access and a socialised model of filmmaking in which participation in the process could be more important than the production values or the wider distribution potential of the product.

Most of the workshops' output was issue-based documentary designed mainly for local, non-broadcast distribution. However, both EFWT and, to a lesser extent VIP, secured funding from and broadcast by Channel 4 under the 'Workshop Declaration'. This ground-breaking agreement dissolved traditional demarcation boundaries between roles in return for a minimum number of full-time salaried staff employed in a not-for-profit structure and with a commitment to socially engaged practice. As with the wider Scottish film sector, Channel 4 was thus instrumental in financially underwriting alternative filmmaking and securing it a larger audience not just in Scotland but across the UK.

From 1989, Channel 4 progressively withdrew its support of UK workshops and other forms of alternative filmmaking. Combined with cuts to a historically low level of local government funding, this hit the Scottish workshop sector particularly hard. Having failed to convince first the SFPF then Scottish Screen of the sector's merits, by the late 1990s only Pilton Video and GFVW continued to provide significant support to alternative filmmakers. Despite isolated explorations of drama or less didactic forms of documentary, Scottish alternative filmmakers generally stayed close to their community video roots. Unlike many of the English workshops, they were thus poorly positioned to engage with increasingly mainstream-orientated film funds or broadcasters. With local filmmakers lacking the experience or credibility to mount them, fiction films with a radical perspective continued to depend on visiting filmmakers such as Ken Loach and the five films he made in Scotland between 1997 and 2012 from scripts by Scottish screenwriter Paul Laverty.

Long-form documentary, having a lower 'entry cost' than fiction and amenable to a more iterative production/financing process, provided more opportunities for alternative filmmakers. Several emerged from the workshops, the strengthening practical film courses in further and higher education (Petrie and Stoneman, 2014) or escaping the increasingly prescriptive and populist confines of ratings and commissioner-led television. Aided by the establishment of the Scottish Documentary Institute in 2004 and growing European links, Scottish documentaries moved onto the international stage, securing co-production finance and distribution and reaching audiences through the burgeoning documentary festival circuit, DVD or the more receptive European broadcasters. However, the international documentary market favours international or at least large scale over local issues. Thus, for example, films by Scottish documentarians on Nicaragua in the 1980s to Venezuela in the 2000s have been more marketable than films addressing domestic experiences. A recent case in point is the difficulty filmmaker Anthony Baxter faced in securing finance for *You've been Trumped* (2011), a documentary on local opposition to Donald Trump's despoliation of part of Scotland's Aberdeenshire coast with a luxury golf course/hotel development. The film was only made possible through the use of crowdfunding, a development which though clearly helpful in many ways also marks a deeper and more problematic shift in the landscape of alternative film.

In the first decade of the twenty-first century, the radical and collectivist documentary tradition established by the 1930s and reprised in the 1980s resurfaced though groups such the 'Camcorder Guerrillas' and 'Media co-op' in Glasgow and in the community engagement model of fiction filmmaking revived by Edinburgh's Theatre Workshop. Although such practices in Scotland have declined substantially since their 1980s peak, over the same period the availability and consumption of 'engaged' film and video has reached the point where it is arguably higher than at any time since the 1930s. A revived distribution chain aided by online and social media marketing tools, the much improved availability of films on DVD or online and initiatives such as the Document International Human Rights Festival (est. 2003) or the Take One Action Film Festival (est. 2008) is promoting the kind of active audience engagement that would be familiar to the Kino film groups of the 1930s or the workshops of the 1980s. However, this engagement is largely driven by interest in global issues so, with little local/national content on offer, alternative cinema in Scotland, as with cinema as a whole, remains overwhelmingly a consumption rather than production activity (MacPherson, forthcoming 2015).

Three theses on mainstream alternatives and alternative mainstreams

In this brief account of the development of alternative film in Scotland, I have tried to show how Scotland's subordinate position within the political economy of British media has shaped the mainstream and alternative filmmaking in a 'combined and uneven' way. Of course, to produce a comprehensive account of alternative media in this or any other national context, we would need to examine other dimensions as well. Writing of the alternative press in 1970s Scotland, for example, David Hutchison argued that "the Presbyterian climate would not encourage any kind of hippy culture and the size of the population ensured that a determined minority of counter culture addicts would be insignificant" (Hutchison, 1978: 43). Similar socio-cultural factors may well have inhibited Scots from embracing countercultural film with the same enthusiasm as their metropolitan counterparts. We also need to be careful about attributing agency to abstractions or neglecting the subjective reality of social actors, i.e., the habitus of filmmakers influenced by multiple and sometimes contradictory frames of reference. Nonetheless, in the last instance I believe we cannot fully understand why Scotland has the alternative media it does without examining the dynamic of political and economic subordination which has shaped the media field. To conclude, then, I want to put forward three propositions which may have currency in similar contexts to Scotland (i.e. where national media may function – albeit only temporarily or partially – as both mainstream and alternative).

1. The centre of mainstream media is where alternatives develop most easily

In England the alternative film sector developed largely continuously from the 1950s to the 1980s out of the critical mass of industry, filmmakers and cultural activists in and around London. By the mid-1970s, they were able to exert considerable influence on the film union ACTT, regional arts bodies and the BFI, the latter being sufficiently responsive to accommodate divergent filmmaking ideologies in its policies (Dupin, 2012). And in the late 1970s and early 1980s, they were able, as part of the wider 'independent sector', to influence the formation and policies of Channel 4, ensuring further substantial support for alternative film not just in London but across the UK.

By comparison, in 1970s Scotland the handful of alternative filmmakers on the margins of an only slightly better off mainstream lacked material infrastructure, professional experience or institutional influence. Notwithstanding the Edinburgh Film Festival's prominent national, indeed international profile as a centre of radical film theory (Lloyd, 2011), Scotland's cultural bodies were much less receptive to the ideological underpinnings of radical film practice than, say, the BFI. At the critical juncture of the early 1980s, when alternative filmmakers in England captured significant state funding, their equivalents in Scotland simply lacked the organisational leverage or programmatic coherence to secure a place in the emerging national film discourse.

2. A deficit of indigenous media can precipitate a progressive 'national alternative', but this in turn may displace more radical alternatives

The fragile Scottish film production sector of the 1970s constituted a national cinema in waiting. Its champions were on the whole genuinely motivated to change and expand representations of Scotland on the screen, if not the practices or social relationships through which they were produced. To that extent, then, they did indeed pose a challenge to mainstream media whose economic and discursive centre of power had always been in London. Located on the periphery of an already struggling UK industry, however, they could only mount that challenge with public funding. Established and alternative filmmakers alike lobbied for new funds, but the institutions' limited resources pitted the two tendencies against each other. The institutional view was that "oppositional film-making needs something to oppose, and my own view is that we must also have an indigenous mainstream Scottish Cinema, as an even higher priority" (Brown, 1982).

Posed as an either/or, building a mainstream Scottish cinema perhaps not surprisingly captured the screen policy agenda in 1982 and has held it ever since. In the 1990s, it expanded to include the understandable aim of attracting location-based productions and increasing Scotland's share of UK television commissions. The twenty-first-century ascendancy of creative industries discourse in cultural policy cemented 'producti-vism' as the driving force of screen policy, pushing alternative filmmaking values to the very margins of visibility. They have largely also disappeared from contemporary critical or academic discourse, implying a shared assumption of the centrality of the national-as-alternative. Just as "[c]ultural imperialism rests on the power to universalise particu-larisms linked to a single historical tradition by causing them to be misrecognised as such" (Bourdieu and Wacquant, 1999: 41), the very idea of alternative *systems* of film production, distribution and exhibition has become unthinkable.

3. Extra-national forces can be a progressive influence but still act to reinforce centre-periphery dependency

The rapid expansion of Scottish independent production that Channel 4 enabled in the 1980s benefited both mainstream and alternative. However, whereas the former grew and diversified with expanding access to Scottish and network broadcasters, alternative filmmakers remained dependent on the lifeline from London. Channel 4 supported not just individual filmmakers but also the development of an alternative infra-structure. When it withdrew from workshops and alternative film more generally in the 1990s, Scotland suffered disproportionally compared to the more diversified English organisations because it had been unable to develop alternative sources of income either in the market or from public subsidy. Just as the culturally con-servative national cinema policies of Scotland's film bodies maintained alternative film's underdevelopment and over-reliance on external supports, so too Scottish broadcasters' limited capacity or appetite for more diverse forms of programming beyond the 'national alternative' reinforced its dependency on a London broadcaster. In both cases the opening up of alternatives within Scotland was disabled.

Conclusion

The landscape of alternative media has changed considerably in the past two decades as the rapid evolution of digital technologies has reduced the entry cost of making films and, more significantly, vastly increased their *potential* distribution and reach. Ease of access to the means of production and distribution and the rise of the 'just do it', 'indymedia' culture appear to have dissolved the barriers to active participa-tion in media production and engagement with audiences which earlier generations of film activists set out to overcome through appropriation of state funding and interventions in institutional policies and structures.

A key difference between Scottish and indeed UK alternative filmmaking in the twenty-first century and the preceding two decades is, for better or worse, a return to a less state-mediated film culture, closer to the 1930s than the 1980s. The price of this relative independence from the state, however, is much greater reliance on resources generated transactionally in the marketplace or the public sphere. It may well be the case that it is no longer necessary or productive to directly challenge film policy or media institutions in order to enlarge the sphere of alternative media. On the other hand, this could be a variant of the 'myth of digital democracy' (Hindeman, 2009) in which the contest to secure the attention and involvement of viewers/users remains stacked in favour of the same few mediators as in the past. In any event, there appears at least to be renewed interest both in the history and future of alternative film with expanding numbers of screenings and discussion events in Scotland and the rest of the UK and growing linkages through, e.g., the Radical Film Network, and of course there is, inevitably, a great deal of further research to be done.

Further reading

Atton (2000) is the first and thus far only analytical treatment of alternative media in Scotland. Bauer and Kidner (2013) provide an invaluable collection of source material and commentary on English and Welsh experiences. Dickinson (1999) is the definitive account of radical film in Britain, though Scotland has only a brief mention. The most recent all-round view of Scottish cinema appears in Murray, Farley and Stoneman. Luxonline (www.luxonline.org.uk/histories/index.html) provides a very useful resource charting much of the development of UK alternative film. MacPherson (forthcoming 2015) offers a historical overview of a century of radical filmmaking in Scotland.

References

Allen, D. (1982) "Workers' films: Scotland's Hidden film culture." In C. McArthur (ed.), *Scotch Reels: Scotland in Cinema and Television*. London: British Film Institute.

Atton, C. (2000) "Alternative media in Scotland: Problems, position and 'product'." *Critical Quarterly*, 42(5), 40–46.

——(2002) *Alternative Media*. London: SAGE.

——(2003) "Alternative media: A case for development." *Scottish Left Review*, 14, 10–11.

Bauer, P. and Kidner, D. (2013) *Working Together: Notes on British Film Collectives in the 1970s*. Southend-on-Sea: Focal Point Gallery.

Blain, N. and Hutchison, D. (eds.) (2008) *The Media in Scotland*. Edinburgh: Edinburgh University Press.

Blandford, S. (2007) *Film, Drama and the Break-Up of Britain*. Bristol: Intellect.

BOP Consulting (2014) *Review of the Film Sector in Scotland*. Glasgow: Creative Scotland.

Bourdieu, P. and Wacquant, L. (1999) "On the cunning of imperialist reason." *Theory, Culture & Society*, 16(1), 41–58.

Brown, J. (1982) "How to spend £80,000 on film-making." *Glasgow Herald*, 13 July.

Deane, J. (2007) "Alternative and participatory media in developing countries." In K. Coyer, T. Dowmunt and A. Fountain (eds), *The Alternative Media Handbook*. London: Routledge (pp. 206–11).

Dickinson, M. (1999) *Rogue Reels: Oppositional Film in Britain, 1945–1990*. London: British Film Institute.

Dupin, C. (2012) "The BFI and film production." In G. Nowell-Smith and C. Dupin (eds), *The British Film Institute, the Government and Film Culture, 1933–2000*. Manchester: Manchester University Press (pp. 69–86).

Featherstone, S. (2005) *Postcolonial Cultures*. Edinburgh: Edinburgh University Press.

Gardiner, M. (2005) *Modern Scottish Culture*. Edinburgh: Edinburgh University Press.

Griffiths, T. (2012) *The Cinema and Cinema-Going in Scotland 1896–1950*. Edinburgh: Edinburgh University Press.

Hindeman, M. (2009) *The Myth of Digital Democracy*. Princeton, NJ: Princeton University Press.

Hogenkamp, B. (1986) *Deadly Parallels: Film and the Left in Britain, 1929–1939*. London: Lawrence and Wishart.

——(2000) *Film, Television and the Left 1950–1970*. London: Lawrence and Wishart.

Hutchison, D. (1978) "The alternative press." In D. Hutchison (ed.), *Headlines: The Media in Scotland*. Edinburgh: EUSPB (pp. 39–50).

Lloyd, M. (2011) *How the Movie Brats Took over Edinburgh: The Impact of Cinéphilia on the Edinburgh International Film Festival, 1968–1980*. St. Andrews: St. Andrews University Press.

MacPherson, R. (2009) "Shape-shifters: Independent producers in Scotland and the journey from cultural entrepreneur to entrepreneurial culture." In J. Murray, F. Farley and R. Stoneman (eds), *Scottish Cinema Now*. Newcastle: Cambridge Scholars Publishing (pp. 222–39).

——(2010) "Is bigger better? Film success in small countries: The case of Scotland, Ireland and Denmark." Retrieved from http://researchrepository.napier.ac.uk/3752/1/Is_bigger_better._R_MacPherson_31May2010.pdf (accessed 3 June 2014).

——(forthcoming) "Radical and engaged." In B. Nowlan and Z. Finch (eds), *Directory of World Cinema: Scotland*. Bristol and Chicago: Intellect.

Maley, W. (1994) "Cultural devolution? Representing Scotland in the 1970s." In B. Moore-Gilbert (ed.), *The Arts in the 1970s: Cultural Closure*. London: Taylor and Francis (pp. 78–98).

Martin, M. (1999) Interview in M. Dickinson (ed.), *Rogue Reels: Oppositional Film in Britain, 1945–1990*. London: British Film Institute (pp. 247–62).

Martin-Jones, D. (2009) *Scotland: Global Cinema, Genres Modes and Identities*. Edinburgh: Edinburgh University Press.

McIntyre, S. (1994) "Vanishing point: Feature film production in a small country." In J. Hill, M. McLoone and P. Hainsworth (eds), *Border Crossing: Film in Ireland, Britain and Europe*. Belfast: Institute of Irish Studies, Queen's University (pp. 88–111).

Murray, J., Farley. F. and R. Stoneman (eds) (2009) *Scottish Cinema Now*. Newcastle: Cambridge Scholars Publishing.

Neely, S. (2008) "Stalking the image: Margaret Tait and intimate filmmaking practices." *SCREEN*, 49(2), 216–21.

Neely, S. and Riach, A. (2009) "Demons in the machine: Experimental film, poetry and modernism in twentieth-century Scotland." In J. Murray, F. Farley and R. Stoneman (eds), *Scottish Cinema Now*. Newcastle: Cambridge Scholars Publishing (pp. 1–19).

Petrie, D. (2000) *Screening Scotland*. London: British Film Institute.

Petrie, D. and Stoneman, R. (2014) *Educating Film-Makers Past, Present and Future*. Bristol: Intellect.

Porter, V. (2010) "Alternative film exhibition in the English regions during the 1970s." In P. Newland (ed.), *Don't Look Now: British Cinema in the 1970s*. Bristol: Intellect (pp. 57–70).

Scott, A. (2009) "What's the point of film school, or, what did Beaconsfield Studios ever do for the Scottish film industry?" In J. Murray, F. Farley and R. Stoneman (eds), *Scottish Cinema Now*. Newcastle: Cambridge Scholars Publishing (pp. 206–21).

Shohat, E. and Stam, R. (2003) *Multiculturalism, Postcoloniality, and Transnational Media*. Princeton, NJ: Rutgers University Press.

Stewart (n.d.) "Biography of Dawn Cine Group." Retrieved from http://ssa.nls.uk/biography.cfm?bid=10035 (accessed 3 June 2014).

Wade, G. (1980) *Street Video: An Account of Five Video Groups*. Leicester: Blackthorn Press.

Warren, J. (1973) "Community video, its Canadian roots and beginnings in Scotland." *Scottish International*, December, 15–17.

24

BETWEEN ASPIRATION AND REALITY

A study of contemporary third-sector media production

Daniel H. Mutibwa

Most research on third-sector media organisations, by which I mean companies representing a sector of media production understood to be relatively autonomous of state and commercial interests, and operating in the interests of community and public life, has tended to focus on how they are bounded by socio-political imperatives. Key examples include providing news and other informational content specifically tailored to meet the requirements of audiences un-catered to by mainstream media, encouraging wider participation in the making of such content and functioning as both a critique of and a corrective to the dominance of mainstream media. In doing so, it is argued, third-sector media organisations demonstrate distinctive social and cultural value in facilitating informed and inclusive debate.

However, my research shows that as socio-political and socio-economic circumstances have gradually changed, other ascendant imperatives – especially of a professional and commercial nature – now play an equally important role in third-sector media production. The interplay between socio-political imperatives and professional and commercial ones can be conflicting, thereby pulling producers in different directions. Moreover, producers can be subjected to systemic pressures such as demands from subsidy and politics, all of which have an impact on third-sector media work. Producers respond in ways that have not been sufficiently studied.

Drawing on perspectives from the political economy of communication tradition, alternative media scholarship and other relevant social and political theories, and using ethnographic research, I address this gap by analysing three key issues, namely the response of producers to the divergent imperatives and to systemic pressures, and producers' perceptions of their work following competing imperatives and systemic influences. I argue that the evolving environment in which third-sector media organisations operate sometimes compels producers to prioritise professional and commercial imperatives over socio-political ones and to give in to systemic pressures, thereby contradicting claims for their distinctiveness in democratic communication. In light of this empirical evidence, I emphasise the need to update the theoretical propositions guiding our field and to contemplate sustainable funding strategies for the sector.

My research is based on semi-structured interviews, participant observation and the study of documentary evidence conducted between 2009 and 2011 at five third-sector media organisations – four of which I focus on in this chapter, namely two newspapers (*AsiaNet* and *Ummah Post*) and a radio station (Radio Shannakay) in Britain, and a newspaper (*Shalom News*) in Germany. I selected these organisations based on the following criteria: longevity, claims to subscription to socio-political goals, adoption of professional and commercial values and a reliance on some sort of public support and politics. Although these organisations are by no means representative of the British and German third-sector media spheres, they nonetheless reflect contemporary practice in both contexts. I use pseudonyms to refer to each of these organisations in accordance with conventional ethical norms.

Theorising third-sector media

Although most third-sector media companies exhibit characteristics similar to the media projects defined as alternative media by Atton (2002), my research showed three key differences between them: first, third-sector media companies do not necessarily see themselves as appendages to social movement activity, while alternative media tend to view themselves as part of such activity. Second, and as we shall see below, third-sector media organisations tend to attach great importance to professional journalistic routine competencies such as factual accuracy, speed at meeting deadlines and the use of the objective reporting style in media production, while alternative media projects do not lay claim to such professionalism. Third, and following on from the second point, third-sector media companies appear to exploit professionalism to make profit and see no contradiction in this, while alternative media tend to be anathema to profit-making, which they associate with capitalist excesses.

Regardless of these differences, the distinctiveness of third-sector media organisations – like alternative media – consists in facilitating democratic communication through providing relevant content and encouraging broader involvement in its creation (ibid.). Such content is playing a key part in filling the gap left by mainstream media, namely public service and commercial media, which are proving unable to provide a full range of programming that adequately serves diverse groups in society. Scholars have attributed this to two key developments.

First, from the 1980s onwards, mainstream public service media have faced multiple challenges as a result of deregulation, fierce competition in a multi-channel environment, audience segmentation and technological transformation (Curran and Seaton, 2010). These factors gradually compelled mainstream public service media to restructure their organisation and operations in order to adapt to and remain competitive in the newly deregulated media landscape. Arguably, this led to the abandoning of many public service obligations considered less profitable yet crucial in facilitating democratic communication, examples of which include the provision of local news and other relevant informational content and the facilitation of informed and rational debate (Murdoch and Golding, 2005). In essence, these obligations "give priority to public affairs programmes, reasoned discussion and ... pluralistic representation" and in doing so, "put the needs of democracy before those of profit" (Curran, 2002: 227).

Second, the ownership of commercial media has tended to be concentrated in the hands of a few corporations. Political economists of communication argue that the power accruing from such concentration of ownership can be exercised to control the production and distribution of ideas, values and beliefs inherent in media and cultural content (Hesmondhalgh, 2006), a scenario that has three dire consequences for democratic communication. First, audiences are primarily viewed as consumers – rather than as citizens – to be delivered to advertisers and sponsors through packaging selected events and products that pass as news (McManus, 1994). Second, control facilitates the exposure and reproduction of the interests and perspectives of media owners and privileged elites rather than those of the public and diverse groups (Curran, 2002). Subsequently, the voices and perspectives expressed in mainstream media are likely to be limited, discredited or excluded altogether, especially if they are perceived to threaten dominant commercial and political interests through dissent (Herman and Chomsky, 1988). Third, according to political economists of communication, the facilitation of monopolistic tendencies not only limits competition but also tends to foster the production of populist, profitable and de-contextualised content that replaces the more relevant informational and cultural outputs perceived to be significant in helping make informed civic decisions (Hesmondhalgh, 2006).

In light of these developments and the subsequent constraints on full and wider participation in public debate in mainstream media, key studies have drawn on social and political theory to highlight the need of 'non-mainstream' media – including third-sector media – to maintain their own communicative spaces. In such spaces, these media organisations should aim to prioritise relevant, civic content and to facilitate inclusive debate outside the control of dominant groups (Downing, 2001). In doing so, such organisations are said to enhance what Habermas called the "communicative rationality" necessary for democratic communication to thrive outside the "re-feudalised" (1989[1962]: 150[175–78]) mainstream media in an attempt to counter the naturalisation of dominant discourses and practices (Eley, 1992).

I find it useful here to build on these theoretical propositions by drawing on Atton's (2002) characterisation of alternative media projects that is similar to what third-sector media companies claim to stand for. What Atton (2002: 25) argues for alternative media, I argue for third-sector media, that for democratic communication to happen effectively, such organisations "must be de-professionalised", meaning that "they must be available to ordinary people without the necessity of professional training". Furthermore, such companies must be "de-capitalised", ensuring that they are "without excessive capital outlay", and also "de-institutionalised", compelling them to "take place in settings other than media institutions or similar settings". The rationale for this is to avert the sort of dominant control inherent in mainstream media from being replicated in third-sector media organisations. As we shall see, contemporary third-sector media companies in Britain and Germany are far from being "de-professionalised", "de-capitalised" or even "de-institutionalised". If anything, many of them have actually been moving in the opposite direction, owing to the dynamics of changing socio-political and economic circumstances.

The dynamics of third-sector media production

Alternative media scholars have found that such projects tend to be more responsive to the needs and interests of diverse groups in society than their mainstream counterparts (Bailey, Cammaerts and Carpentier, 2008). For Atton, such projects make their own news, whether by appearing in it as significant actors or by creating news relevant to their situation (2002: 11). He invokes the idea of native reporting, whereby alternative media producers create outputs "from a position of engagement with the event or process that is their subject" (Atton, 2003: 46), and which is characterised by collaboration and support from their audiences. In Philip Elliot's words, such communicators "are concerned about the social relevance … of their work, [t]heir aim [being] to stimulate and explain things to the audience in a more active way than is allowed for by the established [media organisations]" (1977: 149). My research shows that this applies as much to third-sector media producers. It is in this way that I conceptualise socio-political imperatives.

Professional imperatives require third-sector media producers to abide by a routine characterised by inter-relationships with advertisers, other institutions and sources (Tuchman, 1997), and by objectivity as a style of presentation with its related norms of balance and impartiality (Schudson, 2005). For third-sector media producers, being professional or being seen to be so is crucial not only in invoking a close association with authoritativeness, skilfulness and credibility, but as we shall see, professionalism is also used to attract advertisers and sponsors, a position I portray as problematic.

Commercial imperatives in third-sector media production derive from the desire to build audiences in order to generate income in similar fashion to mainstream media corporations. Their ideal would be to generate income while providing content that aims to serve citizens' interests and needs. But the reality is more complex than that, mainly because the quest to make profits has a significant impact not only on how events are assembled and presented, but also on which events are chosen as news. Furthermore, news producers who rely on advertising revenue might give in to the pressure of advertisers to select and package news accounts that promote the interests of the latter (McManus, 1994).

In addition to these imperatives, there are systemic pressures generated by public policy and politics. Progressive policymakers tend to provide subsidies on the condition that such support contributes to facilitating economic and social objectives such as transmitting associated skills and bringing communities and regions together around shared interests, respectively. However, subsidies might be attached to controls that pressure producers to conform to political interests.

Competing imperatives: Tensions, contradictions and interplays

Between the early 1970s and late 1980s, the evidence I gathered shows that the organisations under study subscribed predominantly to socio-political goals. For example, *AsiaNet* – founded in 1972 – covered news stories that focused on racism and discrimination experienced by resident Gujarati and Hindu communities in

London. In the late 1980s, *Ummah Post* was established as a direct response to what Malik – the chief editor – perceived to be "biased mainstream media news reporting on the *Satanic Verses* controversy and also other issues concerning Muslims in London" at the time.

From the late 1980s onwards, changing socio-political and socio-economic circumstances led these organisations to cover broader subject matter that reflected the dynamics in society and that responded to the needs and interests of diverse, hitherto neglected audience groups. Although partly explained by socio-political imperatives, the move was motivated by the desire to tap into new audience markets with a view to boosting circulation in tune with commercial imperatives. The move was also based on the pursuit of an authoritative and professional journalistic voice on specific issues concerning particular community groups both nationally and internationally.

AsiaNet

For example, in the 1980s *AsiaNet* addressed wider South Asian communities (Pakistani, Bangladeshi and Sri Lankan) across Britain. The paper opened its headquarters in India with a view to serving the huge interest in news from the subcontinent. This move ushered in the trend towards professionalisation, and in doing so, altered *AsiaNet*'s content and its presentation significantly. For instance, the paper gradually moved from focusing solely on issues of interest and concern to resident South Asian communities in London to widening its news coverage across numerous regions in Britain, particularly the West Midlands and Yorkshire, with large Asian communities. This move led the paper to adopt both an objective style of news presentation and a layout associated with professional imperatives. Today, the paper comprises eleven sections. Of these, the Media section, for instance, is a single page and summarises prominent stories with an Asian angle to them extracted from other media outlets, while the Community Voice and Upcoming Events sections are also single pages and accommodate the contributions of community members. The biggest section of all is the three-page Finance section, which covers Asian businesses in Britain.

My fieldwork at the paper coincided with the period during which *AsiaNet* showcased the contribution of British Asian businesses to the economy of London. Its campaign had been sparked off a few weeks earlier by a ferocious debate on the role of immigrants, especially during difficult economic times. The paper underlined the significant contribution made by the approximately 40,000 registered Asian-owned businesses in London which boast an annual turnover of nearly £60 billion and offer employment to almost 300,000 people. The paper's campaign demonstrated how *Asia-Net* was responsive to contemporary developments within both the Asian business community and the wider British public through its news coverage, foregrounding socio-political imperatives. In its coverage, the paper selected six Asian enterprises featured as best-practice examples.

However, a closer look at these businesses indicated that most of them were regular advertisers in the paper and were showcased because they had a longstanding 'client' relationship with *AsiaNet* and that their "contribution was worth coverage". What was meant by 'coverage' here in the context of the campaign is revealing: each of the six businesses was asked to send a brief outline indicating the trajectory of their enterprise from conception through to future plans. The outlines sent were then edited into news stories.

For all the campaign's laudable aim to portray the achievements of Asian businesses in London, it is hard to ignore the influence of commercial imperatives in putting together the business news stories. Additionally, although *AsiaNet* boasts over thirty pages providing "the latest news with in-depth reports and analysis on issues of particular importance to British Asians", there were two aspects that could not be overlooked. First, the brevity of the news articles prevented any detailed analysis. An explanation for this could be the weekly nature of the paper, which might have prompted producers to want to cover many stories in brief rather than report on a few in-depth stories. Second, the paper displayed a high number of advertisements. It seemed that news stories were kept short or withdrawn altogether in order to make space for as many advertisements as possible.

Moreover, some of the short news stories were couched in one-line statements from elite sources (Blumler and Gurevitch, 1995: 103), while others were characterised by "vivid and graphic presentations" (McManus, 1994: 7). Such 'presentations' constituted numerous photographs that resemble the "technically uniform, visually sophisticated, easy-to-understand, fast-paced, people-oriented stories that are produced in a minimum amount of time" (Bantz, McCorkle and Baade, 1997: 273). Not only does such content replace civic information, but the tightly organised, standardised routines within which it is generated inhibit wider involvement, suggesting a dominance of professional and commercial imperatives over socio-political ones in newsmaking at *AsiaNet*.

Ummah Post

Ummah Post strove to establish itself as a leading Muslim newspaper from the early 1990s onwards by widening its coverage to address a global readership, for example by reporting on the first Gulf War and the Bosnian conflict. Given the heterogeneity of its readership, the paper aspired to balance objectivity (which harmonises with professional imperatives) and 'native reporting' (which foregrounds socio-political ones): two styles of news presentation that tend to conflict with each other. Malik narrates that *Ummah Post* "reported critically on what was happening even though [it] empathised with Muslim concerns", suggesting a successful interaction between the two reporting styles. Also, documentary evidence revealed that producers at the paper were sought out for consultation and collaboration on Muslim themes by mainstream journalists, a demonstration of their authoritative status.

However, the paper's perceived balanced and critical position on Muslim issues has occasionally drawn harsh reactions from parts of the readership which, it seems, expect a presentation style that explicitly promotes a Muslim stance. According to Malik, "[s]ome very conservative voices in the Muslim community ... think that if you are a true Muslim person, you should not criticise Islam because that is what non-Muslims do anyway [and] that these are hard times and solidarity should be what matters". Malik contends that this does not deter *Ummah Post* from "keeping [its] line". Interestingly, I found that the paper does not live up to its aspiration in many cases. Its news stories on state funding for Muslim schools and the handling of Muslim terrorist suspects in Britain appeared to have been written in an emotive style that seems to echo more the notion of native reporting – where producers' accounts of events were conveyed in a personal and intimate manner, the ultimate goal of which was to try to reflect reality in a way that people experience it rather than a reality framed on their behalf (Atton, 2003).

Producers at *Ummah Post* find themselves in a position where they are considerably influenced by their cultural values and norms in the process of meaning-making. Schudson captures this well when he notes that "among the resources journalists work with are the traditions of story-telling, picture-making, and sentence construction they inherit from their own cultures, with a number of vital assumptions about the world built in" (2005: 189–90). Such 'cultural maps' help news workers make sense of events by facilitating the assignment of selected events to specific cultural and social contexts familiar to the audience (Hall et al., 1981: 337). However, cultural maps are so deeply entrenched within news workers that even professional journalistic values are no bulwark against a bias inherent in them (Schudson, 2005: 185). This exposes a contradiction between aspiration and reality at *Ummah Post* in the attempt to provide balanced and critical news.

Radio Shannakay

During the first three years of broadcasting up to 2007, Radio Shannakay relied solely on public subsidies and volunteer support to operate. It sourced its news and other informational content from both the regional BBC broadcaster and native reporters based in the communities and regions served in the south of England. Producers obtain most of the news material from a BBC news feed which they re-edit to prioritise local stories that may not appear on the BBC and then merge with accounts from native reporters who – according to Ashley – the station manager at the radio

> will go out and find stories ..., find out what's going on in the community, who's making things happen in the community and having that one-to-one discussion with them. It's not just the news articles. It's getting those people in and having the debates and discussions with them.

The dependence on an institutional source in this way merged with broader involvement in newsmaking displays a successful interplay between socio-political and professional imperatives. From 2008, when Radio Shannakay experienced successive cuts to its subsidy like most third-sector radio stations in Britain, the station sought alternative sources of income in order to maintain operations. Documentary evidence revealed that the need for funds resulted in the development of a "programme sponsorship", which was "an exciting way [for local businesses] to build a special relationship with listeners through association with ... sponsoring the news". Furthermore, "businesses [are] credited with a phrase along the lines of 'Brought to you by', 'Supported by', or 'In association with'". Consequently, a tense interplay between commercial and socio-political imperatives resulted from the gradual increase in advertising which increasingly consumed more airtime, constraining the provision of informational programmes and public debate.

Today, the station pre-records its news and current affairs programmes from which amateurish fluffs and gaffes are omitted in an effort to sound more "professional" with a view to attracting even more advertisers. Although the contentious relationship between commercial and socio-political imperatives still permits expression and discussion to take place, there is a strong likelihood that this could trigger a gradual erosion of socio-political imperatives, which would undermine the social value of Radio Shannakay.

Shalom News

Shalom News – which has addressed the German–Jewish community in Berlin since its inception in 2005 – appears to balance the different imperatives in the provision of news most successfully. Although owned by a holding company, its day-to-day operations are managed by four editors in collaboration with community members. Newsmaking at *Shalom News* thrives on contributions from diverse members of the readership, particularly community elites, academics, politicians and ordinary individuals. That professional editors grant community members a significant role in helping make sense of community and public life around them arguably reflects a successful interplay between socio-political and professional imperatives. This is reminiscent of studies on citizen journalism which found that many news producers showed a willingness to involve citizens in media production processes (Ornebring, 2008; Thurman, 2008).

However, participant contributions were usually edited not only to fit the space available but also to conform to professional journalistic norms to which contributors had been socialised. Although this helps ensure quality and ethical standards, it also appears to constrict contributors in the meaning-making process on their own terms. Intriguingly, although *Shalom News* has been boycotted on occasion for its overly critical reporting on issues within the Jewish community in Berlin, the holding company does not intervene in the paper's editorial policy. In this respect, *Shalom News* appears to favour socio-political and professional imperatives over commercial ones, a phenomenon that seems unique given studies that have found that proprietors regularly interfere in the day-to-day operations of newspapers to maximise profit (McManus, 1994; Keeble, 1998).

Systemic pressures and producers' responses

Systemic pressures in the form of public policy and subsidy can enable but also significantly constrain third-sector media production processes. In much the same way that advertisers influence producers' news decisions, policymakers may have an impact on the autonomy of producers. Illustrative of this is *Ummah Post* which, prior to 9/11 and the 2005 London bombings, received government support in the form of printing subsidies and public service advertisements. These were instrumental in keeping production costs relatively low and in generating revenue. In the aftermath of both events, especially after *Ummah Post* directed sharp critique at the government for what many in the Muslim community in Britain perceived as 'draconian anti-terror laws' aimed at targeting and discriminating Muslims in general, the paper had this support removed, according to Malik. Threatened with closure due to lack of funds, the paper dispensed with its overly critical reporting tone, a move that – although it later helped reinstate public support – amounted to self-censorship. Malik notes that " [t]his decision was not easy [b]ut continuing in that way as one of us put it was … a recipe for self-destruction".

This is reminiscent of political controls, either covert or overt, identified by commentators as significantly impacting newsmaking. It is not surprising that such controls – in the form of restrictive laws and regulations, encouragement of self-censorship, refusals to increase public funding, threat of privatisation or the loss of franchises (Curran, 2002: 222–3) – steer news producers away from covering less favoured news stories. In his examination of the boundaries of journalistic autonomy, Altschull (1997) argues that news producers will always face the pressure to conform to state or commercial interests. He argues that "no newspaper, magazine or broadcasting outlet exceeds the boundaries of autonomy acceptable to those who meet the costs that enable them to survive" (ibid.: 260). Renouncing the overly critical stance at *Ummah Post* seems a calculated and pragmatic move to remain in receipt of subsidy.

Despite competing imperatives and systemic pressures, most producers highlighted a passionate attachment to their work that derives from the desire to make an impact on public life in society in alignment with socio-political goals. The only exception was producers at *AsiaNet*, who appeared more preoccupied with achieving 'set sales targets' and even 'aiming higher' in tune with commercial and professional imperatives than socio-political ones. Most producers indicated they would not 'give up' or 'swap' their work for any other job despite persistent challenges such as long working hours and self-exploitation which characterise much work in third-sector media organisations and help subsidise operational costs, thereby enabling survival in the marketplace. Some producers admitted to a need for self-censorship, thereby acknowledging the pressures exerted by proprietary and political interests similar to those faced by their mainstream counterparts.

Conclusion

Contemporary third-sector media organisations appear to attend to public service obligations most successfully when either emphasising socio-political imperatives or balancing these with professional imperatives. An emphasis on professional imperatives over socio-political ones tends to foster the adoption of routinised newsmaking practices which not only tend to inhibit wider involvement, but also limit the range of ideas, perspectives and experiences portrayed. When commercial imperatives come into play, the content generated tends to be bland, populist and superficial, invariably putting profits before public service goals. If left unchecked, this threatens to undermine the social and cultural value of third-sector media organisations in facilitating democratic practice.

This chapter points to two important insights: first, the need to update the theoretical perspectives guiding this field in order to reflect current practice, particularly the revelations that third-sector media organisations are not necessarily appended to social movement activity, that they attach great importance to professionalism which they exploit to make profit and that they suffer from proprietary and political pressures as their mainstream counterparts. Second, there is a need for sustainable funding strategies or business models which would enable these companies to operate on a financially sound base if they are to fulfil their public service remit. As Picard (2008: 212) argues in his study of the economic and social forces affecting media companies, if "conditions are stable and companies are financially secure, they tend to exhibit more willingness to attend to public functions than when conditions are turbulent and their financial performance is poor".

Further reading

Chapters 9 and 11 by Chris Atton and Tamara Witschge, respectively, in part 3 of Peters and Broersma's (2013) *Rethinking Journalism*. The former provides illustrative examples that demonstrate how traditional journalistic craft skill can be brought together with other forms of storytelling to empower citizens, while the latter provides interesting accounts of how news producers sometimes struggle to live up to the journalistic standards they set themselves. Witschge, Fenton and Freedman (2010) offer an interesting and detailed account of possible but not necessarily viable funding models for third-sector media organisations in part 3 of their report.

References

Altschull, H. J. (1997). "Boundaries of journalistic autonomy." In D. Berkowitz (ed.), *Social Meanings of News: A Text Reader*. Thousand Oaks, CA: Sage (pp. 259–68).

Atton, C. (2002) *Alternative Media*. London: Sage.

——(2003) "Organisation and production in alternative media." In S. Cottle (ed.), *Media Organization and Production*. London: Sage (pp. 41–55).

Bailey, O. G., Cammaerts, B. and Carpentier, N. (2008). *Understanding Alternative Media*. Maidenhead: Open University Press.

Bantz, C. R., McCorkle, S. and Baade, R. C. (1997) "The news factory." In D. Berkowitz (ed.), *Social Meanings of News: A Text Reader*. Thousand Oaks, CA: Sage (pp. 269–85).

Blumler, J. and Gurevitch, M. (1995) *The Crisis of Public Communication*. London: Routledge.

Curran, J. (2002) *Media and Power*. London: Routledge.

Curran, J. and Seaton, J. (2010) *Power Without Responsibility: The Press, Broadcasting and the Internet in Britain*. 7th ed. London: Routledge.

Downing, J. (with Villareal-Ford, T., Gil, G. and Stein, L.) (2001) *Radical Media: Rebellious Communication and Social Movements*. Thousand Oaks, CA: Sage.

Eley, G. (1992) "Nations, publics, and political cultures: Placing Habermas in the nineteenth century." In C. Calhoun (ed.), *Habermas and the Public Sphere*. Massachusetts: MIT Press (pp. 289–339).

Elliot, P. (1977) "Media organisations and occupations: An overview." In J. Curran et al. (eds), *Mass Communication and Society*. London: Edward Arnold (pp. 142–73).

Habermas, J. (1989[1962]) *The Structural Transformation of the Public Sphere: An Inquiry into a Category of Bourgeois Society*. Cambridge: Polity Press.

Hall, S., Critcher, C., Jefferson, T., Clarke, J. N. and Roberts, B. (1981) "The social production of news: Mugging in the media." In S. Cohen and J. Young (eds), *The Manufacture of News: Social Problems, Deviance and the Mass Media*. London: Sage (pp. 335–67).

Herman, E. and Chomsky, N. (1988) *Manufacturing Consent: The Political Economy of the Mass Media*. New York: Pantheon.

Hesmondhalgh, D. (2006) *Media Production*. Maidenhead: Open University Press.

Keeble, R. (1998) *The Newspaper Handbook* (2nd edn). London: Routledge.

McManus, J. (1994) *Market-Driven Journalism: Let the Citizen Beware?* Thousand Oaks, CA: Sage.

Murdock, G. and Golding, P. (2005) "Culture, communications and political economy." In J. Curran and M. Gurevitch (eds), *Mass Media and Society*. 4th ed. London: Hodder Arnold (pp. 60–83).

Ornebring, H. (2008) "The consumer as producer – Of what?" *Journalism Studies*, 9(5), 771– 85.

Peters, C. and Broersma, M. (2013) *Rethinking Journalism: Trust and Participation in a Transformed News Landscape*. Abingdon: Routledge.

Picard, R. G. (2008) "The challenges of public functions and commercialised media." In D. A. Graber et al. (eds), *The Politics of News, The News of Politics*. 2nd ed. Washington, DC: CQ Press (pp. 211–29).

Schudson, M. (2005) "Four approaches to the sociology of news." In J. Curran and M. Gurevitch (eds), *Mass Media and Society*. 4th ed. London: Hodder Arnold (pp. 172–97).

Thurman, N. (2008) "Forums for citizen journalists? Adoption of user-generated content initiatives by online news media." *New Media and Society*, 10(1), 139–57.

Tuchman, G. (1997) "Making news by doing work: Routinizing the unexpected." In D. Berkowitz (ed.), *Social Meanings of News: A Text Reader*. Thousand Oaks, CA: Sage (pp. 173–92).

Witschge, T., Fenton, N. and Freedman, D. (2010) *Protecting the News: Civil Society and the Media*. London: Goldsmiths.

Part IV

DOING ALTERNATIVE JOURNALISM

25
POLITICS, PARTICIPATION AND THE PEOPLE
Alternative journalism around the world

Susan Forde

Introduction

Recent work in the field of community and alternative media studies identifies a unique form of journalism operating within these broader outlets (Atton and Hamilton, 2008; Harcup, 2013; Forde, 2011). The nature of the journalism produced in the alternative sector varies considerably – depending on many factors, including target audience, the medium and original purpose – and this diversity is amplified when considered across national and cultural borders. The alternative journalism we see, for example, in the community media of developing nations differs in both its motivations and its content from, say, a radical online newspaper coming out of New York City. There is purpose in examining the variety of practices occurring across these different nations and in these different formats in efforts to discover the essence of the journalism produced. To that end, this chapter intends to go some way towards an overview and an analysis of international forms of alternative journalism.

The alternative (community, independent, citizens') journalism that exists in advanced Western democracies has been the key focus of research and theorisation to date. In particular, these discussions centre around the role of alternative journalism in democracy; its contribution to broadening public spheres and empowering minority voices; and its role in giving air to ideas which are anathema to the political and economic frameworks of commercial media (see McChesney, 2008, for a detailed discussion of the latter). A second site of examination is the alternative journalism emerging in non-Western nations. In some cases, this may be in advanced Asian nations such as Singapore, Malaysia and Indonesia, where there are clear and established 'alternative' journalists operating to disrupt the existing power structures (*Citizen Nades* in Malaysia, for example, or *OhmyNews* in South Korea), whether they be dominant democratic or commercial power structures or authoritarian regimes. Seneviratne notes that a large number of universities and NGOs have more recently established community radio stations in Indonesia, primarily setting these up as alternative media sites which are "a part of a civil society movement for generating grassroots democracy" (2012: 16). In some instances, the alternative journalism we see here has much in common with the forms established in Western democracies; in other instances, it more closely resembles participatory journalism and 'communication for development' (C4D). Developing nations are most closely associated with participatory journalism (indeed, the terms 'community' and 'participatory' journalism seem synonymous in the developmental journalism context), and evidence from Australia suggests that the essence of successful community media also hinges on the participation of its audiences in content production (Meadows et al., 2007). Essentially, for a community media outlet to be properly grounded in its community and to distinguish itself from other *local* commercial outlets, the audience-producer boundary that exists so starkly in the local commercial outlet must be 'down' in the community outlet. Is the common ground in alternative journalism, across different nations, the disappearance of the audience-producer boundary? Or is it, as many scholars examining alternative media in the context of social movements (old and new; see Gerbaudo, 2012) suggest, their drive to bring people into the civic conversation, and in some cases to motivate for collective action that we see in many international approaches to alternative journalism?

This chapter will explore these issues to provide both an overview of alternative journalism practices and forms in various parts of the world; and to inform discussion about the 'ties that bind' alternative journalists, wherever they are.

Defining issues

As with many subsectors in the alternative and community media field, there is ongoing discussion about what we mean when we discuss 'alternative journalism'. Attempts to define alternative journalism (also variously referred to, with some nuances, as grassroots journalism, citizens' journalism, participatory journalism, radical journalism, community journalism, independent journalism) invariably define the media it belongs to, and so discussions about 'what it is' alternative journalists do often begin with a consideration of what alternative/community/grassroots media do. Given that a substantial portion of this broad volume is given over to consideration about the nature and character of alternative and community media, this chapter will keep considerations of definition relatively brief. Importantly, the chapter will focus specifically on the *journalism* of alternative media – the news-gathering practices and routines, motivations and umbrella structures that might impact the work alternative journalists carry out and produce for their broader media outlet.

Atton and Hamilton note in the opening pages of their 2008 work that the lack of definition around alternative journalism is "infuriatingly vague" (2008: 1). They define it in large part by what it is not, in the sense that alternative journalism's critique "emphasises alternatives to, *inter alia*, conventions of news sources and representation; the inverted pyramid of news texts; the hierarchical and capitalized economy of commercial journalism; the professional, elite basis of journalism as a practice; the professional norm of objectivity; and the subordinate role of audience as receiver" (ibid.: 1). For Atton and Hamilton, alternative journalism is produced outside mainstream media institutions, often by amateurs, and it may or may not be political in its content. At the core of alternative journalism, however, is its essential challenge to media power. That challenge may be focused on political and social alternatives; or more apolitical cultural alternatives, "popular culture and the everyday". Alternative journalism, in this iteration, "may be home to explorations of individual enthusiasm and sub-cultural identity just as much as to radical visions of society and the polity" (2008: 2).

Former alternative journalist Tony Harcup concludes that alternative journalism sets out to "privilege the powerless and the marginal; to offer a perspective 'from below' and to say the 'unspoken'" (2003: 371). He also confirms Atton and Hamilton's identification of the lack of an audience/producer boundary in alternative journalism (as does Skjerdal, 2012, in some African alternative journalism genres; Poell and Borra, 2012; Rodríguez, 2001, in describing 'citizens' media'; see also Rodríguez, 2010, and Forde, Foxwell and Meadows, 2009, among many others). In later work, Harcup (2011) illuminates the connections between alternative journalism and active citizenship – essentially, the role of alternative media outlets and their journalists in activating their audiences, encouraging civic participation and action. While he recognises that 'alternatives' may appear in a range of environments – minority right-wing or racist publications may be an alternative in some contexts – Harcup's most recent work narrows his focus to publications that are "left-of-centre politically, anti-racist, anti-sexist, not produced for profit, and they operate along (more or less) non-hierarchical lines" (2013: 8). Understanding alternative media and journalism as a form of 'active citizenship' acknowledges the empowerment that results when social and political collectives come together to produce their own media (Harcup, 2011).

I have suggested elsewhere (Forde, 2011: 3) that the definitions of alternative journalism usually offered are too broad, and there is evidence that alternative journalism can be recognised as an enduring form, with a set of traits identifiable across time. These "enduring characteristics" are identified as resonating with the unrepresented; working outside established societal power structures; being overwhelmingly dedicated to the role of journalism in society; and existing primarily at the margins of the mediascape, as something of an "endangered species" (ibid.: 53). At their core, all of these characteristics have a political implication and so, under this framing, alternative journalism is a political act concerned with the role of journalism in local and national life – whether that be in an advanced democracy, an emerging or a developing nation.

In the development context, 'communication for development' or 'communication for social change' are far more strategic concepts specific to the communities involved. These terms are built into major international discourses about sustainable development which, it is argued, can only succeed where community participation is paramount as a means to empower and capacity-build individuals and communities (see, for example, Tacchi, 2009; Servaes et al., 2012). Tacchi and Kiran found participation, capacity-building, local solutions and recognising the holistic nature of 'poverty' (the need for higher income and access to better food and education sits alongside the need to be empowered and listened to) to be key to the success and long-term sustainability of community media initiatives in Sri Lanka, Nepal, India and Indonesia (2008) (see also Pavarala and Malik, 2007, for more on the development of community media in India). This suggests an entirely different purpose for alternative journalism in a communication for development project, for example, than that which might be undertaken by long-standing British alternative publication *Peace News*, or by the US investigative online news site, *ConsortiumNews.com*.

The historical development of alternative journalism at a few different international sites provides some clearer indications of the trajectory of alternative and community journalism, and will assist efforts to find the common themes that exist in alternative journalism around the world.

Historical perspectives

There are identifiable 'defining moments' in the history of alternative and community-based journalism in the Western world, focusing on the nineteenth-century radical and working-class press; the pre– and post–World War I era which, in many nations, revolved around the growth of socialist and labour movements which fought the increasing dominance of capitalism; the counter-culture movement of the 1960s and 1970s; and the contemporary 'internet' era which is witnessing a near-saturation of alternative and independent journalism sites available to the public online. These moments, while originating in the Australian context, certainly translate to the experience in other Western democracies such as the United Kingdom, Canada, the United States and parts of Europe. They differ, however, from the key moments that might be identified in developing nations, the Middle East, the former Soviet bloc and in some parts of the Asia-Pacific region. Certainly, if we accept the foundational assumption that alternative/citizens' journalism emerges whenever "non-mainstream groups … contest legitimate discourses" (Bosch, 2008: 72) and also that alternative media can be understood as "a social, political and cultural phenomenon" (Rodríguez, 2001: 3–4), then we accept that the history of alternative journalism is tied to the political and social environment in which it operates. I would argue that this does not mean that alternative journalism is entirely *dependent* upon the environment it exists within – but that the political ambience and the conditions of its location will often determine some of its content and the key milestones in its development.

Downing's analysis focuses on radical media's connections to social movements, which are "the lifeblood of these media, and they are the movements' oxygen" (2001: 390), and any historical tracking of alternative journalism and its broader media outlets will identify the peaks and troughs that occur, depending upon the strength and visibility of the movements from which they emanate. Atton and Hamilton note, for example, the connection Vladimir Lenin identified between the growing socialist movement in Russia and the publication of a political newspaper that would act as an agitator and organiser for the revolution (Lenin, cited in Atton and Hamilton, 2008: 28). They report: "Lenin saw the relationship of a newspaper to the movement as analogous to that of scaffolding to a building … Although critics argued that Lenin had it backwards and that the political movement was the condition for and not the result of the newspaper, Lenin insisted that the newspaper was the formative condition for organization and not its outcome" (ibid.). Meyers's examination of the radical Israeli weekly *Haolam Hazeh* reaffirms the importance of the various international contexts that alternative and community journalism occurs within – indeed, the specific 'meaning' of the terms varies across nations and cultures and depends upon structural contexts as well as political and historical matters (Meyers, 2008: 375). Understanding alternative journalism in its different contexts "broadens the overall comprehension of what alternative and mainstream media are and how they interact" (ibid.: 375).

Irawonto identifies the post-Suharto era as a key moment of historical importance for the Indonesian alternative media. Focusing particularly on the rise of community-based media reflecting the views of traditional Muslims, Irawonto reports that the Muslim press played a key role in giving a voice to 'oppressed' groups in post-authoritarian Indonesia. The masthead *Sabili* was identified as "a radical publication, with a much segmented readership" (Irawonto, 2011: 75), while fellow alternative publications such *Suara Hidayatullah* and *Media Dakwah* were run by Muslim activists whose political and moral views were not 'popular' enough to receive space in major commercial media. The more conservative Islamic press, which reached a relatively small audience in Indonesia compared to the commercial, popular press, fulfilled a political and cultural role at times when Indonesian Muslims felt they had no media reflecting their religious values and morality (ibid.: 75–8). Jurriens more broadly notes that the fall of Suharto's 'New Order' regime gave rise to a new sense of freedom of expression, with many community and alternative media outlets rising in opposition to the dominant commercial and public media (2013). While the growth of Indonesian community media developed in parallel to the death of authoritarianism, "(a)t the same time, they have their roots in a long tradition of social commitment and participation in a variety of Indonesian cultural genres" (ibid.: 8).

Briefly, Skjerdal (2012) notes that colonialism has paid a particularly important role in the way African journalism is constructed and deconstructed. Forms of African journalism appear to be resisting the continued adoption of Western journalism norms in favour of African-based cultural and philosophical underpinnings that more closely reflect alternative or community journalism norms. And on the southern tip of the African continent, the apartheid era in South Africa gave oxygen to a wide and diverse radical movement with a raft of associated alternative and radical political publications. Keyan Tomaselli identified education, access and community organisation as the key functions of the anti-apartheid alternative press in 1980s South Africa, when 80 percent of the nation was denied access to proper housing, education and opportunity (1991: 9, 167). This period of the 'booming' 1980s represented a general lull in the alternative press in many Western nations compared to previous eras (O'Lincoln, 1993: 182), but in contrast, the momentum of the anti-apartheid movement in South Africa ensured this was a fertile time for alternative press in that country.

Finding alternative journalism

If we examine the reasons why alternative and community and citizens' media arise and the motivations of the people involved, we see some essential and important consistencies. Atton and Hamilton, clarify, for example, that alternative journalism in capitalist democracies "is a response most generally to capitalism as a social, cultural and economic means of organizing societies, and to imperialism as a global dynamic of domination and consolidation" (2008: 4). Couldry and Curran identify that the dominant media is not just there to "guard us against the overweening influence of other forms of power" (i.e., to act as the Fourth Estate or the watchdog), but that "media power itself is part of what power watchers need to watch" (2003: 3). Alternative media and its journalists have fulfilled this role of *watching* and warning against mainstream media power and political power. This role, to be the 'watcher' of those in control (of both media and politics), is a key characteristic of alternative journalism and emerges as a key theme in historical accounts. The consistent traits – perhaps the 'ties that bind' – journalists of alternative and grassroots media across time and place are many but can be summarised. They are unique to the sector, and can be transferred and understood within a range of political and economic environments.

First, alternative journalists are committed to encouraging their readers to participate, in broader social campaigns and political activity. They provide information designed to motivate, and activate citizenship. Second, alternative journalists prioritise local news or news immediately relevant to their specific audience over other news. It is this focus which often facilitates strong community connections and which may, in many cases, lead to the breakdown of the audience-producer barrier. Third, alternative journalists choose stories that fill the gaps in the information coming from dominant media. Downing (2001) suggests that this form of radical news will often be about the unrepresented, the voiceless, the downtrodden, but it may also be a more contextualised or a politicised take on news 'events'. Finally, alternative journalists understand the key issues canvassed by the dominant media, and they critique that news and its processes. They have an ongoing role as the 'watchers' of media and political power.

Critical issues for alternative journalism

Critical thinking about alternative media and the activities of its journalists must, to some extent, take into account the changes brought to alternative journalism by the internet, and particularly social media. While there has been significant attention to the impact social media had on revolutionary protest movements during the Arab Spring, the Occupy protests, the Indignado in Spain and so on (see Wolfsfeld, Segev and Sheafer, 2013; Sreberny, 2011; Radsch, 2011; and broadly Cammaerts, Mattoni and McCurdy, 2013), this work has primarily focused on the impact on democracy, the potential for social media to liberate and voice oppressed peoples and subgroups in society. There has been less attention on what happens to alternative journalism when it uses social media as its primary platform, and in this section I want to interrogate this as one of the key critical issues facing alternative and community journalism moving forward.

Platon and Deuze provide a good analysis of the Indymedia concept in their 2003 work, as do Atton (2007) and Hyde (2002), with the latter proudly trumpeting the success and democratising power of Indymedia. John Downing, known as the 'father' of radical media (see early work, Downing, 1984), also recognised the empowering *potential* of Indymedia in 2003, although subsequent research has certainly identified the open publishing system's weaknesses and Indymedia has faded somewhat as an alternative or radical journalism experiment in recent years. Taking its place is social media, and with it a commensurate growth in media scholarship which analyses both the phenomenon and the democratic potential of activists and alternative journalists' use of social media as an organising and dissemination tool.

Poell and Barra (2012) examine alternative journalism as it occurs in the social media outlets of Twitter, Flickr and YouTube in an effort to assess social media's ability to provide a contemporary and accessible outlet for alternative journalism with high audience participation. Poell and Barra identify several critical concerns in their analysis of 'alternative' social media coverage of the G20 protests in Toronto, Canada, in 2009, which they collected through monitoring the alternative media's hashtag #g20report. Most importantly, the protest social media coverage which used the alternative journalism hashtag of #g20report was overwhelmingly dominated by events-based coverage focused on police conflict, rather than on the issues protesters were trying to highlight. That is, the research indicates that in this case, alternative journalism occurring through social media was just as likely to be events and conflict-focused as the mainstream media coverage rather than offering the usual alternative journalism perspective – and analysing the issues and revealing the reasons *behind* the protests which might *encourage action* – that we might expect (ibid.: 705ff). Wolfsfeld, Segev and Sheafer's (2013) comprehensive study of social media use in the Arab Spring – which examined 20 Arab countries and the Palestinian Authority – further found a "consistently negative correlation between the extent of social media penetration and the amount of protests". Their overall findings were that much research seems to "overemphasize the centrality of social media in protest. As always the 'real' question is not whether this or that type of media plays a major role but how that role varies over time and circumstance" (ibid.: 132).

Bennett offers an important insight here that helps assess more objectively the importance of digital media, internet access and its accompanying social media forms to the future of alternative media and journalism. He reminds us that it is the context of the technology, and not the technology itself, that needs to be evaluated if we are to understand the true power of the internet as an empowering tool (Bennett, 2003: 19). Bennett notes that the recognised rise in global activism, demonstrated by a range of events involving mass protest organised primarily through the capabilities of new tech-nologies, cannot be wholly attributed to the reduced costs of the Internet and its potential to coordinate campaigns and actions across geographic borders with the click of a mouse on social media (see Pepe and Gennaro, 2007). More, it is the "social and political dynamics of protest" that have changed, "due to the ways in which economic globalization has refigured politics, social institutions, and identity formation within societies" (Bennett, 2003: 25).

Some current research, then, fires a warning shot for practitioners to temper their excitement over the use of social media as a publishing outlet and to ensure that the principles and traits of alternative journalism are reflected in their use of social media tools. Gerbaudo suggests that "social media can be seen as the contemporary equivalent of what the newspaper, the poster, the leaflet or direct mail were for the labour movement" (2012: 4). There is little doubt that the potential networking and campaign opportunities that social media provides will form part of the work – perhaps a core part of the work – of alternative and community media journalists and producers from this point on. For this reason, the way the technology is used, and the impact it has on the work of alternative journalists, needs ongoing analysis and critique.

Future directions

Annual international gatherings of community and alternative media scholars at various conferences and symposia highlight the ever-present need to revisit what it is that alternative and community media does; and in this context, what it is, specifically, that alternative and community media *journalists* do. The increasing internationalisation of news and media has to some extent caused a counter-movement towards locali-sation, and production of media for niche communities and audiences. Some of this new development is genuine alternative and community media – it might be new media established to help Sudanese migrants find their feet in a new country; it might be a crowd-sourced online alternative news site which emerges from a current political or social movement. There are media outlets emerging, however, which are not alternative or community media in the sense that is meant here, and in the sense that this field acknowledges. They might be Facebook groups or blogs for young mothers, amateur online news sites about craft and knitting, and so on. These are niche media serving specialist audiences, but they are not necessarily 'alternative' media – and the evidence here suggests that the *political act* that underpins alternative and community journalism is the missing key.

Future research requires scholars to continually report on new projects, uses of new media, uses of old media and indeed to revisit past historical examples which might illuminate the true nature of alternative and community media. There has been recent work, some of it referred to here, which examines the audiences of alternative media – but this is an area that requires substantial additional research. While there is a growing understanding of the role of the 'audience member as producer', and this is particularly highlighted in the citizens' media described by Rodríguez and in some community radio outlets, there is very little research which interrogates the alternative and community media audience member who is not a producer, a volunteer, a part-time journalist. There are many heroes of alternative and independent journalism around the world – to risk naming a few, I. F. Stone, Wilfred Burchett, John Pilger, J. A. Wayland and many more in other parts of the world. There is insufficient work that unpacks these heroes of alternative journalism, investigators who sacrifice much – often careers and futures – to pursue information and news that our societies need, but that others will not publish. Future work that crosses into media history and identifies the pioneers of alternative and community journalism is a fertile future research field.

Further reading

Atton, C. and Hamilton, J. (2008). *Alternative Journalism*. London: Sage. The first in-depth examination of 'alternative journalism', important for both the theoretical constructs and options it offers for researchers, and the case studies presented.

Cammaerts, B., Mattoni, A. and McCurdy, P. (eds.) (2013) *Mediation and Protest Movements*. Bristol: Intellect. Edited collection which provides a comprehensive recent overview of connections between social movements, media, internet protest and social media.

Harcup, T. (2013) *Alternative Journalism, Alternative Voices*. Oxon and New York: Routledge. A collection of Tony Harcup's past work with some new contributions, featuring interviews with alternative journalists and case studies. Focuses on alternative journalism in advanced democracies.

Seneviratne, K. (ed.) (2012) *'Peoples' Voices, Peoples' Empowerment: Community Radio in Asia and Beyond*. Singapore: Asian Media Information and Communication Centre. Edited collection which features chapters from most parts of Asia on community radio, internet protest, participatory communication. Contributions also from Australia, New Zealand and parts of Europe.

Skjerdal, T. (2012) "The three alternative journalisms of Africa." *International Communication Gazette*, 74(7), 636–74. Provides a sound literature review on much of the existing research and theorising around African journalistic approaches as an alternative to Western journalism.

References

Atton, C. (2007) "A brief history: The Web and interactive media." In K. Coyer, T. Dowmunt and A. Fountain (eds), *The Alternative Media Handbook*. New York: Routledge (pp. 59–65).

Atton, C. and Hamilton, J. (2008) *Alternative Journalism*. Sage: London.

Bennett, W. L. (2003) "New media power: The internet and global activism." In N. Couldry and J. Curran (eds), *Contesting Media Power: Alternative Media in a Networked World*. Lanham, MD: Rowman and Littlefield (pp. 17–37).

Bosch, T. (2008) "Theorizing citizens' media: A rhizomatic approach." In D. Kidd, C. Rodríguez and L. Stein (eds), Making Our Media: Global Initiatives Toward a Democratic Public Sphere, vol. I. Cresskill, NJ: Hampton Press (pp. 71–89).

Cammaerts, B., Mattoni, A. and McCurdy, P. (eds.) (2013) *Mediation and Protest Movements*. Bristol: Intellect.

Couldry, N. and Curran, J. (2003) "The paradox of media power." In N. Couldry and J. Curran (eds), *Contesting Media Power: Alternative Media in a Networked World*. Lanham, MD: Rowman and Littlefield (pp. 3–16).

Downing, J. (1984) *Radical Media: The Political Experience of Alternative Communication*. Boston, MA: South End Press.

——(with T. Villarreal Ford, G. Gil and L. Stein) (2001) *Radical Media: Rebellious Communication and Social Movements*. Thousand Oaks, CA: Sage.

——(2003) "The Independent Media Center movement and the anarchist socialist tradition." In N. Couldry and J. Curran (eds), *Contesting Media Power: Alternative Media in a Networked World*. Lanham, MD: Rowman and Littlefield (pp. 243–57).

Forde, S. (2011) *Challenging the News: The Journalism of Alternative and Community Media*. London: Palgrave Macmillan.

Forde, S., Foxwell, K. and Meadows, M. (2009) *Developing Dialogues: Indigenous and Ethnic Community Broadcasting in Australia*. Bristol: Intellect.

Gerbaudo, P. (2012) *Tweets and the Streets*. London: Pluto Press.

Harcup, T. (2003). "The unspoken 'said': The journalism of alternative media." *Journalism*, 4(3), 356–76.

——(2011) "Alternative journalism as active citizenship." *Journalism*, 12(1), 15–31.

——(2013) *Alternative Journalism, Alternative Voices*. Oxon and New York: Routledge.

Hyde, G. (2002) "Independent Media Centers: Subversion and the alternative press." *First Monday*, 7(4). Retrieved from http://firstmonday.org/htbin/cgiwrap/bin/ojs/index.php/fm/article/view/944/866 (accessed 18 February 2010).

Irawonto, B. (2011) "Riding waves of change: Islamic press in post-authoritarian Indonesia." In K. Sen and D. Hill (eds), *Politics and the Media in Twenty-First Century Indonesia*. Abingdon, Oxon: Routledge (pp. 67–84).

Jurriens, E. (2013). "Social participation in Indonesian media and art: Echoes from the past, visions for the future." *Journal of the Humanities and Social Sciences of Southeast Asia*, 169(1), 7–36.

McChesney, R. (2008) *The Political Economy of Media: Enduring Issues, Emerging Dilemmas*. New York: Monthly Review Press.

Meadows, M., Forde, S. Ewart, J. and Foxwell, K. (2007) *Community Media Matters: An Audience Study of the Australian Community Broadcasting Sector*. Brisbane: Griffith University.

Meyers, O. (2008) "Contextualizing alternative journalism." *Journalism Studies*, 9(3), 374–91.

O'Lincoln, T. (1993) *Years of Rage: Social Conflicts in the Fraser Era*. Melbourne: Bookmarks.

Pavarala, V. and Malik, K. (2007) *Other Voices: The Struggle for Community Radio in India*. Thousand Oaks, CA: Sage.

Pepe, A. and Gennaro, C. (2007) "Political protest Italian-style: The blogosphere and mainstream media in the promotion and coverage of Beppe Grillo's V-Day." *First Monday*, 14(12). Retrieved from http://firstmonday.org/htbin/cgiwrap/bin/ojs/index.php/fm/article/view/2740/2406 (accessed 18 February 2010).

Platon, S. and Deuze, M. (2003) "Indymedia journalism: A radical way of making, selecting and sharing news?" *Journalism*, 4(3), 336–55.

Poell, T. and Borra, E. (2012) "Twitter, YouTube and Flickr as platforms of alternative journalism: The social media account of the 2010 Toronto G20 protests." *Journalism*, 13(6), 695–713.

Radsch, C. (2011) "Arab bloggers as citizen journalists (transnational)." In J. Downing (ed.), *Encyclopedia of Social Movement Media*. London and Thousand Oaks, CA: Sage (pp. 61–4).

Rodríguez, C. (2001) *Fissures in the Mediascape: An International Study of Citizen's Media*. Cresskill, NJ: Hampton Press.

——(2010) "Knowledges in dialogue: A participatory evaluation study of citizens' radio stations in Magdalena Medio, Colombia." In C. Rodríguez, D. Kidd and L. Stein (eds), *Making Our Media: Global Initiatives Toward a Democratic Public Sphere*. Cresskill, NJ: Hampton Press (pp. 131–54).

Seneviratne, K. (2012) "Community radio in Asia: Slowly coming out of the shadows." In K. Seneviratne (ed.), *Peoples' Voices, Peoples' Empowerment: Community Radio in Asia and Beyond*. Singapore: Asian Media Information and Communication Centre (pp. 1–24).

Servaes, J., Polk, E., Shi, S., Reilly, D. and Yakupitijage, T. (2012) "Towards a framework of sustainability indicators for 'Communication for Development and Social Change' projects." *International Communication Gazette*, 74 (2), 99–123.

Skjerdal, T. (2012) "The three alternative journalisms of Africa." *International Communication Gazette*, 74(7), 636–74.

Sreberny, A. (2011) "Social movement media in 2009 crisis (Iran)." In J. Downing (ed.), *Encyclopedia of Social Movement Media*. London and Thousand Oaks, CA: Sage (pp. 497–9).

Tacchi, J. (2009) "Finding a voice: Participatory development in Southeast Asia." In J. Hartley and K. McWilliams (eds), *Story Circle: Digital Storytelling around the World*. Oxford: Wiley-Blackwell (pp. 167–75).

Tacchi, J. and Kiran, M. S. (2008) *Finding a Voice: Themes and Discussions*. New Delhi: UNESCO.

Tomaselli, K. (1991) "The progressive press: Extending the struggle, 1980–86." In K. Tomaselli and P. Eric Louw (eds), *The Alternative Press in South Africa*. Belville: Anthropos (pp. 155–74).

Wolfsfeld, G., Segev, E. and Sheafer, T. (2013). "Social media and the Arab Spring: Politics comes first." *International Journal of Press/Politics*, 18(2), 115–37.

26
DIGITAL MEDIA AND NEWS

Leah A. Lievrouw

There is broad agreement today about the transformative consequences of networked computing and digital telecommunications – new media and information technologies – in virtually every sector of the economy and aspect of everyday life and culture. Nowhere has the disruption been more profound – or a corresponding sense of 'crisis' more acute – than in the traditional media, entertainment and news industries, whose production methods, markets, cultural practices and modes of consumption and readership[1] have depended so much on the technologies and logic of mass production and mass media. From the seventeenth century onwards, news served as something of a 'killer app' for mass-produced print, attracting unprecedented mass audiences, spurring technological innovations in response to increasing demands for news and reflecting and fostering political and economic upheavals throughout the modern era. In the twentieth century, broadcasting further concentrated news production along mass-production lines, and extended the reach and institutional power of the news industry. "Just as the creation of the mass-market automobile was the result of industrial logic brought to transportation, the rise of the mass press was the result of industrial logic *brought to information*" (Peters and Broersma, 2013: 4; emphasis in original).[2]

Given this trajectory, it is difficult to overstate the scale and scope of change, and journalists' and news organisations' deep sense of rupture and dislocation, associated with the transition to digital technologies since the 1970s, when the first 'video display terminals' began to appear in newsrooms. The disruption has affected news in all its manifestations: as an industry turning out products for consumption in markets; as an institution with norms and values that imposes standards and mediates between the public/civil society and the state; and as a profession practiced by reporters and editors in their efforts to create faithful, reliable accounts and interpretations of events.

The present chapter considers three main themes or dynamics that have emerged from the often uneasy integration of digital technologies and news: *news as process*; the *segmentation and segregation* of content and readers; and changing news *ethics and values*. Each of these has affected news as an institution, as an industry and as a practice. The chapter concludes with a discussion of their implications for alternative and community media.

News as process

The first theme is a growing view of news as process, rather than as an industrially manufactured media 'product'. The adoption of digital platforms and infrastructures in every aspect of reporting and news circulation has evoked an 'always-on', emergent quality that heightens the disposable character of news and the sense of contemporary culture as being in a state of continuous flux. Historically, the *form* of news has always been shaped by the technological tools used to produce and circulate it: news is rendered as recordings or documents in fixed form for distribution to readers, viewers or listeners. Newsworthy events are authoritatively documented for posterity, as by a 'newspaper of record'. Through this process, news becomes a *product*, subject to the same market demands and pricing as other manufactured goods.

The difficulty with recordings and documents, however, is that they interrupt the continuous, time-sensitive nature of the news itself. Although traditional media technologies like printing and photography have been adapted to speed up production, as long as news organisations have produced fixed recordings and documents, they have remained time-bound to the "periodicity of publication" (Bensman and Lilienfeld, 1971: 131). While the routines of reporting and editing might go on continuously, much like the events being covered, those routines are also punctuated by a strict schedule of deadlines that are largely determined by the limits of technology. Thus, conventionally, news has been produced in the form of *periodicals*.

Digital technologies also shape the form of news. Many prestigious online news sites, particularly those associated with 'legacy' media like daily newspapers and news weeklies, still create 'editions' and adhere to regular publication schedules. Photos, graphics, video and text are still composed, edited and published. However, these digital elements can also be browsed and incorporated into far more heterogeneous, dynamic flows of information with 'no fixed address' or firm attribution – borrowed, remixed, linked, re-tweeted, commented, annotated, recommended by anyone according to purpose or interest, without necessarily involving professional journalists and editors (raising serious ethical concerns about the authenticity, sourcing and manipulation of online content; see Pavlik, 2001; Willis, 1994). In a sense, news and the practice of journalism online are more time sensitive than ever. The incessant, globalised demand for information leaves little time for the reflection and contexualisation once afforded by the fixed schedules, deadlines and periodicity of physical documents. In the digital era, news has become a *process*, a kind of reservoir of possibility, as much as a definitive stock of information goods.

Of course, the shrinking news cycle did not originate with the internet. From nineteenth-century news agencies and wire services, to mobile 'electronic news gathering' (ENG) methods in the 1970s that replaced reel-to-reel audiotape and 16mm film, to the introduction of 24-hour cable television news channels in the 1980s, news organisations have sought ways to make news production more immediate. Nonetheless, there is no question that digital technologies have accelerated these time pressures. The capacity for continuous composition, revision and posting of text, images, video and sound has fostered a 'feed the beast' sensibility among journalists and worrying risks of exploitation and burnout, particularly among younger, tech-savvy reporters and editors (Carr, 2014; Keller, 2013; Paulussen, 2012; Peters, 2010; Reinardy, 2011). Growing reliance on freelancers and the resulting lack of long-term career prospects has eroded institutional loyalty and encouraged a more self-interested, adversarial and 'liquid' attitude among young journalists (Kantola, 2013). Crucially, however, this volatile environment has also allowed informed amateurs with special interests and community-based 'citizen journalists' to play a larger role in the news process (e.g., the *Empty Wheel* blog, www.emptywheel.net, is written by Marcy Wheeler, who has a PhD in comparative literature; it is a daily must-read among journalists and policymakers dealing with US national security issues).

The sheer volume of information circulating online has also encouraged new approaches to content production. Online journalists – some of whom may only produce an occasional blog post or commentary – may select and aggregate sundry pieces of material from disparate sources, a process popularly characterised as 'curation' (minus its professional connotations of scholarly depth, connoisseurship, authentication or interpretation). The point is to shape or direct patterns of information flows rather than to create a definitive, reliable, stable or 'true' account of events. Many online journalists are paid according to how many hits their pieces receive; those who can nurture successful 'memes' (bits of cultural discourse that attract bursts of popular interest) or 'click bait' may find them more lucrative than work on an award-winning, long-form investigative story that attracts few readers (Carr, 2014).

Data visualisation is another important tactic for managing and representing relentless event streams and global-scale data flows. Graphics and animation can help 'tell the story' when it involves complex quantitative data or trends over time (McGhee, 2010; Rogers, 2013; Segel and Heer, 2010). 'Data journalism' requires that journalists and editors develop new competencies and practices of search, statistical analysis and graphic visualisation in order to present and make sense of what early twentieth-century journalist and cultural critic Walter Lippmann (1922: 358) called "a picture of reality upon which men [sic] can act" – even if the picture is now a multichannel, continuous, remixed stream of images, sound, text and data accessed via myriad digital devices.

Fact-checking – the verification of information via multiple sources, reliable data or interviews with experts or witnesses – is a core journalistic practice. But it is time consuming, and two developments suggest how fact-checking routines have adapted to the new online context. The first inverts the traditional process. Rather than waiting to publish until all details have been sourced and confirmed (per the editorial adage 'Get it first, but first get it right'), online journalists may post a story that is unconfirmed or incomplete, revising and reposting as new information comes in, whether from reporters or readers (Gillmor, 2004; Pavlik, 2001). A second development is the immediate public feedback afforded by online publishing platforms and the proliferation of dedicated fact-checking sites like Snopes.com, FactCheck.org, PolitiFact.com and WhoWhatWhy.com. These sites comprise a 'meta' ecology of news that performs some traditional fact-checking functions, as well as a watchdog-type function on news production itself (both on- and offline). For readers, they can also serve as trusted aggregators and gatekeepers. Indeed, readers' trust in fact-checking sites has motivated partisan groups to set up imitation sites that question stories they seek to delegitimise or refute.

In this landscape of new modes of curation, storytelling and fact-checking, the nature of sources is shifting as well. Traditional sources – spokespersons, experts, public officials, eyewitnesses, participants, authoritative documents, and so on – still figure prominently; however, digital technologies have highlighted the importance of risk-taking whistleblowers and the journalists they work with. Scale is critical here: digital technologies make it relatively easy to obtain, duplicate and share vast collections of information. Millions of electronic files can be located and retrieved in seconds, duplicated and moved among multiple secure sites to evade discovery and confiscation, transmitted to journalists on tiny flash drives or via secure Internet connections and searched and analysed at length for their relevance to a range of newsworthy issues.

Archetypal examples include the cache of diplomatic cables and classified military documents obtained by WikiLeaks and shared with the *New York Times*, the *Guardian*, *Le Monde*, *Der Spiegel*, and *El País* in 2010–11; and former security contractor Edward Snowden's release of classified materials documenting the unprecedented scope of the US National Security Agency's collection of the personal electronic communications of foreign nationals, their political leaders, as well as US citizens and even members of Congress. In both cases the document collections are huge, providing source material for months or even years of investigative reporting. As sources, Snowden and WikiLeaks founder Julian Assange have helped redirect public debates about government activities and policies, and prompted fresh looks at the ethics, politics and legal regimes governing surveillance. Despite having to go into hiding or self-imposed exile to escape criminal prosecution, Assange and Snowden have (at least to date) successfully employed digital technologies to safeguard the incriminating materials and make them available to journalists and the public, at their discretion and on their own terms – becoming sources perfectly suited to news-as-process.

Segmentation and segregation

The second theme is the growing segmentation and segregation of both news streams and readers afforded by digital technologies, who use them to shape and recombine the variety of news and information available online according to their interests, preferences or viewpoints. Segmentation strategies vary. Some sites focus exclusively on coverage of special-interest topics (law, politics, environment, technology, entertainment), while general-interest media such as the *New York Times* or CNN offer online 'feeds' of proprietary content selected for narrowly targeted, segmented groups of readers. For their part, readers facing a blizzard of choices employ digital filtering and aggregation applications that limit feeds to pre-selected topics.

Again, segmentation is not a new phenomenon; general-interest newspapers and magazines customarily assign reporters to specialised beats and divide their publications into sections for different categories of news (international, politics, business) or reader interests (style/society, arts and entertainment, sports, 'women's' sections). Broadcast news dedicates strictly timed segments to 'hard' news, features, weather, traffic, sports, and so on. The advent of cable television sparked the rise of news-only television channels, which in turn spun off more specialised channels for business, entertainment and political news.

Historically, mass media-driven business models of news have been predicated on comprehensive coverage of just the most newsworthy events during a given news cycle, which are selected to attract the largest possible audience and thus the most lucrative advertisers. In contrast, digital platforms have prompted new business models based on relationships with a vast variety of niche markets. Instead of the wide swath of 'average' readers/viewers at the centre of the mass-market bell curve, news sites online seek to attract various small, narrowly focused segments of a 'long tail' in a heavily skewed but essentially limitless distribution of potential reader groups. The relatively low cost of online news production allows news sites to focus on topics with specific demographic, political, social or cultural appeal. And increasingly, through their "obsession and hyperfocus", these smaller sites and communities are as likely to uncover "big" stories as major news organisations are (Carr, 2013: B1).

Online, then, readers can choose from dozens of news and information sites that cover the topics they care the most about. But even for such specific interests, there can be far more content online than any reader can follow. So a second technique, news aggregation, provides automated updates on collections of sites and sources. Some aggregators 'curate' content, using human editors, readers' pre-set preferences (e.g. Really Simple Syndication, or RSS feeds) or fully automated algorithms (e.g., Google News) that select and present web content based on readers' previous searches, online reading habits, or what others in their social networks are reading. Advocates of aggregation suggest that it gives readers an unprecedented ability to streamline and focus the blur of continuous information streams into a kind of 'daily me' (Negroponte, 1995).

However, critics charge that such highly personalised 'tailoring' encourages readers to seek only information and news that conforms to their particular interests, experiences or biases, and to disregard contradictory or challenging ideas. Readers may become more isolated, polarised or intolerant (Harper, 1997; Kristof, 2009). Civic discourse and the public sphere may suffer as readers avoid exposure to and engagement with different perspectives (Sunstein, 2007). Algorithmic aggregators may severely limit the selection of 'relevant' material served to readers, creating a 'filter bubble' (Pariser, 2011).

Segregation and segmentation are often revenue driven. So-called pay walls, 'walled garden' strategies and restrictive intellectual property regimes exclude non-paying readers, or confine paying readers to restricted domains of content. Digital rights management (DRM) technologies block certain users from accessing certain types of content, or curtail uses of content (linking, copying, sharing, and so on) that would ordinarily be allowed under fair-use or first-sale provisions of copyright law with conventional media forms. Readers' fair-use and first-sale rights may be eliminated entirely by licensing contracts or 'end-user' agreements imposed by content owners as a condition for readers to obtain the work. Such agreements may deliberately induce readers to 'click through' to content without closely reviewing their densely written terms and provisions, which often require readers to surrender extensive information about their online activities in exchange for access. Some sites withhold their content from aggregators and publicly available news streams or collections; it can only be retrieved directly from the publisher's site.

These techniques serve to preserve the owner's control over content availability and pricing, and a degree of mass media-style market power and incumbency. Critics see them as bald attempts to prop up failing business models in which a few dominant producers deliver media products to large, and largely passive, audiences of consumers with few alternatives. They subvert provisions of copyright law meant to encourage the circulation and sharing of knowledge, and the cultivation of informed citizens able to make their own political and economic decisions. Thus, they may also undermine the very 'public' that journalism and the press are meant to serve – and the very reason for speech and press protections in the first place.

Ethics and values

The third theme concerns the ethics and values of news. The data and information flows that have helped shift news from product to process, and new techniques for managing and redirecting those flows into ever more finely tuned and segregated streams for segmented readerships, have intersected with a growing climate of public scepticism towards knowledge authorities and institutions. Together, these factors have created new strains for the ethos of news and professional journalism (especially American journalism) as it has been practiced since the Progressive Era (Schudson, 1990). This dynamic has sparked debates about journalists' professional prerogatives and the social and political role of the press, and a growing recognition that journalistic ethics are not the sole preserve of media institutions or credentialed reporters and editors. It has also prompted increasingly restrictive attempts by governments and media industry players to redefine who 'counts' as a journalist, as these powerful institutions seek new limits on the press and its role in democratic societies as a watchdog and mediator between civil society and the state.

As the centrepiece of traditional journalistic ethics and news values, objectivity (and related concepts of fairness, accuracy and reliability) has been especially susceptible to challenges that it is, variously, an unrealistic, unattainable ideal in practice, a public trust betrayed or a cynical cover for the economic and political alliances of powerful media organisations (Pavlik, 2001). Over time, a new repertoire of news values and journalistic ethics has been negotiated that more closely reflects the sensibility of online culture. Many amateur, volunteer and 'citizen journalists' working in both online and traditional media – "the people formerly known as the audience" (Rosen, 2006) – have come to consider connectivity, participation, community and voice to be as important ethically as objectivity and accuracy *per se*. In the profoundly networked conditions of new media, "transparency is the new objectivity" (Weinberger, 2009). Journalists gain the public's trust by revealing their own processes, stakes and interests in a story, rather than claiming disinterestedness or objectivity.

From this perspective, reader perceptions of credibility, reliability and fairness require that reporters and editors convey a clear, authentic point of view and reputation. Dedicated readers and commenters are often as knowledgeable about complicated, controversial issues as journalists themselves, so journalists may involve community members and amateur colleagues more directly in the process of reporting and commentary (despite reservations in some quarters about amateurs' presumed lack of ethical grounding, disinterested expertise and authority and greater susceptibility to economic and political pressure; Maher, 2005).

Broadly speaking, we might say that in the post-browser internet era, journalistic ethics and news values have become less a matter of standardised ethical codes promulgated and enforced by entrenched institutions (e.g., news organisations, professional societies, educational programs, courts, the state) than a process of engagement with more complex commitments and relationships among participants with diversified experiences, interests, agendas and worldviews, who often mistrust institutional authority and "explicitly separate the practice of journalism from the institutional role and interests of traditional news and media industries" (Lievrouw, 2011: 121).

At the same time, the broad-based participation enabled by new technological platforms has exposed both new entrants and established news organisations to growing challenges from government and private-sector actors seeking to undermine the institutional role and legitimacy of the press. Notably, law enforcement and elected officials in the US have sought to restrict the definition of 'who is a journalist', particularly by establishing credentialing regimes that disqualify independent or investigative journalists, those working for online or multiplatform outlets, or unpaid volunteers (Fry, 2011; Stearns, 2013). The 'phone hacking' scandal in the UK has prompted similar efforts by politicians to define and regulate news organisations and publishers (BBC News UK, 2013).

The changing economics of news have also had ethical/normative repercussions. News production and distribution have dispersed beyond a handful of major industry players that once trained and employed professional journalists, to a diversified ecosystem of projects, sites, feeds, collectives and even 'labs' staffed by experienced journalists, novices, amateurs, independents and activists. In retrospect, it might be argued that objectivity was a news value perfectly suited to the late twentieth-century era of highly concentrated mass media ownership and markets, reduced competition and a dwindling diversity of voices and viewpoints. From this perspective, even one 'truly objective' news organisation could plausibly provide comprehensive, unbiased, fair and fully representative news coverage in a given market. As the number of US news outlets shrank in a wave of sell-offs and mergers in the 1970s and 1980s, critics charged that increased concentration of media ownership and unprecedented shareholder demands for profit ultimately and fatally undermined the public-interest mission and responsibilities of the American press (Bagdikian, 1983). The scene was set for subsequent waves of technological and economic upheaval that battered the industry in the 1990s and early 2000s.

As legacy news organisations have continued to lay off newsroom staff, close foreign bureaus and reduce print editions to a few days a week, new organisational forms and funding models have emerged, including subscription-based or crowd-funded projects like ProPublica, Truthdig, the *Texas Tribune* and PolitiFact.com. News collectives ranging from the countercultural Independent Media Centers (www.indymedia.org) to the market-driven *Huffington Post* are staffed by a mix of professional and amateur contributors. Some traditional newspapers have reorganised as non-profits or branches of academic programs, or rely on philanthropic support, including the *St. Petersburg Times*, the *Anniston* (Alabama) *Star* and the *New Hampshire Union Leader*. The recession has been an important factor in the rise of non-profit news; of 172 non-profit news outlets in the US in 2013, 71 per cent used unpaid volunteers or contributors. Nearly half were launched at the start of the economic downturn in 2008–9 (Mitchell and Jurkowitz, 2013).

Two closely watched recent developments may defy this trend. In 2013, Amazon CEO Jeff Bezos bought the *Washington Post* from its long-time owners, the Graham family. Pierre Omidyar, founder and chair of eBay, has launched an omnibus online news platform, First Look Media, including a flagship site, *The Intercept*, which employs a roster of high-profile professional journalists and academic advisors (see www.firstlook.org/theintercept). Whether these projects mark a return to a venerable dynastic tradition of closely held private enterprises in American publishing, genuinely new models for the news or only stopgap attempts to slow the inevitable slide of the for-profit news industry remains to be seen.

Challenges for alternative and community media

The three dynamics explored here – news-as-process, segmentation/segregation and shifting ethics and values – provide important lessons for alternative and community media as they adopt digital technologies and enter the wider network of online information and news. First, it is clear that many such projects are fundamentally journalistic in approach and method. They document and comment on events from the perspectives of particular communities or specialised interests, especially those that are often marginalised by mainstream news outlets. They emphasise participation and diverse viewpoints rather than standardised or authoritative knowledge and editorial gatekeeping. They certainly fit Chris Atton's (2002) defining characteristics of 'alternative' media as non-commercial, anti-institutional and oppositional, with an emancipatory outlook. They provide 'authentic' venues for representing community interests, and combine "creative expression and social responsibility" (Atton, 2002: 13–14). They also fit the definition of *participatory journalism* as "local and special-interest reporting, editing and opinion that simultaneously uphold and critique the traditional values of journalism and the press" (Lievrouw, 2011: 120).

Thus, alternative and community media projects may also be subject to the three dynamics, if in a different register or on a different scale. The continuous flows, immediacy and diversity of information sources and voices online are invaluable resources for alternative and community media. Small-scale, community-based projects have virtually the same access to constant streams of information online as major media organisations do (what one observer has called "the jailbreak on information" (Carr, 2013: B1), and real potential for 'going viral' and attracting worldwide readership. At the same time, alternative and community media online may also be just as prone to the burnout and 'feed the beast' pressures noted previously. The accelerating pace and always-on culture of the internet can tax overstretched volunteer staffs, and turn a strong community outlet with a clear voice into an incoherent pastiche of fragmentary ideas and agendas.

The problem is not necessarily solved by imposing a single editorial viewpoint or vision. Rather, the challenge is to favour inclusion over exclusion (including dissenting or contrary perspectives) *and* to identify compelling patterns in the flows of information, to connect the disparate dots. For alternative and community media, as for mainstream online media, the key – and the value for readers – is *navigation*, combining informed search, information literacy and well-documented, persuasive interpretation with a clear point of view, and the creation of spaces for conversation, debate and action.

Given their niche constituencies, concerns and readerships, alternative and community media projects are segmented almost by definition. Of course, one of the great strengths of the internet is that it enables people with highly specialised, countercultural or marginalised interests to find and interact with one another on a global scale. It can be an effective platform for both local and widely dispersed communities of interest to mobilise, grow and foster solidarity and collaboration. However, it can also act as a kind of echo chamber (Weinberger, 2004). Technological platforms and features allow participants to exclude opposing views, disengage from pluralistic debates and reinforce their own beliefs with little fear of challenge or contradiction. These features, combined with most people's tendency to seek information that confirms what they already believe, can limit the visibility and relevance of such closed venues. Online, alternative and community media projects may unwittingly court the very insularity and marginalisation they seek to overcome in society and culture at large.

In many ways, the shifting ethos of online journalism and news, from objectivity to a greater emphasis on participation, transparency and authenticity, is ideally suited to the values of alternative and community media. It resonates with their emancipatory aims, mistrust of institutional authority and power, and authenticity and credibility grounded in the diversity of voices who debate it rather than the expert authorities who create it. But we might ask, what about the ultimate goals that objectivity was meant to achieve? In the early twentieth century, Walter Lippmann and his journalistic colleagues worried that citizens were becoming less informed, and public opinion too easily swayed, by jingoistic politicians, advertising and public relations and government propagandists, often with the complicity of powerful, self-interested publishers (a remarkably familiar situation today). What values should the press adopt in order to be an effective watchdog on powerful private interests and the state, and to foster an informed, self-governing citizenry?

It should be said that the rejection of objectivity as a news value and journalistic ethic is not the same as rejecting the aims and responsibilities of the press in a democracy. Nor does it suggest that the press can or should abandon corollary values of fairness, accuracy and reliability. Those who advance transparency, interaction, voice and community as alternatives to objectivity may actually agree with Lippmann that the press must create "a picture of reality upon which men can act", but which is fairer, more accurate and more reliable than one based on objectivity alone.

To conclude, the developments and innovations recounted here suggest that journalism and the press have survived the direst predictions of a decade ago. Some observers cautiously predict a kind of renaissance for the practice of journalism, particularly "public interest-oriented, mission-driven" news (Stearns, 2012). The three dynamics at the intersection of digital media and news – news-as-process, segmentation and segregation, changing ethics and values – may continue to help chart the way ahead for journalism and the press.

Notes

1 The terms 'reading' and 'reader' are used here to denote the whole range of engagement with news. Unlike 'audience', it does not suggest limited feedback or mass-scale reception; unlike 'consumer', it does not reduce engagement to an economic transaction. 'Citizen' suggests broader political agency beyond reading the news. Thus, 'reading' includes viewing, hearing, searching, writing, interpreting, critiquing or any other ways that people generate, use, share and understand news.
2 Due to the author's familiarity with American media policy, journalism history and technology in US media, the present discussion focuses primarily on the US context.

Further reading

David Ryfe and Donica Mensing (2008) make an excellent historical argument for two competing philosophies of American journalism: Lippmann-influenced 'journalism-as-transmission-of-information' versus John Dewey-influenced 'journalism-as-participation'. Michael Schudson's classic study (1990) charts the rise of objectivity as the core of journalism ethics. David Carr's weekly *New York Times* column, 'The media equation', is an incisive, ongoing commentary on the news industry, particularly the economic and ethical challenges of digital technology. Cullen Hoback's amusing, chilling documentary *Terms and Conditions May Apply* (2013) shows how restrictive intellectual property agreements (licensing, clearances and end-user agreements) restrict open information access, extort users' personal information and abrogate the public domain, fair-use and first-sale provisions of copyright law. Simon Rogers, editor of *The Guardian*'s Datablog and Datastore sites, offers an excellent primer on data journalism in his richly illustrated *Facts Are Sacred: The Power of Data* (2013). Geoff McGhee's documentary, *Journalism in the Age of Data* (2010), shows how data visualisation is being used to create new forms of journalistic storytelling.

References

Atton, C. (2002) *Alternative Media*. London: Sage.

Bagdikian, B. (1983) *The Media Monopoly*. Boston, MA: Beacon Press.

BBC News UK (2013) "Q&A: Press regulation." 30 October. Retrieved from http://www.bbc.com/news/uk-21797513 (accessed 14 January 2015).

Bensman, J. and Lilienfeld, R. (1971) "The journalistic attitude." In B. Rosenberg and D. M. White (eds), *Mass Culture Revisited*. New York: Van Nostrand Reinhold (pp. 131–49).

Carr, D. (2013) "Big news forges its own path." *New York Times*, June 16, B1.

——(2014) "Risks abound as reporters play in traffic." *New York Times*, March 23, B1. Retrieved from http://nyti.ms/1fSUYdc (accessed 14 January 2015).

Fry, E. (2011) "Who's a journalist?" *Columbia Journalism Review*, October 7. Retrieved from http://www.cjr.org/behind_the_news/whos_a_journalist_1.php?page=all (accessed 14 January 2015).

Gillmor, D. (2004) *We the Media*. Sebastopol, CA: O'Reilly Media.

Harper, C. (1997) "The daily me." *American Journalism Review*, April. Retrieved from http://ajrarchive.org/article.asp?id=268 (accessed 14 January 2015).

Hoback, C. (2013) *Terms and Conditions May Apply* (video). Retrieved from http://www.tacma.net (accessed 14 January 2015).

Kantola, A. (2013) "From gardeners to revolutionaries: The rise of the liquid ethos in political journalism." *Journalism*, 14(5), 606–26.

Keller, B. (2013) "It's the golden age of news (but not if you're a freelance reporter being held captive in Syria)." *New York Times*, November 4, A25. Retrieved from http://www.nytimes.com/2013/11/04/opinion/keller-its-the-golden-age-of-news.html?smid=pl-share (accessed 14 January 2015).

Kristof, N.D. (2009) "The daily me." *New York Times*, March 18, A31. Retrieved from http://www.nytimes.com/2009/03/19/opinion/19kristof.html (accessed 14 January 2015).

Lievrouw, L. A. (2011) *Alternative and Activist New Media*. Cambridge: Polity.

Lippmann, W. (1922) *Public Opinion*. New York: Harcourt, Brace & Co.

Maher, V. (2005) *Citizen Media Is Dead*. Blog posting, May 8. Retrieved from http://www.vincentmaher.com/?p=400 (accessed 14 January 2015).

McGhee, G. (2010) *Journalism in the Age of Data* (video). Stanford University Department of Journalism. Retrieved from http://datajournalism.stanford.edu (accessed 14 January 2015).

Mitchell, A. and Jurkowitz, M. (2013) *Nonprofit Journalism: A Growing but Fragile Part of the US News System*. Washington, DC: Pew Research Center. Retrieved from http://www.journalism.org/files/legacy/NonprofitNewsStudy.pdf (accessed 14 January 2015).

Negroponte, N. (1995) *Being Digital*. New York: Knopf.

Pariser, E. (2011) *The Filter Bubble: How the New Personalized Web Is Changing What We Read and How We Think*. New York: Penguin Press.

Paulussen, S. (2012) "Technology and the transformation of news work: Are labor conditions in (online) journalism changing?" In E. Siapera and A. Veglis (eds), *The Handbook of Global Online Journalism*. New York: John Wiley & Sons (pp. 192–208).

Pavlik, J. V. (2001) *Journalism and New Media*. New York: Columbia University Press.

Peters, C. and Broersma, M. J. (eds.) (2013) *Rethinking Journalism: Trust and Participation in a Transformed News Landscape*. Abingdon and New York: Routledge.

Peters, J. W. (2010) "In a world of online news, burnout starts younger." *New York Times*, July 18, B1. Retrieved from http://www.nytimes.com/2010/07/19/business/media/19press.html (accessed 14 January 2015).

Reinardy, S. (2011) "Newspaper journalism in crisis: Burnout on the rise, eroding young journalists' career commitment." *Journalism*, 12(1), 33–50.

Rogers, S. (2013) *Facts Are Sacred: The Power of Data*. London: Faber & Faber.

Rosen, J. (2006) "The people formerly known as the audience." *PressThink* blog, June 27. Retrieved from: http://archive.pressthink.org/2006/06/27/ppl_frmr.html (accessed 14 January 2015).

Ryfe, D. and Mensing, D. (2008) "Participatory journalism and the transformation of news." Paper presented at the Annual Meeting of the Association for Education in Journalism and Mass Communication (AEJMC), Chicago. Retrieved from http://citation.allacademic.com//meta/p_mla_apa_research_citation/2/7/1/5/8/pages271585/p271585-1.php (accessed 14 January 2015).

Schudson, M. (1990) *Origins of the Ideal of Objectivity in the Professions: Studies in the History of American Journalism and American Law, 1830–1940*. New York: Garland.

Segel, E. and Heer, J. (2010) "Narrative visualization: Telling stories with data." *IEEE Transactions on Visualization and Computer Graphics*, 16(6), 1139–1148. Retrieved from http://vis.stanford.edu/files/2010-Narrative-InfoVis.pdf (accessed 14 January 2015).

Stearns, J. (2012) "The case for unity among non-profit, community and public media." *MediaShift* blog, October 3. Retrieved from http://www.pbs.org/mediashift/2012/10/the-case-for-unity-among-non-profit-community-and-publi-media277.html (accessed 14 January 2015).

——(2013) *Acts of Journalism: Defining Press Freedom in the Digital Age.* Freepress.net, October. Retrieved from http://www.freepress.net/sites/default/files/resources/Acts_of_Journalism_October_2013.pdf (accessed 14 January 2015).

Sunstein, C. (2007) *Republic.com 2.0.* Princeton, NJ: Princeton University Press.

Weinberger, D. (2004) "Is there an echo in here?" *Salon.com*, 21 February. Retrieved from http://www.salon.com/2004/02/21/echo_chamber/ (accessed 14 January 2015).

——(2009) "Transparency is the new objectivity." Blog post, *JoHo the Blog*, July 19. Retrieved from http://www.hyperorg.com/blogger/2009/07/19/transparency-is-the-new-objectivity/ (accessed 14 January 2015).

Willis, J. (1994) *The Age of Multimedia and Turbonews.* Westport, CT, and London: Praeger.

27
LISTENING TO THE VOICELESS
The practices and ethics of alternative journalism

Tony Harcup

It has become something of a cliché, perhaps even a truism, to describe alternative media as existing to give 'voice to the voiceless'. The phrase is widely used among both scholars and practitioners (this author among them) because it seems to express why some people feel compelled to create such media in the first place; its alliterative and rhetorical qualities no doubt help too. However, although declaring an intention to give voice to the voiceless may produce an attractive motto or slogan, we must dig deeper if we are to discover how such an ethos might be put into practice within media projects that entail "becoming one's own storyteller, regaining one's own voice" (Rodríguez, 2001: 3). Crucial to such an exploration, certainly when we focus more narrowly on the practices and ethics of alternative journalism (rather than wider forms of alternative media production), is what might be described as the fundamentally ethical practice of empathic, active *listening*.

"Listen to the loons"

Giving voice to the voiceless was something that the English radical journalist and activist Paul Foot tried to do, although he preferred to operate under two alternative mottos: "Listen to the loons" and "Never believe anything until it is officially denied" (Foot, 1999: 82). By the first he meant that reporters ought not immediately dismiss someone just because their story initially appears outlandish or unbelievable; the second conveyed the sceptical mindset necessary for independent-minded reporting, whether in alternative or mainstream media. Foot himself worked variously for the mainstream UK tabloid *Daily Mirror*, the left-wing party mouthpiece *Socialist Worker* (the Leninist theory of the press made flesh or, at least, newsprint) and the hybrid alternative-commercial satirical magazine *Private Eye*. For whichever of those three very different publications he happened to be working at the time, he made a point of listening to those dismissed by many others as 'loons', challenging official versions of events, championing those ordinary people who were seeking some kind of social justice and encouraging all kinds of "whistleblowers, grasses and finks" to contact him directly (ibid.: 83). When he died, many tributes were paid by the everyday people at the centre of his stories who said that he had been one of the few journalists to have genuinely listened to what they had to say; many pointed out that not only did he listen to them, but he would routinely read out his draft story over the phone to check for accuracy, something that is far from the norm in mainstream journalism (*Private Eye*, 2004).

Foot's sources – whistleblowers, campaigners, victims and people who simply found themselves "on the other side of the railway line, breadline, the picket line, the barbed wire fence" from those holding power (Wasserman, 2013: 80) – were those who are written out of much mainstream journalism, just as they tend to be written out of the versions of history that are narrated from the perspective of the victors. There are exceptions, with Paul Foot's period at the *Daily Mirror* merely being one of the more high-profile ones, but the tendency of mainstream newsroom sourcing and reporting practices is to produce journalism that in effect often "sides with power" while presenting such a position as "neutral" (Wasserman, 2013: 69). The practices and ethics of alternative journalism offer something quite different precisely by placing the marginalised centre stage and by amplifying their voices rather than silencing them.

Both "Listen to the loons" and "Never believe anything until it is officially denied" were passed on to Foot as guiding journalistic principles in the early days of *Private Eye* by Claud Cockburn (Foot, 1999: 82). Something of a veteran troublemaker, Cockburn had several decades earlier left his job as a *Times* journalist to publish his own alternative duplicated newssheet, *The Week*, as well as report for the communist *Daily Worker* (Cockburn, 1967: 128–52). Clearly having a way with words, Cockburn is also credited with suggesting the name for a new feminist magazine that was being planned in 1972: *Spare Rib*, which survived for two decades, during which time it gave voice to women who had felt silenced on multiple levels, including those marginalised within the male-dominated 'underground' press, women who rejected the consumerist approach of commercial women's magazines and women who were either ignored or patronised by mainstream news and current affairs media (BBC Radio 4, 2013; Rowe, 1982: 13–19).

Reporting from below

Alternative media and alternative journalism come in many forms and do many things, but Susan Forde identifies a "consistent message", which is:

> to give a voice to the voiceless, to fill the gaps left by the mainstream, to empower ordinary people to participate in democracy, and in many instances, to educate people with information they cannot access elsewhere.
>
> (Forde, 2011: 45)

Over the centuries, countless examples of non-commercial, ideas-driven media predicated on the democratised practices of "alternative media activism" (Hesmondhalgh,

2000: 108) have sprung up to allow alternative voices, alternative modes of expression, alternative experiences and alternative ideas to circulate within what has been described variously as a public sphere (Habermas, 1989), a plebeian public sphere (Habermas, 1992: 430), an alternative public sphere (Atton, 2002: 35) and a "subaltern counterpublic sphere" (Pavarala and Malik, 2010; after Fraser, 1992). Sometimes long-lived and relatively popular, sometimes short-lived and marginal, and more often a mixture of the above, alternative media can open up a gap – a "fissure", to use Clemencia Rodríguez's term – through which citizens' voices "can have a presence in the public realm" (Rodríguez, 2001: 165).

Examples within the UK alone might include:

- Eighteenth-century campaigners against the slave trade being given voice in radical journals.
- The Chartist press of the nineteenth century articulating the pro-democracy demands of the organised working class.
- The women's suffrage press of the late 19th and early 20th centuries influencing second-wave feminism in the late 20th century and, in turn, a third wave of feminist media in the twentyfirst century.

In these and numerous other cases, alternative journalists have been prepared to think the otherwise unthinkable and report on those who are saying the otherwise unsayable. In rejecting a top-down approach to social issues, they have adopted a bottom-up approach to journalism. As the feminist and socialist activist and alternative journalist Sylvia Pankhurst put it, when describing her *Woman's Dreadnought* newspaper:

> Our volunteer working women reporters, when investigating conditions, produced far truer accounts than any Fleet Street journalist, for they knew what to ask and how to win the confidence of the sufferers.
>
> (Pankhurst, 1977 [1931]: 526)

As South African academic Herman Wasserman (2013: 79) put it in a different century, on another continent: "Journalists who listen can facilitate a politics from the ground up." Such an approach entails listening to Pankhurst's "sufferers" even when nobody else appears to be doing so; or rather, especially when nobody else is doing so. That is precisely what appears to have happened with a story that was reported by one of the hundreds of alternative local newspapers that emerged in the UK from the late 1960s through to the mid-1980s.

When *Rochdale's Alternative Paper*, known as *RAP*, appeared in that working-class northern English town in 1971, its first cover featured what might today be described as a mission statement but was more a statement of intent. *RAP*'s manifesto of alternative journalism read:

    Questions ... Asked
    Bubbles ... Pricked
    Information ... Open

Workers ... Heard
Issues ... Debated
Rights ... Explained
Bosses ... Challenged
The Unspoken ... Said
Life ... Explored

(*RAP* no. 1, November 1971)

Alongside those words was a caricature of powerful local politician Cyril Smith, known in the mainstream media as Mr Rochdale, in the shape of a giant inflated balloon: a bubble ready to be pricked. Smith was on the cover of *RAP* again eight years later when he was the subject of a substantial piece of investigative journalism into claims that he had abused his power and influence to gain access to vulnerable teenage boys living in a hostel in the town – boys whom he went on to physically and sexually abuse. *RAP* reported how some of the victims had given statements to police years earlier, how the police had gathered sufficient evidence for charges to be laid but how no charge or prosecution ever resulted. The paper tracked down and interviewed many of the boys (who were adults by then), and it was their stories (with their identities protected) that formed the centrepiece of *RAP*'s investigation into Smith (*RAP* No. 78, May 1979). The story was immediately followed up in *Private Eye* – and nowhere else.

Smith, who by that time had become a familiar face on the national as well as local political scene, denied any wrongdoing and threatened legal action against anyone publishing the allegations (although he never did sue). National newspaper news-rooms all bought copies of *RAP* No. 78, but none published a word about the abuse despite the meticulous, multi-sourced and measured way in which the story had been researched and presented. That is, none published a word for the next few decades. It was not until two years after Smith's death in 2010 that, in the wake of the unrelated Jimmy Savile sex abuse scandal, the Smith story was revisited by 21st-century alternative media *Northern Voices*, politics blogger Paul Waugh and *Private Eye* (again), which belatedly prompted mainstream media to report the story, safe in the knowledge that a dead man cannot sue (Walker, 2013: 3; Waugh, 2012). This time, both the Crown Prosecution Service (2012) and even the police felt the need to issue public statements on the case, with the latter going so far as to state as fact that "young boys were victims of physical and sexual abuse committed by Smith" (Greater Manchester Police, 2012). The 'boys' had finally been listened to, although it had taken until the perpetrator was dead and the victims were of pensionable age for that to happen beyond the pages of the alternative media.

The question arises: why had their voices been ignored by the bulk of the media back in 1979? There is no shortage of internet warriors out there who will insist it was because of some high-powered conspiracy to protect a senior national politician, but the reality is probably more prosaic. After all, compared to resource-rich organisations boasting sophisticated public relations operations, "ordinary people" can be "difficult, expensive and inefficient sources" (Whitaker, 1981: 38). All the more so, perhaps, if those ordinary people have been damaged by troubled backgrounds or by being subjected to abuse by those in power. Why would a mainstream news organisation invest in a labour-intensive and legally risky piece of investigative journalism that would stand or fall on the perceived reliability of a group of victims on the margins of society? Whatever the 'truth' of the matter might be, whose version was more likely to be believed if the matter ever came to court: a former Lord Mayor of Rochdale who became a member of Parliament and was a frequent guest on the sofas of TV chat shows, or former boys' home residents who, almost by definition, had experienced dysfunctional lives?

In this sense, it was not a special alternative journalistic toolkit that was used to craft the Smith story, but the application of fairly standard reporting practices to a story (and to a group of people) that the mainstream media either did not recognise as a story or did not believe was worth the risk. It was the determination of *RAP* (and *Private Eye*) to listen to and amplify the voices of a marginalised and (up until then) silenced group of victims that could be said to exemplify the ethics as well as the practices of alternative journalism. John Walker, one of the *RAP* journalists who worked on the original investigation, told a television documentary 34 years later:

> These lads were triply abused. Firstly, many of them had pretty tough upbringings. Secondly, they were abused by Smith. And thirdly, they were each told in no uncertain terms that complaining about it would go nowhere because no one would believe them … This was the untold story and so we felt that we owed it to those lads, to that town, and to ourselves, that we should at least have a go.
>
> (Channel 4, 2013)

The fact that Walker and his colleagues spent more than six months on the story before they were ready to publish is an indication that alternative journalism and listening to the 'loons' is not a question of merely reproducing unsubstantiated rumours or indiscriminately amplifying each and every voice spouting any old rubbish. Just as *RAP* felt it 'owed' it to Smith's victims to look into their stories, so alternative journalism owes it to its community of producers and audience (who are sometimes the same people) to not publish stories or allegations that do not stand up to scrutiny. In this sense, ethical alternative journalism can involve taking people's stories seriously, endeavouring to check them out and ultimately *not* publishing anything about those stories that do not stack up.

Not that reporting from below is confined to recording the lives of 'sufferers' or victims. It is also about listening to, and amplifying, the voices of those actively involved in seeking social change; active agents, not just passive victims. As *Leeds Other Paper* put it in 1975: "We are not aligned to any particular political party but try to support groups and individuals struggling to take control over their own lives – whether it's in the factory, the housing estate, or the home" (cited in Harcup, 2013: 54). Or, indeed, groups and individuals struggling to take control of their own representation in the media. A similar ethos can be seen at work four decades on, informing the practice of the activist video collective *Reel News*, among others:

> *Reel News* will try and cover it all, from pensioners protesting against cuts in voluntary services, artists and musicians looking at the world in a different

way, through strikes against privatisation, right up to the astonishing social movements in Latin America which have brought down governments through uprisings, mass direct action and general strikes. *Reel News* is intended as a two-way resource, so let us know about your campaigns. Better still, film them yourself and send us the video.

(*Reel News*, 2011)

Many of the collective's DVD current affairs bulletins and online video reports consist of extensive footage of protests and demonstrations in which numerous participants are allowed to speak at some length, and in some detail, about whatever issue has brought them onto the streets (see *Reel News*, 2012 and 2013). Such reports would undoubtedly be dismissed as too dull or boring to be considered for broadcast on most mainstream media because they do not feature dramatic shots of confrontation: nobody burns a flag and no masked figures kick in the windows of a bank or a McDonald's restaurant. What they do feature are the voices of people struggling to take control of their own lives, speaking for themselves. These voices are not wholly unmediated because they have been recorded, selected and edited into watchable packages but, to the extent that it is possible in any form of journalism, the speakers' voices are largely allowed to speak for themselves.

Citizens, not consumers

The privileging of the voices of marginalised people or activist communities stems from an attitude that conceives of people primarily as citizens – not primarily as consumers. Such an approach connects the practices of alternative journalism such as "oppositional reporting" (Harcup, 2013: 164) to the ideal of supporting democratic participation (Forde, 2011: 174) and of serving some kind of "public interest" in a way that is more deeply rooted than tends to be the case in much mainstream journalism (Harcup, 2013: 15), despite the latter also drawing on the rhetoric of acting as the people's watchdog (Harcup, 2007: 33–47). If by the public interest we mean something along the lines suggested by the National Union of Journalists, for example – protecting public safety, preventing people from being misled and exposing crime, corruption, conflicts of interest, hypocrisy and corporate greed (ibid.: 153) – then it could be argued that a higher proportion of the journalism found within alternative media is imbued with the public interest than that found within the commercial mainstream. In this sense, alternative journalism – at least, the more open and less propagandistic varieties of alternative journalism as practised by *Spare Rib*, *RAP* and myriad other projects – can be seen as an expression of active citizenship (Harcup, 2011).

Central to such citizenship is what Susan Bickford (1996: 2) terms "political listening", whereby democratic participation within the public sphere requires citizens not merely to allow others to speak but actually to listen to one another. This may not necessarily always result in sweetness and light or eradicate social conflict but, she argues, it can at least enable more informed democratic deliberation on issues of public concern: "Deciding democratically means deciding, under conditions in which all voices are *heard*, what course of action makes sense" (Bickford, 1996: 2; my emphasis). Such an ethic of listening is about people being treated with dignity in a fundamental sense, for Wasserman (2013: 77), who insists that "to treat people with dignity primarily means taking their stories seriously", rather than regarding people's stories as not worth listening to if they cannot be turned into a piece of entertainment that might help boost advertising income.

Feminist thinkers in recent decades have contributed much to our understanding of how ideas such as democratic participation, active citizenship and the ethics not only of giving voice to the voiceless but of listening to such voices can inform the approach of alternative media, including alternative journalism. An ethical approach to listening, informed by such feminist thinking, implies more of a dialogic relationship rather than the one-way transmission of messages, even alternative or radical ones. For Fiona Robinson:

> Listening in this sense means not just hearing the words that are spoken, but being attentive to and understanding the concerns, needs and aims of others in the dialogue.
>
> (Robinson, 2011: 847)

Furthermore, such dialogue may need a sustained period of time to develop and deepen; it is not so much an event or a one-off exchange of views as a "long process" that "does not have a clear beginning or end" (Robinson, 2011: 855). Feminist scholar Carol Gilligan has argued along similar lines that people who are not listened to – attentively, deeply, empathetically – do not really have a voice even when they speak, because the acts of speaking and listening are so closely related, "like breathing out and breathing in"; the trouble starts if people hold their breath and either stop speaking or stop listening (Kiegelmann, 2009). As she explains:

> To have a voice is to be human. To have something to say is to be a person. But speaking depends on listening and being heard; it is an intensely relational act.
>
> (Gilligan, 1993: xvi)

Such listening goes way beyond what might be thought of as mere "politeness", and is "a political process that is potentially difficult, conflictual and aimed at justice", argues Tanja Dreher (2009: 448), just as alternative journalism itself is an essentially *political* activity for Susan Forde (2011: 45). In this sense, it may not be sufficient to ask "Who speaks?" when a more pertinent question may be "Who is heard?"

Practices and ethics can be the same

It would of course be simplistic to claim that all alternative media contain alternative journalism, that all alternative journalism is produced while in listening mode or that all mainstream journalism merely amplifies the voices of the rich and powerful. It has been observed that there can be "hybridity" (Atton, 2003: 26) or a "continuum"

(Harcup, 2013: 114) of journalistic practice, and it ill serves the cause of alternative media to paint the mainstream as a monolithic entity. Both mainstream and alternative journalism are heterogeneous categories and both are subject to change; neither can be understood as if it is a homogeneous sector within which journalists adopt a uniform approach. That mainstream journalism ignored the victimised Rochdale boys for so many decades does not tell the full story, because the voices of another group of children on the margins of the same town did later find an empathic ear on a mainstream national newspaper; *Times* reporter Andrew Norfolk even won the 2012 Paul Foot Award for his investigation into the systematic sexual abuse of vulnerable teenage girls by gangs of men in Rochdale (*Private Eye*, 2013). It was painstaking reporting that, arguably, had more in common with the 1979 *RAP* story than some of the output of more hectoring alternative media. That Norfolk won an award set up in the name of the late Paul Foot lends credence to the argument that the *Times*'s reporting of this later Rochdale case was the exception rather than the rule. In contrast, seeking out, listening to, and then reporting the voices of the sufferers – alongside the voices of activists – is the very purpose of alternative journalism. Such active listening is fundamental to the practices and ethics of alternative journalism. In this sense, the practices and ethics of alternative journalism can perhaps best be understood as being one and the same thing.

There has long been a tendency within much mainstream journalism, especially in the UK, to regard ethics either as a matter primarily concerned with industry regulation or as a series of discrete issues capable of being ticked off a checklist. This can result in ethics being regarded as "crises that pop up from time to time" rather than as issues that need to be "dealt with almost on a minute-by-minute basis" (Frost, 2011: 4). Journalism within alternative media tends to be less concerned with regulatory mechanisms or with following formal codes of practice on issues such as privacy, intrusion, harassment and suchlike; rather, the ethical approach of (much) alternative journalism within alternative media is more about an attitude and approach towards the people who may be a story's subject, source, narrator or audience, sometimes all at the same time. As a result, the 'ordinary people' are afforded dignity not because of legalistic or commercial considerations but because that is the very reason for such media to exist.

The ethics of active listening can subvert traditional perceptions of journalists as "gatekeepers", suggests Wasserman, "by turning them into 'gate-openers' who decentralise the power structure inherent in media production and involve news subjects as equal partners in the production process" (2013: 79). Similarly, by listening to and amplifying the voices of media audiences that are otherwise unheard except in the "banal" sense of so-called user-generated content, "the self-reflexive activities of alternative media production thus perform radical critiques on what it means to be 'in the news', what it means to be an audience and what it means to be a journalist" (Atton, 2013: xi).

It is worth recalling that, when the WikiLeaks source Private Bradley/Chelsea Manning began thinking about blowing the whistle on US military activities in Iraq and leaking information that "would have enormous value to the American public", his/her first thought was to approach mainstream rather than alternative media. Manning telephoned the *Washington Post* and spoke to a reporter, but "I do not believe she took me seriously" and that was the end of that. Manning's own account continues:

> I then decided to contact the largest and most popular newspaper, the *New York Times*. I called the public editor number on the *New York Times* website. The phone rang and was answered by a machine. I went through the menu section for news tips. I was routed to an answering machine. I left a message stating I had access to information about Iraq and Afghanistan that I believed was very important. However, despite leaving my Skype phone number and personal email address, I never received a reply from the *New York Times*.
>
> (Manning, 2013)

Only then did he/she approach the alternative media in the form of WikiLeaks; the result was a series of leaks during 2010 that amounted to the most extensive release of secret information – and perhaps the most extreme form of 'gate-opening' – that the world had ever seen. Whether on a global or local scale, for the previously voiceless to be listened to can be an empowering experience. "We can talk now," as one of the women involved in a small community radio station in rural India put it (quoted in Pavarala and Malik, 2010: 107): "We used to sit silent. Government officials will come and we let them talk. Now we question them."

Further reading

Susan Forde, *Challenging the News: The Journalism of Alternative and Community Media* (Basingstoke: Palgrave Macmillan, 2011). Forde's focus is very much on the journalism of alternative media – a journalism that, she argues, can be seen as a form of political intervention.

Tony Harcup, *Alternative Journalism, Alternative Voices* (London: Routledge, 2013). A collection of studies of alternative journalism at a local level with an emphasis on how such media aim to report 'the voices of the voiceless'.

Herman Wasserman (2013), "Journalism in a new democracy: The ethics of listening" (*Communicatio: South African Journal for Communication Theory and Research*, 39(1), 67–84). Wasserman argues for the ethics of active listening to be taken as seriously within journalism as the act of speaking.

References

Atton, C. (2002) *Alternative Media*. London: Sage.

——(2003) "Ethical issues in alternative journalism." *Ethical Space*, 1(1), 26–31.

——(2013) "Foreword: Local journalism, radical reporting and the everyday." In T. Harcup (ed.), *Alternative Journalism, Alternative Voices*. London: Routledge (pp. xi–xvi).

BBC Radio 4 (2013) *The Reunion: Spare Rib*, produced by Kate Taylor, 15 September. Retrieved from http://www.bbc.co.uk/programmes/b039yz4x (accessed 10 January 2015).

Bickford, S. (1996) *The Dissonance of Democracy: Listening, Conflict, and Citizenship*. New York: Cornell University Press.

Channel 4 (2013) *Dispatches: The Paedophile MP*, directed by Richard Denton, 12 September.

Cockburn, C. (1967) *I, Claud.* Harmondsworth: Penguin.

Crown Prosecution Service (2012) "CPS statement in relation to Cyril Smith," 27 November. Retrieved from http://www.cps.gov.uk/news/latest_news/cps_statement_in_relation_to_cyril_smith/index.html (accessed 25 October 2013).

Dreher, T. (2009) "Listening across difference: Media and multiculturalism beyond the politics of voice." *Continuum,* 23(4), 445–58.

Foot, P. (1999) "The slow death of investigative journalism." In S. Glover (ed.), *Secrets of the Press.* London: Penguin (pp. 79–89).

Forde, S. (2011) *Challenging the News: The Journalism of Alternative and Community Media.* Basingstoke: Palgrave Macmillan.

Fraser, N. (1992) "Rethinking the public sphere." In C. Calhoun (ed.) *Habermas and the Public Sphere.* London: MIT Press (pp. 109–42).

Frost, C. (2011) *Journalism Ethics and Regulation.* Harlow: Longman.

Gilligan, C. (1993) *In a Different Voice.* Cambridge and London: Harvard University Press.

Greater Manchester Police (2012) "Statement regarding Sir Cyril Smith," 27 November. Retrieved from www.gmp.police.uk/Content/WebsitePages/A22934C753EF3F0380257AC300607543?OpenDocument (accessed 25 October 2013).

Habermas, J. (1989) *The Structural Transformation of the Public Sphere: An Inquiry into a Category of Bourgeois Society.* Cambridge: Polity Press.

——(1992) "Further reflections on the public sphere." In C. Calhoun (ed.), *Habermas and the Public Sphere.* London: MIT Press (pp. 421–61).

Harcup, T. (2007) *The Ethical Journalist.* London: Sage.

——(2011) "Alternative journalism as active citizenship." *Journalism: Theory, Practice and Criticism,* 12(1), 15–31.

——(2013) *Alternative Journalism, Alternative Voices.* London: Routledge.

Hesmondhalgh, D. (2000) "Alternative media, alternative texts? Rethinking democratisation in the cultural industries." In J. Curran (ed.), *Media Organisations in Society.* London: Arnold (pp. 107–25).

Kiegelmann, M. (2009) "Making oneself vulnerable to discovery: Carol Gilligan in conversation with Mechthild Kiegelmann." *Forum: Qualitative Social Research,* 10(2). Retrieved from http://nbn-resolving.de/urn:nbn:de:0114-fqs090234 (accessed 10 January 2015).

Manning, B. (2013) "Bradley Manning's statement taking responsibility for releasing documents to *WikiLeaks,*" 28 February. Retrieved from http://www.bradleymanning.org/news/bradley-mannings-statement-taking-responsibility-for-releasing-documents-to-wikileaks (accessed 10 September 2013).

Pankhurst, S. (1977 [1931]) *The Suffragette Movement.* London: Virago.

Pavarala, V. and K. M. Malik (2010) "Community radio and women: Forging subaltern counterpublics." In C. Rodríguez, D. Kidd and L. Stein (eds), *Making Our Media: Global Initiatives toward a Democratic Public Sphere.* Creskill, NJ: Hampton Press (pp. 95–113).

Private Eye (2004) "Paul Foot." Retrieved from http://www.private-eye.co.uk/content/showitem.cfm/issue.1116/section.footie (accessed 30 September 2004).

——(2013) "The Paul Foot Award 2012." Retrieved from http://www.private-eye.co.uk/paul_foot.php?archive=2012 (accessed 27 October 2013).

Reel News (2011) "About," 14 November. Retrieved from http://reelnews.co.uk/about/ (accessed 25 October 2013).

——(2012) "Huge demonstrations in Spain as unions call for a Europe-wide general strike," 12 October. Retrieved from http://reelnews.co.uk/huge-demonstrations-in-spain-as-unions-call-for-a-europe-wide-general-strike/ (accessed 25 October 2013).

——(2013) "5,000 firefighters march through London," 17 October. Retrieved from http://reelnews.co.uk/5000-firefighters-march-through-london/ (accessed 25 October 2013).

Robinson, F. (2011) "Stop talking and listen: Discourse ethics and feminist care ethics in international political theory." *Millennium*, 39(3), 845–60.

Rodríguez, C. (2001) *Fissures in the Mediascape: An International Study of Citizens' Media.* Cresskill, NJ: Hampton Press.

Rowe, M. (ed.) (1982) *Spare Rib Reader.* Harmondsworth: Penguin.

Walker, J. (2013) "Sir Cyril Smith: Our part in his downfall!" *Northern Voices*, 14(Summer/Autumn), 1–13.

Wasserman, H. (2013) "Journalism in a new democracy: The ethics of listening." *Communicatio: South African Journal for Communication Theory and Research*, 39(1), 67–84.

Waugh, P. (2012) "Cyril Smith – some justice at last?" *Politics Home*, 27 November. Retrieved from http://politicshome.com/uk/article/66789/cyril_some_justice_at_last%3F.html (accessed 23 October 2013).

Whitaker, B. (1981) *News Ltd.: Why You Can't Read All about It.* London: Minority Press Group.

28

HAITI GRASSROOTS WATCH

Daring to be more than alternative

Jane Regan

An experimental, collaborative watchdog project arose in post-earthquake Haiti, incorporating concepts and practices from the broad collection of media experiences known as 'alternative and community media', but also drawing heavily on classical journalism traditions and practices, and on more recent developments in US journalism education. Taking a look at its theory and practice adds to the debate on the term 'alternative', and helps make the case for leaving it behind.

Haiti Grassroots Watch (HGW) was co-founded in 2010 by several well-established actors in Haiti's community and alternative media movement: two media institutions, members of community radio stations from the earthquake zone, and this author. The two institutions together account for a good portion of the movement today. The first, AlterPresse, self-identifies as an 'alternative' online news agency and website. Staffed by four to six journalists, a network of correspondents and an editorial team, it says it is guided by the ideals of 'the right to information and communication'. Editors prioritise 'social movement actors', human rights, development and women's rights issues, as well as breaking news "from a democratic perspective and based on alternative research" (AlterPresse, 2013a). The second is the Society for the Animation of Social Communications, or SAKS (*Sosyete Animasyon Kominikasyon Sosyal* in Haitian Creole), which says it promotes "popular [i.e., 'people's'] communications", which it defines as communication by democratically organised associations that have as a goal the promotion of "social change, cultural development and democracy for the majority" (SAKS, 2013).

Local commercial media not up to watchdogging

Fearing that billions of aid dollars would go unwatched, and noting the lack of sound, in-depth journalism in Haiti, the founding partners set out to create Haiti Grassroots Watch (or *Ayiti Kale Je* ['Haiti Eyes Peeled'] in Haitian Creole), an investigative journalism partnership that would also build the capacity of participating journalists. The idea arose about a month after the 2010 earthquake, which killed perhaps 200,000 and left another 1.3 million homeless. This author, a former SAKS employee and collaborator of AlterPresse, met in Haiti with staff from the two institutions, with other journalists and with professors from the State University of Haiti. All agreed that there were no media outlets or journalists in Haiti with the capacity and – perhaps more importantly – the will to watchdog the over $10 billion in recovery and reconstruction monies slated for the devastated country. Indeed, had there been, these newsrooms would have been reporting for years on drug-trafficking, child slavery, rising hunger and the waste, graft and corruption in what many call "the Republic of NGOs" (Klarreich and Polman, 2012).

Although Haiti is 30 years beyond the brutal Duvalier dictatorship (1957–86), boasts a constitution that promises freedom of the press and has hundreds of media outlets, the country has no tradition of investigative or even in-depth journalism. One exception was Radio Haïti Inter under owner-journalist Jean Dominique. Dominique and his journalists asked questions and went into the field, but his brutal assassination on April 3, 2000 (Jean-Pierre, 2000), put an end to that tradition and to the radio itself, which closed a few years later. Indeed, Haiti's news ecosystem is perhaps the bleakest in the hemisphere. Even the largest media owners' association has deplored a "general decline in quality", calling its journalists "irresponsible" and saying their reports were often full of errors, were too "friendly" to their sources and lacked depth (cited in Geffrard, 2009). Haiti has no university-level journalism program and likely the lowest university graduation rate in the hemisphere: about one percent of the population (Downie, 2012: A8). At best, most young journalists have some high school, but have not necessarily completed their Bacalauréat. They may also have spent a few months at one of the unregulated, for-profit 'journalism schools'.

Canadian journalists Barnabé and Breton (2007), in Haiti to do training seminars, reported that journalists have "insufficient" general knowledge, lack transportation and access to basic reference books like dictionaries and are generally "content to be simple conveyor belts" of information from the government, the UN and other authorities (ibid.: 387). Studying radio news broadcasts of the three most popular radio stations, Sérant (2007), himself a journalist and a co-founder of AlterPresse, found that most national radio news was characterised by "a preponderance of the political". Worse, he noted that half of all "news" programming was "impressions, reactions, accusations and denunciations", with only a miniscule percentage of time (between 2.2 and 0.78 per cent) devoted to "original reporting" (ibid.: 84–5).

Another challenge in Haiti comes from the lack of deontology. The country's major media associations recently signed a Code of Ethics, but on-the-ground practices like accepting all-expenses-paid trips to the countryside or abroad continue. Many Haiti media-watchers, including Décimé (2013), an AlterPresse staffer, and Barnabé and Breton (2007: 388), report that newsroom directors consent to and sometimes even encourage their journalists "to accept the per diems, envelopes containing hundreds or even thousands of gourdes" (100 gourdes = about US$2.30). "Decisions that may seem unethical elsewhere in the world are status quo here", long-time Haiti correspondent Klarreich noted (2012).

While dominated by commercial media and the propaganda-laden state outlets, Haiti is also home to not-for-profit media like AlterPresse and SAKS, literary, academic and activist bulletins and magazines, blogs and websites, and several dozen community radio stations, run mostly by peasant, youth and women's associations. Staffed mostly by volunteers, the small, often solar-powered stations have mostly rudimentary production standards, minimal funding and high staff turnover, but they remain important grassroots actors in their communities (Regan, 2008). HGW partner SAKS works with many, providing training, news programs, educational series and some financial support.

Some student associations, church-based institutions, farmers' groups, local non-profits, unions and others produce print bulletins and/or run blogs or news websites. Some, like the monthly Catholic Church-funded *Bon Nouvèl* (Good News), whose building and press were destroyed in the earthquake, last many years (see www. bonnouvel.org), but most are short-lived, folding after funding runs out. One example is *Bri Kouri, Nouvèl Gaye* ('Noise Travels, News Spreads'), a post-earthquake print and online bulletin that lasted only about two years (Let Haiti Live, 2012).

Lack of sound journalism education and commercial media interest in pursuing investigative journalism are not the only challenges to potential watchdoggers in Haiti. Transparency International (2012) puts the country at the bottom of its 'Corruption Perceptions Index', at 165 out of 174 countries. In addition, Haiti has no open-records laws, and a 2012 report on press freedom notes that journalists regularly face "intimidation, threats, destruction of their media equipment, and retaliation by President [Michel] Martelly and his administration against progressive journalists for critical reporting" and "'stonewalling', wherein journalists critical of the government were consistently denied interviews with governmental officials and access to public information" (Institute for Justice and Democracy In Haiti, 2012: 1).

Designing a watchdog to serve many publics

Despite the challenges, the HGW collaborative set out to 'follow the money' and produce investigative reports on the reconstruction that would inform citizens and decision-makers, perhaps inspiring better and more participatory projects along the way. Because decisions about Haiti are often made by foreigners or in conjunction with foreign consultants or entities like the World Bank (indeed, the Interim Haiti Recovery Commission was co-chaired by former US President Bill Clinton), the partners decided that all texts would be produced in English as well as French.

The partners also recognised that text was not sufficient, not least because the country's sole daily paper, *Le Nouvelliste*, printed only 15,000 copies for a population of 10 million, with a "very cautious" editorial line (INFOASAID, 2012: 121). Although there were also several weeklies printing about 5,000 copies each, which also maintained websites, fewer than ten percent of Haitians had regular access to the internet. Of those, only six percent reported getting news and information online.

In contrast, Haiti had some 375 radio stations, most of them commercial, with at least 50 in Port-au-Prince. The overwhelming majority of Haitians got their news via the radio, on traditional radios or, increasingly, on their mobile telephones (ibid.: 41), with 96 per cent of Port-au-Prince residents listening to the radio, mostly news, every day (ibid.: 44). Thus, HGW vowed to also produce each investigation as a radio documentary in Haitian Creole, the only language spoken by all Haitians. (Haiti has two official languages, French and Creole, but an estimated 90 percent of the population speaks and understands Creole only.)

Finally, because many, if not most, Haitians cannot read or write – figures for adult literacy vary, from about 38 per cent to about 51 per cent – television and video are also important ways of relaying news and information. From 2010 through 2013, about one-third of the investigations were produced as videos, with Creole- and English-subtitled versions. In addition to providing DVDs to commercial stations in the capital and some provincial cities, HGW staff and interns organised screenings around the country.

Inspirations

The journalism beacons guiding HGW were in large part based on the same ones that have inspired 250 years of determined and courageous reporting in the West: the understanding that freedom of speech and access to information play crucial roles in democracies, that important exposés only come from digging into the 'muck' of political and business deals, and that sometimes only journalists can 'speak truth to power' when abuses are suspected. But HGW's approach was also influenced by the broad set of concepts and practices known in Latin America as *comunicación popular*, or 'popular communications'. Indeed, institutional partner SAKS is its leading proponent in Haiti. But the HGW coordination team took its understanding from the more specific, and perhaps more militant, definitions common in early writings from the Latin American community radio movement, specifically *radios populares*, or 'popular radios'. Drawing a distinction between 'community' and 'popular' radio, Geerts and van Oeyen (2001) say the latter are "more explicit in their political objectives", are "eminently educational", are "critical and consciousness-raising", should "be participatory" and should work for "change" and "social transformation" (ibid.: 22).

Not surprisingly, because of its emphasis on capacity building, HGW was also influenced by the writings of, and traditions inspired by, Paulo Freire. Teaching was incorporated into almost every aspect of reporting and content creation, from coaching sessions on the dirt floors of makeshift radio stations rebuilt after the earthquake, to the trainings at AlterPresse or SAKS, to the one-on-one accompaniment of journalism students.

Early into the HGW experiment, the coordination team, SAKS and AlterPresse noted that they did not have adequate staff to carry out all the investigations envisaged. The State University of Haiti's Faculty of Human Sciences was persuaded to allow this author to teach the country's first-ever course in investigative journalism. In addition to training about 100 students, final student projects were sometimes upgraded into HGW investigations, and the best students were recruited to work as interns. In the four iterations of the course, and at training sessions for community radio members and journalists from SAKS and AlterPresse, the pedagogy was as dialogic and participatory as possible, since "[o]nly dialogue, which requires critical thinking, is also capable of generating critical thinking" (Freire, 1970: 81). While dialogic capacity building slowed reporting processes considerably, it assured that community radio members, students and journalists increased their skill sets as well as their capacities for critical thinking.

HGW staff and community radio volunteers were also guided by Freirian methods when presenting videos at screenings they organised around the country. In addition to discussing the investigations, audience members were urged to suggest subjects for future investigations in what could be called 'low-tech crowd-sourcing'.

HGW practice was also informed by the writing and thinking on two relatively new trends in the US: one in journalism education and the other involving partnerships between media outlets. The first trend is the 'teaching hospital' model for journalism education, where the classroom becomes a newsroom. While there are many versions of this new approach (as detailed by Francisco, Lenhoff and Schudson, 2012), most involve enabling journalism students to work with professors and/ or working journalists to produce content for the public. These 'new newsrooms', as some have called them, allow for service learning at the same time as they provide a public service, often while engaging in public interest journalism that helps make up for the information deficit created by the ever-shrinking number of commercial media outlets. Jan Schaffer of the Institute for Interactive Journalism or J-Lab at American University holds that these 'labs' can be a place where all students, not just journalism students, can learn "how to hold democratic institutions accountable, how to help citizens do their jobs as citizens, and how to foster new information paradigms" (Schaffer, 2012b: 2676). The second trend that influenced HGW practices is 'networked journalism'. As defined by the J-Lab, it is the partnering of 'legacy' newsrooms with "hyperlocal news sites" (Schaffer, 2012a). Since HGW was engaged in what could be called 'progressive journalism' – in other words, journalism which sought to contribute to social progress (Clark and Van Slyke, 2010: 3) – the collaboration was also informed by a study of networked US progressive media (Clark and Van Slyke, 2010). In their book, the authors looked at outlets and journalists who "risk[ed] career and credibility to speak truth to power" from 2004 to 2008 (ibid.: 4). By working together, sometimes via joint distribution, other times with collaborative reporting, small media outlets found "new pathways to impact and influence" (ibid.: 6).

Results: 'Eyes peeled' and journalists trained

By drawing on the theories, concepts and practices outlined above, and by following the UNESCO 'hypothesis-based inquiry' investigative journalism method (Hunter, 2011), the partnership succeeded in producing in-depth journalism in a participatory, capacity-building manner, with a progressive editorial line. Over 40 months, from late 2010 through 2013, the consortium produced 39 investigations that were read, listened to and/or viewed by the tens of thousands of patrons of the HGW website or the several dozen media outlets across Haiti, the Caribbean, the Americas and Europe that frequently relayed HGW content. Texts were written in both French and English, with about a dozen also in Spanish, and almost all investigations also generated Haitian Creole radio documentaries of about 20–30 minutes. In addition, 11 of the 40 were accompanied by video documentaries in Creole with English subtitles. These were aired on local TV stations and also at over two dozen screenings across the country for audiences totalling well over 2,000 people. Thirteen of the dossiers were reported in conjunction with community radio station members, and over 30 were carried out in part by university students. HGW succeeded in raising about $100,000 per year in 2011, 2012 and 2013. Originally managed by a single journalist (this author), by 2013, HGW had a coordination staff of three and was juggling about four investigations at a time.

The two institutional partners had specific tasks. AlterPresse provided editing and distribution for the French text versions, and occasionally participated in an investigation via the part-time work of one journalist. SAKS was responsible for assuring the production and distribution of the Creole audio versions: to one commercial and about 40 community or local radio stations. In addition to being carried by AlterPresse, in Haiti the texts were regularly run by two or three Haitian newspapers, including *Le Nouvelliste* (the aforementioned 'very cautious' commercial paper), as well as Haitian weeklies in the diaspora. The articles were also frequently used by commercial Haitian radio news programs and their websites, by numerous other sites in Haiti and in the Haitian diaspora and by French-language sites focusing on the Caribbean or on humanitarian and development issues. The texts were also compiled by HGW in a periodically updated *Anthologie*, photocopied and sold at cost or, in the case of screenings, distributed free of charge – five copies each – to the host organisation(s).

The English-text versions were relayed by numerous websites like *Truthout!*, *Global Voices*, *Reliefweb*, *Free Speech Radio News* and other outlets. More importantly, about two-thirds of the English versions went out worldwide on the *Inter Press Service* (IPS) newswire once they had been edited for length and form. These were also sometimes translated by IPS into Spanish and other languages. Creole-language audio versions were posted online for Haitian diaspora radio and for the few community stations in the country with access to the internet, and they also went to about 40 stations across the country on CDs, carried via taxi or a friend. During 2013, HGW also produced short Spanish-language audio versions of ten investigations for PULSAR, the news website of the Latin American chapter of the World Association of Community Radio Broadcasters (AMARC). The video documentaries were also seen abroad. They were embedded in websites, and portions were used by *Democracy Now!*, *Al Jazeera English*, *The Real News Network* and a few other outlets.

HGW investigations have had discernible impact, from exposing and contributing to a temporary halt in secretive gold mining in the North (Regan, 2013), to outing sex for work schemes run by NGO workers (CHF International, 2011), to being frequently cited by foreign journalists and researchers. Perhaps most importantly, HGW helped found a tradition of investigative journalism and educated over 130 journalists in courses and seminars. In addition to the four university investigative journalism courses, HGW coordination staff led a dozen training sessions and seminars in the capital and at partner radio stations in the countryside.

Community? Alternative?

In 2014, however, HGW faced significant challenges related to funding, to its transition to a new coordinator chosen from among AlterPresse staff and also to a challenge that likely stems from the experiment's very underpinnings. HGW was founded as a collaboration dominated by this author and two institutions. Each of the three brought different skill sets and experiences, as well as differing ideologies and priorities. Unnoticed during the founding months, the differences between the commitments and ideological orientations of the coordination team on the one hand, and the two partners on the other, became increasingly clear as the project advanced. And whereas the coordination was focused solely on HGW, the two institutional partners also ran other projects, their own newsrooms and were frequently bogged down with other tasks which sometimes included executing revenue-generating contracts for the very organisations HGW was supposed to be watchdogging, such as UNICEF and the European Union.

Did the differing commitments stem from differing definitions of 'popular communications' and 'alternative' journalism? Perhaps. This 'ideological misalignment' undoubtedly resulted in part from the fact that, at its founding, the partners never specifically defined what *kind* of investigative journalism the HGW would practice: 'alternative', 'progressive', 'rebellious', 'grassroots', 'radical' or even something else. The HGW website only says that reports would seek out "Haitian academics, technicians and specialists" to "add their voices to the voices of the Haitian people and their associations and organizations" and would focus "on 'watchdogging' the aid and reconstruction from the point of view of Haiti's majority, at the same time as it also provides historical and political context, examines structural causes and challenges" (Haiti Grassroots Watch, 2010). The 2010 Memorandum of Understanding (MOU) signed by SAKS, AlterPresse, a representative of women community radio workers and this author says much the same thing, noting that HGW would "enable different actors to hear the voices of the Haitian people, institutions working for social justice, human rights, democratic and popular organizations, youth, women, academics, etc." (Ayiti Kale Je, 2010). Neither the website nor the MOU use terms like 'progressive', 'alternative', 'popular communications or even community'.

Neither of the two institutional partners define these terms very specifically in their theory or practice. AlterPresse self-defines as a practitioner of 'alternative' journalism, but does not always provide readers with what might be considered good examples of that genre. During any given week, at least some of the agency's articles are little more than rewrites of press releases from government ministries, multilateral agencies or local organisations. More alarming, AlterPresse sometimes softened HGW texts. On one occasion, an editor went so far as to change language related to the unconstitutional ouster of President Jean-Bertrand Aristide in 2004, turning the phrase 'coup d'état' into saying the president "had to leave the country due to a protest movement" (AlterPresse, 2013c). AlterPresse also sometimes succumbed to pressure from critics. For example, in 2013 it ran a lengthy (longer than the original article) response to an HGW investigation from a public relations firm concerning an industrial park and a South Korean clothing firm, even though the original article contained no errors (AlterPresse, 2013b). SAKS never altered the editorial line of HGW audio scripts, but on multiple occasions, audio versions were delayed for up to weeks at a time while the institution hustled to fulfil overdue contracts.

These observations are not meant as condemnations. Nor are they comprehensive analyses of 40 months of largely fruitful collaboration. They do, however, provide inklings about the differences between the three major partners of the HGW collaborative: AlterPresse, SAKS and the coordination team headed by this author. The experiment's coordination was lean and nimble, run out of a knapsack for the first year, able to react to changes in the political landscape and/or increases or decreases in funding. But the two institutions were not. And over the years, the words and actions of both have grown slightly less militant as they institutionalised and – coincidentally? – went from being largely voluntary efforts to increasingly reliant on foundation and development money. They may have fallen victim – at least in part – to what Schuller (2012) calls "trickle-down imperialism," where organisations succumb, consciously or unconsciously, to diverse pressures that tend to push them away from their more radical roots. Schuller posits that "the moment an NGO director steps out of the sphere of allowable actions, the organization can be disciplined" (ibid.: 184). Petras (1997) goes further:

> NGOs foster a new type of cultural and economic colonialism and dependency. Projects are designed, or at least approved, based on the "guidelines" and priorities of the imperial centers and their institutions ... Everything and everybody is increasingly disciplined to comply with the donors and project evaluators' demands.

Have SAKS and AlterPresse ever been 'disciplined' or do they fear such a possibility? This study does not have the data necessary to judge. But some of the challenges faced by the partnership in 2012 and 2013, as well as at present, shed light on what can happen when definitions – and commitments – are not strictly demarcated.

Under AlterPresse leadership since early 2014, for the first six months of that year HGW was dormant, sitting on three investigations that were completely reported and ready for editing and publication. AlterPresse was waiting for funding to land in its account: An indication that 'pay to play' was as important as the public interest? The months and years to come – and the content of future investigative reports – will tell.

Hybrid or patchwork?

The HGW collaboration could be termed what Atton and Hamilton call "hybrid", or "mixed economy ... alternative journalism" (2008: 45). Indeed, in their book, the authors discuss concepts and practices that partially describe HGW theory and practice, especially in their sketch of "native reporting", whereby people become journalists via "the application of their own, amateur knowledge to the issues being reported" using their "specialist, local community knowledge" (ibid.: 126–7).

While the concepts of 'mixed economy' or 'hybrid' are interesting, they only partially describe the Haiti collaborative. And HGW can only be seen as 'hybrid' if one draws a line between mainstream and all other journalism, including 'alternative' journalism. Drawing such a line creates a false dichotomy between elements of a much more complex landscape. The HGW experiment drew and *grew* from various media and journalism experiences, some of which self-define as 'alternative' and others which sit firmly in mainstream journalism traditions. In fact, HGW is more of an evolution than a hybrid. Indeed, as Nerone (2013: 456) notes, "[j]ournalisms are never invented out of whole cloth; they are always patchworks of older traditions". In the HGW case, pieces were borrowed from across two centuries and across the globe.

Given its broad and deep conceptual roots, what is the correct label? Isn't 'alternative' too nondescript? And doesn't such a fluid term – which might just as easily apply to form as to content – leave too many details up to the imagination? Finally, given that HGW relied on ideas dating back to early Western journalism, before the label 'alternative' arose, is it fair to place it in opposition to one of its inspirations, dividing the experiment from its origins?

In her study, Forde (2011: 173) calls alternative journalism "a political act", but *all* journalism is a political act. Unfortunately, the 'political acts' of commercial or mainstream journalisms often tend to at least subtly reinforce, rather than question, the status quo. Would it not be useful to leave behind the term 'alternative' – and, while we are at it, 'community' – and to define journalism and media experiences more by their content, as some have already suggested? Downing (2001: ix) says it well when he notes, "to speak simply of *alternative* media is almost oxymoronic. Everything, at some point, is alternative to something else."

In their book, Clark and Van Slyke (2010) skip the term 'alternative'. They use 'progressive', also a relative expression but one that at least implies a tinge of struggle and social change. Inter Press Service (2013) does not use the word 'alternative' either, choosing instead to say it gives "voice to the voiceless" and serves as "a communication channel that privileges the voices and the concerns of the poorest and creates a climate of understanding, accountability and participation around development, promoting a new international information order". That definition might not be tweetable, but it at least gives a hint of what the agency and its journalists hope to accomplish.

Further reading

The 39 Haiti Grassroots Watch investigations produced from 2010 through 2013 can be found at http://www.haitigrassrootswatch.org. The website also has links to several articles and webpages about HGW. Nerone (2013) offers an interesting exploration of the contributions and shortcomings of Western "hegemonic journalism" models and proposes rethinking. Atton and Hamilton (2008) and Downing (2001) remain key texts for those hoping to understand the theory and/or practice of what could be called 'anti-hegemonic journalism', while Geerts and Van Oeyen (2001) offer an incisive overview of Latin American *radios populares* in the 1980s and 1990s.

References

AlterPresse (2013a) Retrieved from http://www.alterpresse.org/ (accessed 24 April 2013).
——(2013b) *Haïti-Le Parc Industriel de Caracol: Précisions apportées par la Wellcom*. Retrieved from http://www.alterpresse.org/spip.php?article14341#.UaH6uOC3Kc9 (accessed 30 April 2013).
——(2013c) *La faim en Haïti: Des causes multiples*. Retrieved from http://www.alterpresse.org/spip.php?article15306#.UwC23yi3Lnt (accessed 15 February 2014).

Atton, C. and Hamilton, J. (2008) *Alternative Journalism – Journalism Studies: Key Texts Series*. London: Sage Publications.

Ayiti Kale Je. (2010) *Pwotokòl dakò*. Unpublished manuscript.

Barnabé, R. and Breton, P. (2007) Le coaching: une approche respectueuse des journalistes et des gestionnaires de médias haïtiens. *Les cahiers du journalisme*, 17, 384–400.

CHF International (2011) Note from David Humphries, director of communications. *Haiti Grassroots Watch*, 20 July. Retrieved from http://www.ayitikaleje.org/8cfwreax (accessed 12 May 2013).

CIPER (Centro de Investigación Periodistica) (2009) *Más (y mejor) periodismo de investigación en América Latina*. Retrieved from http://ciperchile.cl/2009/12/03/mas-y-mejor-periodismo-de-investigacion-en-america-latina/ (accessed 27 April 2013).

Clark, J. and Van Slyke, T. (2010) *Beyond the Echo Chamber: Reshaping Politics Through Networked Progressive Media*. New York: New Press.

Décimé, E. (2013) "Haiti-Presse: La pratique du journalisme à Port-au-Prince, entre 'journalisme de marché' et Éthique." *AlterPresse*, 3 May. Retrieved from http://www.alterpresse.org/spip.php?article14485 (accessed 4 May 2013).

Downie, A. (2012) "Haitian universities struggle to rebound." *Chronicle of Higher Education*, 6 January, A1, A8–10.

Downing, J. (with others) (2001) *Radical Media: Rebellious Communication and Social Movements*. Thousand Oaks, CA: Sage.

Forde, S. (2011) *Challenging the News – The Journalism of Alternative and Community Media*. Basingstoke: Palgrave McMillan.

Francisco, T., Lenhoff, A. and Schudson, M. (2012) "The classroom as newsroom: Leveraging university resources for public affairs reporting." *International Journal of Communication*, 6, 2677–97. Retrieved from http://ijoc.org/ojs/index.php/ijoc/article/viewDownloadInterstitial/1636/818 (accessed 22 December 2012).

Freire, P. (1970) *Pedagogy of the Oppressed*. Translated from Portuguese by Myra Bergman Ramos. New York: Seabury Press.

Geerts, A. and Van Oeyen, V. (2001) *Informe General – Estudio Vigencia e Incidencia Radio Popular 2000*. Quito: Asociación Latinoamericana de Educación Radiofónica (ALER).

Geffrard, R. (2009) "Baisse générale de niveau dans les médias." *Le Nouvelliste*, 9 September. Retrieved from http://www.lenouvelliste.com/article4.php?newsid=74043 (accessed 28 April 2013).

Haiti Grassroots Watch (2010) "About us." Retrieved from http://www.ayitikaleje.org/about-us/ (accessed 15 February 2014).

Hunter, M. (2011) "Story-based inquiry – A manual for investigative journalists." Paris: UNESCO. Retrieved from http://unesdoc.unesco.org/images/0019/001930/193078e.pdf (accessed 30 April 2013).

INFOASAID (2012) "Haiti – Media and telecoms landscape guide." Retrieved from http://infoasaid.org/sites/infoasaid.org/files/haiti_media_guide_final_211012_0.pdf (accessed 3 May 2013).

Institute for Justice and Democracy in Haiti (2012) "Freedom of the press in Haiti – The chilling effect on journalists critical of the government," 27 September. Retrieved from http://ijdh.org/wordpress/wp-content/uploads/2012/09/IJDH_FreedomOfExpression.pdf (accessed 22 December 2012).

Inter Press Service (2013) "About us." Retrieved from http://www.ipsnews.net/about-us/ (accessed 28 April 2013).

Jean-Pierre, J. (2000) "The sound of silence – killing hope in Haiti." *The Village Voice*, 11 April 2000. Retrieved from http://www.villagevoice.com/2000-04-11/news/the-sound-of-silence/ (accessed 15 February 2014).

Klarreich, K. (2012) "On the ground: Journalism ethics in Haiti." *Caribbean Journal*, 9 April. Retrieved from http://www.caribjournal.com/2012/04/09/on-the-ground-journalism-ethics-in-haiti/ (accessed 22 December 2012).

Klarreich, K. and Polman, L. (2012) "The NGO Republic of Haiti." *The Nation*, 12 November. Retrieved from http://www.thenation.com/article/170929/ngo-republic-haiti# (accessed 22 December 2012).

Let Haiti Live (2014) "About Bri Kouri Nouvèl Gaye. Let Haiti Live." Retrieved from http://www.lethaitilive.org/bri-kouri/ (accessed 15 February 2014).

Nerone, J. (2013) "The historical roots of the normative model of journalism." *Journalism*, 14 (4), 446–58. Retrieved from http://jou.sagepub.com/content/14/4/446 (accessed 29 August 2013).

Petras, J. (1997) "Imperialism and NGOs in the Americas." *Monthly Review*, 49(7). Retrieved from http://monthlyreview.org/1997/12/01/imperialism-and-ngos-in-latin-america (accessed 25 May 2013).

Regan, J. (2008) Baboukèt la tonbe – The muzzle has fallen! *Media Development*, 2, 12–17.

——(2013) "Haitian Senate calls for Halt to mining activities." Inter Press Service, 24 February. Retrieved from http://www.ipsnews.net/2013/02/haitian-senate-calls-for-halt-to-mining-activities/ (accessed 12 May 2013).

SAKS (2013) Homepage for Sosyete Animasyon Kominikasyon Sosyal. Retrieved from http://www.saks-haiti.org/ (accessed 6 April 2013).

Schaffer, J. (2012a) *Networked Journalism: What Works – Lessons from Nine Collaborative Journalism Pilot Projects*. Washington, DC: J-Lab: Institute for Interactive Journalism.

——(2012b) "University news sites: Investments in civic entrepreneurship – response to Francisco, Lenoff and Schudson." *International Journal of Communication*, 6, 2674–2676. Retrieved from http://www.j-lab.org/_uploads/ideas/blogically_thinking/schafferresponse.pdf accessed 22 December 2012).

Schuller, M. (2012) *Killing with Kindness – Haiti, International Aid and NGOs*. New Brunswick, NJ: Rutgers University Press.

Sérant, V. (2007) *Sauver l'information en Haïti*. Port-au-Prince: Media-textes.

Transparency International (2012) "Corruption Perceptions Index." Retrieved from http://cpi.transparency.org/cpi2012/results/ (Accessed 24 September 2013).

29
GIVING PEACE
JOURNALISM A CHANCE

Richard Lance Keeble

Introduction

Since the 1970s, a movement has emerged among academics and social movement activists promoting the theory of peace journalism (PJ) – and aiming to inspire further activities. This chapter will argue that the theory has inappropriately prioritised mainstream activities – and failed to acknowledge adequately the role of the alternative media – both historically and today. Such a debate raises a number of important questions. For instance, how are both the peace movement and journalism defined? Is there not a danger of exaggerating the distinctions between alternative and mainstream media? Are there not some progressive spaces within the mainstream to be exploited by peace journalists?

This chapter seeks to highlight the corporate media's historic function to promote overall the dominant political, military, economic, ideological and cultural interests in society. Research has confirmed that the mainstream, professionalised media, given its close ties to the military/industrial/entertainment complex, tends to support warfare and downplays opportunities for the peaceful resolution of conflicts (e.g. Carruthers, 2000; Andersen, 2006). In this context, it can be seen that, historically, the non-corporate, alternative media have played a crucial role in promoting the interests of the peace movement globally – thus providing a voice to the otherwise marginalised or silenced. The chapter will provide a brief history of PJ, a survey of the overall state of PJ today – and a brief focus on two major, contemporary examples of PJ.

The emergence of peace journalism theory and its focus on the mainstream

Peace journalism theory emerged during the 1970s among peace researchers, activists and academics, but the activities of the alternative media were hardly acknowledged (Shinar and Kempf, 2007: 9). The seminal theoretical study was conducted by Johan

Galtung (1998; see also Lynch, 1998: 44), one of the founders of the academic subject of Peace Studies, who essentially contrasted the elements of what he described as 'peace/conflict journalism' with those of 'war/violence journalism'. The theory, then, emerged as a critique of the dominant mode of covering conflict in the mainstream media – and solutions were sought from within the mainstream.

PJ, according to Galtung, 'gave a voice to all parties', emphasised the invisible effects of violence (psychological trauma, damage of social structures), aimed to 'expose untruths on all sides', was 'people oriented', 'gave a 'voice to the voiceless' and was solution oriented. In contrast, war journalism dehumanised the enemy, focused on only the visible effects of violence, was propaganda oriented, elite focused and victory obsessed – and tended to concentrate on institutions (the 'controlled society'). Another seminal text, by Jake Lynch and Annabel McGoldrick, offers a 17-point plan for developing PJ (Lynch and McGoldrick, 2005: 28–31), in which improving professional practice within the mainstream remains the priority. Their points include:

- avoid concentrating always on what divides parties, on the differences between what each say they want. Instead, try asking questions which may reveal areas of common ground;
- avoid focusing on the suffering, fears and grievances of only one party … Instead, treat as equally newsworthy the suffering, fears and grievances of all parties.

In keeping with their stress on professional media, Lynch and McGoldrick suggest the London-based *Independent* as one of the best examples of peace journalism. While the newspaper carries the outstanding reports of veteran reporters Robert Fisk (see Keeble, 2009) and Patrick Cockburn, critical research suggests that the newspaper tends to reproduce Fleet Street's dominant news values (Keeble, 1997, 1999, 2000 and 2004). Another important text, *Peace Journalism: The State of the Art* (Shinar and Wilhelm Kempf, 2007), contains the work of some of the leading theorists in the field, though most concentrate on professional issues and only rarely acknowledge any 'alternative' outlets. Susan Dente Ross ends a highly detailed overview of peace journalism literature by suggesting that no 'revolutionary' changes are needed: "Peace journalism does not involve any radical departure from contemporary journalism practice. Rather peace journalism requires numerous subtle and cumulative shifts in seeing, thinking, sourcing, narrating and financing the news" (Dente Ross, 2007: 74).

The dominant strand of peace journalism theory views journalism as a privileged, professional activity. It has failed to acknowledge the critical intellectual tradition which considers professions as essentially occupational groupings with a legal monopoly of social and economic opportunities in the marketplace, underwritten by the state (Althusser, 1969; Illich, 1973; Parkin, 1979; Collins, 1990). PJ theory, in short, has been too elitist and too utopian in suggesting that improvements in professional routines and reforms in journalistic training can bring about significant changes (Keeble, 2010). And it has been too reluctant to acknowledge the crucial role played by the alternative media – both historically and today – in promoting peace.

Is change possible from within the mainstream?

Yet, PJ theory and practice should not totally exclude the mainstream. Its closeness to dominant economic, cultural and ideological forces means that the mainstream largely functions to promote the interests of the military/industrial/political/entertainment complex (Herman and Chomsky, 1988; Der Derian, 2001). Yet, within advanced capitalist economies, currently suffering acute downturns following the 2008 crisis (which, to a large extent, stemmed from the over-resourcing of US/UK military and imperial adventurism), the contradictions within corporate media have provided certain spaces for progressive journalism.

Chris Atton (2004: 10) warns against presenting a polarised vision of the mainstream and alternative spheres, positing a 'hegemonic approach' that "suggests a complexity of relationships between radical and mainstream that previous binary models have been unable to identify". Robert Hackett (2007) suggests that a way ahead for PJ is to reform mainstream journalism from within. Herman and Chomsky's propaganda model (1988: 2) stresses the role of the corporate media in forming a single propaganda system where "money and power are able to filter out the news fit to print, marginalise dissent and allow the government and dominant private interests to get their message across to the public". But for Hackett, their model is too deterministic. It thus fails to "identify the scope and conditions under which newsworkers could exercise the kind of choices called for by PJ" and to acknowledge that individual journalists are "active and creative agents" able to combine an involvement in the corporate media with regular contributions to alternative, partisan, campaigning media (Hackett, 2007: 93).[1]

Hackett also draws on the 'hierarchy of influences' model of Shoemaker and Reese (1996) and Bourdieu's notion of the media as a relatively autonomous institutional sphere (1998) to further theorise the activities of progressive newsworkers within the corporate media to promote the interests of the peace movement. Arguing that both models suggest some degree of agency for newsworkers, Hackett stresses: "There is, indeed, a necessary role for dedicated journalists to take the lead" (2007: 93). At the same time, he acknowledges the severe constraints on progressive journalists operating within the mainstream: "Ultimately it seems probable that in Western corporate media at least, journalists have neither sufficient incentives nor autonomy *vis-à-vis* their employers to transform the way news is done without support from powerful external allies" (ibid.). Oliver Boyd-Barrett (2010) also highlights the propaganda model's failure to acknowledge journalists' individual agency, though his focus is more on the penetration of corporate media by covert intelligence and their sympathisers.

The historical role of the alternative media

Conventional histories of the media tend to marginalise or ignore altogether the non-corporate media. This should not come as a surprise: the essential ideological function of the dominant political and cultural spheres is to silence the voices of progressive and revolutionary social movements (Keeble, 1997). Yet, the historic role of the alternative media (of which the peace movement media is a part) in the formation of a counter or oppositional public sphere is considerable both in the UK and internationally, and as has been highlighted by scholars (see, for example, Atton and Hamilton, 2008; Couldry and Curran, 2003; Downing, 1984; Forde, 2011; Harcup, 2003 and 2013; Nelson, 1989; Rodríguez, 2001; Sparks, 1985; and Waltz, 2005).

To take just a few specific examples: John Hartley (1996) has highlighted the importance of journalists such as Robespierre, Marat, Danton and Hébert to the French Revolution of the 1790s (see also Chapman, 2008). In the first half of the nineteenth century in the UK, a popular, radical, unstamped (and hence illegal) press played a crucial role in the campaign for trade union rights and social and political reforms (Black, 2001; Conboy, 2004; Curran and Seaton, 2004). Many feminists and suffragettes (such as Sylvia Pankhurst: see Davis, 1999) were radical journalists, pacifists and political agitators. Most studies of the Vietnam War (1965–73) have failed to identify the role of the many anti-war newspapers that cropped up in the armed services during the course of the conflict in both reflecting and inspiring opposition to the conflict. On the other hand, Jonathan Neale (2001: 122–30) identified around 300 anti-war newspapers: for instance, a small group of Trotskyists was behind *Vietnam GI*, which was produced in Chicago with a print run of 15,000 and a mailing list of 3,000 in Vietnam. At Fort Bragg, a chapter of GIs United Against the War put out *Bragg Briefs.*

After the 1964 Gulf of Tonkin incident (in which a US naval destroyer was allegedly attacked by North Vietnamese torpedo boats, providing President Johnson the pretext to launch the war on the North) the corporate media were either hawkish or believers in the 'official word'. I. F. Stone, self-publisher of the *I. F. Stone Weekly*, was alone in highlighting the administration's lies and in running the views of the two lone senators who opposed the war, Wayne Morse and Ernst Gruening (MacPherson, 2006). Moreover, for many, the greatest scoop of the Vietnam conflict was Seymour Hersh's exposure of the Mai Lai massacre of up to 500 women and children by US soldiers in March 1968 – significantly, this was first published by the alternative news agency, the Despatch News Service (Knightley, 1982: 259–60).

Defining the global contemporary peace movement

Consideration of contemporary PJ needs to begin with a definition of the global peace movement which it is aiming to inform, inspire and, indeed, entertain. One of the most useful overviews appears in *Housmans Peace Diary*, produced over the past 61 years by the Housmans radical bookshop in London. In its 2014 edition there is a listing of around 1,500 peace groups from around the world. It begins with international organisations: from Abolition 2000 International Secretariat through the European Bureau for Conscientious Objection, the Global Anabaptist Peace and Justice Network and Mayors for Peace through to the South Asia Peace Alliance, War Resisters' International and the World Peace Council. It moves on to national organisations in 136 countries: from the Women, Peace and Security Research Institute of Afghanistan and Footprints for Peace of Australia, through Britain's Campaign for a Nuclear-Free Middle East and Coalition of Resistance to Zimbabwe's Institute of Peace, Leadership and Governance.

The list highlights the global breadth of the peace movement. It is hardly a distinct, unified grouping, but one closely intertwined with broader (and often competing) social, environmental, religious, feminist, gay rights, educational and human rights movements. Thus, in the Canada section, Toronto Action for Social Change/Homes not Bombs is listed; in Rwanda, there is Shalom: Educating for Peace; and in the US, Psychologists for Social Responsibility (among more than 180 entries). To complicate the issue even further, within these individual organisations there are often factions competing for prominence. Despite its enormity and complexity, the list might even be seen as failing to convey the full picture since trade unions and political parties are excluded – even though those (particularly of the Left, such as the Socialist Workers Party, the Socialist Equality Party, the Communist Party and their international affiliates) can play important roles in peace movements.

All of the organisations listed have internet sites, newsletters or journals and email contacts. Many have a presence on YouTube and Facebook. In other words, via the web and blogosphere – far beyond Jürgen Habermas's original conception of a national public sphere (1974) – it could be argued that a global alternative public sphere (with all its internal contradictions and complexities) has emerged. Indeed, PJ activities are perhaps best understood as operating in this counter-public sphere and global network society (Castells, 2009). Certainly, the activities of this extraordinarily dynamic, diverse, imaginative and global alternative peace movement (and its associated media activities) have been almost totally ignored by mainstream journalists and the academy.

Peace journalism: Broadening the definitions of journalism and journalist

Peace movement media, like other non-corporate outlets, have always tended to rely on the work of non-professional journalists: citizens and community/political activists. As in Chris Atton's definition of alternative media (2002: 25): "They typically go beyond simply providing a platform for radical or alternative points of view: they emphasise the organisation of media to enable wider social participation in their creation, production and dissemination than is possible in the mass media." Thus, these well-established working arrangements long pre-dated recent discussions about the nature of journalism – provoked by the emergence of the internet and its many communicative forms. Stuart Allan, for instance, celebrates the bloggers and the "extraordinary contribution made by ordinary citizens offering their first-hand reports, digital photographs, camcorder video footage, mobile telephone snapshots or audio clips" (2006: 7). John Hartley (2008: 42) even draws on Article 19 of the Universal Declaration of Human Rights to proclaim the radical, utopian-liberal ideal that everyone has the right not only to seek and receive but also to 'impart' (in other words, communicate) information and ideas.

Alternative journalists

This broadened definition of journalism certainly helps incorporate a wide range of media and political activists into the discussion on PJ. For instance, it could include radical, progressive journalists and their associated media such as, in the US, Democracy Now!, an alternative broadcast station (with allied website) run by the

award-winning Amy Goodman, which is overtly committed to peace journalism. As
its website stresses:

> Democracy Now!'s War and Peace Report provides our audience with access
> to people and perspectives rarely heard in the US corporate-sponsored media,
> including independent and international journalists, ordinary people from
> around the world who are directly affected by US foreign policy, grassroots
> leaders and peace activists, artists, academics and independent analysts. In
> addition, Democracy Now! hosts real debates – debates between people who
> substantially disagree, such as between the White House or the Pentagon
> spokespeople on the one hand, and grassroots activists on the other.
>
> (www.democracynow.org)

Other peace-oriented, progressive journals include *Middle East Report* (www.merip.org),
Nation (www.thenation.com), *Mother Jones* (www.motherjones.com), *Z Magazine* (www.
zcommunications.org/zmag) and *In These Times* (www.inthesetimes.com). In Chennai,
India, there is *Frontline* (www.frontline.in), while in London we have the investigative
website Corporate Watch (www.corporatewatch.org). Media such as these often
draw inspiration from Noam Chomsky's critique (1989) of the corporate myths of
'balance' and 'objectivity' and emphasise instead their explicitly partisan character.
Moreover, they seek to "invert the hierarchy of access" to the news by explicitly
foregrounding the viewpoints of 'ordinary' people (activists, protestors, local residents), citizens whose visibility in the mainstream media tends to be obscured by the
presence of elite groups and individuals (Atton, 2002: 20).

The role of progressive intellectuals

A broadened definition of journalist should also acknowledge the role of progressive
intellectuals within peace journalism. For instance, the American historian Tom
Engelhardt, with his colleague Nick Turse, runs the radical, investigative website
tomdispatch.com. Other radical intellectuals prominent in the blogosphere have
included the late Edward Saïd, Noam Chomsky, Norman Solomon, James Winter,
Mark Curtis and the late African intellectual, campaigner and journalist Tajudeen
Abdul-Raheem. The website Coldtype.net publishes the work of many of these writers
in PDF magazine format. In the UK, Professor David Miller and William Dinan are
part of a collective running Spinwatch (www.spinwatch.org), which critiques the PR
industry from a radical peace perspective. Academics David Edwards and David
Cromwell edit the radical media monitoring site Media Lens (www.medialens.org.),
which maintains a constant critique of the mainstream print and broadcast media
from a radical Chomskyite, Buddhist perspective and in support of the global peace
movement. It also seeks to encourage peace activists to be inspired by their critiques
to engage in follow-up protest activities (such as letter writing and demonstrating)
against the mainstream media. As its website states:

> Since 2001, we have been describing how mainstream newspapers and broad-
> casters operate as a propaganda system for the elite interests that dominate

modern society. The costs of their disinformation in terms of human and animal suffering, and environmental breakdown, are incalculable. We show how news and commentary are "filtered" by the media's profit-orientation, by its dependence on advertisers, parent companies, wealthy owners and official news sources. We check the media's version of events against credible facts and opinion provided by journalists, academics and specialist researchers. We then publish both versions, together with our commentary, in free Media Alerts and invite readers to deliver their verdict both to us and to mainstream journalists through the email addresses provided in our "Suggested Action" at the end of each alert. We urge correspondents to adopt a polite, rational and respectful tone at all times – we strongly oppose all abuse and personal attack.

The website globalresearch.ca is run by the Centre for Research and Globalisation, an independent media and research group based in Montreal, Canada. It carries articles by Michel Chossudovsky, Professor of Economics at the University of Ottawa, among other prominent activist academics. Special thematic sections on the site have focused on '9/11 and the "War on Terrorism"', 'Crimes against humanity', 'Media disinformation', 'Militarisation and WMD', 'Poverty and social inequality' and 'Women's rights'. Subjects of in-depth reports include 'Syria: Nato's next war?', the 'Arab Protest War' and 'Occupy Wall Street'.

Human rights and peace journalism

Ibrahim Seaga Shaw (2012) extends the debate over peace journalism with a special focus on human rights reporting. Drawing on Johan Galtung's (1998) theories relating to visible and invisible violence, his concerns embrace:

> direct physical violence – such as genocide, arbitrary arrest and detentions, extra-judicial killings, rape, torture, ethnic cleansing and the mistreatment of prisoners – or indirect forms of cultural and structural violence such as hate speech, racism, xenophobia, poverty, famine, corruption, colonialism, slavery, unfair trade, forced migration, forced labour, human trafficking, marginalisation or the exclusion of minorities.
>
> (Shaw, 2012: 11)

From this perspective, international human rights organisations that produce campaigning sites and publications (reports, magazines, leaflets) can be seen as practising activist peace journalism. Reprieve (www.reprieve.org.uk) campaigns on behalf of those often unlawfully detained by the US and UK in the 'War on Terror', and its director Clive Stafford Smith writes regular pieces for the 'quality' press and the leftist *New Statesman* magazine. Amnesty International (AI, www.amnesty.org.uk) highlights human rights abuses, and members are active in peace movement activities globally. While many in the peace movement denounce Israel as a 'terrorist' and apartheid state, on the Israel/Palestine conflict, AI stresses:

> The innocent imprisoned. Movement restricted. Homes demolished. Human Rights abuses are rife in Israel and the Occupied Territories. We do

not take up a position on issues of statehood. We stand with those demanding that all sides respect human rights and that the perpetrators of human rights abuses are brought to justice.

(www.amnesty.org.uk)

In the US, both the American Civil Liberties Union (www.aclu.org) and Human Rights Watch (www.hrw.org) have consistently campaigned to expose the human rights abuses that have accompanied the 'War on Terror' and produced a number of important reports on the subject.

Peace News and CounterPunch: peace journalism in action

Since its founding in early 1936, *Peace News* has been a site of citizen journalism for the promotion of peace and social justice. Take a look at the back pages of any edition of *Peace News* (http://peacenews.info). Listed there are scores of events happening all across the UK: in September 2012, for example, in Liverpool there was a concert for peace; in Leeds, a talk by Chris Cole, of the Drones Campaign Network; in Bromley, a Peace Day event. All this is evidence of an imaginative, vast, committed and growing progressive and alternative community whose activities (most significantly) are almost totally ignored by the corporate media. A co-editor of *Peace News*, Milan Rai, comments:

> For *Peace News*, citizen journalism has meant activist journalism, with self-reporting by large numbers of social movement activists through the years … Throughout the past thirty years, a staple of *PN* coverage has been the self-documentation by members of various peace camps around Britain, most famously Greenham Common Women's Peace Camp in the 1980s and now including Faslane nuclear submarine base in Scotland and the Atomic Weapons Establishment in Aldermaston, Berkshire. The number of *PN* street sellers may have shrunk over the years, but the number of journalist-activists has increased correspondingly.
>
> (Rai, 2011: 211)

Rai argues that *Peace News*'s primary function is "to assist and encourage people who are seeking to make positive social changes through non-violent means" (cited in Forde, 2011: 84). The November 2013 edition is typical in the way it highlights the work of peace movement activists. Its front-page lead story reports on a new nonviolence campaign in the US, *Pace e Bene*, which is calling for an end to drone warfare, extreme poverty and environmental destruction. Inside, a whole page is devoted to the case of the 'Waddington Six': peace activists found guilty of criminal damage during a protest at the drone base at RAF Waddington, Lincolnshire. Other items focus on the actions of Stop the Arms Fair activists, peaceful anti-fracking protests in Balcombe, West Sussex, and peace activists facing 30-year sentences for breaking into a US nuclear bomb–making factory in Oak Ridge, California, in July 2012.

Another function of media such as *Peace News* is to promote a form of 'counter-journalism'. Rai provides an example of a report on a poll in Iraq in 2007 which suggested a total of 1,220,580 deaths since 2003, a finding which was almost totally ignored by the mainstream media (2011: 216–20). For Rai, the aim of counter-journalism is

> to search the output of the mass media with diligence and a sceptical eye, cutting through the mass of misrepresentation and fraud to discover nuggets that can help citizens to better understand – and to more effectively alter the world in which we are living and acting.
>
> (Rai, 2011: 217)

Another example of PJ as 'counter-journalism' is CounterPunch (www.counter-punch.org), a regularly updated investigative website with an associated printed monthly journal sent to subscribers and a book imprint. Run since 1996 by Jeffery St Clair and, until his death in 2012, Alexander Cockburn, from its Washington, DC, base, it depends entirely on donations from readers and subscriptions – so it is entirely free from corporate pressure (though almost permanently financially insecure). It is firmly in the American 'muckraking' tradition and has consistently opposed US/Western imperialistic adventures, Israel's oppression of the Palestinians, the military/industrial/surveillance complex, the corporate destruction of the environment and global threats to civil liberties.

Many of its pieces are contributed by activist academics and specialist journalists – they provide not only alternative perspectives but information missed by the mainstream. For instance, in the August 2013 issue of the magazine, Jennifer Loewenstein – a faculty associate in Middle Eastern Studies at the University of Wisconsin–Madison, as a well as a freelance journalist and human rights activist – locates the current Syrian crisis in its historical, colonial context. Focusing at the end of her long article on the 'extreme Islamist organisation' Jabhat al-Nusra, and countering the coverage in the corporate media – which is so reluctant to investigate in depth the US government's global ties with supposed 'terrorists' – she concludes: "In its hurry to rid the region of the Assad regime, US policy makers helped fuel the creation of the very type of organization it views as one of its biggest threats."

Conclusion

In Britain, a predictable media panic erupted in 2011 after Fleet Street journalists were discovered hacking into the phones of celebrities, top politicians, royals and the occasional 'ordinary' person, such as missing schoolgirl Milly Dowler (see Keeble and Mair, 2012). An expensive inquiry was then launched into the ethics of the corporate press. Not surprisingly, then, the alternative sector was entirely ignored. Yet, as this chapter has attempted to show, the importance of the alternative media both historically and today as a site for 'good' journalism cannot be under-estimated. Tony Dowmunt draws our attention to the term 'alternative media', noting that it might be thought of as denoting activities of secondary importance to the mainstream. Yet this need not be the case: "In that they provide resistance, opposition and counterexamples to tired and reactionary mainstream uses of media, they are of primary social, cultural and political importance. Nevertheless they remain, by definition, significantly less powerful and privileged than the mainstream" (Dowmunt, 2007: 10). There are, though, as I hope this chapter has shown, reasons for optimism. Beyond the gaze of the elite, a global counter-public sphere (though full of tensions) is bursting with people constantly challenging the lies and mystifications of the powerful and their propaganda media, bravely protesting (through the alternative media and in so many other imaginative ways) against the warmongers – and for peace.

Note

1 Peace journalists of this important hybrid group in the US, UK and India might include Barbara Ehrenreich, Susan George, Phillip Knightley, John Pilger, Arundhati Roy and Jonathan Steele.

Further reading

Three important sites for academic discussions on peace journalism globally are www.cco.regener-online.de, http://globalmedia.emu.edu.tr and Johan Galtung's www.transcend.org. For a more detailed history of the alternative media, see Richard Lance Keeble, "Peace journalism as political practice: A new, radical look at the theory", in Richard Lance Keeble, John Tulloch and Florian Zollmann (eds.) *Peace Journalism, War and Conflict Resolution* (New York: Peter Lang, 2010, pp. 49–67). For the alternative media in the US, see Lauren Kessler, *The Dissident Press: Alternative Journalism in American History* (Newbury Park, London: Sage Publications, 1984) and Bob Ostertag, *People's Movements, People's Press: The Journalism of Social Justice Movements* (Boston: Beacon Press, 2006). Geoffrey Rips, *The Campaign against the Underground Press* (San Francisco: City Lights Books, 1981), is also an invaluable source. Following a three-year study of government documents acquired through the Freedom of Information Act, Rips concluded that the alternative, peace movement press was the target of "surveillance, harassment and unlawful search and seizure by US government agencies".

References

Allan, S. (2006) *Online News: Journalism and the Internet*. Maidenhead: Open University Press.
Althusser, L. (1969) *For Marx*. London: Penguin.
Andersen, R. (2006) *A Century of Media, a Century of War*. New York: Peter Lang.
Atton, C. (2002) *Alternative Media*. London: Sage.
——(2004) *An Alternative Internet: Radical Media, Politics and Creativity*. Edinburgh: Edinburgh University Press.
Atton, C. and Hamilton, J. F. (2008) *Alternative Journalism*. London: Sage.
Black, J. (2001) *The English Press 1621–1861*. Stroud: Sutton Publishing.
Bourdieu, P. (1998) *On Television*. London: Pluto Press.

Boyd-Barrett, O. (2010) "Recovering agency for the propaganda model: The implications for reporting war and peace." In R. L. Keeble, J. Tulloch and F. Zollmann (eds), *Peace Journalism, War and Conflict Resolution*. New York: Peter Lang (pp. 31–48).

Carruthers, S. L. (2000) *The Media at War: Communication and Conflict in the Twentieth Century*. London: Macmillan Press.

Castells, M. (2009) *Communicative Power*. Oxford: Oxford University Press.

Chapman, J. (2008) "Republican citizenship, ethics and the French revolutionary press." In R. Keeble (ed.), *Communication Ethics Now*. Leicester: Troubador (pp. 131–41).

Chomsky, N. (1989) *Necessary Illusions: Thought Control in Democratic Societies*. London: Pluto.

Collins, R. (1990) "Market closure and the conflict theory of professions." In M. Burrage and R. Torstendahl (eds), *Professions in Theory and History: Rethinking the Study of Professions*. London, Newbury Park and New Delhi: Sage (pp. 24–42).

Conboy, M. (2004) *Journalism: A Critical History*. London: Sage.

Couldry, N. and Curran, J. (eds.) (2003) *Contesting Media Power: Alternative Media in a Networked World*. Lanham, MD: Rowman & Littlefield Publishers.

Curran, J. and Seaton, J. (2004) *Power Without Responsibility: The Press, Broadcasting and New Media in Britain*. London: Routledge (7th ed.).

Davis, M. (1999) *Sylvia Pankhurst: A Life in Radical Politics*. London: Pluto.

Dente Ross, S. (2007) "(De-)constructing conflict: A focused review of war and peace journalism." In D. Shinar and W. Kempf (eds), *Peace Journalism: The State of the Art*. Berlin: Regener (pp. 53–74).

Der Derian, J. (2001) *Virtuous War: Mapping the Military-Industrial-Media-Entertainment Network*. New York: Basic Books.

Dowmunt, T. (2007) "Introduction." In K. Coyer, T. Dowmunt and A. Fountain (eds), *The Alternative Media Handbook*. New York: Routledge (pp. 1–12).

Downing, J. (1984) *Radical Media: The Political Experience of Alternative Communication*. Boston, MA: South End Press.

Forde, S. (2011) *Challenging the News: The Journalism of Alternative and Community Media*. Basingstoke: Palgrave Macmillan.

Galtung, J. (1998) "High road – low road: Charting the course for peace journalism." *Track Two*, 7(4). Centre for Conflict Resolution: South Africa. Retrieved from http://ccrweb.ccr.uct.ac.za/archive/two/7_4/p07_highroad_lowroad.html (accessed 7 April 2009).

Habermas, J. (1974) "The public sphere." *New German Critique*, 3, 49–59.

Hackett, R. A. (2007) "Is peace journalism possible?" In D. Shinar and W. Kempf (eds), *Peace Journalism: The State of the Art*. Berlin: Regener (pp. 75–94).

Harcup, T. (2003) "The unspoken – said: The journalism of the alternative media." *Journalism*, 4(3), 356–76.

——(2013) *Alternative Journalism: Alternative Voices*. London: Routledge.

Hartley, J. (1996) *Popular Reality: Journalism, Modernity and Popular Culture*. London and New York: Arnold.

——(2008) "Journalism as a human right: The cultural approach to journalism." In M. Loffelholz and D. Weaver (eds), *Global Journalism Research: Theories, Methods, Findings, Future*. Oxford: Blackwell (pp. 39–51).

Herman, E. S. and Chomsky, N. (1988) *Manufacturing Consent: The Political Economy of the Mass Media*. New York: Pantheon Books.

Illich, I. (1973) "The professions as a form of imperialism." *New Society*, 13 September, 633–35.

Keeble, R. L. (1997) *Secret State, Silent Press: New Militarism, the Gulf and the Modern Image of Warfare*. Luton: John Libbey.

——(1999) "A Balkan birthday for NATO." *British Journalism Review*, 10(2), 16–20.

——(2000) "New militarism and the manufacture of warfare." In P. Hammond and E. S. Herman (eds), *Degraded Capability: The Media and the Kosovo Crisis*. London: Pluto Press (pp. 59–69).

——(2004) "Information warfare in an age of hyper-militarism.'" In S. Allan and B. Zeliger (eds), *Reporting War*. London: Routledge (pp. 43–58).

——(2010) "Peace journalism as political practice: A new, radical look at the theory." In R. L. Keeble, J. Tulloch and F. Zollmann (eds), *Peace Journalism, War and Conflict Resolution*. New York: Peter Lang (pp. 49–67).

Keeble, R. L. and Mair, J. (eds.) (2012) *The Phone Hacking Scandal: Journalism on Trial*. Bury St Edmunds: Abramis.

Knightley, P. (1982) *The First Casualty: The War Correspondent as Hero, Propagandist and Myth Maker*. London: Quartet.

Lynch, J. (1998) *The Peace Journalism Option*. Taplow: Conflict and Peace Forums.

Lynch, J. and McGoldrick, A. (2005) *Peace Journalism*. Stroud: Hawthorn Press.

MacPherson, M. (2006) *All Government's Lie: The Life and Times of Rebel Journalist I. F. Stone*. New York: Simon & Schuster.

Neale, J. (2001) *The American War: Vietnam 1960–75*. London: Bookmarks.

Nelson, E. (1989) *The British Counter-Culture, 1966–73: A Study of the Underground Press*. London: Macmillan.

Parkin, F. (1979) *Marxism and Class Theory: A Bourgeois Critique*. London: Tavistock Publications.

Rai, M. (2011) 'Peace journalism in practice – *Peace News*: For non-violent revolution.' In R. L. Keeble, J. Tulloch and F. Zollmann (eds), *Peace Journalism, War and Conflict Resolution*. New York: Peter Lang (pp. 207–21).

Rodríguez, C. (2001) *Fissures in the Mediascape: An International Study of Citizen's Media*. Cresskill, NJ: Hampton Press.

Shaw, I. S. (2012) *Human Rights Journalism: Advances in Reporting Distant Humanitarian Interventions*. Houndmills, Basingstoke: Palgrave Macmillan.

Shinar, D. and Kempf, W. (eds.) (2007) *Peace Journalism: The State of the Art*. Berlin: Regener.

Shoemaker, P. J. and Reese, S. D. (1996) *Mediating the Message: Theories of Influences on Mass Media Content*. New York: Longman.

Sparks, C. (1985) "The working-class press: Radical and revolutionary alternatives." *Media, Culture and Society*, 7, 133–46.

Waltz, M. (2005) *Alternative and Activist Media*. Edinburgh: Edinburgh University Press.

30
BEYOND THE FIRST STORY
Developing the citizen journalist identity

Mary Angela Bock

In this era of the smartphone, coffee shop wifi and YouTube, the question of the twenty-first century may not be 'Who is a journalist?' but 'Who *isn't?*' Citizen witnesses provided some of the most immediate visual coverage of the Sumatran tsunami of 2004 and the London subway bombings of 2007 (Gordon, 2007). Iran's 'green' revolution of 2009 and the Egyptian Spring were also said to be fuelled by the sharing of information via social media (Ali and Fahmy, 2013). In one generation, television news has gone from an expensive skill speciality to an arena in which children can participate. Welcome to post-modernity's Tower of Babel, where everyone can be a journalist, many commit journalistic acts, a few are paid and still others take pride in contributing to the public sphere as permanent, unpaid outsiders –alternative journalists, to use Atton's (2009) term.

Much of the scholarship on this complex set of circumstances has focused on the *product* of such enterprises, the blogs, stories and photos that result from non-professional media work (Domingo and Heinonen, 2008; Singer, 2005). Some have taken an ethnographic approach and studied the ways professionals and non-professionals interact, and how professionals have attempted to discursively maintain their boundaries (Deuze, 2005; Garcelon, 2006; Platon and Deuze, 2003). This chapter attempts to do both, looking at stories and at human activity, but using a slightly different theoretical lens, to look not at typologies of occupations and professions, but at notions of identity and practice. I argue that citizen journalism can be conceived of as a form of routine truth-telling, one that is shaping its own practices for fact-finding, narrative-composing and audience-building.

My argument is derived from a research project that has employed ethnographic methods (interviews and observations) to explore the development of journalistic identity for those outsiders, some of whom call themselves 'citizen journalists', but others who identify primarily as activists and a few who consider themselves to be alternative press journalists. What sorts of practices, both material and discursive, are associated with these various activities? My material was collected in two American cities: Philadelphia, Pennsylvania, and Austin, Texas. The former was the site of a video workshop for citizen media activism. The latter is the geographic centre of a media anomaly: a generally liberal enclave of progressive activism located in the

middle of a politically conservative state and home to a wide variety of citizen journalism, activist media and alternative news outlets. While the chapter is limited by
its American context, by approaching the subject through the wide lens of citizen
journalism as routine truth-telling, I hope that the argument adds value to a broader
international conversation about alternative journalism.

Witnessing

Witnessing is historically a foundational part of the journalistic impulse. Zelizer
(2007) identified it as a 'key word' of the sort canonised by Raymond Williams
(1976). Peters (2001) created a typology that teased out the ways witnessing is performed ritualistically, corporeally or in mediated ways. In his overview of new
media, witnessing and contemporary journalism, Allan (2013) describes a wide and
variable conceptual territory and pushes back against 'old binaries' that often mark
the debates about citizen journalism. For, while witnessing is one of its foundational
concepts, journalism does not own this keyword. To bear witness, particularly in
times of crisis, is considered a sacred responsibility. Religious rituals often focus on
texts that recorded the witnessing of saints and martyrs. Courtroom witnesses place
their hands on Bibles, their hearts or, in ancient times, their testes, as they swear to
bear witness truthfully.

Though journalism could once claim routine practices of publicly bearing witness
to human events, this claim is no longer exclusive (Allan, 2013; Atton, 2009; Gordon,
2007). Journalistic witnessing was problematic even before today's technology emerged.
Zelizer's work on TV news (1990), for example, pointed to numerous ways the
notion was abused in journalistic discourse. Some of the early sociological studies of
news practices pointed out the way routines and official accounts could obscure
eyewitness accounts (Lang and Lang, 1953; Molotch and Lester, 1974; Tuchman,
1972). For most of the twentieth century, journalists dominated a form of what
Peters (2001) calls 'second order' or mediated witnessing. But even here, journalists
themselves were often apart from what they saw, using pool feeds and press hand-
outs while still claiming the authority of witnessing (Bock, 2009; Cook, 2005).
Mobile media, especially smartphone cameras and technologies that enable live
video streaming, have encroached upon this territory, inspiring confusion, intro-
spection and critique by professional journalists as they try to redraw the borders.
Non-professional bloggers have also attacked the vagaries of second-order witnesses,
notably in the coverage of the Mumbai bombing of 2008 (Allan, 2013). The act of
eye-witnessing, of attending to events with one's body on location, while always
valued in public discourse, seems to be emerging as the discursive 'gold standard' in
the digital realm.

Journalism may not 'own' witnessing, but it has drawn its borders in other ways,
largely through practices designed to support an ideology of truth-telling. The journalistic ideology varies across cultures, though research by Hanitzsh et al. (2010) and
Deuze (2005) points to significant common values, such as detachment and government
monitoring, but variable adherence to notions of objectivity and interventionism. In
her application of the notion of the interpretive community to journalism, Zelizer

(1993) has explained how journalists maintain their authority through discourse *about* their work and through the discursive practices *of* their work. Sociologists have noted that the boundaries of professional journalism are considerably vulnerable because of the work's discursive nature (Reich and Lahav, 2011).

But those working outside the mainstream media organisations are not merely pushing at the border; they are not necessarily 'reporter wannabes'. My project's interviews and observations indicate that alternative journalists seem to be developing their own interpretative community, with their own ways of talking *about* and of *doing* that work. Such practices may be what separate the accidental witness from the person who goes beyond that first story.

Truth-telling as a routine

The individuals who participated in this research may be divided into three categories: alternative publication journalists, writing for a niche audience; self-described citizen journalists; and 'accountability activists' who do not claim to be journalists but whose activity and discourse bear close similarity to newswork. Most of the participants used video cameras as part of their work, though the alternative press journalists (significantly, as I will discuss) work primarily with text or audio. Like the international sample of professionals surveyed by Hanitzsh et al. (2010), these subjects vary in their appreciation of 'objectivity' (particularly in its traditional American form) while still making claims to truth. As Atton has suggested:

> Alternative journalism suggests that authority does not need to be located institutionally or professionally; that credibility and trustworthiness can be derived from accounts of lived experience, not only from objectively detached reporting; and that there need be no imperative to separate facts from values.
>
> (Atton, 2009: 284)

All participants present themselves as practitioners of routine truth-telling, whether they are taxi drivers learning to shoot and edit, veteran reporters trying to maintain a hyper-local web product or the so-called 'cop watchers' who routinely monitor police activity. The differences between them lie in their divergence from mainstream journalism in how they construct and utilise what Tuchman (1978) called the "web of facticity". Three dimensions have emerged from this work thus far: differences in how facts are gathered (which changes what facts are gathered); how those facts are narrativised; and how the audience is sought and addressed.

Fact-finding

The participants in my study were generally motivated by a critique of the mainstream's methods for finding and choosing facts, reflecting an impulse to rely less on official sources and more on the realities they see and experience. Ostertag and Tuchman (2012) suggested that citizen journalists might even be better suited for this type of fact-gathering than professionals, by virtue of their everyday life and social networks. Beyond their 'street-level' knowledge, though, the participants in this study spoke of a distinct desire to regularly cover stories they believe are neglected in mainstream news. Significantly, the younger subjects who are involved in police-accountability activism or citizen journalism consider their cameras to be part of their fact-finding.

In Philadelphia, 'Lynda' explained that she signed up to learn video storytelling so she could fill in where she saw mainstream media fall short:

> Video lets you show what you feel is more important. 'Cause you watch some things, you read things and it don't have all the necessary information sometimes. Sometimes it's just a little bit of this and not enough of that.

'Ron', for example, often covers the very same events as mainstream television stations in his city, but says he stays longer, gets more interviews and does more to capture the nature of the event. He tries to let the activists speak for themselves. His colleague, 'Hope', started out covering protests on behalf of the Palestinian activists, but soon realised that peace activism was related to other progressive causes, such as workers' rights or immigration reform. She spends her spare time covering events with her own video camera: "I got interested in the other things because I needed also more things to spread the word through video," she explained, "so I was just going to many different events." Yet another independent activist filmmaker says he spends nearly all his free time covering events related to the Occupy movement, creating long-form videos designed to give viewers a richer look at events.

The police-accountability activists also use the camera as a fact-finding tool, and they are developing unique video techniques. At one workshop, a leader explained about the danger of stepping into a police officer's periphery and the need for camera operators to triangulate their positions in order to obtain adequate angles. Smartphones are their preferred technology, because members are expected to respond whenever they see police activity:

> It's not the old days where you'd have to have the two spools hanging off your side and you have this big camera. So that's very, very powerful.
>
> ('Jesse')

> You needed the 5 o'clock news back in the day to get a story out. Now anybody can be the reporter the journalist and with no swing or bias in any way it's like turn the camera on here we are my actions, your actions, and you bring everybody to that scenario.
>
> ('Lance')

One graduate of the Philadelphia workshop, a taxi driver, has taken to keeping a camera in his cab to cover news as he finds it. Much like a traditional reporter might cover a beat, police-accountability activists in Austin make regular rounds of the city's nightclub district to monitor the way officers clear the street when the bars close.

Members of the alternative press were less likely to use cameras for their fact-finding, and instead chose the more conventional methods of reporting. They are using social media to deliver information, but conceive of fact-finding in the traditional sense, as a discursive, question-driven process. A former underground newspaper editor spoke of a fellow blogger this way:

> [He's] one of those committed investigative reporters who goes out and does all of his stuff and he has a few other people that work with him but it's mostly that's one guy who's learned over a long period of time how to dig up information and he's in some ways, even though he works online, he's kind of like an old fashioned you know investigative reporter.
>
> ('Frank')

That same former editor builds his blog and community radio show around his source network from past activism, runs stories written from former and new colleagues online and produces a downloadable talk show. Nevertheless, 'Frank' is not completely comfortable with the new media world:

> I have trouble understanding twitter as a communication mechanism, even though it's probably the most powerful one out there right now. I just don't understand like condensing information into such short chunks.

The editor of an online alternative news source says his volunteer hyper-local writers tend to write more opinion than traditional news, and usually do not interview multiple sources the way mainstream reporters might. He continues to look for and nurture good writers for the site.

The three categories of activity collected here reflect a spectrum of a journalistic epistemology that is significant for its shift from word to image. The most conventional of the participants remain "word-people", to use Lowrey's (2002) phrase, while the activists and self-described citizen journalists draw their authority from the technical perfection of their cameras. These differences in turn shape the way these alternative practitioners compose their stories.

Composing narratives

Alternative presses have a long tradition of representing marginalised groups, and historically they have tended to adopt discursive techniques of storytelling similar to those in the mainstream. Stories in the *Village Voice*, for example, might have had a different ideological bent than the *Wall Street Journal*, but they still apply the third-person declarative voice, maintain a certain linguistic distance from the subject and clearly separate the writer from those being quoted. This was reflected by the alternative press journalists interviewed for this project, who emphasised their own writing credentials or, in the case of the online editor, the need to attract local volunteers with good linguistic skills:

> I bury the stuff that isn't good and I promote the stuff that is. I don't get enough. The way it works for me more is that certain community writers who are good, I encourage them to keep continue writing and then they grow to like that exposure.
>
> ('Bob')

John tried to train volunteers in investigative journalism, and found himself frustrated:

> The only product that ever came out of any of those people was the free-lancers in the group that are paid to do something. Other than that I never got anything that was useable.
>
> ('John')

The police-accountability activists and citizen journalists, however, are using their cameras and deploying documentary-style filmic narrative:

> So immediately when I am filming a traffic stop, my actual intention, my philosophy when I'm filming isn't just to film a police officer it's to hold everybody accountable that my camera's in view of, and including myself.
>
> ('Lance')

> And we will give our own narrative, as we're filming, but we're not trying to influence the scene other than letting the cops know that we're there so that they modify their behaviour so that they dampen any aggressive behaviour that they may have.
>
> ('Jesse')

'Ron' and 'Hope' do not record their own voices into their reports, and describe their pieces as a variant of a music video:

> But then I started from doing just really basic shots with the camera to actually like panning or zooming to having a creative eye, develop over that period of time where I could see what would be an interesting shot do with the camera, like, creatively.
>
> ('Hope')

Some of the members of the Philadelphia workshop did record their own voices, but in a sort of linguistic collage, switching narrators without warning, and in one case incorporating chants into their conclusion. As with the differences in fact-finding, the differences in compositional style seem related to the use of visual media. The younger subjects in the project seem unworried about scripting or language; instead, they weave diegetic narratives with images, in keeping with a reliance on the camera as a source of authority in place of institutional support (Bock, 2012). The alternative press journalists, already more accustomed to traditional discursive reportage, utilise the associated traditional form of writing. The split is significant in the way it associates a more conventional form of journalism with writing skills, a dimension often lost in discussions about professionalism, which usually centre on ideologies of objectivity. The influence of technology (and the individuals' comfort with using technology) is also evident in another dimension of practice, audience construction.

Building audiences

Whether they called themselves activists, cop-watchers or citizen journalists, participants in this research are all seeking to be heard or seen by a larger, unknown public.

While it is true that friends and sympathisers are their mostly likely followers, the transcripts reveal a desire to construct a larger, public audience. Participants pointed to the power of social media as a means to seek out new supporters, viewers and readers. 'Accidental' journalists use these tools too, of course, to share their moments. But these routine truth-tellers are deliberately seeking more listeners, viewers and readers. Again, however, being comfortable with new media made a difference in how these subjects constructed their audience. The younger cohort uses social media to seek new followers:

> I believe that still the strongest aspect of [the organization] is that it's decentralized. We're a one stop shop for people sharing ideas and then furthermore people saying this was good this is bad and then learning from one another about how to either fix and hold police accountable more or highlight and document the wrongdoing more thoroughly.
>
> ('Lance')

> We don't have a formal membership. We have people who are extremely engaged, where they're doing stuff on a weekly basis. I would say that that amounts to about a dozen people. And there are people who get engaged for very big events and I would say that that number is probably in the low hundreds. Like one hundred to two hundred. And then there are people who just are willing to post a lot, calling the radio shows who donate money to us and I don't, I've never been able to try to calculate how many those people are.
>
> ('Jesse')

In contrast, the more 'traditional' of these non-traditional journalists seemed comfortable with using the internet to reach the existing audience and maintain ties with an established base.

> If [the website] becomes a desirable thing, like if people think it's cool, think its works, it will grow and then it will create more demand, um you know it's um. The strongest motivator for community journalists will be um having somewhere to post their thoughts that may perceive to be you know the thing, you know like something that people read.
>
> ('Bob')

> There's the connection because a lot of the people do write for us, are people who we've known or have been involved since those days. So it actually has extended that community and so there's a sense of perspective, a sense of historical perspective to a lot of what we do.
>
> ('Frank')

The emerging practices of citizen journalism seem to be derived from two impulses: the use of technology either as a source of authority or as a means to build the audience and a desire to provide a new perspective. All three categories of subjects for this research shared the latter, seeing themselves to varying degrees as a foil to the mainstream. But technology split these participants according to their comfort level and their reliance on image-based discourse as evidence for their perspective.

Conclusion

Early in the citizen journalism movement, one newcomer commented that "I wish I'd known how hard it is to do journalism well. I've now learned by doing it how time-consuming it is to report, write, edit and fact-check news stories with integrity" (Parr, 2005). Everyone in my study reported their attempts to do some of this type of work, but only the ones most wedded to traditional practice, the alternative press participants, expressed frustration about the work. Members of the alternative press also found themselves struggling for financial resources. Yet, while they were work-ing as volunteers, they did not necessarily describe themselves as citizen journalists, but as *journalists*:

> We had certain standards that we were trying to maintain. So you separate the citizen from the journalist and I think that's an advanced way of thinking about what is citizen journalism as opposed to what is professional journalism.
>
> ('John')

In contrast, the newer players, the self-described citizen journalists and the police accountability activists, expressed frustration only with mainstream representations of reality. Unlike the alternative press group, which attempts to tell different stories using traditional methods, this younger, more image-centred group, is trying to shed light on different stories with new methods. Those doing what would be considered the most 'subjective' work, the police-accountability activists, conceive of themselves as routine truth-tellers, comfortable with the idea that what they do could be considered a form of journalism:

> I do believe that every single person who has a video camera or an audio device or anything, when they're documenting what the police are doing, that at the moment they are a citizen journalist and I don't think you have to be a credentialed member of the press to be considered a journalist.
>
> ('Jesse')

Not all witnessing is journalism, and Allan correctly warns us that witnessing is not always truthful (2013). Yet, if truth remains elusive, sincerity can be located in the individual actor. Without institutional support, that individual actor might rely on the camera for authoritative power, using the image in context of a truth claim. Alternative journalism, with its varied practices, forms and labels, seems to share a common intent to tell the truth as seen by the viewer. That the practices and forms diverge somewhat from traditional journalism may reflect, in part, this epistemological shift. Atton (2009) argues that while the academy had started to contend with the significance of citizen journalism, details about its practice were as yet neglected. This chapter attempted to fill that gap by examining how some practices of alternative journalism are taking shape. Based on interviews with a variety of subjects, three dimensions of practice emerged, with the forms of practice shaped by facility with new technology.

In a world that delivers an information tsunami, not merely a 'tide' (as Graber, 1988, has it), it may seem more important than ever to identify what is journalism and what is not. And yet, for those citizen journalists, alternative press writers, documentary activists and all the others involved in this wild, wild web of truth-seeking: if a photo is not retouched, if the quotes are accurate, if the facts can be confirmed, then might the work not speak for itself? Focusing attention on who is and is not a journalist also can and does invite frustration in a world that can deliver a global audience to anyone with a smartphone and a wifi connection. While scholars and journalists might debate about the use of various labels, these individuals are making a routine habit of documenting their world and telling the truth as they see it. When someone claims to be telling the truth to a public audience, perhaps it is most useful to attend to what they are doing, rather than who they are.

Acknowledgements

All names of participants have been changed for the sake of anonymity in accordance with a protocol approved by the Institutional Review Board of the University of Texas at Austin.

Further reading

John Durham Peters's (2001) typology from *Media, Culture and Society* is a good place to start thinking about witnessing and its connection to truthfulness, as is Barbie Zelizer's (2007) article about eye-witnessing and journalism, "On having been there." Readers might also want to consult *Media Witnessing*, an edited volume by Paul Frosh and Amit Pinchevski (2009). In particular, chapter 2 by Frosh, "Telling presences", is helpful in terms of theory, and chapter 7, "From danger to trauma", by Carrie Rentschler, in terms of practice. Finally, for more on visual citizen journalism specifically, readers should look to M. A. Bock's chapter "Little brother is watching" in S. Allan and E. Thorson's *Citizen Journalism: Global Perspectives*, vol. 2 (2014), and Mette Mortenson's (2011) case study of the Neda Soltan video.

References

Ali, S. R. and Fahmy, S. (2013) "Gatekeeping and citizen journalism: The use of social media during the recent uprisings in Iran, Egypt, and Libya." *Media, War and Conflict*, 6, 55–69.

Allan, S. (2013) *Citizen Witnessing*. Cambridge: Polity Press.

Atton, C. (2009) "Why alternative journalism matters." *Journalism: Theory, Practice, Criticism*, 10, 283–85.

Bock, M. A. (2009) "Who's minding the gate? Pool feeds, video subsidies and political images." *International Journal of Press and Politics*, 14, 257–78.

——(2012) "Citizen video journalists and truthful authority: Reviving the role of the witness." *Journalism: Theory, Practice and Criticism*, 13, 639–53.

——(2014) "Little brother is watching: Citizen video journalists and witness narratives." In S. Allan and E. Thorson (eds), *Citizen Journalism: Global Perspectives*, vol. 2. New York: Peter Lang (pp. 349–60).

Cook, T. E. (2005) *Governing the News: The News Media as a Political Institution*. Chicago: University of Chicago Press.

Deuze, M. (2005) What is journalism? *Journalism*, 6(4), 442–64.

Domingo, D. and Heinonen, A. (2008). "Weblogs and journalism: A typology to explore the blurring boundaries." *NORDICOM Review*, 29, 3–15.

Frosh, P. and Pinchevski, A. (eds) (2009). *Media Witnessing: Testimony in the Age of Mass Communication*. Basingstoke: Palgrave Macmillan.

Garcelon, M. (2006) "The 'Indymedia' experiment: The internet as movement facilitator against institutional control." *Convergence*, 12, 55–82.

Gordon, J. (2007) "The mobile phone and the public sphere: Mobile phone usage in three critical situations." *Convergence*, 13, 307–319.

Graber, D. A. (1988) *Processing the News: How People Tame the Information Tide*. White Plains, NY: Longman.

Hanitzsh, T. F. H. et al. (2010) "Mapping journalism cultures across nations." *Journalism Studies*, 12(3), 273–93.

Lang, K. and Lang, G. (1953) "The unique perspective of television and its effect: A pilot study." *American Sociological Review*, 18, 3–12.

Lowrey, W. (2002) "Word people vs. picture people: Normative differences and strategies for control over work among newsroom subgroups." *Mass Communication and Society*, 5, 411–32.

Molotch, H. and Lester, M. (1974) "News as purposive behaviour: On the strategic use of routine events, accidents and scandals." *American Sociological Review*, 39, 101–12.

Mortensen, M. (2011) "When citizen photojournalism sets the news agenda: Neda Agha Soltan as a Web 2.0 icon of post-election unrest in Iran." *Global Media and Communication*, 7, 4–16.

Ostertag, S. F. and Tuchman, G. (2012) "When innovation meets legacy." *Information, Communication and Society*, 15, 909–31.

Parr, B. (2005) "Things I wish I'd known before I became a citizen journalist." *Neiman Reports*, 59(4), 29–31.

Peters, J. D. (2001) "Witnessing." *Media, Culture and Society*, 23, 707–23.

Platon, S. and Deuze, M. (2003) "Indymedia journalism." *Journalism*, 4, 336–55.

Reich, Z. and Lahav, H. (2011) "Are reporters replaceable? Literary authors produce a daily newspaper." *Journalism: Theory, Practice and Criticism*, 13, 417–34.

Singer, J. B. (2005) "The political J-blogger: 'Normalizing' a new media form to fit old norms and practices." *Journalism*, 6, 173–98.

Tuchman, G. (1972) "Objectivity as strategic ritual: An examination of newsmen's notions of objectivity." *American Journal of Sociology*, 77, 660–79.

——(1978). *Making News: A Study in the Construction of Reality*. London: Free Press.

Williams, R. (1976) *Keywords: A Vocabulary of Culture and Society*. Oxford: Oxford University Press.

Zelizer, B. (1990) "Where is the author in American TV news? On the construction and presentation of proximity, authorship and journalistic authority." *Semiotica*, 80, 37.

——(1993) "Journalists as interpretive communities." *Critical Studies in Mass Communication*, 10, 219–37.

——(2007) "On 'Having been there': Eyewitnessing as a journalistic key word." *Critical Studies in Media Communication*, 24, 408.

31
'IPHONE-WIELDING AMATEURS'
The rise of citizen photojournalism

Stuart Allan

In July 2000, an Air France Concorde jet on its way to New York crashed shortly after taking off from Charles de Gaulle Airport in Paris, killing 109 people on board and four more on the ground. News organisations, moving swiftly to put together a major breaking story, quickly discovered that they were reliant on citizen witnesses for descriptions of what they had seen and heard, as well as for any imagery they were able to contribute. "The sight of Concorde, the world's fastest passenger aircraft, making its doomed ascent into French skies trailing a plume of fire seconds before exploding in a ball of flame, is certain to be one of the defining news images of the 21st century," journalist Valerie Darroch (2000) wrote at the time. The image in question, which she suggested was likely to be "indelibly etched on the collective memory", had been taken by an amateur photographer. Hungarian engineering student Andras Kisgergely, enjoying his hobby of plane-spotting with a friend, had been near the scene with a small Canon Reflex 35mm camera. Reuters purchased the rights to Kisgergely's image – Brian MacArthur (2000) of *The Times* having dubbed him "the newspaper hero of the night" for his photo-reportage – relaying it around the world in time for it to feature prominently on front pages the next day. Toshihiko Sato, a Japanese businessperson waiting to board a flight, also happened to shoot a newsworthy image, capturing the instant the engine burst into flames. Rights for its use were secured by a British picture agency, Buzz Pictures, which in turn negotiated exclusive terms with a London newspaper, the *Mirror* (Rees, 2000).

"Now, everyone is a potential cameraman", Jonathan Duffy (2000) reported for BBC News Online at the time. Crediting amateurs with capturing the most significant images of the crash, he described what proved to be "the most dramatic evidence of all", namely a video shot by the wife of a Spanish lorry driver – her name was kept anonymous – as the two drove past the perimeter of the airport. "The grainy, 15-second piece of footage, in which the flames appear to have engulfed the rear of the jet," Duffy observed, "is a reminder of how everyday technology has brought a chilling reality to television news." Evidently the couple were paid a 'generous' amount by a Madrid television station, Antena 3 (later revealed to be £200), which in turn negotiated the global rights with the Associated Press Television News agency for a more substantial sum. The 'amateur footage' was vividly described in press reports, including details such as "The camera pans to the left and the truck's driver in the next seat is caught in profile. Behind him through the window, the grainy, shaky picture shows bright, orange-and-white fire enveloping the left side of the plane" (*Ottawa Citizen*, 2000). A report for AP by Paul Ames (2000) continued: "Like some monstrous, wounded bird, the great white plane struggles to gain height as a bubbling, blazing spout of flame and black smoke bellows behind." While critics such as Madeleine Bunting (2000) in *The Guardian* decried the news media's "appetite for catastrophe", the "saturation" coverage of the crash "exposing our voyeurism" as members of "ghoulish crowds" fascinated by "dramatic immediacy" for its own sake, a bidding war for this video of the airplane's final seconds underscored its commercial value. "The amount paid for the Concorde film is by no means the highest paid for amateur video footage," Julian Lee (2000) remarked in *The Times*, "but it underlines the increasingly important role that members of the public are playing in news-gathering."

Fast-forward to contemporary crisis events, and what was considered to be the extraordinary nature of citizens' contributions to a major breaking news story have become ordinary, even routine features of daily reportage for news organisations around the globe. A telling comparison with the Concorde incident would be the way vital details regarding the crash landing of Asiana Flight 214 at San Francisco International Airport on 6 July 2013 were being relayed by citizen witnesses almost instantly (see also Thorsen and Allan, 2014). For television networks and online news sites hurriedly marshalling video imagery for special reports piecing the news story together, most of what could be secured by their own journalists arriving after the crash featured long-range shots of the wrecked passenger jet stranded on the runway. Appreciably more compelling in visual terms – echoing Concorde thirteen years earlier – were the short clips of precipitous footage provided by citizen witnesses who happened to be near the scene at the time. Not surprisingly, their impromptu forms of reportage were swiftly appropriated as material from "actual non-journalistic sources", in the words of one CNN reporter, who then added that "this really is the rise of citizen journalism" (Avlon, 2013). In marked contrast with the Concorde crisis, social networking platforms rendered these diverse forms of reportage almost instantly available to publics near and far without journalistic mediation by news organisations.

YouTube user Alek Yoo (sfprepper415) recorded black smoke billowing from the airplane resting on the tarmac, its rear fuselage torn away, from where he stood in the airport terminal. On the third floor of a nearby hotel, 18-year-old Jennifer Solis – described by ABC News in its report as an amateur videographer– recorded the moment the emergency chutes were deployed from the exit doors, as well as the efforts of firefighters trying to dowse the fire ignited in the cabin. Having heard the sound of the crash, she had quickly grabbed her digital camera, later recalling: "I immediately went outside; I saw the big cloud of dirt, and I started recording immediately." Solis said she could not believe the surreal scene occurring before her, remarking: "[It] was just the first time I ever experienced something like this. I usually see things like this on the news" (cited in Louie, 2013). Even more remarkable was the amateur video shot by aircraft buff Fred Hayes, who happened to be videoing airplanes landing as he walked along San Francisco Bay with his wife during a weekend visit. "When I caught the plane coming into view, everything looked fine at first until I kind of fixed my gaze on him, and I seen his nose up in the air," Hayes told CNN. "And then I just totally locked on him. I thought he was going to take off and go up, and then he just kept going down" (cited in Smith and Hall, 2013). Hayes's harrowing footage captured the airplane's descent leading to the violent moment of impact with the seawall and the ensuing carnage, thereby helping resolve divergent views – "a maelstrom of conflicting information", in the words of one news commentator – regarding what had actually transpired. The 40-second clip, obtained exclusively by CNN, also included the audio recording of the couple's anguished responses as they looked on, lending an emotive sense of the personal distress they were experiencing.

The significance of these and related forms of citizen witnessing being uploaded across fluidly ad hoc collaborative networks, where the resources of sites such as Twitter, Facebook, Path, Flickr, Instagram, Tumblr and YouTube were mobilised to considerable journalistic advantage, seldom received more than passing comment in mainstream press reports. In marked contrast with how the 'amateur video footage' of the Concorde crash was heralded for its transformative potential more than a decade earlier, this blurring of reportorial boundaries may be read as being indicative of the relative extent to which citizen journalism has been effectively normalised where breaking news of crisis events is concerned. Remarkably, the recent decade has seen the gradual unfolding of a profound shift in public perceptions, namely that contributions of citizens who happen to be first at the scene have become so commonplace as to be almost expected (indeed, explanations for the absence of such material may well be necessary in ensuing news accounts). Citizens – be they victims, bystanders, first-responders, officials, law enforcement, combatants, activists or the like – together are actively engaging in newsmaking by crafting for their own purposes a diverse array of tools, methods and strategies to relay first-person reports, increasingly in real time as crisis events progress.

Such spontaneous, spur-of-the-moment responses, so often motivated by a desire to connect with others, go to the heart of current debates about citizen journalism, one of the most challenging issues confronting mainstream news organisations today. Accordingly, our mode of enquiry here will be conceptually driven in order to contribute to theory-building for future research in citizen-centred newsmaking. In striving to de-familiarise the familiar tenets of these dynamics, our attention turns in the first instance to illustrate how wider factors, particularly economic ones, are recasting news organisations' commitments to photojournalism. It is by situating citizen news photography within these evolving contexts, I argue, that we can secure an effective vantage point from which to examine how its relative affordances and possibilities are slowly, unevenly consolidating in journalistic terms. Next, the chapter will proceed to elaborate a conceptual basis for critical explorations of the wider implications being engendered, not least for our changing conceptions of photojournalism's civic responsibilities within wider participatory cultures.

Professionalism under threat

Calls for the reinvention of photojournalism have been resounding ever louder over recent years, the traditional definitional boundaries demarcating the amateur from the professional news photographer proving increasingly problematic. Searching questions are being asked within multimedia newsrooms about how best to re-profile their visual news provision within this climate of uncertainty. More often than not in recent years, it seems, the person first on the scene of a crisis event with a camera has been an ordinary citizen. The active participation of amateur photographers in news-gathering processes corresponds to the growing ubiquity of cheaper, easier-to-handle digital cameraphones, as well as the ease with which ensuing imagery can be uploaded and shared across social networking sites. For varied reasons, priorities and motivations, so-called 'accidental photojournalists' have been widely perceived to be redefining the nature of news photography.

A telling case in point was the sudden announcement made by managers at the Chicago *Sun-Times* in May 2013 that the newspaper would be eliminating its entire photography department, thereby terminating the employment of 28 photographers and photo editors. The day of the announcement, *Sun-Times* reporters received a memo from Managing Editor Craig Newman (2013) informing them that they would be undergoing 'mandatory' training in 'iPhone photography basics' in order to supplement the work of freelance photographers (and, it was presumed, contributions from members of the public as well) wherever possible. "In the coming days and weeks," he stated, "we'll be working with all editorial employees to train and outfit you as much as possible to produce the content we need." The *Sun-Times*'s 'knee-jerk reaction' to financial difficulties, as it was characterised by some critics, appears to be consistent with a growing pattern to 'outsource' photographic responsibilities in order to better ensure the viability of news organisations under threat of closure by anxious investors. "It's not common, but it's not unprecedented either," Kenny Irby of the Poynter Institute observed at the time. "This is part of an ongoing trend that has been happening for the last 10 years or so in American newsrooms, with the downsizing and devaluing of professional photojournalism" (cited in Marek, 2013). The price such organisations are paying is proving to be considerable, not least with regard to sustaining a reputation – or 'brand', in managerial discourse – based upon public trust to inspire loyalty among readers. "While our reporters are doing the best they can to take photos with their iPhones and still trying to deliver quality stories, visually, the story has taken a big hit," Beth Kramer of Chicago's Newspaper Guild told ABC News two months after the *Sun-Times* decision. In Pulitzer Prize winner John H. White's case, it was a 35-year career at the *Sun-Times* that came to an abrupt end. "It was as if they pushed a button and deleted a whole culture of photojournalism," he surmised. "Humanity is being robbed," he added, "by people with money on their minds" (cited in Irby, 2013).

Photojournalism's 'death spiral' is gaining momentum, several commentators have been warning since, with its status as a professional craft in danger of unravelling. While the *Sun Times* has quietly re-instated a small number of the photographers it abruptly dismissed, elsewhere other news organisations have invoked similarly drastic cost-cutting measures. In Australia, for example, the Fairfax media company – owner of newspapers, magazines, radio and digital media operating there and in New Zealand – announced in May 2014 that 80 posts would be terminated, initially including three-quarters of the photography staff in Sydney and Melbourne. Despite strong revenue performance for the company overall (it reported net profits after tax of $193 million in February 2014), it was argued that the perceived savings from outsourcing photography to Getty Images, a stock photo agency, would be in the interests of shareholders. Few readers would notice the difference, managers insisted, when defending the 'restructure' plan in the face of vocal opposition over professional photographers being made redundant. "These people have put their lives on the line, year in, year out," photojournalist Tamara Dean of the *Sydney Morning Herald* (a Fairfax title) pointed out. "When so many journalists have to work on the phone these days, the photographers are the eyes, the witnesses to history in the making," she added. "Removing those eyes will mean becoming even less a witness to real news" (cited in ABC News, 2014). Evidently Fairfax's new 'sourcing model' presumed readers themselves would be relied upon to generate news imagery to complement Getty's efforts, further helping push costs down. "The age of the camera phone has probably bluffed media management into believing that photojournalism is a luxury," former Fairfax photographer Chris Beck (2014) said at the time. "Blurry amateur phone video and pictures of fights and fires on the news and internet are becoming more pervasive because they are immediate."

While this re-inflection of journalistic values to prioritise economic factors is hardly a new phenomenon, warnings about the impact of outsourcing on standards of quality would seem to be going unheeded in many news organisations around the world. "In an age when we are assaulted by a blizzard of imagery, you need skilful and dedicated professionals to lift your publication above the ordinary," veteran news photographer Mike Bowers (2014) contends, yet "quality" was "not a word that had much sway with managers" under financial pressure, at least in his experience as a managing editor of photography for daily newspapers. Time and again, in my reading, sharp criticisms of 'iPhone-wielding amateurs' and the like figure conspicuously in grim prognostications of photojournalism's impending demise, while broader structural imperatives – typically framed via discourses of 'fiscal responsibility', 'economic competitiveness', 'global patterns and trends', and so forth – elude sustained attention. Evidence of public concern is readily apparent, such as in the case of the petition to save the Fairfax photography jobs that garnered more than 11,000 signatures in 48 hours (Bodey, 2014), but also on a more regular basis, not least in the comment sections of news sites (Allan, 2014). Still, sweeping claims about citizen journalism persist, with direct correlations frequently drawn between the rise of the camera-equipped cell or mobile telephones and the fall of professional photojournalism.

'Everyone becomes a photojournalist'

Disputes over what counts as photojournalism, and thereby who qualifies to be a photojournalist, are hardly new, of course. Such tensions have long reverberated in popular accounts of the rise of the cameraphone and its perceived impact – both celebratory and condemnatory alike – on the reportorial world. The anticipated implications for the fledgling device – 'everyone becomes a photojournalist' – have proven to be surprisingly close to the mark, with the capacity for the real-time conveyance of recorded moments of personal significance to the user engendering intense interest.

In striving to document events unfolding before them, citizens are generating first-hand, embodied forms of 'truth telling' – via digital photographs, camcorder video, mobile telephone footage and the like – of intense interest to news organisations while, at the same time, undercutting the proclaimed epistemic certainties of professionalised norms, values and protocols (see also Atton, 2012; Blaagaard, 2013; Cottle, 2013; Thorsen and Allan, 2014). Breaking news of crisis events, in particular, have recurrently highlighted the extent to which photo editors find themselves relying upon imagery shot by non-professionals to convey first-hand perspectives. Recent examples abound, encompassing citizen photo-reportage shot in war and conflict zones (Allan, 2013a; Alper, 2014; Kristensen and Mortensen, 2013; Matheson and Allan, 2009; Wall and El Zahed, 2014), as well as from the chaotic scenes of natural disasters, such as earthquakes, hurricanes, tornadoes or floods (Liu et al., 2009; Chouliaraki, 2012; Pantti, Wahl-Jorgensen and Cottle, 2012; Sheller, 2015), as well as accidents, violent incidents or 'terror' attacks (Allan, 2014, Meikle, 2014; Mortensen, T. M., 2014; Reading, 2009; Yaschur, 2012; Zelizer, 2011), among many others. In each instance, to varying degrees, the very amateurishness of citizen imagery tempers normalised conventions of journalistic authority, its up-close invocation of presence, 'I am here' and this is 'what it means to be there', intimately intertwining time, space and place to claim an emotional, often poignant purchase (Allan, 2013a, 2013b; Becker, 2013; Caple, 2014; Mortensen, M., 2014).

Indeed, the frequently astonishing array of images suddenly available when a crisis event unfolds constitutes a vital documentary resource, one typically transgressing traditional conventions of journalistic objectivity – the photojournalist as dispassionate witness – in visual storytelling. Precisely what it means 'to document' is increasingly open to re-interpretation, the ostensibly codified ethics of facticity unsettled by first-person narratives alert to their partial, provisional contingencies. At the same time, social media – Facebook, Twitter, YouTube, Flickr, Instagram and the like – open up potential spaces for dialogic partnership between image-makers, subjects and their viewers. "The open subjectivity of these amateurs, their explicit involvement and the lack of financial incentives can help them reach an audience that is in sympathy with the motives of these ordinary citizens, which may be similar to their own," former *New York Times* photography editor Fred Ritchin (2014) contends. "These images are, to some extent, a shared dialect, created by sharing images via mobile phones and capable of capturing many more details." It is in this fluid interweaving of details that subjectivity displaces objectivity, in his view, and thereby disrupts the "usual pretence of standard journalism" (see also Ritchin, 2013).

Alternative futures

Revisioning photojournalism as a much more collaborative project invites dialogue and debate about how to best develop an alternative ethos of 'standards' consistent with its democratising potentials. The news photographer's ethical imperative to bear witness is an epistemic conviction of professionalism, yet its subtly tacit affirmation in accustomed norms, values and protocols requires self-reflexive attention to be sustained – and, increasingly, safeguarded – in light of challenges posed to its discursive authority, not least by citizens who suddenly find themselves compelled to generate their own first-hand, embodied forms of visual reportage. With this in mind, we need to open up for analysis and critique the ways in which myriad modes of reportorial form, practice and epistemology – all too often obscured by apparent 'revolutions' in technology – are being crafted through the exigencies of citizen-centred photo-reportage. Here we need to delve into the reportage of real-world events with the aim of elucidating the basis for thinking through the imperative of citizen witnessing precisely as it is taken up and re-inflected in wider discourses of journalism.

Such an approach might usefully begin with the observation that prevalent conceptualisations of citizen journalism – and, by extension, citizen photojournalism – typically overlook the fact that it is relatively rare for the individuals under scrutiny to self-identify with such terms in the first place. Instead, what has become a highly polarised debate, one where the rhetorical clash of claim and counterclaim risk reifying into place assertions as self-evident facts. In some instances, citizen journalism is to be championed for its transformative potential, namely to democratise what was once considered the exclusive domain of the seasoned professional and, in so doing, to rehabilitate a fading commitment to fourth-estate priorities. For many of its critics, in marked contrast, citizen-centred journalism is either disparaged as a passing fad, or reduced to simply the latest form of user-generated content in the long history of amateur involvement in news reporting. Many of them insist that images provided by amateurs, typically for free, compromise the craft's viability, leaving its guiding principles on the verge of collapse in a climate of managerial indifference, if not outright neglect. "What newspapers and professional journalists need to realize, and the world has to realize, is that we are news photographers, not somebody out there with an iPhone and a camera, jumping over people to put images on YouTube," John Tlumacki (2013) of the *Boston Globe* observed in the aftermath of the Boston Marathon bombings (see also Allan, 2014). Despite the ubiquity of citizen imagery, he insisted, the news photographer's specialist role remains vital. "I'm so sick of citizen journalism, which kind of dilutes the real professionals' work. I am promoting real journalism, because I think that what we do is kind of unappreciated and slips into the background."

It is in such charged circumstances that we recognise the concept of citizen witnessing is a contested one, which is to acknowledge that it is socially and historically contingent in its inflection across diverse journalistic contexts. Efforts to disentangle 'citizen' from 'witnessing', so as to rethink one in relation to the other, will help us establish a conceptual basis that is distinctive from more conventional approaches to citizen journalism. A first step, in my view, is to engage with pejorative dismissals of the individuals involved. Idealised, self-romanticising configurations of the 'citizen photojournalist' will not withstand closer scrutiny, of course, nor will sweeping dismissals of the individuals involved, particularly where it is alleged they are naive, untrustworthy or irresponsible due to personal motivations revolving around everything from reckless money-making to idle, frivolous spectatorship, or even gratuitous voyeurism. One need not believe that citizen witnesses are compelled by a singular desire to perform their civic duty to democracy to recognise the extent to which such contemptuous, folk, devil-like stereotypes do so many of them a disservice. At the same time, my alignment of the word 'citizen' with 'witnessing' is intended to tease out some of the tacit tensions besetting journalism's investment in certain normative ideals, namely by calling for further consideration not only of the citizen as journalist but also of the journalist as citizen.

Looking ahead, news organisations willing to recast photojournalism anew, namely by making the most of this potential to forge co-operative relationships between professionals and their citizen counterparts, will secure opportunities to rethink its forms, practices and epistemologies at a time of considerable scepticism about future prospects. Collaboration necessarily demands mutual respect through open dialogue, encouraging innovation through experimentation in new modes of photo-based storytelling (see also Allan, 2013a, 2013b; Frosh and Pinchevski, 2009; Lister, 2013; Pantti, Wahl-Jorgensen and Cottle, 2012; Peters and Broersma, 2012). Despite the attendant risks, then, news organisations' purposeful appropriation of the profusion of citizen imagery enables them to narrativise component elements of a news story that would otherwise be impossible to secure by professionals arriving on the scene afterwards. This authority of presence recurrently throws into sharp relief the extent to which these shifting, uneven conditions for visual participation are being pried open for re-negotiation, with an ensuing "ethics of showing" (Linfield, 2010) coalescing into alternative, vernacular modalities of reportorial evidence. In marked contrast with the professional's priorities, citizen imagery typically invites unruly, disruptive ways of seeing, its impulsive materiality threatening to disobey more conventionalised rules of inclusion and exclusion consistent with mainstream journalism's preferred framings. Indeed, it is the professional's valorisation of impersonal detachment, underwritten by the sustaining rituals of craft, which risks appearing outmoded – or worse – in comparison with the 'raw' immediacy of the citizen's precipitous photo-reportage. It is in refashioning social contracts of collaboration, it follows, that photojournalism will enrich through renewal its relationships with its interpretive communities.

Further reading

Chouliaraki (2012) examines how media imagery risks turning "us into the ironic spectators of other people's suffering". Ellis (2012) investigates how documentary genres are being transformed by digital technologies, including with respect to witnessing. Martin and von Pape's (2012) collection of essays focuses on the deployment of images in mobile or smartphone usage. An exploration of how photojournalism's forms and practices are being recast in digital contexts, not least by citizen photographers, is provided by Ritchin (2013).

References

ABC News (2014) "The future of Fairfax photographers." Media Watch, Australian Broadcasting Corporation, 8 May.
Allan, S. (2013a) Citizen Witnessing: Revisioning Journalism in Times of Crisis. Cambridge: Polity Press.

——(2013b) "Blurring boundaries: Professional and citizen photojournalism in a digital age." In M. Lister (ed.) *The Photographic Image in Digital Culture* (2nd edn). London and New York: Routledge (pp. 183–200).

——(2014) "Witnessing in crisis: Photo-reportage of terror attacks in Boston and London." *Media, War and Conflict*, 7(2), 131–51.

Alper, M. (2014) 'War on Instagram: Framing conflict photojournalism with mobile photography apps.' *New Media and Society*, 16(8), 1233–1248.

Ames, P. (2000) "Amateur video captures horror of Concorde Crash with BC-France-Concorde crash." *Associated Press International*, 26 July.

Atton, C. (2012) "Separate, supplementary or seamless? Alternative news and professional journalism." In C. Peters and M. Broersma (eds), *Rethinking Journalism: Trust and Participation in a Transformed News Landscape*. London: Routledge (pp. 131–43).

Avlon, J. (2013) Cited in transcript, CNN Reliable Sources, broadcast 11:00 am EST on 7 July.

Beck, C. (2014) "When photographers were always part of the story at Fairfax." First Digital Media, 8 May.

Becker, K. (2013) "Gestures of seeing: Amateur photographers in the news." *Journalism*. Retrieved from http://jou.sagepub.com/content/early/2013/12/11/1464884913511566.full.pdf +html (accessed 1 December 2013).

Blaagaard, B. (2013) "Post-human viewing: A discussion of the ethics of mobile phone imagery." *Visual Communication*, 13(3), 359–74.

Bodey, M. (2014) 'Fairfax reduces job losses to 60 after union talks." *The Australian*, 2 June.

Bowers, M. (2014) "Photography requires skill." *The Guardian*, 7 May.

Bunting, M. (2000) "The ghoulish crowds." *The Guardian*, 27 July.

Caple, H. (2014) "Anyone can take a photo, but: Is there space for the professional photographer in the twenty-first century newsroom?" *Digital Journalism*, 2(3), 355–65.

Chouliaraki, L (2012) *The Ironic Spectator: Solidarity in the Age of Post-Humanitarianism*. Cambridge: Polity.

Cottle, S. (2013) "Journalists witnessing disasters: From the calculus of death to the injunction to care." *Journalism Studies*, 14(2), 232–48.

Darroch, V. (2000) "The six million words a day man: The anonymous communicator." *Scotland on Sunday*, 13 August.

Duffy, J. (2000) "The amateurs capturing history." BBC News Online, 28 July.

Ellis, J. (2012) *Documentary: Witness and Self-Revelation*. London and New York: Routledge.

Frosh, P. and Pinchevski, A. (eds.) (2009) *Media Witnessing: Testimony in the Age of Mass Communication*. Basingstoke: Palgrave Macmillan.

Irby, K. (2013) "John White on *Sun-Times* layoffs." Poynter, 31 May.

Kristensen, N. N. and Mortensen, M. (2013) "Amateur sources breaking the news, metasources authorizing the news of Gaddafi's death." *Digital Journalism*, 1(3), 352–67.

Lee, J. (2000) "Point, shoot and coin it." *The Times*, 4 August.

Linfield, S. (2010) *The Cruel Radiance: Photography and Political Violence*. Chicago: University of Chicago Press.

Lister, M. (2013) *The Photographic Image in Digital Culture* (2nd edn). London and New York: Routledge.

Liu, S. B., Palen, L., Sutton, J., Hughes, A. L. and Vieweg, S. (2009) "Citizen photojournalism during crisis events." In S. Allan and E. Thorsen (eds), *Citizen Journalism: Global Perspectives*. New York: Peter Lang (pp. 43–63).

Louie, D. (2013) "Video shows SFO crash passengers' escape from plane." abc7news.com, 8 July.

MacArthur, B. (2000) "An appetite for catastrophe." *The Times*, 28 July.

Marek, L. (2013) "Chicago *Sun-Times* cuts entire photography staff." Crain's Chicago Business. com, 30 May.

Martin, C. and von Pape, T. (eds.) (2012) *Images in Mobile Communication*. Wiesbaden: VS Research.

Matheson, D. and Allan, S. (2009) *Digital War Reporting*. Cambridge: Polity Press.

Meikle, G. (2014) "Citizen journalism, sharing, and the ethics of visibility." In E. Thorsen and S. Allan (eds), *Citizen Journalism: Global Perspectives*, vol. 2. New York: Peter Lang (pp. 171–82).

Mortensen, M. (2014) "Eyewitness images as a genre of crisis reporting." In E. Thorsen and S. Allan (eds), *Citizen Journalism: Global Perspectives*, vol. 2. New York: Peter Lang (pp. 143–54).

Mortensen, T. M. (2014) "Blurry and centered or clear and balanced? Citizen photojournalists and professional photojournalists' understanding of each other's visual values." *Journalism Practice*, 8(6), 704–25.

Newman, C. (2013) "Memo to *Sun-Times* editorial staff from Managing Editor Craig Newman." Posted on the Facebook page of Robert Feder, 30 May.

Ottawa Citizen (2000) "Video captures Concorde horror." *The Ottawa Citizen*, 27 July.

Pantti, M., Wahl-Jorgensen, K. and Cottle, S. (2012) *Disasters and the Media*. New York: Peter Lang.

Peters, C. and Broersma, M. (eds.) (2012) *Rethinking Journalism: Trust and Participation in a Transformed Media Landscape*. London and New York: Routledge.

Reading, A. (2009) "Mobile witnessing: Ethics and the camera phone in the 'War on Terror'." *Globalizations*, 6(1), 61–76.

Rees, J. (2000) "Snapshots that froze history." *Sunday Business*, 30 July.

Ritchin, F. (2013) *Bending the Frame: Photojournalism, Documentary, and the Citizen*. New York: Aperture.

——(2014) "Photojournalism in crisis? In conversation with Revista ZUM." Retrieved from https://www.oximity.com/article/Photojournalism-in-crisis-1 (accessed 8 July 2014).

Sheller, M. (2015) "News now: Interface, ambience, flow, and the disruptive spatio-temporalities of mobile news media." *Journalism Studies*, 16(1), 12–26.

Smith, M. and Hall, L. (2013) "Oh, Lord have mercy: Witness captures fatal jet crash." CNN.com, 8 July.

Thorsen, E. and Allan, S. (2014) "Introduction." In E. Thorsen and S. Allan (eds), *Citizen Journalism: Global Perspectives*, vol. 2. New York: Peter Lang (pp. 1–12).

Tlumacki, J. (2013) Interview with K. Irby, 22 April. Retrieved from Poynter.org

Wall, M. and El Zahed, S. (2014) "Embedding content from Syrian citizen journalists: The rise of the collaborative news clip." *Journalism*. Retrieved from http://jou.sagepub.com/content/early/2014/04/22/1464884914529213.full.pdf+html (accessed 1 May 2014).

Yaschur, C. (2012) "Shooting the shooter: How experience level affects photojournalistic coverage of a breaking news event." *Visual Communication Quarterly*, 19(3), 161–77.

Zelizer, B. (2011) "Photography, journalism, trauma." In B. Zelizer and S. Allan (eds), *Journalism after September 11* (2nd edn). London and New York: Routledge (pp. 55–74).

32
INDEPENDENT CITIZEN JOURNALISM AND TERRORISM

From blogs to Twitter

Hayley Watson and Kush Wadhwa

Where does the news come from? In contemporary society, with complex, layered mechanisms for the production and distribution of news, this continues to be a relevant sociological question that demands an answer. As indicated by the influential German sociologist Max Weber (1998[1910]), who in 1910 called for a "survey of the press", it is vital for social scientists to understand the ways in which the press functions, for the news media plays an influential role in not only informing the public about current events, but also as an essential communication medium that influences public perceptions (as argued by Lippmann, 2008). With vast transformations in the news media and advances in technology over the past decade, it is necessary for sociologists to continue their efforts to understand the workings of those who contribute to producing and sharing the news, particularly as content is increasingly fed and shaped by members of the public via acts of citizen journalism (i.e. the involvement of the public in the news production process).

In recent years, much attention has been focused on how citizen journalists are contributing to the construction of news, for instance by submitting their photographs or videos to the news media for publication (Allan, 2006, 2007, 2009; Domingo et al., 2008). However, rather than examining the functionality of the relationship between citizen journalists and the traditional media, this chapter seeks to identify how those members of the public who are self-published and therefore not reliant on the news media to publish their insights are functioning. We say these members of the public produce independent citizen journalism (ICJ). Accordingly, by drawing on acts of terrorism for illustrative purposes, we will examine how ICJ producers have developed their news-gathering practices, what challenges they face, what problems they might pose and where future research ought to be concentrated to widen our understanding of the role of ICJ in a security-related incident that impacts the community. First, however, let us clarify what we mean by ICJ.

What is independent citizen journalism?

Within the study of the public's involvement in the production and distribution of the news, there are numerous terms being employed. As seen in Figure 32.1, researchers have used different terms to clarify the nature of involvement by the public in the production of news.

Within this chapter, we will refer to the involvement of the public in the reporting of a terror attack as an act of citizen journalism, following leading scholars including Allan (2007) and Rosen (2008). However, in terms of analysing the impact of citizen journalism on the reporting of a terrorist attack and examining the various tools that citizens use, we will focus on those acts of citizen journalism that are self-published. In this way, we will address *independent* forms of citizen journalism. Examining ICJ enables us to study a form of citizen involvement in the production and distribution of news that does not involve editorial control by the professional news industry.

Tools of the trade: From blogs to Twitter

Understanding how ICJ contributes to the news involves an understanding of the various distribution tools at their disposal. Following the attacks in the US on New York City and Washington, DC, in September 2001 (9/11), Zoidberg (2001) used a blog hosted by LiveJournal to post a text-based piece titled 'Rage like a fist'. A blog

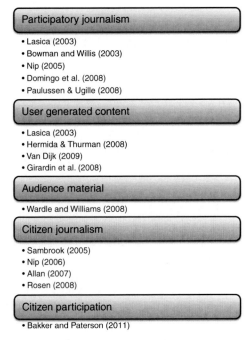

Figure 32.1 The various terms used to describe the involvement of the public in the production of news.

is a "personal webpage in a journal format, using software that automatically puts new entries ('posts') at the top of the page, and shifts old entries to archives after a specified time, or when the number of posts becomes too large for convenient scrolling" (Quiggin, 2006: 482). The post by Zoidberg contained a personalised response to 9/11, with the author discussing how he had heard about the attacks, recounting the news to his colleagues, watching updates on television, and later holding a memorial service for friends and family. Kottner (2001) also wrote a blog post on 9/11. The blog was hosted by TypePad; during the piece, Kottner discussed his own 'near miss' experience of the attacks. Neither of the posts included images or links to help supply visual evidence of events. At the time of publication, users of these blogs would have been able to include links to other news items and images; instead, authors relied on text rather than other multimedia aides to tell their story, demonstrating emphasis on the written word over visual content, perhaps a result of the (then) restrictions in terms of easily being able to upload and share pictures/videos online.

As demonstrated by Watson (2012), the terror attacks on the London transport network on 7 July 2005 (07/07) brought citizen journalism following an act of terrorism into the spotlight. In addition to submitting footage to news organisations such as the British Broadcasting Corporation (BBC), members of the public used new media applications such as blogs for the self-publication of their material, where they shared links, images and text to construct and portray their own interpretation of the attacks. As also argued by Stuart Allan:

> Members of the London blogging community were mobilizing to provide whatever news and information they possessed, in the form of typed statements, photographs or video clips, as well as via survivors' diaries, roll-calls of possible victims, emergency-response instructions, safety advice, travel tips, links to maps pinpointing the reported blasts locations, and so forth.
>
> (Allan, 2006: 15)

Allan notes that the blog tracking website Technorati identified more than 1,300 blog posts relating to the 07/07 attacks by 10:15 am (the attacks took place at approximately 8:50 am).

Not only were blogs used to report 07/07, but there were also instances of ICJs using their blogs to discuss the contributions of other citizens and their role in portraying the news. For instance, Porter (2005), whose wife was in London on the day of the attacks, compiled a post that charted his attempts to find his wife in London; in addition, he provided information relating to the reporting activities by members of the public online and argued for professional news organisations to recognise the efforts and contributions by citizen journalists in their coverage:

> What do I want in my *Wall Street Journal*, *New York Times* and *San Francisco Chronicle* when I pick them up from the porch tomorrow? I want the type of reporting that professionals can still do better than citizens, but also points to the best of the citizen work.

Unlike the activities of bloggers following 9/11, Porter and other ICJ writers were using text as well as providing links and images to supply further details of the attacks. Our analysis of blogging during 07/07, using an Advanced Google Blog Search, revealed that of 169 blog posts, 34 contained images (17.4%), 86 contained links to other blog sites (44.1%) and 76 included links to the news media (39%), demonstrating ICJ's engagement with digital tools including links and the embedding of images into content.

The continuing presence of ICJ and the use of blogs can be seen following the 2007 Glasgow airport attacks. A Google Blog Search for the day of the attacks revealed that approximately 1,288 posts were written. The attacks also represent the first noticeable use of Flickr (a photo-sharing social networking website) by the public, to upload and store photographs of the event. Following an advanced search on Flickr for the term 'Glasgow airport attacks', 90 photos were identified; however, only eight of these were found to be of any relevance to the attacks, three of which contained photographs of television screens announcing the attacks (one of BBC, one of CNN and one of Sky News).

Other photos were taken by James A. Moore, a member of the public and professional wildlife photographer, who made his way to the airport to capture photographs of the event, offering live photographic evidence of the unfolding situation. Moore's rationale for placing the photographs on Flickr was as a log, and also as a way of distributing the images had they been needed. However, as of March 2010, the photographs had not been used elsewhere. Following the uploading of images onto Flickr, Moore felt he was subjected to some hostility from audiences, questioning why he felt it necessary to upload photographs of such events: "I did get a bit of flack for posting them on Flickr – but I guess this was before the times of TwitPic and the like and maybe then was still frowned upon. The term 'sicko' I believe was used." This reaction raises an interesting question as to how members of the public feel about the content produced and shared by the public, which would be a fruitful area for future research.

Of particular importance to ICJ following an act of terrorism are the 2008 Mumbai attacks, which are renowned for the central role that citizen journalists (including ICJs) played in the up-to-date commentary of news reports and photography of the unfolding attacks. Due to the large volume of content produced, reports of the power of social media, particularly social networking websites, were highlighted across the web. The UK's *Daily Telegraph* claimed that throughout the attacks the "social web came of age" (Beaumont, 2008), and *NowPublic* declared "crowd-powered news reports of terrorist attacks in Mumbai as a climactic moment in a year in which citizen journalism proved its mettle" (Kioskea, 2008).

One ICJ, Vinukumar Ranganathan (2008), uploaded 112 photographs to Flickr. The photographs were taken in Colaba and consist of images of destruction to vehicles and buildings from a series of blasts. The vast range and quantity of images provide a comprehensive visual presentation of the devastation caused by the blasts. Having uploaded them to Flickr, Ranganathan's ICJ efforts were recognised by various news establishments. For example, *Digital Journal*, a citizen journalism–based news organisation, stated:

> *Digital Journal* is pleased to recognize the hard work of photographer Vinukumar Ranganathan, whose photos of the attacks' aftermath are spread

throughout the news network. His album is definitely worth a long look, and the articles using his photos shed light into a chaotic week in India; from useful updates to opinion pieces on sliding investor confidence.

(Silverberg, 2008)

As of 5 May 2010, there were 159,958 views of the photo set taken by Ranganathan, illustrating that ICJ-based material does indeed attract an audience. While photography is a powerful form of ICJ, others used their blogs to provide descriptive accounts of their experiences during the Mumbai attacks, as well as for reporting and discussing other instances of citizen journalism (as also seen following 07/07). For example, Gauravonomics (2008) provided an in-depth account of different ICJ activities taking place via the social networking website Twitter and personal blogs. Elsewhere, Hongyan (2009) discusses the use of the blogosphere for help-related information, for instance, 'Mumbai help' provided useful information such as contact details for embassy and consulate hotlines, as well as acting as a service to help individuals get in touch with families/friends in Mumbai.

A distinctive feature of the Mumbai attacks, compared to the other crises discussed in this chapter, is the use of the social networking website Twitter. Information in the form of 'tweets' included the number of casualties and fatalities, as well as more extensive tweets concerning action that was taking place on the ground. As Stelter and Cohen (2008) reported: "at the peak of the violence more than one message per second with the word 'Mumbai' in it was being posted onto Twitter". Twitter was not only a popular platform for ICJ; for some, it was a means of staying up-to-date with unfolding events and therefore a key resource for the public (ibid.).

More recently, the use of Twitter, as well as other social networking sites including Reddit and Facebook, has been used by ICJs to participate in the sharing and discussion of news, as was widely seen following the April 2013 Boston Marathon attacks (Papadimitriou et al., 2013). An analysis of tweets in the first 20 minutes of the attacks (which took place at 14:49 EDT) by Cassa et al. (2013) revealed that within three minutes of the attacks, word stems containing 'explos*' and 'explod*' appeared on Twitter. Many of these tweets stemmed from those eyewitnesses at the scene of the attacks.

An aspiring journalist, @Boston_to_a_T, posted an image of one of the explosions via his Twitter account. Since the attacks, the photo has been retweeted (passed on by other Twitter users) 2,065 times. Twitter was also seen to play a key role in the dissemination of updates by ICJ, including those responsible, throughout the siege on the Westgate shopping mall in Kenya in September 2013 (Ensor, 2013; Khera, 2013). An analysis of 732,386 tweets by Card, MacKinnon and Meier (2013) revealed that among others (e.g. local and international media, civil society organisations, etc.), eyewitnesses provided the second largest amount of tweets (17.9%), and the greatest number of tweets were by civilians (75.8%). Tweets were also identified to be composed and published by hostages caught up in the crisis, and by those involved in conducting the attacks, the terrorists. Tweets by eyewitnesses were "defined as tweets authored by a bystander, someone in the vicinity or an eyewitness to events relating to the attacks. In total 151 tweets were considered to be authored by eyewitnesses, with 100 unique eyewitnesses responsible for the 151 tweets" (ibid.: 6). Of the tweets analysed, 85.7 per cent contained a relevant picture and 14.3 per cent included a relevant video, illustrating the power of providing visual material to discuss an event.

Lessons learned and future research

What then, have we learnt about the activities of the public during a security-related event by reviewing instances of ICJ following an act of terrorism? The most striking observation is the noticeable development in technology, particularly social media and its role in enabling citizens to contribute to crisis reporting, particularly in their abilities to share visual content. Over time, new media applications used for ICJ have evolved from blogs to social networking sites, particularly Twitter. However, developments in technology do not automatically bring about changes in audience interaction; rather, as argued by Watson (2011), there is also a need for citizens to participate in the sharing of news content as active audiences, and thus, to have a desire to be involved in producing and sharing the news. Notably, as depicted in the timeline (Figure 32.2), there is a time lag before new platforms are adopted for reporting purposes following an act of terror.

In February 2004, prior to the Madrid attacks (March 2004), two fundamentally important social network sites, Facebook and Flickr, were launched. Facebook is now (as of May 2013) one of the largest social networking sites in the world, with approximately 1.11 billion monthly users (Associated Press, 2013). Just 16 days after the launch of Facebook, on 20 February 2004, Ludicorp, a private company interested in developing interactive technology online, launched Flickr, a social networking site for uploading and sharing photographs online (Ludicorp, 2004). Each of these social networking sites enables individuals to connect to other people worldwide, enabling them to share information, photographs and, in the case of Facebook, video. From the perspective of ICJ, social networking sites not only serve as platforms for the self-publication of news, but can also be seen as agents, attracting and engaging audience use of the internet on a daily basis. In this way they serve to enable citizens to become accustomed to sharing information with others in their social networks (Watson, 2011).

The use of Flickr and Facebook by the public for reporting an act of terror was not apparent during the 2004 Madrid attacks, showing that it can take time for a new medium of communication to be adopted by members of the public. In examining the use of social media following an act of terror, it was not until 07/07 that it became clear that social networking websites began to be used as a tool for dissemination purposes. The true potential for Flickr appears to have been realised during the Mumbai attacks when ICJs used the site to publish photographs. As with Flickr and Facebook, it was not until over a year following its launch that Twitter was forced into the spotlight with the Mumbai attacks in November 2008, and its continued use to report news of terror attacks, as seen following other attacks, including the Boston Marathon attacks (2013) and the Kenyan shopping mall attacks (2013), shows its continued use for ICJ (as well as its increasing use by the news media) as a news forum for reporting purposes following a crisis.

How can we understand the continued use of social networking sites by ICJs? Over time, in relation to crisis management, our analysis revealed that a number of

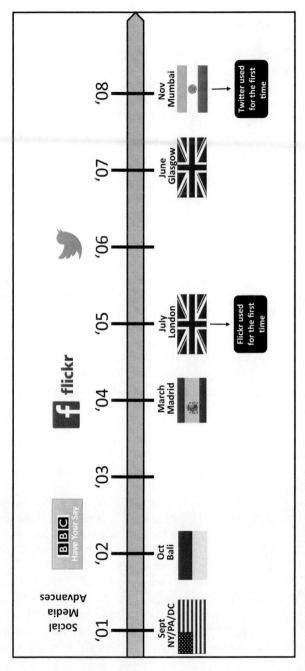

Figure 32.2 Timeline: Advances in new media for reporting terrorism by the public.

new media applications have been developed, encouraging individuals to share their insights, as well as enabling them to communicate with others. An example is the American Red Cross suite of six disaster applications (such as the Hurricane App), which encourages individuals to participate in one-way communication, request or offer assistance, organise themselves and contribute to any Red Cross campaigns that might be taking place. Currently, we are limited in our understanding of the extent of the use of these applications, primarily as a result of the lack of primary data freely available which provide information on usage (Watson et al., 2013). However, we do know that as social networking sites, including Facebook and Twitter, have grown in popularity, and are used on a regular basis, they appear to be regarded as suitable for sharing news-related content following a security event. Thus, existing applications seem to fit the needs of the ICJ in recording, producing and sharing news content with their wider social networks.

It is evident that ICJs are currently playing a role in the construction of the news and are doing so by using a range of new media tools to help them with the self-publication of news. Within the social sciences and other fields, debates have circulated over what citizen journalism means for the news industry and the social construction of news (e.g., Singer, 2006; Hermida and Thurman, 2008; Bruns, 2008). However, in addition to examining the impact of citizen journalism on the news industry, it is necessary to consider some of the other impacts and challenges associated with ICJ in relation to security. As we note elsewhere, citizen journalism, particularly ICJ, not only plays a crucial role in enabling members of the public to participate in sharing information about the news, but these contributions are also of use when the activities of ICJ are taken into consideration for the purpose of managing a crisis (Watson and Wadhwa, 2014).

Some challenges

While ICJs are able to play an important role in providing and sharing up-to-date crisis-related information, such contributions are not without challenges. An important challenge is how the public should manage such vast amounts of information, particularly information that may be inaccurate. Youngs (2009: 135) argues that the blogosphere's vast audience, which is made up of individuals with very different backgrounds, can mean that the consumption of information does not necessarily "guarantee effective and clear communication". The wealth of information available on the internet brings with it issues to do with whether the information is "trustworthy, reliable or relevant" (Youngs, 2009: 136; see also Keen, 2007).

Unreliable information can lead to confusion and, in some situations, misunderstanding (Watson and Wadhwa, 2014). In the case of a crisis such as an act of terrorism, misunderstanding can stem from misleading information being shared, which can potentially lead to problems relating to confusion, unnecessary concern and alarm on the part of the public, which in turn could prohibit their capacity to respond, in a resilient manner, to a crisis. Youngs (2009) argues that it is necessary for audiences within the blogosphere to be critically active: rather than consuming information passively, individuals must sift through the mountain of information that is available to them and use their knowledge and intuition to decipher its meaning. Such a point is also relevant for those utilising social networking sites as a source for information.

Another way of viewing the challenges associated with ICJ (as well as those reliant on the news media for publication) is by developing an understanding of whether such behaviour is anti-social (Bakker and Paterson, 2011: 191). Bakker and Paterson refer to the work of Glaser (2005), who following 07/07 investigated the idea of citizen journalists acting as 'citizen paparazzi'. Glaser points to Jardin, a freelance technology journalist, who raises the question of the ethical implications of citizen journalist behaviour; if we are able to utilise technology to capture people in their 'direst times', we therefore have an ethical obligation to consider our actions, particularly in relation to norms such as compassion and responsibility. It is essential, therefore, to question what ICJ means for community morals in certain security-related situations.

Another challenge associated with ICJ is the implication of activities and shared content on the security of communities. For instance, do ICJ writers respect data protection implications of their activities (i.e. protecting the identity and ensuring the anonymity of those who may be part of their reporting, such as the images of others and vehicle license plates)? This is particularly important when considering ICJ activities in politically volatile areas, where remaining anonymous may be a central concern for ensuring an individual's safety (Kotsiopoulos et al., 2013). Furthermore, it is worth considering how material created and shared via ICJ may impact the security of citizens in the event of an ongoing act of terror as a result of the sharing of tactical information. For instance, following the 2008 Mumbai attacks, citizens were asked to stop tweeting so as to avoid divulging critical tactical information to those responsible, which could have further threatened the security of those caught up in the attacks. To illustrate, Reed (2008) points to the posting of a message on Global Dashboard by *BBC* reporter 'Alex' that the Indian government had asked for all live tweets from the scene to "cease immediately":

> A tweet reading as follows is proliferating on *Twitter* as users re-post it on their feeds: "ALL LIVE UPDATES – PLEASE STOP TWEETING about #Mumbai police and military operations." Various *Twitter*ers reply indignantly that if they're to stop posting the details, the broadcast media should do the same.

In relation to the effects of ICJ following an act of terror, it would be beneficial to understand the effects of citizen contributions to the news on the tactical response to an attack. Crucial questions include whether material from ICJ is more efficient and reliable than material from formal press at the beginning of an event. Do ongoing contributions from ICJ impact the outcome of an event? Following the siege on the Westgate shopping mall in Kenya, Meier (2013) raises the important question as to whether the terrorists used Twitter to increase their situational awareness. Accordingly, researchers ought to further understand the ways in which terrorist organisations are using social media for their own means, not only for tactical gains, but in addition, whether their engagement with social media helps them fulfil their need and goal for gaining further publicity for their deeds (Watson, 2012).

Conclusion

Independent citizen journalism consists of the self-publication of news content by members of the public, who use a range of tools from blogs to social networking sites, particularly Twitter, for publication purposes. When considering the involvement of the public in producing and sharing the news during a security-related event, there are many areas of future research that are required to advance our understanding of the impact of community participation on our understanding of the news. This is particularly important in the case of unregulated and unedited contributions from ICJs, in relation to how these individuals can contribute to the response efforts of a security-related incident. Crucially, stakeholders who might find ICJ content useful, such as those first-responders involved in mining data from citizens to use for their own crisis response efforts in order to enhance their situational awareness, must carefully consider how to engage citizens and their wider social networks to make their contributions more effective and useful in helping them meet their goals.

Acknowledgements

This chapter is partly based on research from the lead author's PhD thesis (awarded in 2011) as well as from the European Commission-funded Contribution of Social Media In Crisis management (COSMIC) project, under grant agreement No. 312737. The views in this paper are those of the authors alone and are in no way intended to reflect those of the European Commission and/or other partners.

Further reading

Allan, S. and Thorson, E. (eds.) *Citizen Journalism Global Perspectives*, vol. 2 (2014) offers an overview of key developments in citizen journalism since 2008. Many of the chapters in this volume continue to consider the role of the community, particularly in the form of citizen journalism in relation to security.

References

Allan, S. (2006) *Online News*. Maidenhead: Open University Press.
——(2007) "Citizen journalism and the rise of 'mass self-communication'." *Global Media Journal Australian Edition*, 1(1), 1–20.
——(2009) "Histories of citizen journalism." In S. Allan and E. Thorson (eds), *Citizen Journalism Global Perspectives*. New York: Peter Lang.
Allan, S. and Thorsen, E. (2014) *Citizen Journalism: Global Perspectives* (2nd edn). Oxford: Peter Lang Publishing.
Associated Press. (2013) "Number of active users at Facebook over the years." *Yahoo News*. Retrieved from http://news.yahoo.com/number-active-users-facebook-over-230449748.html (accessed 15 October 2013).

Bakker, T. and Paterson, C. (2011) "The new frontiers of journalism: Citizen participation in the United Kingdom and the Netherlands." In K. Brants and K. Voltmer (eds), *Political Communication in Postmodern Democracy: Challenging the Primacy of Ethics*. Hampshire: Palgrave Macmillan.

Beaumont, C. (2008) "Mumbai attacks: Twitter and Flickr used to break news." *Telegraph*. Retrieved from http://www.telegraph.co.uk/news/worldnews/asia/india/3530640/Mumbai-attacks-Twitter-and-Flickr-used-to-break-news-Bombay-India.html (accessed 20 May 2010).

Bruns, A. (2008) "The active audience: Transforming journalism from gatekeeping to gate-watching." In C. Paterson and D. Domingo (eds), *Making Online News: The Ethnography of New Media Production*. Oxford: Peter Lang.

Card, B., MacKinnon, J. and Meier, P. (2013) "#Westgate tweets: A detailed study in information forensics." *Qatar Computing Group*. Retrieved from http://irevolution.files.wordpress.com/2013/11/westgate-analysis-in-info-forensics.pdf (accessed 22 November 2013).

Cassa, C., Chunara, R., Mandl, K. and Brownstein, J. S. (2013) "Twitter as a sentinel in emergency situations: Lessons from the Boston Marathon explosions." *PLoS Currents*. Retrieved from http://currents.plos.org/disasters/article/twitter-as-a-sentinel-in-emergency-situations-lessons-from-the-boston-marathon-explosions/ (accessed 22 November 2013).

Domingo, D., Quandt, T., Heinonen, A., Paulussen, S., Singer, J. B. and Vujnovic, M. (2008). "Participatory journalism practices in the media and beyond." *Journalism Practice*, 2(3), 326–42.

Ensor, J. (2013) "Nairobi shopping mall attack: As it happened." *Telegraph.co.uk*. Retrieved from http://www.telegraph.co.uk/news/worldnews/africaandindianocean/kenya/10326548/Nairobi-shopping-mall-attack-live.html (accessed 15 October 2013).

Gauravonomics (2008). "Real-time citizen journalism in Mumbai terror attacks." *Gauravonomics.com*. Retrieved from http://www.gauravonomics.com/blog/real-time-citizen-journalism-in-mumbai-terrorist-attacks/ (accessed 10 September 2010).

Glaser, M. (2005) "Did London bombings turn citizen journalists into citizen paparazzi?" *Online Journalism Review*. Retrieved from http://www.ojr.org/ojr/stories/050712glaser/ (accessed 23 June 2011).

Hermida, A. and Thurman, N. (2008) "A clash of cultures: The integration of user-generated content within professional journalistic frameworks at British newspaper websites." *Journalism Practice*, 2(3), 343–56.

Hongyan, J. (2009) "Mumbai attacks: A new wave of citizen journalism." *RSIS Commentaries*. Retrieved from http://dr.ntu.edu.sg/bitstream/handle/10220/4530/RSIS1302008.pdf?sequence=2 (accessed 5 January 2011).

Keen, A. (2007) *The Cult of the Amateur* (Kindle ed.). London: Nicholas Brealey Publishing.

Khera, J. (2013) "Authorities and militants take Nairobi battle to Twitter." *BBC*. Retrieved from http://www.bbc.co.uk/news/world-africa-24218276 (accessed 15 October 2013).

Kioskea. (2008) "Mumbai attacks caps year for citizen journalism." *Now Public*. Retrieved from http://en.kioskea.net/news/11086-mumbai-attacks-caps-year-for-citizen-journalism-nowpublic (accessed 20 May 2010).

Kotsiopoulos, I., Yannopoulos, A., Watson, H., Finn, R., Wadhwa, K. and Papadimitriou, A. (2013) "Political, social and industrial opportunities arising from the use of emerging technologies." *Deliverable 3.21 of the COSMIC Project*. Retrieved from http://www.cosmic-project.eu/node/24 (accessed 25 November 2013).

Kottner, L. (2001) "The 9/11 journals: Introduction." *Lee Kottner Blog*. Retrieved from http://leekottner.typepad.com/the_911_journals/2001/09/introduction.html (accessed 26 May 2010).

Lippmann, W. (2008) *Public Opinion*. Miami, FL: BN Publishing.

Ludicorp (2004) "Flickr launches." *Ludicorp*. Retrieved from http://www.ludicorp.com/news_item_display.php?id=36 (accessed 12 February 2010).

Meier, P. (2013) "Did terrorists use Twitter to increase situational awareness?" *iRevolution*. Retrieved from http://irevolution.net/2013/02/14/terrorists-used-twitter/ (accessed 15 October 2013).

Papadimitriou, A., Yannopoulos, A., Kotsiopoulos, I., Finn, R., Wadhwa, K., Watson, H. and Baruh, L. (2013) "Case studies of communication media and their use in crisis situations." *Deliverable 2.2 of the COSMIC Project*. Retrieved from http://www.cosmic-project.eu/node/24 (accessed 25 November 2013).

Porter, S. (2005) "London bombings: The unread newspaper." *First Draft*. Retrieved from http://www.timporter.com/firstdraft/archives/000468.html (accessed 10 September 2010).

Quiggin, J. (2006) "Blogs, wikis and creative innovation." *International Journal of Cultural Studies*, 9(4), 481–96.

Ranganathan, V. (2008) "Bombay blast." *Flickr*. Retrieved from http://www3.Flickr.com/photos/vinu/sets/72157610144709049/ (accessed 20 May 2010).

Reed, J. (2008) "Mumbai attacks: Citizen journalism round-up." *The Guardian*. Retrieved from http://www.guardian.co.uk/commentisfree/2008/nov/27/mumbai-terror-attacks-india (accessed 10 September 2010).

Rosen, J. (2008) "A most useful definition of citizen journalism." *Press Think*. Retrieved from http://journalism.nyu.edu/pubzone/weblogs/pressthink/2008/07/14/a_most_useful_d.html#more (accessed 12 August 2009).

Silverberg, D. (2008) "TopFinds: Citizen journalism shines in Mumbai coverage, international events." *Digital Journal*. Retrieved from http://www.digitaljournal.com/article/262752 (accessed 10 September 2010).

Singer, J. B. (2006) "Stepping back from the gate: Online newspaper editors and the co-production of content in Campaign 2004." *Journalism and Mass Communication Quarterly*, 83(2), 265–80.

Stelter, B. and Cohen, N. (2008) "Citizen journalists provide glimpses of Mumbai attacks." *New York Times*. Retrieved from http://www.nytimes.com/2008/11/30/world/asia/30Twitter.html (accessed 10 September 2010).

Watson, H. (2011) "Preconditions for citizen journalism: A sociological assessment." *Sociological Research Online*, 16(3). Retrieved from http://www.socresonline.org.uk/16/3/6.html (accessed 15 October 2013).

——(2012) "Dependent citizen journalism and the publicity of terror." *Terrorism and Political Violence*, 24(3), 465–82.

Watson, H., Finn, R., Wadhwa, K. and Yannopoulos, A. (2013) "Baseline analysis of communication technologies and their applications." ·*Deliverable 2.1 of the COSMIC Project*. Retrieved from http://www.cosmic-project.eu/node/24 (accessed 25 November 2013).

Watson, H. and Wadhwa, K. (2014) "The evolution of citizen journalism in crises: From crisis reporting to crisis management." In S. Allan and E. Thorsen (eds), *Citizen Journalism: Global Perspectives*, vol. 2. New York: Peter Lang (pp. 321–32).

Weber, M. (1998)[1910] "Preliminary report on a proposed survey for a sociology of the press." *History of Human Sciences*, 11(2), 111–20.

Youngs, G. (2009) "Blogging and globalization: The blurring of the public/private spheres." *Aslib Proceedings: New Information Perspectives*, 61(2), 127–38.

Zoidberg (2001) "Rage like a fist." *Zoidberg*. Retrieved from http://zoidberg.livejournal.com/2001/09/11/ (accessed 28 January 2010).

33
WORKING THE STORY
News curation in social media as a second wave of citizen journalism

Axel Bruns

The first wave of citizen journalism

The story of citizen journalism as a social and cultural practice is in many ways tightly intertwined with the story of the technologies that are used to *do* citizen journalism. One of the founding myths of citizen journalism (see for example Meikle, 2002 and 2003; Platon and Deuze, 2003; Bruns, 2005) is the introduction of the first Indymedia publishing platform, just in time for the 1999 Seattle World Trade Organization summit and the 'alternative globalisation' activities and demonstrations which accompanied it. Supported by the then brand-new 'Web 2.0' publishing technologies that enabled the rapid publication of updates in text, audio and video from the summit, the Seattle Independent Media Center (IMC) became a first highly visible example of citizen journalism, and inspired a substantial number of follow-on projects (not least the global Indymedia movement itself): "In the ten months following Seattle, a network of more than 30 such IMCs had been set up, each using the same freely circulated software, and each relying on individual participants or visitors to submit content" (Meikle, 2002: 90).

This chapter traces the development and transformations of citizen journalism from these early beginnings through the heyday of stand-alone citizen journalism sites and news blogs to the present-day revival of collective news curation practices in social media environments, paying special attention to the online platforms which underpin such activities. To highlight this connection between the practice of citizen journalism and its technological frameworks is by no means to fall into the trap of technological determinism: in a variety of forms, and without using the term itself, citizen journalism had been practiced – often less visibly so – for decades, even centuries; the pamphleteers of the American struggle for independence may be considered to have practiced a form of proto-citizen journalism (and some of them, indeed, later founded the United States' first newspapers), using another then brand-new publishing technology: the commercial printing presses which had recently become available in many of the colonies. Citizen journalism as a social practice always draws on the publishing tools at hand; the emerging Web 2.0 simply became the latest and particularly powerful set of tools with which to engage in an alternative form of newswriting and commentary – tools so versatile that the term 'citizen journalism' itself was born.

The Indymedia publishing platform did not remain the only major support technology for citizen journalism, of course – other user-controlled publishing platforms, and especially Weblogs, became important for the further development and mainstreaming of citizen journalism. Contrary to the work done by the Seattle Independent Media Center in 1999, such efforts often shifted from first-hand reporting towards news commentary, however (Bruns, 2006; Singer, 2006). Outside major local events, most citizen journalists and news bloggers remained dependent on the material published in conventional news outlets, and were able only to provide alternative interpretations and analyses of such news reports. As a direct consequence, contrary to the gatekeeping of traditional news outlets, forms of 'gatewatching' emerged (Bruns, 2005): citizen journalists followed and observed the material published by mainstream news organisations, government and NGO bodies, industry, research centres and civil society groups – compiling, collating and curating the material from these information sources in their own publications. Leading citizen journalists also conducted their own background research – such fact-checking at times became crucial for debunking the spin put on stories by political players and some partisan journalists. This posed a substantial, critical challenge to journalism-as-usual, as Walsh points out: "once the 'news', which journalism traditionally presents as the objective truth, was revealed to be a manufactured product – a product manufactured, moreover, by methods that seemed cynical and manipulative to many outsiders – the knowledge hegemony of journalism began to show cracks" (2003: 369).

If the majority of such user-led engagement with the news might better be described as 'citizen commentary' than citizen journalism, it nonetheless had a significant impact on the established journalism industry, and on society as such. Key episodes in the story of citizen journalism include the resignation of US Republican leader Trent Lott over apparently pro-segregationist comments, and the retirement of veteran US news anchor Dan Rather following CBS's bungled handling of dubious documents about George W. Bush's service record in the National Guard; in both cases, citizen journalists drove the news commentary and analysis when mainstream media failed to fully engage with these stories.

News bloggers and citizen journalists also provided an important alternative perspective in the lead-up to the 2003 Iraq War, at a time when a mistaken sense of 'patriotism' led to a "spiral of silence" (Noelle-Neumann, 1974) that effectively silenced voices critical of US government policy in the mainstream US media. By that time, even some professional journalists had begun to see blogs as alternative outlets "through which they could share their more candid responses to the bigger questions of the war. Journalists' personal entries provided a much broader range of opinions ... than were available, particularly to Americans, on broadcast and cable television" (Rushkoff, 2003: 17). Disenchanted with the state of the contemporary news industry, in other words, professional journalists were turning to citizen journalism – one even raised some US$10,000 through crowdfunding to finance his travel to northern Iraq as an independent war journalist (Allbritton, 2003).

Elsewhere, too, citizen journalists with specific expertise filled the gaps which mainstream news organisations could or would not address: in the 2007 Australian federal election, the electoral predictions made on their blogs by independent opinion poll analysts came much closer to the mark than those by influential mainstream journalists and commentators, in spite of the latter's thunderous indignation at being thus outdone by amateurs who "wouldn't get a job at a real newspaper" (*Australian*, 2007) – amateurs who were in fact experts in their own fields (cf. Bruns, 2012). This foreshadowed the role that analyst Nate Silver would come to play in the 2008 and 2012 US elections.

But while such examples serve to demonstrate the truth in early blogger-journalist Dan Gillmor's widely cited statement that "my readers know more than I do" (2003: vi), they also show that such superior knowledge tends to be the result of a para-professional dedication to specific themes and topics, which is far from universal among citizen journalists and news bloggers in general, or indeed among the broader readership base for journalism in both its 'professional' and 'citizen' forms. A more precise variation on Gillmor's statement would be that '*some* of my readers know more than I do', and that some of these knowledgeable readers in turn may write for citizen journalism sites and news blogs.

To the extent that the term 'citizen journalism' evokes hopes of a widespread, democratic participation in the journalistic process, such hopes have tended to remain unfulfilled: citizen journalists *are* citizens, of course (as indeed are professional journalists), but they are far from representative of the overall population. The demographics of citizen journalism are often hardly different from those of professional (political) journalism: for the most part, citizen journalists are likely to be news enthusiasts and what Stephen Coleman has described as "political junkies" (2006), much like their opposite numbers in the news industry. Contrary to the 'armchair journalist' accusations, many citizen journalists probably *would* get a job at a real newspaper, if they could be bothered to earn the formal professional qualifications required (and if real newspapers were still hiring new staff).

From sites to networks: The decline of the imprint

The publishing logic behind citizen journalism sites of the post-Indymedia generation, including news blogs, is in many aspects not particularly different from that of newspapers (and newspaper websites). Although citizen journalism sites tend to introduce a greater openness to participation by a wider range of contributors, and although the scope and style of news coverage and commentary in these sites may differ from conventional industry practice, one fundamental characteristic that unites the two is that they remain *sites*: distinct publications. Even if citizen journalism sites and news blogs do not seek to replace newspapers and other news publications altogether, as the latter have at times suspected, many of them have certainly sought to establish themselves as viable and recognised sources of news and commentary alongside the imprints of the mainstream news media.

The speed with which several key sites with roots in the citizen journalism movement – the *Huffington Post* in the US, *Crikey* in Australia, *OhmyNews* in South Korea – were able to establish themselves as accepted journalistic or quasi-journalistic imprints in their respective mediaspheres demonstrates this point. Each may look different in content and style from its more venerable news industry colleagues and competitors, but they match them, crucially, in the fact that each serves as a recognisable masthead to signal a unified editorial philosophy and style. The impact of this incarnation of citizen journalism is comparable perhaps with that of the pirate radio stations in the 1960s and 1970s, which thoroughly revitalised the stale content formats at the time, but which over the years gradually transmogrified into accepted, legalised members of the industry establishment.

One key explanation for why these sites, many of which ostensibly started out to address what they perceived as shortcomings in the mainstream media industry, ended up replicating so many of mainstream news's features lies in the technological foundations available at the time. To operate a citizen journalism site, or even to run a one-person news blog, initially tended to mean setting up a stand-alone content management system – or coding the system from scratch. Later entrants were able to bypass the most onerous aspects of this process by opting for a ready-made hosting solution (such as Blogger, for blogs, or one of the many providers offering pre-installed Wordpress or Drupal sites ready for customisation), but the end result in each case was a stand-alone site, ready to be filled with content and to be promoted to readers.

This is largely because the early heyday of citizen journalism, in the afterglow of Seattle, coincided with a period of heightened individualism in participatory online media environments (Bruns, 2013). Earlier social and networked spaces for user-generated content, such as AOL and GeoCities, had begun to lose favour with users, while the blogs and other content management systems which gained popularity in the early 2000s were based inherently around individual users. The operators of sites based on this latest generation of 'Web 2.0' tools sought to overcome such fragmentation by linking to each other in posts and blogrolls, but fundamentally remained micro-proprietors – each operating independent sites which were at best loosely confederated.

Over the course of the past ten years, however, this loosely networked individualism has given way in turn to a new, much more strongly connected and networked online environment, driven chiefly by the advent of what we now refer to as social media, from early platforms such as MySpace to the current international market leaders Facebook and Twitter. Twitter, which due to its flat and open network structure has lent itself especially well to the rapid distribution of breaking news across a wide population of participants, has emerged as a key new space for professional as well as citizen journalists; the vast majority of local and global news organisations as well as many individual journalists now operate Twitter accounts.

The adoption of social media such as Twitter fundamentally alters the logic of the institutional imprint, however: in sharp contrast to the previous phase, where mainstream and alternative news organisations were able to carve out their own online spaces in the form of their independently operated websites, they are now all participating within a third space which offers only limited opportunities for customisation and is ultimately subject to the rules set by a third-party proprietor. Functionally, the Twitter account of an @nytimes or @abcnews is no different from the accounts of individual journalists, news enthusiasts or everyday users.

Furthermore, the social networking logic upon which such sites are built means that individual posts from any of these accounts are effectively detached from their imprints as they are disseminated through the network. Most social media users no longer encounter a news story because they follow the news imprint it originates from, but encounter the imprint because they follow an unfolding story by tracking relevant posts as they circulate through social media channels. Whether local, national or global, any story on social media is now built, tweet by tweet, from the incremental news and updates and running commentary originating from a diverse coalition of news organisations, individual professional and citizen journalists, domain experts and stakeholders and more or less knowledgeable other users. Who these contributors are still matters, to be sure, but the track record of individual accounts in covering a story becomes more important than the news brand with which these accounts may be affiliated.

This shift marks the gradual closure of what Thomas Pettitt has described as the "Gutenberg Parenthesis" (2013). The primacy of print on paper as the leading news medium since Gutenberg's invention of the printing press also meant the primacy of the newspaper format as the least bad compromise between speed of dissemination and financial viability. To package news stories in the form of a daily newspaper was necessary because a greater frequency of publication would have been organisation-ally and economically unsustainable (although for major news events, such as the outbreak and conclusion of wars, special issues would at times be printed to reduce the time lag between daily editions), and a lower frequency would have failed to address the needs of the audience for timely news.

With the shift from print to online, however, and the corresponding gains in the possible speed and reach of news dissemination, the packaging of news in daily editions is no longer necessary, and even becomes counterproductive. Most newspaper sites now publish stories as they come to hand rather than coordinating their release with the publication of their print counterparts. But the closure of the Gutenberg Parenthesis not only transforms the provision of news from a product (the physical newspaper, in a daily edition) to a service (the newspaper site, constantly updated), but results in even more far-reaching changes: it enables audiences to pick and choose individual items from a variety of competing news services, rather than subscribe to one service among many.

The increasing use of social media as alerting services through which brief pointers to newly published news articles are disseminated only serves to further boost this global, instant, real-time attention market: in their network activity feeds, social media users are now almost immediately faced with a choice of news coverage for any one story that ranges from ABC News to Die Zeit, and from venerable institutions to upstart citizen journalists. A number of legacy news providers have sought to prevent such per-story customer choices by instituting online 'paywall' systems that require users to commit to the imprint by paying a monthly or yearly access fee – often only with the result that audiences now bypass such paywalled sites altogether. Behind the withdrawing of their content from open circulation and comparison against competing news coverage may be a belief that enough readers still value the unified and consistent editorial agenda which a specific imprint can provide, but the very limited success of paywall systems to date suggests that contemporary news audiences, at least on social media, relish the opportunity to compare coverage across diverse news outlets.

The atomisation of the news

In the post-Gutenberg, online environment news imprints – of conventional news organisations, or of their citizen journalist counterparts – have not disappeared, but they have begun to matter a great deal less because audiences are able to choose from a much greater range of reports on the same story. As Katharine Viner, editor-in-chief of *The Guardian*'s Australian edition, puts it, information has become "something liquid and free-flowing". She suggests that the newspaper in its conventional form "is complete. It is finished, sure of itself, certain. By contrast, digital news is constantly updated, improved upon, changed, moved, developed, an ongoing conversation and collaboration. It is living, evolving, limitless, relentless" (2013). In this state, the news is atomised: news topics are broken down into their constituent stories, and those stories themselves are dissembled into continuous streams of updates and additions, in 140 characters or less.

Such updates, in turn, may originate from a variety of possible and sometimes competing and contradicting sources: from the diverse professional and citizen journalists and news organisations covering the story, from the news actors (politicians, businesses, celebrities, organisations) featured in the story or from a diverse group of commentators, analysts and experts able to provide further background information – and increasingly, these news updates are created in or at least disseminated widely through social media, with news coverage in other media (radio, television, print) breathlessly attempting to keep up with the real-time flow of information across Twitter and Facebook. This process can be observed especially clearly in the context of acute breaking news, associated on Twitter often with the emergence of topical hashtags associated with the unfolding story. Hashtags enable the rapid formation of ad hoc publics (Bruns and Burgess, 2011) which enable their contributors and followers to come together to jointly "work the story" (cf. Bruns and Highfield, 2012) by sharing and compiling all relevant information as it comes to hand.

In such communities we encounter a reformulation of the original citizen journalism practice of gatewatching, conducted now as a collective exercise rather than as the core activity of a handful of news enthusiasts only. Contrary to the individualised spaces of citizen journalism sites and news blogs with their considerable barriers to participation, to become a gatewatcher in a social media space like Twitter requires no more than the use of the appropriate hashtag to tweet a link to a new piece of information about an unfolding story, or the use of the retweet or share buttons to pass on another user's recent update to one's own group of followers or friends, perhaps with added commentary. This puts participation in citizen journalism–related activities within reach of a considerably larger group of users, and finally approaches the ideal of myriad 'random acts of journalism' that combine into an unprecedentedly detailed and multifaceted coverage of the news, as J. D. Lasica envisaged it in 2003. Indeed, where a criticism of earlier forms of citizen journalism was that they failed to broaden the demographics of journalistic activity beyond the already active 'usual suspects', the problem with the coverage of major breaking news events on Twitter is that, at times, so many users actively contribute that the sheer volume of hashtagged tweets becomes overwhelming. Yet, even when the speed of updates increases to a point where not every tweet can be read, not every link can be clicked on, such hashtags usually still provide a valuable source of real-time updates on the story as it unfolds.

Outside acute events and hashtags, collective gatewatching plays an important role in social media, too. Communities of interest are supported by networks of mutual connection within social media spaces (through friend or follower relationship mechanisms), enabling the messages posted by any one community member to reach the entire group; the reposting of relevant messages affords them even greater visibility. Such collective practices further serve to undermine the dominance of any one organisational or individual participant or of any one news imprint or journalist, as the community collectively compiles news and information from a broad range of sources.

What emerges is a new practice of communal news curation, building on individual participants' gatewatching efforts. Social media provide the space for a much broader range of practices than those related to news and journalism only (much in the same way that news blogging is only one possible use of blogs: cf. Bruns and Jacobs, 2006; Walker Rettberg, 2008), but such news curation nonetheless constitutes one key use of social media at present. As a form of (citizen) journalism, news curation foregrounds the input rather than output aspects of the journalistic process: it is at its core more an exercise of research and compilation than one of interpretation and publication. This enables it to retain strong communal aspects, since the finding and sharing of information can more easily be conducted communally than the development of an interpretive perspective built on such information.

In spite of such strong communal aspects, however, leading drivers of the news curation process emerge, frequently due to the speed, volume or quality of their information-sharing activities. These lead users are the present-day equivalents of the prominent citizen journalists of the previous decade, and are at times indeed recruited from similar backgrounds – however, a number of particularly social media-savvy professional journalists have also begun to reposition themselves by serving in such news curation functions: US-based National Public Radio journalist Andy Carvin, for example, came to prominence through his ad hoc news curation work on Twitter during the Arab Spring uprisings in 2011 and 2012, when he took to Twitter (cf. Hermida, Lewis and Zamith, 2014).

News curation in social media spaces is also being formally recognised and supported as a distinct role for professional journalists. News organisations are beginning to position some of their staff as news curators (if not always using that title) by devoting part of their workload to such curation activities, even if they take place away from the formal online spaces (chiefly, the website) established by the news organisation itself, and even if they are conducted by the journalist through their personal social media account rather than an organisational presence. One prominent example for this trend is Australian journalist Latika Bourke, who was employed by the leading public broadcaster, the Australian Broadcasting Corporation, in 2010 to be its first "social media reporter" (ABC TV Blog, 2010) – that is, as a professional journalist whose primary medium for covering the news was not the radio, television or online channels operated by the ABC, but a third-party social media space (in this case, chiefly Twitter).

A crucial step in the move towards news curation is the acceptance that it is necessary to link to external sources, even if to do so appears to weaken one's own imprint. Although citizen journalists have long practiced this inclusive approach to information dissemination (indeed, with the rise of gatewatching the idea of citizen journalism was largely built on this practice), *Guardian Australia*'s Katharine Viner describes the long struggle which established news organisations have had to undergo before they could accept this approach:

> If you look at the idea of linking out to external sources with an old media, newspaper perspective, of course you'd never do it. They're a competitor, why on earth would you give them traffic? It's only when you adjust to the logic of new media that you see that linking out to a source is essential.
>
> (Viner, 2013)

Taking this approach – as *The Guardian* has done, especially when running its popular 'live blogs' that accompany major unfolding events – means valuing leadership in news curation over the ownership of a news agenda. At the same time, by positioning its live blogs as curated, real-time, inclusive spaces of news coverage which resemble a more carefully filtered and moderated social media feed, *The Guardian* can reimpose its imprint onto that 'liquid and free-flowing' space of online news: the imprint is reborn as a nexus of news coverage because it has proven to be especially adept at collating and curating coverage from all over the Web, all over the world, in a single stream of updates which offers a valuable service to readers.

Conclusion: News curation as core practice

Notably, public broadcasters like BBC and ABC, and other organisations with more limited exposure to market forces, like the Scott Trust-funded *Guardian*, have been among the earlier movers towards such internet-age practices (e.g., BBC Press Office, 2004): it takes a great deal less rethinking for these organisations to acknowledge the good work done by their competition. By contrast, as they seek to protect legacy business models inherited from the age of print, purely commercial news organisations have tended to make their own content even harder to link to by erecting more or less impenetrable paywalls around their sites. It is therefore not without considerable irony that the perennially underfunded Australian Broadcasting Corporation can now introduce its out-linking trial as an initiative designed to support the country's imperilled commercial news industry: "by providing these links, given the great trust the public places in the ABC, I hope we'll provide a real boost to local news media. The ABC may not be able to halt the disruption that comes with the digital age but it can help deliver the dividends" (Scott, 2013).

It seems, then, that the gatewatching and news curation practices which emerged with citizen journalism in the late 1990s and which were turbo-charged with the decentralisation of information sharing and the consequent atomisation of news stories through social media in the first decade of the twenty-first century have now become core practices of journalistic activity at both 'professional' and 'citizen' levels – and that news curation, even where it recognises and links to the coverage published by competitors in the market, can become the basis of new business models.

What is taking shape is a media ecology – or more precisely, a news ecology – which features a number of news imprints that are reborn not as monolithic, stand-alone organisations with the pretension to provide 'all the news that's fit to print' from in-house resources, but as smarter, networked organisations which in equal measure compete and collaborate with their peers as they engage both in news coverage and in news curation. In this new form, the imprint is no longer homologous with the publication (the newspaper, the news website), but extends also to the activities of journalistic staff that take place in third-party social media spaces, where journalists such as Carvin or Bourke provide both first-hand reporting and news curation services that are backed up by institutional as well as personal authority.

It is in these third-party spaces which act as a neutral ground between the various news organisations, journalists and other stakeholders that the core of the communal, collective gatewatching and news curation activity now takes place. It may have taken the best part of two decades, but the network logic of citizen journalism, allied with technological frameworks of social media as drivers of its second wave, has begun to substantially alter news practices as we knew them.

Further reading

Hermida, Lewis and Zamith (2014) offer an excellent in-depth account of news curation in a social media space, using the example of Andy Carvin's work during the Arab Spring. Bruns's *Gatewatching* (2005) defines and explores the concept of gatewatching, as an alternative to conventional gatekeeping. Readers interested in online news and citizen journalism are well served by a number of recent collections, such as *News Online: Transformations & Continuities* (edited by Graham Meikle and Guy Redden; Houndmills: Palgrave Macmillan, 2011) and *Citizen Journalism: Global Perspectives* (edited by Stuart Allan and Einar Thorsen; New York: Peter Lang, 2009).

References

ABC TV Blog (2010) "ABC news appoints social media reporter – Latika Bourke," 13 December. Retrieved from http://blogs.abc.net.au/abc_tv/2010/12/abc-news-appoints-social-media-reporter-latika-bourke.html (accessed 19 October 2013).

Allbritton, C. (2003) "Blogging from Iraq." *Nieman Reports*, 57(3), 82–85.

Australian (2007) "History a better guide than bias." *The Australian*, 12 July. Retrieved from http://www.theaustralian.com.au/opinion/editorial-history-a-better-guide-than-bias/story-e6frg6 zo-1111113937838 (accessed 19 October 2013).

BBC Press Office (2004) "BBC launches newstracker." Retrieved from http://www.bbc.co.uk/ pressoffice/pressreleases/stories/2004/10_october/01/newstracker.shtml (accessed 19 October 2013).

Bruns, A. (2005) *Gatewatching: Collaborative Online News Production*. New York: Peter Lang.

——(2006) "The practice of news blogging." In A. Bruns and J. Jacobs (eds), *Uses of Blogs*. New York: Peter Lang (pp. 11–22).

——(2012) "Journalists and Twitter: How Australian news organisations adapt to a new medium." *Media International Australia*, 144, 97–107.

——(2013) "From homepages to network profiles: Balancing personal and social identity." In J. Hartley, J. Burgess, and A. Bruns (eds), *A Companion to New Media Dynamics*. London: Blackwell (pp. 417–26).

Bruns, A. and Burgess, J. (2011) "The use of Twitter hashtags in the formation of *ad hoc* publics." Paper presented at the European Consortium for Political Research Conference, Reykjavík, 25–27 August 2011. Retrieved from http://eprints.qut.edu.au/46515/ (accessed 19 October 2013).

Bruns, A., Burgess, J. Crawford, K. and Shaw, F. (2012) *#qldfloods and @QPSMedia: Crisis Communication on Twitter in the 2011 South East Queensland Floods*. Brisbane: Arc Centre of Excellence for Creative Industries and Innovation. Retrieved from http://cci.edu.au/flood $sreport.pdf (accessed 19 October 2013).

Bruns, A. and Highfield, T. (2012) "Blogs, Twitter, and breaking news: The produsage of citizen journalism." In R. A. Lind (ed.), *Produsing Theory in a Digital World: The Intersection of Audiences and Production*. New York: Peter Lang (pp. 15–32).

Bruns, A. and Jacobs, J. (eds.) (2006) *Uses of Blogs*. New York: Peter Lang.

Coleman, S. (2006) "How the other half votes: *Big Brother* viewers and the 2005 general election." *International Journal of Cultural Studies*, 9(4), 457–79.

Gillmor, D. (2003) "Foreword." In S. Bowman and C. Willis, *We Media: How Audiences Are Shaping the Future of News and Information*. Reston, VA: Media Center at the American Press Institute (p. vi). Retrieved from http://www.hypergene.net/wemedia/download/we_media.pdf (accessed 19 October 2013).

Hermida, A., Lewis, S. and Zamith, R. (2014) "Sourcing the Arab Spring: A case study of Andy Carvin's sources on Twitter during the Tunisian and Egyptian revolutions." *Journal of Computer-Mediated Communication*, 19(3), 479–99.

Lasica, J. D. (2003) "Blogs and journalism need each other." *Nieman Reports*, Fall, 70–74. Retrieved from http://www.nieman.harvard.edu/reports/03-3NRfall/V57N3.pdf (accessed 19 October 2013).

Meikle, G. (2002) *Future Active: Media Activism and the Internet*. New York: Routledge.

——(2003) "Indymedia and the new Net news." *M/C Journal*, 6(2). Retrieved from http://journal.media-culture.org.au/0304/02-feature.php (accessed 19 October 2013).

Noelle-Neumann, E. (1974) "The spiral of silence: A theory of public opinion." *Journal of Communication*, 24(2), 43–51.

Pettitt, T. (2013) "Media dynamics and the lessons of history: The 'Gutenberg parenthesis' as restoration topos." In J. Hartley, J. Burgess and A. Bruns (eds), *A Companion to New Media Dynamics*. London: Blackwell (pp. 53–72).

Platon, S. and Deuze, M. (2003) "Indymedia journalism: A radical way of making, selecting and sharing news?" *Journalism*, 4(3), 336–55.

Rushkoff, D. (2003) *Open Source Democracy: How Online Communication Is Changing Offline Politics*. London: Demos. Retrieved from http://www.demos.co.uk/files/OpenSourceDemocracy.pdf (accessed 19 October 2013).

Scott, M. (2013) "The ABC in the media ecosystem." Speech to the American Chamber of Commerce in Australia, Sydney, 25 July. Retrieved from http://about.abc.net.au/speeches/the-abc-in-the-media-ecosystem/ (accessed 19 October 2013).

Singer, J. B. (2006) "Journalists and news bloggers: Complements, contradictions, and challenges." In A. Bruns and J. Jacobs (eds.) *Uses of Blogs*. New York: Peter Lang (pp. 23–32).

Viner, K. (2013) "The rise of the reader: Journalism in the age of the open web." *Guardian Australia*. Retrieved from http://www.theguardian.com/commentisfree/2013/oct/09/the-rise-of-the-reader-katharine-viner-an-smith-lecture (accessed 19 October 2013).

Walker Rettberg, J. (2008) *Blogging*. Cambridge: Polity.

Walsh, P. (2003) "That withered paradigm: The web, the expert, and the information hegemony." In H. Jenkins and D. Thorburn (eds), *Democracy and New Media*. Cambridge, MA: MIT Press (pp. 365–72).

34

COMMUNITY AND ALTERNATIVE MEDIA

Prospects for twenty-first-century
environmental issues

Kerrie Foxwell-Norton

Introduction

The 1992 United Nations Rio Earth Summit and the publication of its Agenda 21 heralded a united international response to global environmental issues, bringing the concept of Ecologically Sustainable Development (ESD) to the fore of public consciousness and government policymaking. Agenda 21, as the action plan for ESD, was reaffirmed at the 2012 Rio+20 Conference by the 192 governments in attendance. Much criticism has been made of the lack of action arising from Agenda 21 over the past 20 years and the need for a far more urgent response to the key environmental issues – including that of fossil fuel depletion and climate change (UN, 2012). Agenda 21 shares with other international, regional and national statements a commitment to the critical value of communities in protecting local environments – and additionally points to the strength and potential of the collective efforts of local communities worldwide to fulfil the promise of producing an ecologically sustainable society. This shares much with the global community and alternative media movement, and its reliance on local community participation to deliver communicative democracy. While environmental policy statements appeal to a sense of local ownership of environments, in a similar vein, community and alternative media appeal to local ownership of media. Both are reliant in a very fundamental sense on local participation and action – broadly dissolving the boundaries between the 'experts' and citizens.

In this chapter, I would like to begin to trace the normative pursuit of citizen participation in natural resource management so ubiquitous in environmental policy, alongside the passionate and salient ethos of participation typical of alternative and community media. I am interested in exploring the synergies between ecological democracy – defined as citizen participation in decisions relating to our natural environments – and media democracy – defined as citizen participation in the production, representation and distribution of media. Citizen participation is a problematic concept for policy generally (see Arnstein, 1969) and for alternative and community media scholars specifically. Carpentier (2011: 31) has drawn attention to the ways in which different articulations of democracy lead to variants of participation, distinguishing between 'access', 'interaction' and 'participation'. Similar discussions have taken place around citizen participation in natural resource management – broadly advocating for 'power-sharing' with communities, debating top-down or bottom-up approaches and what makes participation 'meaningful' (Ellsworth, Hildebrand and Glover, 1997) rather than a 'tick-box'.

The pursuit of community participation in both media and environmental management shares many core characteristics not the least of which is a belief in the value of local and contextual responses by active citizens to conserve and protect both environmental and, in the case of media, cultural diversity. In short, discourses of media and environment collide at our relationships to place, privileging local ownership/stewardship as critical to justice and positive social and environmental change. Further, both seek at least to disturb the status quo between 'experts' and 'citizens', opening a space to empower community voices and action to be valued and legitimised (Fischer, 2000; Meadows et al., 2007; Foxwell et al., 2008). This synergy opens a host of possibilities and opportunities for the communication of environmental issues, capitalising on the nexus of local action in environment and media.

My discussion here is in part informed by my research with colleagues on the Australian community broadcasting sector (Forde, Meadows and Foxwell, 2002; Meadows et al., 2007; Forde, Foxwell and Meadows, 2009) alongside an ongoing investigation of local communities and environmental issues (see Foxwell-Norton, 2013). Throughout 2011–12, I accepted an honorary consultancy to assess local opinion on a local and state government-proposed 'Tourist Park'. This development proposal led to a very public role for me in my local coastal community of Cabarita Beach/Bogangar. Cabarita Beach/Bogangar is a small coastal village of about 3,000 residents on the east coast of Australia. The nearest major city is Brisbane, approximately 90 minutes away, while the backpacker mecca of Byron Bay is about 30 minutes to the south. In the past decade, this area has been under substantial development pressure. It is the fourth time a tourist park has been proposed, and each time it has been met with a passionate and vehement response of opposition from locals (see www.cabaritabeach.org/community-plan.html). The Cabarita Beach/Bogangar Community Plan (Foxwell-Norton, 2011; hereafter Community Plan) sought citizen participation in local environmental decision-making, with local media playing a significant role in representing these issues in the local community public sphere (Forde, Meadows and Foxwell, 2002).

The Community Plan was established as a proactive response to the tourist park proposal, gathering public opinion through a survey of local residents which was also made available more widely via online options ($n = 785$), focus groups and a critical analysis of the public submissions and processes adopted by local and state government authorities. My fieldwork was supplemented with a series of interviews, post–Community Plan delivery with local activists, politicians, journalists and bureaucrats ($n = 6$) to reflect on the role of communities in coastal management and the role of local media in representing coastal development, conflict and management issues. The newsworthiness of this local clash between citizens and governments (and aspects of the business community) is obvious – conflict being the most obvious news value at play. The issue appeared 66 times across only five local newspaper publications (published exclusively for the local shire) in a 12-month period. A Facebook group, 'No Tourist Park at Southbeach Cabarita', still active, has 800 members and was used extensively during the Community Plan and broader campaign to advise residents of events and to direct them to local media coverage. In a village of approximately 3,000 people, 785 surveys were completed, overwhelmingly by residents keen to have their say. The results of this survey confirmed anecdotal evidence that there was not only opposition to the tourist park proposal, but moreover there was no significant support either. While the Community Plan report contained a number of development recommendations that would receive community support, the focus here is on community participation in local environmental issues and the role of local media.

Community and alternative media: Local definition

In pursuing this confluence of participation in media and participation in environmental issues, definitions of community and alternative media require some limitations. In this context, definitions of community media relate to 'place' – community media that have a local physical presence in communities and are best positioned to communicate community participation in local environmental management and issues. I am defining 'community media' in a geographical sense as media that represent local people and issues, because this is where the collision of environmental policy and community media possibilities occurs. Meadows (2013: 44) uses the term 'community media' to describe 'media produced in an environment where there are strong connections with either a local community or a particular community of interest', citing the relationship between producers and audience members as defining. Following Meadows (ibid.), this might include 'alternative' (Atton, 2002), 'radical' (Downing, 2001), 'citizens' (Rodríguez, 2001), 'grassroots', 'independent' and so on media, but not necessarily. Howley (2005: 266) argues that this community media "create knowable communities", engendering at the local level an awareness of belonging to, and responsibility toward community – and here this is specifically extended to an awareness of local environmental issues. It is their capacity and intent (however successful) to represent and reproduce the everyday lived experiences of community at the local level – from local sporting events, to party politics, crime, natural disaster, local heroes and achievements, businesses and so on – which offers a plethora of opportunities for the communication of local and global environmental issues.

Community media outlets claim to be in touch with local people and local issues – media owned by locals, for locals. Investigations of Australia's community media sector have highlighted the role the local media performs in the life of communities, providing locally relevant news and information to a diversity of audiences, and thus contributing to the development of a 'community public sphere' (Forde, Meadows and Foxwell, 2002; Meadows et al., 2006), where citizens are empowered via the media to engage and participate in public debate and decision-making. Similarly, a key component of ecological democracy is that technological development and economic development are debated before key decisions are made (Beck, 1992), though this does not guarantee positive environmental outcomes (Dryzek, 2012: 243). Ostensibly, then, *local* ownership and local relations have power and currency in both discourses of the media and discourses of the environment. Local relationships to place are critical to the protection and preservation of communities *and* their environments – understood as a site where significant change can happen. With regard to the Community Plan, a senior local councillor summed up the nature of this relationship thus:

> Well, the media kind of have an important gate keeping role as informants, they don't always get it right and that's my experience. They want to make a story sometimes where there's no story, by and large, let's assume we have a balanced media and they are totally objective, they are going to be important ingredients to ensure that these things stay up the agenda. Community views, community engagement issues are high on the agenda because if they can give voice to community opinion that matters and changes things. People power works at local government level, I think.
>
> (Interview, 25 July 2013)

Relations between locals and their environment are pervasive and assumed in this mix of community media impacts. The representation of relations to place that are characteristic and indeed typical of much local community media are so 'ordinary' that this critical role – in representing and communicating relations between communities and their environments – is almost lost in 'common sense'. This is perhaps particularly so for environmental policymakers, where the pursuit of ESD deems knowledges not based in economics and environmental sciences (i.e. the discourses of ESD) marginalised from any legitimate or meaningful position in environmental decisions and policy-making. Local cultures and local values are, ironically enough, often absent from policies designed to incite their participation in or awareness of local environmental issues. The rhetoric is that the local communities are at the fore of policy-making, but the reality is that local efforts are circumscribed long before public appeals for citizen participation (Foxwell-Norton, 2013). Local community media is often assumed to have a 'special relationship' due to its proximity to local people and issues (Ewart and Massey, 2005), and as such offers a host of possibilities in representing and asserting local relationships to place. In his comparative study of regional and rural journalism in Australia and Canada, Richards found that local media:

> facilitate communication between journalists and non-journalists to the benefit of the local community. In each region, local people rely on "their" media for news and information about local happenings and assume that this news and information will be presented in ways which support the common interests of the region.
>
> (Richards, 2013: 638)

Richard echoes previous research about local community broadcasters in Australia but also globally (Forde, Meadows and Foxwell, 2002; Meadows et al., 2007). A local journalist who had been reporting on my recent experience with the Community Plan articulated his role in reporting local relationships to place:

> Journalism is ... reporting, sure the day-to-day issues, you have hard issues, you've got tsunamis, car accidents, etc., they'll have to be reported, that's fine but it's also the issues that are just as important for communities is the sense of place, it's where they live and how they want to live because that's a big part of democracy.
>
> (Interview with local journalist, 15 June 2013)

The critical dimension of 'place' narrows the focus of the alternative and community media to which I refer – and is a critical point in connecting trends between environmental policy and journalism and community and alternative media. In many ways, this media is 'alternative' inasmuch as it is local and specific – asserting local difference and significance at a historical moment when the 'global' is both the threat and the 'fashion' (see Howley, 2005: 39). Arguably, 'place-based' alternative and community media are implicitly sites of political contest and challenge in a similar though not the same way to publications, which are more explicit in their environmental focus and dedication to radical social and environmental change. In their everyday representation of local relationships to place, these media assert the significance of the specificities and subtleties of local cultures and experiences. This is a clear challenge to globalising discourses that too often easily brush over local differences.

Local place, local media

Globally, local communities are recognised as the vanguard of conservation and protection efforts. Local, national and international environmental policy and conservation campaigns consistently cite the importance of local environmental stewardship and participation – a special local relationship to place – as a critical aspect of environment conservation measures (Foxwell-Norton, 2013; Dovers, 2005). At the local level of Cabarita Beach/Bogangar, the local shire pursues community engagement strategies with gusto, especially in relation to coastal zone management. The most recent coastal management plan is clear, declaring community input as

> fundamental in ensuring that the wide range of community views are taken into consideration and that a sense of ownership is developed amongst community members.

There exists an inescapable relationship between the ways in which we frame or think our environments, our actions therein and our environment as a natural entity unto itself (Cox, 2013; Jagtenberg and McKie, 1997). Communities do not just live in their local environment; they also 'think' their environments, bringing a host of cultural frameworks to their place – a relationship between the 'semiosphere' and the 'biosphere' (Jagtenberg and McKie, 1997), which guides thoughts and actions in relation to our environment. We develop a 'sense of place' that is the lived human experience of our natural environment – and accounts for the complexity of human relations to place. Local media have a very specific role to perform in relation to their place, articulating and representing the nature of relations between locals and their place. These ideas direct critical attention to the 'where' of journalism and the media, beyond spelling and other copy edits, and even beyond media ownership to the cultural dimension of representations of place (Griffin, 1999).

Barbie Zelizer (1993: 269) refers to 'place' as not only a physical location but also a "culturally negotiated term by which journalists draw upon larger ideological discourses in relating the news." In the case of small towns, she concludes that "it may be that notions of place consolidate communities" (ibid.: 283). Similarly, Griffin asserts that

> Journalists [and media] are becoming more involved (also *will* become even more involved or perhaps *should* become even more involved) in the reporting and representation of place and that this involvement, while being part of a broad tendency towards a new recognition of the importance of space and place in our perception of the world, is also a "localising" phenomenon in which media interact with local government and local communities.
>
> (Griffin, 1999: 19–20)

Previous research on Australia's Indigenous and ethnic community radio sector has found that community media provide ways to re/connect with community and country through "creating a sense of belonging and place in a space predominantly defined by dominant white Anglo culture" (Foxwell, Forde and Meadows, 2012). Place-based community media are well poised to foster relations to place that will empower local citizens with a sense of stewardship sought by environmental policy. This is happening regardless of recognition by authorities and with various environmental outcomes across publications, with varying degrees of reputation and success. This has certainly been the experience with reporting the Community Plan and associated development proposals. The most popular source of information for survey respondents ($n = 785$) was local media, followed by conversations with family and friends – presumably informed in part by local media. Further research here needs to emphasise the local and the contextual; it needs to consider the normative and qualitative intent of community media, alongside content and audience reception analyses. Following Cottle, I argue that the most important aspect of understanding local media coverage is understanding the "interactions between different institutional arenas and how these influence the discourses and representations of environmental news" (Cottle, 2009: 77).

There has been a substantial amount of research investigating the ways in which mainstream journalism and media variously construct, frame, represent or otherwise mediate and mediatise the environment and environmental issues or protest (for example, Boycoff, 2011; Carvalho and Peterson, 2012; Eide and Kunelius, 2012; Cottle, 2008; Lester and Hutchins, 2011; Lester, 2007, 2010; Lester and Cottle, 2009; Lewis and Boyce, 2009; Hansen, 2010). Questions of the 'environment' and 'environmental issues' are also found in alternative and community media scholarship. In

2001, Downing identified the ecological movement as a 'New Social Movement' in his seminal discussion of radical media and social movements (Downing, 2001: 24). In 2002, Atton investigated a range of "environmental anarchist" publications, citing them as a "distinguishing feature of the British alternative press in the 1990s" (Atton, 2002: 83). The performance of alternative media in response to climate change has also received attention. Gunster (2011, 2012) has investigated the Canadian context, arguing that in the case of climate change, it is the communication of the politics rather than the science which is at issue. He concludes that, at its best, alternative media position citizens with the power to impact climate change mitigation (Gunster, 2012: 274). In Malaysia, Smeltzer (2008) distinguished between mainstream state-controlled media and online alternative media, where the latter fills a gap in informing citizens about environmental issues. In El Salvador, Hopke (2012: 377–8) has traced the way in which alternative media there functioned to support the anti-mining social movement, acting as a 'counter-narrative', elevating community interests of human rights and environmental justice.

In light of the contemporary policy enthusiasm for community participation in environmental management, alongside the increasing acknowledgment that the public is disempowered by grand 'doomsday' messages about environmental catastrophe, community media may be a site where local empowerment and action can be fostered. While mainstream 'big' media articulate relations to our places that are global and overwhelming in magnitude and stature, community media can and do represent relations that are smaller, visible and possible to effect. Community media are a local response to a global environmental issue even when not framed as such – avoiding the larger issues may be more conducive to citizen action and participation. For example, climate change was rarely mentioned during the Community Plan, but the debate and indeed the outcome stymied the development of a tourist park. The tourist park development exemplifies many of the threats associated with contemporary industrial capitalist society, broadly prioritising profits over the conservation of a coastal ecosystem treasured by local people. This is a local instance of a global issue. Indeed, the biggest challenge of climate change mitigation is to shift and reorient the relentless pursuit of development so fundamental to our society to something which will thwart environmental catastrophe and support our environments and planet. In part, then, the local efforts relating to the Community Plan disrupt hegemonic development discourses – and local media have an important role to play in communicating this challenge and prospect for change in the local community public sphere. Beck's (1992) risk society thesis describes our contemporary global condition, characterised by an anxiety borne of the sheer scope and scale of manufactured environmental risks, which are a direct consequence of modern industrial society and progress. Beck (ibid.: 22–3) contends that the mass media (alongside the scientific and legal professions) have "key social and political positions" in the social definition and construction of these risks. Community media are sites where active responses to these enormous and unfathomable risks – of climate change, fossil fuel depletion, pollution, deforestation and so on – can be made possible, and thus enchant communities so disenchanted (in the sense identified by Max Weber and others) by communication which disconnects local communities from their places.

Conclusion

I remain seduced by the idea that local-level resistance has the capacity to have an impact on larger social structures. Following Foucault, community media have the power to be a part of local resistance to environmental destruction. His insistence that we look to the local everyday operation of power, knowledge and practices illuminates the potential of community media to respond to twenty-first-century environmental issues. For Foucault (1980: 98), 'power' is something which circulates; "it is never localised here or there, never in anybody's hands, never appropriated as a commodity or piece of wealth ... individuals are the vehicles of power, not its points of application". Foucault's re/conceptualisation of power as a 'network' rather than the 'wielding sword of the powerful' can show how communities and their media might respond to global environmental challenges. Fischer understands Foucault's conceptualisation of power as

> multiple and ubiquitous – the struggle against it must be localised resistance designed to combat interventions into specific sites of civil society. Because such power is organised as a network rather than a collection of isolated points, each localised struggle induces effects on the entire network. Struggles cannot be totalised; there can be no single centralised hierarchical organisation capable of seizing a centralised power.
>
> (Fischer, 2000: 27)

Following Foucault, the power to instigate social and environmental change may be found in the everyday relations of power and knowledge – and it may be that the collation of these strategic local interventions are able to produce the structural shifts necessary for positive environmental futures. This theoretical approach concurs with recent applications of radical democratic theory to community media (Rodríguez, 2001, 2011), where power is enacted and citizenship expressed in a multiplicity of forums, including political action in the quotidian.

The environment and environmental issues represent specific challenges and opportunities for community and alternative media, though the challenges are complex. We know that the collective efforts of a "community mass media" (Foxwell, 2012: 133) have had substantial impacts in the lives of communities, be they based on geography or interest. If the environment is to have a 'voice', there is some agreement that community media are the places where it will be broadcast to where it really counts: our local places. It is through the work of active citizens, engaged and participating in the production, distribution and consumption of their own media, where the voice of the environment will be heard.

The challenge is to support and/or extend the commitment to cultural and communicative rights characteristic of much alternative and community media practice and scholarship to the non-human – merging ecological and media democracy. I do not underestimate the magnitude of this task and acknowledge that this chapter may have raised more questions than it has answered. There is much work to be done in investigating media formats, journalism practices and the myriad of local experiences, which give context to the transformative processes, and the potential of community media and environmental issues. It is clear, however, that for environmental policy and action, the idea of community holds just as much force as it does in discussions of media. The architecture and the imagination exist in these ostensibly disparate fields of environmental policy and community media – both embrace active citizens, and meaningful participation and debate in the local community public sphere. The challenge is to best capitalise on the potential of both local ownership of media and local environments to secure a brighter future for humanity and our planet.

Further reading

Atton's (2002) *Alternative Media*, particularly chapter 4, is a great starting point to begin an exploration of alternative media and environmental issues. More recently, Gunster's (2012) chapter "Visions of climate politics in alternative media" provides insight into the possibilities of alternative media representations of climate change via case studies which highlight civic engagement and participation. Gunster's chapter appears in an edited volume, *Climate Change Politics: Communication and Public Engagement* (Carvalho and Petersen, 2012), all of which will be useful to those interested in the intersection of environmental issues, communication and the public. Readers interested in a comprehensive introduction to media and environmental conflict are directed to Lester's *Media and Environment* (2010) and her subsequent works.

References

Arnstein, S. R. (1969) "A ladder of citizen participation." *JAIP*, 35(4) (July), 216–24.

Atton, C. (2002) *Alternative Media*. Sage: London.

Beck, U. (1992) *Risk Society: Towards a New Modernity*. Newbury Park, CA: Sage.

Boycoff, M. T. (2011) *Who Speaks for the Climate? Making Sense of Media Reporting on Climate Change*. Cambridge: Cambridge University Press.

Carpentier, N. (2011) *Media and Participation. A Site of Ideological-Democratic Struggle*. Bristol: Intellect.

Carvalho, A. and Peterson, T. R. (eds.) (2012) *Climate Change Politics: Communication and Public Engagement*. New York: Cambria Press.

Cottle, S. (2008) "Reporting demonstrations: The changing media politics of dissent." *Media, Culture and Society*, 28(2), 853–72.

——(2009) *Global Crisis Reporting: Journalism in the Global Age*. Maidenhead: Open University Press.

Cox, R. (2013) *Environmental Communication and the Public Sphere* (3rd edn). Thousand Oaks, CA: Sage Publications.

Dovers, S. (2005) "Clarifying the imperative of integration research for sustainable environmental management." *Journal of Research Practice*, 1(2), Article M1. Retrieved from http://jrp.icaap.org (accessed 12 April 2006).

Downing, J. (with others) (2001) *Radical Media: Rebellious Communication and Social Movements*. Thousand Oaks, CA: Sage.

Dryzek, J. (2012) "Ecological democracy." In R. DeYoung and T. Princen (eds), *The Localisation Reader: Adapting to the Coming Downshift*. Cambridge, MA: MIT Press (pp. 243–56).

Eide, E. and Kunelius, R. (eds.) (2012) *Media Meets Climate: The Global Challenge for Journalism*. Gothenburg, Sweden: Nordicom.

Ellsworth, J. P., Hildebrand, L. P. and Glover, E. A. (1997) "Canada's Atlantic coastal action program: A community-based approach to collective governance." *Ocean and Coastal Management*, 36(1–3), 121–42.

Ewart, J. and Massey, B. L. (2005) "'Local (people) mean the world to us': Australia's regional newspapers and the 'closer to readers' assumption." *Media International Australia*, No. 115 (May), 94–108.

Fischer, F. (2000) *Citizens, Experts and the Environment – The Politics of Local Knowledge*. Durham, NC: Duke University Press.

Forde, S., Foxwell, K. and Meadows, M. (2009) *Developing Dialogues: Indigenous and Ethnic Community Broadcasting in Australia*. London: Intellect.

Forde, S., Meadows, M. and Foxwell, K. (2002) "Creating a community public sphere: Community radio as a cultural resource." *Media International Australia*, 103, 56–67.

Foucault, M. (1980) *Power and Knowledge: Selected Interviews and Other Writings 1972–1977*. London: Harvester Press.

Foxwell, K., Ewart, J., Forde, S. and Meadows, M. (2008) "Sounds like a whisper: Australian Community Broadcasting hosts a quiet revolution." *Westminster Papers in Communication and Culture*, 5(1), 5–25. University of Westminster, London.

Foxwell, K., Forde, S. and Meadows, M. (2012) " Australian Indigenous and ethnic community radio: Public spaces, familiar places," In K. Seneviratne (ed.), *Community Radio in Asia and the Pacific*. Singapore: Hampton Press.

Foxwell-Norton, K. (2011) *Cabarita Beach/Bogangar Community Plan: Final Report*. Gold Coast: Griffith University.

——(2012) "The rise of community mass media – Some implications for classic media theory." In J. Gordon (ed.) *Community Radio in the 21st Century*. Berg, Switzerland: Peter Lang (pp. 133–52).

——(2013) "Communication, culture, community and country: The lost seas of environmental policy." *Continuum: Journal of Media and Cultural Studies*, 27(2), 267–82.

Griffin, G. (1999) "Local journalist makes good: Cultural geography and contemporary journalism." *Australian Journalism Review*, 21(1), 17–36.

Gunster, S. (2011) "Covering Copenhagen: Climate change in BC media." *Canadian Journal of Communication*, 36(3), 477–502.

——(2012) "Visions of climate politics in alternative media." In A. Carvalho and T. R. Peterson (eds), *Climate Change Politics: Communication and Public Engagement*. New York: Cambria Press (pp. 247–76).

Hansen, A. (2010) *Environment, Media and Communication*. New York: Routledge.

Hopke, J. E. (2012) "Water gives life: Framing an environmental justice movement in the mainstream and alternative Salvadoran press." *Environmental Communication: A Journal of Nature and Culture*, 6(3), 365–82.

Howley, K. (2005) *Community Media People, Places and Communication Technologies*. Cambridge: Cambridge University Press.

Jagtenberg, T. and McKie, D. (1997) *Eco-Impacts and the Greening of Postmodernity – New Maps for Communication Studies, Cultural Studies and Sociology*. Thousand Oaks, CA: Sage Publications.

Lester, L. (2007) *Giving Ground: Media and Environmental Conflict in Tasmania*. Hobart: Quintus Publishing.

——(2010) *Media and Environment: Conflict, Politics and the News*. Cambridge: Polity.

Lester, L. and Cottle, S. (2009) "Visualising climate change: TV news and ecological citizenship." *International Journal of Communication*, 3, 920–36.

Lester, L. and Hutchins, B. (2011) "Soft journalism, politics and environmental risk: An Australian story." *Journalism*, 12(7) (October), 1–14.

Lewis, J. and Boyce, T. (eds.) (2009) *Media and Climate Change*. New York: Peter Lang Publishing.

Meadows, M. (2013) "Putting the citizen back in journalism." *Journalism*, 14(1) (January), 43–60.

Meadows, M., Forde, S., Ewart, J. and Foxwell, K. (2007) *Community Media Matters: An Audience Study of the Australian Community Broadcasting Sector*. Brisbane: Griffith University.

——(2006) "Creating an Australian community public sphere: The role of community radio." *The Radio Journal – International Studies in Broadcast and Audio Media*, 3(3), 171–87.

Richards, I. (2013) "Beyond city limits: Regional journalism and social capital." *Journalism: Theory, Practice and Criticism*, 14(5), 627–42.

Rodríguez, C. (2001) *Fissures in the Mediascape: An International Study of Citizens' Media*. Cresskill, NJ: Hampton Press.

——(2011) *Citizens' Media Against Armed Conflict: Disrupting Violence in Colombia*. Minneapolis: University of Minnesota Press.

Smeltzer, S. (2008) "Biotechnology, the environment, and alternative media in Malaysia." *Canadian Journal of Communication*, 33(1), 5–20.

United Nations (1992) *Agenda 21: The United Nation's programme of action from Rio*, New York.

——(2012) UN Conference on Sustainable Development. *The Future We Want*. Conference Outcome, Rio De Janeiro, 20–22 June.

Zelizer, B. (1993) "Pioneers and plain folks: Cultural constructions of place in radio news." *Semiotica*, 93(3–4), 269–85.

Part V
COMMUNITIES AND IDENTITIES

35

MAKING MEDIA PARTICIPATORY

Digital storytelling

Christina Spurgeon and Jean Burgess

What is digital storytelling?

Common sense suggests that digital storytelling encompasses all kinds of computer-mediated activity, from the user-generated content of YouTube to digital journalism, blogging and the commercial transmedia franchises that followed in the wake of blockbusters such as *Star Wars* and *The Matrix* (Jenkins, 2006: 93ff) but that are now increasingly standard in the media industry (Edwards, 2012). Such a generic under-standing of digital storytelling also extends to non-linear media such as computer games, where players co-create the narrative action through gameplay. In media studies, all these possibilities have pointed to the disruptive influence of the 'digital' qualifier in the control architectures of communications systems, the interpersonal sender-receiver relations of 'storytelling' practices and the political economies of media institutions, markets and networks, as well as broad transformations taking place in human culture, communication and cognition (Erstad and Wertsch, 2008: 26).

Oral traditions of storytelling are being recovered and fused with emergent narrative practices in the expanding social spaces and identity-centred politics of contemporary digital media cultures. From journalism to social media, the practices of our profes-sional storytellers continue to evolve and change (Hartley, 2008, 2009a), along with our storytelling institutions and their functions. Comprehending these developments is a key problem of contemporary media and cultural studies (Burgess, 2006: 201ff). Are the politics of representation giving way to a new progressive politics of self-representation and direct participation? Or, instead, are these new genres of 'self-representation' (Thumim, 2012: 72) part of a more general 'demotic' turn in the function of contemporary media (Turner, 2010)? Do media merely mediate or amplify cultural identities, or is media functionality becoming "closer to that of a translator or even an author of identities" (ibid.: 3)? How can we know if the changing actor-networks of storytelling "contribute to a wider democratisation, a reshaping of the hierarchies of voice and agency" (Couldry, 2008b: 51)? This chapter considers the place of one specific critical participatory media production practice known as 'digital storytelling' in addressing these larger questions of socio-cultural change. The workshop-based method of digital storytelling that has been associated with the Center for Digital Storytelling (CDS) in Berkeley, California, since the mid-1990s (Meadows, 2003) now has a substantial recent history of use by media and cultural studies researchers for a range of purposes, including understanding the problems of making media participatory, among other things.

Participatory media production has flourished with the growth of consumer markets for digital media technologies, but many critical participatory media movements pre-date digital media (Carpentier et al., 2013; Jenkins, 2009). In many respects these movements, variously theorised as radical (Downing, 2001), citizens' (Rodríguez, 2001), alternative (Atton, 2002), tactical (Cubitt, 2006) community and 'third sector' (Rennie, 2006) media, anticipated the conversational affordances of digital media. The critical concerns of these movements for the social relations of media continue to distinguish them from other participatory media. These movements continue to question the authority and legitimacy of established storytelling institutions (including commercial news and entertainment enterprises, public service broadcasters, journalism, advertising and national cinema) and seek to expand possibilities for media participation and inclusive representation. They have helped qualitatively and quantitatively diversify media systems around the world, not just in terms of what can be seen and heard, but also in terms of how media is made (Spurgeon, 2013). Through the development and use of participatory techniques for generating and sharing knowledge about media production and distribution, these movements have helped de-mystify media and reduce barriers to social inclusion and participation in a number of crucial ways. They have also provided media and cultural studies scholars with valuable sites for researching the sociocultural transformations afforded by the population-wide availability of 'new' media and communication technologies, as well as their limitations.

The critical participatory media movement of digital storytelling

What is now recognised as the particular 'branded methodology' (Lambert, 2013: 34) of digital storytelling was developed in San Francisco in the early 1990s at the intersection of community theatre and digital media arts. The 'moment' of digital storytelling configured in this way was made possible by the intersection of technology and values: a particular West Coast formation of alternative media ideology was articulated with the increased multimedia affordances of the 1990s personal computer (including faster memory, video and 16-bit sound cards), and the liberatory potential rhetorically associated with personal computing in general. Over a decade of intensive practice, Joe Lambert and various collaborators conceived, formalised and standardised a participatory pedagogy for digital storytelling, and established the CDS as an organisational vehicle for propagating and institutionalising the practice. The centrepiece of the CDS method is a collaborative, workshop-based process for creating digital stories. Through peer-based learning in small groups, the CDS method aims to build trust, solidarity and narrative capacity. It is intended to help 'ordinary people' (Thumim, 2012: 21ff), especially those whose perspectives are otherwise marginalised in dominant media cultures, to reveal and use their 'authentic voice' (Podkalicka, 2009: 563). Workshop facilitators encourage participants to embark on a reflexive journey of self-discovery through personal storytelling and creative expression. The method aims to balance "the ethics of democratic 'access' with an aesthetic that aims to maximise relevance and impact" (Burgess, 2006: 208). To this end, it seeks to develop skills in executing a compelling, unique story in a digital media form, usually made by combining a script written and recorded in the first person with a small selection of still images in a movie-making application. The most faithful applications of the CDS method privilege the assumedly transformative process of making individual stories over the potential cultural or social uses of the products themselves (Lambert, 2013: 84). However, the method is also concerned with contextualising stories for sharing within the group, as well as real and imagined publics beyond.

The CDS method of digital storytelling is a knowingly facilitated rather than 'DIY' practice. Both the CDS and its digital storytelling method are grounded in an 'open' (Hartley, 2009b: 143), critical orientation to fostering inclusive participatory digital media cultures. The method has been taken up in a range of North American and international contexts (Lambert, 2013: 126ff; Hartley and McWilliam, 2009). The CDS has made important and influential contributions to the education and professional development of digital storytelling facilitators. Knowledge of the CDS method has been explicitly codified and practiced in ways that have aided the method's extensive and intensive transfer and uptake in many different contexts, so that it might indeed be just as well framed as an alternative media 'movement' as a method. The method was first taken to England and Scandinavia through CDS collaborations with community-based arts and media practitioners, academics and public broadcasters in the early 2000s. It was then taken up in other parts of Europe, Australia and other "mostly rich and digitally saturated" countries (Lundby, 2008: 2), and then to numerous other places, including South America and Southeast Asia. This rapid international diffusion was one of many features of the growing movement that caught the attention of media studies scholars (Hartley and McWilliam, 2009) and drew them into an international digital storytelling movement. The movement is led by its own "activist intellectuals" (Atton, 2002: 106) who have built an international praxis community. This community consists of networks of practitioners, students, scholars and researchers, and even meets at dedicated international conferences. A substantial multidisciplinary body of scholarly literature, as well as practitioner-centred 'how to' and 'best practice' guides, have been generated and circulate in this milieu, and have helped legitimate the CDS method as a strategy for building community-based participatory capacity.

The central focus of the CDS method is on the art of storytelling. Core practitioners of the practice are associated with, but are not limited to, community arts and participatory media movements. Applications and adaptations of the CDS method have been enormously varied and motivated by a gamut of intrinsic, aesthetic and instrumental interests in storytelling. They have included professional development, team building, planning and evaluation in health and education services; community cultural development through support for intergenerational connection, recognition of indigenous cultures, cultural difference and diversity, understanding disability, creative expression of youth identity, dealing with experiences of migration, loss, abuse and social and economic development including poverty reduction, urban planning and organisational storytelling; social awareness and activism around violence prevention, gender and sexual identity and equality, environmental conservation and justice, and truth and reconciliation; formal learning in primary, secondary, tertiary and further education settings; as well as informal acquisition of digital media competencies and literacies in social learning settings. Digital storytelling has also been used in the professional development of journalists, and adapted for use in training citizen-journalists as 'witnesses' to human and environmental rights violations, and advocates for social change (Lambert, 2013; Watkins and Tacchi, 2008: 13–33). The involvement of participatory media movements, such as digital storytelling, in facilitating international social solidarity is a theme that bears further investigation.

The CDS method has also been taken up in formal institutions of public culture such as museums, galleries and libraries for a variety of purposes (Thumim, 2012). It has been used to update and extend pre-existing methods and interests in self-representation and cultural participation, including the core methods deployed by the oral history movement in pursuit of more diverse official narratives of nation and community (Burgess and Klaebe, 2009; Clark, 2009; Simondson, 2009). One of the method's most visible moments came between 2001 and 2008, when BBC Wales ran a seven-year digital storytelling project (Thumim, 2012; Meadows and Kidd, 2009). The Capture Wales project did more than simply create opportunities for BBC Wales's constituent audiences to access the expertise of the public service broadcaster and directly participate in content creation. It also aimed to "make an original and sustainable contribution to community self-expression … a new way for the BBC in Wales to connect with communities, not in a top-down corporate manner but through a project which depends for its delivery and success upon action within communities" (Meadows and Kidd, 2009: 98). The project's legacy included more than 600 stories that had been created in community-based workshops and curated for web publication and screening in other BBC windows. It also included a "vibrant digital storytelling culture … with more than thirty groups across the country running their own projects" (ibid.: 92).

Digital storytelling in media studies research

In the main, however, and as has been observed in relation to other critical media movements (Atton, 2002; Rennie, 2006), digital storytelling is not as visible in media studies or further afield as the reach of the practice might otherwise warrant (Hartley and McWilliam, 2009). Nonetheless, digital storytelling has been taken up in scholarly studies of media, often in the traditions of media sociology, cultural studies and literary and narrative theory. Media studies scholars have found the CDS method to be a useful research tool and departure point for thinking about how participatory media cultures are made. It has provided a platform for theorising the politics and practices of self-representation in a digital cultural context (Lundby, 2008; Thumim, 2012). It has also been used to generate insights into how 'bottom-up' narrative practices can shape and change organisational cultures, and media systems more generally (Hartley, 2009a). Digital storytelling projects have been used as sites for qualitative data collection, using established methods such as interviews and textual analysis (Thumim, 2012) and participant observation and practitioner reflection (Lambert, 2013). Digital storytelling has also been used to address methodological problems of media research, and led to the development of collaborative participatory action research methods, informed by media anthropology and ethnography (Hearn et al., 2009). Advocates of the CDS method have criticised instrumental and emotionally exploitative adaptations of the CDS method (Lambert, 2009: 82) for their superficiality, if not the actual harm they may do to the wider critical project of making media participatory. However, Jo Tacchi's work in particular has demonstrated the ethical as well as pragmatic case for adaptation, particularly in settings where the media cultures of participants are not digital (Tacchi, 2009). The 'adaptation/adoption' tension has also helped media scholars understand how textual and contextual factors constrain and enable the open-ended variation of 'vernacular creativity', as well as the discourses of user-generated media (Burgess, 2006).

Some attempts have been made to comprehensively map and quantify the field of digital storytelling in order to improve the visibility of the practice (see McWilliam, 2009, for one such project). However, quantitative analysis is limited by complications that arise from the disconnection between the production and publication of stories. Not all stories are put into circulation, and where publication does occur, it is often in tactical, offline contexts, such as festivals, closed screenings or limited circulation using stand-alone media such as DVDs. Indeed, US liberal advocates of the CDS method are unapologetic about the individualistic intent of the method to first and foremost facilitate the production of 'private' media (Lambert, 2013: 15) for self-expression, identity formation and dialogue within the immediate production context. For this reason, digital stories are more like 'folk art' than television (Burgess, 2006). They are produced as a result of small-scale activity by groups of people and organisations, in localised contexts for highly specific purposes. While public cultural institutions and community media arts organisations may assist in the production, collection and curating of digital stories, full archives are not necessarily accessible or maintained.

Digital storytelling also resists empirical methods of classification. The practices of digital storytelling are not neatly bounded or isolated from other user-generated and participatory media practices. This in turn highlights a paradox: on the one hand, "the potential, whether realised or not, for cultural participation and self-representation" has become "ordinary" and "everyday" in contemporary digital media cultures (Burgess, 2006: 204); while on the other, facilitation is a necessary pre-condition to widening participation in "the apparently autonomous new media cultures ... that are so loudly and frequently celebrated" (ibid.: 209). This foregrounding of facilitation has also supported breakthroughs for theorising the roles of amateurism and expertise in participatory media in dialogic and open systemic terms, rather than as closed, deficit models of mechanical communication (Hartley, 2008). These developments also mark a break with constructivist philosophies of agency in which the CDS method itself was founded and a turn to approaches influenced by science and technology studies (STS). The CDS method nonetheless continues to invigorate important debates about the politics of 'voice' (Tacchi, 2009; Podkalicka, 2009). It has also provoked the challenge for cultural studies to become a facilitator of participation, "rather than to speak heroically on *behalf* of ordinary voices" (Burgess, 2006: 212). It has also contributed to a renewed critical interest in conversational media and the mediation of difference (Couldry, 2008a) and the place of listening in public discourse and media practice (Podkalicka, 2009; O'Donnell, Lloyd and Dreher, 2009).

This focus on the ethics and politics of media consumption also holds the key to solving one of the most pressing problems for critical media movements in the present period of 'mass conversation' (Spurgeon, 2008); that is, whether the critical project of participatory media is exhausted once the possibilities of media participation are universally 'everyday' (Rennie, 2006). When diminution of the distance between producer and consumer is the norm, is the possibility of participatory content creation enough to sufficiently differentiate critical participatory media from other, demotic forms of user-generated media? The problem is interesting to illustrate with reference to digital storytelling. Digital storytelling, like participatory media more generally, pre-supposes the possibility of producers and audiences being fully interchangeable. However, unlike many other forms of user-generated media, and in spite of its una-pologetic privileging of self-expression and self-awareness over concerns of publica-tion and audience (Lambert, 2013), digital storytelling is also premised on mutual communicative reciprocity between storytellers and listeners.

Active listening is an integral part of the digital storytelling production process. Even though the method is preoccupied with self-realisation for individualised authors through processes of creative expression and textual production, it also intentionally makes productive use of the dialogic qualities of storytelling as a matter of ethical practice. The method similarly insists that storytellers exercise creative control over their stories and that they retain ultimate authority in decision-making about sharing beyond the workshop. The practical reality, however, is often somewhat different. The CDS digital storytelling method offers surprisingly little guidance when it comes to the challenges of cultivating active listening beyond the workshop setting, relying heavily instead on the skill and capacities of well-intentioned adopters (Vivienne and Burgess, 2012). Choices about the platforms used for downstream communication and sharing of stories are something of a methodological after-thought, even though in practice these decisions are often pre-determined and aligned with dominant interests in the outcomes of digital storytelling projects (usually funders) as well as the cultural, community and organisational contexts in which production takes place. While many sponsors of digital storytelling work-shops are principally interested in the therapeutic benefits of the workshop process, this is not always the case (and, arguably, nor should it be). Proceeding from the presumption that stories are created to be shared (Lundby, 2008: 3), participation in many projects is also often contingent upon a willingness to make stories available for wider publication, usually on the internet. Facilitators (often community-based artists or independent digital media producers) need to routinely negotiate issues of consent, safety, risk and emotional support with individual storytellers and the often divergent interests of wider communities of solidarity, and funding sources, in the ownership of digital story outputs as well their wider circulation (Lambert, 2013: 41). Careful curation of digital stories is necessary in order to optimise empathetic reception and active listening to stories as well as social and systemic change beyond the production context (Vivienne and Burgess, 2012; Simondson, 2009). These factors are under-researched areas of participatory media.

Facilitating and enabling access to the means of media production is a defining feature of critical participatory media movements, including digital storytelling. The CDS method provides a window into the facilitation functions of participatory media movements and related subterranean tensions of participatory media cultures more generally. The method is producer-centred, but its reliance on facilitation of informal learning and vernacular creativity draws attention to the material and cultural conditions of participatory media cultures. It also provides opportunities to see how participatory media contribute to the destabilisation of modern ideas of individual authorship (Friedlander, 2008). The CDS method approaches storytelling as a shared human cultural practice rather than an isolated individual effort (Couldry, 2008b). It is "deeply rooted in the collaborative process of the story circle of the production workshop, and maybe in the template narratives in the overall culture" (Lundby, 2008: 6). Yet, it reinforces the authority of individual authors by insisting that storytellers retain individual ownership (if not control) of their stories. This particular 'do no harm' (Lambert, 2013: 117) ethic of collaboration is informed by the professional sensibilities of human services as well as those of critical social documentary. It is intended to guard against the potential for story-tellers to be alienated from their own stories and identities through unethical appropriation, described as story 'theft' in practitioner-led 'best practice' debates (Cuddell, 2012).

Also reflected in the producer-centred orientation of participatory media move-ments, including digital storytelling, are "some of the blindspots of Marxist theorists" (Rennie, 2013: 596) on questions of audiences and consumption. As Rennie has argued in relation to community media, this is reflected in policy, scholarly and practitioner malaise about questions of ethical media consumption choices. It is not simply enough that producers have an interest in 'ethical media'. It is important that 'consuming/producing' media publics can pursue their interests in locating and identifying 'ethical' media (ibid.: 597). Expressed in terms of 'communication rights' discourse, Rennie maintains that this problem requires theoretical and prac-tical solutions that recognise the mutual inter-dependence of individual, minority and collective rights of producers and the publics they seek to invoke, to be heard, seen and informed. The CDS method proceeds from the assumption (probably correctly) that the capacity for active listening capacity (Crawford, 2009) is a scarce resource beyond the immediate context of production, but to what extent can it be assumed to be completely non-existent, or overlooked? How can active listening be systematically supported beyond the safety nets of ethical collaborative pro-duction practice (of the kind intended to be provided in the Story Circle)? This is the nub of the problems of scalability and visibility for digital storytelling, but also its value for addressing the larger problem of listening in participatory media. How do critical participatory media facilitators and producers collaborate to increase the value of their activities for active listeners? "To begin to listen," as Rennie observes, "audiences need to know what ethical media systems already exist; they need to be able to find what it is they are looking for and to enjoy it when they do" (2013: 594).

Beyond media and cultural studies

Speculation about the significance of storytelling to human systems of knowledge and culture is no longer confined to discussions of qualitative methods and interpretive traditions in the humanities and social sciences (Hartley, 2009a). Similarly, the use of digital storytelling in research is not confined to media and cultural studies. A full consideration of other disciplinary uses of digital storytelling is beyond the scope of this chapter. Nonetheless, it is important to note some of the major multidisciplinary conversations that occur around digital storytelling, particularly in education, community health and allied services. In education, digital storytelling has provided a meeting point for multidisciplinary engagement in how learning and literacy for competent citizenship in digital media cultural contexts might be reflexively theorised, researched and practised (Drotner, 2008). This has generated important insights into the limits and potential of storytelling in organisational and institutional learning and as a tool for transforming the social institutions, spaces and professional practices of education. Similar insights have been generated in relation to community and public health where therapeutic uses are also made of digital storytelling. It is not unusual for there to be claims asserted in relation to digital storytelling about the therapeutic and transformative effects of storytelling, and its implications for individual and collective wellness and healing.

The CDS method draws upon group creative processes used in therapeutic expressive arts (Lambert, 2013: 72), and although it does not claim any therapeutic value, Lambert also argues that "it would be inconceivable, incomprehensible, and irresponsible if we did not recognize the emotional and spiritual consequence of this work" (Lambert, 2013: 83). While much is made of the informal therapeutic benefits of facilitated digital storytelling, especially in community health contexts, the empirical foundation of this particular form of narrative therapy remains under-researched.

Conclusion

The CDS method of digital storytelling deliberately exposes the micro-processes of storytelling and media-making to critical examination by participants. For this reason, the method also lends itself as a platform for scholarly research into how changes to human communication tools are implicated in broader processes of socio-cultural change. These changes to human consciousness, culture and social organisation are often only detected with the benefit of historical hindsight (for example, Carey, 1992). It supports research into the implications and consequences of changes to the ways in which stories are created, mediatised and mediated for collective, not just individual, human action (Erstad and Wertsch, 2008). It has also provided a means for researching the impact of self-representation and mediated social participation on the status of marginalised groups and individuals. Indeed, the participatory media movement that has developed around the CDS method has provided an accessible and valuable starting point for critically engaging media students, scholars and practitioners in the politics of how and why participatory media is made.

Further reading

Two edited collections are dedicated to digital storytelling and provide informative international and interdisciplinary perspectives on the practice. *Story Circle: Digital Storytelling Around the World* (Malden, MA and Oxford: Wiley-Blackwell, 2009), edited by John Hartley and Kelly McWilliam, situates the development and rapid transfer of digital storytelling in the ongoing evolution of storytelling institutions and practices. Contributors consider the foundational practices in the English-speaking world, and survey adaptations and emergent practices in South American, southeast Asian and European settings. Contributors to *Digital Storytelling, Mediatized Stories: Self-Representation in New Media* (New York: Peter Lang, 2008), edited by Knut Lundby, bring a broad range of disciplinary perspectives to bear upon practices of self-narration. Joe Lambert's landmark book (New York: Routledge, 2013), now in its fourth edition, anchors a detailed discussion of the CDS method, rationale and formative influences in the rich experiences of critical media praxis.

References

Atton, C. (2002) *Alternative Media*. London: Sage Publications.

Burgess, J. (2006) "Hearing ordinary voices: Cultural studies, vernacular creativity and digital storytelling." *Continuum: Journal of Media and Cultural Studies*, 20(2), 201–14.

Burgess, J. and Klaebe, H. (2009) "Digital storytelling as participatory public history in Australia." In J. Hartley and K. McWilliam (eds), *Story Circle: Digital Storytelling Around the World*. Malden, MA and Oxford: Wiley-Blackwell (pp. 155–66).

Carey, J. (1992) *Communication as Culture: Essays on Media and Society*. New York: Routledge.

Carpentier, N., Dahlgren, P. and Pasquali, F. (2013) "Waves of media democratization: A brief history of contemporary participatory practices in the media sphere." *Convergence*, 19(3) (August), 287–94.

Clark, M. A. (2009) "Developing digital storytelling in Brazil." In J. Hartley and K. McWilliam (eds), *Story Circle: Digital Storytelling Around the World*. Malden, MA, and Oxford: Wiley-Blackwell (pp. 144–54).

Couldry, N. (2008a) "Mediatization or mediation? Alternative understandings of the emergent space of digital storytelling." *New Media and Society*, 10(3) (June), 373–91.

——(2008b) "Digital storytelling, media research and democracy: Conceptual choices and alternative futures." In K. Lundby (ed.), *Digital Storytelling, Mediatized Stories: Self-Representation in New Media*. New York: Peter Lang (pp. 41–60).

Crawford, K. (2009) "Following you: Disciplines of listening in social media." *Continuum: Journal of Media & Cultural Studies*, 23(4), 525–35.

Cubitt, S. (2006) "Tactical media." In K. Sarikakis and D. K. Thussu (eds), *Ideologies of the Internet*. Cresskill, NJ: IAMCR/Hampton Press (pp. 35–46).

Cuddell, C. (2012) "Impacts, effects, evaluation." Session 2, Co-Creative Communities: Storytelling Futures for Community Arts and Media. ACMI, 8 November. Transcript. Retrieved from http://digitalstorytelling.ci.qut.edu.au/index.php/events (accessed 7 March 2014).

Downing, J. D. H. (with others) (2001) *Radical Media: Rebellious Communication and Social Movements*. London: Sage.

Drotner, K. (2008) "Boundaries and bridges: Digital storytelling in education studies and media studies." In K. Lundby (ed.), *Digital Storytelling, Mediatized Stories: Self-Representation in New Media*. New York: Peter Lang (pp. 61–84).

Edwards, L. H. (2012) "Transmedia storytelling, corporate synergy, and audience expression." *Global Media Journal*, 12(20), 1–12.

Erstad, O. and Wertsch, J. V. (2008) "Tales of mediation: Narrative and digital media as cultural tools." In K. Lundby (ed.), *Digital Storytelling, Mediatized Stories: Self-Representation in New Media*. New York: Peter Lang (pp. 21–40).

Friedlander, L. (2008) "Narrative strategies in a digital age: Authorship and authority." In K. Lundby (ed.), *Digital Storytelling, Mediatized Stories: Self-Representation in New Media*. New York: Peter Lang (pp. 177–97).

Hartley, J. (2009a) "TV stories: From representation to productivity." In J. Hartley and K. McWilliam (eds), *Story Circle: Digital Storytelling Around the World*. Malden, MA, and Oxford: Wiley-Blackwell (pp. 15–36).

——(2009b) "Uses of YouTube: Digital literacy and the growth of knowledge." In J. Burgess and J. Green (eds), *YouTube: Online Video and Participatory Culture*. Cambridge: Polity Press (pp. 126–43).

——(2008) "Problems of expertise and scalability in self-made media." In K. Lundby (ed.), *Digital Storytelling, Mediatized Stories: Self-Representation in New Media*. New York: Peter Lang (pp. 197–212).

Hartley, J. and McWilliam, K. (eds.) (2009) *Story Circle: Digital Storytelling Around the World*. Malden, MA, and Oxford: Wiley-Blackwell.

Hearn, G., Tacchi, J., Foth, M. and Lennie, J. (2009) *Action Research and New Media*. Cresskill, NJ: Hampton Press.

Jenkins, H. (2006) *Convergence Culture: Where Old and New Media Collide*. New York: New York University Press.

——(2009) "What happened before YouTube." In J. Burgess and J. Green (eds), *YouTube: Online Video and Participatory Culture*. Cambridge: Polity Press (pp. 109–25).

Lambert, J. (2009) "Where it all started: The Center for Digital Storytelling in California." In J. Hartley and K. McWilliam (eds), *Story Circle. Digital Storytelling Around the World*. Malden, MA, and Oxford: Wiley-Blackwell (pp. 80–90).

——(2013) *Digital Storytelling: Capturing Lives, Creating Community* (4th edn). London and New York: Routledge.

Lundby, K. (ed.) (2008) *Digital Storytelling, Mediatized Stories: Self-Representations in New Media*. New York: Peter Lang.

McWilliam, K. (2009) "The global diffusion of a community media practice: Digital story-telling online." In J. Hartley and K. McWilliam (eds), *Story Circle: Digital Storytelling Around the World*. Malden, MA, and Oxford: Wiley-Blackwell (pp. 37–76).

Meadows, D. (2003) "Digital storytelling: Research-based practice in new media." *Visual Communication*, 2(2), 189–93.

Meadows, D. and Kidd, J. (2009) In J. Hartley and K. McWilliam (eds), *Story Circle: Digital Storytelling Around the World*. Malden, MA, and Oxford: Wiley-Blackwell (pp. 91–117).

O'Donnell, P., Lloyd, J. and Dreher, T. (2009) "Listening, pathbuilding and continuations: A research agenda for the analysis of listening." *Continuum: Journal of Media and Cultural Studies*, 23(4), 423–39.

Podkalicka, A. (2009) "Young listening: An ethnography of YouthWorx Media's radio project." *Continuum: Journal of Media and Cultural Studies*, 23(4), 561–72.

Rennie, E. (2013) "Community media production: Access, institutions, and ethics." In N. V. Angharad and V. Mayer (eds), *The International Encyclopedia of Media Studies, Volume II: Media Production*. Malden, MA: John Wiley and Sons (pp. 582–600).

——(2006) *Community Media: A Global Introduction*. Lanham, MD: Rowman & Littlefield.

Rodríguez, C. (2001) *Fissures in the Mediascape: An International Study of Citizens' Media*. Creskill, NJ: Hampton Press.

Simondson, H. (2009) "Connecting through digital storytelling: 3CMedia." *Journal of Community, Citizens, and Third Sector Media*, 5(October), 61–73.

Spurgeon, C. (2013) "The art of co-creative media: An Australian survey." *Cultural Science*, 6(1), 4–21.

——(2008) *Advertising and New Media*. New York: Routledge.

Tacchi, J. (2009) "Finding a voice: Participatory development in Southeast Asia." In J. Hartley and K. McWilliam (eds), *Story Circle: Digital Storytelling Around the World*. Malden, MA, and Oxford: Wiley-Blackwell (pp. 167–75).

Thumim, N. (2012) *Self-Representation and Digital Culture*. London: Palgrave Macmillan.

Turner, G. (2010) *Ordinary People and the Media: The Demotic Turn*. London: Sage.

Vivienne, S. and Burgess, J. (2012) "The digital storyteller's stage: Queer everyday activists negotiating privacy and publicness." *Journal of Broadcasting and Electronic Media*, 56(3), 362–77.

Watkins, J. and Tacchi, J. (eds.) (2008) *Participatory Content Creation for Development: Principles and Practices*. New Delhi: UNESCO.

36

DIASPORIC MEDIA IN MULTICULTURAL SOCIETIES

Olga Guedes Bailey

Introduction

In Western multicultural societies, the political claims of diasporas and minority groups[1] on redistribution and cultural recognition have been intensified. Nation-states have had to accept difference and, in many instances, have granted a variety of measures to counter social and political marginalisation (Song, 2007). But this does not mean that institutional practices and everyday social relations have changed. For example, while there has been an increase in levels of participation of multi-ethnic groups in European multicultural societies, and a more positive approach to difference and diversity in official policy on race, ethnicity and culture, there has also been an increase of quite intolerant public discourse and migration policies (Lentin and Titley, 2011).

The tensions of the politics of multiculturalism highlight Nancy Fraser's (1995) contention that the politics of multiculturalism includes both cultural difference and redistributive justice. Diasporas and minority groups have become important actors in the struggle for economic redistribution and cultural and political 'recognition' (Fraser, 2008). Fraser argues that as cultural injustices are entangled and support those of a socio-economic nature, redistributive solutions should include a conception of recognition and vice versa that encompasses the complex formation of social identities rather than one that endorses reification. Fraser's concepts are relevant to this discussion to situate the struggles, particularly for cultural and social recognition of these groups, including media and communication access and participation.

Among the myriad political, ethical and theoretical questions that arise from these developments is that of the constitution of multicultural states, and of communities within such states that on the one hand proclaim their 'difference' from the national mainstream, and on the other are marginalised and/or misrepresented on the basis of perceived cultural or religious 'difference'.

Multiculturalism presents a paradox in dealing with the question of how to construct a society that reconciles universal rights with the rights of minority groups. As

Fish (1997) indicates, the dilemma of implementing multiculturalism leads to the challenge of creating a social and political frame that can envisage diversity as different, however equal, without threatening national unity and social consistency in the process. This contested debate within multiculturalism (Kymlicka, 1995; Young, 1997) shows the challenges that diversity and contemporary identities represent to liberal democracy and the modern nation-state. In keeping with patterns of migration from the developing world, multiculturalism has been a perspective that has clearly increased in visibility and importance across Western societies in the past five decades.

The contested nature of multiculturalism is significant to any analysis of diasporas and minority groups' access and participation in the media sphere, particularly the role of alternative media in this process. The right of diasporic peoples and minorities to political participation includes rights of communication, information and representation, which are part of the wider debate on integration and inclusion in liberal democracies.

There is a multitude of ethical–political concerns surrounding the debate on multiculturalism. In the context of this chapter, the focus is briefly on the politics of 'recognition', participation and representation of diasporic and minority groups. Intrinsic to this is the matter of the role of mainstream and, in particular, of alternative media in multicultural societies. The chapter argues that alternative media are potentially productive as a space of cultural expression enabling a dialogue across and within cultures – both minority and 'majorities' – on what constitutes their commonalities and differences regarding values and rights. Essential to this is the question of participatory and representational politics, in particular the inclusion of their voices in the public sphere, including the media.

The chapter is divided into three sections. The first briefly contextualises the role of mainstream and alternative media in multicultural societies; the second will attempt to examine what constitutes alternative media in order to position diasporic media on the continuum of the communication landscape in multicultural societies; the third part will attempt to explore the development and practices of transnational diasporic media.

Media, diasporas and minorities

How can we understand the role of mainstream media in the complex landscape of multicultural societies? What constitutes an inclusive and multicultural media? How do alternative media function in the media landscape of multicultural societies?

The media have the potential to facilitate the exercise of critical citizenship, and to provide a forum for debate and deliberation as well as to restrain the powers of the state. In the context of multicultural societies, where diasporas and minorities struggle for the right of political participation, including the right to symbolic representation, the media can be understood as both a space to communicate, propagate and interact, as well as a battlefield – a 'symbolic arena' – a site for contested struggles over different meanings and identities. Such politics make the media into a site for a "new form of governmentality, concerned with the rules by which groups may claim new subjectivities-status" (Patton, 1993: 161).

The media are thus fundamental in debates on liberal democracy as they play a crucial role in the different struggles for the extension of citizenship rights and political participation (Meyer and Minkoff, 2004). The value of the media lies in making visible issues, identities and needs that are not readily aired in more formal arenas of public debate and decision-making. Sen argues that "as one element in an institutional complex of plural representation, free expression, and rights to participation, media institutions are therefore crucial to the instrumental realisation of normative principles of democracy, equality and social justice" (1999: 65).

However, it could be argued that some of the views on media roles in liberal democracies are based on a liberal-humanist 'colour-blindness' argument; that is, not paying much attention to the 'politics of difference' of diasporas and minority groups, or to the neutrality of liberal policy and the notion of a singular public sphere.[2] Nevertheless, the multidimensionality of diasporic media cultures are articulated by different media – big and small – suggesting that the articulation of their cultural and political identities is highly constructed by different forms of media and differentiated by the specificity of media appropriation of each group (Hepp, Bozdag and Suna, 2012).

In this context of multidimensional diasporic media cultures in Western societies, it could also be claimed that there has been a process of methodical exclusion of diasporas, ethnic and religious minorities from the public sphere, including the mainstream media. Their misrepresentation, under-representation and invisibility have generated an ongoing struggle over meaning, between those at the margins of society and of the mainstream media. A great number of these groups have reacted by producing their 'alternative media'. The presence of diasporas as active social actors in the communicative landscape can perhaps be associated with Mark Poster's suggestion that the change from a "mode of production to a mode of information" has consequences beyond the political and economic realms and into the everyday life of ordinary people (Poster, 1990).

This discussion takes the view that the alternative community media practices of diasporic groups might support the creation of spaces of inclusion, participation and political activism, and produce a sense of belonging[3] for many of those groups. This argument is in line with Fuchs's contention that "alternative media should not only be understood as alternative media practices, but also as critical media that question dominative society" (Fuchs, 2010: 173).

The possibility of producing their own media is the result, among other elements, of processes of migration, of media misrepresentation of minority groups and of changes in the media landscape mostly generated by new communication and information technologies. In an interesting article on "Ethnic media, community media and participatory culture," Deuze (2006) suggests that the popularity of ethnic/minority/ diasporic (news) media should be located in a wider social trend: that of the worldwide emergence of a progressively more participatory and regional media culture in multicultural societies which includes "all kinds of community, alternative, oppositional, participatory and collaborative media practices", and the global market forces, stimulating the proliferation of regional, relatively small-scale enterprises targeting niche audiences, as well as transnational media targeting a wider audience. He points out that the development of such media in the context of journalism has been dominated by the increase of community media (Jankowski and Prehn, 2002), "we media" (Bowman and Willis, 2003), citizen's media (Rodríguez, 2001; Rodríguez, Kidd and Stein, 2010), grassroots journalism (Gillmor, 2004) and other relatively radical alternatives to mainstream journalistic practice emerging both online (Atton, 2004), and offline (Howley, 2005, 2010).

Alternative community media

In this discussion, diasporic media is conceived as a type of alternative community media which are not necessarily radical, but fulfil for their audiences a fairly significant social and, occasionally, political role. Community media is defined as a site

> where grassroots or locally oriented media access initiatives predicated on a profound sense of dissatisfaction with mainstream media form and content, dedicated to the principles of free expression and participatory democracy, and committed to enhancing community relations and promoting community solidarity.
>
> (Howley, 2005: 2)

Diasporic media are sites permeated by local and global forces and conditions, thus creating one of the many "heterogeneous dialogues" related to globalisation (Appadurai, 1996), and becoming part of "a complex form of resistance and accommodation to transnational flows" (Howley, 2005: 33; Martin-Barbero, 1993). These "public sphericules" (Cunningham, 2001) challenge essentialist notions of community. That is, diasporic minority community, through its socialisation around media events, is, to a degree, constituted through media (cf. Hartley and McKee, 2000: 84).

The contemporary diasporic and minority media landscape is characterised by a mixture of non-commercial and commercial enterprises, with some of the latter being able to achieve stable positions in the alternative market. In addition, many of these are on online media platforms, which dissipate the problems of circulation and distribution inherent in the traditional media. Diasporic and minority media journalistic practice has hybrid features, combining mainstream media production elements with innovative ones. They do not necessarily mirror the mainstream, and might have a more meaningful and distinctive journalistic ethos; that is, a political mission and/or social conscience in relation to their specific communities. Diasporic media vary in their political and social aims, management, professionalism, communicative strategies, media technologies, nature (commercial or not) size and lifespan. They may represent a specific community, defend particularistic identities and mediate a group's participation in national and transnational public spheres, thus functioning to create and sustain transnational communities and networks of diasporic groups, particularly in locations where they represent minorities. They may be minorities in their countries of residence, but they are at the same time part of a wider imagined community with whom they have a common culture, language and history. Furthermore, "diasporic media address those audiences both in their particularity, and also in the universality of their (imaginary) cultural existence (e.g. Somalis in London share commonality with Somalis in France)" (Georgiou, 2005: 483). Taken together in their diversity, diasporic media constitute an important element in the communicative landscape of diasporas, not only for their re-imagining of the self and belonging within and across spaces, but for their struggle for pluralistic representation and recognition.

The reconfiguration of the media landscape coupled with the ongoing politics of recognition for ethnic difference (Cecil, 2000) provide an argument for a conception of alternative diasporic media that goes beyond existing views and becomes inclusive of alternative formations which differ and cross borders in new ways. That is to say, the common assumption that commercial alternative media – and their journalistic practices – necessarily undermine the critical, oppositional stance of the established press is questionable (Benson, 2003). Although most diasporic media rely on advertising and/or subscriptions, they can offer news and views ignored by the mainstream media, and might encourage democratic debate and, in some cases, active political involvement. In fact, as suggested by Deuze, (alternative) minority community media function "sometimes as a commercial yet also a communal and a reciprocal link between media makers and media users" in the context of a participatory culture (2006: 269). The changing mediascape, characterised by new forms of alternative media and journalistic practices, suggests an approach to alternative media and journalism beyond the traditional dichotomy of mainstream versus alternative, less "either ... or" (Harcup, 2005), and more acceptable to new hybrid forms and practices (Atton, 2004) – a form of alternative rhizomatic media (Bailey, Cammaerts and Carpentier, 2008).

Transnational diasporic media

According to commentators on international communication, there is a shift taking place towards a transnational media order, which is "remapping media spaces and involving new media practices, flows and products" (Chalaby, 2005). The accessibility of these technologies has advanced cultural diversity and heterogeneity across diasporic communities. Moreover, the confluence of these factors has allowed diasporic groups to use the potential of diasporic media for the affirmation and articulation of their cultures and as a way of reaffirming difference (Gilroy, 1997). Most transnational diasporic media (e.g. satellite television) is mainstream media in the home country providing programmes specifically related to the national culture, which are then rebranded as minority/diasporic/ethnic media (e.g. satellite television) for transnational consumption. In some cases, as in the Brazilian satellite television channel Record, the only local element is the adverts. In multicultural urban spaces, diasporic groups and their media interactions, although local in many ways, are also permeated by the diversity of diasporic media available to them, local or transnational. The creation of such communicative 'sphericules' or alternative spaces of communication, such as websites, community radio, and web-based and transnational television, are proliferating all across Britain, Europe, the US and Australia. Immigrants such as Arabs, Chinese, Indians, Afro-Caribbeans and Latin Americans are accessing satellite channels that are broadcasting programmes from their country of origins.

Nacify (1993), for example, in his analysis of the role of transnational diasporic television, categorises them into three types: 'exilic' television functions to create new solidarities within the community and to mediate identity negotiation, positioning themselves in the 'spaces of liminality' where they "struggle for authenticity and identity, deterritorialization and reterritorialization" in longing for the homeland and stabilised individual subjectivity and cultural identity, while raising contradictions, uncertainties, and insecurities; 'minority television' produced by indigenous minorities "located here and now, not over there and then"; and transnational television, which combines programmes produced in the homeland with those produced by different transnational commercial media corporations catering for specific ethnic groups (ibid.: 165, 347). It could be suggested that although transnational media provide a more complex cultural sphere, they do not necessarily promote a 'transnational identity', as these media continue to present images and meanings that are specific of historic, economic and cultural conditions tied to their place of production, and audience reactions reflect their own responses to these specificities.

Most users of diasporic media are those who are in a continuous process of cultural negotiation (i.e. migrants living dual lives, who speak more than one language, and whose family – and sometimes work – involves transnational travel; Portes et al., 1999). "Their reasons for using these media vary from sustaining a bond with their home countries or connecting with the new country, reconfirming the multipositionality of their diasporic home and its connection to numerous publics" (Georgiou, 2006: 90) to simply engaging with the pleasures and ordinariness attached to media consumption, to overcoming social and cultural exclusion through the process of identity negotiation, which the diasporic media partly facilitate. Most importantly, consumption varies within diasporas according to their different generational, gender, linguistic and ethnic differences, and distinct reasons for migration. Likewise the media practices of diasporic groups not only constitute "diasporic media"; they have a quite diverse "staple media diet" (Bailey, 2007).

The space of transnational media might be considered a 'contact zone' for diasporic groups, providing them with transnational bonding – transporting them home as well as bringing home to them. Pratt (1992: 4) describes contact zones as "social spaces where disparate cultures meet, clash and grapple with each other, often in highly asymmetrical relations of domination and subordination". Her concept describes the contact of two cultures with a clear hierarchy and subjugation relationship. This might be the case with transnational media. However, she refers to a space where people who are usually separated geographically meet, create and establish regular relationships. Her perspective stresses the interaction dimension and the manner by which subjects are defined in and by their relationship with others and, it could be added, to their relationship with media. Classic colonial contexts limit the analytic scope of the 'contact-zone'. If the cultures or spatial imaginations that interact are stressed, the symbolic spaces that are not necessarily physical, or colonial in the territorial sense, will be seen. This modification of Pratt's contact-zone directs us when looking for 'diasporic space', 'no diasporic space' and contact between them. This contact may not depend on concrete common ground; it may be found in interactions about meanings and in personal encounters. Cultural contact-zones may indeed be colonial; however, space – physical or metaphoric – may be contested wherever it is constructed. In terms of transnational media, it could be suggested that they are spaces of transnational and cross-cultural encounter, sites of creativity, discussion and representation and a space for cultural dialogue and translation where imagination guides its constant social construction of space (Shields, 1992). The same imagination guides the constant social construction of space (ibid.), and contributes to processes of imagined communities (Anderson, 1991).

For Appadurai (1996), the power of transnational media resides in their ability to produce transnational imaginaries capable of creating and sustaining new forms of transnational publics. Comparing these transnational media forms to the powers of print capitalism in creating the imagined communities of the nation-state (Anderson, 1991), he suggests a similar development is happening with the development of modern identities, helped by transnational media that connect individual and social groups to new types of cultural experiences and spaces. The diasporic symbolic communicative space generated by transnational media provides a complex cultural sphere where cultural identities are articulated by what Schlesinger calls an "audio-visual space" (in relation to European identity), that needs to be understood in combination with an analysis of cultural identities, as they are not oppositional terms (cf. Schlesinger, 1994). Morley and Robins propose that in the context of globalisation, a new "electronic space" has been created, which is a "placeless geography of image and simulation" (1995).

The literature on media and diaspora (Nacify, 1993; Gillespie, 2000; Sreberny, 2000; Cunningham and Sinclair, 2001; Christiansen, 2004; Bailey, 2008) seems to suggest that hybrid cultural expression is part of the everyday routines of diasporic subjects in which the diasporic, transnational media provide links maintaining new kinds of long-distance imagined communities, and consequently sustaining identities and culture. The media are also among the integral resources that shape diasporic experiences and identities. Because of the multiplicity of the forms in which they appear and the rapid way in which they move through daily routines, the media provide resources for self-imagining and engines for the formation of diasporic spheres (Appadurai, 1996). The internet and television, for example, create key spaces where people are variously invited to construct a sense of self – whether as 'us' and 'them', 'insider' and 'outsider', 'citizen' and 'foreigner', 'normal' and 'deviant', 'the West' and 'the rest' (Cottle, 2000). Diasporic media space is a "transnational site of contestation, in which nation, race, gender, class, culture and language continuously interrelate to produce complex identities" (Kim, 2011: 136).

A different take on transnationalism is offered by Aksoy and Robins (2003), who have argued that this assumption – imagined community – is based on a 'national mentality' with its categories of community, identity and belonging, which overlooks new possibilities of transnationalism. Based on their research on Turkish-speaking groups in London, they point out that media consumption is determined socially rather than by ethnicity. For them, the television experience of Turkish audiences is related to its ordinariness, familiarity and everydayness – "banal transnationalism". They also point out that Turkish television is an agent of "cultural de-mythologisation"; i.e., the ordinariness of Turkish television, of bringing the everyday of Turkish life to them, works to demystify ideas of the homeland (Robins and Aksoy, 2005; Aksoy and Robins, 2003). This in turn leads to the argument of 'de-ethnicisation' developed by Milikowski. Her analysis is centred on how Turkish satellite television could further ethnicise or de-ethnicise Turkish immigrants in the Netherlands, and argues that Turkish television 'de-ethnicises' rather than 'ethnicises' viewers' perception of cultural difference. While "ethnicization refers to the formation of social boundaries created to protect ethnic-cultural heritages, de-ethnicization refers to the 'undoing' of such boundaries" (Milikowski, 2000: 444). In this construct, the concept of ethnic-cultural boundaries related to post-immigration is paramount in clarifying how different groups establish their own subjectivity and dynamics (ibid.). It could be contended that cultural and media practices – mainstream and alternative – constitute both processes of bridging and binding diasporic groups across transnational nodes of relationships as well as demystifying fixed notions of identity and home. More importantly, perhaps, is to understand transnational diasporic media as a network space which might provide experiential mediations that strengthen diasporic people's understanding of their "multi-locationality, facilitate the fostering of belonging, perform identification that might help develop a civic engagement in the multicultural societies where they live and perhaps improve their conditions for cultural and social recognition" (Bailey, 2011: 259).

It is relevant to point out the limited political strength of diasporic media, as market forces within a multicultural society, will not themselves generate a fair multi-ethnic public sphere or politically significant 'public sphericules' (Downing and Husband, 2005). One could argue that diasporic and minority media may foster the growth of transnational, national and local communities of great value, but their value depends ultimately on the level of influence they obtain in the mainstream media and their capacity to influence public opinion and policy-makers beyond their alternative media/'public sphericules'.

Final notes

The study of diasporic alternative media reveals the contradictory nature of 'multi-culturalism' in Western societies and the dependent politics of difference (i.e. the inclusion or exclusion of different groups from the public sphere), since minority media are, in part, a result of 'multicultural' media policies. The point to be made about multiculturalism and the politics of media is that rather than embracing the other in an inclusive form of dialogue, multicultural media policies currently continue to marginalise minorities' voices. Their invisibility and marginalisation in mainstream media has helped create a new ghetto of 'diasporic media' where they find a voice, but in a circumscribed social space. In other words, diasporic and minority groups might have found a space to express their cultural difference and contend for recognition and influence, but it is a space that, in most cases, seems to have little recognition outside their own community. Therefore, their chances of political mobilisation and participation are reduced.

Perhaps what is needed is not only the recognition of the role of diasporic-minority media in multicultural Western societies but their political and material inclusion in a multi-ethnic public sphere, or a more complex multiculturalism where the quest for 'differentiated citizenship' can be articulated, and a 'multiculti' (cf. Baumann, 1999: 141) media environment can flourish. In this context, the power of diasporic and minority media in multicultural societies to bring changes regarding these groups demands' for social and political recognition should be considered with caution. There are relevant questions still not fully answered; what is the nature of the public spheres initiated around diasporic media as a specific form of public communication in multicultural social formations? Has the existence of multiple public spheres increased diasporic groups' power in gaining cultural and political recognition, or boosted their visibility in the public arena and their capacity for challenging dominant discourse?

The question that remains unclear with regard to the political motivation of diasporic-ethnic media is whether they are challenging the dominant public sphere, being independent (or excluded) from it, or absorbed by it. Cunningham, for instance, emphasises the value of public sphericules as constituted beyond the nation-state, as "global narrow casting of polity and culture, assists in restoring them to a place – not necessarily counter hegemonic but certainly culturally plural and dynamically contending with western forms of recognition of indisputable importance for plural societies" (Cunningham, 2001: 134). Yet, he acknowledges that they are "social fragments", though they provide a central space for public communication in globally dispersed communities. If they are 'fragmented', it is not clear whether he is somehow reinforcing the dualism of the public sphere debate, and/or presenting them as a space constrained by its own 'ethnic' boundaries (i.e. a communicative space contained by its 'minority' status that does not challenge the relations of power of the mainstream politics of communication). Appadurai (1996) too celebrates the "diasporic public sphere" through his confidence in the political efficacy of transnational virtual communities, which offer the chance of engagement in global movements for cultural autonomy and sustainable justice. For him, those sphericules offer the possibility not only to perform new identities but also to re-connect the displaced (ibid.: 33–4). Alternative media as public sphericules are indeed vital to plural societies, but the proliferation of diasporic-minority alternative spheres does not lead necessarily to a multiplication of political forces. The political success of alternative diasporic community media in multicultural societies remains to be seen.

Notes

1 Diasporic subjects' experiences are lived 'outside' and 'inside' a 'diaspora space' which is constructed by several axes of differentiation and inequality – nationality, class, gender, ethnicity. They face discrimination, antagonism, celebration, as well as 'internal-group' pressures to resist and/or comply with a defined 'cultural identity'. They network with others in permanent or temporary alliances in a changeable and liminal zone that becomes 'home'; a space where cultural affinities and differences are constantly negotiated.

2 The public sphere is used here as a metaphor for understanding the potential of the media in extending the political debate and enhancing the inclusion of diasporic and minority groups.

3 Belonging has a number of dimensions, as it refers, among other things, to cultural identity, to the material conditions in terms of 'preconditions for quality of life' and to an affective dimension related to social ties. See Anthias (2007).

Further reading

Bailey (2007) examines a case study of alternative community media (*Quoran* magazine), which provides information and analysis of current affairs relevant to the Muslim community in the UK. O'Neal (2007) presents a case study of an African community radio that supports the needs of the elderly and youth for non-formal education, as well as providing information relevant to the community, such as environment, health and social welfare. Hopkins (2009) offers an important review of the main advances on the area of media and migration from a global perspective, arguing that the production and consumption of media content by migrants are shaped by material, social and individual parameters, and not simply by ethnicity or migration. The text discusses issues of poor representation and the exclusion of minorities in main-stream national media and the responses from these communities; the importation of media content from the homeland or elsewhere; and the creation of local migrant media (the "migrant mediasphere").

References

Aksoy, A. and Robins, K. (2003) "Banal transnationalism: The difference that television makes." In K. H. Karim (ed.), *The Media of Diaspora*. Routledge: London (pp. 89–105).

Anderson, B. (1991) *Imagined Communities: Reflections on the Origin and Spread of Nationalism*. London: Verso.

Anthias, F. (2007) "Belonging in a globalising and unequal world: Rethinking translocations." In N. Yoval-Davis, N. Kannabiran and U. M. Vieten (eds), *The Situated Politics of Belonging*. London: Sage (pp. 17-31).

Appadurai, A. (1996) *Modernity at Large: Cultural Dimensions of Globalization*. Minneapolis: Minnesota University Press.

Atton, C. (2004) *An Alternative Internet*. Edinburgh: Edinburgh University Press.

Bailey, O. G. (2007) "Transnational identities and the media." In O. Bailey et al. (eds), *Transnational Lives and the Media. Re-Imagining Diasporas*. London: Palgrave.

——(2008) "Diasporic identities and mediated experiences in everyday life." In I. Rydin and U. Sjoberg (eds), *Mediated Crossroads: Identity, Youth Culture and Ethnicity*. Gothenburg, Sweden: Nordicom Press.

——(2011) "Reconfiguring diasporic-ethnic identities: The web as technology of representation and resistance." In M. Christensen, A. Jasson and C. Christensen (eds), *Online Territories: Globalization, Mediated Practice and Social Space*. New York: Peter Lang (pp. 256–72).

Bailey, O. G., Cammaerts, B. and Carpentier, N. (2008) *Understanding Alternative Media*. Maidenhead: Open University Press.

Baumann, G. (1999) *The Multicultural Riddle*. London: Routledge.

Benson, R. (2003) "Commercialism and critique: California's alternative weeklies." In N. Couldry and J. Curran (eds), *Contesting Media Power: Alternative Media in a Networked World*. Lanham, MD: Rowman and Littlefield (pp. 111–28).

Bowman, S. and Willis, C. (2003) *We Media: How Audiences Are Shaping the Future of News and Information*. Arlington, VA: Media Centre, America Press Institute.

Cecil, M. (2000) "Editor's introduction." *Journal of Communication Inquiry*, 24(4), 355–56.

Chalaby, J. (2005) "From internationalization to transnationalization." *Global Media and Communication*, 1(1), 28–33.

Christiansen, C. (2004) "New media consumption among immigrants in Europe: The relevance of diasporas." *Ethnicities*, 4(2), 185–207.

Cottle, S. (ed.) (2000) *Ethnic Minorities and the Media*. Buckingham: Open University Press.

Cunningham, S. (2001) "Popular media as public 'sphericules' for diasporic communities." *International Journal of Cultural Studies*, 4(2), 131–47.

Cunningham, S. and Sinclair, J. (2001) *Floating Lives: The Media and Asian Diasporas*. Lanham, MD: Rowman & Littlefield.

Deuze, M. (2006) "Ethnic media, community media, and participatory culture." *Journalism*, 7(3), 262–80.

Downing, J. and Husband, C. (2005) *Representing Race: Racisms, Ethnicity and the Media*. London: Sage.

Fish, S. (1997) "Boutique multiculturalism, or why liberals are incapable of thinking about hate speech." *Critical Inquiry*, Winter, 378–94.

Fraser, N. (1995) "From redistribution to recognition? Dilemmas of justice in a 'postsocialist' age." *New Left Review*, 212, 68–93.

——(2008) "From redistribution to recognition? Dilemmas of justice in a 'postsocialist' age." In Kevin Oslom (ed.), *Adding Insult to Injury: Nancy Fraser Debates Her Critics*. London: Verso (pp. 9–41)

Fuchs, C. (2010) "Alternative media as critical media." *European Journal of Social Theory*, 13(2), 173–92.

Georgiou, M. (2005) "Diasporic media across Europe: Multicultural societies and the universalism-particularism continuum." *Journal of Ethnic and Migration Studies*, 31(3), 481–98.

——(2006) *Diaspora, Identity and the Media*. Cresskill, NJ: Hampton Press.

Gillespie, M. (2000) "Transnational communications and diaspora communities." In S. Cottle (ed.), *Ethnic Minorities and the Media*. Buckingham: Open University Press (pp. 164–79).

Gillmor, D. (2004) *We the Media: Grassroots Journalism by the People, for the People*. Sebastopol, CA: O'Reilly Media.

Gilroy, P. (1997) "Diaspora and the detours of identity." In E. Woodward (ed.), *Identity and Difference*. London: Sage.

Harcup, T. (2005) "'I'm doing this to change the world': Journalism in alternative and mainstream media." *Journalism Studies*, 6(3), 361–74.

Hartley, J. and McKee, A. (2000) *The Indigenous Public Sphere*. Oxford: Oxford University Press.

Hepp, A. Bozdag, C. and Suna, L. (2012) *Cultural Identity and Communicative Connectivity in Diasporas: Origin-Ethno- and World-Oriented Migrants*. Retrieved from http://www.academia.edu/920072/Cultural_identity_and_communicative_connectivity_in_diasporas_Origin-_ethno-and_world-oriented_migrants (accessed 9 December 2013).

Hopkins, L. (2009) "Media and migration: A review of the field." *Australian Journal of Communication*, 36(2), 36–54.

Howley, K. (2005) *Community Media, People, Places, and Communication Technologies*. Cambridge: Cambridge University Press.

——(ed.) (2010) *Understanding Community Media*. London: Sage.

Jankowski, N. and Prehn, O. (2002) *Community Media in the Information Age: Perspectives and Prospects*. Cresskill, NJ: Hampton Press.

Kim, Y. (2011) "Diasporic nationalism and the media: Asian women on the move." *International Journal of Cultural Studies*, 14(2), 136–51.

Kymlicka, W. (1995) *Multicultural Citizenship*. Oxford: Oxford University Press.

Lentin, A. and Titley, G. (2011) *The Crisis of Multiculturalism: Racism in a Neoliberal Age*. London: Zed Books.

Martin-Barbero, J. (1993) *Communication, Culture and Hegemony: From Media to Mediations.* London: Sage.

Meyer, D. S. and Minkoff, D. C. (2004) "Conceptualizing political opportunity." *Social Forces,* 82(4), 1457–1492.

Milikowski, M. (2000) "Exploring a model of de-ethnicization: The case of Turkish in the Netherlands." *European Journal of Communication,* 15(4), 443–68.

Morley, D. and Robins, K. (1995) *Spaces of Identity: Global Media, Electronic Landscapes and Cultural Boundaries.* London: Routledge.

Nacify, H. (1993) *The Making of Exile Culture: Iranian Television in Los Angeles.* Minneapolis: University of Minnesota Press.

O'Neal, C. H. (2007) "Community radio: *Milango* for lives." In K. Coyer, T. Dowmunt and A. Fountain (eds), *The Alternative Media Handbook.* London: Routledge (pp. 123–25).

Patton, C. (1993) "Tremble, hetero swine!" In M. Warner (ed.), *Fear of a Queer Planet.* Minneapolis: University of Minnesota Press (pp. 143–77).

Portes, A., Guarnizo, L. E and Landot, P. (1999) "The study of transnationalism: Pitfalls and promise of an emergent research field." *Ethnic and Racial Studies,* 22(2), 217–37.

Poster, M. (1990) *The Mode of Information: Post-Structuralism and Social Context.* Chicago: Chicago University Press.

Pratt, M. (1992) *Imperial Eyes: Travel Writing and Transculturation.* London and New York: Routledge.

Robins, K. and Aksoy, A. (2005) "Whoever looks always finds: Transnational viewing and knowledge-experience." In J. Chalaby (ed.), *Transnational Television Worldwide: Towards a New Media Order.* London: I. B. Tauris (pp. 14–42).

Rodríguez, C. (2001) *Fissures in the Mediascape: An International Study of Citizens' Media.* Cresskill, NJ: Hampton Press.

Rodríguez, C., Kidd, D. and Stein, L. (eds) (2010) *Creating New Communication Spaces.* Volume I of *Making Our Media: Global Initiatives toward a Democratic Public Sphere.* New York: Euricom Monographs, Hampton Press.

Schlesinger, P. (1994) "Europe's contradictory communicative space." *Daedalus,* 123(2), 28–55.

Sen, A. (1999) *Development as Freedom.* Oxford: Oxford University Press.

Shields, R. (1992) *Places of the Margin: Alternative Geographies of Modernity.* London: Routledge.

Song, S. (2007) *Justice, Gender, and the Politics of Multiculturalism.* Cambridge: Cambridge University Press.

Sreberny, A (2000) "Media and diasporic consciousness: An exploration among Iranians in London." In S. Cottle (ed.), *Ethnic Minorities and the Media: Changing Cultural Boundaries.* London: Open University Press (pp. 154–63).

Young, I. M. (1997) *Intersecting Voices.* Princeton, NJ: Princeton University Press.

37

PRISONERS' RADIO

Connecting communities through alternative discourse

Heather Anderson

You're listening to Locked In on 4ZZZ 102.1FM. We're your weekly prisoners' request show and don't forget, if you're offended by strong language or adult concepts, please tune out for the next two hours. First up we have a letter from Arthur Gorrie Correctional Centre ... Dear Locked In, how the fuck are yas?

(*Locked In*, 21 October 2013, 6:03 pm)

Welcome to the world of prisoners' radio, where prisoners, ex-prisoners, and their friends and families, as well as activists and community broadcasters, discuss public and private elements of life behind bars. This chapter explores how prisoners' radio engages prisoners' voices and fosters their connections to community while producing alternative discourses that enrich the wider public sphere. While there are many different aspects of prisoners' radio worthy of research and discussion, there are two aspects of particular significance. First, as isolated institutions, prisons do not appear conducive to fostering connections between prisoners and the wider community to which the majority of them will return. Prisoners' radio provides such a conduit. Second, again due to the private and insulated nature of correctional services, very little is known about this stage of the justice system. Prisoners' radio provides one way to generate alternative discourses and understandings about the incarcerated. But first we need to paint a picture of the genre itself.

What is prisoners' radio?

Prisoners' radio is a broad term, referring to any type of radio broadcast by or for a 'prisoner community of interest', that can be heard by the general public. Beyond that simple statement, this media type offers itself through a wide variety of formats. Prisoners' radio may broadcast as a regular programme or an annual special feature. It may be presented by prisoners inside prison, but more often than not is facilitated through community or public radio stations 'on the outside'. Programmes may focus on the personal lives of prisoners and play music requests and dedications, or present news and current affairs relating to prison issues and other related themes – and sometimes they do a mixture of both. Excluded from this definition are internal prison radio stations ('prison radio') that can only be received within the perimeter of the correctional centre in which it broadcasts. While there is a need for research into prison radio stations themselves, it is a different type of medium and, as such, it is important to maintain a distinction between the two. Prison radio is an even less researched area than prisoners' radio programming, mostly due to practicalities – prisons are very isolated, secretive places and little public information is available to what goes on inside these institutions. There are, however, a number of well-known prison radio stations and training projects that will be mentioned during this chapter.

The majority of prisoners' radio programmes broadcast from outside prison; however, there are some exceptions. *Beyond the Bars* is an Australian project that broadcasts annually to coincide with NAIDOC Week – a celebration of the survival and strength of Aboriginal and Torres Strait Islander culture. Broadcasters conduct prison workshops in the weeks leading up to NAIDOC Week that culminate in live programs from a number of institutions, broadcast locally through Melbourne community stations 3CR and 3KND, and nationally through the National Indigenous Radio Service. Another more regular programme, *Souverains Anonymes*, is produced by prisoners from Bordeaux Jail, in Montreal, Canada, and broadcast by several community radio stations in Quebec.

A more common approach is where the broadcasts are produced outside prison with contributions from the prisoner population. The Australian programme *Prison Radio* in Adelaide reads prisoners' letters every week, along with song dedications. The San Francisco–based *Prison Radio Project* produces documentaries and the commentaries of several prisoners, including well-known political prisoner Mumia Abul Jamal, working with radio stations to disseminate their content. On the Gaza Strip, *The Prisoners' Radio* fosters contact between Palestinian families and their loved ones in Israeli prisons, whom they are unable to visit due to the blockades.

Broadly, prisoners' radio aims to provide audiences with alternative discourse on prison issues as well as to connect prisoners with the wider community through their participation in media. It includes the voices of "prisoners, former prisoners, their friends and family, social justice activists and/or government representatives as well as community radio broadcasters and the occasional prison staff member" (Anderson, 2012: 15).

Examining prisoners' radio

Prisoners' radio shows tend to be broadcast on community radio stations, and while it is difficult to produce an exhaustive list of programmes due to their transient nature, at the time of writing there is prisoners' radio programming in Jamaica, South Africa, the Gaza Strip, Australia, Canada, the United States, Spain and the United Kingdom (though most Spanish and UK radio is in the form of prison radio rather than content broadcasting to the wider community).

Australia and Canada appear to have the most established regular and long-running prisoners' radio programmes, more than likely because both of these countries also have long-standing community radio sectors. The United Kingdom and United

States, it seems, operate more internal prison radio stations, and also have national networks such as Inside Job Productions and the Prison Radio Association (UK) that coordinate training and resources for these prison radio stations. Other national networks include the Prison Radio project in the United States and the Prison Broadcasting Network in South Africa, which has a strong Christian emphasis.

A broader inventory of prisoners' radio can be found in Anderson (2012), and this chapter is not the place to replicate this. It does, however, seem appropriate to share a few more examples before moving on to discuss two major themes relating to this distinct form of broadcast. As already mentioned, there appear to be two main types of prisoners' radio programme – request shows and information shows – although the two can sometimes combine. Alternatively, we might consider programmes that focus on facilitating prisoners' participation and those that emphasise the dissemination of information and alternative discourses on law and order issues (again, there are hybrid forms).

Canada has a large number of prisoners' radio shows in the second category that mostly focus on providing news and information. *Stark Raven* on Co-Op Radio in Vancouver is one long-running example that broadcasts regularly (at the time of writing, three times a week for one hour) and focuses on prisons and criminalisation locally, nationally and internationally. The program has a significant activist contribution and is produced by a collective that also posts news on the Prison Justice website (www.prisonjustice.ca). CKUT in Montreal has two separate prison news and current affairs programmes and also coordinates national community radio broadcasting for Prisoners' Justice Day. The station's newsroom has also facilitated documentary-making with prisoners, circumventing a ban on taking recording equipment into prisons by acting as a conduit for the participants. The newsroom coordinator would conduct interviews on behalf of prisoners who would then listen back to the content to make editorial and production decisions that, once again, would be carried out by the newsroom coordinator. This way the prisoners were able to produce their own media working around situations of non-access (Anderson, 2012).

In Australia there is a mix of request-based programmes, such as the *Prison Show* mentioned earlier, and information-based programmes, such as 3CR's weekly *Doin' Time*. Request programmes also dominate Indigenous broadcasting in Australia. Another approach to prisoners' broadcasting comes in the form of the 30-minute programme *Jailbreak*, broadcast in Sydney on 2SER but also nationally via the Community Radio Network. *Jailbreak* is funded by a government body (South East Health) and managed by a community organisation that supports prisoners and their families (the Community Restorative Centre). The programme is funded to broadcast harm minimisation and health promotion messages that focus on lived experiences and is produced through project-based workshops inside and out of prison (Minc, Butler and Gahan, 2007).

The United States hosts many prisoners' programmes. *The Prison Show* broadcasts on KPFT in Houston, Texas, and divides its broadcasts between one hour of news and information and two hours of recordings of messages from friends and family. These recordings were used to successfully lobby for changes in Texas legislation allowing for contact between prisoners and their children; the radio show's main host and producer is a former prisoner and jailhouse lawyer. Also in Texas, this time from Livingstone, we find the Christian/family station KDOL that broadcasts three programmes as part of its All Life Is Precious Ministries. One of these programmes airs the night before a prisoner's execution, playing their favourite requested music and relaying messages from friends and family. The impact, not to mention controversy, of such programming is somewhat incomprehensible.

The academic study of prisoners' radio

There has been little academic attention given to prisoners' radio programming, beyond my own work (Anderson, 2012, 2013b, 2008). One exception is that of anthropologist Daniel Fisher (2009), whose research on mediating kinship in Northern Australia looks in part at Indigenous "call-in request shows" and how these address the "geographical and institutional boundaries of (incarcerated) Indigenous people from kin and community" (Fisher, 2009: 281). He describes request shows as cultural practices that resonate "with media activists' efforts to link up incarcerated men and women with their families and communities" (ibid.: 282). This, he says, is particularly important considering the dispersed nature of many Indigenous families due to the 'stolen generations', taken as children to foster homes and state institutions, as well as the disproportionately high number of Indigenous prisoners.

There are a small number of studies that describe the work of particular radio stations and their programmes. Minc, Butler and Gahan (2007) describe the work of *Jailbreak* within a health policy context, explaining the strategies used to successfully promote healthy lifestyles among prisoners in New South Wales. *Radio Wanno*, at HMP Wandsworth (a project of Inside Job Productions in the United Kingdom), is described by McDermott (2004) in terms of its innovative training and contribution to prisoner rehabilitation, from a criminology studies perspective. Other studies describe the listening patterns of radio audiences in prison (Bonini and Perrotta, 2007; Jewkes, 2002) but do not focus specifically on radio programming produced for and/or by prison communities of interest.

Connecting to community

It is important to consider the effect prison life has on a person's sense of belonging to the outside world. Prisons are isolated institutions with limited communications with the outside world that not only restrict the ability for healthy public debate on prison issues to exist, but also challenge any opportunities for prisoners to a maintain sense of connection with their communities. Prison life has the very real potential to damage the bonds that connect people to society (Stern, 1998: 11), and yet most prisoners will return to their communities within a relatively short period of time.[1]

Unfortunately, prisons are not typically successful in preparing prisoners for their resumption of their status as ordinary citizens – the very nature of incarceration can fracture family and social networks, undermine employment opportunities and introduce criminal alternatives to life in open society (Hogg, 2002), and numerous studies have emphasised the value of outside relationships (Culhane, 1988; Toch,

1996) to assist with avoiding such fracturing. The prison system itself can also discourage contact through visits. Many visitors find their treatment by prison officers, as well as the physical accessibility of many prisons, has a negative influence on the frequency of contact between prisoners and their loved ones on the outside (Toch, 1996). Issues of isolation are compounded for Indigenous prisoners and other marginalised populations. Socio-economic conditions often limit family and friends from visiting prisoners who are incarcerated away from their home areas.

Meadows et al. (2007) identified prisoners' radio to be addressing issues of isolation through the Central Australian Aboriginal Media Association (CAAMA) and National Indigenous Radio Service (NIRS) that broadcast request shows and other prisoners' radio broadcasting. We might expect similar issues to be faced by prisoners in remote locations around the world, and it is possible that prisoners' radio programmes are able to assist in lessening isolation by providing a link between listeners inside and out. The founder of *Beyond the Bars*, Jay Estorninho, supports this, arguing that for Indigenous people the programmes play a vital role in assisting prisoners to feel part of their community during NAIDOC week, while facilitating contact between those inside and outside prison:

> It's just so important for the community ... how much this means on both sides, the blokes and the women inside prison ... and the feedback you get from the audience is, you know, they really appreciate hearing from people who are important to them, whether it be family or friend or just people they know in the community.
>
> (Estorninho, telephone interview, 20 December 2007)

A particularly challenging time for many prisoners (at least in Western societies) is Christmas. In Queensland, Australia (and similarly elsewhere), there are no visits on Christmas Day, and any programs or activities are cancelled, as many staff are on leave during this time. According to Catholic Prison Ministry coordinator Dave Martin (personal correspondence, 28 October 2013), many prisoners prefer to treat it as an 'ordinary' day so they don't feel the pain of being apart from those on the outside. There is a high degree of loneliness in prison, highlighted around significant days like Christmas.

Prisoners' radio shows attempt to address these problems in different ways. Some programmes, such as *Jailbreak* and *Locked In* (Brisbane, Australia), host live Christmas Day specials, regardless of what day of the week this holiday falls on. The presenter of the *Sunday Night Request Show* on 98.9FM (an Indigenous station also in Brisbane, Australia) has, in the past, visited correctional centres in the weeks leading up to Christmas to record messages from the prisoners to their loved ones on the outside.

In Whitesburg, Kentucky, *Calls from Home*, based at community radio station WMMT, produces a Christmas special made up of the voices of friends and families of those inside, "sharing the intimate power of families speaking directly to their incarcerated loved ones" (*Calls from Home*, 2013). A toll-free number is set up for people to record their messages, and the pre-produced programme is distributed to community radio stations across the country. National syndication is particularly important due to the high number of urban prisoners being relocated to correctional centres in remote rural areas (such as the coalfields of Appalachia, where WMMT is based).

Locked In uses a talkback system only on Christmas Day, which enables callers to speak live-to-air. The following is a transcript from one of these calls that went to air in 2012:

FIRST CALLER: Merry Christmas Guy, I'm up at Woodford, love you babe, wish you were here today ... (voice starts to break) ... yeah. I'm with your mum and your sisters, they wanna say a quick hello.

MUM: Merry Christmas Guy-Guy from me and Dad, hope you have a good one and we'll see ya soon.

YOUNG CHILD: Hello, merry Christmas uncle, love you uncle Guy-Guy, ok see ya.

Another three or four different people – younger and older – all speak into the phone at the same time, with various Christmas messages.

FIRST CALLER: That's from all your family from Mildura ... love you ... call me Friday when you can ... And I'll ring back soon and your father can do a shout out to you.

(*Locked In*, 25 December 2012)

The impact of this broadcast was captured in prisoners' letters in the following weeks, with one describing how it brought a tear to his eye. Other feedback to *Locked In* (with which the author volunteers) demonstrates the effect the Christmas Day broadcast has on other listeners, who might not otherwise even consider the impact of having a loved one incarcerated on such a traditionally family-orientated day. This leads us to think about how prisoners' radio shows provide alternative discourses within which to consider prisons issues more broadly. Alternative constructions come not only from information, but also from the perspectives that are generated through the personalisation fostered when people tell their own stories, in their own voices, and human interest, as a news value, can be a "united force in reminding people of their shared humanity" (Conley, 1997: 71). The Christmas Day broadcasts are certainly very humanising in this sense and encourage listeners unfamiliar with the prison experience to frame prisoners as individual family members rather than nameless criminals. As one listener described:

> In essence, *Locked In* humanises people in jail. [It's] no easy task to remind the greater community that prisoners are Mothers, Fathers, Sons, Daughters, Brothers and Sisters to people everywhere, in all walks of life, when many people would prefer to think of them as persona non grata.
>
> (M. Trembath, email correspondence, 7 November 2007)

Alternative discourses

Inside prison, people live outside the media's unblinking eye (Lumby, 2002), and the general public probably knows less about imprisonment than about any other stage of the justice system (Roberts and Hough, 2005; Surette, 2007). Because the majority of people have never been to a prison, either as visitor, 'resident', or staff member, other sources need to be drawn upon for understandings about the prison system.

A wide range of cultural products "feed the popular imaginary with representations of life in prison" (Ek, 2005), and Hollywood especially can be viewed as a discursive practice that fixes the meaning of prison itself (Mason, 2006). Fictional representations of the prison certainly have a significant effect on wider understandings of prison issues, so much so that Ek (2005) found the international public is more aware of crime and punishment 'US-style' than it is of actual procedures and legislation in home countries – such is the "power of cultural import" (ibid.: 113).

From a non-fiction perspective, there is plenty of research that points to minimal reporting on prison issues compared to other layers of law enforcement (Ericson, Baranek and Chan 1991; Roberts and Hough, 2005) yet, at the same time, law and order issues consistently dominate electoral politics and are a staple in everyday public debate (Hogg and Brown, 1998). Despite this, the public appears poorly informed about the effectiveness of different types of sentences, and crime is framed through the lens of individual pathologies rather than structural crises such as the collapse of the welfare state (Cheliotis, 2010).

The mass media play a decisive role in the formation of punishment among the public (ibid.); the increase in incarceration rates in Britain and Europe has been linked to media reporting of high-profile dramatic and isolated events (Walmsley, 2000). Media coverage of prisons and prison life is often inadequate and sensational; mass culture seems to make it easier for those in power to disseminate their views "but harder for marginal voices to talk back" (Warner, 2002: 49). Robert Gaucher, an activist working with both prisoners and prisoners' advocacy groups, is critical of the mainstream media's ability or willingness to cover prison issues and laments the absence of prisoners' own views and perspectives in the public sphere:

> I have yet to encounter any Canadian prisoners' views on this [Tough on Crime] legislation … "agencies" et al. do not achieve much media coverage or generate much public debate over criminal justice issues, let alone provide prisoners' positions in Canada.
>
> (Gaucher, email interview, 21 December 2007)

There is a clear and urgent need for alternative discourses on law and order issues that speak through the voices of those experiencing, or with experience of, the prison system, as well as for representations that place incarceration within a broader societal context. The majority of information imparted through prisoners' radio is produced by activists, community organisations and the broadcasters themselves, with prisoners' radio acting as an alternative, not only through choices of content and angle, but also through the wide range of voices presented which might often not otherwise receive significant airplay or media space. Prisoners' radio programmes can be thought of as establishing counter-publics, in the sense that they expose alternative ideas and discourses about prison and criminal justice issues to a wider audience. They also act as enclaves (see Squires, 2002), fostering the internal dialogues and debates that occur between prisoners themselves, as well as within the prisoners' radio 'community of interest'. Programmes with a focus on the dissemination of information for wider public discussion include *Stark Raven*, *Prison Radio* (Canada), Prisoners' Justice Day programming, *Doing Time*, *Jailbreak*, and the various syndicated shows produced in the United States. Some radio programs, such as *Stark Raven* and *Off the Hour* in Canada, are explicit about the way they directly position themselves in opposition to the mainstream:

> We provide news that blasts through the sensationalism and sound bites of the mainstream media.
>
> (CKUT, 2007)

> We're trying to be politically conscious and counter information, trying to counter mainstream information. We're presenting ideas and having people think in a different way.
>
> (*Stark Raven* presenter, Aspinwall, 2007)

Increasing communication between the public and the prisoner has been found to be an effective way of avoiding prison disturbances, because prisoner dissatisfaction may be appeased when they believe that they are reaching someone outside (Irwin in Martin and Sussman, 1993: 209). Prisoners in my own research (Anderson, 2012) took the opportunity to act as political commentators and demonstrated an awareness of a wider listening public, producing their own news or commentary in the letters that they wrote for broadcast. One prisoner, writing to *Locked In* for on-air broadcast, had the following comment to make on alleged corruption within Queensland Corrective Services and the need for a Royal Commission:

> The system has plummeted into the bowels of hell, and the reality of it is we can all have ideas of advocate groups having a voice for us but without a royal commission into this shit, or setting the state alight, fuck all and plenty of it is all the future holds for crimes doing time … It's heartening in the moment to hear supporters of us fire up, but come tomorrow we are not better off.
>
> (*Locked In*, 16 March 2007)

Conclusion

The perspectives of prisoners are able to enhance the quality of public discussion surrounding prison and criminal justice issues. Prisoners themselves also often rely on prisoners' radio to receive news from and about their local prison environments. Information is not always available through mainstream outlets, and prisoners may be hindered in their own efforts to find information; newspapers are not available to general prison populations. Correctional services may use the internet as the predominant means of promoting their initiatives, a media outlet not readily accessible to those who are incarcerated.

Prisoners' radio programmes also provide alternative content in the ways in which particular topics are treated, often examining causes rather than effects. Alternative constructions may come not only from information and context, but also through the personalisation engendered when people tell their own stories in their own voices. Prisoners' programmes can be humanising in this sense, where very private topics are discussed through a completely public medium and allow other listeners to consider prison life through different perspectives. Listeners may be reminded that prisoners are people, only temporarily removed from society (Anderson, 2012). Prisoners are traditionally defined and treated as a group in society whose voices are considered less moral and less deserving of attention (Culhane, 1988). Community media production can challenge these assumptions by providing alternative opportunities to participate in debate and discussion relevant to prisoners' lives (Anderson, 2008).

Further research is needed to consider the effects of media production on prisoner populations, for example through prison radio projects that provide formal educational qualifications alongside experiences of working in radio. We might also consider the benefits of viewing prisoners as community radio volunteers; the importance of prisoners being able to practice altruism is gaining recognition as a way to encourage prisoners "to develop their own personal qualities such as concern for others and not just to have the identity of a thief, a burglar or a hooligan" (Stern, 2005: 12). Strong links between community radio volunteering and empowerment (Meadows et al., 2007) could be extended to the concept of the prisoner broadcaster. There is a certain empowerment that comes from producing one's own media that allows prisoners a voice, where they might otherwise be considered as unworthy of our attention or even invisible.

Note

1 Average sentences across Western countries vary (Australia – 2 years and 2.1 months for women, Canada – up to six months, United States – 5 to 10 years, United Kingdom – up to four years; Australian Bureau of Statistics, 2011; Kilroy and Warner, 2002; Thomas, 2010; Federal Bureau of Prisons, 2013; Berman and Dar, 2013), but even with the higher statistics from the USA and UK, it is apparent that most prisoners are only in custody temporarily.

Further reading

Anderson (2012) is currently the only comprehensive work on prisoners' radio worldwide and includes an international inventory of prisoners' radio programmes and stations as well as four detailed case studies from Canada and Australia. There are also journal articles (for example Anderson 2013b, 2008) that deal with specific issues raised by this media type, while Anderson (2013a) uses the Australian project *Beyond the Bars* to look at relationships between prisoners' radio and community. Fisher (2009) examines how radio (including prisoners' request shows) mediates kinship in Indigenous communities in Northern Australia. McDermott (2004) focuses on *Radio Wanno* in the UK from a criminal justice perspective, and Minc, Butler and Gahan (2007) use the Australian program *Jailbreak* to explore drug policy.

References

Anderson, H. (2008) "Engaging the civil dead: Citizens' media and prisoners' radio." *Global Media Journal*, 2, 1–11. Retrieved from http://www.hca.uws.edu.au/gmjau/archive/iss2_2008/heather_anderson.html (accessed 18 January 2015).

——(2012) *Raising the Civil Dead: Prisoners and Community Radio*. Bern, Switzerland: Peter Lang.

——(2013a) "Beyond the bars: Prisoners' radio strengthening community." *Media International Australia*, 149 (November), 112–27.

——(2013b) "Facilitating active citizenship: Participating in prisoners' radio." *Critical Studies in Media Communication*, 30(4), 292–306.

Aspinwall, E. (2007) Interview with author, Vancouver, Canada, 16 July.

Australian Bureau of Statistics (2011) *Prisoners in Australia 4517.0*. Commonwealth of Australia, Canberra.

Berman, G. and Dar, A. (2013) *Prison Population Statistics*. House of Commons Library, London.

Bonini, T. and Perrotta, M. (2007) "On and off the air: Radio-listening experiences in the San Vittore prison." *Media, Culture and Society*, 29, 179–193.

Calls from Home (2013) *Join the Campaign*. Retrieved from http://nationinside.org/campaign/calls-from-homeholiday/ (accessed 18 January 2015).

Cheliotis, L. K. (2010) "The ambivalent consequences of visibility: Crime and prisons in the mass media." *Crime, Media, Culture*, 6 (August), 169–84.

CKUT (2007) "CKUT 90.3 FM news collective blog." Retrieved from http://ckut.ca/news.php (accessed 31 January 2008).

Conley, D. (1997) *The Daily Miracle: An Introduction to Journalism*. Oxford: Oxford University Press.

Culhane, C. (1988) *Still Barred from Prison: Social Injustice in Canada* (vol. 3). Montreal: Black Rose Books.

Ek, A. (2005) *Race and Masculinity in Contemporary American Prison Narratives*. New York: Taylor and Francis Group.

Ericson, R. V., Baranek, P. M. and Chan, J. (1991) *Representing Order: Crime, Law, and Justice in the News Media*. Toronto: University of Toronto Press.

Federal Bureau of Prisons (2013) *Quick Facts about the Bureau of Prisons*. Retrieved from http://www.bop.gov/news/quick.jsp#3 (accessed 18 January 2015).

Fisher, D. (2009) "Mediating kinship: Country, family, and radio in Northern Australia." *Cultural Anthropology*, 24, 280–312.

Hogg, R. (2002) "Prisoners and the penal estate in Australia." In D. Brown and M. Wilkie (eds.) *Prisoners as Citizens, Human Rights in Australian Prisons*. Annandale, Australia: Federation Press.

Hogg, R. and Brown, D. (1998) *Rethinking Law and Order*. Annandale, Australia: Pluto Press.

Jewkes, Y. (2002) "The use of media in constructing identities in the masculine environment of men's prisons." *European Journal of Communication*, 17(2), 205–25.

Kilroy, D. and Warner, A. (2002) "Deprivation of liberty – Deprivation of rights." In D. Brown and M. Wilkie (eds.) *Prisoners as Citizens, Human Rights in Australian Prisons*. Annandale, Australia: Federation Press.

Lumby, C. (2002) "Televising the invisible: Prisoners, prison reform and the media." In D. Brown and M. Wilkie (eds), *Prisoners as Citizens, Human Rights in Australian Prisons*. Annandale: Federation Press.

Martin, D. M. and Sussman, P. Y. (1993) *Committing Journalism: The Prison Writings of Red Hog*. New York: W.W. Norton and Company.

Mason, P. (2006) *Captured by the Media: Prison Discourse in Popular Culture*. Cullompton, Devon: Willan Publishing.

McDermott, N. (2004) The 'word' on education in prison: Radio Wanno." *Criminal Justice Matters*, 56(1), 38–39.

Meadows, M., Forde, S., Ewart, J. and Foxwell, K. (2007) *Community Media Matters: An Audience Study of the Australian Community Broadcasting Sector*. Brisbane: Griffith University.

Minc, A., Butler, T. and Gahan, G. (2007) "The Jailbreak Health Project – Incorporating a unique radio programme for prisoners." *International Journal of Drug Policy*, 18, 444–6.

Roberts, J. V. and Hough, M. (2005) "The state of prisons: Exploring public knowledge and opinion." *Howard Journal of Criminal Justice*, 44(3), 286–306.

Squires, C. R. (2002) "Rethinking the Black public sphere: An alternative vocabulary for multiple spheres." *Communication Theory*, 12(4), 446–69.

Stern, V. (1998) *A Sin against the Future: Imprisonment in the World*. Boston: Northeastern University Press.

——(2005) *Prisons and Their Communities: Testing a New Approach*. London: International Centre for Prison Studies.

Surette, R. (2007) *Media, Crime, and Criminal Justice: Images, Realities and Policies* (3rd edn). Belmont, CA: Thomson Wadsworth.

Thomas, J. (2010) *Adult Criminal Court Statistics, 2008/2009*. Ontario: Statistics Canada.

Toch, H. (1996) *Living in Prison: The Ecology of Survival* (rev. edn). Washington, DC: American Psychological Association.

Walmsley, R. (2000) "The world prison population situation: Growth, trends, issues and challenges." Paper presented at the Association of Parole Officers International Conference, Ottawa. Retrieved from www.apaintl.org/Pub-Conf2000-PlenaryWalmsley-En.html (accessed 19 September 2007).

Warner, M. (2002) *Publics and Counterpublics*. New York: Zone Books.

38
FANZINES
Enthusiastic production through popular culture

Chris Atton

This chapter explores the nature and scope of fanzines in broad terms: the sheer numbers and diversity of titles make it impossible to provide anything but a general introduction. Examples of specific titles tend to draw on popular music, an indication of the focus of most research into fanzines. (This is not to deny the great deal of attention paid to other fan communities, for example in science fiction; there is, however, relatively little work on fanzines in those communities.)

I use the term 'fanzine' throughout the chapter, for reasons of clarity. The term 'zine' is also often found in both academic studies and popular commentary to refer generally to the same class of amateur publishing. It is important, though, to distinguish between zine and fanzine, for conceptual reasons. The term 'zine' seems to have been established in the 1980s to refer to an extremely wide range of amateur publications, often written, edited and published by one person (Duncombe, 1997). The word itself is a truncation of 'fanzine', a strategy deemed useful by the publishing community itself to indicate positions and interests different from fanzine producers. Fanzines are primarily concerned with the object of their attention (works of literature, music, films or other cultural activities). This is not to say that they are solely about consumption: John Fiske (1991 [1989]: 151) argues that fans are "cultural producers, not cultural consumers". The creativity of fans in the social setting of the fanzine is described by Henry Jenkins (1992: 213) as forming "an alternative social community" where cultural production is employed "as a means of building and maintaining solidarity within the fan community".

In the case of zines, we find a similar impulse towards community, though there is less focus on primary texts (television programmes, films, music, sport and so on). In many cases, those who produce zines turn to themselves, to their own lives and experiences: they turn these into the subjects of their writing. At the heart of zine culture is not the study of the 'other' (celebrity, cultural object or activity) but the study of self, of personal expression and the building of community (Duncombe, 1997). Given that the production of zines arises from what we might term a "fanzine culture" (Rutherford, 1992), it inevitable that the two practices will share some features. This is particularly the case where printed titles have moved online, as we shall see later in the chapter. First, though, we will examine the nature and scope of the fanzine, before exploring the cultural significance of fanzine production and its social settings.

The nature and scope of fanzines

The fanzine is an amateur form of publishing, one that is prompted less by commercial gain than by an enthusiasm for its subject. It is written, edited and produced by fans. The portmanteau term 'fanzine' (combining 'fan' and 'magazine') has its origins in the American science fiction magazines of the 1930s. According to Teal Triggs (1995: 77), it was coined by Russ Chauvenet in 1941 "to describe a mimeographed publication devoted primarily to science fiction and superhero comic enthusiasts". Titles such as *Amazing Stories* and the *Comet* in the US and *Novae Terrae* in the UK not only presented short stories in the genre, but also provided space for readers to discuss the science upon which the stories were premised. It is possible to locate the roots of fanzine publishing even earlier, in the amateur journalism of the second half of the 1800s and, in particular, in the establishment in the United States of amateur press associations (Rau, 1994). However, the publications that have come to be known as fanzines tend to have their origins in the amateur science fiction magazines of the early twentieth century.

These early science fiction magazines brought together professional writers and fans of their writing to create and sustain a cultural community for a literary genre that was at that time largely disregarded or dismissed by elite literary groups (critics, academics and readers). As such, they sustained a contemporary cultural form that was deemed to be marginalised by mainstream cultural agents. This is a significant function of the fanzine that persists to the present: we see its continuation through fanzines devoted to horror films, 'B' movies, science fiction television series, as well as in avant-garde and experimental forms of popular music.

In the 1950s and 1960s, while publications such as *Melody Maker* and *New Musical Express* in the United Kingdom sought to embrace emerging musical styles and began to take popular music seriously, the need for fanzines remained significant. The British fanzines *Blues Unlimited* (1963) and *Blues and Soul* (1968) appeared at critical moments in popular music; in both cases, the attention of the mainstream music press was drawn by syntheses of existing genres. The musicians who provided the raw material – the 'roots music' – tended to be forgotten. Along with folk movement fanzines such as *Sing Out!* (1950), such titles developed and sustained interest in these genres and kept enthusiasts informed.

Fanzines also sustain aspects of popular culture that have either passed into history or are in a process of emergence. Examples of the former in popular music include titles that cover the rock 'n' roll of the 1950s and garage bands of the 1960s; the latter have included publications devoted to emerging punk scenes across the world, free improvisation and German rock music. Perhaps paradoxically, fanzines may provide detailed commentary of very visible aspects of popular culture. Numerous fanzines have dealt with the work and life of such rock stalwarts as Elvis Presley, the Rolling Stones, Bruce Springsteen and Pink Floyd. Fans of rock auteurs such as Bob Dylan have continued to find the oeuvres of their favourite artists inexhaustible as sites for criticism, documentation and speculation. The fanzine is typically found in the evolution of a genre in order to validate music that is generally ignored or reviled by the mainstream critics. In some cases, as in jazz, it existed to provide more detailed and reflective coverage than was available within the confines of the daily newspaper or general-interest magazine. Paul Stump (1997: 339) has talked of music fanzines keeping certain musics alive, "in much the same way artisanal crafts or endangered wildfowl survive: through the selfless, financially unremunerative toil of devotees".

Ideology and cultural politics

Fanzines challenge critical orthodoxy: as we have seen, they often arise because their contributors believe that 'their' culture is marginalised or misrepresented by mainstream tastes. Fanzine writers are less interested in reaching out to broader audiences, preferring to cultivate and consolidate specialist audiences. Seen in this way, fanzines have an ideological foundation. Simon Frith has even termed music fanzines "ideological magazines" and has argued that they are extremely effective spaces for establishing "ideological musical communities" (2002: 240). It is in these spaces that a "democratic conversation [takes place] between music lovers, a social celebration of a particular kind of musical attention and commitment'" (Frith, 2002: 241). This conversation becomes possible because, as Frith argues, "critics of popular forms (TV, film and to some extent pop) need know nothing about such forms except as consumers; their skill is to be able to write about ordinary experience" (1996: 38, n. 40).

The conversation is democratic because the knowledge and authority on which it is based come not from formal education or professional training but primarily from autodidactic, amateur enthusiasm. Fanzines "focus on the accumulation and display of detailed information about a topic. [...] fans come to perform their own detailed critiques of their chosen subjects. Such displays of specialised knowledge are common across the range of fanzines" (Atton, 2004: 139–40). Such accumulation and display of expert knowledge has the capacity to challenge professionalised notions of authority and expertise. To be considered an expert by readers means that the fanzine writer accrues a high degree of cultural capital. This expertise is typically displayed directly and not through the mediation of other sources (such as professional writers or other experts). It is from this direct display of expert knowledge that the writer achieves credibility.

Turning to cultural politics, when the fanzine is considered from within cultural studies or cultural sociology, it is most often characterised as a "site for cultural contestation" (Jary, Horne and Bucke, 1991), where identities may be formed and communities developed. Fanzines thus become, it may be argued, major sites of cultural production that represent or stand in for, activate or establish a community. The dominant sociological understanding of the fanzine is that the power of 'amateur' work lies in its subcultural location (Hebdige, 1979). Jary, Horne and Bucke (1991: 584) see in football fanzines the "same orientation to contradiction, the oppositional stance, mentioned by Hebdige". Here, the primary function of the fanzine is to stand in for a social relationship.

Cultural homology and the demographics of fanzines

For many cultural commentators and academics alike, the punk movement of 1976–7 represents the defining cultural moment of the fanzine. Here, we find the argument that the fanzine is not merely a medium for a marginalised cultural activity, but that it is

CHRIS ATTON

definitively subcultural in its origins and intent. Arguably there has been an over-emphasis on theorising the fanzine in subcultural terms: in her survey of British fanzines, Teal Triggs (1995: 74) argues that "[f]anzines are vehicles of subcultural communication".

Dick Hebdige argued that the punk fanzine can be seen as "homologous with punk's subterranean and anarchic style" (Hebdige, 1979: 112) through what have since been considered the classic features of fanzine production: stencilled lettering or Letraset type for headlines; primitive cut-and-paste page layouts based on typewritten (not typeset) copy and articles photocopied from newspapers and magazines; photocopied photographs (rather than half-tone reproductions); and the use of handwritten copy among a variety of typefaces. The form and the production values of the punk fanzine have endured as stereotypical of the fanzine. More significantly, though, in terms of fanzine practices, the anti-design aesthetic of the punk fanzine has become the norm, regardless of the subcultural origins of the music, its musicians and its fans. The homological argument finds in these features a reaction against professionalism and a refusal to accord to the conventions of magazine layout and design. It assumes a symbolic fit between the fanzine and the lifestyle and experiences of its producers.

According to this argument, the fanzine would tend to have been produced by unskilled (in a conventional sense) working-class youth. In the case of punk, this often seems to have been the case, but the assumption does not withstand close scrutiny. For example, while *Sniffin' Glue* was edited and written by a working-class Londoner (Mark Perry), Scotland's first punk fanzine (*Hanging Around*) was put together by middle-class students at the University of Edinburgh. The post-punk fanzine *Stabmental* was produced by pupils of Oundle School, an English public school (Atton, 2006a).

Because the fanzine does not require professional experience of either journalism or publishing, nor any advanced educational attainment, it does make it amenable – in principle, at least – to a far wider range of people than we would expect to see as professional critics. In practice, though, this range is quite restricted: it is young white males who seem to be responsible for most music fanzines. Some of the most significant fanzines in the history of rock writing fall into this category, such as Paul Williams's *Crawdaddy!* (founded in 1966 and not only the first rock fanzine but arguably the first rock magazine), Greg Shaw's *Who Put the Bomp!* (1970), Paul Morley's *Out There* and *Girl Trouble*, and Jon Savage's *London's Outrage* (Atton, 2003). There are exceptions: Sarah Champion published her first fanzine, *Alarm*, when she was a fourteen-year-old schoolgirl. She went on to produce *Scam* and *Bop City*, two influential publications in the British post-punk and dance scenes of the late 1980s (Dickinson, 1997). The prominence of men reflects the gendered nature of much of the popular culture under discussion in fanzines. For example, though women are not entirely absent from football fanzines, they do comprise a very small minority of contributors (Atton, 2006b); by contrast, feminist cultures produce fanzines that are wholly edited and written by women (such as *Riot Grrrl*; Duncombe, 1997: ch. 7).

The special pleading for punk as the progenitor of late-twentieth-century fanzine production also makes it difficult to consider – and seems to exclude – those people who produced fanzines that dealt with other musical forms, whose publications were more clearly professional or which had relationships with the mainstream that are not straightforwardly 'oppositional'. Progressive rock fanzines, for example, seem to favour tidy, professional-like layouts that permit the reader to read through them – rather than against them – to their subject matter (Atton, 2001). The anti-design of the punk fanzine can be explained by the exigencies of funding, rather than by an appeal to ideology. For fanzines, there have been few opportunities for external funding (at least in the early days of publication); for many, there may be no desire even to seek such funding, in order to remain independent of advertising revenue (an ideological position shared by many alternative and community media projects). Consequently, production values are often very different from those of mainstream magazines. Until the 1970s, it was common for copy to be hammered out on old typewriters, headlines hand-lettered (in some cases, entire issues were hand-written) and illustrations etched onto duplicating stencils. As the photocopier became more widely available, original illustrations and graphics 'borrowed' from professional sources (including the commercial press) could easily be incorporated into the text. Although not all fanzines were as resolutely amateurish as these methods suggest, all had at their heart what we might call a domesticity of production that predates punk. The US jazz magazine *Coda* began in 1958 as a 12-page mimeographed fanzine, put together by its editor and a team of volunteers working for beer and pizza. *Mojo Navigator Rock 'n' Roll News*, the predecessor to Greg Shaw's *Who Put the Bomp!*, began in 1966 as a stapled, two-page mimeographed newsletter.

Fanzines around the world

So far this chapter has focused on fanzines from the US and the UK, but fanzine production is international. Of particular interest here are the ways in which fanzines engage with popular cultural forms that originate in the US and the UK, and how fanzine discourse is able to assign value to these forms that is very different from their origins. In the 1980s, the German fanzine *Gorilla Beat* explored the music of artists as diverse as the Pretty Things, Procol Harum, the Pink Fairies and Joy Division in part because the editor loved these musics, and in part because these musical associations made sense to a particular German audience in a way they would not have to a British or a North American audience of the same time. Similarly, some Japanese fanzines are sites for heterogeneous musical appreciation, where genres and artists are shorn of their original cultural contexts. Elsewhere, the fanzine is employed to sustain indigenous musical cultures in the face of a mainstream press obsessed with the current North American or British stars. These cultures are not necessarily 'folk' in origin; they might just as easily draw from rock music or jazz, as in the French fanzines *Notes* and *Improjazz*. In other cases, fanzines might have a sociopolitical dimension, as in the numerous fanzines published in Japan and South America that deal with extreme musics (such as industrial music, grindcore and death metal) that are in contrast to the dominant mores of the societies within which they are produced. Before 1989, the production of a fanzine anywhere in Eastern Europe was a political act even more significant than these. Fanzines in the Eastern bloc have been little researched, but there are examples from Poland, Hungary and the former Czechoslovakia that derive much from the aesthetic and subcultural values of punk and might be considered forms of dissident publishing, as serious an undertaking as any explicitly political *samizdat*. In common with most *samizdat* publishing, such publications have diminished in number and importance with the liberalisation of government and markets in these countries.

Online fanzines

Fanzines are always created from the available technological resources of the present. They offer a space for the creation, development and enacting of a community of interest. In the case of online fanzines, it may be argued that such opportunities are further enhanced: freed from the physical limits of the printed publication, contributors are able to post immediate impressions of cultural experiences or requests for information. Long-form writing, whether in the shape of biographical and historical essays, discographies or catalogues, may be promoted without the restrictions of page lengths. The collaborative possibilities of online communication enable fan communities to actively participate in and share the development of encyclopaedia-like resources. The personal web page may be employed as a fanzine. Seen in this light, the internet has become an extension of fanzine culture, enabling individuals to write and communicate as often or as rarely as they wish, unconstrained even by the rather flexible notions of frequency, circulation and production values of the printed fanzine.

The movement of many fanzines to the internet offers a number of advantages, therefore. Printing costs and the limits of voluntary labour (time and numbers of people involved) have chronically affected the frequency and, more generally, the longevity of the printed publication. The reliance on the efforts of a small group of dedicated fans, together with financial limits, makes the move to web-based publication very tempting. Printing costs, the labour of layout and the effort involved in distribution are, if not entirely absent (printing, of course, is absent), significantly reduced. Many fanzine editors, however, prefer to maintain a printed title, using a web presence as advertising for the printed form and to encourage subscriptions. The British football fanzine is one example, where a tradition persists of selling a football club's fanzine on match days outside the football ground, on the terraces and in pubs. The commercial potential of the football fanzine has not gone unnoticed by marketers. Content aggregators and web hosts have recognised this since the 1990s and provide space for football fanzines that is supported by advertising, typically for sports-related goods and services such as club souvenirs, sporting equipment and club strips and gaming and betting services (Atton, 2006b).

There is evidence to suggest, however, that the online fanzine is not an equal replacement for its printed precursor. When the editor of *For the Clerisy* moved his publication to the internet, he found that he not only lost readers who lacked access to the technology, he also lost readers who preferred the tactile and portable nature of the printed publication (Atton, 2002). After a few issues of the *Clerisy* e-zine, readership had dropped so low that it returned to print. While access to the technology is now far more common than it was in the 1990s, the arguments about portability and physical familiarity persist and are familiar to any champion of the printed page. While fanzines survive in printed form and show no signs of disappearing, in cyberspace it is often difficult to separate online fanzines 'proper' from other forms of personal publishing. The rise of social networking sites in the 2000s has arguably refocused the energies of individuals to explore their own identities and to seek out like-minded others. The standardised layout of the Facebook page reduces the possibility of individual creativity. Where radical media so often fail due to poor circulation and small audiences, paradoxically the printed fanzine might well survive because of its marginality, its limited reach and its rather antiquated physicality.

Influences and connections

The untutored enthusiasm that is common to fanzine writers and professional rock critics (however different the texts they produce might be, however different their motives and their audiences) has made possible the frequent movement of fanzine writers to the professional music press, particularly in Britain. Professional rock journalists are fans too; the roots of their profession lie in the 1960s, with the fanzines and specialist music magazines of the US and the underground press of the UK, where many writers began as amateurs and non-professionals. Those that became professional journalists "posit[ed] themselves as enlightened fans" (Gudmundsson et al., 2002: 60). The amateur status of the music fanzine does not prevent it from making significant inroads into mainstream music culture. Some fanzine writers and editors (Paul Morley and Jon Savage are conspicuous examples in the United Kingdom) have gone on to become established, professional music journalists and cultural critics. *Crawdaddy!* and *Who Put the Bomp!* became places where rock journalism was significantly developed: writers such as Lester Bangs, Greil Marcus and Dave Marsh used these titles to experiment with new styles and perspectives. In terms of significance, such titles as these heralded the birth of the specialist music magazine.

Further reading

As perhaps befits such an eclectic enterprise as the fanzine, there is no single definitive text to consult. There are instead a large number of case studies. Some explore a specific time period (Sabin and Triggs, 2001; Triggs, 1995) or a specific culture (Atton, 2001; Haynes, 1995). Dickinson (1997) is unusual in considering fanzines as part of a wider tradition of radical community media. Duncombe's (1997) emphasis on identity and community suggests connections between alternative cultures and the kind of fan practices presented in Gray, Sandvoss and Harrington (2007), though Duncombe is less interested in fanzines than zines, as defined in this chapter.

References

Atton, C. (2001) "'Living in the past'? Value discourses in progressive rock fanzines." *Popular Music* 20(1), 29–46.

——(2002) *Alternative Media*. London: Sage.

——(2003) "Fanzines." In J. Shepherd et al. (eds), *The Continuum Encyclopedia of Popular Music of the World, Volume One: Media, Industry and Society*. London: Continuum (pp. 226–8).

——(2004) *An Alternative Internet: Radical Media, Politics and Creativity*. Edinburgh: Edinburgh University Press; New York: Columbia University Press.

——(2006a) "Sociologie de la Presse Musicale Alternative en Grande Bretagne." *Volume! La Revue des Musiques Populaires*, 5(1), 7–25.

——(2006b) "Football fanzines as local news." In B. Franklin (ed.), *Local Journalism and Local Media: Making the Local News*. London: Routledge (pp. 280–89).

Dickinson, R. (1997) *Imprinting the Sticks: The Alternative Press outside London*. Aldershot: Arena.

Duncombe, S. (1997) *Notes from Underground: Zines and the Politics of Alternative Culture*. London: Verso.

Fiske, J. (1991[1989]) *Understanding Popular Culture*, London: Routledge. Originally published by Unwin Hyman.

Frith, S. (1996) *Performing Rites: Evaluating Popular Music*. Oxford: Oxford University Press.

——(2002) "Fragments of a sociology of rock criticism." In S. Jones (ed.), *Pop Music and the Press*. Philadelphia: Temple University Press (pp. 235–46).

Gray, J., Sandvoss, C. and Harrington, C. L. (2007) *Fandom: Identities and Communities in a Mediated World*. New York and London: New York University Press.

Gudmundsson, G., Lindberg, U., Michelsen, M. and Weisethaunet, H. (2002) "Brit crit: Turning points in British rock criticism, 1960–1990." In S. Jones (ed.), *Pop Music and the Press*. Philadelphia: Temple University Press (pp. 41–64).

Haynes, R. (1995) *The Football Imagination: The Rise of Football Fanzine Culture*. Aldershot: Arena.

Hebdige, D. (1979) *Subculture: The Meaning of Style*. London: Routledge.

Jary, D., Horne, J. and Bucke, T. (1991) "Football 'fanzines' and football culture: A case of successful 'cultural contestation'." *Sociological Review*, 39(3), 581–97.

Jenkins, H. (1992) "'Strangers no more, we sing': Filking and the social construction of the science fiction fan community." In L. A. Lewis (ed.), *The Adoring Audience: Fan Culture and Popular Media*. London: Routledge (pp. 208–36).

Rau, M. (1994) "Towards a history of fanzine publishing: From APA to zines." *Alternative Press Review*, Spring/Summer, 10–13.

Rutherford, P. (1992) *Fanzine Culture*. Glasgow: Clydeside Press.

Sabin, R. and Triggs, T. (eds.) (2001) *Below Critical Radar: Fanzines and Alternative Comics from 1976 to Now*. Hove: Slab-O-Concrete.

Stump, P. (1997) *The Music's All That Matters: A History of Progressive Rock*. London: Quartet.

Triggs, T. (1995) "Alphabet soup: Reading British fanzines." *Visible Language*, 29(1), 72–87.

39
MOVEMENT MEDIA AS TECHNOLOGIES OF SELF-MEDIATION

Bart Cammaerts

Introduction

In the social movement literature, 'movement media' are often described as independent channels of communication set up by activists and social movement organisations "to spread their word, to reframe their goals and demands, to change their forms of action and/or to re-orient their media strategies so that they become more attractive to the media" (Rucht, 2004: 29). Their emergence, it is argued, is the result of a distinct reaction to "a lack of interest, or bias, on the part of the established media" (ibid.: 37).

In the field of media and communication studies, we can also observe a distinct focus on the mainstream media framing of protest and of social movements more generally (Halloran, Elliott and Murdock, 1970; Gitlin, 1980; Eldridge, 1995; Cottle, 2008; Cammaerts, 2013a). Besides this, the broader phenomenon of alternative media, which is juxtaposed to mainstream media, has also received increased attention in recent years (Downing, 2001; Atton, 2002; Bailey, Cammaerts and Carpentier, 2008). In this work, a much deeper appreciation and valuation for alternative channels of communication can be felt.

In this chapter, through the adoption of the Foucauldian notion of technologies of the self, it will be argued that the adoption and use of movement media by activists is not merely the result of a lack of mainstream media resonance, but is on the contrary a set of self-mediation practices constitutive of social movements.

Movement media as technologies of self-mediation

It is often assumed that movement media are "inward looking" (see Rucht, 2004) and that they are instrumental in the building of collective identities inherent to movements, but also in terms of the gradual articulation of the various movement frames, whether diagnostic, prognostic or motivational (Snow and Benford, 1988). Movement media are also considered to be inward looking because the audiences of movement media are usually those that already sympathise with the movement – "the like-minded", as Gamson and Wolfsfeld (1993) call them. Depending on the cause and popularity of the movement, movement media often have what could be called niche or micro-audiences. Movement media thus tend to be less successful at reaching the broad public. Hence, it is argued, there is a persistent dependence on mainstream media to reinforce and disseminate movement frames to the public at large. As Rucht (2013: 262) contends, despite the emergence of the internet "[t]o reach the public at large, the key channel was and is getting access to and coverage by the established media".

While the disproportionate attention on the internet in research on social movements has to some extent downplayed the remaining importance of traditional media, it could also be argued that there is often too much emphasis on mainstream media, to the detriment of movement media. When it comes to articulating what constitutes 'movement media', I contend that we should consider traditional media such as print and broadcasting, as well as the telephone, mobile communication and the internet.

Movement media is theorised here through the Foucauldian concept of *technologies of the self*. In his later work on technologies, Foucault (1997: 225) distinguished technologies of production, technologies of sign systems, technologies of power and technologies of the self. When speaking about technologies of the self, Foucault referred to devices, methods or 'tools' that enable the social construction of personal identities and make it possible for individuals to transform themselves as well as constitute themselves as a subject. It is thus through technologies of the self and the constitution of identities that self-compliance to the structures of coercion is being instilled, but it is also the space where resistance can be given shape and is exercised. By approaching movement media as technologies of the self and as a means for self-mediation, which I will define below as more than mere self-representation, I argue that movement media are not per se merely inward looking, but can also be outward looking.

Mediation

When proposing the notion of technologies of self-mediation, mediation is as important a concept as technologies of the self. In this regard, it is important to understand that while self-mediation processes are in part about self-representation, it is also about much more than that. As a theoretical concept, mediation enables us to capture diverging articulations between media, communication, protest and activism. The Latin American scholar Martín-Barbero (1993) led the way by explicitly linking mediation(s) to social movements. He spoke of matrices of communication, culture and hegemony, and in doing so shifted the debate from the media as an institution towards dialectical processes which position "the media in the field of mediations" (ibid.: 139).

Mediations thus occur as a cultural process negotiated between the dominant actors in a given society and the subordinate actors who in turn develop bottom-up (communicative) strategies to resist. Power is considered to be central and inherent to processes of mediations, and while we can see power relations as asymmetrical, they are not totalising (i.e. there is room for counter-hegemonies, for the building of collective identities and for the waging social and political struggles).

The concept of mediation also enables us to bridge the symbolic – as expressed through meaning-making and through struggles for and the management of visibility (Thompson, 1995: 134–48) – and the material, the tools, "the technologically driven and embedded" (Silverstone, 2005: 189). When speaking about technologies in this context, we can refer both to the Foucauldian approach to technologies as abstract processes and to the material attributes of communication technologies that enable and constrain.

At the level of technologies and technological innovation, theories that attempt to understand the relationship between the social and technology are useful in this regard. Emphasising the "social shaping of technology" approach, which foregrounds a more dialectical relationship between structure and agency, Silverstone talks of the way in which media and communication technologies are being domesticated in everyday practices of individuals:

> The more recent history of home computing indicates that individuals in the household construct and affirm their own identities through their appropriation of the machine via processes of acceptance, resistance, and negotiation. What individuals do, and how they do it, depends on both cultural and material resources.
>
> (Silverstone, 1999: 252)

Technology is not considered to be neutral here: designers and companies develop technologies with pre-conceived goals and aims, but at the same time its introduction in society leads to a process of negotiation, which can result in the appropriation of technology within everyday life practices, but likewise strategies of resistance, either through the rejection of technology or through re-configuration of innovative user-patterns unforeseen by the developers of the technology.

A relevant recent example is the use of text messaging, Twitter, Facebook or other digital tools and platforms by activists to mobilise for and coordinate direct actions, to garner support or to recruit active members (Cammaerts, 2012). These technologies/platforms were, however, not necessarily designed with the intention to facilitate protest, dissent and resistance. While much of the theorisation in this regard has focused on new media and ICTs, similar processes of appropriation and adaptation of then new communication technologies such as print and radio into the communicative repertoire of social movements have taken place in the past.

Technologies of self and of self-mediation

As outlined above, it is fruitful to approach movement media as technologies of self-mediation, with reference to technologies of the self. Foucault (1997) identified three Stoic technologies of the self, which apply equally to technologies of self-mediation.

- Disclosure or "the cultivation of the self" (ibid.: 234)
- Examination or "taking stock" (ibid.: 237)
- Remembrance or the "memorizations of deeds and their correspondence with rules" (ibid.: 247)

Technologies of self-mediation point to movement media as potentially constitutive of collective identities and highly relevant in view of disseminating, communicating and recording a variety of movement frames. They are the tools through which a social movement becomes self-conscious. A historical example of this would be the way in which silk-screen printing technology played a pivotal role during the May 1968 student protests in France. The iconic imagery produced by the *ateliers populaires* in Paris, but also in cities such as Toulouse, Marseille and Bordeaux, produced during the May 1968 protests and strikes came to define that movement (Rohan, 1988). The iconic radical posters, quite rough, usually monochrome, with striking images and playful slogans, were to a large extent determined by the technique of silk-screen printing and played a pivotal role in the construction of the collective identity and public image of that movement.

This particular use of silk-screen printing as a technology of self-mediation neatly fits the first Stoic technology of the self identified by Foucault (1997), namely the *disclosure of self*; here, movements use movement media to construct and sustain collective identities, to articulate a set of demands and ideas and to in effect become self-conscious as a movement. However, Foucault (1997) differentiated two other Stoic technologies of the self which are equally – if not more – relevant to social movements and their self-mediation practices:

- *The examination of self*: self-reflexivity, making transformation and change within a movement possible.
- *The remembering of self*: archiving the past, and transmitting practices, tactics and ideas across space and time.

In the May 1968 example, the examination of self largely took place unmediated. At various points in the day general assemblies would be held at the *ateliers populaires*, where decisions were made as to what would get printed. The ideological content of the posters differed depending on who was physically present at these general assemblies. As one participant recalled, "certain posters were passed at certain times because there were more pro-Chinese and fewer Trotskyites, or the other way around" (Eric Seydoux, quoted in Tempest, 2006). There were, however, also mediated forms of examination, through newsletters and newspapers (Rohan, 1988). Furthermore, the Sorbonne students who instigated the May '68 uprisings would have been acutely aware of a more global climate of contestation and student protests, for example the violent anti-Vietnam protests at Columbia University in the US a month earlier.

In terms of remembrance, the legacy of the posters themselves and their *agit-prop* style influenced the imagery of many other movements across the world for decades after 1968. The posters were cheap to produce, and once the screen was ready, large numbers could be printed relatively quickly. For these reasons, screen-printing or serigraphy was for a long time the preferred way to reproduce textual and visual content in various underground subcultures across the world.

Affordances and constraints of technologies of self-mediation

Insofar as we approach media and communication technologies as objects that can do things – devices or tools – it matters how we as (political) subjects perceive them and attribute use-values to them, how we objectify the things around us. The notion of affordances has in recent years been foregrounded as a more complex theorisation of how we embed technologies into our everyday practices through an assessment of what these technologies enable us to do and also through the constraints they place upon us. In what follows, I present an analytical approach to these affordances, but also to the constraints of technologies of self-mediation.

Affordances

Gibson (1977) argues that affordances represent opportunities or rather potentialities for a set of actions. As we use objects, they become an extension of ourselves, disrupting the subject-object dichotomy. The notion of affordances became popular in fields such as ergonomics, technology design and innovation studies in order to make sense of our relationship with and our shaping of technologies. Print technologies, tele-communication technologies, broadcasting technologies and finally the more recent information and communication technologies each provide social movements with different affordances at the level of disclosure, examination and remembrance, and together they constitute a sorts of repertoire – a communicative toolbox – out of which activists and movements choose depending on their specific needs.

In the toolbox we might find a range of communication technologies, such as radio, telephones and TV, but with the internet as well as print technologies there is a need to delineate a number of more specific formats or applications. For example, the internet enables emailing, online chatting, streaming, social media and text messaging, all of which hold different affordances. Within print we need to differentiate between posters, stickers, photographs, flyers, letters, manifestos, between texts and visual images.

The affordances of technologies of self-mediation revolve around two sets of tensions: one between public and private, or between outward and inward forms of communication, and the second between immediacy and asynchronicity, between the fleeting and the permanent. In Table 39.1, these two sets of affordances are juxtaposed to provide a matrix of technologies of self-mediation.

Table 39.1 Matrix of technologies of self-mediation.

	Real time/fleeting	Asynchronous/permanent
Public/outward	Radio TV Streaming Social media	Essays/manifesto Posters Stickers and flyers Paintings/murals Film/video Photographs Social media Website
Private/inward	Telephone Internet relay chat VoIP	Letters Email Text messages Private messages on SNS

We also expect activists to consider the recipients of their message, which can be related to the intentionality of communication. For example, organising or coordinating a direct action through independent channels of communication will require different communicative practices and technologies than when activists wish to disseminate movement frames through independent channels. Some communication technologies enable more private forms of communication (such as letters, telecommunications or email), while others make possible a more public form of communication (radio, twitter or a website). In terms of the Foucauldian technologies of self, the inward and the private often, but not exclusively, relate to strategies of examination, while outward and public forms of communication have more salience with respect to the disclosure of self.

The innovative use of pamphlets, telephones and cassette tapes or what Srebreny-Mohammadi and Mohammadi (1994) called "small media" in the run-up to the Iranian revolution of 1979 was a good example of the complex interconnections of private forms of communication with public ones, and is illustrative of how the use of these small media served a disseminating role at the level of disclosure, a coordinating self-reflexive role at the level of examination as well as an archival role in line with strategies of remembrance. Ayatollah Khomeini's speeches were recorded in Paris, transmitted through the telephone and re-recorded on cassette tapes in Tehran. Algar (1983: 105) called cassette tapes the "technological symbol" of the 1979 Iranian revolution, but as pointed out, the telephone also proved to be an important tool.

The speed of communication also plays an important role: does it have to be immediate, linking several actors in a direct way, enabling 'live' in real-time communication, or can communication be indirect or asynchronous? This maps onto the differences between on the one hand live radio or online chatting, and on the other hand a printed manifesto or a poster. The distinction between the immediate and the delayed foregrounds the distinction between communication that is fleeting and communication patterns that are more permanent and can thus be recorded for posterity. The latter form part of the collective long-term memory of dissent and contentious politics, while the former are ephemeral. Inevitably there exists an interplay between the ephemeral and that which is more permanent. In Foucauldian terms, it could be argued that the fleeting is more redolent of practices centred on examining the self, while permanency has more relevance for the remembrance of self.

Remembrance is of particular importance when considering social movements. Social movements build on ideas developed and tactics enacted by past and current movements, and are often involved in inventive imitation or a "fruitful interference of repetitions" (Tarde, 1903: 382). Communication and mediations play an important role in movement spill-overs or the way in which ideas, symbols or tactics of contention travel and transgress from one movement to another (Meyer and Whittier, 1994). The permanent nature of protest artefacts, for example, enables symbols and discourses embedded in them to be culturally transmitted on a long-term basis, feeding future struggles and effectively becoming epistemic communities.

Illustrations of movement spill-overs can be witnessed in: (1) the Jasmine Revolution in Tunisia (2010), spreading to other Arab countries such as Egypt, Libya and Syria, partly fuelled by regional broadcasters, but also the internet; (2) the way in which the occupation of a public space such as Tahrir Square was appropriated first by the

Indignados in Spain (2011–12) and later by the Occupy movement (2011); (3) the 'V for Vendetta' Guy Fawkes masks, first used by the online hacktivist collective Anonymous and subsequently appropriated by activists during the Arab Spring by the Indignados and Occupy movement, as well as by Julian Assange of WikiLeaks, Beppe Grillo of the MoVimento 5 Stelle and activists in the so-called 'V for Vinegar' protests in Turkey and Brazil in 2013.

Constraints

Technologies of self-mediation not only afford, they also constrain and limit. These constraints should, however, not exclusively be defined in negative terms, but can also be viewed as productive in a Foucauldian sense, whereby structural constraints also have productive capacities, and whereby the exercise of power inevitably invokes strategies of resistance (Foucault, 1978).

At the level of disclosure, communication tools primarily raise issues relating to access and skills. Different media at different times in history presented different challenges for activists and movements as well as the dominant powers they fought. For example, prior to the French Revolution, measures of censorship such as the screening of content prior to publication, a license to operate printing presses, a monopolistic printing guild or tight controls on distribution of paper, as well as post-factum forms of censorship such as police repression against illegal presses or the regulation and surveillance of the booksellers, were commonplace (Darnton, 1982; Roche, 1989). All of this was implemented to counter the "dangerous power of the written word to subvert social order by entering into collective processes of political contestation" (Baker, 1987: 208).

Similarly, radio broadcasting has a long legacy of regulation and restrictions enforced through a system of licensing which tends to impede access to the airwaves for oppositional forces and social movements. In Western democracies, so-called third-sector radios, operating between the state-owned broadcasting system and the commercial broadcasting sector, are seen as autonomous media that constitute "vehicles of social movements" to disseminate alternative content (Langlois and Dubois, 2005: 9–10). Social movements are thus keen to

> create media that break down hierarchies of access to meaning-making, therefore allowing those typically found at the grassroots to have a voice and to define reality.
>
> (Ibid.: 10)

Alternative and oppositional radio stations have a long history of struggle for recognition in Western democracies, as well as beyond. In the West, radical radio stations often had to contend with heavy-handed state repression, including the impounding of broadcasting material, hefty fines and in some instances even arrests (Cammaerts, 2009). In non-Western contexts, repression was also rife and went much further. Fanon (1965) describes how radio transformed from a hegemonic instrument in the hands of the French colonisers into an instrument of resistance for those fighting against the colonial power. At first, the rejection of radio by the Algerian population was very much an act of defiance against the French oppressors. However, as Fanon (ibid.: 82) pointed out, after the start of *La Voix de l'Algérie Libre* – "bringing to all Algeria the great message of the Revolution" – owning a radio suddenly became a patriotic duty. In 20 days' time, all the radio sets in the whole of Algeria were sold out. The French authorities did everything they could to disrupt the broadcasts of the Voice of Free Algeria, from jamming their signal to banning batteries and battery chargers and seizing radio sets (see also Downing, 2001).

Skills may also act as constraints, in terms of both production and reception. At the level of production, knowledge and technical skills of how to produce media, be it textual, visual or audio, are an important factor in the struggles for visibility of activists. Thompson (1995: 23) speaks of the technical skills and competences required to produce and transmit information linked to symbolic power and the management of visibility. At the level of reception, text requires the ability to read and can in certain contexts exclude. This is also pertinent to the internet and other ICTs, where in addition to the ability to read, other forms of communication and technical literacies are required as well (Livingstone, 2008). This explains why at times visual images such as murals or sound transmitted through radio matter more than the textual when it comes to self-mediation. As Downing (2001: 181) reminds us, "[i]n nations with substantial illiteracy, including major nations such as India and Brazil, radio has predictably played a more important role than the press". There is a strong tradition of murals in Latin America as a way to communicate movement frames (Coffey, 2002). Skills and literacy also explain why the Soviet samizdat was mainly an affair of intellectuals:

> It must be borne in mind that dissent and samizdat are still mainly phenomena of the intelligentsia, those employed in occupations for which a higher education is normally a prerequisite and those receiving a higher education.
>
> (Duncan, 1982: 155)

A further constraint is situated at the intersection between production and reception, and concerns the reach of different media and communication tools. Some media reach a much broader audience than others. At the same time, some media are precisely geared to communicate with the few rather than with the many, enabling processes of examination rather than disclosure (I shall return to these later). Reach is important in terms of disclosure. It is in the activists' interest that the resonance of their messages and frames is as wide as possible. Mainstream media seem to be more effective at providing access to the public at large, while movement media tend to have much smaller audiences and are geared towards communicating with those that are already (more or less) aligned with the movement frames (Gamson and Wolfsfeld, 1993; Rucht, 2013). Even though the internet potentially enables activists to reach large, transnational audiences, this is not easily achieved. Much of the communicative activity undertaken online by social movements is limited to those that choose to 'tune in', producing an "echo-chamber" effect (Boutyline and Willer, 2013). Maximising reach and resonance remains a particular challenge for social movement media.

Furthermore, the current popularity of social media among activists also comes with its own constraints. There is an intrinsic tension between the individualistic nature of social media platforms and the need for movements to build and sustain collective identities and to organise collective actions. Social media are mostly corporate capitalist spaces, which also raises the question to what extent they can still be considered alternative or movement media.

As the examples above attest, the dominant forces in society that also occupy state institutions and own communication infrastructures will often attempt to disrupt the strategies of disclosure by social movements, particularly if they are anti-systemic. Another way, however, in which the state attempts to disrupt tactics of disruption is by targeting strategies of self-reflexive examination, mainly through surveillance and infiltration (O'Reilly, 1989; Cammaerts, 2013b).

There are also constraints on remembrance. Paper-based archives of protest artefacts and movement media tend to be fragmented and can be difficult to access. Many are kept by private individuals or in university libraries and are not generally easily accessible. While online archives are now available to many people and enable movement spill-over, even these can be ephemeral and precarious. For example, in 2011, Facebook closed down more than 60 political groups without prior warning (Open Rights Group n.d.), resulting in the disappearance of much of these groups' archives.

Conclusion

In this chapter, I have argued that movement media and strategies of self-mediation serve a variety of functions for social movements and for activists. These functions can be mapped onto Foucault's three Stoic technologies of the self: disclosure, examination and remembrance. Disclosure refers to ways in which movement frames are produced and disseminated; examination refers to the coordination of movements and the need for self-reflexivity; remembrance refers to ways in which movement frames and protest tactics are recorded and archived, potentially leading to movement spill-over. Considered broadly to include print, broadcasting and digital telecommunication tools, movement media afford real-time as well as asynchronous communicative practices which can be directed outwardly at a variety of publics through disclosure or inwardly through examination. Media practices can also be directed towards archiving and memorialising, through strategies of remembrance.

We also need to acknowledge constraints. Strategies of disclosure can be constrained at the point of production by the regulation of access to media and communication technologies. They can also be limited by the technical skills required to produce media artefacts. At the point of reception, reading skills and media literacies are crucial in receiving and decoding movement frames through movement media. The mediation of self-examination is highly susceptible to surveillance and disciplining tactics by the state and corporate actors. Strategies of remembrance may also be compromised due to the fragmentation of archives, archives not being in the public domain or the ephemeral nature of some movement media.

Considered as technologies of self-mediation, movement media afford and constrain at the same time. The relationship between affordances and constraints should be seen as productive; innovation creates new opportunities which can be (and often are) closed down by dominant actors in their attempts to control the means of communication that are at the disposal of activists, but at the same time new opportunities emerge.

Further reading

Downing, J. (2008) "Social movement theories and alternative media: An evaluation and critique." *Communication, Culture and Critique*, 1(1), 40–50. An overview, as well as critique, of the lack of attention for alternative media and communication in social movement theory.
　Cammaerts, B. (2012) "Protest logics and the mediation opportunity structure." *European Journal of Communication*, 27(2), 117–34. A response to Downing's critique from the field of media and communication, introducing mediation in social movement theory.
　Rucht, D. (2013) "Protest movements and their media usages." In B. Cammaerts, A. Matoni and P. McCurdy (eds), *Mediation and Protest Movements* Bristol: Intellect (pp. 249–68). An engagement with issues relating to media and communication and protest from the field of social movement studies.

References

Algar, H. (1983) *Roots of the Iranian Revolution*. London: Open Press.
Atton, C. (2002) *Alternative Media*. London: Sage.
Bailey, O., Cammaerts, B. and Carpentier, N. (2008) *Understanding Alternative Media*. Maidenhead: Open University Press/McGraw Hill.
Baker, K. M. (1987) "Politics and public opinion under the old regime: Some reflections." In J. R. Senser and J. D. Popkin (eds), *Out of Print: Press and Politics in Pre-Revolutionary France*. Berkeley: University of California Press (pp. 204–46).
Boutyline, A. and Willer, R. (2013) "The social structure of political echo chambers: Ideology and political homophily in online communication networks." Working Paper. Retrieved from http://www.ocf.berkeley.edu/~andrei/EchoChambers.pdf (accessed 10 January 2015).
Cammaerts, B. (2009) "Community radio in the West: A legacy of struggle for survival in a state and capitalist controlled media environment." *International Communication Gazette*, 71(8), 1–20.
——(2012) "Protest logics and the mediation opportunity structure." *European Journal of Communication*, 27(2), 117–34.
——(2013a) "The mediation of insurrectionary symbolic damage: The 2010 UK student protests." *International Journal of Press/Politics*, 18(4), 525–48.
——(2013b) "Networked resistance: The case of WikiLeaks." *Journal of Computer-Mediated Communication*, 18(4), 420–36.
Coffey, M. K. (2002) "Muralism and the people: Culture, popular citizenship, and government in post-revolutionary Mexico." *Communication Review*, 5(1), 7–38.
Cottle, S. (2008) "Reporting demonstrations: The changing media politics of dissent." *Media, Culture and Society*, 30(6), 853–72.

Darnton, R. (1982) *The Literary Underground of the Old Regime*. Cambridge, MA: Harvard University Press.

Downing, J. D. (with T. V. Ford, G. Gil and L. Stein) (2001) *Radical Media: Rebellious Communication and Social Movements*. London: Sage.

Duncan, P. J. S. (1982) "Russian intellectual dissent: Marxism, liberalism and nationalism." *Critique: Journal of Socialist Theory*, 13(1), 154–63.

Eldridge, J. (1995) *Glasgow Media Group Reader, Volume One: News Content, Language and Visuals*. London: Routledge.

Fanon, F. (1965) *A Dying Colonialism*. New York: Grove Press.

Foucault, M. (1978) *History of Sexuality, Part 1: An Introduction*. New York: Pantheon.

——(1997) "Technologies of the self." In P. Rabinow (ed.), *Essential Works, Volume 1: Ethics, Subjectivity, and Truth*. New York: New Press (pp. 223–51).

Gamson, W. A. and Wolfsfeld, G. (1993) "Movements and media as interacting systems." *Annals of the American Academy of Political and Social Science*, 528, 114–27.

Gibson, J. J. (1977) "The theory of affordances." In R. Shaw and J. Bransford (eds), *Perceiving, Acting, and Knowing: Toward an Ecological Psychology*. Hillsdale, NJ: Lawrence Erlbaum Associates (pp. 67–82).

Gitlin, T. (1980) *The Whole World Is Watching: Mass Media in the Making and Unmaking of the New Left*. Berkeley: University of California Press.

Halloran, J. D., Elliott, P. and Murdock, G. (1970) *Demonstrations and Communication: A Case Study*. Harmondsworth: Penguin Books.

Langlois, A. and Dubois, F. (eds.) (2005) *Autonomous Media: Activating Resistance and Dissent*. Gatineau, Quebec: Cumulus Press.

Livingstone, S. (2008) "Internet literacy: Young people's negotiation of new online opportunities." In T. McPherson (ed.), *Unexpected Outcomes and Innovative Uses of Digital Media by Youth*. Cambridge, MA: MIT Press (pp. 101–21).

Martín-Barbero, J. (1993) *Communication, Culture and Hegemony: From the Media to Mediation*. London: Sage.

Meyer, D. S. and Whittier, N. (1994) "Social movement spillover." *Social Problems*, 41, 277–98.

Open Rights Group (n.d.) "FB takedowns." Retrieved from http://wiki.openrightsgroup.org/wiki/FB_takedowns (accessed 20 March 2015).

O'Reilly, K. (1989) *"Racial Matters": The FBI's Secret File on Black America, 1960–1972*. New York: Free Press.

Roche, D. (1989) "Censorship and the publishing industry." In R. Darnton and D. Roche (eds), *Revolution in Print: The Press in France, 1775–1800*. Berkeley: University of California Press (pp. 3–26).

Rohan, M. (1988) *Paris '68: Graffiti, Posters, Newspapers and Poems of the Events of May 1968*. London: Impact.

Rucht, D. (2004) "The quadruple 'A': Media strategies of protest movements since the 1960s." In W. van de Donk, B. D. Loader, P. G. Nixon and D. Rucht (eds.) *Cyberprotest: New Media, Citizens, and Social Movements*. London: Routledge (pp. 29–58).

——(2013) "Protest movements and their media usages." In B. Cammaerts, A. Matoni and P. McCurdy (eds), *Mediation and Protest Movements*. Bristol: Intellect (pp. 249–68).

Silverstone, R. (1999) "Domesticating ICTs." In W. Dutton (ed.), *Society on the Line: Information Politics in the Digital Age*. Oxford: Oxford University Press (pp. 251–53).

——(2005) "The sociology of mediation and communication." In C. Calhoun, C. Rojek and B. S. Turner (eds), *The Sage Handbook of Sociology*. London: Sage (pp. 188–207).

Snow, D. A. and Benford, R. D. (1988) "Ideology, frame resonance, and participant mobilization." *International Social Movement Research*, 1(1), 197–217.

Sreberny-Mohammadi, A. and Mohammadi, A. (1994) *Small Media, Big Revolution: Communication, Culture, and the Iranian Revolution.* Minneapolis: University of Minnesota Press.

Tarde, G. (1903) *The Laws of Imitation.* Translated by E. C. Parsons with introduction by F. H. Giddings. New York: Henry, Holt and Co.

Tempest, G. M. (2006) "Anti-Nazism and the *ateliers populaires*: The memory of Nazi collaboration in the posters of Mai '68." BA thesis, University of California at Berkeley. Retrieved from http://www.docspopuli.org/articles/Paris1968_Tempest/AfficheParis1968_Tempest.html (accessed 10 January 2015).

Thompson, J. B. (1995) *The Media and Modernity: A Social Theory of the Media.* Cambridge: Polity.

40
OCCUPY AND SOCIAL MOVEMENT COMMUNICATION

Dorothy Kidd

Introduction

On 17 September 2011, several hundred people took over Zucotti Park near the New York Stock Exchange on Wall Street. Over the following weeks, Occupy Wall Street expanded to a trans-local movement known simply as Occupy, in which tens of thousands took over public squares and streets and participated in allied off- and online actions, in 951 cities in 82 countries. Inspired by the uprisings in Egypt, Greece, Spain and Mexico, Occupy was far from spontaneous; it converged many singular struggles of students, artists, trade unionists, anti-poverty groups, media activists and hackers, which then in combination scaled up further than any other (Gamson and Sifry, 2013: 162).

Adbusters, the Vancouver-based culture-jamming magazine, set the initial date on the anniversary of the signing of the American Constitution with one single demand, "a presidential commission to separate money from politics". Nevertheless, the Occupy movement refused to make any specific claims of the US or other national governments. Instead, under the inclusive banner of the '99%', they employed an extensive repertoire of participatory communications practices to call out the inequities of corporate and government policies which had impoverished millions through home foreclosures and rising debt. More significantly, they set about to build a social movement based on self-care and self-representation, community dialogue and collective deliberation.

Many commentators from across the political spectrum have dismissed the Occupy movement because of its lack of long-term impact on Washington politics, or corporate power. The record in these realms is indeed spotty, as, aided by government bail-outs, finance capital has rebounded with renewed force and continues in its exalted place in government decision-making around the world. However, in this chapter I instead focus on Occupy's contribution to participatory communications. I argue that Occupy's programmatic goal was not to change state or corporate institutions, but was inward, to prefigure direct grassroots democracy through the cultivation of democratic communications.

The movement garnered much higher levels of US commercial news coverage, much more of it positive, than earlier movements for political, economic and social justice (Bennett and Segerberg, 2012). More significantly, and with distinct local variations, Occupy "renovate[d] and democratized virtually all aspects of the communication process: the definition of communication, of what social actors may participate, the employment of new media technology, the democratization of existing technology, the redefinition of 'media professionalism', the development of new codes of ethics and new values" (White, 1995: 93).

A short history of social movement communications

Describing the historical role of oppositional movements within the dominant culture, Raymond Williams posited that each epoch consists of different variations and stages, and at every point there are dynamic, contradictory relationships in the interplay of *dominant, residual* and *emergent* forms (1977). Occupy's repertoire of communications practices was not a pre-packaged set of software from a dominant research organisation. Instead, we can see their DNA emergent in the historical cycles of residual social movements, three of which were oft-cited by Occupy participants, and which I briefly rehearse. The first was the student and new left movements of the 1960s. The US Students for a Democratic Society (SDS), and other groups, advocated 'participatory democracy', where decisions were made by those affected by them (Polletta, 2013: 41). Much of the new left's strategic repertoire was within the field of culture and communications. Angela Davis reminded us of this historical thread, when she spoke about the "long march through the institutions" before leading a street demonstration to Occupy Philadelphia on 28 October 2011. Drawn from Antonio Gramsci, and modified by the German student leader Rudi Dutschke, the strategy was for political movements to peacefully take control of "the switch-points of social power" in the field of cultural values.

During the 1970s, one set of activists took up this call and founded alternative media organisations (variously called community media, radical media or grassroots media). Their goals were to challenge the hegemonic control of the means of communications, and prefigure the kinds of social values they sought by facilitating a plurality of expression, especially from groups systemically excluded from constituted power. During the 1980s, activists formed national, regional and transnational media networks, including community and social movement–based computer networks, long before the birth of the World Wide Web (Murphy, 2002). Nevertheless, this vision of non-hierarchical practice was constrained by the cost and accessibility of the means of media production and circulation, and as Atton notes, a small corps of paid and volunteer producers ran most alternative media (2002).

The second historical moment, from which Occupy drew, was the Zapatista uprising against the North American Free Trade Agreement (NAFTA) in 1993 in Chiapas, Mexico. Protesting NAFTA's policy of enclosing the *ejidos*, or the common lands guaranteed by the Mexican Revolution, they succeeded in holding off the Mexican

Army and gaining world attention, with a very short-lived show of arms, and a powerful war of "images, words, legitimation and moral authority" (Martinez-Torres, 2001: 348). The Zapatistas represented a paradox: high-tech information technologies, crucial to a globalising capitalism, turned against it by a rural, and primarily indigenous, guerrilla movement. With few electronic or digital communications resources of their own, the Zapatistas drew instead on the network of alternative and social movement media dubbed the "electronic fabric of struggle" by Harry Cleaver (1995). The Zapatistas inspired civil society in Mexico, and a growing transnational anti-corporate globalisation movement with their inclusive and more Gramscian war of position, which focused on strengthening participatory democracy, creative engagement in the cultural realm and intercultural dialogues through *encuentros*, or face-to-face public assemblies.

The third historical moment took place in December 1999 in Seattle, Washington, when a coalition of coalitions opposed to neo-liberal globalisation used their own means of information and communication to mobilise tens of thousands to disrupt the meeting of the World Trade Organisation (WTO). Inspired by the Zapatistas' model of *horizontal* direct action, and recognizing that there would be little positive US corporate news media coverage of the protests, alternative media producers, artists and radical software designers launched the Independent Media Center (IMC) (Kidd, 2003).

The IMC represented a qualitative shift in the scope and scale of media power. The IMC do-it-ourselves ethos not only by-passed the gate-keepers of the corporate news media, but also the *vertical* approach of the established NGOs, whose spokes-people framed specific policy in terms friendly to the commercial news media, as well as the *institutional* approach of the established alternative media with their commitment to brick and mortar operations, permanent staff and relations with established community organisations. The IMC's open-source platform was much more nimble: it allowed anyone with internet access to download and upload any genre of content, pre-dating blogging, YouTubing and Web 2.0 by several years. Very quickly, the global IMC grew to 150 autonomous media collectives around the world that functioned as the go-to medium for news reports for what began to be called the global justice movement. Nevertheless, the long-term viability of the IMC was limited by a lack of economic resources, and continuing tensions over the cultural capital of gender, race, class and rich country/poor country, all of which were harbingers of Occupy.

Theorising social movement communications

In 1995, drawing primarily from the Latin American experience, Robert White argued that the kinds of social changes implied in the democratisation of communication are best explained in terms of the process of social movements (White, 1995: 92). After Seattle, there was an outburst of academic literature; however, much of it neglected the long, slow and south-to-north build-up of the global justice movement, and instead attributed the success in Seattle to the decentralised, flexible and distributed networks of the internet. For example, in one oft-cited article by Naomi Klein, she wrote that the activist model "mirrors the organic, decentralized, interlinked pathways of the Internet" (Klein, 2001). Less reported was her important caveat: "all this talk of radical decentralization conceals a very real hierarchy based on who owns, understands and controls the computer networks linking the activists to one another … a geek adhocracy" (ibid.).

A decade later, the uprisings, beginning in Iran in 2009, and including Occupy in 2011, led to another uptick in commercial news reports and academic studies, this time most narrowly focused on young people's use of Twitter, Facebook and other digital social media, neglecting the contribution of residual social movements and processes, and the continuing use of face-to-face and electronic communications, and of the dominant media. As Clemencia Rodríguez et al. have noted, the complex repertoires of social movement communications are thus reduced to the singular interface between individuals and the latest US corporate brands (Rodríguez, Ferron and Shamas, 2014).

Fortunately, a growing interdisciplinary scholarship provides a more comprehensive, holistic and longitudinal approach. J. D. Downing explicitly designed the *Encyclopedia of Social Movement Media* to include historical and contemporary practices, from graffiti to the internet, and especially from movements of the global south (Downing, 2011: xxv). Cammaerts, Mattoni and McCurdy encompass the entirety of social movement media and communication processes and practices in what they term the *media ecology* (2013: 3), whose long history, Lievrouw suggests, involves "divides, diversities, networks, communities and literacies" (2011: 1–3). Treré (2011) examines activist media use as *a diverse system* of inter-related and inter-dependent parts and relationships, including *keystone species*, which *co-evolve* with a sense of *locality*.

These scholars use the theoretical lens of *mediation* to attribute a degree of agency to audiences, users, citizens and subordinate or marginalised groups (Cammaerts, Mattoni and McCurdy 2013: 4). It combines interpersonal processes of creation and sharing of meaning and the use of technological channels to extend, or enhance human communication (Lievrouw, 2011: 4). *Mediation* includes *reconfiguration*, in which users modify and adapt media technologies and systems as needed; and *remediation*, which consists of borrowing, adapting and remixing existing processes of communications and media making (ibid.).

All these authors recognise a major change in media power, or the direct control over the means of media production (Couldry and Curran, 2003: 4). The almost complete domination of media and information during the twentieth century by a handful of global corporations is no longer assured, their commercial success and business models not only contested by an array of capitalist rivals, but by social movement challengers. Since the mid-1990s, social movements have effectively directed their own media to mobilise communities of support and action, reach out to allies and broker space in the corporate commercial news media (Hunter et al., 2013). Some social movements take a *transmedia mobilisation* approach, using a multitude of participatory media-making practices across multiple platforms, and producing multimodal narratives to reach and involve diverse audiences (Costanza-Chock, 2013: 97). Significantly, as we see below, they take advantage of the growing dissemination of read/write digital literacies, and the consequent emergence of *mass self-communication* networks in most regions of the world (Castells, 2007: 249), to create and share content, aggregate, curate, remix and circulate rich media texts among their social, cultural and political networks.

The Occupy movement represented a complex of ecologies, which combined hundreds of autonomous local encampments, allied campaigns and off- and online projects, linked by the Occupy name, values, communications repertoires and frames of meaning. Each local site varied depended on their local balance of social actors, existing histories of contention, social and communication divides and dominant media ecologies (Uitermark and Nicholls, 2012; Kidd, 2013), with InterOccupy developed to bridge the gap between the various groups by using online tools and conference calls (Donovan, 2013).

Composition of Occupy

The Occupy movement built on residual social movements and alternative communications groups such as Indymedia. For example, in New York City, the national Nurses' Union, students' organisations and artists groups, the Right to the City coalition, and the hacker group Anonymous had all organised protests in New York, and many became keystone members of Occupy. Many camps then actively reached out to existing community-based organisations to organise joint actions, educational forums and working groups.

The Occupy Research Network (ORN), a collaboration formed by the Oakland-based DataCenter.org, Indymedia activists and other scholar activists, reported that half the participants had been involved before in another social movement (Costanza-Chock, 2012: 6). Their research report provides a more nuanced examination of the make-up of Occupy than is often reported. Large numbers of white, male, college-educated and Net-savvy young people were indeed involved (ibid.). However, at least half identified as working or lower middle class, with incomes at the median level of Americans, and with only a third employed full-time. There were slightly more women than men. Significant contingents of trade unionists, US military, working-class people and urban poor participated.

The communications practices and platforms reported by participants complicate a simplistic image of white youth leashed to social media. The digital divides that shape and are in turn shaped by existing US class, race and gendered inequalities were also prominent in Occupy. The novelty for many was the opportunity for face-to-face public dialogue, disrupting the contemporary norm of social fragmentation and isolation. Although 64 per cent reported using Facebook to gather information and 74 per cent to post information, nearly half reported discussing Occupy face-to-face, a quarter used newspapers and 42 per cent email. Overall, participants used a combination of "off-line, analog, poster and print-based and 'low-tech' forms of media production", in parallel with high-tech "autonomous wireless networks, hackathons and the creation of new tools and platforms" (ibid.: 4–5).

Residual movements and practices

Occupy's communicative innovation was not any particular technology or practice but its remediation and reconfiguration of earlier practices of residual social change movements. The rules of consensus for decision-making came from the feminist and anarchist traditions; the hand signals from the Disability Justice Movement

461

(Costanza-Chock, 2012: 7); the human mic from anti-nuclear rallies and the global justice movement (Desiriis, 2013); the posters, street theatre, and street puppets from Reclaim the Streets (T. Rosenberg, interview, 18 May 2012); the attention to daily care from the feminist movements (Haiven, 2011); and the story-telling from African American, Latin American and women's movements. Each of these face-to-face practices was then remediated and circulated across the Occupy network via web-based conversations, YouTube videos or social media.

Experienced media activists also helped out at many sites. For example, the Global Revolution stream provided DIY real-time coverage from sites around the world; initiated by activists with Los Indignados experience, it was supported by Indymedia and other long-time media activists. Other experienced hands helped set up working media, tech and press groups, which organised print publications, produced and circulated video narratives, designed and coded websites and wikis, built Occupy media platforms, liaised with alternative and commercial media outlets and supported social media presence (Costanza-Chock, 2012: 4). The commercial social media platforms were by no means universally embraced, as many were critical of the constraints of their corporate ownership, and instead set up their own local websites (Caren and Gaby, 2011).

Horizontalism

If the global justice movement had uneasily negotiated an alliance between the vertical and horizontal approaches to organisation (Kavada, 2013), Occupy represented themselves as horizontals, with consensual participation "part of the *myth* of the movement, portending the kind of communication and the kind of reformed society they promise to bring into existence" (White, 1995: 105). The primary medium for deliberation and self-governance was the general assemblies, drawn from the Zapatista *encuentros* and convergences of the counter-globalisation movement, with elaborate rules designed for "participation, consensus, consultation of membership, articulation of felt desires, [and] building solidarity" (ibid.: 106). The human mic, in which participants repeated speakers' statements en masse, allowed for greater participation as it enabled all voices to be heard in the same way, and reinforced everyone's active engagement. The general assembly and the human mic became Occupy's "most crucial identity symbols", dramatising to members that they are "part of the cultural capital" of the movement (ibid.).

The inclusiveness and attempts to unite the 99% were by no means realised. There were constant tensions over tactical differences, power fissures of race and gender, between 'hard core' and less frequent participants, and between professional class and those without permanent housing. Residual community-based organisations of working-class and poor people, inspired by the scope and scale of the uprisings, often provided material support and helped negotiate relations with city officials; however, they sometimes clashed over continuing stereotypes about poverty, race, class and gender, and especially over the camp-directed orientation and their own longer-term community-based approaches to policy and electoral reform (Williams, Poblet and Bee, 2011).

The tensions over the overarching narrative of horizontalism echoed debates in the new left of the 1960s. Jo Freeman had warned that the elimination of formal structures and establishment of horizontal ones does not automatically remove the power of dominant individuals and cliques, and this article was again cited to challenge the myths of "open-ness" (Costanza-Chock, 2012: 9) and horizontalism (Gerbaudo, 2012: 24). Gerbaudo argued against horizontalism full-stop, writing that that Occupy instead represented a "choreography of assembly" in which a smaller number of facilitators set the scene and scripted people's physical assembly in public space (ibid.: 40). In contrast, for Costanza-Chock, Occupy represented a tension between "openings" for participation, and strong forces towards "closed cultures". He characterised Occupy as a "leaderful" movement (2012: 9–10), especially cataloguing the leadership of working groups formed by women, people of color and LGBTQ people to support one another and each other's participation.

The commons in the square

Occupy represented a renewed attention to local, public spaces and territories (Halvorsen, 2012: 5), providing unconventional intersections in which people come together to create new kinds of connections and solidarities (Atlas, 2012: 152). Many described this collective reclamation of public space and time away from waged work as a *commons*, in opposition to the *enclosure* or privatisation and commercialisation of downtown cores, in which any non-conforming people (and especially the poor) had been turfed out, and the possibilities of "alternative sociability" and political encounter reduced (Gerbaudo, 2012: 105). Occupy's politics of the commons was not a call to reinvigorate public institutions of the welfare state but to create an alternative domain of collective production and social reproduction. Occupy provided the collective practice space for untold numbers of artists and cultural producers, and as Sylvia Federici has argued, placed the "creation of more cooperative and egalitarian forms of human, social and economic relationships at the center of political work" (Haiven, 2011). They prefiguratively set up working groups to attend to people's daily needs, such as food, shelter, health and safety, and activities for kids; and to represent a diversity of collective imaginaries through arts and media projects.

Story-telling and self-expression

The encampments provided a glue of physical proximity, close working relationships and common obstacles and hardships, fostering "strong reciprocal trust and mutual support" (Marcuse, 2011). Rather than focusing outward, in reaction against state or corporate policies, or framing claims for ever-narrower constituencies that had become the trend for US NGOs, the focus was on group-generated needs. Occupy took "people out of their own silos, forcing more cooperation. A whole lot of cross-fertilization happened" (T. Rosenberg, interview, 18 May 2012).

Occupy provided multiple places of encounter, and a plastic sense of time, that facilitated rich dialogical exchanges and collective production of knowledge. Echoing the consciousness-raising of the women's movement, and the Freirian notion of conscientisation, participants reflected on their life conditions and listened to one another, allowing for the articulation of private problems as collective and public issues (Sziarto and Leitner, 2010: 383). The mutual emotions that were unleashed created a "space for new identifications to emerge" (ibid.: 384), and allowed participants to recognise some of the deep social, economic and cultural divisions among them, and understand their relationship with other participants.

Story-telling was one of the primary modes of expression, used in interpersonal conversations, protest rallies and social media dialogues. Unlike formal deliberative genres, story-telling allows speakers to provide a richer lived account of their own experience, to articulate situations, issues and values usually marginalised by the dominant culture (Polletta and Lee, 2006). A more open, less structured genre, story-telling encourages listeners to reconsider established ideas, stereotypes and social remedies, and to share their own narrative.

Occupy participants used every form of artistic medium, from posters to music, ballet and flash-mob dance, street theatre, stand-up comedy and film. Sometimes art was employed tactically: singing en masse to stop foreclosure auctions, dancing flash-mob style to take over bank lobbies, or using masks to maintain anonymity in face of security cameras and police surveillance. Drawing from the carnival traditions of street protest, they combined the element of surprise with the critique of the status quo through role reversal, subversive humour, and full-bodied mass participation. On other occasions, the art practices were part of strategic interventions with existing organisations or neighbourhood groups that highlighted structural problems of unemployment and precarity, or celebrated and memorialised existing neighbourhoods (Atlas, 2012; Treibitz, 2012).

Occupy and the news ecology

The Occupy movement changed the news ecology. Rather than focusing on media-friendly protests and sound bites, participants documented protests, reported on individuals' stories and provided the analyses themselves. They by-passed the residual commercial media gate-keepers by circulating their news on a number of different media platforms. Teams produced regular reports for news sites such as New York's 'Occupy *Wall Street Journal*', and the live 'Global Revolution' video stream, and thousands of individuals created YouTube video reports. Over 170,000 people in the US alone shared live reports, news about police arrests and personal stories over 400 pages of Facebook. Hundreds wrote blog posts such as 'We are the 99 percent' on Tumblr, or posted news stories to an Occupy Reddit site. The total views of all these postings were in the millions. Independent and alternative media organisations, with platforms in print, radio and television, then re-assembled the reports and stories for audiences off the web.

Nevertheless, Occupy depended on the mainstream news media to get the attention of the wider public and policy-makers, especially in the first week of Occupy Wall Street. In fact, it took a photograph of a police commander pepper-spraying a trio of young blonde women during a street demonstration before the dominant news media provided much coverage. The resultant mainstream news coverage and the viral circulation of the video of the women screaming in pain led to a rapid expansion of Occupy encampments around the world. The Occupy movements' circulation of that image set the pace; after that, the commercial news media often struggled to keep up with the movement's news flow.

Occupy not only garnered much higher levels of US dominant news coverage, much more of it positive, than earlier movements for political, economic and social justice (Bennett and Segerberg, 2012). The dominant news frame changed, re-introducing long-silenced debates about class and systemic inequality (Stelter, 2011), and renewed visibility to social movements, and their capacity for "upending governments and conventional wisdom", as *Time* magazine put it (Stengel, 2011). The coverage reversed a long downturn in which few news reports featured the role of community organisations in remedying local problems and injustices (Barker-Plummer and Kidd, 2009). To be sure, the dominant genre of local commercial news continued; many of the stories featured incidents of violence. However, the strength of the #Occupy news flow meant that alternative narratives were "established in the public imagination", according to Oakland media activist Tracy Rosenberg: "Injustice, inequality, homelessness is not invisible and can't be swept away. The police can attack with flash grenades but we all have to see that. That makes a difference" (interview, 18 May 2012).

Post-Occupy

The Occupy movement involved more people, worldwide, than any public mobilisations since the global protests against the US and their allies' invasion of Iraq, and represented a new cycle of social movement media power, renovating and democratising virtually all aspects of communication. Occupy represented a perfect storm which cannot be easily replicated. Its impact was due to many factors – the element of surprise, the beginnings in New York, one of the globe's primary media hubs, the multiple spaces and extended times of encounter outside normal capitalist relations, the contribution of residual movements and activists, the harnessing of a wide diversity of cultural and communications practices and the openness of its platform for others to engage. Nevertheless, there are some lessons we can take away about social movement communications.

The movement modelled a transmedia approach, combining a fluid mix of practices that considered different cultures, literacies and strengths; social media were in fact mundane, everyday tools (Nielsen, 2013). The Occupy movement did not succeed because of its adaptation of computer applications, nor a particular horizontal or networked social formation. Rather than a flat architecture, the movement was constitutively ridden with imbalances and assymetries (Bergaudo, 2012: 19), troubling the "easy distinction between vertical and horizontal organizational structures" and showing more hybridised forms (Berger, Funke and Wolfson, 2011: 189). Creating a temporary spatial and temporal zone allowed the Occupy movement to develop a new "social ethic of democratic communication" (White, 1995: 112) that has been remediated in both old and new community-based political and cultural initiatives (Khatib, Killjoy and McGuire, 2012), and new social movement campaigns of immigrants, students, low-wage workers. During the heady days of the movement, Occupy participants did not wait for the commercial news media to tell their story; since then, they are not waiting for scholarly consideration, but are recording their own histories and analyses of the movement (Williams, Poblet and Bee, 2011; Writers for the 99%, 2012; Shiffman et al., 2012).

Further reading

Chapter 6, "Occupy Wall Street: Harvesting the salt of the earth," in Manuel Castells's *Networks of Outrage and Hope: Social Movements in the Internet Age* (2012), examines the demographic components, ideas and values and communications repertoires of the Occupy movement in the US. Chapter 4, "'The hashtag which did (not) start a revolution': The laborious adding up to the 99%", of Paolo Gerbaudo's *Tweets and the Streets: Social Media and Contemporary Activism* (2012) provides a detailed account of the cultural mediation of face-to-face communications, and social media at Occupy Wall Street in New York City. The "New political spaces" edition of *Race, Poverty and the Environment* (http://reimaginerpe.org/node/6924) provides a deeper before-and-after examination of social movements at one site, Occupy Oakland.

Readers interested in a historical and global mapping of Occupy should read the special Occupy issue of *Social Movement Studies: Journal of Social, Cultural and Political Protest*, 11(3–4), 2012, which provides case studies of related movements (Los Indignados, Arab Spring, Chilean student movement, Israel), uneasy relationships to residual movements (North American indigenous movements, homeless peoples), specific Occupy encampments (Pittsburgh, London, El Paso, Los Angeles and Amsterdam) and theoretical discussions of its legacy.

References

Atlas, C. (2012) "Radical imagination." In R. Shiffman et al. (eds), *Beyond Zucotti Park: Freedom of Assembly and the Occupation of Public Space*. Oakland, CA: New Village Press (pp. 146–55).

Atton, C. (2002) *Alternative Media*. London: Sage.

Barker-Plummer, B. and Kidd, D. (2009) "Closings and openings: Media restructuring and the public sphere." In K. Howley (ed.), *The Community Media Reader*. Thousand Oaks, CA: Sage Books (pp. 318–27).

Bennett, W. L. and Segerberg, A. (2012) "The logic of connective action." *Information, Communication and Society*, 15(5), 739–68.

Bergaudo, P. (2012) *Tweets and the Streets: Social Media and Contemporary Activism*. London: Pluto Press.

Berger, D., Funke, P. and Wolfson, T. (2011) "Communications networks, movements and the neoliberal city: The Media Mobilizing Project in Philadelphia." *Transforming Anthropology*, 19(2), 187–201.

Cammaerts, B., Mattoni, A. and McCurdy, P. (eds.) (2013) *Mediation and Protest Movements*. Bristol: Intellect Books.

Caren, N. and Gaby, S. (2011) "Occupy Online: Facebook and the Spread of Occupy Wall Street." 24 October. SSRN: http://dx.doi.org/10.2139/ssrn.1943168.

Castells, M. (2007) "Communication, power and counter-power in the network society." *International Journal of Communication*, 1, 238–66.

——(2012) *Networks of Outrage and Hope: Social Movements in the Internet Age*. Cambridge: Polity Press.

Cleaver, H. (1995) "The Zapatistas and the electronic fabric of struggle." Retrieved from http://libcom.org/library/zapatistas-electronic-fabric-struggle-draft-cleaver (accessed 2 June 2014).

Costanza-Chock, S. (2012) "Mic check! Media cultures and the Occupy movement." *Social Movement Studies: Journal of Social, Cultural and Political Protest*, 11(3–4), 375–85.

——(2013) "Transmedia mobilization in the Popular Association of the Oaxacan Peoples, Los Angeles." In B. Cammaerts, A. Mattoni and P. McCurdy (eds), *Mediation and Protest Movements*. Bristol: Intellect Books (95–114).

Couldry, N. and Curran, J. (2003) "The paradox of media power." In N. Couldry and J. Curran (eds), *Contesting Media Power: Alternative Media in a Networked World*. Lanham, MD: Rowman & Littlefield (pp. 3–15).

Deseriis, M. (2013) "The people's mic as a medium in its own right: A pharmacological reading." *Communication and Critical/Cultural Studies* 11(1), 42–51.

Donovan, J. (2013) "Occupy 3.0 – A slow network movement." *Waging Non Violence: People Powered News and Analysis*, 18 September. Retrieved from http://wagingnonviolence.org/feature/occupy-3-0-slow-network-movement/ (accessed 30 March 2014).

Downing, J. D. (2011) "Introduction." *Encyclopedia of Social Movement Media*. Los Angeles: Sage Reference.

Gamson, W. and Sifry, M. (2013) "The #Occupy movement: An introduction." *Sociological Quarterly*, 54, 159–228.

Gerbaudo, P. (2012) *Tweets and the Streets: Social Media and Contemporary Activism*. London: Pluto Press.

Haiven, M. (2011) "Feminism, finance and the future of #Occupy – An interview with Silvia Federici." *Znet*. Retrieved from http://zcomm.org/znetarticle/feminism-finance-and-the-future-of-occupy-an-interview-with-silvia-federici-by-max-haiven/ (accessed 9 June 2014).

Halvorsen, S. (2012) "Beyond the network? Occupy London and the global movement." *Social Movement Studies: Journal of Social, Cultural and Political Protest*, 11(3–4), 427–33.

Hunter, M. L., Van Wassenhove, L. N., Besiou, M. and Van Halderen, M. (2013) "The agenda-setting power of stake-holder media." *California Management Review*, 56(1) (Fall), 24–49.

Kavada, A. (2013) "Internet cultures and protest movements: The cultural links between strategy, organizing and online communication." In B. Cammaerts et al. (eds), *Mediation and Protest Movements*. Bristol: Intellect Books (pp. 77–94).

Khatib, K., Killjoy, M. and McGuire, M. (2012) *We Are Many: Reflections of Movement Strategy from Occupation to Liberation*. Oakland, CA: AK Press.

Kidd, D. (2003) "Indymedia.org: A new communications commons." In M. McCaughey and M. D. Ayers (eds), *Cyberactivism: Online Activism in Theory and Practice*. New York: Routledge (pp. 47–70).

——(2013) "#Occupy in the San Francisco Bay." *Rethinking Urban Inclusion: Spaces, Mobilisations, Interventions. Cescontexto – Debates*, No. 2. Center for Economic Studies, University of Coimbra, Portugal.

Klein, N. (2001) "Were the DC and Seattle protests unfocused?" Retrieved from http://www.naomiklein.org/articles/2001/07/were-dc-and-seattle-protests-unfocused (accessed 5 June 2014).

Lievrouw, L. (2011) *Alternative and Activist New Media*. Cambridge: Polity Press.

Marcuse, P. (2011) "The purpose of the Occupation movement and the danger of fetishizing space." Blog post, 15 November. Retrieved from http://archive.wikiwix.com/opendemocracy/?url=http://pmarcuse.wordpress.com/2011/11/15/the-purpose-of-the-occupation-movement-and-the-danger-of-fetishizing-space&title=Peter%20Marcuse/ (accessed 6 October 2012).

Martinez-Torres, M. E. (2001) "Civil society, the internet, and the Zapatistas." *Peace Review*, 13(3), 339–46.

Murphy, B. (2002) "A critical history of the internet." In G. Elmer (ed.), *Critical Perspectives on the Internet*. Lanham, MD: Roman & Littlefield.

Nielsen, R. K. (2013) "Mundane internet tools, the risk of exclusion, and reflexive movements – Occupy Wall Street and political uses of digital networked technologies." *Sociological Quarterly*, 54, 173–77.

Polletta, F. (2013) "Participatory democracy in the new millennium." *Contemporary Sociology*, 42(1), 40–50.

Polletta, F. and Lee, J. (2006) "Is telling stories good for democracy? Rhetoric in public deliberation after 9/11." *American Sociological Review*, 71, 699–723.

Rodríguez, C., Ferron, B. and Shamas, K. (2014) "Four challenges in the field of alternative, radical and citizens' media research." *Media, Culture and Society*, 36(2), 150–66.

Shiffman, R., Bell, R., Brown, L. J. and Elizabeth, L., with A. Fisyak and A. Venkataraman (2012) *Beyond Zucotti Park: Freedom of Assembly and the Occupation of Public Space*. Oakland, CA: New Village Press.

Stelter, B. (2011) "Camps are cleared, but '99%' still occupies the lexicon." *New York Times*, 30 November.

Stengel, R. (2011) "Person of the year introduction." *Time*, 14 December. Retrieved from http://content.time.com/time/specials/packages/article/0,28804,2101745_2102139_2102 380,00.html (accessed 30 December 2011).

Sziarto, K. and Leitner, H. (2010) "Immigrant riding for justice: Space-time and emotions in the construction of a counter-public." *Political Geography*, 29, 381–91.

Treibitz, J. (2012) "The art of cultural resistance." In K. Khatib, M. Killjoy and M. McGuire (eds), *We Are Many: Reflections on Movement Strategy from Occupation to Liberation*. Oakland, CA: AK Press.

Treré, E. (2011) "Studying media practices in social movements." CIRN Prato Community Informatics Conference, Refereed Stream.

Uitermark, J. and Nicholls, W. (2012) "How local networks shape a global movement: Comparing Occupy in Amsterdam and Los Angeles." *Social Movement Studies*, 11(3–4), 295–301.

White, R. (1995) "Democratization of communication as a social movement process." In P. Lee (ed.), *The Democratization of Communication*. Cardiff: University of Wales Press.

Williams, R. (1977) *Marxism and Literature*. London: Oxford University Press.

Williams, S., Poblet, M. and Bee, N. (2011) "On Occupy: A roundtable discussion." *Race, Poverty and the Environment*, 18(2). Retrieved from http://reimaginerpe.org/radio/rpe/williams-poblet (accessed 10 June 2014).

Writers for the 99% (2012) *Occupying Wall Street: The Inside Story of an Action that Changed America*. New York: OR Books.

41

WILL IT HARM THE SHEEP?

Developments and disputes in central Australian indigenous media

Tony Dowmunt

There's a famous story from half a century ago that Sol Worth and Jon Adair tell about their negotiations with a Navajo elder, Sam Yazzie, to enable them to make films with Navaho people in the US:

> Adair explained that we wanted to teach some Navaho to make movies ... When Adair finished Sam thought for a while, and then turned to Worth and asked a lengthy question which was interpreted as, "Will making movies do the sheep any harm?" Worth was happy to explain that as far as he knew, there was no chance that making movies would harm the sheep. Sam thought this over and then asked, "Will making movies do the sheep good?" Worth was forced to reply that as far as he knew making movies wouldn't do the sheep any good. Sam thought this over for a moment, then, looking round at us, he said, "Then why make movies?"
>
> (Worth and Adair, 1972: 5)

Yazzie's question "Why make movies?" is intriguing because it makes us ask: are there real benefits that media use brings to indigenous communities? And perhaps, by implication, does this work bring more benefits to its champions in the over-developed world – people like myself and maybe some readers of this book – than it does to indigenous populations? These questions preoccupied me during a research trip to Alice Springs in Central Australia that I made in October–November 2011. My aim had been to follow up a Channel 4 programme – *Satellite Dreaming* (CAAMA Productions, 1991) – which I was involved in making 20 years earlier as a co-production with the indigenous media organisation CAAMA (the Central Australian Aboriginal Media Association). I was interested to find out what developments and changes had happened in the intervening years, and to see what lessons those changes might hold for those of us interested in alternative and indigenous people's media now.

Twenty years ago the answers to both my questions seemed very clear to me ('yes' and 'no', respectively), but since then there have been a number of insightful critiques of indigenous peoples' media, some of which I'll cite later in relation to the Central Australian experience. I'll mention just two now. Just over 20 years ago Rachel Moore questioned the way in which academic visual anthropologists celebrated indigenous videos for the "rock solid fact of their authenticity" (Moore, 1994: 128), suggesting that "in its first world reception" this work becomes "one long performance" of the defining contact myth "between primitive and civilised" (ibid.: 132). She was talking about the reception of this cultural work in an academic context – as was Toby Miller, who wrote about the way in which "Aborigines have been the most important exporters of social theory and cultural production to the northern hemisphere over the past century" (Miller, 1995: 7). He satirises the "lengthy history of First World people writing about tribal Aboriginal forms of life and then exporting them back home, with a subsequent elevation of status for themselves and a renewal of critique for Academic theorisation" (ibid.: 14) – a useful caution for me as I write this now.

Satellite Dreaming was shown in 1993 on both the ABC in Australia and Channel 4 in the UK – the latter was part of a series of programmes, with an accompanying book called *Channels of Resistance* (Dowmunt, 1993). *Satellite Dreaming* began with a sequence depicting the launch of AUSSAT – the satellite system which was to deliver phone and TV signals to the remote Australian outback – followed by a graphic representation of an indigenous man protecting the centre of the continent from the satellite signal with a traditional wooden shield, then a sequence depicting indigenous video production and playback in the desert. Our intentions are probably clear from this sequence of images, a depiction of modern technology meeting traditional Aboriginal life in the outback (our version, perhaps, of the "contact myth" that Moore describes), and then of traditional culture fighting back against the technology, resisting the media invasion with their own productions. This 'resistance' model – indigenous people resisting media invasion – is one of the binaristic simplifications that I've come to question since making *Satellite Dreaming*.

What took me to Central Australia 20 years ago to make this programme? And then what drew me back again at the end of last year? My interest was stimulated in the mid-1980s when I first heard about CAAMA winning – against all the odds – the licence to run a TV station for the whole Central Australian footprint which the AUSSAT system covered. This was real David and Goliath stuff – all the more inspiring for a media activist like myself in mid-1980s Thatcherite Britain (a few years after the Falklands War, the miners' defeat, the abolition of the GLC and other socialist metropolitan councils). It was obvious that the alternative media project in the UK was unlikely to get much purchase in the mainstream media world in that particular political climate, but out there in Central Australia it seemed a small and marginalised group was doing just that.

I went to Alice Springs for the first time in 1986, mainly to meet up with Philip Batty – a 'whitefella' who had co-founded CAAMA a few years earlier with his Aboriginal colleague John Macumba. Philip was the person perhaps most responsible for winning CAAMA the license. He had started his work as a media activist in the late 1970s in Papunya. After moving to Alice Springs and working on the first radio programme for aboriginal people with John Macumba, they set up CAAMA – which originally they had wanted, in the spirit of the times, to call something like the "black revolutionary media organisation" (P. Batty, interview, 2011).

While still in Papunya, Philip had become aware of the AUSSAT satellite project. The government's plan was to cover the continent with three satellites to provide TV and phone signals in even the most remote areas – the areas where large numbers of Aboriginal people still led more 'traditional' lives, and where many indigenous languages were still spoken. A delegation from Canberra had come to Papunya to do a consultation exercise on the introduction of these new media technologies into remote desert communities, which bewildered the local people – not least because, Philip pointed out, most of them didn't understand English (P. Batty, interview, 2011).

The anthropologist Eric Michaels had also started to work at Yuendumu (a settlement 293km northwest of Alice Springs) a few years after this, with an anthropological brief to investigate the potential effects of the satellite on Aboriginal communities – which he then departed substantially from. In partnership with Francis Juppurula Kelly, a local Warlpiri man, and under the direction of a local committee of elders, he established Warlpiri Media, "to get protection for Aboriginal people", as Kelly has since described it: "We are lucky we started Warlpiri Media in this community, if not we could have lost our culture and language" (Kelly, 1988). The 'protection' they provided was local programming, initially shown in the community via a pirate TV transmitter. Eric Michaels suggested the work was a response to

> the problem of social diversity that introduced media pose for indigenous peoples everywhere: how to respond to the insistent pressure towards standardization, the homogenizing tendencies of contemporary world culture?
> (Michaels, 1994: 100)

Michaels's question was being asked by a large number of people in Central Australia in response to AUSSAT, and fairly rapidly in the early 1980s a campaign developed – led by CAAMA but with the participation of Ernabella Video Television (now PY Media) and Warlpiri Media, both of which were already running pirate TV stations for cultural maintenance and 'protection'. This work was among that described by Faye Ginsburg in an influential article published in 1991, where she argued that "indigenous and minority people have been using a variety of media as new vehicles for self-determination, and for resistance to outside cultural domination" (Ginsburg, 1991: 92).

The campaign culminated in CAAMA bidding for the license to run the AUSSAT Central Australian footprint, at a public government tribunal in Alice Springs. They were successful, after a long fight.

Freda Glynn, an Aboriginal woman who was at that time running CAAMA with Philip Batty, had made the case to the Tribunal by talking about "the emergency that has arisen with Aboriginal people" (Bell, 2008: 257) – which included many of the young people in remote communities who were self-harming and glue sniffing. She suggested that satellite television was "the third wave": first was the invasion by Europeans, then the introduction of alcohol into the communities and now television: "we may be able to use it or it may destroy that very strong culture in the communities" (ibid.: 154). Glynn and others saw this perceived threat of 'culture-cide' by the satellite broadcasting – its potentially destructive social effects on communities, and on indigenous languages – as being best countered by indigenous media: vehicles for 'self-determination', and for 'resistance' to outside cultural domination – in Faye Ginsburg's language. As it turned out, Imparja TV – the station that was established by CAAMA as a result of winning the licence – was a failure in terms of CAAMA's (or more exactly Philip and Freda's) ambitions for it – a long story, but principally because it was forced to compete in the marketplace as a commercial broadcasting organisation, with the result that it produced very little of the Aboriginal programming that was promised in its licence application – a story we told in *Satellite Dreaming*, showing how Aboriginal programming didn't generate sufficient advertising revenue to 'justify' its costs. In the end, Philip was forced out of CAAMA, along with Freda, primarily because they disagreed with the governing board (of CAAMA and Imparja) about the commercial direction Imparja TV was travelling in.

In the years since then, Philip has developed an analysis of this history in which he tried to go beyond the 'resistance' model. For instance, he critiqued a sentence in the introduction to *Channels of Resistance*, where I wrote about how groups all over the world were beginning to resist "dominant television forms" (Dowmunt, 1993: 14). He responded:

> there is little point in deploying crude binary logic in analyzing these exceedingly complex events in terms off a contest between the dominated and the dominant. Rather, there were numerous points of resistance dispersed across a broad field of activity ...
>
> (Batty, 2001: 1)

He later elaborated his critique of the resistance model in his PhD thesis – which strove to understand the role of the state in determining what had gone wrong with Imparja:

> in failing to address the problematic relationship between the development of Aboriginal broadcasting and government, many of these writers not only demonstrate a certain naïveté about the state's project of "Aboriginal self-determination", but take an intellectually barren approach in its analysis ... Here, the government is simply seen as part of the "natural" social and political order in which these developments occurred. Furthermore, the propensity to render invisible the role of government in the development of Aboriginal broadcasting is ... directly connected to the narrowly-defined ideologies that underpin such work.
>
> (Batty, 2003: 16–17)

The project of 'Aboriginal self-determination' to which Batty refers here began in the early 1970s, partly in response to demands from Aboriginal activists that the federal government give them the right to administer their own communities. The government agreed, and appointed the Aboriginal and Torres Strait Islander Commission to allocate and distribute funds to Aboriginal communities and to liaise with the federal government in relation to funding policies. So the project from the start was heavily enmeshed in state power. Batty goes on to suggest that the selves deployed by self-determination were themselves shaped by state power:

> Throughout the era of Aboriginal "self-determination" … the state has sought to constitute a range of differing Aboriginal "selves" … Perhaps the most ambiguous feature of the Aboriginal self-determinationist project has been its desire to constitute – in certain contexts – what I will describe as a "resistant Aboriginal self". Here I will focus on the "culturally authentic" and "resistant" Aboriginal "self", since their formation was of central importance in the formation of an Aboriginal agency capable of establishing an Aboriginal broadcasting service.
>
> (Batty, 2003: 42)

So he saw the policy of self-determination much more as a project of the state than of autonomous, 'self-determined' action by the Aboriginal community, and argued that the state was integrally involved in the mobilisation of the various Aboriginal 'selves' that served their policy needs. He concludes that

> the "culturally authentic" and "resistant" Aboriginal "self" … was of central importance in the formation of an Aboriginal agency capable of establishing an Aboriginal broadcasting service.
>
> (Batty, 2003: 42)

Batty critiqued Eric Michaels's work, most vigorously for his perceived championing of the 'culturally authentic' Aboriginal 'self' – in effect, for having too simple, even an essentialist view of traditional Aboriginal communities. The widespread critiquing of Michaels's work started soon after his death, in a special issue of *Continuum* (O'Regan, 1990) in which, for instance, Tim Rowse suggests that Michaels was too committed to the notion of "communicating community" in a situation in which "community as such may not exist as a unified entity" (1990: 115), and Robert Hodge accuses his work of expressing "a ghostly survival of Aboriginalism [akin to Saïd's 'Orientalism'] in [his] own core premises" (ibid.: 141).

More recently, Melinda Hinkson has written that Michaels's focus on the uses of video and television for "cultural maintenance" fostered a "false dichotomy … between traditional and modern, culture and lifestyle and indeed local and global – that assumes cultural production to be a static process" (2002: 205). Her view is that this focus enabled him to ignore the fundamentally "inter-cultural" (ibid.: 213) nature of his media work in Yuendumu, disregarding his own role as a European in an encounter with his Aboriginal collaborators. Finally, Jennifer Deger makes the point that "the kind of cultural future envisioned by Michaels … is, in a profound sense, his own" (2006: 41). She suggests that "the defiant tone that infuses these [Michaels's and others'] accounts of indigenous empowerment through technology has proven to have a widespread and … somewhat romantic appeal" (ibid.: 47).

I appreciate the weight of some of the criticisms levelled against Michaels, as I'm conscious that I am someone who was also thoroughly seduced by this 'romantic appeal' in the 1980s and 1990s – and that it provided some of my motivation for wanting to return to Australia recently. In the intervening years I'd kept in touch with what was happening in Central Australia, including following the progress of Warwick Thornton's first feature film *Samson and Delilah*, which he shot and directed and which won the Camera d'Or (best first feature) at the Cannes Film Festival in 2009. In 1992 Warwick was 19, an Aboriginal trainee at CAAMA and the cameraman on *Satellite Dreaming*. In *Samson and Delilah* (2009), Thornton used his own experience as a young Aboriginal man growing up in and around Alice Springs to inform the story of his two young lovers and their harsh encounters with their own culture, and with white Australia. It is a film that, despite an apparently optimistic ending, presents as bleak a picture of life for young Aboriginal people as Freda Glynn had at the AUSSAT tribunal over 20 years before. However it does end with the two protagonists apparently trying to re-forge their lives on an 'outstation' in the remote landscape of Delilah's family's 'country' – a way of life which affirms traditional Aboriginal culture and its sacred relationship with the land.

The earlier bleakness in the film reflects the fact that there has been very little social or economic progress in remote Aboriginal communities since my visit 20 years ago. In November 2011 another 'whitefella' and I were filming in the Todd River Basin in Alice Springs, which is traditionally a camping ground for Aboriginal people visiting from the bush, but also a congenial place to drink. Consequently it has become a regular stomping ground for non-indigenous film crews who want cutaways for their documentaries on the Aboriginal 'problem' in Alice Springs.[1] We were actually after shots that showed the contrast of the graffiti-covered bridge with the shiny new Imparja TV building – just across the road from the Todd River – but an Aboriginal man whom we could just glimpse in the background of the shot saw we were filming and approached us to protest, with more sadness than aggression, explaining: "We are not animals in zoo."

Prominent in the graffiti on the bridge was an anti-intervention slogan – 'Respect: Stop the Intervention' – scrawled over a black, yellow and red Aboriginal flag. In the 20 years since I had been in Alice Springs, the 'self-determination' policies that prevailed then have been substantially reversed, not least by the recent so-called 'Intervention'. The 'Intervention' (or to give it its official name, 'Northern Territory National Emergency Response') was an attempt by the state to regulate life in remote communities in the Northern Territory in response to widespread reports of increased alcohol use, domestic violence and child sexual abuse, a response that initially involved sending the army into these communities, in 2007. This, of course, was massively controversial with both indigenous and non-indigenous peoples.

The Aboriginal activist Rosalie Kunoth-Monks was a strong opponent of the Intervention, describing it as being like "Australia declaring war on us, and in the process they demonised and dehumanized Aboriginal [people]" (Kunoth-Monks, 2013). She lives in a Northern Territory community called 'Utopia', which became the irony-saturated title of John Pilger's (2013) film, in which he convincingly makes the case that the demonising of the Northern Territories by the Intervention masked what, in effect, was a state land-grab of previously semi-autonomous Aboriginal territory to make it easier to acquire and exploit mineral rights. However, there also are a number of Aboriginal supporters of the Intervention. On my recent visit I met a young woman from Yuendumu in Alice Springs who saw it as an appropriate way to combat domestic violence in her community, and the lawyer and activist Noel Pearson and the anthropologist Marcia Langton both have argued strongly in favour of the emergency response in the Northern Territory. In many ways the 'Intervention' also represented a final nail in the coffin of the 'self-determination' policies that white Australia had pursued in relation to Aboriginal people since the 1960s, and some writers have argued that self-determination as a policy had been a (well-meaning) failure from the start:

> Self-determination was to herald a radical change to a new era of racial equality. But equality could not be suddenly conjured into being by brave words. Differences which had been constructed and confirmed by inequality at every level through inter-racial history were in fact constitutive of the black and white people being governed.
>
> (Cowlishaw, 1999: 217)

This was compounded by the opposition to the policy by its many white critics, who deployed

> an aggressive public rhetoric which decried self-determination as "waste", ridiculed the enterprises and openly predicted disaster. To protect the projects from this hostile discourse, many involved whitefellas muted their own anxiety that Aboriginal alienation from the ordinary processes of modern society was so extensive as to represent an insuperable barrier.
>
> (Cowlishaw, 1999: 237)

This anxiety was becoming more evident and expressed during my time in Australia, and explains some of what I heard from white people in Alice Springs and elsewhere, about Aboriginal work with video. For instance, one filmmaker told me that it was "sad what's happening". Twenty years ago whitefellas like him thought they'd work themselves out of jobs by training Aboriginals, but this hasn't happened and his conclusion was that the "Western way of life" was "too much for bush people".

******

Given that the 'resistance model' is no longer apparently so useful and the project of 'self-determination' is so damaged, what is still meaningful and important about the Central Australian experience with media? One of the lessons for me has been that it's important to look beyond the binaries – both those between oppression and resistance, and between the modern and the traditional: the work is to discover "not 'their' culture and not 'our culture' but something in between" (Cowlishaw, 1999: 5). I still think that the space between our (Western and Aboriginal) experiences of media can be illuminating, and we can still usefully examine our assumptions about media through understanding our projections onto the indigenous other. In the West we are all still, I'd say, in "the belly of the beast" – in Eric Michaels's resonant phrase characterising modern mass media[2] – and this can induce a claustrophobia that inhibits our seeing alternatives.

In *Satellite Dreaming* there's an interview with Pantjiti Mckenzie, who worked with Ernabella Video Television. Ernabella is a Pitjantjatjara community 200km or so southwest of Alice Springs, and the site, as I've already mentioned, of a pirate TV experiment. She describes her work recording women's sacred 'business': "I record women's secret ceremonies in the bush. We bring it back and put it in a special cupboard. It's for private viewing, not for making programmes. It's good." 'Private viewing' means that these tapes can only be seen by groups of initiated women. I very much enjoy her satisfaction with a use of video and TV that is at complete variance with how we in the West have come to see the meaning and function of television as a mass medium – centre out, to an undifferentiated audience. She celebrates her videos for being local, made for a highly differentiated and restricted audience.

Jennifer Deger works in a community in Arnhem Land making videos with Yolgu people, and makes a similar point:

> for Yolngu there is no generic idea of a person or audience – everyone is already constructed in kin relationships [which] determine the mode of address, style of language, and even the subject matter of conversation. Thus the notion of an intimate yet undifferentiated audience that informs Western broadcasting models is fundamentally at odds with Yolngu modes of communication.
>
> (Deger, 2006: 17)

Deger argues that Aboriginal-produced media (in her experience with the Yolngu) contribute to our debates in the West about the limitations of the notion of *representation* in our understanding of how media operate. Borrowing from writers like Laura Marks and Vivian Sobchack, she proposes "a different sense of the relationship between the image and the imaged. It is this that I mean by 'presencing' – the sense in which so-called representing re-presents in material, tangible terms what it purports to simply copy" (ibid.: 100)

There's an example of this kind of thinking about the relationship between the image and the imaged in a sequence from *Satellite Dreaming*, depicting EVTV filming the sacred story of Nyiru and the Seven Sisters. At night around a campfire at Kuruala (the sacred site of the featured part of the story), the traditional custodian of the site, Noli Roberts, is giving his reasons for inviting us – the CAAMA crew and myself – to film the re-enactment of the Seven Sisters songline at one of its sacred sites: "When people see it they will say: 'It's true. I see how Nyiru and the Seven Sisters came to Kuruala.'" For him – and in most traditional Aboriginal culture – there is no distinction between fiction and fact – so everything you film is 'true'. It's 'true' that Nyiru came to Kuruala, because the videoing process 'presences' Nyiru and the Seven Sisters – makes them present and real, not 'fictional'.

This absence of the category of 'fiction' has very material consequences for Indigenous uses of contemporary digital technologies and, of course, the 'virtual reality' of the internet is certainly having some influence in communities in Central Australia too. I learned on my visit last year that Pantjiti McKenzie is currently involved with a web-based cultural maintenance project called Ara Iritija – "a community-based, multimedia digital archive, designed at the request of Ngaanyatjarra, Pitjantjatjara and Yankunytjatjara (Anangu) communities", as they describe themselves on their website.[3] Apparently the Anangu consultants on the project were alarmed when they discovered that men's and women's business was being stored in the same database.

They insisted not just that they were separated virtually, but physically too, stored on different computers – a contemporary version of the locked cupboard of videos only accessible to initiated women.

While in the era of self-determination this kind of traditional cultural maintenance work – alongside more obviously political struggles around land rights – was seen as unproblematically progressive, in more recent years it has become more contested. At the time of my first visit twenty years ago, the reclaiming of traditional lands (the struggle for 'land rights') was analogous to the reclaiming of traditional culture through the kinds of practices described by Noli Roberts. But now the ideological underpinnings of both projects are being questioned, perhaps most clearly in the 'culture crisis' in Australianist anthropology – provoked by the Intervention – which positions those still committed to self-determination against those who think that ethnography has, in Marcia Langton's words, been destructively

> governed by a gerontocracy and supported by hunter-gatherer economies and ways of life. This world no longer exists in much of Australia, and where these institutions survive, they are compromised and altered by welfare dependency, modern consumerism and a range of conditions associated with the rapid transition to modernity.
>
> (Langton, 2010: 92)

Some of these intellectuals – including Langton and Philip Batty – support the Intervention as (as they see it) an appropriate mechanism to check some of these 'conditions' – notably, domestic violence, child abuse and drug and alcohol dependency – that are still endemic in many remote Aboriginal communities. Traditional, gerontocratic culture, in which the elders hold sway, is seen as hostile to people's well-being – particularly to women and young people. This view may be supported by statistics which show that "those Indigenous Australians with the most language and culture are precisely those with the worst health" (Kowal, 2010: 184), and so "the more remote you are, the worse your health is" (ibid.: 185). Kowal, however, also points to statistics on 'outstation' health which might undermine this connection between remoteness and ill health, statistics which suggest that people living 'authentically' in the outstations (like the protagonists of Samson and Delilah at the end of the film) may have better health than those living in the more regulated communities in the outback. As she says "very, very remote" people may have better health than the merely "very remote" (ibid.).

However, for me the fundamental point is not about tradition versus modernity – or even about cultural and ethnic differences – but more about media power. I still agree with Eric Michaels's conclusion to his essay on 'Aboriginal content' – a criterion which the AUSSAT tribunal was anxiously trying to define to help its decision about which applicant to award the license to (CAAMA or its opponents). Michaels thought the definition of 'Aboriginal content' was much less urgent than the issue of who was going to make and control the media productions that were going to end up on the satellite. He concluded that

> What we need is an adequate program for local community television. If we take "community" rather than "Aboriginality" to be the subject, and make

"local" the qualifier, only then do we avoid the traps of racism and paternalism in our rhetoric and practice.

(Michaels, 1994: 44, 42)

What is clear from my recent visit is that the desire in traditional indigenous communities in Central Australia to make their own media is still very much alive – not only in Ara Iritija or *Samson and Delilah*. To take just two examples, Noli Roberts and others had just finished recording the final leg of the Seven Sisters story, and Francis Kelly was shooting a new version of the story of the Coniston massacre – a project he had begun with Eric Michaels in the 1980s (Michaels, 1994: 110–15). These communities clearly do not doubt that their use of media and television brings real benefits, and the work continues to fascinate me as a rare example of local, community control over media representation.

Notes

1 See, for instance, *Unreported World: Australia's Hidden Valley*, broadcast in the UK on Channel 4 while I was in Australia (Unreported World, 2011).
2 Michaels, quoted by Ruby (2000: 221).
3 See http://www.irititja.com/the_archive/index.html (accessed 29 January 2014).

Further reading (and viewing)

Satellite Dreaming is available at www.satellitedreaming.com – a website which also has other research material and relevant links. There is no one book that describes Indigenous media work in Central Australia as a whole, but Bell (2008) gives a full and balanced account of the history of Imparja TV, and Eric Michaels's writings are collected in *Bad Aboriginal Art* (1994). *Shimmering Screens* (Deger, 2006) centres on media work with a Yolgu community in the north of Australia, and *Culture Crisis* (Altman and Hinkson, 2010) gives a range of responses to the Northern Territory 'Intervention' from anthropological perspectives.

References

Altman J. and Hinkson, M. (eds.) (2010) *Culture Crisis*. Sydney: University of New South Wales Press.
Batty, P. (2001) "Enlisting the Aboriginal subject: The state invention of Aboriginal broadcasting." Power of knowledge, the resonance of tradition, Australian Institute of Aboriginal and Torres Strait Islander Studies Conference, Australian National University.
——(2003) *Governing Cultural Difference*. Retrieved from http://ura.unisa.edu.au/R/?func=dbin-jump-full&object_id=unisa28408 (accessed 31 May 2014).
Bell, W. (2008) *A Remote Possibility: The Battle for Imparja Television*. Alice Springs, NT: IAD Press.
CAAMA Productions (1991) *Satellite Dreaming*. Retrieved from http://www.satellitedreaming.com/ (accessed 30 May 2014).

Cowlishaw, G. (1999) *Redheads, Eggheads and Blackfellas: A Study of Racial Power and Intimacy in Australia*. Ann Arbor: University of Michigan Press.

Deger, J. (2006) *Shimmering Screens: Making Media in an Aboriginal Community*. Minneapolis: University of Minnesota Press.

Dowmunt, T. (ed.) (1993) *Channels of Resistance: Global Television and Local Empowerment*. London: BFI.

Ginsburg, F. (1991) "Indigenous media: Faustian contract or global village?" *Cultural Anthropology*, 6(1), 92–112.

Hinkson, M. (2002) "New media projects at Yuendumu: Intercultural engagement and self-determination in an era of accelerated globalization." *Continuum*, 16(2), 201–20.

Hodge, R. (1990) "Aboriginal truth and White media: Eric Michaels meets the Spirit of Aboriginalism." In T. O'Regan (ed.) *Continuum*, 3(2), 138–58.

Kelly, F. J. (1988) "Warlpiri media history." Retrieved from http://www.pawmedia.com.au/library/warlpiri-media-history-by-francis-jupurrurla-kelly-520 (accessed 12 November 2013).

Kowal, E. (2010) "Is culture the problem or the solution? Outstation health and the politics of remoteness." In J. Altman and M. Hinkson (eds), *Culture Crisis*. Sydney: University of New South Wales Press (pp. 179–94).

Kunoth-Monks, R. (2013) Audio interview by Jeff McMullen with Rosalie Kunoth-Monks. Retrieved from http://www.respectandlisten.org/miscellaneous/rosalie-kunoth-monks.html (accessed 26 January 2014).

Langton, M. (2010) "The shock of the new: A post-colonial dilemma for Australianist anthropology." In J. Altman and M. Hinkson (eds), *Culture Crisis*. Sydney: University of New South Wales Press (pp. 91–115).

Michaels, E. (1994) *Bad Aboriginal Art*. Minneapolis: University of Minnesota Press.

Miller, T. (1995) "Exporting truth from Aboriginal Australia." *Media Information Australia*, 76(), 7–17.

Moore, R. (1994) "Marketing alterity." In L. Taylor (ed.), *Visualizing Theory: Selected Essays from V.A.R., 1990–1994*. New York: Routledge (pp. 126–41).

O'Regan, T. (ed.) (1990) *Continuum*, 3(2).

Pilger, J. (2013) *Utopia*. DVD available from http://www.moviemail.com/film/dvd/Utopia-Pilger-2013/ (accessed 23 January 2014).

Rowse, T. (1990) "Enlisting the Warlpiri." In T. O'Regan (ed.) *Continuum*, 3(2), 114–37.

Ruby, J. (2000) *Picturing Culture: Explorations of Film and Anthropology*. Chicago, IL: University of Chicago Press.

Unreported World (2011) "Australia's hidden valley." http://www.channel4.com/programmes/unreported-world/videos/all/australias-hidden-valley (accessed 23 January 2014).

Worth, S. and Adair, J. (1972) *Through Navaho Eyes – An Exploration in Film Communication and Anthropology*. Bloomington: Indiana University Press.

Part VI
CULTURES OF TECHNOLOGY

42
TECHNOLOGICAL STRUGGLES IN COMMUNITY MEDIA

Nico Carpentier, Vaia Doudaki and Yiannis Christidis

Introduction

Community media are frequently, and for good reason, seen as organisations that allow the democratic to be translated into everyday life. As civil society organisations, they are locations where internal participatory-democratic cultures and horizontal decision-making structures are realised. As media organisations, in contrast to commercial and public broadcasters, they allow communities to participate in self-representational processes.

This chapter aims to confront community media's participatory potentialities and realities with a strand of political theory that sees conflict as the main characteristic of the social. The aim of this confrontation is to further enrich community media theory with a perspective that takes difference as a starting point, and that avoids homogenising particular social fields. The question then becomes how conflict, struggle and difference become managed within a participatory setting, which we shall explore through Mouffe's (2005, 2013) notion of agonism.

In our analysis, we want to focus on technology, which is omnipresent in community media at the most material level of the production and distribution process, but also as a condition of possibility for its existence and realisation of its objectives. As broadcasters are (often) also objects of regulation, the technological becomes an area of contestation and, because of their dependence on technology, a possible threat. This chapter will look at both levels, and illustrate the sometimes abstract discussion with two case studies, based on research performed in 2013, one on the everyday technological struggles within one particular radio station (the Cypriot community radio station CUT-Radio) and one on the struggles of Community Media Forum Europe (CMFE) to achieve a digital radio regulatory environment that will enable the community media field to continue broadcasting in the digital era.

Technology, participation and power

When Feenberg (2010: 80) wrote about the democratisation of technology, he was making a much more general point, pleading for "broadly constituted technical alliances [that] would take into account destructive effects of technology on the natural environment as well on human beings". Despite the fact that Feenberg did not focus on community media,[1] these media organisations nevertheless structurally contribute to this democratisation of technology, by making media production and distribution technologies available to non-professionals. This argument is one of the reasons why community media organisations are deemed socially relevant. This can be argued in more detail by examining the four approaches used in the literature for the study of community media (discussed in Carpentier, Lie and Servaes, 2003; see also Bailey, Cammaerts and Carpentier, 2007). Taken together, these four approaches allow us to theorise the complexity and rich diversity of community media, but they also show the role of participation and technology:

- The community approach to community media focuses on access by, and participation of, the community; the opportunity given to 'ordinary people' to use media technologies to have their voices heard; and the empowerment of community members through valuing their skills and views.
- The alternative approach stresses that these media have alternative ways of organising, alternative ways of using technologies, carry alternative discourses and representations, make use of alternative formats and genres and remain independent from market and state.
- The civil society approach incorporates aspects of civil society theory to emphasise that citizens are being enabled to be active in one of many (micro-)spheres relevant to everyday life, using media technologies to exert their rights to communicate.
- Finally, the rhizomatic approach uses Deleuze and Guattari's (1987) metaphor to focus on three aspects: community media's elusiveness, their interconnections (among each other and [mainly] with civil society), and the linkages with market and state. In this perspective, community media are seen to act as meeting points and catalysts for a variety of organisations and movements.

As the above overview shows, community media organisations allow non-professionals (and sometimes semi-professionals) to participate in these media organisations (and use their production and distribution technologies), and to participate through these organisations to have their voices heard. As one of us has argued extensively (Carpentier, 2011), to talk about participation implies talking about actors and their power positions towards each other and towards production and distribution infrastructures and technologies, in the context of their specific social, political, historical and economic conditions. This argument then brings us unavoidably to the issue of power, and the complexities of this concept. One way of approaching this complexity is through Foucault's work, who defined power in his work in the 1970s as "a general matrix of force relations at a given time, in a given society" (Dreyfus and Rabinow, 1983: 186). Foucault focuses on power *relations*, which he sees as mobile and multi-directional: power is practiced and not possessed (Kendall and Wickham, 1999: 50).

At the same time, Foucault (1978: 94) explicitly stresses that this does not imply that power relations are necessarily egalitarian, but that domination should simply not be considered to be the 'essence' of power. Instead, the social is characterised by a multitude of strategies that form a complex power-game.

Chantal Mouffe places even more emphasis on the discursive struggles that originate from the continuous interplay of power strategies. This antagonistic dimension of the social, or its "context of conflictuality" (Mouffe, 2005: 9), is characteristic for the political, and as such is a "dimension that is inherent to every human society and that determines our very ontological condition" (Mouffe, 1997: 3). Mouffe's position arises from her post-structuralist emphasis on contingency and difference, starting from the idea that re-articulations and reconfigurations of the social are always possible. While the social is structurally contingent and susceptible to change, Mouffe still recognises that stability and fixity exist, and she emphasises that these fixations are not natural, but the result of political interventions. When a particular order becomes especially fixed, benefitting from the luxury of normalisation and taken-for-grantedness, Mouffe uses the concept of hegemony to describe this order. Hegemony is never total, though, as she writes: "Every hegemonic order is susceptible of being challenged by counterhegemonic practices" (Mouffe, 2005: 18).

Community media, struggle and agonism

Within the framework of this chapter, two issues then arise. First, community media tend towards more maximalist participatory processes, characterised by more horizontal and egalitarian power relations. Community media are organisations that articulate people and objects (including technological objects) within a particular entity, with the ambition to realise their participatory objectives, at the levels of (1) decision-making procedures, (2) control over technological objects and (3) production practices. Community media offer an organisational shelter (and often a material space where technologies can be accessed) for these (maximalist) participatory practices, in a societal context that is not always appreciative of more maximalist forms of participation.

But care should be taken not to romanticise community media as participatory heaven. What the Foucauldian analytics of power, together with Mouffe's approach towards the political, enable us to show is that participatory organisations are not outside the workings of conflict, struggle and difference. The maintenance of egalitarian and horizontal structures and practices requires almost continuous effort, and challenges to this power balance constantly lurk around the corner. The existence of these more horizontal decision-making structures does not exclude the possibility that these horizontal structures are altered, that different positions, such as staff members and volunteers, affect the power balance or that strong individual (informal) power positions disrupt the horizontality of the decision-making processes. In some cases, as the conflict-ridden US-based Pacifica Network shows (Dunaway, 2005), these power imbalances can be very disruptive (see also Atton, 2002: 98ff). This debate is not only found in the world of community media, but is part of a much broader debate on workings of informal power in civil society and new social movements.

One seminal article here is Freeman's (1971–73) study of (what she calls) the structurelessness of feminist movement groups and organisations, and how this produces power imbalances.

The second issue that arises from this discussion is that a power struggle exists *over* the (maximalist) participatory model and community media's empowering usage of technology. The signification of participation can be seen as part of a "politics of definition" (Fierlbeck, 1998: 177), since its specific articulation shifts depending on the ideological framework that makes use of it. This implies that the concept of participation is contingent and itself part of power struggles in society, which might also have a hegemonic dimension. In other words, in all fields of democratic societies we see a struggle between minimalist and maximalist forms, which also impacts the intensity of participation. The media field is not outside this struggle (Carpentier, 2011). At the same time, in contemporary Western societies we tend to lean towards more minimalist forms of participation, although what Mouffe (2000) has called the democratic revolution – spanning a history of 200 years – has intensified levels of participation over time. Nevertheless, the minimalist forms of participation can still be seen as dominant, while radical-maximalist models of participation take a much more counter-hegemonic position. This again also applies to the media field. The dominant model of present-day mainstream media remains based on a set of key characteristics. Mainstream media are large scale, use advanced technology and are geared towards large, homogeneous (segments of) audiences. They are either state-owned organisations or commercial companies; they are vertically structured, staffed by professionals and carriers of dominant discourses and representations. With their different organisational structures and cultures, and by producing non-dominant representations, community media form a counter-hegemonic alternative towards this hegemonic model (Carpentier, Lie and Servaes, 2003).

If conflict is taken as a starting point, the question then becomes how to deal with this omnipresence of conflict and struggle. Learning from Carl Schmitt, Mouffe (1990: 58–9) warned us against the "dangerous dream of a perfect consensus, of a harmonious collective will". From this perspective, hegemony forms a potential danger, as it tends to remove some diversity from our sight. But on the other hand, there is always the threat that the 'we/they', which structures political conflict, turns into an antagonism where the 'they' becomes the enemy (Mouffe, 2005: 15). This construction of the enemy is again not restricted to traditional politics; it also affects non-mainstream broadcasters who have been prosecuted, have had their equipment confiscated, were shut down and (in the worst case) had their staff members injured or even killed.[2] The answer that Mouffe provides, to respect difference and to democratically contain conflict, is based on the concept of agonism. For Mouffe (ibid.: 20), agonism describes a "we/they relation where the conflicting parties, although acknowledging that there is no rational solution to their conflict, nevertheless recognise the legitimacy of their opponents" (ibid.: 20). An agonistic relationship does not hide the differences in position and interest between the involved parties; they are "in conflict" but "share a common symbolic space within which the conflict takes places" (ibid.: 20; see also Mouffe, 2013: 7). Nevertheless, we need to point to the risk that hegemony transforms agonism into antagonism, as hegemony always contains the risk that the other (the 'they') becomes excluded from the political. In this sense, agonism includes a striving for hegemony, but its full realisation may jeopardise that very same agonism.

These logics of struggle, and the need to contain these struggles through agonism, apply directly to the field of community media. First, within community media organisations, it is necessary to acknowledge the existing struggles, despite (or thanks to) their maximalist participatory nature. Agonism allows for recognising the existence of adversaries, conflict, struggle and difference, in combination with the existence of strategies that attempt to equalise the power position of actors involved in the participatory process. Here, one should keep in mind that these conflicts and struggles need not always involve intense emotions or major issues. Many struggles are based on the existence of different viewpoints in relation to everyday practices that appear to be banal (at least at first sight). Second, agonism also allows us to study how the community media movement enters into a struggle with mainstream political and technological actors, in defence of the interest of the community media sector and in resistance of the hegemonic position of these mainstream political and technological actors. Each scenario of agonistic conflict will now be illustrated by a case study that focuses on the technological as the location of these struggles.

Everyday struggles at CUT-Radio

The first case study focuses on everyday struggles over technology within a particular community radio station, CUT-Radio, and on how these tensions are resolved agonistically. CUT-Radio is the community radio station of the Cyprus University of Technology, based in the city of Limassol. It started broadcasting in March 2013, and combines music, news, entertainment and educational shows, mostly produced by university students. The radio station is administered by a Radio Team from the Communication and Internet Studies Department of the university, while the overall responsibility lies with the University Council. As the declaration in its website states, CUT-Radio focuses "on the participation and representation among the university community members, in the public sphere and the active inclusion of its members in the society" and "helps to highlight innovative platforms for experimentation with new ideas and concepts" (CUT-Radio, 2013).

The case study combines auto-ethnography[3] with interviewing,[4] inspired by Fals-Borda's (1998) participatory action research. One of the radio station's staff members, Yiannis Christidis, was invited into the research team, and – in dialogue with the other authors – performed an auto-ethnography, combining the writing elements of autobiography and ethnography (Ellis, Adams and Bochner, 2010; Bruner, 1993). The auto-ethnography locates several tensions and conflicts in three areas: establishment, management and everyday operations. First, the phase where the radio station was established was characterised by a series of struggles and conflicts. The first struggle was for the radio station to get its licence, as there was (and still is) no specific community media legislation. Instead, the proposers had to apply with the Radio Television Authority for a "small local radio station" licence. The initiative started in 2008, but after a planning phase of several years (also necessary to gather knowledge about the procedures and requirements), further delays occurred because of additional requests for information from the administration and elections within the Council of the Audiovisual Committee of Cyprus. One of the consequences of the 18-month delay was that the technology that was purchased had to be stored for a considerable amount of time before it could be used. Moreover, when the studio became operational, some of the technological material had grown outdated and is now underused.

Another set of struggles in the establishment phase was related to the construction of the studios, and the way the technology was arranged within the premises of the radio station. Within the university different perspectives existed on where the radio should be located. Moreover, the decision was taken to "have a room that a passer-by could easily look into – through a large window – so that CUT-Radio would obtain an 'urban' look and was 'self-promoted'." The spatial openness also had a symbolic dimension, signifying that the radio was "not closed and for a few people" (interview with Angeliki Gazi, 4 November 2013). The actual construction produced several structural problems. For instance, when the antenna was installed, a television cable was accidentally used, which had to be replaced. The way the technology was arranged within the main studio was (afterwards) not considered optimal: "the two speakers-monitors on the producer's desk occupy almost the 30% of the desk's space, which makes it uncomfortable for any radio producer to place a piece of paper, a tablet, or even more impossible, a laptop computer".

The second area – management – has a very different type of struggle, with different actors. Some of the main issues here, the lack of student involvement in the managerial levels of the radio station (despite the Radio Team's efforts), or the way that the radio's regulations are implemented, are beyond the scope of this technology-focused analysis. More relevant here is the struggle over financial resources between the Radio Team and the department on the one hand and the university management on the other. The economic situation of Cyprus, and of the university, does not produce a luxurious situation for CUT-Radio, and requests to raise the budget and hire more staff have been rejected, with the exception of three people who are employed at the radio station for six months within the framework of a European project.

Third, at the level of everyday operations we again find a very different pattern of struggles. One area is the training of the radio producers in using the technology according to particular quality standards.[5] The producers are 'self-technicians', which requires them to master the use of microphones and the console (which they tend to learn quickly) but also to achieve much more difficult skills, such as multi-tasking. This learning process is supported by staff members, but also by other producers: "it often happens that the most experienced teach the newcomers". Crucial to the functioning of the radio station is the care of its technology, avoiding that it gets damaged. Everyday technology, like headsets, is fairly fragile and needs to be treated carefully. In one case, the staff refused to replace two broken headsets (which still could be used) to make this point, only to find that the headsets had been fixed with tape. None of the producers complained, and nobody knows who fixed them. Other – even more straightforward – technologies play a significant role in the everyday operation of the radio station, such as the door and its locks: "every producer is responsible for allowing the next one to enter, when the Radio Team is absent".

As the radio station is also dependent on other university departments, some of the everyday technological struggles are with the technical department of the university and other service providers. For example, it "is common that sometimes the streaming service goes down due to server or even electricity issues". In such cases, it is difficult to get other departments to respond. The everyday struggles within the radio station thus become a struggle between staff members and students, among students and between students and technologies. Technology (and its deployment) turns out to be quite obstinate, not making the life of staff members any easier, but the analysis also shows that these struggles and conflicts are resolved in a friendly way, where other positions are accepted, understood and brought agonistically into the functioning of the radio station.

The macro-struggles at CMFE

The second case study takes a broader perspective. It focuses on the struggle over digital radio standards between community media, and more specifically one of its representatives, the Community Media Forum Europe (CMFE), as well as mainstream political actors and main stakeholders of the industry. CMFE, founded in 2004, is a European community media network of policy experts, organisations and federations, which aims to support and represent the interests of community media at the European level. CMFE currently has 118 members from 26 European countries. To examine the lobby work of the CMFE, the 27 documents that are related to the topic of digital radio broadcasting, spanning a period of nine years (2005–2013), were downloaded from CMFE's online archive[6] and analysed through a qualitative content analysis (Wester, 1987).

Digital radio broadcasting has become an area of struggle after the first standard, the European DAB, failed to become accepted as the worldwide system for digital radio, and both Japan and the US developed their own systems (respectively, ISDB-TSB and IBOC). Later, DAB was improved and transformed into DAB+. A fourth standard, DRM, originally developed for AM, was altered in the early 2000s for use on the FM band, and labelled DRM+ (Ala-Fossi et al., 2008; O'Neill, 2009). In May 2011, all four standards were accepted by the International Telecommunications Union (Recommendation ITU-R BS.1894). Digital radio has been actively promoted since the 1990s (Ala-Fossi et al., 2008) to offer the possibility for more radio broadcasters in a given spectrum, better audio quality, and less power and transmitters required to cover a region. As the European Union does not currently enforce a common policy on radio broadcasting, the struggle over the digitisation of radio is mostly, but not exclusively, conducted at the level of the member states (O'Neill, 2009), involving also the industry and other media organisations. Arguably, there are two main areas of contestation: the switch-off of analogue FM broadcasting and the use of a particular standard for digital radio broadcasting.

Different actors take different positions on these issues. For instance, the European Broadcasting Union (EBU) launched, on 13 February 2013, Recommendation R138,[7] which favours the use of DAB+, places DRM at a secondary position and calls for a joint decision for an analogue FM switch-off date. At the same time, the EBU runs the so-called 'Euro-Chip campaign', arguing for a minimum requirement of the main radio transmission technology standards that allow for analogue FM, DAB, DAB+ and DMB(+). Earlier, the Norwegian Ministry of Culture, on 4 February 2011, had published a time path for the digital (radio) switchover, with a preference for DAB(+).[8] Later, Denmark (in 2012) and Sweden (in 2013) made similar decisions. In contrast, Finland stopped its DAB broadcasts in 2005.

CMFE intervenes in these debates in a number of ways. The analysis of the CMFE documents shows that their struggle is structured around three main positions. First, on the allocation of sufficient number of frequencies, CMFE argues that the number of frequencies on analogue FM for community radio stations is inadequate. CMFE states that frequencies are mainly used by (and technically planned for) public and/or commercial radios, and that there is a lack of proper legal recognition and planning mechanisms to meet the needs of FM frequencies for (often small-scale) community radios.

Second, CMFE avoids an antagonistic perspective and recognises that "digitization of terrestrial radio helps to overcome existing scarcity in the analogue spectre" (CMFE letter to European Commissioner Neelie Kroes, 19 December 2011), agreeing that it "is making terrestrial radio much less power consuming offering high reception and audio quality". But at the same time, CMFE still resists an analogue FM switch-off, "before the new digital system is fully accepted by audiences" and demands a period of both analogue and digital broadcasting that will be safeguarded by the EU.

CMFE's third struggle is for the adoption of the DRM+ standard. Again, CMFE holds an agonistic position. It does not oppose DAB(+), which is promoted by and put in operation by large-scale broadcasters in different European countries. At the same time CMFE pleads and lobbies for the necessity of introducing DRM+. Its main arguments for the introduction of DRM+ is that it is relatively simple and cheap to implement, and that DRM+ allows community radios to both own and operate their own transmission systems (CMFE letter to Fatih Yurdal of the European Communications Office, 29 December 2009). CMFE does not propose to privilege one system over the other, but argues for multi-standard, hybrid radio receivers. According to the organisation, new radio receivers should be "futureproof", that is, compatible with all European digital standards (and with the analogue FM standard during the transition period), "since digital-only receivers for years to come threaten to cut off listeners from their local radio stations" (CMFE letter to Neelie Kroes, 19 December 2011).

Establishing the effectiveness of these CMFE initiatives is extremely difficult. When asked, one of the CMFE board members, Christer Hederström, pointed to the role of the CMFE in Sweden in placing community media ('närradio') on the agenda and in strengthening the position of the national community media association, NRO.[9] Hederström also stated that "the digital [switchover] coordinator has been given directive to find solutions especially geared for CR" (personal communication, 6 November 2013), in consultation with the representatives of the Swedish community media field (Dir. 2013:76[10]). At the European level, CMFE has been recognised in a number of more formal ways. In 2013, the European Commission invited CMFE to become part of a "new High Level Group of the mobile and broadcasting industry to advise the European Commission on political and technical aspects regarding the future use of the UHF broadcasting band in the EU" (personal communication, Nadia Bellardi, vice president of CMFE, 12 November 2013). At the same time, CMFE and the European community media generally find themselves in a rather weak power position, in a European political context which is not geared towards maximalist participatory organisations, and which does not apply these principles itself. Nevertheless, and despite their unequal power position, CMFE maintains a position towards the different technologies and towards the different political, media and industry actors, that is clearly agonistic and that does not define these others as their enemies.

Conclusion

The aura of democracy that surrounds community media can be in many cases substantiated, but more problematically this aura also provides implicit support for the myth of community media as ultimate realms of consensuality, where conflict has been structurally overcome and erased. In contrast, participatory democracy requires hard work to agonistically deal with the many struggles and conflicts that characterise the social. These struggles enter into the organisational context of community media, where different actors and groups, with sometimes different interests, need to resolve these internal differences, including the emancipatory use of technology. Community media organisations are not isolated from the social, but are part of a complex network of other organisations, such as universities and their departments, civil society organisations, suppliers, regulators, ministries, and so on. These networked relations are structured in particular and various ways, opening up the possibility for conflict. At a European level we can see the presence of conflict, where the counter-hegemonic community media field, despite its legal recognition and considerable numbers, finds it extremely difficult to have its interests preserved in a political context which is less agonistic than its own.

The democratic importance of community media lies in the way that they allow non-professionals to participate in media production, distribution and management, but also in how their agonistic problem-solving strategies enhance a wider democratic culture. Despite the often banal nature of these issues, we should acknowledge the strength of community media in dealing with struggle, conflict and difference in an agonistic way. We should not ignore these apparently trivial conflicts, but understand how much they are part of the everyday experience of community media. More importantly, and without romanticising community media, we should look at how conflicts are resolved while remaining within the maximalist participatory configuration, because that is where one of their main democratic strengths lies.

Notes

1 More in general, Feenberg (2010: 81) uses a rather negative perspective on the media.
2 Troubling examples can be found on the IFEX website.
3 Citations in this part are based on Yiannis Christidis's auto-ethnography unless otherwise indicated.

4 Two interviews with Angeliki Gazi, the main initiator of the project, were organised on 30 October and 4 November 2013.
5 These are not necessarily defined in the same way as mainstream media; see Carpentier (2011: 337ff).
6 They were downloaded from the "Documents" section of http://www.cmfe.eu.
7 See http://tech.ebu.ch/Jahia/site/tech/cache/offonce/news/crystal-clear-recommendation-from-the-di-13feb13 and http://tech.ebu.ch/docs/r/r138.pdf.
8 See http://www.regjeringen.no/upload/KUD/Medier/Rapporter/V-0951E-SummaryReport No8_2010-11.pdf.
9 See http://www.nro.se/.
10 Dir. 2013:76 Branschsamordnare für digitalisering av ljudradion [Dir. 2013:76 Industry coordinator for the digitalisation of radio]; see http://www.opengov.se/govtrack/dir/2013:76.

Further reading

Olga Bailey, Bart Cammaerts and Nico Carpentier, *Understanding Alternative Media* (Maidenhead: Open University Press/McGraw-Hill, 2007), provides a detailed overview of the four approaches to community media. Kevin Howley's *Understanding Community Media* (Thousand Oaks, CA: Sage, 2010) and John D. H. Downing's *Encyclopedia of Social Movement Media* (Thousand Oaks, CA: Sage, 2010) offer good discussions on community media, also in relation to the digital. A good introduction into the work of Chantal Mouffe is *New Theories of Discourse: Laclau, Mouffe and Žižek*, by Jacob Torfing (Oxford: Wiley, 1999). An interview with Chantal Mouffe appears in "Hegemony, democracy, agonism, and journalism" by Nico Carpentier and Bart Cammaerts, in *Journalism Studies*, 2006, 7(6), 964–75.

References

Ala-Fossi, M., Lax, S., O'Neill, B., Jauert, P. and Shaw, H. (2008) "The future of radio is still digital – But which one? Expert perspectives and future scenarios for radio media in 2015." *Journal of Radio and Audio Media*, 15(1), 4–25.
Atton, C. (2002) *Alternative Media*. London: Sage.
Bailey, O., Cammaerts, B. and Carpentier, N. (2007) *Understanding Alternative Media*. Maidenhead: Open University Press/McGraw & Hill.
Bruner, J. (1993) "The autobiographical process." In R. Folkenflik (ed.), *The Culture of Autobiography: Constructions of Self-Representation*. Stanford, CA: Stanford University Press (pp. 38–56).
Carpentier, N. (2011) *Media and Participation: A Site of Ideological-Democratic Struggle*. Bristol: Intellect.
Carpentier, N., Lie, R. and Servaes, J. (2003) "Community media – Muting the democratic media discourse?" *Continuum: Journal of Media and Cultural Studies*, 17(1), 51–68.
CUT-Radio (2013) *Declaration*. Retrieved from http://www.cut-radio.org/declaration (accessed 10 January 2015).
Deleuze, G. and Guattari, F. (1987) *A Thousand Plateaus: Capitalism and Schizophrenia*. Minneapolis: University of Minnesota Press.
Dreyfus, H. L. and Rabinow, P. (1983) *Michel Foucault: Beyond Structuralism and Hermeneutics*. Chicago: University of Chicago Press.

Dunaway, D. K. (2005) "Pacifica Radio and community broadcasting." *Journal of Radio and Audio Media*, 12(2), 240–55.

Ellis, C., Adams, T. E., Bochner, A. P. (2010) "Autoethnography: An overview." *Forum Qualitative Sozialforschung/Forum: Qualitative Social Research*, 12(1). Retrieved from http://www.qualitative-research.net/index.php/fqs/article/view/1589/3095 (accessed 10 January 2015).

Fals-Borda, O. (1998) *People's Participation. Challenges Ahead. A Synthesis of the World Congress of Participatory Convergence, Cartagena, Columbia, 1997.* London: Intermediate Technology Publications.

Feenberg, A. (2010) *Between Reason and Experience: Essays in Technology and Modernity.* Cambridge, MA: MIT Press.

Fierlbeck, K. (1998) *Globalizing Democracy: Power, Legitimacy and the Interpretation of Democratic Ideas.* Manchester, UK: Manchester University Press.

Foucault, M. (1978) *History of Sexuality, Part 1: An Introduction.* New York: Pantheon.

Freeman, J. (1971–73) "The tyranny of structurelessness (online version based on three previous versions)." Retrieved from http://www.jofreeman.com/joreen/tyranny.htm (accessed 10 January 2015).

Kendall, G. and Wickham, G. (1999) *Using Foucault's Methods.* London: Sage.

Mouffe, C. (1990) "Radical Democracy or Liberal Democracy?," *Socialist Review* 20(2): 57–66.

——(1997) *The Return of the Political.* London: Verso.

——(2000) *The Democratic Paradox.* London: Verso.

——(2005) *On the Political.* London: Routledge.

——(2013) *Agonistics: Thinking the World Politically.* London: Verso.

O'Neill, B. (2009) "DAB Eureka-147: A European vision for digital radio." *New Media and Society*, 11(1–2), 261–78.

Wester, F. (1987) *Strategieën voor kwalitatief onderzoek [Stategies for qualitative research].* Muiderberg: Couthinho.

43

A CLASH OF CULTURES

Pirate radio convergence and reception in Africa

Hayes Mawindi Mabweazara

Introduction

Sustained threats to democratic communicative spaces in most African countries have led to the resurgence of underground forms of communication, commonly associated with the historical struggles for independence from colonial power. Among these reincarnating alternative forms of communication are 'pirate' radio stations, also variously known as 'clandestine' or 'exile' radio. They largely beam their signals from outside the political jurisdiction of their target countries as a crucial means of providing information "in opposition to government-controlled airwaves" (Coyer, 2007: 15).

The 21st-century model of these stations, however, represents a 'paradigmatic shift' from traditional underground radio culture. They can no longer merely be defined as subversive offshore radio stations broadcasting from sympathetic countries in unidirectional, predominantly non-participatory formats. Rather, as with most contemporary forms of communication, they are heavily influenced and shaped by processes of convergence associated with interactive digital technologies. The majority of the stations have set up interactive news websites on which they post news bulletins as well as offer programming on demand through podcasting and live audio streaming. In addition, programmes are archived and available for downloading from the websites. The websites have thus become a key avenue for the stations to interact and engage with their audiences alongside various other *multimedia* platforms, which include social media, email and the mobile phone. Collectively, these platforms provide new ways of evading pervasive government censorship.

Thus, pirate radio as a technology or medium in Africa has transformed significantly. It is "is now a virtual space, network space and mobile space while at the same time remaining a physical space" (L. Moyo, 2014: 50) associated with the studio, whence 'counter-hegemonic' news discourses are packaged and disseminated. This pluralisation of spaces by new media technologies, as Moyo further argues, "is subverting the old notion of [pirate] radio as a unified and bounded medium". The new platforms "traverse the traditional methods of radio access and consumption" (ibid.) and render the radio stations widely distributed and accessible. These changes engender "greater potential for active, individualized, and interactive usage" of pirate radio content, thus reinforcing its capacity as "an alternative platform that is truly informed by community involvement" (L. Moyo, 2012: 489–90).

Against this backdrop, this chapter uses two prominent pirate radio stations, Short Wave (SW) Radio Africa[1] and Voice of America's Studio 7, beaming into Zimbabwe (and the wider world) from the UK and the US, respectively (via short-wave, the internet and mobile phones), as a focal point for illuminating how digital technologies have radically transformed the production, transmission as well as reception practices of traditional pirate radio in Africa. Like most underground radio stations on the continent, the two stations emerged as a direct response to the state's protracted and fossilised culture of political and ideological control of the country's broadcasting services. They were both set up by disgruntled exiled journalists who defiantly sought to wage war against the state's tight control on the media and sustained negative responses to calls for the liberalisation of the country's broadcast sector.

The study draws its insights from qualitative interviews with a selection of the two stations' audiences drawn from Zimbabwe's three key cities – Harare (the capital), Bulawayo (the second largest city) and Gweru (located in the midlands), as well as document analysis and internet research. Although there are obviously several other examples of pirate radio stations "broadcasting into dozens of African countries, including Libya, Madagascar, Sudan, Western Sahara and all the states in the Horn of Africa" (Smith, 2013: 13), SW Radio Africa and Studio 7 can fairly be seen as offering typical examples of contemporary pirate radio culture in Africa. However, it needs to be stated that by drawing on insights from Zimbabwe, I am by no means suggesting that perspectives from one African country are generalisable or representative of emerging 'digital pirate radio' cultures in other African countries. Rather, the attempt here is to offer localised insights from a country that can fairly be seen as providing archetypal examples of contemporary underground radio in Africa, albeit in its own qualitatively unique ways. Thus, while largely attempting the difficult task of contributing an African perspective on contemporary pirate radio reception, the study remains alert to the fact that the continent is far from exhibiting a collective singular identity – it is culturally, politically and economically fragmented.

In exploring how the convergence strategies appropriated by SW Radio Africa and Studio 7 are transforming the stations' production and reception practices, I highlight the ambiguities and complexities associated with the era of convergence in Africa. The chapter submits that while the convergence strategies adopted by the radio stations broaden and expand the range of options available for the reception of their programming (albeit in disproportionate ways), traditional forms of reception (through shortwave) remain in force. This is largely because of enduring questions of access to digital technologies (especially the internet), and the lasting connections between traditional live radio and the oral traditions of local culture.

Thus, the popularity of live 'over the air' shortwave radio demonstrates not only the intricacies of the socio-economic and political context in which the new model of pirate radio operates, but also the very peculiarities of the cultural realities in which radio, and indeed, digital technologies in general, are used in Africa. Consequently, rather than see the changes ushered by digital technologies as displacing old practices, we need to see the transformations as "evidence of an ecological reconfiguration" (Gurevitch, Coleman and Blumler, 2009: 167), taking place alongside traditional reception practices. Fundamental to the traditional forms of reception is the extant oral communication tradition, which contributes significantly to the impact of radio on the African continent. This points to the fact that in Africa *convergence* can indeed assume unique forms, shaped by an intricate combination of local socio-economic, political and cultural factors.

Theoretical approach: Invoking the 'active audience' tradition

To explore the issues raised above, the study draws on the "active audience tradition", which emphasises the "ways in which the haphazard and contingent details of people's daily lives provide the context in which media are engaged with and responded to" (Livingstone, 1998). Through emphasising the "interpretive relations between audi-ence and medium" (ibid.), this body of theory has reinvigorated theoretical as well as political discussions on the issue of 'impact', raised by the early traditions of audience research. Its starting point is that the meaning or 'impact' of media texts is not something fixed, or inherent, within the text. Rather, media texts acquire meaning only at the moment of reception; that is, audiences are seen as producers of meaning, not just consumers of media content. They decode or interpret media texts in ways that are related to their social and cultural circumstances and to the way in which they subjectively experience those circumstances (Ang, 1990). In support of this view, Ruddock (2001) argues that communication is culturally specific and as such can only be understood as a process from the point of view of the people involved. In general, therefore, reception researchers aim to uncover how people in their own social and historical contexts make sense of media texts in ways that are meaningful, suitable and accessible to them.

Ang (1990) observes that some reception researchers have used terms such as 'interpretive communities' and 'subcultures' to denote groups of people who make common interpretations of media texts. Such groups of people do not have to be physically united in one location, but can be geographically dispersed and can consist of many different kinds of people who do not know each other but are symbolically connected by their shared interest in particular media forms and content. In the same vein, Jensen (1988: 4) notes that "the central locus of analysis is the interface between medium and audience, and the interface itself is a social form rather than a direct consequence of the specific technology".

The active audience theory therefore sensitises us to the importance of viewing audiences' engagement with technologies "in social rather than purely technical terms" (Livingstone, 2002: 19). It enables us to see technologies as acquiring "meanings in the heterogeneity of social interactions" (Bijker, 1995: 6), and therefore open to qualita-tive or interpretive investigations. Although the broader conceptualisation of the 'active audience' tradition took shape well before the 'new media era', it retains its relevance as a 'tool' for closely examining media use, reception and consumption in the digital era. Its constructivist thrust accommodates the radical changes to the concept of the audience emerging with the interactivity of digital technologies. In particular, it accommodates the fact that audiences and users of new media "are increasingly active – selective, self-directed, producers as well as receivers of texts"

(Livingstone, 2004: 79). This explicit emphasis on users' active engagement with media emerging with interactive digital technologies crucially extends the scope of "arguments in 'active audience' theory by transforming hitherto marginal (and marginalized) tendencies into the very mainstream of media use" (Livingstone, 2004: 79).

The sections that follow discuss the findings of the study, highlighting how digital technologies have radically transformed the production, transmission as well as reception of traditional pirate radio in Africa.

Convergence and the changing nature of pirate radio reception

Despite the well-known limitations of access to the internet in Africa, SW Radio Africa and Studio 7's websites are seen as complementing traditional live broadcasts by providing alternative space for accessing their content 'on demand'. The expediency and flexibility engendered by the radio stations' websites was particularly noted in contexts where conflicting political positions within families or busy work schedules made it difficult to listen to the stations' live broadcasts. This emancipatory potential of the internet has turned pirate radio in Africa into a far more pervasive and accessible form of 'online journalism'. The flexibility further highlights the fact that "the meaning of a particular technology is not pre-given but constructed as the technology figures in practices of consumption and becomes embedded in everyday life" (Silverstone and Hirsch, in Spitulnick, 2000: 146). This 'social shaping' conception of the radio station's websites also draws attention to the more general question about how communication technologies are understood as continuous with and embedded in existing social realities and dynamics in Africa. As Spitulnick (2000: 145) writes: "the impact of a media technology changes with both its context and the activities that accompany it". Thus, as Mudhai (2011: 253) puts it: "although radio's survival as a major cultural phenomenon [in Africa] may appear to be under threat from new media technologies, convergence [only] makes it possible for it to remain a significant arena of information dissemination".

The *interactivity* of the stations' websites was also described as central to the redefinition of how their audiences engage with their news content. It provides one of the main avenues for audiences to engage directly with the stations' programming, hence leading to erstwhile rare audience participation. The opportunity to comment on stories and (indirectly) contribute to the generation of news content has turned the radio stations into socially engaging 'communal' forms of journalism, which as one respondent put it: "*represents [their] own interests, ideas, observations and opinions*". In this sense, users of the radio stations' websites are becoming *active, selective* and *self-directed* participants as well as addressees of the stations' mass circulating messages (Livingstone, 2004). The boundaries of traditional pirate radio, as we have known it, have thus been broken, transforming it from a routinely centralised monomodal news outlet into a pluralised alternative form of communication.

It is important, however, to highlight that these profound 'changes' to the reception of SW Radio Africa and Studio 7 only mirror an ecological recasting of the stations' traditional transmission strategy, as opposed to introducing entirely new forces that radically break from old ways (I return to this point shortly). Highlighting this view with respect to daily email news alerts circulated by the stations, interviewees high-lighted that the alerts only provided a cursory 'preview' of the detailed stories in the evening's live broadcasts.

This trend in the use of email was also manifest in the use of social networking sites such as Facebook, which, as noted earlier, the radio stations use to mobilise and engage their audiences, especially by alerting them to topical live programmes. For a number of respondents, social media also played a key role in circulating and continuing the radical and subversive political discourses generated by the radio stations. The viral energy of Facebook's interactivity thus amounted to "a new flow of incessantly circulating publicity" in which "messages are debated, rumours floated, tested, and even discarded" (Gurevitch, Coleman and Blumler, 2009: 170).

While the study generally revealed that the radio stations' web-based platforms are mainly used by an 'elite' group of audiences, especially those with occupations that allow for unlimited access to the internet, the explosion of mobile phone own-ership among both elite and poor has facilitated a wide and expansive distribution of the radio stations' content. Capitalising on the pervasiveness of the technology in the country, both SW Radio Africa and Studio 7 openly invite listeners to phone in or send SMS messages with comments on news and current affairs. Most participants in this study described this practice as enabling them to engage and contribute directly to the radio stations' content in unprecedented ways, thus inverting the traditional 'top-down' practice associated with 'old' monomodal pirate radio channels (D. Moyo, 2009).

While the foregoing appropriations of digital technologies in the reception of pirate radio can collectively be seen as pointing to the emergence of an alternative multi-layered assemblage of platforms whose transmissions straddle social divides, this should not, however, mask the complexities and contradictions associated with the reception of 'digital pirate' radio in Africa as discussed in the sections that follow.

Challenges of access to 'digital pirate radio'

Although on the surface the convergence strategies noted above seem to reflect a widened scope of the platforms through which both SW Radio Africa and Studio 7 reach out to their audiences, the study also shows that the stations' digital transmission platforms, especially those associated with internet connectivity, are mainly used by an 'elite' group of audiences with regular and unrestricted access. The disparities in 'access' are also manifest in the audiences' disproportionate abilities to effectively exploit the multiple digital platforms for the reception of content from the radio stations. Consequently, the potential empowering effects that follow from the creative convergence of new and old media are selective and confined to an elite group.

A number of participants pointed to the persistent structural problem of internet connectivity and its implications for downloading or streaming live programmes on the web. Similarly, some participants pointed to their reliance on antiquated com-puters at their workplaces – the only places they could access reasonably faster internet. These challenges highlight the significance of the popular 'technicist' understanding of the digital divide. As van Dijk (2005: 49) puts it: "physical and conditional access … make a tremendous difference to the potential application and the level of inequality between users" of digital technologies. This has prompted some writers to surmise that while future developments in the convergence of radio are exciting, "internet based radio, pod casting and 'any time any place' radio listening via mobile devices such as MP3 players are some way off [in Africa]" (Myers, 2008).

For a number of interviewees, limited economic power made it a matter of hard choice to use the internet in public access points such as internet cafes, hence preventing them from taking advantage of the stations' web-based transmission platforms. These observations reinforce Hambuba's (2010: 138) view that most people in Africa, particularly women, "face the dilemma of choosing whether to spend their money on use of ICTs or to buy food for their families and meet other very basic needs of survival". Therefore, in examining the implications of convergence processes on the reception of underground radio in Africa, it is important to consider the shaping impact of the socio-economic context inhabited by its audiences.

However, while 'access' challenges are predominantly defined in terms of well-known physical and economic conditions, a number of interviewees pointed to the fears associated with using public spaces to browse content from SW Radio Africa and Studio 7, radio stations deemed subversive and illegal by the state (D. Moyo, 2010: 28). The Zimbabwe government is, for instance, known to confiscate shortwave radio sets from people caught listening to what it defines as 'offensive' broadcasts from the pirate stations. These actions inevitably drive listeners of the radio stations 'underground' (D. Moyo, 2010).

These challenges not only highlight the complex and multifaceted nature of the digital divide in Africa, but also point to the contingent and ambiguous nature of (pirate) radio reception in the digital era. They further provide evidence for the need "to reframe the overly technical concept of the digital divide" (van Dijk, 2006: 223) by paying more attention to socio-economic, physiological, cultural and political influences to the adoption and use of digital technologies. This understanding extends the notion of 'access' to include "(digital) skills or competencies in media or technology use and applications" (ibid.: 224) which have a bearing on the Zimbabwean audience's appropriation of the digital platforms used by both SW Radio Africa and Studio 7.

'A clash of cultures': Local culture in contention with digital culture

While there is no doubt that the adoption of digital technologies by both SW Radio Africa and Studio 7 has broadened the options available for the reception of their content (albeit in disproportionate ways), one of the central findings of this study is that traditional forms of pirate radio reception remain in force among both 'mass' and 'elite'. This was due in part to the enduring questions of 'access' to digital technologies as discussed above, as well as deeply rooted in the lasting connections between local cultural traditions of orality and radio as a traditionally monomodal "medium of the spoken word" (Ceesay, 2000). Thus, the cultural context of radio reception in Africa sustains consumption practices that differ markedly from contemporary practices in the economically developed world of the North, where digital technologies have radically redefined radio, turning it into an "'asocial ... solo medium which is isolationist rather than communal" (Barnett and Morrison, 1989: 1). Participants in this study highlighted that traditional (pirate) radio remained their preferred source of news, stressing that while they occasionally browse through the radio stations' websites at work, their main interest was in the live broadcasts, as using the internet is a completely different experience. Consequently, even with unlimited access to the radio stations' digital platforms, live broadcasts have remained the default setting for accessing the stations' content.

This preference for live radio broadly suggests that radio as a technology in Africa has inherent properties that predispose it to particular kinds of uses. Primarily, it connects with an extant oral tradition and culture, which has resisted displacement from various forces, including new digital technologies. This has led some scholars to conclude that radio in Africa has survived the perceived threats of new digital technologies (Mudhai, 2011). As *the* medium of the spoken word, radio replicates and extends an already existing oral culture (Ceesay, 2000), which forms the base of communicative practices in Africa. As Myers (1998: 201) aptly puts it: "In many ways radio is the tangible modern extension of [Africa's] oral tradition." This observation was cogently expressed by one follower of SW Radio Africa:

> the thing about listening to live radio broadcasts is that, it is very personal and immediate. It speaks directly and instantaneously to your lived existence, *whereas on the web, it is about taking time to read the news or, perchance, download podcasts* if the Internet connection is good ... *It is very different to our notion of radio ...*

Highlighting the significance of the oral nature of radio, Hayman and Tomaselli (1989: 2) contend that "The act of listening to the radio (switching on the receiver in the family home, with one or more members of the family present) could be considered as a daily habit or ritual in which ideology is present." One respondent reinforced this point by referring to the 'unsaid practice' in which his family gathers around a radio receiver in the evenings as they "collectively appreciate alternative voices" on Studio 7. This idea of appreciating news as a family points to the political effectiveness of the domestic context of pirate radio consumption, as the home environment is turned "into the world of real dialogue with the listener" (Ceesay, 2000: 107) as well as a "centre from where individuals bridge the distance with the world" (Winocur, 2005: 319). Further, communal listenership in the home environment facilitates instantaneous reflections on the news content, as it is immediately 'commented upon, reinterpreted, and reinforced' (Daloz and Verrier-Frechette, 2000: 181) in discursive transactions that sometimes transcend the confines of the home context.

The preference for live radio in the domestic context was also closely linked to the flexibility and immediacy that live audio offers. While digital platforms were predominantly described as sources of news outside the home environment (mostly at work), live radio was seen as most valuable in the home context, not least because of the privacy and safety it provides (when listening to what is generally considered subversive by the state), but also because of the flexibility and intimacy associated with the context. The conception of (pirate) radio as an accompaniment to daily routine in the home context is not a new one; it resonates with early studies, which described radio as "inextricably woven into people's lives" (Barnett and Morrison, 1989: 3).

The interface between radio as a medium of the spoken word with the local traditions of orality has resulted in consumption practices that differ radically from the situation in the global North where, as Mudhai (2011) observes, new media have significantly redefined the reception and consumption of radio. Consequently, while 'access' is central to the appropriation of digital technologies in the reception of underground radio in Africa, there is a sense in which it is somewhat inconsequential in the overall determination of the impact of digital technologies on (pirate) radio reception. Thus, when examining the impact of digital technologies on radio listenership patterns in Zimbabwe and, indeed, Africa at large, the extent to which radio has inherent properties that predispose it to certain kinds of uses and interpretations has to be taken into consideration. In doing so, however, caution must be taken to avoid lapsing into a simplistic notion of technological determinism, which sees technology as the only relevant explanatory variable of its appropriation in society. As Wasserman (2005: 165) rightly puts it, digital technologies only serve to "enlarge and accelerate processes already in place in societies ... rather than create entirely new forces" that radically break from old ways. Expressing similar sentiments, Gurevitch, Coleman and Blumler (2009: 167) contend that the changes ushered by digital technologies only provide "evidence of an ecological reconfiguration [and a] recasting of roles and relationships within an evolving media landscape".

These views direct attention to the fact that the multiple digital transmission strategies used by both SW Radio Africa and Studio 7 complement and enhance rather than replace conventional or established culturally rooted patterns of (pirate) radio reception (Mudhai, 2011). We therefore need to see the transformations as "evidence of an ecological reconfiguration" (Gurevitch, Coleman and Blumler, 2009: 167), taking place alongside traditional reception practices. Further, as noted earlier, the popularity of live shortwave radio points to the complexities as well as the idiosyncrasies of the socio-political, economic and cultural context in which (clandestine) radio and digital technologies are appropriated in Africa. Thus, while *convergence* is often thought of in technological terms, from the findings above, we can contend that in Africa convergence can indeed take unique, socially shaped forms.

Conclusion

From the findings discussed above, the convergence of technologies has clearly reconfigured the operations of contemporary 'pirate' radio in Africa at a number of levels, including widening the options for accessing the stations' programming and reformulating reception practices. It can no longer be defined simply in terms of the traditional monomodal 'underground' radio that eschews allowing listeners to 'speak back' to its content or to actively participate in the generation of its content.

However, despite this "ecological reconfiguration" (Gurevitch, Coleman and Blumler, 2009: 167), traditional forms of reception and consumption remain in force largely because of the enduring intersections between radio as *the* medium of the voice and the oral traditions of local culture. As L. Moyo (2014), reminds us, whereas the convergence of media and communication technologies has been largely a characteristic of the economically developed countries of the North, "Africa has a slightly different experience. Radio remains, at the very best, traditional for most people *who still receive it through the simple mode of traditional broadcasts*" (ibid.: 51).

In the same way, the majority of radio audiences in Africa are in parts of the world where the simplest means of radio transmissions remain the best way to get messages to the masses. Thus, the disproportionate access to digital technologies, especially the internet, has significant implications on how underground radio audiences use the stations' digital platforms to access their content. In this sense, we can conclude that the value of new technologies in the reception of underground radio in Africa, therefore, lies in the extent to which they enmesh with old reception practices rather than in supplanting the 'socially shaped' traditional ways of (pirate) radio reception. In fact, radio convergence in Africa needs to be seen as assuming unique forms that go beyond the simple ability of digital technologies to carry similar kinds of services at one go.

Finally, while the evidence used in this study is predominantly drawn from an examination of practices and cultures related to developments in one country, there is a sense in which these find resonance in wider sub-Saharan Africa, precisely because of connected socio-political, economic and cultural factors – all of which shape and constrain the appropriations of new digital technologies in the context of underground radio.

Note

1 SW Radio Africa ceased broadcasting in August 2014 – just before this study went to press – due to financial constraints. The station relied entirely on donations for its operations, and its founder, Gerry Jackson, surmised that the continued bleak state of the political situation in Zimbabwe gradually took a toll on the generosity of donors. However, its 13-year multimedia archive is hosted at: http://web.archive.org/web/20140819182956/http://www.swradioafrica.com/2014/08/11/sw-radio-africa-has-now-shut-down/#sthash.eZruaOt8.dpuf

Further reading

Gunner et al.'s edited book *Radio in Africa: Publics, Cultures, Communities* (Johannesburg: Wits University Press, 2011) offers a detailed exploration of contemporary radio cultures in Africa. Dumisani Moyo's chapter 3 in particular focuses on clandestine radio. In chapter 6, Mano delves into why radio remains a medium of choice in the 'Global Age' on the African continent. Chapters 3 and 13 of Mabweazara et al.'s edited book *Online Journalism in Africa: Trends, Practices and Emerging Cultures* (New York: Routledge, 2014) provide critical insights into how radio production and reception practices in Africa (Malawi and Kenya specifically), are transforming with the adoption and appropriation of interactive digital technologies. Readers interested in further exploring the impact of interactive digital technologies on the institutional and organisational practices of radio in Africa should also consult Dumisani Moyo's edited special issue of *Telematics and Informatics*, 30(3) (2013), titled "The digital turn in radio: Understanding convergence in radio news cultures."

References

Ang, I. (1990) "The nature of the audience." In J. Downing, A. Mohammadi and A. Sreberny-Mohammadi (eds), *Questioning the Media: A Critical Introduction*. London: Sage (pp. 155–65).

Barnett, S. and Morrison, D. (1989) *The Listener Speaks: The Radio Audience and the Future of Radio*. London: Her Majesty's Stationary Office.

Bijker, W. E. (1995) *Of Bicycles, Bakelite and Bulbs: Towards a Theory of Sociotechnical Change*. Cambridge, MA: MIT Press.

Ceesay, C. N. (2000) "Radio in Niger: Central control versus local cultures." In R. Fardon and G. Furniss (eds), *Africa in African Broadcast Cultures: Radio in Transition*. Oxford: James Currey.

Coyer, K. (2007) "Mysteries of the black box unbound: An alternative history of radio." In K. Coyer, T. Dowmunt and A. Fountain (eds), *The Alternative Media Handbook*. London: Routledge (pp. 15–28).

Daloz, J. P. and Verrier-Frechette, K. (2000) "Is radio pluralism an instrument of political change? Insights from Zambia." In R. Fardon and G. Furniss (eds), *African Broadcast Cultures: Radio in Transition*. Oxford: James Currey (pp. 180–87).

Gurevitch, M., Coleman, S. and Blumler, J. G. (2009) "Political communication – Old and new media relationships." *ANNALS of the American Academy of Political and Social Science*, 625, 164–81.

Hambuba, C. (2010) "Women and ICTs in Africa." *Gender and Media Diversity Journal*, 8, 137–46.

Hayman, G. and Tomaselli, R. (1989) "Broadcasting technology as an ideological terrain: Some concepts, problems and assumptions." In R. Tomaselli, K. Tomaselli and J. Muller (eds), *Currents of Power: State Broadcasting in South Africa*. Bellville: Anthropos (pp. 1–22).

Jensen, K. B. (1988) "Answering the question: What is reception analysis?" *Nordicom Review*, 9(1), 2–5.

Livingstone, S. (1998) "Relationships between media and audiences: Prospects for future audience reception studies." In T. Liebes and J. Curran (eds), *Media, Ritual and Identity: Essays in Honor of Elihu Katz*. London: Routledge (pp. 237–55).

——(2002) *Young People and New Media*. London: Sage.

——(2004) "The challenge of changing audiences: Or, what is the audience researcher to do in the age of the internet?' *European Journal of Communication*, 19(1), 75–86.

Moyo, D. (2009) "Citizen journalism and the parallel market of information in Zimbabwe's 2008 elections." *Journalism Studies*, 10(4), 551–67.

——(2010) "Reincarnating clandestine radio in post-independent Zimbabwe." *The Radio Journal – International Studies in Broadcast and Audio Media*, 8(1), 23–36.

Moyo, L. (2012) "Participation, citizenship, and pirate radio as empowerment: The case of radio dialogue in Zimbabwe." *International Journal of Communication*, 6, 484–500.

——(2014) "Converging technologies, converging spaces, converging practices: The shaping of digital cultures and practices on radio." In H. M. Mabweazara, O. F. Mudhai and J. Whittaker (eds), *Online Journalism in Africa: Trends, Practices and Emerging Cultures*. New York: Routledge (pp. 47–64).

Mudhai, O. F. (2011) "Survival of 'radio culture' in a converged networked new media environment." In H. Wasserman (ed.), *Popular Media, Democracy and Development in Africa*. New York: Routledge (pp. 253–68).

Myers, M. (1998) "The promotion of democracy at the grassroots: The example of radio in Mali." In V. Randall (ed.), *Democratization and the Media*. London: Routledge (pp. 200–216).

——(2008) "Radio and development in Africa: A concept paper." Prepared for the International Development Research Centre (IDRC) of Canada.

Ruddock, A. (2001) *Understanding Audiences: Theory and Method*. Sage: London.

Smith, D. (2013) "Digital didn't kill the radio star: Shortwave and satellite help radio reign supreme." *Rhodes Journalism Review Alive*, 1, 12–14. Retrieved from http://www.rjr.ru.ac.za/rjrpdf/rjralive/viva_radio.pdf (accessed 24 January 2014).

Spitulnick, D. (2000) "Documenting radio culture as lived experience: Reception studies and the mobile machine in Zambia." In R. Fardon and G. Furniss (eds), *African Broadcast Cultures: Radio in Transition*. Oxford: James Currey (pp. 144–63).

van Dijk, J. G. M. (2005) *The Deepening Divide: Inequality in the Information Society*. London: Sage.

——(2006) "Digital divide research, achievements and shortcomings." *Poetics*, 34(4–5), 221–35.

Wasserman, H. (2005) "Connecting African Activism with global networks: ICTs and South African social movements." *Africa Development*, 30(1–2), 163–82.

Winocur, R. (2005) "Radio and everyday life: Uses and meanings in the domestic sphere." *Television and New Media*, 6(3), 319–32.

44

I FILM THEREFORE I AM

Process and participation, networks and
knowledge – examples from Scottish
community media projects

Kirsten MacLeod

This chapter examines community media projects in Scotland as social processes
that nurture knowledge through participation in production. A visual and media
anthropology framework (Ginsburg, 2005) with an emphasis on the social context of
media production informs the analysis of community media. Drawing on community
media projects in the Govan area of Glasgow and the Isle of Bute, the techniques of
production foreground "the relational aspects of filmmaking" (Grimshaw and Ravetz,
2005: 7) and act as a catalyst for knowledge and networks of relations embedded in time
and place. Community media is defined here as a creative social process, characterised
by an approach to production that is multi-authored, collaborative and informed by
the lives of participants, and which recognises the relevance of networks of relations
to that practice (Caines, 2007: 2). As a networked process, community media production is recognised as existing in collaboration between a director or producer,
such as myself, and organisations, institutions and participants, who are connected
through a range of identities, practices and place. These relations born of the production process reflect a complex area of practice and participation that brings together
"parallel and overlapping public spheres" (Meadows et al., 2002: 3). This relates to
broader concerns with networks (Carpentier, Servaes and Lie, 2003; Rodríguez,
2001), both revealed during the process of production and enhanced by it, and how
they can be described with reference to the knowledge practice of community media.

This chapter suggests that community media production can be described as both
a site of knowledge production and a form of practice. It draws on Grimshaw and
Ravetz's (2009) critique of the techniques of production of observational film, which
they describe as a locus of knowledge, to frame participatory community media as a
"knowledge practice" (Grimshaw, 2011). It is suggested here that the "ways of knowing"
(Grimshaw and Ravetz, 2005: 25) that "emerge through the very grain of filmmaking"
(MacDougall, 1998: 76) in community media production emphasise relationships
and social knowledge, where experience, social interaction and the relations between
people can be recognised as creating knowledge. Community-based media production

is explored here as a process which nurtures this embedded social knowledge, which is part of and connected to place and the communities to which participants belong (Cohen, 1982).

As the productions described below suggest, community media practice draws on participatory, dialogic (Bruzzi, 2006; Elder, 1995) and collaborative techniques of production that privilege knowledge that is personal, subjective and experiential rather than knowledge that is objective, specialised or expert (Grimshaw, 2001: 170). The 'knowledge' of community media production is provoked by and through the process of filming, embedded in webs of relationships, reflecting context and place and embodied in and through practice (Grimshaw and Ravetz, 2009: 132).

Networks and knowledge: Community media production in Govan

The production of the participatory documentary *You Play Your Part* (2011) is discussed here as an example of the networked knowledge practice of community-based media. I produced and directed the documentary in association with Govan-based community media organisation Plantation Productions and the University of the West of Scotland. Participants took part through a senior citizens' group, the Govan Seniors Film Group, which is hosted by Plantation along with individuals from mental health support services in Govan. The short documentary film is about campaigning women in Govan and the surrounding areas and drew on the experiences, networks and knowledge of participants. My practice as a director, facilitated through Plantation Productions, reflects a combination of participatory techniques and local networks of relations, connecting me, participants, organisations and institutions to each other, to Govan and to the broader themes pursued in the film such as politics, campaigning and work.

While Atton (2007) has described how community media have been recognised for their social, economic and cultural benefits and for the diversity such media offer, official discourses on community media as offering "local content services" (Ofcom, 2006: 4) barely seem to scratch the surface of the lively, mainly non-broadcast sector in Scotland, which combines a range of working practices, organisations and funding models as well as encompassing a range of individual filmmakers' and artists' practice. Since 2007, I have worked with Plantation Productions as a freelance director, producer and workshop leader. Plantation's aims are to use the arts and media as a tool for community development.

Although Govan is home to one of the last of the Clyde shipyards, as a post-industrial area it has suffered significant depopulation since the mid-twentieth century with high levels of unemployment and low income. Since 2003, Govan has been targeted for social and economic regeneration and redevelopment (Brown, 2006; Glasgow City Council, 2006; Daily, 2005). According to Moya Crowley (2010), who established Plantation Productions in a disused school in 2001, being based in their current venue the Portal, a community arts centre on Govan's High Street, is central to the organisation's approach: "We are embedded in the community.Through that the projects have been informed by the community."

You Play Your Part drew on networks of relations established during previous productions I had directed, such as with the Govan Seniors on *The Govan Banners*

(2010), a documentary about Govan and the Spanish Civil War, and with the mental health service users on participatory productions that were screened at the Scottish Mental Health Arts and Film Festivals in 2009 and 2010. These networks of relations connected participants, Plantation Productions and me with individuals, community groups and organisations, such as libraries, archives and film festivals. As the production process continued and went into distribution, these networks continued to feed into an ongoing process of production.

By examining the production process of *You Play Your Part*, workshops, interviews and screenings are described here as examples of participatory techniques and knowledge practice. This develops the concept of workshops as an organisational frame to describe a range of alternative media practices, such as the video workshop movement in the UK during the 1980s (Dickinson, 1999; Fountain, 2007). Here, workshops are framed as techniques within the production process and as a form of participatory practice characterised by regular participation, discussion and negotiation.

An example of workshops as practice, which also references and connects the production with the video workshop movement, was the screening of and discussion around *Red Skirts on Clydeside* (Woodley and Bellamy, 1984), a documentary film produced by the Sheffield Film Co-Op about the rent strikes led by Mary Barbour and women in Govan in 1915 (Ewan et al., 2006). The workshop screenings gave rise to discussion and debate among the Govan Seniors around issues such as women's emancipation, the First World War, and working conditions in the shipyards of Govan. This further stimulated reflections on growing up in the area, as well as memories and discussions about contributors to the *Red Skirts* film, who were known to members of the group through connections in Govan. This performance of memory (Caines, 2007: 132), within a group context and connected to place, served to provoke affirmations of identity, both collective and individual (Lourenco, 2007; Caines, 2007), regarding Govan as a place of socialist values and political campaigning, and as a place in a shared past which many participants still called home.

As part of the development process of *You Play Your Part*, the screening of *Red Skirts* provoked participants to describe their own lives and memories, reflecting personal concerns and experiences, which were acknowledged and validated by the group. These memories, opinions and stories reflect "unofficial knowledges" (Caines, 2007: 135) where memory is a form of shared and often negotiated social knowledge and where Govan as a place is created and recreated. As well as provoking memories and "personalized histories which disrupt authorized knowledge of the past" (ibid.: 15), the screening of *Red Skirts on Clydeside* also provoked revelations, which connected with personal and political networks. For example, the screening of the film acted as a catalyst for discussions with Seniors' member Cathy about her own involvement in political campaigns (in a way similar to that described in Meadows et al., 2009). Cathy revealed that as a bus conductor in the 1950s she had campaigned for equal pay for women. She had campaigned with Agnes McLean, who had worked and led women on strike at the nearby Rolls Royce factory. Agnes's campaigning in Govan and nationally (Rafeek, 2008: 89; Ewan et al., 2006: 236) became a central thread in *You Play Your Part*, linking participants to campaigns and campaigners across time as well as to political and trade union affiliations, place (Govan and Clydeside), work and gender. Cathy was key to the network of production of the video, connected to people, place, politics and the past, her shared knowledge and experience of campaigning provoked by the screening of the film.

Interviews were another example of the participatory production process (White, 2003; Rodríguez, 2001) as a site of networked knowledge practice. The concern here is not with challenging realist or anti-realist strategies in the techniques of documentary and participatory filmmaking (Waldman and Walker, 1999), but rather in appreciating that in a community media context, techniques such as the interview foreground working-class women's experiences and privilege their voices (Hankin, 2007). Here, interviews were a strategy within the participatory and collaborative framework that created opportunities for women (and men) to speak.

While acknowledging the role of the director in facilitating and directing the interview, in participatory video the interview becomes a site of the co-creation of knowledge. *You Play Your Part*'s production process, and in particular interviews, acted as a process and a place that legitimised participants' knowledge. Far from being marginal, this local knowledge (Fuller, 2007) takes centre stage (Braden, 1998). The interview, in focusing on the life experience of an individual, places Govan and women's history at the centre of the world, of central importance, rather than as peripheral to more important events.

As the production progressed, participants coalesced into a group formed of women from the Govan Seniors and local mental health services users. This production group interviewed two women who further exemplify the networked process and knowledge practice of the film and which validated women's knowledge and experiences. Marion had worked and campaigned in Govan with Agnes McLean, shared political affiliations with Cathy and Seniors' member Jean as members of the Communist party and was married to Duncan, who had joined the Govan Seniors during the previous *Govan Banners* production. Linda, meanwhile, was a friend and colleague of several production members through the mental health support networks in Govan and had been introduced to me at a screening of a Plantation film at the Scottish Mental Health Arts and Film Festival. She also knew Jean through the Scottish Trades Union Council women's committee. Linda had worked in Govan at the Fairfield's Govan shipyard, located less than 100 meters from the Portal. While working there during the 1970s, she had taken part in the Upper Clyde Shipyard (UCS) "Work-In" (Foster and Woolfson, 1986) and been part of the union-led workers' campaign to keep the shipyards open.

During interviews with the women at the Portal, conducted and filmed by members of the group and me, Linda shared her perspective on women's participation in a male-dominated industrial campaign while Marion shared her knowledge and experience of the campaign for equal pay:

> MARION: It was the early 1950s. If you can imagine we had never heard of feminism, of any woman fighting for anything, of equality. We didn't know that the idea was … that you would get married and someone would look after you. I thought, "wait a minute, I've no intention of ever getting married!"

When Marion said this during the interview, the women sitting around her all laughed, empathising with her story. Similarly, when Linda was interviewed, she was able to participate in a supportive environment where her experiences and her identity as a politically active woman were valued (Waldman and Walker, 1999). Like Cathy and Marion's contributions, Linda was able to present through the interview her own personal experience of an iconic national event in Scottish working-class and political history within the context and narrative of the film and women's campaigning in Govan:

> LINDA: We done our bit and we fought as good as the men did, but we never got the recognition that we should have got. I mean there were draughtswomen in there. There were cleaners who scrubbed their nails right in scrubbing decks, scrubbing cabins. You never hear about them; you never hear about the women in the stationary or the secretaries. Who did all that? Where were all these women?

Linda's re-telling of her experience and her analysis of the UCS work-in during the interview process asserted her embedded and experiential knowledge (Grimshaw and Ravetz, 2005) of a previously little known aspect of a historical event, and as such her testimony offers a critique of mainstream media (Meadows et al., 2009: 49) and official knowledge that has bypassed women's contributions to the UCS work-in. The knowledge of campaigning and of specific events was revealed through the production interview process, reflecting the networks of people and place through whom the encounter was produced.

The ongoing process of community media production as a knowledge practice stimulated by networks of participation was evident in the distribution and screenings of the film in Govan and Glasgow, and at conferences and events in the UK and abroad. The screenings of the film brought audience members and participants together in an ongoing dialogic process of production whereby meaning was constructed through the encounters and where the networks and agency of the participants become organising factors in the process. Screenings of the finished film emphasise the "after-life" of community media (Englehart, 2003: 75) and suggest an ongoing process of production "beyond the project" (Sobers, 2010: 27) or the actual film.

You Play Your Part was premiered at the Glasgow Film Theatre on International Women's Day in 2011, where it was included in a double bill with *Red Skirts on Clydeside* as it was subsequently at the Glasgow Women's Library. Engaging public audiences, these screenings served to maintain and reinforce the networked and ongoing process of production between the two films. The screenings highlighted the collaboration between organisations such as Plantation Productions, the University of the West of Scotland, the Glasgow Film Theatre, the Glasgow Women's Library and myself as a producer and director and connected participants with an international network of women, mobilised through International Women's Day, which itself connects with the themes and politics explored in the film.

In bringing networks of people together, the screenings and discussions afterwards offered new perspectives on the apparently familiar, new contexts (Braden, 1998; Tarrant, 2008) in which to situate participants, audience and place. After the Glasgow Women's Library screening, audience member Esther revealed that although she'd known Marion and Linda for some time she had not known about the details they described in the film:

ESTHER: I didn't know that Marion that you'd been so involved, although I'd known you for many years through the WEA (Workers' Educational Association). I think also, that Agnes's story will be lost if this kind of work isn't done. And Linda, I never knew about the women's struggle in the UCS ... I think what you've done is just fantastic. It is a lesson for the rest of us, if we don't do something it just gets lost.

Here, Esther reveals that she is part of the networks of relations of the film's production process (she knew Agnes, Linda and Marion through political and social affiliations), and like Marion is calling the audience to action in response to the film. The presence of the participants from the film at the screening was crucial, opening up new opportunities for networks and knowledge beyond and after the film.

Island identities: The Bute Video Project

The Bute Video Project was a collaborative island-based community video project that I produced and facilitated in 2011 on the Isle of Bute. Bute is located at the mouth of the Firth of Clyde on the West Coast of Scotland. It has a population of approximately 7,200 people, with the bulk of the population living in the main town, Rothesay. The island's principal economies are farming and tourism, the latter of which has been a mainstay of the island's economy since its heyday in the late 19th century (Boyne, Gallagher and Hall, 1999: 121).

I organised and facilitated (Carpentier, 2007) the project and produced four short documentary films about the island that were directed and crewed by participant filmmakers. The project was supported by a network of individuals, institutions and agencies, which included the Scottish Centre for Island Studies, the University of the West of Scotland and Argyll and Bute District Council. As in Govan, workshops were a feature of the participatory and collaborative production processes on Bute. The workshops were characterised by weekly meetings over a period of three months at a community centre in Rothesay. A dialogic process of development for the participants' films involved a process of learning about the techniques of documentary production combined with a framing of ideas for films around practical, ethical and narrative concerns. Through discussion, exercises and watching documentaries, participants were encouraged to think about how to translate their ideas into films. Lourenco (2007) has described this approach as a form of "narrative technique", through which community media re-organise representations of identity.

Four films were developed and produced by the group, as well as 'imagined films' – ideas for films that were discussed and proposed for production, but which were not made. *Rothesay Shops* is a portrait of the independent local shops and shopkeepers on the island; *The Big F – Guitars R Us!* takes a look at guitar playing on the island during a guitar festival; *Rhubodach Forest* features an interview with the manager of a community-owned forest; and *My Rothesay* is a personal short film about the filmmaker's experiences of moving to the island. The imagined films included *The Life of Pie*, about the production process of making 'traditional' Scotch mince pies on and off the island; *Backstreets of Rothesay*, about the less touristic parts of the main town; and *It'll Never Happen*, about negative attitudes to development on the island.

What emerged from these films and ideas for films was not "a single integrated meaning of island place" (Hay, 2006: 34) but rather many 'Butes' formed around individual and shared experiences of place and mediated by individual experience (Cohen, 1985). Production techniques such as the workshops facilitated collaboration and knowledge exchange engaging with a creative storytelling process (Ball-Rokeach, 2001) through which participant filmmakers re-imagined place – their many Isles of Bute. These ideas and films drew on the participants' situated knowledge and networks of relations on the island as well as knowledge and relations within the video project group. Participants shared contacts with each other and drew on their own networks to produce their films or develop their ideas. The guitars film drew on its director, Chris's, networks of friends and fellow musicians on the island, while the shops film was based around the people and shops its director, Ann, visited regularly. Paul's imagined film *The Life of Pie* was based on a farmer and butcher he knew on the island, while Kathryn, who directed *Rhubodach Forest*, was able to use Paul's contact with the forest manager to make her film about the community-owned forest.

The networked process of production, which saw resident filmmakers draw on their own contacts, relations and knowledge of the island in the development and production of their own films, emphasised the ways in which the filmmakers fore-grounded personal experience and relations, situating themselves as local filmmakers within the production of their films and the representation of the island.

As filmmakers filming 'at home', they encountered their own range of issues and production dilemmas, distinct from the experience of media producers who do not live where they film. The Bute filmmakers had to combine production with personal and public roles on the island, which affected their approach to the production process and their representations of their community. For example, *Rothesay Shops* represented the filmmaker's sense of the independence of the shops in Rothesay, in contrast to chains of High Street shops on the mainland. It is a personal video that presents her perspective of the island and what she values about 'island-ness' (Baldacchino, 2008).

The films and the process of their making mediated the filmmakers' identities as islanders (Ginsburg, 1995), drawing on their relationships with people and places, which became embedded in the ways they made their films. As the island filmmakers often shared and juggled multiple roles (Cohen, 1985: 23), such as directing, editing, interviewing, operating camera and recording sound, there were also tensions between their production roles and personal lives. Choices over what equipment to use became obstacles to the filmmakers' priorities of being unobtrusive and not intruding on the physical and social spaces in which they were filming. One of the filmmakers pointed out to me that while I was a professional filmmaker they were not, and as local filmmakers they were less willing to sacrifice relations with contributors who were also part of their daily lives and island networks.

Tensions were further evident in post-production as the filmmakers wrestled with issues of how to represent their contributors, aware of them as individuals with whom they shared networks of relations on the island. For example, Ann, whose *Rothesay Shops* film values the relationships between island shopkeepers and their customers, found that this very closeness to her contributors (the shopkeepers) threatened how she could behave as a filmmaker. Although an 'incomer' to the island, Ann had concerns with representation precisely because of her insider resident status (Burnett, 1997).

As the Bute Video Project productions suggest, community media has the potential to make visible not necessarily 'the community', but rather different notions of community that are personally inscribed by the situated experience and knowledge of the filmmakers (Abu Lughod, 1991). Rather than expecting films to transparently represent a fixed idea of the Isle of Bute, these films open up the multiple meanings and experiences of identity, communities and place (Ginsburg, 2004: 300). The Bute filmmakers foreground their roles as islanders over their roles as filmmakers, their conflicts and approaches to filming asserting the validity of their experience, knowledge and ongoing residence on the island, where relations with other residents and contributors continue long after their films have been made. In this way the ongoing life of the film is manifest in and through the participant filmmaker's approach to the production process.

The Bute Video Project emphasises how relations between participants, facilitators and residents of the island lie at the heart of the community media production process. Collaborative and participatory productions act as agencies through which participants employ a range of strategies and techniques to mediate the complexity of place – the island – and identity – as islanders – and where production roles are foregrounded with experience and situated knowledge.

Conclusion

The Scottish projects discussed here demonstrate the ways in which community media productions might be embedded in networks of relations and considered as ongoing social processes of production. The examples suggest community media production as a collaborative and networked process of activating relations and situated knowledge. These participatory techniques (as knowledge practice) are embedded in and validate place and the personal. Furthermore, the production process operates as a site of knowledge practice across time to connect people, productions and places in the periods before, during and after production.

The knowledge practice of community media production emerges during the production process and is provoked by this process, stimulated by the participation and agency of those engaged in its networks. The participatory process described here is activated by the director or producer in collaboration with organisations and participants. It reveals the situated knowledge and experience of participants and shows these to be central in connecting and disrupting official narratives of place, community and history.

Further reading

Grimshaw and Ravetz's (2009) *Observational Cinema, Anthropology, Film, and the Exploration of Social Life* is insightful for its detailed analysis of the social and production processes of observational documentary. Janey Gordon's (2009) *Notions of Community: An Edited Collection of Community Media Debates and Dilemmas* provides a useful range of examples and approaches to community media, with particular relevance to my research in chapter 4, "Community, cultural resource and media: Reflecting on research practice," by K. A. Burnett and T. Grace.

References

Abu Lughod, L. (1991) "Writing against culture." In R. G. Fox (ed.), *Recapturing Anthropology*. Santa Fe: School of American Research Press (pp. 137–62).

Atton, C. (2007) "Current issues in alternative media research." *Sociology Compass*, 1(1), 17–27.

Baldacchino, G. (2008) "Studying islands on whose terms?" *Islands Studies Journal*, 3(1), 37–56.

Ball-Rokeach, S. J. (2001) "Storytelling neighbourhood." *Communication Research*, 28(4), 392–428.

Boyne, S., Gallagher, C. and Hall, D. (1999) *Restructuring Peripherality: The Reconfiguring of the Isle of Bute*. Research Centre of Bornholm.

Braden, S. (1998) "A study of representation using participatory video in community development, from Freire to Eldorado." PhD thesis, University of Reading, UK.

Brown, B. (2006) *Population 2001 and 2004: Govan Craigton*. Edinburgh: Scottish Executive.

Bruzzi, S. (2006) *New Documentary* (2nd edn). London: Routledge.

Burnett, K. (1997) "Negotiating home: Categorization and representation of identity among indigenous and incoming people of Uist, in the Outer Hebrides." PhD thesis, Glasgow Caledonian University.

Caines, R. (2007) "Troubling spaces: The politics of 'new' community-based guerrilla performance in Australia." PhD thesis, University of New South Wales.

Carpentier, N. (2007) "Theoretical frameworks for participatory media." In N. Carpentier, P. Pruulmann-Vengerfeldt, K. Nordenstreng, M. Hartmann, P. Vihalemm, B. Cammaerts and H. Nieminen (eds), *Media Technologies and Democracies in an Enlarged Europe*. Estonia: Tartu University Press (pp. 105–22).

Carpentier, N., Servaes, J. and Lie, R. (2003) "Community media: Muting the democratic media discourse?" *Continuum: Journal of Media and Cultural Studies*, 17(1), 51–68.

Cohen, A. P. (1982) *Belonging: Identity and Social Organisation in British Rural Cultures*. Manchester, UK: Manchester University Press.

——(1985) *The Symbolic Construction of Community*. London: Routledge.

Crowley, M. (2010) Presentation, *Community Media Networking Day*, Viewpoints Film Festival, 19 November, Centre for Contemporary Arts, Glasgow.

Daily, M. (2005) "Housing policies and community deprivation in Scotland." In *Poverty, Deprivation and Development in Working-Class Communities*. Report of Conference held in Govan, 22 November 2004. Glasgow: Govan Community Council (pp. 5–9). Retrieved from http://www.govanlc.com/govanconf.pdf (accessed 14 January 2015).

Dickinson, M. (1999) *Rogue Reels: Oppositional Film Making in Britain, 1945–90*. British Film Institute.

Elder, S. (1995) "Collaborative filmmaking: An open space for making meaning, a moral ground for ethnographic film." *Visual Anthropology Review*, 11(2), 94–101.

Englehart. L. (2003) "Media activism in the screening room: The significance of viewing locations, facilitation and audience dynamics in the reception of HIV/AIDS films in South Africa." *Visual Anthropology Review*, 19(102), 73–84.

Ewan, E. L., Innes, S., Reynolds, S. and Pipes, R. (eds) (2006) *The Biographical Dictionary of Scottish Women*. Edinburgh: Edinburgh University Press.

Foster, J. and Woolfson, C. (1986) *The Politics of the UCS Work-In*. London: Lawrence and Wishart.

Fountain, A. (2007) "Alternative film, video & television, 1965–2005." In T. Dowmunt, K. Coyer and A. Fountain (eds), *The Alternative Media Handbook*. London: Routledge (pp. 29–46).

Fuller, L. K. (ed.) (2007) *Community Media: International Perspectives*. New York: Palgrave Macmillan.

Ginsburg, F. (1995) "Mediating culture: Indigenous media, ethnographic film, and the production of identity." In L. Deveraux and R. Hillman (eds), *Fields of Vision: Essays in Film Studies, Visual Anthropology and Photography*. Oakland: University of California Press (pp. 256–90).

——(2004) "Shooting back: From ethnographic film to indigenous production/ ethnography of media." In T. Miller and R. Stam (eds), *A Companion to Film Theory*. Oxford: Blackwell Publishing (pp. 295–313).

——(2005) "Media anthropology: An introduction." In E. Rothenbuhler and M. Coman (eds), *Media Anthropology*. Thousand Oaks, CA: Sage (pp. 17–25).

Glasgow City Council (2006) *Central Govan Action Plan*. Report commissioned by Glasgow City Council and partners. Retrieved from http://www.getintogovan.com/content/uploads/Full-CGAP-2006.pdf (accessed) 14 April 2011).

Gordon, J. (ed.) (2009) Notions of Community: An Edited Collection of Community Media Debates and Dilemmas. Oxford: Peter Lang Publications.

Grimshaw, A. (2001) *The Ethnographer's Eye: Ways of Seeing in Anthropology*. Cambridge University Press.

——(2011) "The Bellwether ewe: Recent developments in ethnographic filmmaking and the aesthetics of anthropological inquiry." *Cultural Anthropology*, 26(2), 247–62.

Grimshaw, A and Ravetz, A. (2005) *Visualizing Anthropology*. Bristol: Intellect Books.

——(2009) *Observational Cinema, Anthropology, Film, and the Exploration of Social Life*. Bloomington: Indiana University Press.

Hankin, K. (2007) "And introducing.the female director: Documentaries about women filmmakers as feminist activism." *NWSA Journal*, 19(1), 59–88.

Hay, P. (2006) "A phenomenology of islands." *Island Studies Journal*, 1(1), 19–42.

Lourenco, R. S. (2007) "Video-identity: Images and sounds of citizenship construction in Brazil." In L. K. Fuller (ed.), *Community Media: International Perspectives*. New York: Palgrave Macmillan (pp. 89–99).

MacDougall, D. (1998) *Transcultural Cinema*. Princeton, NJ: Princeton University Press.

Meadows, M., Forde, S., Ewart, J. and Foxwell, K. (2002) "Communicating culture: Community media in Australia." Our Media Not Theirs II, a pre-conference on alternative media at IAMCR, Barcelona.

——(2009) "A catalyst for change? Australian community broadcasting audiences fight back." In J. Gordon (ed.), *Notions of Community: An Edited Collection of Community Media Debates and Dilemmas*. Oxford: Peter Lang Publications (pp. 149–73).

Ofcom (2006) *Digital Local: Options for the Future of Local Video Content and Interactive Services*. London: Office of Communications.

Rafeek, N. (2008) *Communist Women in Scotland*. London: Tauris.

Rodríguez, C. (2001) *Fissures in the Mediascape*. Creskill, NJ: Hampton Press.

Sobers, S. (2010) "The Beyond Project – An ethnographic study in community media education." PhD thesis, University of Bristol.

Tarrant, P. (2008) "Documentary practice in a participatory culture." PhD thesis, Queensland University.

Waldman, D. and Walker, J. (eds.) (1999) *Feminism and Documentary*. Minneapolis: University of Minnesota Press.

White, S. A. (2003) *Participatory Video: Images That Transform and Empower*. Thousand Oaks, CA: Sage.

Filmography

The Big F – Guitars R Us! (2011) DVD, Chris Corin.
The Bute Video Project (2011) DVD, Kirsten MacLeod, the University of the West of Scotland.
The Govan Banners (2010) DVD, Kirsten MacLeod, Plantation Productions.
My Rothesay (2011) DVD, Kathy McLean.
Red Skirts on Clydeside (1984) DVD, Jenny Woodley, Christine Bellamy, Sheffield Film Co-Op.
Rhubodach Forest (2011) DVD, Kathryn Kerr.
Rothesay Shops (2011) DVD, Ann Russell.
You Play Your Part (2011) DVD, Kirsten MacLeod, Plantation Productions and the University of the West of Scotland.

45

FLOSSTV

TV hacking within media arts practice

Adnan Hadzi

This chapter operates in the context of a European political discourse, where the main concern is counter-cultural approaches to non-mandatory collaboration and contractual agreements. FLOSSTV (Free, Libre, Open Source Software TV) covers a broad range of practices, from television via documentary up to media arts productions. This chapter documents the endeavour to formulate a policy for FLOSS culture. FLOSSTV explores methods that can facilitate media and arts practitioners wishing to engage in collaborative media productions. FLOSSTV investigates the theories and histories of collaborative media and arts productions in order to set the ground for an exploration of the tools, technologies and aesthetics of such collaborations. FLOSSTV proposes a set of contracts and policies that allow for such collaborations to develop. It is through practice that this research explores FLOSS culture, including its methods, licencing schemes and technologies. In order to focus the research within the field of FLOSSTV, the pilot project Deptford.TV, which I am a participant of, was initiated as the central research experiment.

Deptford.TV is an online audiovisual database primarily collecting media assets around the Deptford area, in southeast London. Deptford.TV functions as an open, collaborative platform that allows artists, film-makers, researchers and participants of the local workshops in and around Deptford, and also beyond Deptford, to store, share, re-edit and redistribute their footage and projects. The open and collaborative nature of the Deptford.TV project demonstrates a form of shared media practice in two ways: audiences become producers by submitting their own footage, and the database enables the contributors to interact with each other. Through the Deptford. TV project I argue that, by supporting collaborative methods and practices, FLOSS (Free, Libre, Open Source Software) can empower media and arts practitioners to collaborate in production and distribution processes of media and arts practices.

Case study: Deptford.TV

Deptford.TV was established in 2005, in collaboration with James Stevens's initiatives *Deckspace* media lab (2001) and the *Open Wireless Network, OWN* (2009), as well as with the media art collective !Mediengruppe Bitnik (2002). Deptford.TV exists as an intervention into the public sphere and the public domain. Researchers work together with artists, film-makers, students and people living and working in Deptford. All of these people can join the project not only as audiences but also as co-producers, in order to collectively document the process of change in the Deptford area, and/or to produce media art beyond the historical borders of Deptford. The Deptford.TV practice produces 'copylefted' content (i.e. content allowing for participants to use each other's assets and share their project files). The sharing of the project files (found footage) becomes a remixing of post-production processes.

For the Deptford.TV project, participants become hackers: in the same way that hackers and coders of the open source/free software movement are sharing the source codes of their programs under a 'copyleft' license (Liang, 2004), the participants of the Deptford.TV project share their video source codes. By the term 'video source code' or 'TV code', I refer to the raw film material plus the metadata created by logging and editing this raw material. The various Deptford.TV projects, together with their raw materials and metadata, become the source code of Deptford.TV, which undergoes an editing process, or a digital bricolage, at the hands of its participants. Janet Harbord discusses the bricolage within the post-production process in her book *The Evolution of Film: Rethinking Film Studies* (2007) by starting with a quote from Miriam Hansen: "Digital technologies such as computer enhancement, imaging, and editing have shifted the balance increasingly toward the postproduction phase, thus further diminishing the traces of photographic, indexical contingency in the final product" (Hansen, 1997: vii).

The Deptford.TV project experiments with collaborative post-production methods, such as applying TV hacking to media and arts practices, through the use of free and open source software. This collective approach to production merges the processes of script-writing, filming, editing and distribution, as the users are shooting, editing and viewing the productions simultaneously. Some projects never finish with the traditional final-cut version but remain open-ended. Harbord reflects on this notion of editing and refers to it as 'temporal art': "Editing as assemblage, a bringing together of parts into unforeseen relations, requires us to think about film's spatial manipulations, as a fabric that threads itself across space linking atomized images and producing new lines of connection" (2007: 80).

TV hacking is an act of producing television 'together', to "establish a temporary hybrid media lab" (Combiotto and Smoljo, 2004). TV hacking raises the question of how interaction itself might be managed and produced, through the implicit and habitual ways of producing television. If power generates new opportunities rather than simply repressing them, then, following Michel Foucault (1980), more interaction and participation can extend and not simply challenge power relations. So far television has been the most regulated medium and holds enormous power over the field of cultural production and even artistic practices. Nevertheless, following the Snowden revelations, one may think that the internet might become more rigorously regulated, through a heavy commercial re-territorialisation.

New media law and ethics in 'the remix'

FLOSSTV criticises the impact of new intellectual property legislation on media production, as well as conceptions and applications of collective authorship and alternative licensing schemes. Currently the term 'social media' refers to commercial enterprises, such as Facebook, MySpace, YouTube, etc., hosting and serving User Created Content (UCC). One might argue that 'social media' in regards to the notion of User Created Content is a misleading label, as it uses the word 'social', which I propose should be about being 'social', benefiting society, within media practices rather than being 'for profit'. What is common to most of the definitions of 'social media' is that in situations of social interaction, technologies are used in order to collaborate on the creation of value. 'Value' is a critical notion, the meaning of which varies greatly: value for the commercial service provider, as in 'for profit', or value to the community as a 'service provider', as in benefit. Unfortunately, the sharing of knowledge, data and culture might soon be restricted to the 'for profit', centralised commercial services, offering UCC.

The internet is being subjected to various attempts at control by large-scale commercial corporations. The 'information commons' (Besser, 2001) could in these instances be seen as disappearing due to the assertion of strong intellectual property rights. In this respect, the media industry is lobbying for changes in copyright law, in order to benefit from stronger regulation of otherwise unregulated practices. Under this regime it is likely that the use of creative material will become more and more a privilege of those who can afford to pay for its rights – thus restricting the access to living archives. For the FLOSSTV research, I borrow the term 'living archives' from Saul Albert, who defines it as "archives of public interest, providing material or documenting events and processes that are otherwise invisible to official sources of historical and archival authority" (2006). The media industry depicts a future of decreasing profits due to digitisation, in order to force through draconian laws that generally benefit the copyright holders and weaken the public sphere. It is here that the practices of remixing clash with intellectual property laws, as demonstrated in the remix film project *RIP: Remix Manifesto* (Gaylor, 2008). Harbord uses DJ Spooky to illustrate such a remix. Spooky did a critical remix of *The Birth of a Nation* (Griffith 1915), labelled *Rebirth of a Nation* (Miller, 2007), where "parallel actions occurring simultaneously and parallel action occurring in separate temporal frames" provide "a model from which music was to evolve in sampling and cutting" (Harbord, 2007: 91). Spooky's remix criticises the racist tone of *The Birth of a Nation* and its history as the first film to have been screened at the White House, which established the film's long-standing impact on American political life as a "basis for normalisation of racism" (Miller, 2007) within US society.

Manovich (2005) reminds us that the concept of remixing in music became mainstream in the 1980s, when it was used in electronic music through sampling and scratching methods. Manovich continues by identifying the relevance of the term when looking at history, for example the culture of Ancient Rome which, in a sense, 'remixed' Ancient Greek culture, and the Renaissance, which 'remixed' Antiquity. But Manovich argues that the remixes are not transparent in many fields and disciplines because of a lack of access to the libraries, the raw materials. The fields where the remixing culture is open and transparent are mainly in music (through sampling) and in computer programming (where programmers rely on software libraries in order to write new code). The recent emergence of video archives allows for such a transparency within the field of film remixing. Remixing films enables artists to approach films as living archives through their engagement with both historical materials and contemporary raw materials. Remixes, especially when combined with database structures, involve breaking down the classical linear narrative of a film and offer the possibility of viewing society and its history from many perspectives: because the different narratives are "stored digitally, rather than in some permanent material, [those] media elements maintain their separate identity and can be assembled into numerous sequences under program control" (Manovich, 2006).

This leads to an audience producing and "watching databases" (Lovink and Niederer, 2008) such as YouTube, instead of films or TV. But there are also examples of mainstream television producing database films, as the Channel 4 Dispatches documentary *Iraq's Secret War Files* (Sigsworth, 2010), for which Channel 4 fed a database with documents leaked over WikiLeaks of "nearly 400,000 secret military significant activities reports (SIGACTS) logged by the US military in Iraq between 2004 and 2009" (McGreal, 2010). I would argue that this was an unprecedented early confrontation of the public with data coming out of a war which according to US officials had already been declared finished. The data contain 38 million words written by US soldiers in Iraq between 2004 and 2009. Channel 4 states that "the scope of the files is so vast, The Bureau of Investigative Journalism and Channel 4 created a purpose-built database in order to search and correlate the military codes, operational terms and abbreviations" (2014). From the perspective of the FLOSSTV research, it is interesting that these codes start functioning as meta-data offering narratives when queried through a database. A good example for such an engagement with a database is the art work *Endless War* (YoHa and Fuller, 2012), by the collective YoHa and Matthew Fuller (Harwood, 2014), that critically reflects upon the war files created by databases, in the form of a "walk-through the WikiLeaks Afghan War Diaries by NGRAM analyses" (Kunsthal Aarhus, 2013).

FLOSSTV focuses on social software interfaces through which participants can share their audio-visual projects over a database. For the Deptford.TV project, I chose to use software systems which themselves are FLOSS. Deptford.TV uses the content management system *Drupal* (Spreisz, 2007) in order to experiment with collaborative/collective production methods by using a method of version control of the Deptford.TV project files, which are often referred to as the Edit Decision List (EDL), all licensed under the General Public License (Free Software Foundation, 2007). The EDL, together with the raw material and meta-data, becomes the source code of Deptford.TV.

Remixing media arts

The FLOSSTV research is only possible through the recent emergence of new network technologies, a 'copyleft' attitude and culture and a broader acceptance of FLOSS. Today, a significant, and increasing, number of artists and collectives use FLOSS practices, such as the Linux operating system, for their work. In the case of Deptford.TV, those FLOSS practices were represented by the workshops organised in collaboration with the !Mediengruppe Bitnik. For !Mediengruppe Bitnik it was always important to point out to the participants that these workshops were organised in a playful, collaborative manner. The playful state only becomes possible when one admits that one does not have the answers.

What drew my attention to !Mediengrupp Bitnik was their way of practising art. Changes to existing cultural systems are part of the artistic work of !Mediengruppe Bitnik. Bitnik uses the strategies of hacking that are available for a practice of conversion, reorientation and criticism of media systems. For Bitnik, hacking is an artistic intervention into an existing system, to open it for other than its intended purpose. !Mediengruppe Bitnik is especially interested in multimedia systems, mediated realities and live media. Our interests converged in the exploring and opening up of questions around intellectual properties, rights issues and the use of copyleft for media, arts and software productions.

What emerged out of the 'urban change of Deptford' TV hacking workshops was an interest among the participants in the density of CCTV as a consequence of the regeneration process, and how these systems can be used in a creative way offering an 'image of the city' (Lynch, 1960). At the same time, !Mediengruppe Bitnik organised TV hacking workshops around CCTV sniffing, creating a workshop situation in which participants experience the city through a *dérive* ("drift") through the city and search for CCTV signals, transmitted over WiFi signals (!Mediengruppe Bitnik, 2011).

A possible answer to why the Deptford.TV participants had such an interest in these CCTV hacking workshops can be found in "Bilder der Ueberwachung" (images of surveillance), where Dietmar Kammerer (2008) looks into the question of why CCTV is so widely accepted. For Kammerer, CCTV is not only about technology but mainly a social practice (ibid.: 143), meaning that CCTV images have to be seen in order for them to have any influence on our realities. Kammerer argues, as one possible answer to his question, that it is also due to mainstream media that CCTV technologies have gotten a certain flair of pop culture. Surveillance became part of the pop cultural imaginary; thus, Kammerer claims CCTV reached the state of the "spectacle of surveillance" (ibid.: 20). What is of interest for the Deptford.TV CCTV hacking workshops is Kammerer's reflection on the subversion and hacking of these CCTV technologies, which leads him to a Foucauldian conclusion that there is no outside power. "As these kinds of critical practice are operating on an immanent level, they simultaneously react to and perpetuate the always changing modulations of the *dispositif* of surveillance. Thus, the *dispositif* will not be eliminated but reproduced ad infinitum" (Prinz, 2009: 162).

I decided to organise a TV hacking workshop focusing on the topic of CCTV images by inviting !Mediengruppe Bitnik to collaborate on a workshop on how to capture CCTV images. As with the Deptford.TV hacking workshop, the participants worked with found content. In this case, the content comprised the CCTV images that the workshop participants could 'receive' (Parisi, 2008) over consumer wireless TV receivers (Systm and Harrison, 2005; Schwartz, 2002). The participants themselves became 'social hackers' (Kulikauskas, 2004) who witness the previously discussed pseudo-public spaces through CCTV technology. After a short introduction to CCTV film-making, the participants went on a walk through Deptford in order to find CCTV images, practising 'sousveillance'. Sousveillance, French for 'subveillance', describes the reverse process of the habitual surveillance. Normally, state or other privileged institutions take or have the right to survey. With sousveillance, it is the other way around: "watchful vigilance from underneath" (Hyde, 2009). Steve Mann called this "inverse surveillance" (2004b) while researching wearable computing (1997) such as the *EyeTap* (2004a) device, which would allow anyone to record moving images of their surroundings through cyber-glasses.

Equipped with CCTV video signal receivers, the incoming surveillance camera signals led the participants through the city. By using wireless television receivers, which are sold in many electronics shops, the participants could view signals transmitted on the open spectrum of the WiFi frequency. The receivers caught surveillance camera signals in public and private spaces and made them visible: surveillance became sousveillance. My documentary practice and Bitnik's media arts practices joined, and I became a member of !Mediengruppe Bitnik. In May 2009 we gave a TV hacking workshop entitled *CCTV – A Trail of Images* at Goldsmiths, University of London. The Deptford.TV project extended from being a collaborative documentary film project, around the urban change process of Deptford, to a database project that also applies and experiments with artistic practices.

Deptford.TV as living archive

The Deptford.TV project offered participants the know-how required in order to share the raw material and to access each other's project files over the archives stored on the Deptford.TV servers. Archives have always been an important element of a documentary film-maker's practice. Including the Prelinger Film Archives, the Internet Archive holds over 2,000 feature-length films, constituting a 'living archive' and generating new audiences. The Deptford.TV project functions as an open interface for the process of communication through the use of 'many-to-many' media. The outcome of Deptford. TV is an online, often 'locative' (van Oldenborgh and Garcia, 2008) platform connected to existing archives of film and sound content and/or archives with content that defies easy categorisation as fictional or non-fictional. The Deptford.TV media content is simply multiple documentations of a process, while it invites the viewer to make his/her own interventions. The material (the film) can be recombined by the participants, thus giving the viewers control over the interpretative matrix in order for them to construct their own meanings.

An example of a database film is Lev Manovich and Andreas Kratky's *Soft Cinema* (Manovich, 2002; Manovich and Kratky, 2005) project based on Manovich's discussions on database narratives, database as a symbolic form and making art of databases (Manovich, 2000; see also Brouwer and Mulder, 2003). In *Soft Cinema* it is not participants, as in the Deptford.TV project, who decide on the edit, but an algorithm on the computer which is running the *Soft Cinema* software, and which is editing files from the database in real time following rules defined by the authors/ participants. "The liveliness of data as it couples with other forms of life prompts possibilities for a sophisticated computational culture that, as much as it runs with the expansive nature of computing in the present day, begins to reshape what is understood as computing as a way of thinking, sensing and doing" (Fuller, 2009).

In his research on database documentaries, Graham Harwood (2011) takes up the view that databases can also serve as raw materials for film productions. For

Harwood, the database administrator, as director and author, can query the database in order to produce narratives which can form the foundation for film productions. A guiding principle of the FLOSSTV approach is that every time participants read (selected) data from a (general) database, they engage in a documentary practice: an edit is made. Just as the Open Source/Free Software movements share the source code of their programs under copyleft licenses, the raw production materials in FLOSSTV projects are shared as film 'source code' under a copyleft license. The film source code is the raw material plus the metadata created by logging and editing this material. The FLOSSTV method changes the notion of traditional broadcasting. The production and distribution processes merge into one, and the audiences participate actively, undertaking a role traditionally reserved for producers and thus challenging the notion of professional media production. I would argue that FLOSSTV, because it supports collaborative methods and practices, can empower media and arts practitioners to collaborate in the production and distribution processes of media and arts practices. FLOSSTV is a more appropriate solution than using proprietary software, which only allows for the modification of the source codes when restrictive permissions are fulfilled.

In analysing the conditions under which the Deptford.TV project took place, I argue that the method of version control opens up the possibility of collaboration within the field of media and arts productions. By applying version control to art and media productions, artists are enabled to 'deep link' assets and gain access to archives, since the versioning system enables the tracking of updates as well as sources. The Deptford.TV method is applying the idea of 'versioning systems' to media production, by version controlling the Deptford.TV projects. A good example of such a version control system, on a textual basis, is Alexandre Leray and Stefanie Vilayphiou's *Ongoing Manifesto* (2010), which is written with the software Brainch.

The code of the Deptford.TV project that handles the version control of video project files aims to achieve in film-making what *Brainch* achieves for texts, that is, to enable 'critical video editing' (Hadzi, 2013). The participants in the Deptford.TV project use version control on the project files of the edited films. Participants can download a copy of a specific project file, including an edit-log file describing all the assets, which can then be shared, modified and amended. Contributors can add content or delete content. In the case of Deptford.TV, they can re-edit and remix projects. Having done edits on a project file, the contributors upload the files back to the Deptford.TV database. If other contributors have been working on the same project, *Subversion* (Collins-Sussman, Fitzpatrick and Pilato, 2004) remembers every version, every project file, that was ever created and uploaded to the repository, with additional metadata information about who submitted a specific revision, "and even gives you a line by line listing of who changed what when" (Haskel, 2008).

Conclusion

Participatory media practices are of importance for the FLOSSTV practice because participation in 'open' and 'free' media production should be inclusive, available to all interested parties. Eggo Müller explains that television influences the newly established sphere of user-generated video content sites, such as YouTube. User-generated video hosting sites and television do not represent "diametrically opposed concepts, but different institutionalizations of television on a spectrum of cultural forms of television that mutually define each other. One should not underestimate broadcast television's power to shape [this] participatory space of video-sharing sites" (2009: 59). Following Müller, I am critical of the romantic notion of bottom-up user generated video-hosting platforms. Müller draws an analogy to a similarly romanticised notion of utopian versus dystopian cultures within digital media pro-duction which, according to him, brands professional, commercial media practices as repressive and manipulative, while non-professional, non-commercial media practices are seen as empowering and democratic. Müller argues that these different spheres are not imposed upon users but co-created as "formatted spaces of participation" (Müller, 2009: 59). Müller's concept of formatted spaces can be applied to most of Web 2.0, or social networking platforms. Many of these social networks are 'walled off' systems that do not allow for an open exchange between different platforms, and can even take ownership of the data their users are contributing to the networks.

The characteristics of the contingent and situated Deptford.TV method suggest that it is within the field of participatory media and arts practices where researchers and practitioners can apply the FLOSSTV methods to other practices and research contexts. Within the field of participatory media, Deptford.TV critically proposes an open platform in the form of a joint authorship, as a "commons-based peer pro-duction" (Benkler and Nissenbaum, 2006), rethinking and questioning the consumer-versus-producer dichotomies. For researchers and practitioners engaging with the Deptford.TV method, this means co-curating the projects and co-participating in the process, further enhancing the access to such methods and processes, which can be further applied by other artistic and social practices. This 'collaborative culture' signifies a shift from conventional interdisciplinary arts projects towards "a synergy that marginalizes individual contribution over the relational dynamics and emergent possibilities of the collective.that builds and uses media technologies that both reflect upon and engender new types of social interaction" (Doruff, 2003: 70). Those interested in the FLOSSTV research can access all the code and content of the Deptford.TV project, available under a copyleft license, and apply them to other participatory research projects. As a collective, participatory research project, FLOSSTV is as much about its evolving method as it is about its practice, content and its participants. The FLOSSTV method can facilitate media and arts practitioners wishing to engage in collaborative culture, and the practice of participatory media and arts productions, by enabling a discursive environment through critical video editing, remixing and the sharing of media.

Further reading

Hadzi's chapter "Critical video editing" in the book *Media Interventions* (New York: Peter Lang, 2013) provides a more detailed description of the Deptford.TV post-production process. Jonas Andersson Schwarz's book *Online File Sharing: Innovations in Media Consumption* (London: Routledge, 2013) explores the peer-to-peer distribution models briefly discussed in connection to the *Digital Economy Act* (2010). For those interested in FLOSS and art practices, the book *FLOSS+ART* edited by Aymeric Mansoux (London: OpenMute, 2008) gives a good overview of applicable methods.

References

Albert, S. (2006) *Living Archives*. Retrieved from http://so-on.be/?id=823 (accessed 11 May 2014).

Benkler, Y. and Nissenbaum, H. (2006) "Commons-based peer production and virtue." *Journal of Political Philosophy*, 14(4), 394–419.

Besser, H. (2001) "Intellectual property: The attack on public space in cyberspace." *UCLA*. Retrieved from http://besser.tsoa.nyu.edu/howard/Papers/pw-public-spaces.html (accessed 10 May 2014).

Brouwer, J. and Mulder, A. (eds.) 2003 *Making Art of Databases*. Rotterdam: V2.

Channel 4 (2014) "Iraq secret war files, 400,000 leaked." *Channel 4 News*. Retrieved from http://www.channel4.com/news/iraq-secret-war-files (accessed 11 May 2014).

Collins-Sussman, B., Fitzpatrick, B. W. and Pilato, C. M. (2004) *Version Control with Subversion*. Sebastopol, CA: O'Reilly Media.

Combiotto, T. and Smoljo, D. (2004) "RUE-TV – COPYFIGHT!" *PROX/V/S/ON*. Retrieved from http://web.archive.org/web/20041029011945/http://www2.snm-hgkz.ch/~thomas/prox-ivision/index.html (accessed 10 May 2014).

Doruff, S. (2003) "Collaborative culture." In J. Brouwer and A. Mulder (eds), *Making Art of Databases*. Rotterdam: V2 (pp. 70–96).

Foucault, M. (1980) *Power*. Edited by C. Gordon. London: Penguin.

Free Software Foundation (2007) "The GNU General Public License." *GNU Project*. Retrieved from http://www.gnu.org/copyleft/gpl.html (accessed 10 May 2014).

Fuller, M. (2009) "Active data and its afterlives." *SPC.ORG/Fuller*. Retrieved from http://www.spc.org/fuller/texts/active-data-and-its-afterlives/ (accessed 10 May 2014).

Gaylor, B. (2008) *RIP: A Remix Manifesto 2.0*. Retrieved from http://ripremix.com/ (accessed 10 May 2014).

Griffith, D. W. (1915) *The Birth of a Nation*. Retrieved from http://www.archive.org/details/dw_griffith_birth_of_a_nation (accessed 10 May 2014).

Hadzi, A. (2013) "Critical video editing." In K. Howley (ed.), *Media Interventions*. New York: Peter Lang (pp. 323–41).

Hansen, M. B. (1997) "Introduction." In S. Kracauer (ed.), *Theory of Film: The Redemption of Physical Reality*. Princeton, NJ: Princeton University Press.

Harbord, J. (2007) *The Evolution of Film: Rethinking Film Studies*. London: Polity.

Harwood, G. (2011) "Database documentary." *YoHa*. Retrieved from http://yoha.co.uk/node/177 (accessed 10 May 2014).

——(2014) "Endless war: On the database structure of armed conflict." *Rhizome*. Retrieved from http://rhizome.org/editorial/2014/mar/17/endless-war-database-structure-armed-conflict/ (accessed 11 May 2014).

Haskel, L. (2008) "Subversion, a useful FOSS tool." *The Next Layer*. Retrieved from http://www.thenextlayer.org/node/425 (accessed 10 May 2014).

Hyde, M. (2009) "Marina Hyde: Put enough cameras on the police and even the serially deferential wake up." *The Guardian*. Retrieved from http://www.guardian.co.uk/commentisfree/2009/apr/11/police-surveillance-marina-hyde (accessed 10 May 2014).

Kammerer, D. (2008) *Bilder der Überwachung*. Frankfurt am Main: Suhrkamp.

Kulikauskas, A. (2004) "Social hacking: The need for an ethics." *Journal of Hyper(+)drom*, 1 (September). Retrieved from http://journal.hyperdrome.net/issues/issue1/kulikauskas.html (accessed 18 October 2010).

Kunsthal Aarhus (2013) "Endless war." *Kunsthalaarhus*. Retrieved from http://kunsthalaarhus. dk/en/yoha-graham-harwood-matsuko-yokokoji-with-matthew-fuller-endless-war (accessed 11 May 2014).

Leray, A. and Vilayphiou, S. (2010) *An Ongoing Manifesto For Processual Design*. Retrieved from http://beta.brainch.stdin.fr/about/ (accessed 10 May 2014).

Liang, L. (2004) *Guide to Open Content Licenses*. Rotterdam: Piet Zwart Institute. Retrieved from http://www.theartgalleryofknoxville.com/ocl_v1.2.pdf (accessed 10 May 2014).

Lovink, G. and Niederer, S. (eds.) (2008) *Video Vortex – Responses to YouTube*. Amsterdam: Institute of Network Cultures.

Lynch, K. (1960) *The Image of the City*. Cambridge, MA: MIT Press.

Mann, S. (1997) "Wearable computing: A first step toward personal imaging." *Computer*, 30(2), 25–32.

——(2004a) "EyeTap." *Personal Imaging Lab*. Retrieved from http://www.eyetap.org/ (accessed 10 May 2014).

——(2004b) "'Sousveillance': Inverse surveillance in multimedia imaging." Retrieved from http://web.archive.org/web/20130614134144/http://www.idtrail.org/content/view/135/42/ (accessed 10 May 2014).

Manovich, L. (2000) "What is digital cinema?" *Manovich.net*. Retrieved from http://www. manovich.net/TEXT/digital-cinema.html (accessed 10 May 2014).

——(2002) *Soft Cinema: Navigating the Database*. Karlsruhe: ZKM.

——(2005) *Remix and Remixability*. Retrieved from http://www.nettime.org/Lists-Archives/nettime-l-0511/msg00060.html (accessed 10 May 2014).

——(2006) "Cinema by numbers: ASCII films by Vuk Cosic." *Contemporary ASCII*. Retrieved from http://www.ljudmila.org/~vuk/ascii/lev_eng.htm (accessed 10 May 2014).

Manovich, L. and Kratky, A. (2005) *Soft Cinema*. Retrieved from http://www.softcinema.net/? reload (accessed 10 May 2014).

Mansoux, A. (ed.) (2008) *FLOSS+ART*. London: OpenMute.

McGreal, C. (2010) "Who watches WikiLeaks?" *The Guardian*. Retrieved from http://www. guardian.co.uk/media/2010/apr/10/wikileaks-collateral-murder-video-iraq (accessed 10 May 2014).

!Mediengruppe Bitnik (2002) *Bitnik.org*. Retrieved from http://www.bitnik.org/en/ (accessed 10 May 2014).

——(2004) *[Debug] Fwd: Labor und Medien presents: TV HACKING STUDIO WORKSHOP*. Retrieved from http://vnm.zhdk.ch/pipermail/debug/2004-May/000037.html (accessed 6 January 2011).

——(2011) "CCTV – A trail of images." In S. M. Schmidt (ed.), *Hacking the City: Interventionen in öffentlichen und kommunikativen Räumen*. Goettingen: Steidl Gerhard Verlag (pp. 25–34).

Miller, P. (2007) *Rebirth of a Nation*. Starz! Network. Retrieved from http://www.rebirthofanation. com/ (accessed 10 May 2014).

Müller, E. (2009) "Formatted spaces of participation – Interactive television and the changing relationship between production and consumption." In M. van den Boomen et al. (eds), *Digital Material*. Amsterdam: Amsterdam University Press (pp. 49–65).

Parisi, J. (2008) "Video sniffing: Counter-surveillance inquiries." *DataVeillance*. Retrieved from https://web.archive.org/web/20100821224149/http://dataveillance.blogspot.com/2008/02/ video-sniffing-counter-surveillance.html (accessed 10 May 2014).

Prinz, S. (2009) "Review: Bilder der Überwachung." *Foucault Studies*, 7 (September), 159–63.

Schwarz, J. A. (2002) "Nanny-cam may leave a home exposed." *The New York Times*. Retrieved from http://www.nytimes.com/2002/04/14/business/nanny-cam-may-leave-a-home-exposed.html?pagewanted=1 (accessed 10 May 2014).

——(2013) *Online File Sharing: Innovations in Media Consumption*. London: Routledge.

Sigsworth, M. (2010) *Dispatches – Iraq's Secret War Files*. Channel 4. Retrieved from http://www.channel4.com/programmes/dispatches/episode-guide/series-74/episode-1 (accessed 11 May 2014).

Spreisz (2007) "Drupal and Subversion." *SNV Talk*. Retrieved from https://web.archive.org/web/20121104102028/http://www.svntalk.com/node/6 (accessed 10 May 2014).

Stevens, J. (2001) "Deckspace." *SPC.ORG*. Retrieved from http://dek.spc.org/ (accessed 10 May 2014).

Systm and Harrison, K. (2005) "Building a war spying box." *Revision3*. Retrieved from http://revision3.com/systm/warspyingbox (accessed 10 May 2014).

van Oldenborgh, L. and Garcia, D. (2008) "Alternative visions of television." In K. Coyer, T. Dowmunt and A. Fountain (eds), *The Alternative Media Handbook*. London: Routledge (pp. 93–104).

YoHa and Fuller, M. (2012) *Endless War*. Retrieved from http://vimeo.com/61424524 (accessed 11 May 2014).

46

SOCIAL MEDIA
AND ACTIVIST
COMMUNICATION

Thomas Poell and José van Dijck

Introduction

During the 2009 and 2010 protests against G20 summits in London, Pittsburgh and Toronto, the protest coordinators urged activists to report on the demonstrations using major social media platforms, including Twitter, YouTube, Facebook and Flickr (Bennett and Segerberg, 2011; Poell and Borra, 2012). In January and February 2011, the opposition against the dictatorial regimes in Tunisia and Egypt especially used Facebook and text messaging to share reports on the events in the streets, while Twitter played a vital role in the transnational communication on these revolutions (Lim, 2012; Lotan et al., 2011). Inspired by the Arab Spring, large protests subsequently erupted in Spain, the US, Italy and many other countries during the summer and fall of 2011. Again, major social platforms were used for mobilisation and communication purposes (Castells, 2012; Gerbaudo, 2012).

The widespread use of social media in contemporary activism constitutes a new phase in the development of alternative communication. Historically, activists have tried to gain access to the mass media to communicate with larger publics. As Rucht (2004: 27) notices, "from the local to the global levels, movements struggle for public visibility as granted (or refused) by the mass media." Gaining public visibility through mainstream media has always proven difficult, as it forced activists to make concessions about how they present themselves publicly, catering to the mass media's need for spectacle, conflict and flamboyant newsworthy individuals (Gitlin, 1980; Lester and Hutchins, 2009; Rucht, 2004).

In addition, activists have focused on developing and using their own platforms for protest mobilisation and communication to become less dependent on mainstream media (Atton and Hamilton, 2008; Couldry and Curran, 2003). Alternative media, such as SchNEWS and Indymedia, as well as a wide range of NGO websites have been created to counterbalance the dynamic of mainstream reporting, which often disregards the reasons and broader context of protests, focusing instead on its spectacular, newsworthy aspects. These alternative platforms have been considered important, not only because they allow for more issue-focused reporting, but also because alternative journalism tends to explicitly foreground "the viewpoints of 'ordinary people' (activists, protesters, local residents)" (Atton and Hamilton, 2008: 86). However, a major disadvantage of alternative media is that they generally do not allow activists to tap into mass audiences and bring about a shift in media power.

Media power

The rise of social platforms allegedly brought about a significant change in this regard. Research on the Arab Spring revolutions and the Occupy protests shows that hundreds of thousands and occasionally millions of people could be reached through Facebook, Twitter and YouTube. For example, during the Egyptian uprising in 2011, in the week preceding President Mubarak's resignation, the rate of tweets about the protests grew to 230,000 per day (Howard et al., 2011: 4). Even more people appeared to be using Facebook. Most visible was the 'We are all Khaled Said' Facebook page, created in June 2010 to protest against the police-inflicted death of Said, a young middle-class Egyptian man. Several hundred thousand people commented on and 'liked' the posts that were shared through this page (Gerbaudo, 2012; Lim, 2012). To get a sense of the size of the overall public that was reached through these Twitter and Facebook activities, it is important to keep in mind that contributing users each have their own networks of followers or friends, which may include thousands of people. Thus, the actual reach of the social media protest communication was many times larger than the number of people posting, tweeting or commenting on these protests.

Given the vast reach of social media communication, a crucial shift seems to be taking place in the distribution of media power, that is, in "the way social reality itself is defined or named" (Couldry, 2003: 39). Activists have evidently become much less dependent on television and mainstream newspapers to influence public communication. As Tufekci (2013: 867) makes clear, "the 'power-dependency' relationship between media and the social movement actors has been fundamentally altered". Mainstream media are no longer the only available option to reach large audiences. The examples of the Arab Spring revolutions and the Occupy protests show that social media allow activists, under the right conditions, to directly communicate with very large publics. From this perspective, social media appear to resolve the communication predicament in which activists have historically found themselves.

However, as political-economic and software studies research has demonstrated, social media do not simply enable user activity, but very much steer this activity (Fuchs, 2011; Langlois et al., 2009; van Dijck and Poell, 2013). Through technological features such as 'retweeting', 'liking', 'following' and 'friending', as well as algorithmic selection mechanisms, which privilege particular types of content, social platforms shape how users can interact with each other through these platforms. These forms of technological shaping do not necessarily correspond with user interests, let alone with activist interests, but are first and foremost informed by the business models of social media corporations. This chapter will show how social media's techno-commercial mechanisms influence activism in ways that potentially undermine its long-term efficacy.

We will develop a critical perspective on the techno-commercial dynamics of social media in dialogue with the current research on the 2011 protest wave (Bennett and Segerberg, 2012, 2013; Castells, 2012; Gerbaudo, 2012; Lim, 2012, 2013; Lotan et al., 2011). Researchers have examined how activists *use* social media in complex processes of protest communication and mobilisation, providing detailed insights on how online contention is deeply entangled with offline activist practices, and how local and global communication networks are fundamentally connected with each other in contemporary protest. Moreover, protests should be understood within their particular cultural, social and historical contexts. While this research is highly valuable, it leaves unexplored the problematic role of the techno-commercial infrastructure of social media platforms in today's protest configurations.

We argue that it is not just important to examine contemporary activist communication as complex *socio-cultural* processes, as the above-mentioned researchers do, but also as *techno-commercial* processes – that is, the architectures and business models underpinning social platforms. This preliminary exploration focuses on two vital developments in social media-driven contemporary activism: the *acceleration* and *personalisation* of activist communication. Social media greatly enhance the speed and reach of protest communication and mobilisation, elevating their reliance on the mainstream media, while simultaneously undermining the ability of activists to focus public attention on the larger issues at stake in political contestation as well as undermining their attempts to build durable networks and communities around these issues.

Acceleration

The first development we would like to highlight concerns the acceleration of activist communication propelled by social media. In combination with the ubiquitous availability of advanced mobile communication devices, social platforms allow users on the move to massively exchange information in real time. Consequently, the Web is transforming from a relatively static environment primarily focused on information retrieval to a highly dynamic ecology of data streams, which constantly feed users with new information (Berry, 2011; Hermida, 2010).

This transformation greatly speeds up the exchange of information between activists. On the one hand, acceleration can be interpreted as a form of empowerment. Social platforms allow activists to document (almost in real time) unfolding protest events, and massively share their emotions regarding these events (Papacharissi and de Fatima Oliveira, 2012). Examining the social media communication of the 2010 Toronto G20 protests, Poell and Borra (2012), for example, show that by employing various social media platforms, protestors were able to meticulously report and communicate the unfolding events on the streets of Toronto. Omnipresent police activity was documented in particular detail. Exploring Twitter communication during the Egyptian revolution through the most widely used hashtag, #egypt, Papacharissi and de Fatima Oliveira (2012: 273–4) discern a similar 'ambient' information-sharing environment. They use the term 'instantaneity' to describe the instant online recording and reporting of unfolding events, and to capture the tone and urgency of the language individuals used in retweeting and requesting instant updates. Such near real-time and ubiquitous forms of protest communication, which far outstretch the reporting capabilities of mainstream media, can be of strategic importance for activists.

On the other hand, though, protestors' social media reporting practices tend to mirror much criticised mainstream reporting by focusing on the violence and spectacle that accompanies many protests. Historically, alternative activist reporting has been considered especially important because it allowed activists to counterbalance mainstream reporting and highlight the larger issues at stake in political contestation. In the early 2000s, NGO sites and alternative online news outlets, such as Indymedia, were celebrated precisely because they facilitated the long-term articulation and polarisation of protest issues. By reporting on such issues and linking alternative sites to each other as well as to corporate and governmental sites, activists constituted 'issue networks' (Bennett, 2003; Dean, 2002; Marres and Rogers, 2005). As Jodi Dean (2002: 172–3) has pointed out, such networks made it possible to move away from the "drive for spectacle and immediacy that plagues an audience oriented news cycle" as they "work to maintain links among those specifically engaged with a matter of concern". Evidently, the event-oriented focus and 'real-time' nature of social media protest communication runs the risk of shifting the perspective of online activist communication from the actual protest issues to the protest spectacle.

It is crucial to note that the event-oriented focus of social media communication is not merely the result of specific user practices, but is also prompted by the technological architectures underpinning social platforms. Various social media sharing mechanisms, such as 'liking' and 'retweeting', are pushed by the platforms themselves, as well as by many mainstream and alternative news sites in the form of social buttons (Gerlitz and Helmond, 2013). Omnipresent sharing features stimulate users to spread and repeat breaking news. Further adding to the newsy character of social platforms are the 'hashtag' and 'trending topic' features, which are particularly prominent in the Twitter architecture, but have more recently also been taken up by Facebook. Hashtags instigate users to share and search for news on specific subjects, whereas trending topics further highlight breaking news. Especially Twitter has developed their trending feature into a sophisticated popular news barometer by identifying the 'most breaking news', and by allowing users to break down trending topics by region, country and city (Parr, 2010).

To understand how features such as trending topics shape activist communication, it is important to see that these features do not directly translate user interests, but that they algorithmically process combinations of user signals (Bucher, 2012; Gillespie, 2014). By including and excluding particular signals and giving them relative weight, social media algorithms co-determine what is considered 'relevant' or 'trending'. As the Occupy protestors found out, social media's algorithms can conflict with what users themselves consider relevant. In the fall of 2011, at the height of the occupations, these protestors noticed that despite their intense use of #OccupyWallStreet and #OccupyBoston, these hashtags trended almost anywhere in the US except for New York and Boston, whereas less popular Occupy-related terms and hashtags made it into the trending topic lists of the two cities. Suspicious Occupiers subsequently accused

Twitter of manipulating its trending topics. However, as Gilad Lotan (2011) has demonstrated, no censoring appears to have taken place; it was the "outcome of a purely algorithmic mechanism", pointing out that the consistent attention given to #OccupyWallStreet and #OccupyBoston in NYC and Boston did not result in attention spikes. As Lotan explains, trending topics are not simply determined on the basis of the volume of tweets containing a particular hashtag or term. Instead, "the algorithm adapts over time, based on the changing velocity of the usage of the given term in tweets. If we see a systematic rise in volume, but no clear spike, it is possible that the topic will never trend" (ibid.). In other words, Twitter algorithmically privileges breaking news and viral content dissemination over long-term issues of interest. Similar observations can be made concerning Facebook's News Feed algorithms (McGee, 2013).

Given how this event-oriented focus is fundamentally built into social media platforms' architectures, it will be very difficult to reverse or adjust the perspective of social media communication. This becomes especially difficult as activists increasingly build their communication strategies around social platforms' sharing mechanisms and orient these strategies towards the platform's algorithmic selection principles. Occupy protestors' obsession with Twitter's trending topics is symptomatic of this tendency, as is the activists' practice of promoting particular hashtags, such as #g20report in the case of the G20 protests, #sidibouzid during the Tunisian revolution and #25jan in the early stages of the Egyptian revolution.

The real-time dynamic of protest communication is not just constituted through the mutual articulation of social technologies and users practices, but also through the ways in which mainstream and alternative news sites draw from social media data streams. This could be clearly observed in the case of the 2010 Toronto G20 protests. Exploring the online ecology of these protests, Poell (2014) noticed that alternative news sites, such as Rabble.ca and the Toronto and Vancouver Media Co-Ops, picked up the posts and links shared on Twitter and Facebook aimed at reconstructing the confrontations between protestors and police. These sites, just as various Canadian mainstream news outlets, heavily drew from the constant stream of photos, videos and text updates from the major social platforms.

A similar event-oriented dynamic could be observed during the Arab Spring protests. Leading news organisations such as the BBC and Al Jazeera, as well as individual journalists like Andy Carvin from National Public Radio (NPR), directly built on the flood of user-generated content (UGC) shared through social media (Hänska-Ahy and Shapour, 2013; Lewis, Zamith and Hermida, 2013; Lim, 2013). At the same time, activists made concerted efforts to pull together new sources of information and opinions on the uprisings posted on social platforms. Alternative media sites, such as Global Voices and the collective Tunisian blog Nawaat, played a vital role in these efforts and became central information hubs where relevant social media posts were verified, translated and aggregated in a structured fashion, making news from the ground accessible for Al Jazeera and other international media (Poell and Darmoni, 2012; MacKinnon, 2012).

These examples show how, during large protests, online ecologies emerge in which social, alternative and mainstream media are deeply entangled. The central role of social platforms in such configurations offers strategic advantages to activists, who are able to quickly disseminate information throughout the online media landscape. However, it also means that social media impute their logic onto activist communication practices. The instantaneous 'always-on' dynamic of social platforms intensifies mainstream media's focus on breaking news and renders alternative media increasingly event-oriented. As such, alternative reporting effectively becomes more 'mainstream'.

Personalisation

The second development enhancing the reach and speed of activist communication while simultaneously undermining its long-term efficacy is 'personalisation'. Understood from a socio-cultural perspective, the personalisation of activism implies that individuals' own narratives rather than collective identity frames become important in activist mobilisation and communication processes. Moreover, it means that "digitally networked individuals with multiple affiliations" instead of social movement organisations become increasing central to such processes (Bennett and Segerberg, 2011: 772).

This perspective on personalisation has been most extensively developed by Bennett and Segerberg (2011, 2012, 2013), who maintain that the development of social media has enabled a new form of activism termed 'connective action'. Rather than relying on the formal organisations and collective identity frames that traditionally drive activism, connective action revolves around easy-to-personalise ideas, such as 'we are the 99 per cent'; ideas mostly shared through social platforms. Reflecting on the 2011 Spanish 15-M movement, the authors note that this movement, which was not directed by formal organisations, was able to build strength over time using a mix of social media and other online platforms in combination with "face-to-face organizing, encampments in city centers, and marches across the country" (Bennett and Segerberg, 2012: 741).

Scholars interrogating such instances of online connective action notice that the personalisation of activism certainly does not preclude the development of a strong sense of solidarity during protests. In their analysis of #egypt, Papacharissi and de Fatima Oliveira (2012: 275) observed "overwhelming expressions of solidarity" and "camaraderie". Gerbaudo (2012: 159), drawing from several case studies on the 2011 protests, concludes that "social media have become emotional conduits for reconstructing a sense of togetherness among a spatially dispersed constituency, so as to facilitate its physical coming together in public space".

A crucial question is whether such instances of solidarity or togetherness can eventually translate into more durable networks and communities that provide the basis for political contestation in the long run. Community formation has always been considered a central objective of alternative activist communication and more generally of projects of political emancipation (Atton, 2002; Couldry and Curran, 2003; Fraser, 1990). Do social media also facilitate this objective? Taking up this question, Castells suggests that instances of togetherness, generated through a combination of intense social media interaction and the physical occupation of city squares, can very well trigger processes of community formation. He sees contemporary protestors "setting out to discover potential communality in the practice of the movement". Thus, Castells argues, "community is a goal to achieve, but togetherness is a starting point" (2012: 225).

However, if we examine the personalisation of activism from a techno-commercial perspective, it remains questionable whether there is a natural progression from 'togetherness' to 'community'. Personalisation as a techno-commercial process involves social platforms prompting users to explicitly make 'personal' connections through a variety of technological mechanisms. Moreover, personalisation uniquely depends on these platforms' propensity to algorithmically connect users to content, advertisers and each other (van Dijck and Poell, 2013: 9). As such, social media are not simple 'tools' for constructing personal networks or mere 'vehicles' for public sentiments. Instead, social platforms *steer* users towards personalised connections, while at the same time introducing viral mechanisms in public communication that *produce* moments of togetherness.

Major social platforms such as Facebook, Twitter and YouTube personalise the user experience on a number of levels. First, they push users to create and extend their personal networks by 'following' or 'friending'. They also stimulate users to create their own communication spaces, for example through hashtags such as #egypt, #sidibouzid or #OccupyWallStreet, or in the form of Facebook Groups and Pages like 'We are all Khaled Said'. Finally, social platforms algorithmically select for each user the content that is most likely to meet their interests, hence serving customised media diets. Thus, the techno-commercial flipside of personalisation is customised services that steer users towards particular types of connections and content.

Social media corporations have become increasingly sophisticated in personalising the user experience. For example, discussing the 2013 update of Facebook's news feed, one of the corporation's engineering managers, Lars Backstrom, explained that the platform has evolved from considering only a few user signals to assessing more than "100,000 individual weights in the model that produces News Feed" (McGee, 2013). The algorithmic balancing of these user signals determines *which* of the on average 1,500 available stories a user gets to see. Backstrom elucidates how not only individual user signals play a role in this process, but how Facebook also looks at global interactions, which can outweigh the signals of individual users if these interactions are strong enough. In practice, this means that viral protest messages can appear at the top of users' News Feeds, outweighing posts by family and friends.

The particular business models of social media corporations directly inform the technological development of personalisation. These models primarily revolve around user profiling and targeted advertising – the largest source of revenue for most corporations. User profiling is pursued through the systematic collection and analysis of user metadata (Fuchs, 2011). Through personalisation, social platforms are able to profile user interests, allowing both customisation of information and targeted advertising. Identifying trending topics is an essential aspect of social media exchange because these features enable corporations to develop real-time public sentiment tracking services as additional sources of revenue. Since 2010, Twitter has delivered such services through its 'data resellers', such as Topsy, Gnip and DataSift (Dwoskin, 2013). More recently, Facebook started to develop similar data services (Goel, 2013).

In light of these techno-commercial mechanisms, which underpin the socio-cultural forms of personalisation, it should come as no surprise that activist communication and mobilisation processes based on social media have generated loosely connected protest networks, which just as quickly fall apart as they are stitched together. Personalisation, real-timeness and virality are part of social media's DNA. The technological architectures and business models of these media are geared towards the viral dissemination of affective messages through personal networks. For activists, this is both a blessing and a curse. As social media penetrate deeply into day-to-day personal communication in ways alternative media have never been able to do, activists can reach categories of people who would otherwise not be reached by activist communication. At the same time, the interactions and interests that tie dispersed social media users together to form protest movements, generating instant moments of togetherness, inevitably dissolve when social platforms algorithmically connect users to the next wave of trending topics.

Whereas alternative media are technologically and intellectually designed to sustain interest in particular social and political issues and to build communities around such issues, social media are focused on connecting users only momentarily. To sustain their structural commercial appetite for online engagement, social platforms continuously introduce the next set of topics that satisfy user interests, whatever these interests might be. Indeed, social platforms are both technologically and commercially antithetical to community formation. In their pursuit of profiling and targeting users, commercial social platforms have no real interest in community formation except for rhetorical purposes. Hence, there is no natural progression from 'togetherness' to 'community' (as Castells suggests), but rather the reverse appears to be true: in social media-dominated online environments, processes of togetherness are always ephemeral, always already on the point of giving way to the next set of trending topics and related sentiments.

Reconsidering media power

Examining the ways in which social platforms shape personalisation and the instantaneous viral circulation of content forces us to revisit the question of media power. While the rise of social media has made activists much less dependent on television and mainstream newspapers, this certainly does not mean that activists have more control over the media environments in which they operate. Media power has neither been transferred to the public, nor to activists for that matter; instead, power has partly shifted to the technological mechanisms and algorithmic selections operated by large social media corporations (Facebook, Twitter, Google). Through such technological shaping, social media greatly enhance the news-oriented character of activist communication, shifting the focus away from protest issues towards the spectacular, newsworthy and 'conflictual' aspects of protest. Simultaneously, social platforms not only allow users to engage in personal networks but also steer them towards such connections. While personal networks and viral processes of content dissemination can generate strong sentiments of togetherness, they are antithetical to community formation. In sum, the ways in which social media shape and steer activism trigger critical questions regarding the long-term efficacy of social media protest communication.

In the wake of the partial shift towards social media, alternative media are as important for activism as they ever were. They are vital forces providing a counter-balance against dominant media – that is, mainstream press and large social platforms combined. Providing such counterweight has also become increasingly complex. In contrast to traditional mass media, social technologies are intricately intertwined with activist mobilisation and communication processes and hence with alternative reporting practices. Evidently, social media platforms have been greatly beneficial for alternative activist reporting in terms of speed, reach and variety of information sources, so abandoning commercial social media platforms is not an option. At the same time, it is crucial for alternative media to remain at a critical distance from these forms of communication and to provide a genuine alternative to the event-oriented focus of social-media-driven protest communication. The challenge for activists is to profit from the affordances of social platforms while simultaneously gaining public attention for the fundamental issues at stake in contemporary protests, and to continue building communities around these issues. If the recent resurgence of activism is to lead to real political change, it remains important not only to mobilise people, but also to raise their political awareness and tie them into durable networks, which can press for change in the long run.

Further reading

Castells (2012), Gerbaudo (2012) and Bennett and Segerberg (2012, 2013) have produced the main theoretical claims regarding the role of social media in the 2011 protest wave. Lim (2012, 2013), Tufekci and Wilson (2012), Lotan et al. (2011) and Poell and Darmoni (2012) analyse in detail how social platforms are used in the particular political and cultural context of the Tunisian and Egyptian revolutions. Similar studies for the Occupy protests have been provided by Juris (2012), Thorson et al. (2013) and DeLuca, Lawson and Sun (2012). For techno-commercial perspectives on social media and activist communication, readers can consult Youmans and York (2012), Poell (2014) and Langlois et al. (2009).

References

Atton, C. (2002) *Alternative Media*. London: Sage.

Atton, C. and Hamilton, J. F. (2008) *Alternative Journalism*. London: Sage.

Bennett, W. (2003) "Communicating global activism." *Information, Communication and Society*, 6(2), 143–68.

Bennett, W. L. and Segerberg, A. (2011) "Digital media and the personalization of collective action." *Information, Communication & Society*, 14(6), 770–99.

——(2012) "The logic of connective action." *Information, Communication and Society*, 15(5), 739–68.

——(2013) *The Logic of Connective Action: Digital Media and the Personalization of Contentious Politics*. Cambridge: Cambridge University Press.

Berry, D. M. (2011) *The Philosophy of Software*. London: Palgrave Macmillan.

Bucher, T. (2012) "Want to be on the top? Algorithmic power and the threat of invisibility on Facebook." *New Media and Society*, 14(7), 1164–80.

Castells, M. (2012) *Networks of Outrage and Hope: Social Movements in the Internet Age.* Cambridge: Polity.

Couldry, N. (2003) "Beyond the hall of mirrors? Some theoretical reflections on the global contestation of media power." In N. Couldry and J. Curran (eds), *Contesting Media Power: Alternative Media in a Networked World.* Lanham, MD: Rowman and Littlefield.

Couldry, N. and Curran, J. (eds.) (2003) *Contesting Media Power: Alternative Media Power in a Networked World.* Lanham, MD: Rowman and Littlefield.

Dean, J. (2002) *Publicity's Secret: How Technoculture Capitalizes on Democracy.* Chicago: Cornell University Press.

DeLuca, K. M., Lawson, S. and Sun, Y. (2012) "Occupy Wall Street on the public screens of social media: The many framings of the birth of a protest movement." *Communication, Culture and Critique,* 5(4), 483–509.

Dwoskin, E. (2013) "Twitter's data business proves lucrative." *The Wall Street Journal,* October 7. Retrieved from http://online.wsj.com/news/articles/SB10001424052702304441404579118531954483974 (accessed 14 October 2013).

Fraser, N. (1990) "Rethinking the public sphere: A contribution to the critique of actually existing democracy." *Social Text,* 25–26, 56–80.

Fuchs, C. (2011) *Foundations of Critical Media and Information Studies.* New York: Routledge.

Gerbaudo, P. (2012) *Tweets and the Streets: Social Media and Contemporary Activism.* London: Pluto Books.

Gerlitz, C. and Helmond, A. (2013) "The like economy: Social buttons and the data-intensive web." *New Media and Society,* 15(8), 1348–1365

Gillespie, T. (2014) "The relevance of algorithms." In T. Gillespie, P. Boczkowski and K. Foot (eds), *Media Technologies.* Cambridge, MA: MIT Press (pp. 167–94).

Gitlin, T. (1980) *The Whole World Is Watching.* Berkeley: University of California Press.

Goel, V. (2013) "Facebook offers new windows into social conversation." *New York Times,* September 9. Retrieved from http://bits.blogs.nytimes.com/2013/09/09/facebook-offers-new-windows-into-social-conversation/?_r=0 (accessed 12 October 2013).

Hänska-Ahy, M. T. and Shapour, R. (2013) "Who's reporting the protests? Converging practices of citizen journalists and two BBC World Service newsrooms, from Iran's election protests to the Arab uprisings." *Journalism Studies,* 14(1), 29–45.

Hermida, A. (2010) "Twittering the news: The emergence of ambient journalism." *Journalism Practice,* 4(3), 297–308.

Howard, P. N., Duffy, A., Freelon, D., Hussain, M., Mari, W. and Mazaid, M. (2011) *Opening Closed Regimes: What Was the Role of Social Media during the Arab Spring?* Seattle: University of Washington, Project on Information Technology and Political Islam.

Juris, J. S. (2012) "Reflections on #Occupy everywhere: Social media, public space, and emerging logics of aggregation." *American Ethnologist,* 39(2), 259–79.

Langlois, G., Elmer, G., McKelvey, F. and Devereaux, Z. (2009) "Networked publics: The double articulation of code and politics on Facebook." *Canadian Journal of Communication,* 34, 415–34.

Lester, E. A. and Hutchins, B. (2009) "Power games: Environmental protest, news media and the internet." *Media, Culture and Society,* 31(4), 579–95.

Lewis, S. C., Zamith, R. and Hermida, A. (2013) "Content analysis in an era of big data: A hybrid approach to computational and manual methods." *Journal of Broadcasting and Electronic Media,* 57(1), 34–52.

Lim, M. (2012) "Clicks, cabs, and coffee houses: Social media and oppositional movements in Egypt 2004–2011." *Journal of Communication,* 62, 231–48.

——(2013) "Framing Bouazizi: 'White lies', hybrid network, and collective/connective action in the 2010–11 Tunisian uprising." *Journalism,* 14, 921–41.

Lotan, G. (2011) "Data reveals that 'Occupying' Twitter trending topics is harder than it looks!" *SocialFlow*, 12 October. Retrieved from http://blog.socialflow.com/post/712024 4374/data-reveals-that-occupying-twitter-trending-topics-is-harder-than-it-looks (accessed 10 September 2013).

Lotan, G., Graeff, E., Ananny, M., Gaffney, D., Pearce, I. and Boyd, D. (2011) "The revolutions were tweeted: Information flows during the 2011 Tunisian and Egyptian revolutions." *International Journal of Communication*, 5, 1375–1405.

MacKinnon, R. (2012) *Consent of the Networked: The Worldwide Struggle for Internet Freedom.* New York: Basic Books.

Marres, N. and Rogers, R. (2005) "Recipe for tracing the fate of issues and their publics on the web." In B. Latour and P. Weibel (eds), *Making Things Public: Atmospheres of Democracy.* Cambridge, MA: MIT Press (pp. 922–35).

McGee, M. (2013) "EdgeRank is dead: Facebook's news feed algorithm now has close to 100K weight factors." *Marketing Land*, August 16. Retrieved from http://marketingland.com/ edgerank-is-dead-facebooks-news-feed-algorithm-now-has-close-to-100k-weight-factors-55908 (accessed 14 October 2013).

Papacharissi, Z. and de Fatima Oliveira, M. (2012) "Affective news and networked publics: The rhythms of news storytelling on #Egypt." *Journal of Communication*, 62(2), 266–82.

Parr, B. (2010) "Twitter improves trending topic algorithm: Bye bye, Bieber!" *Mashable* [Online]. Retrieved from http://mashable.com/2010/05/14/twitter-improves-trending-topic-algorithm-bye-bye-bieber/ (accessed 7 June 2011).

Poell, T. (2014) "Social media and the transformation of activist communication: Exploring the social media ecology of the 2010 Toronto G20 protests." *Information, Communication and Society*, 17(6), 716–31.

Poell, T. and Borra, E. (2012) "Twitter, YouTube, and Flickr as platforms of alternative journalism: The social media account of the 2010 Toronto G20 protests." *Journalism*, 13(6), 695–713.

Poell, T. and Darmoni, K. (2012) "Twitter as a multilingual space: The articulation of the Tunisian revolution through #sidibouzid." *NECSUS – European Journal of Media Studies*, 1 [Online]. Retrieved from http://www.necsus-ejms.org/twitter-as-a-multilingual-space-the-articulation-of-the-tunisian-revolution-through-sidibouzid-by-thomas-poell-and-kaouthar-darmoni/ (accessed 14 October 2013).

Rucht, D. (2004) "The quadruple 'A': Media strategies of protest movements since the 1960s." In W. van de Donk et al. (eds), *Cyberprotest: New Media, Citizens and Social Movements.* London: Routledge (pp. 25–48).

Thorson, K., Driscoll, K., Ekdale, B., Edgerly, S., Thompson, L. G., Schrock, A., Swartz, L., Vraga, E. K. and Wells, C. (2013) "YouTube, Twitter and the Occupy movement: Connecting content and circulation practices." *Information, Communication and Society*, 16(3), 421–51.

Tufekci, Z. (2013) "Not this one: Social movements, the attention economy, and microcelebrity networked activism." *American Behavioral Scientist*, 57(7), 848–70.

Tufekci, Z. and Wilson, C. (2012) "Social media and the decision to participate in political protest: Observations from Tahrir Square." *Journal of Communication*, 62(2), 363–79.

van Dijck, J. and Poell, T. (2013) "Understanding social media logic." *Media and Communication*, 1(1), 2–14.

Youmans, W. L. and York, J. C. (2012) "Social media and the activist toolkit: User agreements, corporate interests, and the information infrastructure of modern social movements." *Journal of Communication*, 62(2), 315–29.

47
MOTIVATIONS OF ALTERNATIVE MEDIA PRODUCERS
Digital dissent in action

Megan Boler

Introduction

While alternative media have existed and served myriad purposes throughout history, arguably never before has there been such need for contesting accounts of local and global events. The lockstep relationship of many traditional news sources to government/ corporate interests has rendered hopes of a press that serves publics and democracy a nostalgic dream. This chapter offers an analysis of a particular and little-studied area of contemporary digital activist culture: the motivations of independent producers of blogs and web-streamed videos. I focus on the motivations of the producer/ makers of these practices I call 'digital dissent', with the aim of contributing to the literature that seeks to understand the individual's motives, agency and role within the larger productive environment more commonly referenced as 'alternative media'. Within this context, my research shows that those producing alternative media, and specifically interventions into traditional media, are motivated not only by frustration, but out of a desire to *make sense of* the combined forces of corporate owned media with political interests.

In those nascent years of what is sometimes referred to as a Web 2.0 landscape, alternative media exist in a plenitude of forms, access points, points of view and despite the infinite diversity of views, share in their goal of challenging traditional authority and power of state and corporate news in part by providing alternative accounts of diversely determined news agendas.

In Atton's invaluable book *Alternative Media*, he provides one definition as follows: "alternative media argue for social change, seek to involve people (citizens, not elites) in their processes and are committed to innovation in form and content. This set of aims takes into account not only content, but presentation and organizational procedures" (Atton, 2002: 15–16).

Defining 'grassroots media', Atton notes that such "are produced by the same people whose concerns they represent, from a position of engagement and direct participation" (ibid.: 16). Finally, impressing a point of definition central to my research into the production of 'digital dissent' and its myriad forms of public expression, Atton explains: "In arguing for social change alternative media may then not only be understood as producing instrumental discourses (theoretical, expository, organizational) to provoke change: following Duncombe, they are able to enact social change through their own means of production, which are themselves positioned in relation to the dominant means of production" (2002: 18). Thus, to understand 'alternative', one must also understand what such a notion and practice exist in relation to; and, as will be shown in this chapter, the motivation for such alternative production exists in a dynamic relation of frustration with traditional forms of news, frustrations that reflect a significant cultural zeitgeist.

Against this backdrop understanding of alternative media, a central question stands out within existing scholarship: *What motivates people to engage in participatory media and public political expression such as writing news blogs, producing short political videos for public circulation and/or repurposing/remixing corporate content to draw attention to political agendas?* Providing some context to this research, Ekdale et al. (2010) surveyed 66 top 'A-list' political bloggers on their motivations. One of their conclusions for future directions includes urging scholars to examine how lesser-known bloggers' motivations do or don't correspond with their findings. Since 2001, my research has focused centrally on alternative media and the individual's motivations in creative public expression of 'digital dissent'. The mixed-methods research project "Rethinking Media Democracy and Citizenship" (funded by the Canadian Social Science and Humanities Research Council and hereafter referred to as RMD) upon which this essay draws was conducted during 2005–8. This research project focused centrally on the motivations for digital public expression through the forms of blogs, viral videos and online video. The project focused on those engaging web-based media to address issues related to US foreign policy and militarism after September 11, 2001, focusing specifically on dissenters' perceptions of traditional media and its role in relation to then US President George W. Bush and Pentagon policies related to the so-called 'war on terror'. Our research sought those speaking out particularly in the context of US foreign policies after September 11, 2001, and the context of the 'war on terror'.

Our findings are based on the results of an online survey administered to 161 online producers of dissent, which was followed up by 35 semi-structured interviews from the four primary sites or groups, which were then coded for emergent themes. The four sites of study were as follows:

1 Online networks developed about Jon Stewart's *The Daily Show* and appearance on *Crossfire*.
2 Bush in 30 Seconds, MoveOn.org Contest (150 Quicktime movie finalists).
3 Independently produced 'viral videos'.
4 Political blogs addressing media responsibility to democracy following the US invasion of Iraq.

Producers of digital dissent reveal different variations of motivations for engaging, but those we interviewed and surveyed – regardless of political or partisan perspectives or identities – expressed explicit frustration with traditional media coverage during the historically formative years following September 11, 2001. Our research evidenced that frustrations with traditional news media coverage after September 11, 2001, were a significant and major catalyst for everyday citizens to become media makers and producers of digital dissent. A second key finding that this chapter will address, in lesser depth, is how that the distinctive medium (blog, video, meme) chosen by the producer differentially shaped their sense of audience, 'community' and being in conversation and being heard. (Curiously, though not elaborated here given limitations of space, a surprising number of those we interviewed do not identify as 'activists', nor necessarily see themselves as 'political'.) Finally, one notes while hearing the voices of those interviewed, how motivations are distinctively tied to strong emotions – anger and frustration with traditional news sources in particular – and how these affects frequently compel public expressions and production. Most often, the affect is not channelled necessarily into an expression of anger per se, but expressed through the diverse expressions of information, analysis and informed opinion in the different genres represented here.

Current debates on individuation and digital dissent

Stiegler's notion of the 'transindividual' (Crogan, 2010) helps make sense of the complex relationship and flows between the individual and collectivities in tech-related engagement. As this chapter reveals, individuation is not at odds with collective engagement. Indeed, digital contexts and modes are well suited to this multiplicity of engagements and are indeed responding to the growing gap between both forms of existence. The contemporary individual, Stiegler tells us, "is at the same time always *augmented* yet also *diminished* by technological individuation – that is the individuation of the sort of beings that we are, or at least try to be, or that we believe to be in our attempt to share a common future" (2013: 19).

As the new DIY citizenship movement(s) show participants a way to move from youth apathy, disenfranchisement and so-called 'slacktivism' to new hybrid movements, the move from collective to individual activism is exemplary of both digital activism and 21st-century social movements (Ratto and Boler, 2014). Online and off-, social and political are increasingly blurred, in many cases resulting in a disavowal of 'political' identities by many users. Social media represent new hybrid possibilities for grassroots movements that allows people to express themselves both individually and collectively, suggesting new and proliferating forms of participatory democracy. From recent movements such as OWS, Idle No More, Montreal Student Protests and the Arab Spring, these collectivities continue to grapple with challenges of sexism, racism and classism (Boler and Nitsou, 2014).

To what extent can social media can do more than "reflect practices structured around the self even in the nonmainstream world of alternative media"? as Fenton and Barassi ask (2011: 193), and in what ways can social media be of service to activist movements with democratic practices at their core? Intrinsically connected to the self/other divide, alternative media can offer some insights into the pluralistic role of these proliferating forms and their relationship to both the individual and the collective in social action (see, for example, Bimber, 2000). While the individual must drive civic engagement through online media, most often radical change comes about through collective action.

This emergent 'politics of online individuation' points to new directions for future roles and production modes, mirroring multiple roles that arose within the Occupy movement that I have written about elsewhere (see Boler et al., 2014; Boler and Nitsou, 2014), tied to the potential Web 3.0 role of 'new freelance editors' (money to be made, capital to be gained) who connect, filter and prioritise information flows. Questions of the ways in which these roles might vary from bloggers, vloggers and other current digital dissent-makers bring us back to issues concerning truth, identity and increasingly (particularly in an exponential sense since these interviews were conducted in 2005–7), online markets.

Some scholars have even begun to track the agency of the individual versus collective in independent (individual vs. group) blogs, their differences from mainstream media sites and their impact on news production and delivery (see, for example, Hartley, Burgess and Bruns, 2013; Bruns 2005). The ability of individuals versus collectives or lobby groups varies widely; as noted by Bruns (2005: 189), "individual blogs return us to a far more tightly controlled publishing model". Yet, oversimplified binaries of individual/collective risk re-essentialising ways of considering the proliferation of digital dissent. As Bruns reminds us, "Just as the real importance of punk wasn't in the individual songs, the importance of Indymedia isn't in this or that new story posted to this or that site. Instead, it's in its DIY ethos and its commitment to establishing new networks" (ibid.: 84).

For many who create web-based interventions – productions which in themselves may be helping create communities of producers – there does not appear to be a direct correlation between their work and the creation of online communities. Rather, as Sloan remarks, there are individual relationships, but "I have to say I really don't have a sense of communication or community with viral video makers or meme producers" (interview with author). Yet, the ways in which blogs, memes and other digital artefacts and practices get made continues to change apace. Whether they serve as motivators for others' work of creating community, or politicisation or of entertainment and consumption remains to be seen.

Differentiated motivations became clear between the different groups of dissent producers. Bloggers expressed strong and clear desires to change minds, to improve their own arguments, to incite dialogue and to create spaces for agonistic conversation. The 'comment' function of blogs permitted bloggers to experience a sense of dialogic community, something not experienced by the other groups interviewed.

The Bush in 30 Seconds and other video producers engaged what might be termed more 'artistic' representations of dissent – web-based videos or memes/viral videos. These participants expressed a desire to effect audiences and viewers, but because the study took place prior to video-sharing platforms like YouTube, these video makers had fewer experiences of 'hearing back' from viewers and thus little sense of whether their video had been viewed, much less how it might have affected viewers.

The respondents from the subgroup of bloggers engaging *The Daily Show with Jon Stewart* revealed a different set of themes. For those who regularly discussed *TDS*, the themes from the open-ended questions emerged as desires to:

- Share something funny with others.
- Respond to Jon Stewart's infamous *Crossfire* appearance.
- Share *TDS* unique or important perspective.
- Archive and capture specific episodes the bloggers strongly wished others to see for specific political reasons.

Motivations for digital dissent: Overview of survey findings

In terms of motivation, the following themes emerged across all groups in the open-ended questions:

- Make a statement/express myself/be heard.
- Anger and frustration with current events or political issues.
- Desire to influence others (especially to influence election results).
- 'Corrective' function to counter media.

The first group of themes is consistent with survey responses dealing with reasons for participation in online forums.

- Consistent with the first theme, "make a statement/express myself/be heard," 87 per cent of respondents agreed or strongly agreed with the statement "I participate in online forums because I feel that they give me a public voice."
- Consistent with the third theme, "influence others," 76 per cent agreed or strongly agreed with the statement "I participate in online forums because I feel I can influence others' thinking."
- Consistent with the fourth theme, "'corrective' function to counter media," 76 per cent agreed or strongly agreed with the statement "I participate in online forums because I want to supplement mainstream news media." Note, however, that participants tend to disagree that online forums replace traditional news media.
- The influence of friends, family or peers does not appear to be a strong motivator.
- There were no significant differences noted among groups in response to these questions.

Perceptions of bias

Survey results suggest that respondents tend to view the media with some degree of scepticism. Respondents were asked to provide one word to describe mainstream media. The most frequently used words are:

Biased – 10
Corporate – 6
Timid – 6
Lazy – 4
Shallow – 4

The majority of words used by respondents tended to be negative, and clearly suggest an overall impression of disappointment and critique. These results are consistent with responses to survey questions. In response to the query "What do you think mainstream news organizations care about most when deciding what stories to report?" No respondents thought that "keeping the public informed" was the primary motivation. Sixty-nine per cent reported "attracting the biggest audience," while 20.4 per cent reported both of these. Offering interesting insight into the motivations of those surveyed – and who represent but a small portion of the 1,500 thirty-second video contestant submissions to MoveOn.org's "Bush in 30 Seconds" contest held in 2003 – our survey reveals the following information about motives for engaging in the competition. Their written responses revealed their motivations to include:

- We were able to make a pithy political statement in a humorous way.
- I wanted to support MoveOn, as I have been very impressed with their ability to motivate and organize the left.
- Current state of affairs, my absolute disgust of all the 'sheep' who voted for Bush and what he has done to this country.
- I felt infuriated by the activities of the Bush Administration. Also, I have experience in filmmaking so I thought I should do something.
- Ability to change people's minds about the war.
- We wanted to say what we felt about the Bush Administration in a creative way that could potentially be seen by a very large number of people.
- An urgent need to do something – anything – that might help prevent the re-election of George W. Bush
- The creative challenge of presenting a comprehensive case against him in 30 seconds.

The production of videos for online circulation reflects a different kind of creative poesis than do blogging practices, an approach to opening the world to consideration, to provoking critical consideration, and so on, with video-making demonstrating a quite distinct and different sensibility of audience and rhetorical approach from blogging. In the next section, the survey findings are discussed in relation to the project's initial research questions.

On motivations for blogging

Both the survey and interviews revealed that bloggers felt a remarkably strong commitment to dialogue and debate across partisan lines, in efforts to come to truths via processes of agonistic debate, deliberative (Habermasian) dialogue and an investment in pluralism, or diverse views made possible via blogs (Andrea Schmidt and Megan Boler, "Will new media save democracy?" February 2007, *Counterpunch*).

In describing his motivation for blogging, Sloan says, "Almost overnight it became more psychologically rewarding, [and] then emotionally rewarding," citing as reasons "the conversation around it", including reader comments, and second the process of being referred back to or "getting linked up on other blogs" (interview with author).

Motivations for digital political dissent work have strongly affective aspects as well as political or civic ones.

The motivations of people producing alternative media in the context of Web 2.0 vary widely. This section outlines a comparison and contrast of how (primarily amateur) independent bloggers and independent video makers described their motivations for creating alternative accounts of political matters in the context of post-9/11 and the landscape of traditional and corporate-owned media. What was then a newly egalitarian access to the tools of production helped create Sloan and Thompson's EPIC2014 and other self-generated political commentaries that reflected "a people's discourse, [that] certainly did give rise to people asking some interesting questions and have some interesting conversations about 'wait, what does this mean? Do we want this? This is scary, I like it', which is great, a conversation about where we're going, where society is going and what we think about it" (Sloan, interview with author). Participants noted the ways in which blogging and other individual expressions of political engagement or activism helped develop their own individual abilities to think critically, engage rhetorically or discursively and individually set their own pace of engagement with the issues/other agents engaged in these contexts. As a contributor to a prominent US military blog explains, "I like to argue because it helps form my opinion. I'm not bound to any opinion, and arguing with smart people who disagree is the best way to find holes in your own argument."

This view is highly representative of a motivation numerous bloggers described to us throughout the study: a distinct desire for serious dialogue, agonistic debate, a desire to 'hammer out' analyses and exchange views and 'facts' in order to get closest to forms of agora/debate embodied in blogospheres. One blogger writes, "the reason I have comments and I entertain comments is because I'm trying to establish whether my position's coherent". And another interviewee tells us, "I'm looking for something that probably doesn't match my political views and gives me a chance to either embrace it as making a little bit of sense – maybe embrace it completely – or maybe consider it ridiculous" (Jim Hanson, blogger).

Responses to open-ended survey questions are revealing. Blogging, notes one respondent, "allows a level of citizen participation. You have a voice as well as a vote instead of just going and pulling a lever and being an anonymous number, you actually contribute something to the debate." Another writes that motivation is linked, again, to frustration with the media's failures: "I see few, if any, Iraqi voices in the media. When I read op-eds or watch talking heads on TV, the writers and speakers are not Iraqi. The only Iraqis featured are the dead and grieving. As an Iraqi, I find that offensive. Why can't we speak for ourselves? I tried to send op-eds to mainstream papers, few were interested in my opinions. I almost feel as though I had no choice but to start a blog. I hope people read my blog and learn what an Iraqi might think about the war. It's a complicated subject. I hope I can provoke thought by offering a different perspective." Revealing the strong motivations and hopes for positive change through dialogue and debate, this quote reflects the intense (and inspiring) commitment of many bloggers: "I'm not just attempting to influence [readers] while they're online, I'm attempting to influence them for their entire lives."

Emergent and overlapping themes

In this section, the general motivations noted thus far are analysed in greater detail by examining 'co-occurrences' revealed through density and frequency coding of our 30 interviews (coding completed using the QDA software Atlas.ti). Media Bias (19-5) represented a key frustration that motivated the bloggers. According to right-of-centre blogger Pat Santy, "Sometime about the time of 9/11, I became very unhappy with the news media because I began to sense I was not getting the whole story and that there was a lot of information that was out there that somehow was being filtered very carefully and also was being presented more as opinion rather than as factual kinds of information. This disturbed me greatly, being someone who'd been reading newspapers for 20 plus years sort of compulsively."

Pat did not believe she was getting the whole story, in a fair and factual manner; her activism was significantly motivated by her frustration with the ways in which the news is filtered, and filled with an increasing amount of opinion 'filling in' for more factual information, to a greater extent than she had witnessed in her 20 years of 'compulsive' newspaper reading.

Further on, Pat describes with a subdued sense of anger that the lack of in-depth analysis is a motivation to her seeking and producing alternative media:

> Again, I had the sense, what's going on? Why aren't they tell me the details of this? I could only find the details in the reports from the soldiers, in the people who were actually physically there who were sending back stuff via their blogs and I was just totally impressed with how much more information, how much perspective and how much in-depth understanding there was out there that was not getting presented in the regular news media.

Pat could see directly, given her immersion in news, how much more information was possible from an eyewitness and on-the-ground perspective possible through the military blogging. She soon had "50 or 60 different blogs that I read regularly including the military blogs" and cancelled her subscription to the *New York Times*.

> So that was a very profound awakening for me, like I said as a news-aholic and I just started, I mean, I started with Instapundit, pretty soon I had 50 or 60 different blogs that I read regularly including the military blogs, including the government military blogs, including bloggers from the middle east and other places who were giving other kinds of analysis so that's sort of what started off for me so I stopped reading the *New York Times* entirely, in fact I cancelled my subscription because I really felt that I understood pretty much what was going on plus if I wanted anything from then, I could get it online.

Her activism in the form of blogging is closely linked with her recognition that alternative media sources provided more trustworthy and broader perspectives regarding the US invasion of Iraq, analyses required to begin understanding making sense of the war in Iraq yet consistently not provided by traditional news.

Showing the co-occurrence of Motivation_Frustration with Media (16-18) with Media Criticism_Not Doing Their Job (10-3) and additionally with Media Criticism_Corporate Control, indy video producer and director Holly Mosher tells us: "I feel like they completely failed us but of course they're corporate so unfortunately the oversight in this country is failing us because they should not have the licenses to be broadcasting what they are and calling it 'news'" (3:28, 191). Her motivation to act – based on her frustration with the media – stems from her belief that the media's job is to keep the public informed so that informed decision-making can drive a democratic process. In other words, the media's job – as the 'fourth estate' – is to function as a 'watchdog' to limit abuses of power from government and/or corporate interests.

Participants repeatedly cited "Motivation related to Frustration with Media" (16-18), with the specific frustration being their shared critique that media are "Not Doing Their Job" (10-3). As Ben Bryant describes it, his voice escalating with anger: "I mean, the media were completely not doing their job. They weren't investigating stuff, they weren't reporting stuff, they rolled over on their back like a puppy dog. I was really pissed off" (1:44, 234). Our interviews revealed that frustration with the media and criticism of the media not doing their job is also tied to frustrations with then President George W. Bush, and the criticism that Bush was able to get away with his actions because the media did not perform their job of questioning these decisions, thus failing to act in the public interest.

Media Criticism_Not Doing Their Job (10-3) is also associated with Motivation_Frustration with Bush (10-10) in the following example. As Mosher tells us, "I mean it's very easy to look up on the internet and find all the evidence that showed that he was lying yet the media for some reason wasn't telling the truth. Now they are years later and hundreds of thousands of people's deaths later and all the hatred and animosity we've created by this war that was based on lies. So watching the American news I couldn't even watch it seeing the way they were completely not doing their job" (B30HM02 – 06:00). Her frustration with Bush appears to be evenly associated with her criticism that the media was not doing its job. On her analysis, the fact that the media was remiss in their duty to the public as government 'watchdogs' cost 'hundreds of thousands of people's deaths' by not reporting the truths that were readily accessible to challenge Bush's lies.

Conclusion

As social and alternative media scholars continue to point out, individuation has always been a central component of online collectivities, recalling the ways in which social media tools (Facebook, for example) have been intrinsically linked to sexual desire, functioning as a tool of "a libidinal economy [that is] intrinsically individualistic" (Hui, 2011: para 7). This age of networks in which individual and collective digital activism and digital citizenship begin to represent both a depoliticised and a repoliticised notion of collective engagement lets us think in new ways about individual and group participation in social causes.

For Stiegler, "the laborer serves the machine-tool, and it is the latter that has become the technical individual – in the sense that it is within the machine-tool, and within the technical system to which it belongs, that an individuation is produced" (2010: 37). This individuation from (and within) 'the machine' or machine-tool echoes notions of the posthuman and the ways in which technology can continue to co-constitutively expand human potential. For the participants of RMD, this individuation is concerned with converting motivation to become active around issues of political and social concern, into learning digital dissent tools for diverse applications – some individual and some still collective.

The data analysis revealed the following emergent themes as the primary motivations for participants' web-based political and public expressions – what I term 'digital dissent'. Specifically, our findings show that those we surveyed and interviewed are motivated to produce digital dissent by shared desires to

- experience an increased sense of community
- have a public voice
- make a statement / express myself / be heard
- express anger and frustration with current events or political issues
- offer 'corrective' function to counter mainstream media.

The research study from which these findings are drawn investigated people's motivations for becoming involved in such activities, particularly in and through the use of social media.

One of the tensions that is apparent in the data from this study is the way in which seemingly contradictory opportunities made possible by digital dissent and online engagement continue to inform rather than stifle each other. Be it concerns of the individual versus the collective, of 'real' versus 'virtual' newsfeeds and social functions, or of truth versus supposed fictions, the study of individual and collective motivations for engaging interactive digital dissent offers rich futures.

Whether Web 3.0 technologies, or an extension of Web 2.0 digital dissent tools, can create and maintain communities of practice that are both constitutive but also reproductive/redistributive like their hard-copy forebears remains to be seen. However, in the short term, studies like RMD can offer some productive possibilities for better understanding truth, identity and motivation in such online digital dissent.

While alternative media has had a vibrant and robust life for decades, the radically changed access to the means of production and circulation of communication made possible by 'Web 2.0' technologies has broadened what can be considered alternative media and increased the likelihood of everyday readers' exposure to alternative media. It has also given rise to the potential of the 'individual online activist', a subject who may or may not see herself in relation to larger collectivities, either virtual or embodied.

Finally, if Foucault is right that "knowledge is made for cutting" rather than for stable understanding, both individual and collective expressions of digital dissent reflect a potent fracture in our spectacular mediascape that occasions a shift in our concepts of politics, satire and truth, one that lingers after the punchline. We can also use this to better theorise not only outmoded notions of truth but of identity. Without giving up hope on solutions, we are encouraged, with often biting irony, to complicate the discourses of the mainstream media. Such contradictions and discomforts with mainstream media allow new ruptures in constrictive social fabrics, making way for new configurations of democracy, identity and individuation in the interest of 'making sense' of the riddles of truthiness that define our increasingly mediatised landscape.

Acknowledgements

Special thanks to Dr. Anne Harris for her contribution of the discussion on individuation, and for her insights and contribution. Thanks also to Dr. Laura Pinto for her collaboration in the "Rethinking Media and Democracy" (RMD) SSHRC-funded project on the development, administration and analysis of the survey. Thanks to Rawle Agard for his work as a research assistant analysing the interview material for RMD with Atlas.ti software.

Further reading

Two edited volumes especially valuable in their analyses of journalism after September 11, 2001, include *Reporting War: Journalism in Wartime* (Allan and Zelizer (eds.), New York: Taylor and Francis, 2004) and *War and the Media* (Thussu and Freedman (eds.) London: Sage, 2010); for an overview of the role of digital media within this context, see Boler's "Introduction" to *Digital Media and Democracy* (2008). To explore the increasing sense of 'dis-information' connected to news representations of war, see the news essay by Ron Suskind, "Without a doubt," *New York Times* (17 October 2004); Wark's *Virtual Geography: Living with Global Media Events* (Bloomington: Indiana University Press, 1994); and the classic *Manufacturing Consent: The Political Economy of the Mass Media*, by Hermann and Chomsky (New York: Pantheon, 1988). On the significance of political satire and fake news, see Boler with Turpin, "*The Daily Show* and *Crossfire*: Satire and sincerity as truth to power", in Boler (2008).

References

Atton, C. (2002) *Alternative Media*. London: Sage.

Bimber, B. (2000) "The study of information technology and civic engagement." *Political Communication*, 17(4), 329–33.

Boler, M. (ed.) (2008) *Digital Media and Democracy: Tactics in Hard Times*. Cambridge, MA: MIT Press.

Boler, M., Macdonald, A., Nitsou, C. and Harris, A. (2014) "Connective labor and social media: Women's roles in the 'leaderless' Occupy movement." *Convergence: The International Journal of Research into New Media Technologies*, 20(4), 438–60.

Boler, M. and Nitsou, C. (2014) "Women activists within the leaderless Occupy Wall Street: Consciousness-raising and connective action in hybrid social movements." In M. McCaughey (ed.), *Cyberactivism on the Participatory Web* (2nd ed.). New York: Routledge.

Bruns, A. (2005) *Gatewatching: Collaborative Online New Production*. New York: Peter Lang.

Crogan, P. (2010) "Knowledge, care and trans-individuation: An interview with Bernard Stiegler." *Cultural Politics*, 6(2), 157–70.

Duncombe, S. (1997) *Notes from Underground: Zines and the Politics of Alternative Culture.* London: Verso.

Ekdale, B., Namkoong, K., Fung, T. K. and Perlmutter, D. D. (2010) "Why blog? (then and now): Exploring the motivations for blogging by popular American political bloggers." *New Media and Society*, 12(2), 217–34.

Fenton, N. and Barassi, V. (2011) "Alternative media and social networking sites: The politics of individuation and political participation." *Communication Review*, 14(3), 179–96.

Hartley, J., Burgess, J. and Bruns, A. (eds) (2013). *A Companion to New Media Dynamics.* Hoboken, NJ: John Wiley & Sons.

Hui, Y. (2011) "Collective individuation: A new theoretical foundation for social networks." *CCCBlab Research and Innovation in the Cultural Sphere.* Retrieved from http://blogs.cccb.org/lab/en/article_la-individuacio-col·lectiva-una-nova-base-teorica-per-a-les-xarxes-socials/ (accessed 15 October 2014).

Ratto, M. and Boler, M. (eds.) (2014) *DIY Citizenship: Critical Making and Social Media.* Cambridge, MA: MIT Press.

Schmidt, A. and Boler, M. (2007) "Will new media save democracy?" *Counterpunch*, February. Retrieved from http://www.commondreams.org/views07/0222- 29.htm (accessed 15 October 2014).

Sloan, R. and Thompson, M. (2004) *EPIC2014.* Retrieved from http://epic.makingithappen.co.uk (accessed 15 October 2014).

Stiegler, B. (2010) *For a New Critique of Political Economy.* London: Polity Press.

——(2013) "The most precious good in the era of social technologies." *Unlike Us Reader: Social Media Monopolies and Their Alternatives*, 16–30. Retrieved from http://networkcultures.org/wpmu/portal/publication/unlike-us-reader-social-media-monopolies-and-their-alternatives/ (accessed 15 October 2014).

48

HACKTIVISM AS A RADICAL MEDIA PRACTICE

Stefania Milan

Introduction

When in September 1995 President Jacques Chirac announced that France would run a series of nuclear tests in the Polynesian atoll of Mururoa, a group of Italian artists decided to exploit the technical properties of the nascent internet to make a political statement. The call for action invited activists to join "a demonstration of 1,000, 10,000, 100,000 netusers all together making part of a line crossing French Government's sites. The result of this strike will be to stop for an hour the network activities of the French Government" (Tozzi, n.d.). On 21 December, ten websites, including that of the Nuclear Energy Agency, were attacked simultaneously by thousands of users who continuously reloaded the pages, making them temporarily unavailable. It was the first 'netstrike', or network strike, a type of distributed denial of service (DDoS) attack. According to its promoters, a netstrike is "the networked version of a peaceful sit-in. The metaphor that best represents it is that of a number of people that walk on pedestrian crossings with signs and banners, if their number is really big they can stop traffic for a noticeable period of time" (Tozzi, n.d.). A decade later, a decentralised network going under the mass noun of Anonymous launched a disruption campaign on the web in defence of freedom of expression online. These "digital Robin Hoods" (Carter, 2012) engaged in several DDoS attacks against institutional and business websites, including Amazon and Mastercard. The Mururoa netstrike and Anonymous's web disruptions are instances of hacktivism.

Hacktivism indicates collective action in cyberspace that addresses network infrastructure or exploits the infrastructure's technical and ontological features for political or social change. Activists engage in politically motivated use of technical expertise in view of fixing society through software and online action. In short, it is "activism gone electronic" (Jordan and Taylor, 2004: 1). The Texas-based computer underground group known as Cult of the Dead Cow (currently Hacktivismo) claims to have coined the term, a portmanteau of 'hacking' and 'activism', in 1998 (Delio, 2004). Hacktivists emerge from within the so-called civil society, that is to say the relatively autonomous realm of human action outside the remit of the state and the market. However, hacktivism disputes some of our fundamental interpretations of said civil society, more often than not associated with nongovernmental organisations (NGOs). It challenges the increasing professionalisation of transnational activist networks by routinely involving non-professional activists, and points to the disembodiment of contemporary activism by decoupling resistance and physical presence (Wong and Brown, 2013).

Following Couldry, who called for a sociological approach in addressing media as practice, this chapter explores hacktivism focusing on "the open set of practices relating to, or oriented around" technology (Couldry, 2004: 117). In particular, hacktivism positions itself in the long tradition of radical media practices, as defined by Downing (2001). Similarly to radical media practitioners, hacktivists "express an alternative vision to hegemonic politics, priorities, and perspectives"; their tactics "break somebody's rules, although rarely all of them in every aspect" (v–ix). The emergence of hacktivism signals the need to think of liberation as an everyday process that disrupts immediate realities (Downing, 1984). This disruption of the present takes place at two levels: at the level of political participation, and at the level of political contention. In fact, hacktivists see cyberspace as both an arena for civic engagement, and an object of contention in its own right. As an arena for civic engagement and a platform for collective action where alternative views about society are articulated and shared, cyberspace allows activists to practice digital citizenry, to organise and to engage in cyber-specific forms of collective action. As an object of contention, cyberspace is to be defended from tightening state control, restrictive legislation and aggressive commercialisation.

Hacktivism is a highly contested concept, used to label diverse tactics and ethical codes not always compatible with each other. For instance, while Anonymous may not hesitate to deface websites or launch DDoS, other groups may consider these tactics a form of censorship and a breach of freedom of speech, as such counter to the very aims of hacktivism. With this contention in mind, this chapter explores the main features of hacktivism as a radical media practice, looking at the shared history and core values of activists. As we shall see, it adopts an inclusive definition of hacktivism that involves both disruptive and self-organisation tactics. It takes a sociological perspective and asks "what people are doing and how they categorise what they are doing" (Couldry, 2004: 125). It is based on in-depth interviews with radical internet activists collected over the period 2005–12, which gained the author access to "the categorisations of practice that people make themselves" (ibid.: 122). The chapter is structured as follows: first, it offers a historical overview on hacktivism as a radical media practice, illustrating how its understandings and actions have evolved since its inception; second, it offers a sociological analysis of hacktivist organisational patterns; third, it explores hacktivists' tactics and their approach to institutions and social norms. In the conclusion, it delves into the challenges that hacktivism faces in the present and near future, touching upon issues of repression, accountability and impact.

The rise of hacktivism as a political subject

We can identify three main phases in the brief history of hacktivism as a political subject. They follow the gradual recognition of the potential of cyberspace as an arena for collective action, and reflect the increasingly lower cost and availability of internet access and skills. In the pre-internet phase, resourced NGOs joined forces to create their own networking infrastructure. The second phase, which corresponds approximately to the diffusion of the internet in the 1990s, saw the idea of cyberspace as a political arena spreading also to grassroots groups. In the third phase, in the early 2000s, hacktivism became the playground of individual activists too, partially thanks to the increasing readiness of hacktivism tactics.

The first instances of activists appropriating digital technologies for civic engagement date back to the 1980s. Before the diffusion of the internet, the Bulletin Board System (BBS) allowed users to exchange messages and files by means of a common landline. In 1984 a coalition of human rights, development and women's NGOs from four continents signed the Velletri Agreement, committing to use telephone lines to network their computers (Murphy, 2005). With funding from the Canadian International Development Research Centre, they developed their own network, named Interdoc and open to civil society organisations. Several other networks followed between 1985 and 1990, providing progressive activists with cheap systems for sharing text-based information: among them were Fidonet, which relied on BBS technology; the London-based GreenNet, oriented towards the "progressive community working for peace, the environment, gender equality and social justice"; PeaceNet and EcoNet in the US, which later merged into the Institute for Global Communications; and the European Counter Network, based in Italy and connected to the most radical fringes of European social movements. Some still operate today. In 1988 PeaceNet and GreenNet teamed up to establish the first NGO-owned transatlantic cable, implementing "the Internet vision of global communications unfettered by commercial barriers" (Murphy, 2000). In 1990 they joined forces in the Association for Progressive Communications (APC), to ensure that "all people have easy and affordable access to a free and open internet to improve their lives and create a more just world" (Association for Progressive Communications, n.d.).

The second phase of hacktivism follows the spread of the internet in the mid-1990s, which facilitated the emergence of a new type of grassroots activism which had direct action in cyberspace at its core. As an activist put it, "finally technology and politics were talking the same language, and the links between the physical and electronic spaces were becoming real" (Milan, 2010: 89). Hacktivism *stricto sensu* appeared to the scene, exploiting for protest purposes the low cost, speed and flexibility of network-mediated communication. In 1994, the US tactical media collective Critical Art Ensemble (CAE) was the first to theorise electronic civil disobedience "as another option for digital resistance … that would produce multiple currents and trajectories to slow the velocity of capitalist political economy" (Critical Arts Ensemble, 2001: 13–14). In their view, electronic civil disobedience was the most meaningful form of political resistance in times of nomadic and decentralised power. Rather than a mass movement, CAE activists saw electronic disturbance as a cell-based hit-and-run media intervention taking advantage of the decentralisation typical of the information society (Critical Arts Ensemble, 1996). In 1995, the first netstrike targeted the websites of the French government, in retaliation for its nuclear experiments in Polynesia. The following year, the Italian activists credited with having invented the netstrike published a 145-page book designed to spread the tactic. The first chapter, entitled "Net strike starter", included a detailed explanation of how to organise a netstrike, with theoretical premises and practical hints (Strano Network and Tozzi, 1996). Many netstrikes followed across the world, including in Saudi Arabia and South Korea, targeting government websites and protesting, among other things, the war in Yugoslavia and the death penalty. Other hit-and-run media interventions emerged, such as tactical media projects, "media of crisis, criticism and opposition" by "groups and individuals who feel aggrieved by, or excluded from, the wider culture" (Garcia and Lovink, 1997).

In 1994, the Zapatista uprising, an indigenous rights movement, exploited the networking capabilities of the internet to speak for itself, bypassing mainstream media. What was barely a local struggle in the remote state of Chiapas, Mexico, turned into the first global "information guerrilla movement", which gained the support of many transnational networks (Martinez-Torres, 2001). In 1996 the Zapatistas called out for activists around the world to team up to "make a network of communication among all our struggles and resistances" (Hamm, 2005). Inspired by the Zapatistas' call for action, Western activists realised that "grass-roots 'social movements' needed new networks of communication ... but also that the way these networks were created, run and developed, mirrored, as much as possible, the direct, participatory, collective and autonomous nature of the emerging social movement(s) themselves" (Milan, 2010: 88–89). In 1999, activists protesting against the World Trade Organization summit in Seattle, Washington, gave life to the first Independent Media Center, or Indymedia. For the first time in internet history, thanks to an open-source software developed by activists in Sydney, Australia, users could publish content online without editorial filter, prior registration or webmaster skills. Three years after its foundation, Indymedia counted already 89 nodes across six continents (Kidd, 2003).

Do-it-yourself radical communication projects became increasingly popular: they put self-organisation, freedom of speech and grassroots media production at the centre of social change. Networking infrastructure, too, became an object of contention, as activists progressively realised the importance of controlling their own channels of communication. Radical tech activists engaged in the creation of autonomous networking infrastructure independent from the state and the market, recognising the role of the internet as a tool for individual and collective empowerment. With internet connections in households still a rarity, activists offered public access points, often in occupied buildings. When internet became mainstream, they started operating exclusively as noncommercial internet service providers (ISPs), offering at no cost privacy-aware email accounts, mailing lists and web hosting. Popular self-organised servers include Autistici/Inventati in Italy, Riseup and Mayfirst/People's Link in the United States, SO36 and Nadir in Germany and Plentyfact in the UK. They provide the digital backbone for activists to network, communicate and protest: Riseup alone hosts some 50,000 email accounts, and over one million people subscribe to the mailing lists hosted on its servers. In Europe, alternative ISPs emerged in the milieu of the squatted social centres, and maintain strong linkages to the more radical and antagonist scene. Their mission goes well beyond self-organisation in the communication sphere: for example, Riseup's purpose is "to aid in the creation of a free society, a world with freedom from want and freedom of expression, a world without oppression or hierarchy, where power is shared equally" (Riseup, n.d.).

The third phase in the evolution of hacktivism corresponds to the popularisation of hacktivism practices by individuals aligned to Anonymous, whose nuisance campaigns started in 2003 and made the news for the first time in 2008. Anonymous originated in online chat rooms focused on politically incorrect pranks. Later, it mutated into a politically engaged group, maintaining, however, an orientation to the 'lulz', a neologism indicating the fun associated with pranks (Gorenstein Massa, 2010; Coleman, 2013a). Activists mobilise against companies, governments and individuals in retaliation for behaviours that threaten the uncensored internet. Earlier actions included online mobilisation and nuisance campaigns against the Church of Scientology, accused of censoring its members' opinions; the International Federation of the Phonographic Industry for its pro-copyright battles; and child pornography sites. Anonymous mobilised also in support of WikiLeaks, by attacking the websites of companies and security agencies guilty of taking action against the whistle-blower website (Milan, 2013a). Similarly, the now defunct LulzSec, whose motto was "Laughing at your security since 2011", has exposed security concerns with spectacular hacks, attacking companies of the calibre of Sony Pictures and News Corporation.

Thanks to Anonymous and LulzSec, hacktivism is no longer a marginal struggle by a bunch of geeks: what were back in the 1990s sporadic cell-based interventions are now tactics practiced on a regular basis by transnational decentralised networks of individuals seeking to intervene regularly into real-world struggles. While the diffusion of hacktivist exploits is also a consequence of the sheer number of people with access to technology and technical expertise, it was Anonymous who gave hacktivism popularity, encouraging young people who do not care about the consequences to join. However, Anonymous-like disruptive actions co-exist with self-organization efforts. Radical internet activists continue to defend, seek and expand spaces of autonomy in cyberspace, for example by creating encryption tools and alternatives to corporate social networking services in view of protecting user privacy and online dissent. Among the newest projects are Tor, an 'onion routing' encryption system designed to protect users' anonymity in online interactions, and Crabgrass, a Riseup spin-off that offers an open-source social networking platform for activists where users are in control of their data.

Structurelessness and dictatorship of action: Organisational norms and forms

Hacktivist groups include for the most part techno-savvy activists. However, technical expertise is progressively losing relevance, as software makes it easier to engage in disruptive exploits. Organisation norms and forms are strictly interconnected: the ways people organise tend to mirror the values they stand for, such as grassroots autonomy, antagonism and participation. In turn, these principles mirror the features of the technology that is at the core of the mobilisation: the decentralisation of the internet inspires the hacktivist preference for distributed forms of organisation, while internet neutrality, according to which "all bits are created equal", partially explains the activists' inclination towards a participatory approach to decision-making. Grassroots autonomy refers both to the autonomy of the group from the context in which it is embedded (that is to say, actions and decisions are supposedly independent from social norms and even existing legislation), and to the autonomy of the individual within the group. Antagonism indicates an anti-establishment ethos and a political radicalism that translates as a principled scepticism towards power holders and structures. In this respect, hacktivists are subcultural and contentious at the same time: the challenge to authority is a building block of their identity and a recurrent feature in the normative order of groups. Finally, participation entails openness to anybody who is willing to get involved, although it is kept in check by the fact that members tend to share a certain social and political proximity as a prerequisite to action. These principles translate into practice in organisational forms that are also an "ethical statement" *per se* (Jordan, 2002: 74).

Organisational patterns vary in the degree of formalisation and openness, but groups usually share a number of features. First, they are likely to be informal groups of equals, and reject hierarchies in both organisation and representation mechanisms (e.g., spokespersons). They resemble a "community without structure" (Leach, 2009: 1059), characterised by decentralisation and horizontality. Nonetheless, there are mechanisms in place that ensure that some structure is preserved, such the consensus-based division of tasks to ensure the project sustainability. Second, recruitment mechanisms and the focus on action assimilate hacktivist groupings to affinity groups, that is to say small temporary clusters of individuals who gather around a given objective, usually a disruptive action (McDonald, 2002). Like affinity groups, hacktivist groupings are fairly small, and regulated by trust and loyalty. Members share the same values prior to action; new members are recruited over time according to the same affinity principle. Third, hacktivist groupings operate through a division of labour system rooted in individual skills and reputation, which assumes a high degree of personal motivation but flexible individual contributions. Reputation, in particular, regulates interaction within the group of peers and is a critical driving force for engagement. Finally, hacktivist groups are deliberately kept 'invisible' through the use of collective nouns and anonymity in online interactions (e.g. nicknames, encryption). What is visible is the action, which identifies the group and has a performative and expressive function.

Typically, groups implement a participatory decision-making method rooted in consensus, and based on countless virtual meetings to discuss actions and strategies. However, by admission of the same activists, distortions of these non-hierarchical patterns do exist, and translate into actions being occasionally undertaken by individuals without consulting their fellow members. An activist called it "the dictatorship of action", by which "those who decide to organize something, are in charge of their own project and get support of the others of the group" (Milan, 2013b: 94). This mechanism is similar to the so-called "tyranny of structurelessness" (Freeman, 1972): the high consideration for the leaderless nature of the organisation makes it difficult for activists to counterbalance informal and unacknowledged leadership, which is dangerous precisely because it is denied. Hacktivists, however, justify these distortions on the ground that it is essential for the group to 'get things done'. They operate on the basis of a sort of inferred consensus derived from the fact that activists tend to share a set of tacit values as a precondition for joint action.

Hacktivist organisational forms and decision-making patterns identify a tension between collectivism and individualism, which we see at work also in other currents of contemporary social movements (see, for example, McDonald, 2006; Milan, 2013a).

Whereas generally activism is a collective process, hacktivism is experienced through actions like coding and hacking, which remain essentially individual, although they gain meaning in the interaction with peers. This is why we can speak of an "experience movement", which cannot be explained in terms of the relation of the individual to the collective, but where the individual practice takes central stage. Rather than being characterised by "the power to represent", experience movements involve "grammars of embodiment" rooted on the individual (McDonald, 2006: 37).

Beyond laws and social norms: Hacktivism tactics

Tactics adopted by hacktivists range from disruptive protest and direct action to forms of resistance and self-organisation. Protest, in particular, provides a "moral voice", giving activists "an opportunity to articulate, elaborate, alter, or affirm one's moral sensibilities, principles, and allegiances" (Jasper, 1997: 15). Tactics embody a strong contestation ethos, are intentional and rooted in a group's values, but most importantly, they are a reaction to the socio-political context in which activists are embedded. In other words, activists react to and interact with social norms and institutions of a given social system. Many hacktivist actions, such as netstrikes, DDoS attacks and website defacements, fall under the rubric of 'outsider' tactics. Outsider tactics allow activists to apply pressure on institutions and businesses by organising rallies and direct action. They are typical of activists who lack access to institutions and cannot advance their demands from within the system, or who refuse to interact with institutions because they do not consider them to be legitimate political actors (see also Tarrow, 2005).

On the contrary, self-organisation and forms of resistance such as those implemented by encryption developers and alternative ISPs, are examples of tactics that go 'beyond' institutions and social norms. Like those hacktivists who do not accept institutions as legitimate power-holders, hacktivists who engage in beyond tactics reject institutions altogether, thus positioning themselves outside the reform axis (cf. Day, 2005). In addition, they also refuse to stay within the known social system and respect its rules, be it social norms or existing legislation. At the same time, they seek to build a different social order by creating alternative prefigurative realities that attempt to achieve here and now the principles activists stand for. These prefigurative realities take the shape of alternative technology, infrastructure and sets of values. Examples include alternative ISPs and open-source software. As an activist put it, "the political goal is to create counter-power, not to oppose [power] … like in the Indymedia slogan: 'don't hate the media, become the media'" (Milan, 2013b: 127). The main objective is to "by-pass the mainstream by creating living alternatives to it. I don't think we need to focus in 'asking' or 'having a voice'. I think we have 'to do', 'keep doing' and keep building working structures and alternatives … that work regardless of 'their' regulation[s]" (ibid.: 130).

Prefigurative realities "provide staging posts along the way, moments of transformation, however small" (Downing, 2001: 72). They point to the fact that the vision of a fairer society cannot be detached from the process of its making. We can position hacktivist prefigurative political projects in a continuum ranging from concrete and down-to-earth to abstract and utopian. But these projects do not represent the simple withdrawal of activists into a parallel world, insofar as they seek to send an emancipatory revolutionary message to society. Although they are mostly local projects, their aims are much broader in scope: by creating these parallel realities, hacktivists send a signal to contemporary societies and show a possible way out of the current order. It was precisely the recognition of this revolutionary message that prompted Coleman (2013b) to claim that geeks are "the new guardians of our civil liberties".

Whereas hacktivists prefer not to interact with institutions and policy arenas, they do react when laws, regulations or police repression jeopardise their activities and values. Threats act as moral shocks and are able to foster collective action. The hacktivist tactical repertoire then includes avoiding control, creating technical bypasses to evade legislation, hacking norms and conventions and all those "obscure technically savvy ways of circumventing limitations" (Milan, 2013b: 132). It is the "engineering philosophy to 'make things work'" that encounters an "insistence on adopting a technocratic approach to solving societal problems and to bypassing ('hacking') legislative approaches" (Berry, 2008: 102). To say it with an activist, the "main tactic is just avoid all the laws, sneak a way around it" (Milan, 2013b: 132). Hacktivists, for example, bypass data retention regulations by creating cryptographic means of 'hiding' the metadata of electronic communications, or by relocating their servers in countries in which certain regulations do not apply. Further, activists 'hack' norms by envisioning different working rules and implementing them 'by design' in their daily practices and in the software they design. They may also try to change the definition and perception of social practices in view of legitimising them, thus engaging in longer-term norm change strategies.

Conclusion

Hacktivists nowadays face three main challenges: the growing repression of people and actions, the accountability of tactics towards the broader society activists claim to serve and the impact of projects and strategies. Hacktivism is undoubtedly increasingly common. As its popularity grows, so do surveillance and repression of its activities. Whereas earlier generations of activists preferred to remain under the radar in order to protect their projects from law enforcement, Anonymous have included 'making the news' in their tactical repertoire. This strategy came at the price of several imprisonments, and in the long term might have a negative impact on recruitment and the sustainability of projects and campaigns.

As a relatively specialised form of activism, hacktivism lacks widespread support, partially due to the discrepancy between its radical content and form, and a not-so-radical community of internet users. Observers have criticised the lack of transparency of hacktivists groups and projects, and their poor accountability to the people they claim to protect and serve. In addition, hacktivism tactics might occasionally become coercive insofar as activists "assert their moral claims, irrespective of the legality of their protest, by using their bodies to occupy a space" (Doherty, Plows and Wall, 2003: 670). Are these radical media practices without a radical movement? The poor accountability might seem intrinsic to nonprofit dissident practices, as the price to pay for their independence. However, although hacktivists score high in terms of "grassrootedness" (van Rooy, 2004) and do not claim to speak for a third party but for themselves, they should cultivate the relation with their audiences as part of their strategy.

Finally, one might question the impact of hacktivism practices on the wider society. Hacktivists in fact often "create little islands of prefigurative politics with no empirical attention to how these might ever be expanded into the rest of society" (Downing, 2001: 72). However, their projects and actions represent an example to society. As an activist explained, radical media practices "can be very utopian, very experimental. They don't have the pressure to present an outcome at the end … As such, they might have the function of some utopian 'guiding star', the star that provides a fix[ed] point of navigation for sailors, who use it for orientation without attempting to reach it" (Hintz, 2010: 252).

Further reading

Jordan and Taylor (2004) is the first systematic book on hacktivism as a political subject and offers a vivid, even if now slightly outdated, account of hacktivism practices. Milan (2013b) provides an exhaustive sociological analysis of radical internet activism. In particular, chapter 2 places internet activism in relation to other past and present mobilisations, and chapter 3 illustrates cultural and ideological references as well as identity building in technology activism. TVO's broadcast *Attack of the Hacktivists* (*The Agenda with Steve Paikin*, 25 October 2011; see http://theagenda.tvo.org/episode/ 124944/hacktivism-and-the-trouble-with-rim) explores Anonymous from multiple perspectives. *Hacker, Hoaxer, Whistleblower, Spy: The Many Faces of Anonymous* (London: Verso, 2014) by anthropologist Gabriella Coleman brings readers inside the hacktivist subculture, drawing from extensive interviews with key actors. *The Coming Swarm: DDOS Actions, Hacktivism, and Civil Disobedience on the Internet* by Molly Sauter (London: Bloomsbury, 2014) investigates the history, theory and practice of DDoS attacks as a tactic of political activism.

References

Association for Progressive Communications (n.d.) *The APC Vision*. Retrieved from http:// www.apc.org/en/about (accessed 18 January 2015).
Berry, D. M. (2008) *Copy, Rip, Burn: The Politics of Copyleft and Open Source*. London: Pluto Press.
Carter, A. (2012) *From Anonymous to Shuttered Websites, the Evolution of Online Protest*. Retrieved from http://www.cbc.ca/news/canada/story/2012/03/15/f-online-protest.html (accessed 18 January 2015).
Coleman, G. (2013a) "Anonymous and the politics of leaking." In B. Brevini, A. Hintz and P. McCurdy (eds), *Beyond WikiLeaks: Implications for the Future of Communications, Journalism and Society*. Basingstoke: Palgrave Macmillan (pp. 209–28).

——(2013b) "Geeks are the new guardians of our civil liberties." *MIT Technology Review.* Retrieved from http://www.technologyreview.com/news/510641/geeks-are-the-new-guardians-of-our-civil-liberties (accessed 18 January 2015).

Couldry, N. (2004) "Theorising media as practice." *Social Semiotics*, 14, 115–32.

Critical Arts Ensemble (1996) *Electronic Civil Disobedience.* New York: Autonomedia.

——(2001) *Digital Resistance: Explorations in Tactical Media.* New York: Autonomedia.

Day, R. J. F. (2005) *Gramsci Is Dead: Anarchist Currents in the Newest Social Movements.* London: Pluto Press.

Delio, M. (2004) "Hacktivism and how it got here." *Wired.* Retrieved from http://archive.wired.com/techbiz/it/news/2004/07/64193 (accessed 18 January 2015).

Doherty, B., Plows, A. and Wall, D. (2003). "The preferred way of doing things: The British Direct Action Movement." *Parliamentary Affairs*, 56, 669–86.

Downing, J. D. H. (1984) *Radical Media: The Political Experience of Alternative Communication.* Boston: South End Press.

——(with others) (2001) *Radical Media: Rebellious Communication and Social Movements.* Thousand Oaks, CA: Sage.

Freeman, J. (1972) "The tyranny of structurelessness." *Berkeley Journal of Sociology*, 17, 151–65.

Garcia, D. and Lovink, G. (1997) *The ABC of Tactical Media.* Retrieved from http://project.waag.org/tmn/frabc.html (accessed 18 January 2015).

Gorenstein Massa, F. (2010) *Out of Bounds: The Anonymous Online Community's Transition to Collective Action.* Unpublished manuscript, Boston College.

Hamm, M. (2005) *Indymedia – Concatenations of Physical and Virtual Spaces.* Retrieved from http://republicart.net/disc/publicum/hamm04_en.htm (accessed 18 January 2015).

Hintz, A. (2010) *Civil Society Media and Global Governance: Intervening into the World Summit on the Information Society.* Berlin: LIT Verlag.

Jasper, J. (1997) *The Art of Moral Protest: Culture, Biography, and Creativity in Social Movements.* Chicago: University of Chicago Press.

Jordan, T. (2002) *Activism! Direct Action, Hacktivism and the Future of Society.* London: Reaktion Books.

Jordan, T. and Taylor, P. A. (2004) *Hacktivism and Cyberwars: Rebels with a Cause?* London: Routledge.

Kidd, D. (2003) *The Independent Media Center: A New Model. Media Development*, IV. Retrieved from https://docs.indymedia.org/pub/Global/PDFsOfIndymediaGuide/brochure pages.pdf (accessed 18 January 2015).

Leach, D. K. (2009) "An elusive 'we': Anti-dogmatism, democratic practice, and the contradictory identity of the German Autonomen." *American Behavioural Scientist*, 52, 1042–68.

Martinez-Torres, M. E. (2001) "Civil society, the internet, and the Zapatistas." *Peace Review*, 13, 347–55.

McDonald, K. (2002) "From solidarity to fluidarity: Social movements beyond 'collective identity' – The case of globalization conflicts." *Social Movement Studies*, 1, 109–28.

——(2006) *Global Movements: Action and Culture.* Malden, MA, and Oxford: Blackwell.

Milan, S. (2010) "The way is the goal: Interview with Maqui, Indymedia London/IMC-UK Network Activist." *International Journal of E-Politics*, 1, 88–91.

——(2013a) "WikiLeaks, Anonymous, and the exercise of individuality: Protesting in the cloud." In B. Brevini, A. Hintz and P. McCurdy (eds), *Beyond WikiLeaks: Implications for the Future of Communications, Journalism and Society.* Basingstoke, UK: Palgrave Macmillan (pp. 191–208).

——2013b. *Social Movements and Their Technologies: Wiring Social Change.* Basingstoke: Palgrave Macmillan.

Murphy, B. (2000) *The Founding of APC: Coincidences and Logical Steps in Global Civil Society Networking*. Annual Report 2000. Melville, South Africa: Association for Progressive Communications.

——(2005) "Interdoc: The first international non-governmental computer network." *First Monday* 10(5). Retrieved from http://firstmonday.org/ojs/index.php/fm/article/view/1239/1159 (accessed 18 January 2015).

Riseup (n.d.) *About us*. Retrieved from https://help.riseup.net/about-us (accessed 18 January 2015).

Strano Network and Tozzi, T. (1996) *Net strike, no copyright, etc.* Bertiolo: AAA Edizioni.

Tarrow, S. (2005) *The New Transnational Activism*. New York: Cambridge University Press.

Tozzi, T. (n.d.) Netstrike (1995). tommasotozzi.it, http://www.tommasotozzi.it/index.php?title=Netstrike_%281995%29 (accessed 18 January 2015).

van Rooy, A. (2004) *The Global Legitimacy Game: Civil Society, Globalization, and Protest*. New York: Palgrave Macmillan.

Wong, W. H. and Brown, P. A. (2013) "E-bandits in global activism: WikiLeaks, Anonymous, and the politics of no one." *Perspectives on Politics*, 11, 1015–1033.

49
'LOOK @ THIS FUKKEN DOGE'
Internet memes and remix cultures

Victoria Esteves and Graham Meikle

On 26 February 2014, the US government's Department of Health and Human Services posted a new public information campaign message to their Facebook page and Twitter feed. Intended to encourage people to sign up for health insurance, it showed a photo of a Japanese Shiba Inu dog romping in the snow, surrounded by text fragments in a brightly coloured Comic Sans font: *So health insurance. Very benefits. Wow. Many coverage. Much affordable. Such HealthCare.gov*. This particular breed of dog, this particular font and colour scheme, and this particular grammar – *very noun, much adjective, wow* – are the elements of the *doge* internet meme, in which pictures of an identified individual dog are remixed into a more and more elaborate repertoire of references to be shared across social media networks. The use of what was at the time a relatively new internet meme in a government health campaign illustrates how quickly and how widely such practices now circulate. In this case, what began as an in-joke for users of 4Chan, Tumblr and Reddit spread to political campaigning, commercial advertising and a functioning doge-based currency in a matter of months.

This chapter examines such internet memes as forms of text and practice that are native to the social media environment, illustrating that environment's fundamental aesthetic and production logics of remix. Social media are networked platforms that combine public with personal communication. They grow by having their users contribute content, thus building the database that those platforms can exploit for advertising and marketing. Social media are those that allow any user, in principle, to say and make things; to share the things that they or others have said and made; and to make that saying, making and sharing visible to others in contexts where it is often far from clear who is watching or why. The personal relationships and experiences of the individual user take on a public quality, while more familiar forms of media content become the focus of personal communication that is visible to others. So social media can be understood by analysing their uses and affordances in terms of *creativity*, *sharing* and *visibility*.

Internet memes circulate so widely through the social media environment not because they possess some intrinsic infective capacity that people are powerless to resist, but because many different individuals in many different contexts find them meaningful and choose to make them, to share them with others, and in doing so to make both their memes and themselves visible. Users of social media now share ideas, information, meanings – and noise – through networks of mediated sociality. From this perspective, social media communication is an unfinished process of circulation and connection, of relationships and associations, with each link, *like* and share opening up different kinds of connectivity, different possibilities for meaning and different trajectories for further circulation. Each connection both establishes new relations between individuals and makes visible previously invisible connections. Internet memes are forms of easily remixed texts and images that are intrinsic to this social media environment.

This chapter first defines *internet meme*, before returning to the extended example of the *doge* case and setting these twenty-first-century practices in the context of prehistories of the arts, computing and consumer electronics of the twentieth century. Internet memes, while often frivolous and trivial, are also an important index of the ways in which ideas, texts and images are adopted, adapted and shared through social media networks and beyond. And in this they illustrate how once-alternative creative strategies, from collage and *détournement* to sampling and zines, have become the basic mechanics of everyday social media interactions.

What's a meme?

It's important to distinguish between the original sense of the word 'meme', and the more useful contemporary application of the term to particular internet phenomena. The original word 'meme' was coined by zoologist Richard Dawkins in 1976. In his book *The Selfish Gene*, Dawkins proposed meme as "a noun which conveys the idea of a unit of cultural transmission, or a unit of *imitation*" (1976: 206, original emphasis). He offered as examples the following list: "tunes, ideas, catch-phrases, clothes fashions, ways of making pots or of building arches" (ibid.) and suggested that

> Just as genes propagate themselves in the gene pool by leaping from body to body via sperms or eggs, so memes propagate themselves in the meme pool by leaping from brain to brain via a process which, in the broad sense, can be called imitation.
>
> (Ibid.)

As with genes, the chances of survival in a competitive environment depend upon "longevity, fecundity, and copying-fidelity" (ibid.: 208). Psychologist Susan Blackmore developed Dawkins's idea further in *The Meme Machine* (1999), in which she insisted on imitation as the key element, arguing that "a meme is whatever it is that is passed on by imitation" (ibid.: 43). As Blackmore's use of 'whatever' suggests, there are substantial difficulties in deciding what is to count as a meme; and indeed, as communication scholars rather than zoologists, we might wonder why Dawkins saw this as a word that needed to be invented in the first place. One clue is offered on the very first page of *The Selfish Gene*, where he makes a swipe at the humanities, observing that "Philosophy and the subjects known as 'humanities' are still taught almost as if Darwin had never lived" (Dawkins, 1976: 1). So his original purpose may have been to stake a claim for the natural sciences on the terrain of culture; as Andrew Ross observes, "ideas that draw upon the authority of nature nearly always have their origin in ideas about society" (1994: 15). But rather than adding anything new or useful to our understanding of communication, Dawkins's word most often works as an unacknowledged synonym of a perfectly good word that already existed and that still works just fine. That word is 'idea'.

Consider, for example, this passage from Douglas Rushkoff's 1994 book *Media Virus*, which made enthusiastic use of the word 'meme' in exploring its territory of cable TV and nascent online culture:

> Each meme, especially a new or "mutant" meme, must find a carrier – a viral shell – capable of delivering it to ready individuals, even if they are in the minority. The mass media is understandably unwilling to provide passage for memes that will be unpopular with their audiences. They are in business.
> (Rushkoff, 1994: 196)

Replace each use of 'meme' in that passage with the word 'idea', and Rushkoff's point is not only unchanged but also much clearer. His use of the words 'viral shell' also points to the problematic biological equivalence that Dawkins established from the beginning between genes and memes. Human ideas are not viruses, and they do not "propagate themselves ... by leaping from brain to brain". Rather, they circulate through being both adopted and adapted by people. The distinction between so-called 'viral' content, which becomes very popular very quickly, and internet memes, which are not only adopted but adapted and remixed, is, then, an important one (Shifman, 2012; Marwick, 2013).

Later in the 1990s, Canadian culture jammers Adbusters emphasised the word 'meme' in a new sense, one which can now be seen as the emergence of the distinctly different sense of 'internet meme'. On the one hand, they made heavy use of Dawkins's sense of 'meme' in a similar uncritical way to Rushkoff – so Adbusters's founder Kalle Lasn, for example, wrote of how something called 'meme warfare' had become "the geopolitical battle of our information age" (Lasn, 1999: 123), and of the need to identify 'macromemes' and 'metamemes', without which, he wrote, "a sustainable future is unthinkable" (ibid.: 124). But on the other hand, Adbusters, which would later play a role in precipitating the Occupy Wall Street events of 2011 (Castells, 2012), were also a key group in promoting the idea of culture jamming, through which activists were encouraged to rework and remix images in order to highlight the political assumptions through which they worked (Dery, 1993). Culture jamming is to take a familiar sign and to reshape it as a question mark. It can be understood as jamming in the sense of getting in the way, and as jamming in the sense of collaborative improvisation (Meikle, 2007). It's a practice with a pre-web history, but which found a natural home online in a symbolic environment in which any image could be copied, edited and pasted into a new context, so calling into question both that original image and that new context. And this practice offers a bridge from

Dawkins's coinage to the contemporary sense of 'internet meme', as something that users *do* – an active engagement with digital texts and images, a critical understanding of their rules and grammar, the sharing and circulation of remixed ideas and a sense that meanings are to be made, not just taken.

It is in this sense that an internet meme is a shared representation of online interaction. The rules and structures of each instantly recognisable meme are a representation of the communication practices and the particular online space in which it was developed – 4Chan, Tumblr, Reddit or YouTube, for instance – so that each new meme emerges as an in-joke, in which more and more people are able to share as it circulates beyond the space of its initial online mediation. Moreover, those generally simple rules (cats say 'haz', not 'has', there is only one Rick Astley song suitable for use in pranking people, and so on and on) provide a framework within which each internet meme can be remixed by new participants in new contexts. Internet memes, then, are *shared, rule-based representations of online interactions that are not only adopted but also adapted by others.*

Very doge. Such meme. Wow.

In February 2014, the Jamaican national bobsleigh team made it to the Winter Olympics in Sochi, Russia, after supporters raised $30,000 in donations made through the doge-based crypto-currency Dogecoin. Crypto-currencies – Bitcoin is the best known at the time of writing – are experimental media for financial transactions, through which 'coins' or unique digital identifiers are 'mined' or released by expending very high levels of computer-processing power on cracking complex maths problems. The finite number of such identifiers and the 'work' needed to find them create the scarcity from which the coins derive their value. Dogecoin is a doge-themed variant – *much coin, very currency, wow* – and indeed, the remixing of crypto-currency principles into new versions such as Sexcoin, Scotcoin or the Kanye West-themed Coinye indicates that Bitcoin itself is, among other things, an internet meme. The emergence of Dogecoin in December 2013 was a striking indication of how fast the doge meme had circulated, and its use in the Jamaican Olympic bobsleigh appeal – named, inevitably, project Dogesled – made international news (see www.dogesled.net, www.dogecoin.com and www.reddit.com/r/dogecoin).

Though it is hard to measure when an internet meme reaches a point of palpable cultural significance, an undeniable milestone has been reached when a functioning currency is based on a social media joke. Doge's scope is remarkable. The website *Know Your Meme* offers one history of doge's rise to popularity, identifying a 2010 post on Reddit with the title "LMBO LOOK @ THIS FUKKEN DOGE" as a key origin of both the particular image and the particular spelling, and tracing the adoption of the subsequent internet meme across Tumblr, 4Chan and Reddit (http://knowyourmeme.com/memes/doge). Doge reached a certain level of ubiquity in late 2013: "In the great history of the internet," declared *Wired* magazine in December of that year, "2013 will be known as the Year of the Doge" (Watercutter, 2013). By early 2014, it appeared in all sorts of spaces and contexts, from private conversations to public interactions – adopted, adapted and shared. It has appeared as part of a

Subway ad for cheap sandwiches ("Wow. Such deal"). US Republican politician Steve Stockman used doge grammar and the characteristic colours and font in a tweet attacking his electoral rival ("Wow. Such Obamacare funding"). When the popular phone game *Flappy Bird* was withdrawn by its creator in February 2014, a version remixed as *Flappy Doge* appeared within hours. Search for 'doge meme' on YouTube, and the site returns the results in a customised doge font and colour scheme.

By travelling so widely – not through space but through contexts – doge demonstrates that internet memes allow for cultural and social sharing and exchange. The doge meme illustrates the characteristic features of the form. It has rules and codes that can be very easily and quickly learned. It can be easily adapted and shared. And this sharing and adaptation take it into new environments that are far from the original social media spaces in which it emerged as a representation of in-jokes and collaborative cultural practices. Doge is a particularly good example of an internet meme's flexibility, mutability and popularity, evidenced as it makes its way through various spaces and contexts, adapted into the most unpredictable forms.

Dogecoins are worth just fractions of a cent, and crypto-currencies demand a lot of mining time and computing resources in order to yield minimal returns. So, considering these disadvantages, it's worth questioning the motivation behind mining and buying Dogecoins. In this case, and unlike Bitcoin, the reward doesn't appear to be centred on money itself, but rather on the chance to be a part of the cultural aspects of Dogecoin – to participate in something that can be shared and understood with others, albeit now with an added financial dimension. An internet meme begins as an in-joke. As it becomes more widely adopted and adapted, more and more people can share in the joke, making it their own while also participating in something more public (Baym, 2010; Shirky, 2010). Dogecoin miners unite under the phrase "To the moon!", referring to their hopes for the currency, while also serving as encouragement and an extension of the sense of inclusion that is particular to social media meme interactions.

The doge internet meme is not only represented through remixes of the iconic image of a Shiba Inu dog, but also through the accompanying text – doge speak – that follows a particular rule-based logic. In a parallel way to the grammar of lolcats, doge grammar has been detached from the image and is commonly used on its own to represent or refer to the doge meme. This shift towards a purely textual form of the meme has no doubt contributed to its popularity, as textual participation is the lowest of barriers in online interaction – by simply writing "Such doge. Much meme. Wow", one is already engaging with the doge meme even without the use of a Shiba Inu picture. Anything can be remixed into this framework – a private joke, a reference to popular culture, a sandwich ad, a health insurance promotion. Those who recognise the reference may share in a sense of common understanding – that they too are in on the in-joke. At the same time, this sense of exclusivity is countered by the sheer number of people that are in on the joke, since the doge meme has established such a broad reach. In this way, popular internet memes – lolcats, "Harlem Shake" videos, Ellen DeGeneres's 2014 Oscar night group selfie – become global inside jokes that can be tailored to specific types of communication and varied contexts. They allow users to both adopt them, for a sense of inclusion, and adapt them, for a sense of exclusivity, remaking the global former in-joke anew as an actual in-joke.

Ctrl + C, Ctrl + V

Internet memes are built on the act of remixing, which is a recurring practice in online participatory cultures, and indeed one of the essential aspects of daily digital experience (Benkler, 2006; Lessig, 2008; Manovich, 2009). As the product of visual or textual remix – most commonly by the superimposition of text on an existing image, as in a lolcat or a doge image – internet memes can be seen as an extension of existing pre-internet cultures of copy and paste. Despite common associations of mashups and the remix with the digital environment of the twenty-first century, these are practices with long pre-histories (Lessig, 2006).

One pre-history of internet memes involves the remix aesthetics of so much of the arts and popular cultures of the twentieth century (Miller, 2004, 2008; Chandler and Neumark, 2005; Manovich, 2009). From T. S. Eliot and his fragments to DJ Shadow and his fragments, from the Cabaret Voltaire in Zurich to the Cabaret Voltaire from Sheffield, high art and popular cultures were driven by the copy–paste impulse of Ctrl + C, Ctrl + V. In art, Cubism, Dada, Surrealism, the Situationists, Pop Art and Fluxus all remixed and reimagined found objects. In literature, the high modernism of Joyce's *Ulysses* saw the narrative structure of Homer's *Odyssey* remixed with a stylised reimagining of Dublin on 16 June 1904, while later magical realist fiction such as that of Gabriel García Márquez, Toni Morrison or Angela Carter mashed the conventions and concerns of the modern realist novel with the folk cultures of rural Colombians, African American slave narratives or pre-modern European fairy tale traditions. In cinema, Eisenstein's principles of montage, Hollywood continuity editing and the jump cuts of the French New Wave all traded in cutting and pasting to offer new meanings from juxtaposition. In music, jazz brought collaborative improvisations, with each performance a one-off remix of a theme, while the cut-and-paste cultures of punk-inspired zines, and the cut-and-paste cultures of hip-hop and electronic dance musics, find their contemporary digital analogues in the cut-and-paste cultures of YouTube and Tumblr.

These remix aesthetics were augmented by a parallel prehistory of the development of graphically enabled personal computers, from Douglas Engelbart's famous 1968 demonstration of innovations – the mouse, windows, hyperlinks – that pointed towards a future in which computers could be used by the non-specialist, through prototypical graphical user interfaces such as Ivan Sutherland's "Sketchpad" and convergent multimedia devices such as Alan Kay and Adele Goldberg's "Dynabook" and on to the introduction of the Macintosh in 1984. Each of these – and many cognate – developments offered further resources for the non-specialist individual user to manipulate, edit and remix digital texts of all kinds (Packer and Jordan, 2001; Wardrip-Fruin and Montfort, 2003). The widespread domestication of the World Wide Web offered not only limitless access to such texts but also the capacity to share and make visible what one has said or made from them. The emergence of the Web 2.0 business model (O'Reilly, 2005) in the first decade of the twenty-first century made platforms for the circulation of user-generated content near ubiquitous, and also simplified and automated practices of creating, editing and sharing ideas, texts and images.

Moreover, as Henry Jenkins has pointed out (2003), contemporary remix aesthetics also builds upon cultural habits and expectations developed by the adoption and adaptation of earlier innovations in consumer electronics and home entertainment – from the zines made with photocopiers to the personal libraries and edited interpretations of broadcast material enabled by the VCR; from the capacity to customise urban space with a personal soundtrack offered by transistor radios, Walkmans and iPods, to the sense of immersive engagement offered by videogames; and from the ability to create one's own images offered by devices from the Polaroid to the camcorder and the ability to edit those images offered by packages from Photoshop to iPhoto.

Each of these prehistories – in art, in computing, in consumer electronics – provides a different context for the practices of internet memes. While the similarities between, say, Dada and doge might not be very apparent at first, both are products of remix aesthetics and logics, and both appear random, yet operate through rules. As Dada spread from country to country (Richter, 1965; Sanouillet, 2012), some ground rules were established to give this most chaotic of aesthetics a distinct coherence (Lievrouw, 2011: 64). Internet memes too come with rule-based structures that guarantee that the remixing process does not leave the original completely unrecognisable.

The re-appropriation and remix of cultural meanings and objects was also one of the core aspects of the punk movement. Punk didn't merely wish to question mainstream symbols by appropriating them and changing their meaning – punk encouraged everyone and anyone to do it for themselves (Marcus, 1989; Savage, 1991; Ensminger, 2011). By doing so, punk emphasised the importance of being inclusive when it comes to remixing. For punks, creation – whether it be music, fashion, flyers or meanings – was one of the most important values: to go out there and make things with other people, regardless of the quality of the finished product ("Here's three chords, now form a band"). To be active was more important than to be good (Leblanc, 1999: 38; Ensminger, 2011: 49; Jacobson, 2010: 32) – an ethos that echoes in the production and circulation of internet memes.

Conclusion

Internet memes are rule-based representations of particular kinds of online interactions that emerge in particular kinds of social media networks, but they are not confined to such spaces. As the doge example shows, although they may be more prominent in some sections of the internet than others, internet memes also find their way into public platforms and personal emails, into political campaigning and commercial advertising, as they are adopted and adapted into everyday life. Yet, such manifestations of internet memes beyond social media networks point towards more than just their pervasiveness and their value as objects of meaning and humour. Internet memes increasingly feature in posters and slogans that are used in political protests and demonstrations throughout the world (Shifman, 2014). The capacity to both adopt and adapt an internet meme allows for a tailoring of political messages to be crafted by each individual, allowing for personal input, while retaining the underlying recognisable traits of the broader political statement that the meme represents (such as 'We are the 99%').

However, at the same time, this democratic and optimistic view of memes as tools for everyday users to express themselves socially or politically needs to be set against their increasing appropriation by corporations for commercial purposes – as, for example, in Vodafone's take on the "Double Rainbow" meme in an ad campaign.

This commercial appropriation of representations of shared online interactions also situates internet memes within debates about the exploitation of free digital labour (Terranova, 2004; Fuchs, 2014). Internet memes do not focus on ascription of authorship and come instead from a culture where attribution is not prioritised or encouraged (Davison, 2012), which might serve as an encouragement for corporations to use online memes as they wish, since this informal system means that corporations do not have to pay for the use of online memes in their advertisements. Furthermore, this problematic form of circulation may strip internet memes of any counter-cultural meaning that they might have or represent. The explicit circulation of memes in commercial contexts, then, intersects with larger debates regarding digital labour relations and participatory culture, as examples such as the Vodafone or Subway cases connect with critiques of 'produsers' (Bruns, 2008) being exploited by having both their freely made cultural objects and their meanings usurped by commercial enterprises for profit (Terranova, 2004; Andrejevic, 2008; Fuchs, 2014).

Internet memes can be complex, and at times demanding in terms of the cultural literacy needed in order to understand them. Meikle and Young (2012) point to the *Loltheorists* community, which remixes the principles of lolcats with references to the works of social and cultural theorists (http://loltheorists.livejournal.com), as an example of how internet memes operate through in-jokes shared between participants in a particular social media space:

> A staring picture of Foucault, for instance, with the caption "ALL UR SUB-JEKTIVITIES ARE BELONG 2 DISCURSIVE REGIMES UV POWR", rules out anyone unfamiliar with Foucault's work, the "all ur base are belong to us" meme and, indeed, who the guy in the picture actually is.
> (Meikle and Young, 2012: 117)

Internet memes, then, are complex social and cultural acts, and should not be seen as just random images posted on the web – or indeed, "leaping from brain to brain", as Dawkins had it (1976: 206). Behind the manifest silliness of doges and lolcats lies something much more powerful – *intercreativity*, or collaborative processes of making and sharing (Berners-Lee, 1999: 182–3). To make and share internet memes is to make and share meanings. These rule-governed representations of online interaction connect meanings and their makers with others in complex networks of mediated sociality. Internet memes are creative acts done not only for but with others. As products of remix cultures, the creative value of memes might be overlooked, but as this chapter has stressed, the Ctrl + C, Ctrl + V impulse has been central to many artistic and creative phenomena of the past. Users say and make things through internet memes, share the things that they or others have said or made and make all of this visible to new others in new contexts.

Further reading

The standard reference in discussions of memes is Richard Dawkins's *The Selfish Gene*, although we have argued in this chapter that an 'internet meme' is something quite different from Dawkins's original concept. Internet memes have not as yet attracted a critical mass of research attention. The first book-length study is Limor Shifman's *Memes in Digital Culture* (2014). A very brief but useful introductory article is Marwick (2013). Readers interested in the internet meme prehistories of art, multimedia computing and consumer electronics that we sketch in this chapter are referred to Chandler and Neumark (2005), Dery (1993), Jenkins (2003), Lessig (2008) and Packer and Jordan (2001).

References

Andrejevic, M. (2008) "Watching television without pity: The productivity of online fans." *Television and New Media*, 9(1), 24–46.

Baym, N. K. (2010) *Personal Connections in the Digital Age*. Cambridge, UK: Polity.

Benkler, Y. (2006) *The Wealth of Networks*. New Haven, CT: Yale University Press.

Berners-Lee, T. (1999) *Weaving the Web*. London: Orion Business Books.

Blackmore, S. (1999) *The Meme Machine*. Oxford: Oxford University Press.

Bruns, A. (2008) *Blogs, Wikipedia, Second Life, and Beyond: From Production To Produsage*. New York: Peter Lang.

Castells, M. (2012) *Networks of Outrage and Hope*. Cambridge, UK: Polity.

Chandler, A. and Neumark, N. (eds) (2005) *At a Distance: Precursors to Art and Activism on the Internet*. Cambridge, MA: MIT Press.

Davison, P. (2012) "The language of internet memes." In M. Mandiberg (ed.), *The Social Media Reader*. New York: New York University Press (pp. 120–34).

Dawkins, R. (1976) *The Selfish Gene*. Oxford: Oxford University Press.

Dery, M. (1993) *Culture Jamming: Hacking, Slashing and Sniping in the Empire of Signs*. Pamphlet Series, No. 25. Westfield, NJ: Open Magazine.

Ensminger, D. (2011) *Visual Vitriol: The Street Art and Subcultures of the Punk and Hardcore Generation*. Jackson: University Press of Mississippi.

Fuchs, C. (2014) *Social Media: A Critical Introduction*. London: Sage.

Jacobson, E. (2010) "Music remix in the classroom." In M. Knobel and C. Lankshear (eds), *DIY Media: Creating, Sharing and Learning with New Technologies*. New York: Peter Lang (pp. 27–50).

Jenkins, H. (2003) "Quentin Tarantino's *Star Wars*? Digital cinema, media convergence, and participatory culture." In D. Thorburn and H. Jenkins (eds), *Rethinking Media Change*. Cambridge, MA: MIT Press (pp. 281–312).

Lasn, K. (1999) *Culture Jam*. New York: Eagle Brook.

Leblanc, L. (1999) *Pretty in Punk: Girls' Gender Resistance in a Boy's Subculture*. New Brunswick, NJ: Rutgers University Press.

Lessig, L. (2006) "(Re)creativity: How creativity lives." In H. Porsdam (ed.), *Copyright and Other Fairy Tales: Hans Christian Andersen and the Commodification of Creativity*. Cheltenham: Edward Elgar Publishing (pp. 15–22).

——(2008) *Remix*. London: Bloomsbury Academic.

Lievrouw, L. A. (2011) *Alternative and Activist New Media*. Cambridge: Polity.

Manovich, L. (2009) "The practice of everyday (media) life: From mass consumption to mass cultural production?" *Critical Inquiry*, 35, 319–31.

Marcus, G. (1989) *Lipstick Traces: A Secret History of the Twentieth Century*. London: Picador.

Marwick, A. (2013) "Memes." *Contexts*, 12(4), 12–13.

Meikle, G. (2007) "Stop signs: An introduction to culture jamming." In K. Coyer, T. Dowmunt and A. Fountain (eds), *The Alternative Media Handbook*. London: Routledge (pp. 166–79).

Meikle, G. and Young, S. (2012) *Media Convergence: Networked Digital Media in Everyday Life*. Basingstoke: Palgrave Macmillan.

Miller, P. D. (2004) *Rhythm Science*. Cambridge, MA: MIT Press.

——(ed.) (2008) *Sound Unbound: Sampling Digital Music and Culture*. Cambridge, MA: MIT Press.

O'Reilly, T. (2005) "What Is Web 2.0? Design patterns and business models for the next generation of software." *O'Reilly Media*, 30 September. Retrieved from http://oreilly.com/web2/archive/what-is-web-20.html (accessed 10 April 2014).

Packer, R. and Jordan, K. (eds.) (2001) *Multimedia: From Wagner to Virtual Reality*. New York: W. W. Norton.

Richter, H. (1965) *Dada: Art and Anti-Art*. London: Thames and Hudson.

Ross, A. (1994) *The Chicago Gangster Theory of Life*. London: Verso.

Rushkoff, D. (1994) *Media Virus*. New York: Ballantine Books.

Sanouillet, M. (2012) *Dada in Paris*. Cambridge, MA: MIT Press.

Savage, J. (1991) *England's Dreaming*. London: Faber.

Shifman, L. (2012) "An anatomy of a YouTube meme." *New Media and Society*, 14(2), 187–203.

——(2014) *Memes in Digital Culture*. Cambridge, MA: MIT Press.

Shirky, C. (2010) *Cognitive Surplus*. London: Allen Lane.

Terranova, T. (2004) *Network Culture*. London: Pluto.

Wardrip-Fruin, N. and Montfort, N. (eds) (2003) *The New Media Reader*. Cambridge, MA: MIT Press.

Watercutter, A. (2013) "The 10 best memes of 2013." *Wired*. Retrieved from http://www.wired.com/2013/12/best-memes-2013 (accessed 10 April 2014).

50

SLOW MEDIA AS ALTERNATIVE MEDIA

Cultural resistance through print and analogue revivals

Jennifer Rauch

When Elissa Altman inherited her father's vinyl collection, it spurred her to re-evaluate the merits of print and analogue media relative to digital forms – and she noticed that other people were doing the same. "Consider: a close family friend ditches his 12-megapixel camera for a Leica M6 Rangefinder," Altman wrote in *The Huffington Post* (2009). "Culinary anthropologists Naomi Duguid and Jeffrey Alford shoot only film for their magnificent books ... Letter-press printing communities are emerging everywhere, creating original cards and posters in response to their mass-produced counterparts."

Altman is one of many advocates for Slow Media, which emerged at the turn of the millennium as a new iteration of the Slow movement (Rauch, 2011). Popularised by Slow Food, the term 'slow' serves as shorthand for leading a balanced life, pursuing quality over quantity and valuing artisanal skills. The concept taps into transcendentalism, Romanticism, epicurianism, Buddhism and other traditions of Eastern philosophy and Western counterculture. Principles associated with Slowness include mindfulness, humanism, localism, serenity, sensuality, simplicity and self-reliance (see Honoré, 2005; Petrini, 2001). Just as the Slow Food movement recalibrated attitudes towards farming and cooking as social goods, Slow Media theorists and practitioners aim to transform thinking about mediated communication and digital culture.

Slow Media is part of a broader re-appraisal of modern culture taking place in the twenty-first century. It challenges the notion that one's default speed in daily life should be 'as fast as possible' and contends that you can only understand fast, digital media by recognising and appreciating their opposites. From the Slow perspective, shifting between various speeds is more desirable than going slow all the time; there is no universally correct tempo. Many people apply deliberate slowness to media production and consumption through four principles: (1) increasing one's use of print and analogue forms, (2) using digital media in slow ways, (3) reducing one's use of fast media, whether temporarily or permanently, and (4) reducing one's use of all media forms in favour of unmediated activities. People from various walks of life – including many high-tech workers, so-called 'digital natives' and others who value new media – enact such principles in order to preserve a place for slower media alongside faster ones.

One might be tempted to dismiss Slow Media as a Luddite impulse or a lifestyle choice that is merely reactionary, regressive and apolitical. However, its proponents put forth a compelling critique of corporate, commercial culture that deserves closer attention. They also propose some collective, progressive solutions to the cultural domination and commodification that they perceive. In a nutshell: Slow Media are *alternative media*. This category is notoriously difficult to define (see Atton, 2002; Downing, 2001), but people who use alternative media broadly agree that it should: (1) be produced by small organisations rather than big companies, (2) use traditional technologies as well as new ones, (3) not be motivated by profit alone, and (4) advocate for different societal values (Rauch, 2014). Slow Media conforms closely to these precepts, as this essay will illustrate. I briefly introduce philosophies and practices articulated in the Slow Media Manifesto (David, Blumtritt and Kohler, 2010), my own work (Rauch, 2011) and other sources. Drawing upon concepts such as *aura* (Benjamin, 1968[1936]) and *residual media* (Williams, 1977), I consider the appeal of Slow Media in a digital culture and its potential as an alternative media model.

In 2010, a trio of German scholars drafted a "Slow Media Manifesto" that circulated widely on the Internet. Sabria David, Jorg Blumtritt and Benedikt Kohler proposed that some people have grown tired of new, fast technologies that are purportedly cheap, time-saving and easy to use. They described Slow Media in terms familiar to the Slow Food movement: sustainable, local, hand-crafted, community-minded, fair-traded, long-lived and thoughtfully used (David, Blumtritt and Kohler, 2010). The manifesto suggests that, like Slow Food, slowness in media confronts flaws in an industrial system driven by short-term gains, global inequality, shoddy products, unfair labour practices, environmental degradation and unsustainable consumption. Books and records are the only specific print or analogue media mentioned in their 800-word statement.

These theorists proposed that Slow Media forms possess an *aura* that should be associated with present and future-mindedness, not backward-looking nostalgia. For instance, Item No. 12 in the manifesto states that Slow Media are "progressive, not reactionary" and complement speedier forms rather than contradict them (David, Blumtritt and Kohler, 2010). Item No. 11 describes Slow Media as emanating "a special aura. They generate a feeling that the particular medium belongs to just that moment of the user's life" (ibid.). The manifesto suggests that while machine-made Slow Media have less aura than handmade forms do, they have more aura than fast media do: "Despite the fact that [Slow Media] are produced industrially or are partially based on industrial means of production, they are suggestive of being unique and point beyond themselves" (ibid.). Thus, printed zines and vinyl records may be mass-produced but, by virtue of being material, are perceived as more auratic than virtual alternatives.

This conception of Slow Media adapts the ideas of Benjamin, who thought that collectors liberated auratic objects "from the drudgery of usefulness" by investing them with cult value rather than commodity value (1968[1936]: 42). He described aura mystically as a "strange weave of space and time" and as a form of perception that endows an object with the "ability to look back at us" (Benjamin, 1931, in Hansen, 2008: 339). He connected the nostalgic aspects of aura with the hope of social change: "The collector, like the revolutionary, dreams his way into a bygone world and a better one" (Benjamin, 1968[1936]: 42). While Benjamin believed that objects must be originals to have aura, Slow Media thinkers ascribe this invisible substance to print and analogue copies, too.

Another item in the Slow Media Manifesto is particularly relevant to this discussion. Item No. 9 criticises advertising as antithetical to the Slow spirit, proposing word-of-mouth promotion and the gift economy as alternatives. "The success of Slow Media is not based on an overwhelming advertising pressure on all channels but on recommendations from friends, colleagues or family," the theorists write (David, Blumtritt and Kohler, 2010). Thus, Slow Media is imagined as resistance to commercialism, which echoes the critique of product development and marketing made by Altman. "It's about selling us, the consumer, the next big thing, which will be obsolete by the time it hits the stores so that we want the next thing after that. And after that," she writes (Altman, 2009). If the market for fast culture starts feeling too pushy, she proposes pushing back: "Go Slow. Listen to your father's albums. Read a book. A paper one" (ibid.).

As Altman and others have observed, many people in North America, Europe, Australia and elsewhere continue using print and analogue forms, or have adopted them anew. Despite the ubiquity of digital devices and networks, a spectrum of old media forms that seemed endangered, if not extinct, has persisted. For example: young people in New York City refurbish old typewriters for fun and profit (Halpern, 2011). More than 20,000 visitors attend an annual art book fair featuring handmade books and zines (Printed Matter, 2014). Music aficionados such as Sonic Youth's Thurston Moore and Pitchfork's Marc Hogan have waxed poetic over audiocassettes (Hogan, 2010). Some publishers have returned to print, as indie-rock magazine *Magnet* did after disappointment with a digital-only model (Deluca, 2011). Also, many albums from the likes of the Beatles, Bob Dylan and the Rolling Stones, as well as newer acts such as Daft Punk, the National and Vampire Weekend, have been issued or re-issued on vinyl (Kozinn, 2013). I focus here on two case studies of low-tech media that have thrived in recent years: vinyl records and printed zines.

Case study 1: The vinyl 'resurgence'

From the vantage point of Slow Media, strategies to increase profit by reducing costs or to manipulate popular demand through marketing and planned obsolescence become more apparent. Many people who use print and analogue objects perceive consumers as being coerced by the dominant culture into adopting new media. They recognise the extent to which product development is determined by business considerations that do not necessarily align with social needs or consumer preferences, and they recognise that consumers might choose an alternate course of action. Changes in the recorded music industry around the turn of the millennium provide a case in point. Consider the following headlines:

"The death of high fidelity" (*Rolling Stone*)
"Vinyl may be final nail in CD's coffin" (*Wired*)
"Vinyl gets its groove back" (*Time*)
"Weaned on CDs, they're reaching for vinyl" (*The New York Times*).

News events such as these trace the rebound, over a period of three years, from the seeming demise of vinyl records as a musical commodity to their resurrection. When compact discs were first introduced in the 1980s, sales of vinyl records remained steady but no longer provided revenue growth. Regardless of the fact that vinyl was still commercially viable, major labels began to phase it out in the 1990s (see Davis, 2007) and to promote CDs as a great leap forward in convenience and durability. Yet, consumers still resisted switching, partly because CDs were much more expensive than records: on average, $16.98 for a disc versus $9.98 for a record. Compact discs eventually succeeded not because the public wanted them, but because corporations engineered a market for them.

Despite popular preference for vinyl and resistance to CDs, by 1989 records became difficult to find and compact discs were ubiquitous. "We live in a market-driven economy, which every school-kid knows is synonymous with 'democracy,' and the market was demanding more of those excellent, highest-possible-fi compact discs ... right?" some musicians asked facetiously, in offering an alternate explanation for the disappearance of records: major distributors had agreed to cease their long-standing practice of accepting returns on vinyl, which forced record stores to stop carrying vinyl (Negativland, 1996). "Record retailers could not afford the financial risk of carrying anything that was on vinyl because if it didn't sell they would be stuck with it" (ibid.: 30). In addition to charging higher prices, the music industry found other benefits to CDs. Labels continued paying artists a royalty rate based on the lower vinyl price and pocketed the difference. When manufacturing costs declined dramatically, to around $2 per CD, those savings were not passed on to consumers.

The case of CDs demonstrates that media innovations do not always arise from necessity, utility or popular desire. In *Being Digital*, Nicholas Negroponte explains how changes in the media environment do not result from aggregated individual choices (1996) – often misperceived as 'democracy,' as Negativland noted. For instance, high-definition television was developed in the 1990s because manufacturers wanted it, not because the public was clamouring for it. Viewers probably wanted better TV programs more than better picture quality, but selling more equipment offered greater revenue growth than improving content did (ibid.). Media companies are driven "to repurpose their bits at seemingly small marginal cost and at a likely large profit," Negroponte writes (ibid.: 63). Digital content also offers businesses unprecedented control over hardware and software markets through planned obsolescence and fast-paced innovation, where consumers can be compelled to buy new things more quickly than they otherwise might.

Media businesses enhance profitability by decreasing the durability of their goods, not by increasing it – as Slow Media do. Books and records that were made decades ago often still work. E-readers and MP3 players from a few years ago often do not. Although Negroponte asserted that the medium is no longer the message (ibid.: 61), the persistence of Slow Media suggests otherwise. From the perspective of mainstream culture industries, media forms may matter only to the extent that they affect money-making potential, but from the perspective of users and fans, print and analogue forms *per se* do matter.

In contradiction to the eulogies for vinyl, collectors of all ages have increasingly turned to records and the market for CDs has stagnated amid competition with digital downloads, online radio and streaming services.[1] Vinyl sales, which had held steady at around 1 million since the mid-1990s, started to rebound in 2008. The number of record albums sold in the US increased sixfold by 2013, to 6 million – a 33 per cent increase over the previous year (Nielsen, 2014). Digital downloads fell for the first time in 2013; they represented around 40 per cent of the recorded music market, compared to 60 per cent for CDs and 2 per cent for vinyl (ibid.). In 2014, sales of LPs rose another 49 per cent over the previous year, and the aging factories struggled to keep pace with the growing consumer demand (Shah, 2014). In concert with this trend, stores have started selling vinyl alongside stereo equipment, head-phones, coffee, antiques and/or Korean fried chicken. For example, in 2013 the UK label Rough Trade opened an enormous retail store in New York that prominently features vinyl records and music books, along with a concert venue and bar. Per-haps, as a recent *New York Times* article about vinyl enthusiasts said, "Resistance was not futile" (Kozinn, 2013).

Vinyl aficionados comprise a medium-specific group that views the format as Benjamin did: as a quasi-sacred artefact, rather than a market commodity. Many artists and fans consider vinyl a marker of integrity that opposes the commodification of music, as John Davis argues in "Going analogue" (2007). Audiophiles seek out vinyl for its sound quality, warmth, permanence, authenticity and tangibility (McCarthy, 2010). Some collectors, oriented in part towards the past, seek records whose music or packaging evokes personal experience or cultural history (or both). Such symbolic aspects of vinyl fandom are performed by characters in the 1995 book and 2000 movie *High Fidelity*, as independent record store clerks represent life events through analogue artefacts and refuse to sell albums to people they don't like. Analogue music has receded from public visibility since the 1990s, but anecdotal evidence and sales data show that many enthusiasts never abandoned it.

Case study 2: The zine 'resurgence'

Similarly, printed zines have persisted regardless of publicity into the digital age, remaining integral components of 21st-century DIY communities among young and old alike. Influential independent publishers have kept up long-standing printing traditions, such as the not-for-profit *Maximumrocknroll*, which has promoted under-ground culture since the early 1980s by reviewing paper zines and punk-rock records ("physical releases only," according to MMR policy). Other zines have arisen more recently, in what has been described as a "revival" by *New York Times* blogger Jenna Wortham, a former culture reporter for *Wired*. "Lately, it seems, the zine is enjoying something of a comeback among the Web-savvy, partly in reaction to the ubiquity of the Internet," she wrote (2011). A New York public librarian specialising in periodicals seconded the observation. "We're seeing a flowering of print," she said, pointing to zines. "People are drawn to the experience of creating and collecting these physical objects" (ibid.).

Zines – a contraction of 'magazine' or 'fanzine' – are associated with democratic ideals of participation and typified by idiosyncratic themes, noncommercial motives, irregular frequencies, small budgets and low circulations (see Atton, 2002, 2010; Duncombe, 1997; Rauch, 2004; Rauch, 2008). Production is sometimes sophisticated (desktop publishing, offset printing, binding, specialty stock) but often low-tech (hand-writing, typewriters, cut-and-paste, office paper). People often associate the terms 'zines' and 'e-zines,' but the two formats have little in common; the latter are electronic magazines akin to Web pages and blogs that rarely arise in an independent context of production, as the former typically do (Rauch, 2008).

Some online publications, such as BoingBoing and Pitchfork, did grow out of underground communities that also produced zines. This is a recursive process, not a linear one: some printed zines have likewise grown out of digital communities that produce blogs. When a blog writer named David Shapiro launched his printed zine at a party sponsored by Tumblr, some deemed this "ironic" (Berkowitz, 2011) – fallaciously assuming a binary choice between print and digital forms. "It's satisfying to produce something that people can hold and treasure and value partially for its physicality instead of something [online] that gradually disappears," said the 23-year-old writer. "It feels like a rare pleasure to hold up a bunch of pieces of paper that are bound together and read them, instead of reading off a screen" (in Wortham, 2011). Slow Media practitioners often see print and digital media as complementary, not as competing with each other or being mutually exclusive.

This self-publisher's digital experience informed his enjoyment of printed formats, and vice versa. His response resembles other zine producers' whom I interviewed about blogging, which promises an appealing alternative to print: cheaper, more flexible, with broader reach (Rauch, 2004). Many editors were ambivalent towards digital media and talked about having a "love–hate relationship with the Web," finding print "more aesthetically appealing," the excitement of "meeting people in the flesh" rather than online (ibid.: 158–60). One editor said of his fellow zine creators, "Some people do both print and Web versions, but print means more to them" (ibid.: 163). Many of them reported turning to the internet in response to real-world conditions that made it harder to promote and circulate DIY publications: the decline of independent retailers and national franchises such as Tower Books and Records that once supported zines; the disappearance of zine directory *Factsheet Five*, "a central place that everyone could pay attention to" (ibid.: 166); the difficulty of finding distributors and getting paid; and unreliable publicity from the mainstream press. In other words, their individual decisions to stop making zines were influenced not only by personal preferences but also by structural obstacles.

After experimenting with online production, many zine editors had a renewed appreciation for print and predicted that others might someday re-evaluate it, too. "Because of all this Web stuff, people might see that zines published by print are different, and go back to that," one said. "A lot of people like to do whatever stands out, to go against the tide" (Rauch, 2004: 167). They speculated that zine culture might have temporarily ebbed or merely given the appearance of receding because the novelty of digital publishing siphoned away energy and attention. Zines "flow in and out of the public eye but they have always been there in great number," one self-publisher concluded, presaging periodical re-emergences such as the current one (ibid.: 167).

In response to the practical obstacles that led some to abandon print zines, people keen on making and selling them have built new networks, both digital and physical, to support such projects. Communities devoted to handcrafted media have burgeoned alongside the eateries and emporia born of Slow Food's resurrection of artisanal values in farming and dining. In New York City, some independent bookstores and art galleries stock a wide range of zines and comics. A mobile zine shop–gallery reading-room occasionally roams the streets of Brooklyn. A variety of individual artists and collectives offers workshops in zine creation, along with activities such as Coptic binding and postcard making. The creativity of these DIY communities was highlighted in a *New York* magazine story about the "Analogue Underground," a "loosely affiliated network of artists, tinkerers and the merely tech-weary [who] aren't ditching their iPhones or boycotting Facebook just yet, but they are seeking a slower, more hands-on way of doing things" (Halpern, 2011: 53). The article's author, however, characterises her subjects as "neo-Luddite" and "anti-tech" despite contradictory evidence in her interviews (ibid.). She also labels Slow Media such as typewriters and turntables "outdated" while quoting collectors and producers who said their analogue artefacts are still useful, often in perfect working order after more than 50 or 100 years.

Print-media producers in England and Scotland shared similar viewpoints to these US zine editors regarding supposedly out-of-date technologies. For example, a 25-year-old Edinburgh student who writes poems by typewriter thinks that analogue machines are just as "fantastic" tools for creative people as digital ones are. "You don't necessarily have to say, 'That's outdated and we can do better now'," she told *The Observer*. "There's a kind of resurgence of old technology, people realizing that actually, it does still have something to give, and we don't have to leave it all behind. The two can exist happily alongside each other" (O'Hagan, 2011). A main drawback of her typewriter collection: she can't get ribbons or replacement parts for some older ones, which date back a century, yet would still function if an industry existed to support them.

Conclusion

Records, zines and other print and analogue media are often deemed 'obsolete' in the technological sense of being incompatible with widely used digital forms. From the perspective of Slow Media enthusiasts, however, obsolescence is in the eye of the beholder, a discursive construction that involves technological features but is not determined by them. Obsolescence reflects a medium's status – which is shaped by cultural and structural forces, including commercial advertisements, market forces, publicity and community support as well as the availability of local bookstores, product distributors, typewriter ribbons and other material support.

Print and analogue media that were once mainstream have unquestionably been nudged off centre stage. Nonetheless, Slow Media still flourish in the sidelights due to the creative agency of people who share a system of symbolic meanings, an urge to participate in diverse media traditions and access to the requisite materials and knowledge. Slow Media projects have been criticised as commercially non-viable or even elitist, by virtue of their not being mass-produced as cheaply as possible. Small-scale production and physical distribution do limit audiences and potential economies of scale, of course, but this niche status helps insulate Slow Media from commercial pressure and corporate co-optation that could undermine its power as an alternative model.

The discourse about Slow Media that I've discussed underscores many structural concerns voiced by alternative-media scholars (see Atton, 2002; Downing, 2001; Hamilton, 2008; Rauch, 2014). Oppositional, nonconformist, autonomous, anti-capitalist and communitarian principles are woven throughout both the alternative and Slow Media perspectives. While the phrase 'alternative media' was once closely associated with new technologies, recent research shows that alternative-media users also value traditional, familiar forms of media (Rauch, 2014). Those respondents ranked corporate ownership, commercial interests and profit motives as top problems with mainstream media that necessitate alternatives (ibid.) At a time when commercial messages and profit motives exert increasing control over the internet's evolution and threaten the progressive potential of digital media (see McChesney, 2013; Meikle, 2002), print and analogue forms might appear as less hegemonic alternatives.

The question remains of what to call this phenomenon of print and analogue persistence in a digital world. Two possibilities are 'legacy media' and 'residual media' – neither of which connotes desirable objects and positive activities that people deliberately pursue, as opposed to ones that are simply inherited or left over. Legacy media, for example, describes organisations that existed before the rise of the internet; journalists often use it to describe news institutions like NBC and the *New York Times*. Residual media comes from Williams, who envisioned cultural forms moving through historical stages of being emergent, dominant and residual (1977). Scholars of residual media have examined how people reuse, repair and recycle artefacts such as telephones, letters and player pianos before disposing of this "detritus of capital and commodity" (Acland, 2007: xvii).

Like Slow Media, residual media describes a domain of culture beyond the market that remains resistant and relevant. "The residual, by definition, has been effectively formed in the past, but it is still active in the cultural process, not only and often not at all as an element of the past, but as an effective element of the present ... They represent areas of human experience, aspiration and achievement which the dominant culture neglects, undervalues opposes, represses or even cannot recognize" (Williams, 1977: 122–24). Both the Slow and residual concepts challenge what Acland calls the "reigning myth of media": that technological change "consists solely of rupture with the past" (2007: xix). Yet, the linear conception of residual neglects some of the cyclical processes essential to understanding how and why people not only reuse and recycle detritus but also uphold and revive long-standing media traditions, which Slow Media helps explain.

The framework of Slow Media also foregrounds the problem of speed, which plays a central role in capitalist processes of mass manufacturing, disposability and planned obsolescence that emphasise superficiality, efficiency and quantity over other aspects of social life. The Slow movement has fruitfully encouraged people to reassess consumer culture and struggle against artifice, commodification, standardisation and the loss of traditional tastes. Unlike residual media, Slow Media offers solutions and models for action – for instance, in the development of community-supported agriculture and other Slow Food networks. Slow Food founder Carlo Petrini poses his movement as a challenge to the narrative of progress-through-technology put forth by profit-maximising businesses – in his case, industrial food production. "It seems wrong that cultural heritage is discarded due to enthusiasm with false development," Petrini wrote. "A way of living in the world is vanishing because it is no longer compatible with the rhythm of global capital" (2001: 181). In slowing down that rhythm, foodies join conservative impulses with progressive values such as economic justice and environmental sustainability to create an alternative infrastructure.

Some perceive any preference for historical forms and older practices as nostalgia – for an alleged golden age from which civilisation has fallen or for youthful days when life was supposedly simpler. People often treat nostalgia as a suspicious or conservative instinct, overlooking its transformative capacity. Recent research has boosted this oft-maligned reputation, showing that nostalgia makes people more generous with strangers and tolerant of outsiders, makes life seem more meaningful and makes people more optimistic and inspired about the future (e.g. Cheung et al., 2013; Routledge et al., 2011). As Stuart Tannock has observed, historical media are often enjoyed because they generate new experiences; they offer a productive feeling that invokes "a positively evaluated past world in response to a deficient present world" (1996: 454). Some vintage media enthusiasts likely do mourn aspects of the past, but this does not preclude them from looking also at the present or towards the future. Using Slow Media can provide a glimpse of another culture that was, is, will be possible. This is what makes Slow Media *alternative*, and wherein lies its potential for resistance.

Note

1 It is ironic that by popularising CDs, the music industry equipped the public with perfect digital copies of records, which bolstered the file-sharing phenomenon.

Further reading

Readers interested in the concept of Slow Media should read Rauch (2011), who provides a detailed account of its emergence in popular and press discourse. Duncombe (1997) is a comprehensive study of the origins and practices of zine publishing as well as alternative cultural ideals related to identity, community, work and consumption. Rauch (2004) specifically explores zine circulation rituals and the limitations of the Web for self-publishers in terms of social interactivity. Readers interested in the persistence of records should read Acland (2007), especially chapter 6 on "vinyl junkies" and chapter 12 on "going analog."

References

Acland, C. (2007) *Residual Media*. Minneapolis: University of Minnesota.

Altman, E. (2009) "Move over slow food: Introducing Slow Media." *Huffington Post* (29 November). Retrieved from http://huffingtonpost.com/elissa-altman/move-over-slow-food-intro_ b_367517.html (accessed 21 March 2015).

Atton, C. (2002) *Alternative Media*. London: Sage.

——(2010) "Popular music fanzines: Genre, aesthetics and the 'democratic conversation'." *Popular Music and Society*, 33, 517–31.

Benjamin, W. (1968[1936]) *Illuminations* (ed. H. Arendt). New York: Schocken.

Berkowitz, J. (2011) "New media meets zines in the 'world's first perfect' irony." *Fast Company* (21 November). Retrieved from http://www.fastcompany.com/1796016/new-media-meets-zines-worlds-first-perfect-irony (accessed 14 January 2015).

Cheung, W. Y., Wildschut, T., Sedikides, C., Hepper, E. G., Arndt, J. and Vingerhoets, A. J. (2013) "Back to the future: Nostalgia increases optimism." *Personality and Social Psychology Bulletin*, 39, 1484–1496.

David, S., Blumtritt, J. and Kohler, B. (2010) "Slow media manifesto" (2 January). Retrieved from en.slow-media.net/manifesto

Davis, J. (2007) "Going analogue: Vinylphiles and the consumption of the 'obsolete' vinyl record." In C. Acland (ed.), *Residual Media*. Minneapolis: University of Minnesota.

Deluca, D. (2011) "Web-only, indie-rock magazine returns to its roots in print." *Philadelphia Inquirer/Daily News* (16 November). Retrieved from http://articles.philly.com/2011-11-16/news/30405995_1_magnet-magazine-new-music (accessed 14 January 2015).

Downing, J. D. H. (with others) (2001) *Radical Media: Rebellious Communication and Social Movements*. Thousand Oaks, CA: Sage.

Duncombe, S. (1997) *Notes from Underground: Zines and the Politics of Alternative Culture*. New York: Verso.

Halpern, A. (2011) "The analogue underground." *New York* (11 July), 52–59.

Hamilton, J. F. (2008) *Democratic Communications: Formations, Projects, Possibilities*. Washington, DC: Lexington.

Hansen, M. B. (2008) "Benjamin's aura." *Critical Inquiry*, 24, 336–75.

Hogan, M. (2010) "This is not a mixtape." *Pitchfork* (22 February). Retrieved from http://pitchfork.com/features/articles/7764-this-is-not-a-mixtape (accessed 14 January 2015).

Honoré, C. (2005) *In Praise of Slowness*. New York: HarperOne.

Kozinn, A. (2013) "Weaned on CDs, they're reaching for vinyl." *New York Times* (9 June).

McCarthy, A. (2010) "Living with digital, resurrecting analogue, and our shifting search for sound." *Gnovis*, 10.

McChesney, R. (2013) *Digital Disconnect: How Capitalism Is Turning the Internet Away from Democracy*. Boston: New Press.

Meikle, G. (2002) *Future Active: Media Activism and the Internet*. New York: Routledge.

Negativland (1996) "Shiny, aluminum, plastic and digital." *The Baffler*, 8, 29–31.

Negroponte, N. (1996) *Being Digital*. New York: Vintage.

Nielsen (2014) "U.S. music industry year-end Review 2013" (27 January). Retrieved from http://www.nielsen.com/us/en/reports/2014/u-s-music-industry-year-end-review-2013.html (accessed 14 January 2015).

O'Hagan, S. (2011) "Analogue artists defying the digital age." *The Guardian* (23 April). Retrieved from www.theguardian.com/culture/2011/apr/24/mavericks-defying-digital-age

Petrini, C. (2001) *Slow Food: Collected Thoughts on Taste, Tradition and the Honest Pleasures of Food*. White River Junction, VT: Chelsea Green.

Printed Matter (2014) "About the New York Art Book Fair." Retrieved from http://nyart bookfair.com/about (accessed 16 May 2014).

Rauch, J. (2004) "Hands-on communication: Zine circulation rituals and the interactive limitations of web self-publishing." *Popular Communication*, 2, 153–69.

——(2008) "Zines." In W. Donsbach (ed.), *International Encyclopedia of Communication*. Oxford and Malden: Wiley-Blackwell (pp. 5381–5383).

——(2011) "The origin of slow media: Early diffusion of a cultural innovation through popular and press discourse, 2002–2010." *Transformations Journal*, 20. Retrieved from http://www.transformationsjournal.org/journal/issue_20/article_01.shtml (accessed 14 January 2015).

——(2015) "Exploring the alternative-mainstream dialectic: What 'alternative media' means to a hybrid audience." *Communication, Culture and Critique*, 8(1), 124–43.

Routledge, C., Arndt, J., Wildschut, T., Sedikides, C., Hart, C. M., Juhl, J., Vingerhoets, A. J. and Schlotz, W. (2011) "The past makes the present meaningful: Nostalgia as an existential resource." *Journal of Personality and Social Psychology*, 101, 638–52.

Shah, N. (2014) "The biggest music comeback of 2014: Vinyl records." *Wall Street Journal* (11 December). Retrieved from www.wsj.com/.comeback-of-2014-vinyl-records-1418323133 (accessed 14 January 2015).

Tannock, S. (1996) "Nostalgia critique." *Cultural Studies*, 9, 454.

Williams, R. (1977) *Marxism and Literature*. New York: Oxford University.

Wortham, J. (2011) "Raised on the web, but liking a little ink." *New York Times* (22 October).

INDEX